Weimar Prussia, 1918–1925

Dietrich Orlow

WEIMAR PRUSSIA
1918–1925
The Unlikely Rock of Democracy

UNIVERSITY OF PITTSBURGH PRESS

Published by the University of Pittsburgh Press, Pittsburgh, Pa. 15260
Copyright © 1986, University of Pittsburgh Press
All rights reserved
Feffer and Simons, Inc., London
Manufactured in the United States of America

Library of Congress Cataloging in Publication Data

Orlow, Dietrich.
  Weimar Prussia, 1918–1925.

  Bibliography: p. 333.
  Includes index.
  1. Prussia (Germany)—History—
  1918–1933. 2. Democracy. I. Title.
DD453.075 1985   943.085   85-1187
ISBN 0-8229-3519-8

For my parents

Contents

Tables

Acknowledgments

The debts of gratitude accumulated in the course of researching and writing a major work of scholarship are numerous, and it is a pleasant duty to acknowledge the many forms of aid and encouragement that facilitated the emergence of this study.

Above all, I am grateful to the Alexander von Humboldt Foundation for its lengthy and generous fellowship support of my research activities. My tenure as a Humboldt Fellow for more than two years enabled me to carry out the bulk of the necessary archival researches. The American Council of Learned Societies and the Boston University Graduate School provided smaller, but no less appreciated, grants-in-aid. The Boston University Graduate School also provided some funds for the typing of the manuscript.

Because of the upheavals of twentieth-century German history, primary source material is located in a wide variety of institutions and that in turn requires a considerable amount of travel. Research activities are also made more difficult by the dispersal of what were once single sets of papers. (The Otto Braun papers, for example, now reside in three different archives.) I would like to express my gratitude to the numerous institutions which I visited in the course of researching this study (listed in the bibliography). The staffs of all of them were unfailingly helpful and generous in making the materials in their custody available to me.

Unlike our colleagues who work in earlier periods of the past, we who do research in contemporary history are fortunate in having the insight of those who participated in the events themselves at our disposal. In the case of the political history of Prussia, I was able to interview two men who played major roles in the latter years of Weimar Prussia, Professor Herbert Weichmann, in the 1930s Otto Braun's personal assistant and later the lord mayor of Hamburg, and Ernest Hamburger, a former member of the Prussian legislature. In addition, John Caspari who was during the Weimar years the *Landeshauptmann* of Brandenburg, generously answered written questions.

Every piece of research benefits immensely from discussions with colleagues in the field. Some of the cross-fertilization may be so subtle as to remain almost unnoticed, but in my case a number of colleagues deserve a very specific and public acknowledgment. They include Professor Hans Mommsen of Bochum, who originally suggested the topic of this study; Dr. Susanne Miller of Bonn, whose insight particularly into the workings of the German Social Democrats is unparalleled; and above all, Professor Werner

Jochmann of Hamburg. Not only was Dr. Jochmann's constructive criticism instrumental in shaping the organizational format of the study, but his generosity in sharing his unrivaled knowledge of the period in numerous conversations with me greatly facilitated the work's progress. I would also like to thank Professor Hagen Schulze, Berlin, for giving me copies of some interviews which he had conducted in connection with research for his recently published biography of Otto Braun.

At a somewhat more mundane, but no less necessary level, I would like to thank Jennifer Saxton, Patricia Jalbert, and Stephen Chapman, each of whom typed a major portion of the manuscript.

Finally, this book, perhaps more than most, has been a family affair. An earlier version of the manuscript was in German, and my parents, my wife, and my daughter were all instrumental in translating and adapting the manuscript into English. I gratefully acknowledge their arduous (and uncompensated) labors. In addition, my wife and daughter also helped with the typing and editing.

Needless to say, whatever errors and shortcomings remain are my responsibility.

Weimar Prussia, 1918–1925

Introduction

Germany's defeat in the Second World War ended the existence of both the German Reich and the state of Prussia. The Reich, stripped of much of its former territory, was divided first into four zones of Allied occupation and eventually transformed into present-day West and East Germany. The state of Prussia, which especially in Anglo-Saxon eyes had long epitomized the negative aspects of the German nation,[1] was quite literally legislated out of existence. On February 25, 1947, the Allied Control Council issued Law no. 46: Prussia was abolished, its institutions dissolved, its assets confiscated.[2]

Actually, the Allies' decision was redundant. By 1947 Prussia had ceased to have any significance as a government entity, and the later rulers in East and West Germany had no interest in resurrecting the state. Indeed, for some thirty years after World War II the *finis Borussiae* seemed total. Professional historians and other specialists continued to debate Prussia's past significance, but public interest in the two Germanies and outside their boundaries in things Prussian was virtually nonexistent.

Recently, however, there has been a remarkable change, as an avalanche of publications, exhibitions, and films on the history and culture of Prussia has provided evidence of nostalgia and renewed attention in both East and West Germany.[3] In the summer of 1981 a major multimedia exhibition in West Berlin sought to provide a balanced assessment of Prussia's contributions to German and European civilization.[4] On the other side of the border, the East German press for the first time in many years began referring to King Frederick II as "Frederick the Great," while GDR television featured a miniseries celebrating the Prussian reform era in the early years of the nineteenth century.

The revival of interest in Prussia and its history in the two Germanies was not entirely accidental. As the political systems in East and West Germany mature, both the Federal Republic and the German Democratic Republic face the problem of national continuity and identity. Neither is possible without confronting the problem of Prussia in the evolution of Germany. For much of its history, the Reich's largest state was far more than a medium-sized territory with an industrious, if somewhat dour population. "Prussia" was also, for better or worse, an idea and an ideal. To be "Prussian" epitomized a particular mindset and a way of life that, especially after the middle of the nineteenth century, came to be increasingly identified with Germany itself.

3

Prussia's political history must be addressed in the context of the "German problem," that is, the cause and course of modernization in Germany.[5] Students of recent German history constantly confront the problem of the Reich's peculiar patterns of development in evolving from a predominantly agrarian society to a highly industrialized country. The process of modernization has been, of course, a universal phenomenon in European history, but it has become axiomatic to regard Germany's development as unique in at least two ways. On the one hand, the transformation of German society was extremely telescoped—that is, the process took place over a very short time—and on the other, modernization seemingly stopped after altering only part of Germany's premodern social structures and values. Historians have pointed out that especially during the time of the Second Empire (1871–1918) and to a lesser extent during the years of the Weimar Republic as well, German society evolved modern forms of organization and values in economics and technology, while its political structures and value patterns remained typical of preindustrial times.

Contemporary historiography has done much to explore the anomalies of Germany's modernization processes. Specifically, analysts have sought to find the reasons why Germany—in contrast to its major West European neighbors—lagged behind in evolving a viable democratic political system. Debate on the reasons for the "modernization warp" continues, but most researchers would agree that, in addition to such factors as the profound differences in the level of economic development in the eastern and western regions of the country, and the religious split between north and south, the role of Prussia in German history played a major part in shaping the country's paths to modernization.[6]

Especially after the Reich became united in 1871 through the force of Prussian arms, Germany's largest state was essentially a Reich in miniature. Prussia's territory and population made up roughly three-fifths of the Reich as a whole, the state's borders to the east and west were the same as the national frontiers, and Prussia's social structure paralleled that of the Reich. Since after 1871 Prussia's authoritarian political structures also dominated the Reich's political institutions, many historians have treated German and Prussian history before and after 1918 as essentially identical.[7]

There are some good reasons to justify such an approach. At least since the middle of the nineteenth century, German federalism has had both an offensive and a defensive character. For the most part, the German states were "defensive" in their relations with each other and with the central government, anxious to protect their territorial and political autonomy against the encroachments of larger neighbors and whatever Reich authority existed. This form of federalism is perhaps best exemplified by the fear of the southern German states (notably Bavaria) that they would lose their cultural and political independence if the central government were to acquire powers beyond those characteristic of a loose confederation. In contrast, Prussia's attitude toward federalism was more "offensive." After their defeat of the revolution of 1848, the state's Conservative political leaders increasingly identified Prussia's interests with those of the Reich, and they sought to dominate the central government. The ruling Junkers believed that Germany's largest state had a paradigmatic role to play in the future history of the Reich: Prussia was to defend political authoritarianism in all of Germany against the subversive influence of democracy and political pluralism.

The identification of Prussian authoritarianism and the evolution (or lack of it) of German political life seemed so close that most treatments of modern German political history have struck a quasi-deterministic note, a sort of negative historicism. In consequence, both the collapse of 1918 and the later Nazi seizure of power seem inevitable results of ossified structures and rigid mindsets by the Prusso-German political leaders. With the empire and the Weimar Republic acting as precursors with "prefascistic structures"[8] which could not escape their "anonymous fate,"[9] Nazi totalitarianism in many accounts appears as the only logical outcome of modern German history. And with the outcome axiomatic, the historian's task becomes primarily a quest to explain why the tragedy was as inevitable as it has been declared to be.

The search has produced a variety of answers. Many analysts have concentrated on the weakness of the German party system and the inadequacies of the Bismarckian and Weimar constitutions as reasons for the failure of political democracy in Germany. Among the political groups, scholars have understandably focused on the shortcomings of the moderate bourgeois parties and the right-wing Socialists, since it is generally agreed that any significant changes in the authoritarian political structures established after 1871 could come only through the cooperative effort of these reformist forces. It is certainly true that until 1918 profound ideological differences and strong class antagonisms negated all efforts toward systematic cooperation between the moderate bourgeoisie and the working classes, and limited their working together to momentary tactical arrangements.[10] In addition, for the most part neither the moderate bourgeois parties nor the Social Democrats actively sought governmental responsibility before World War I, so that when executive power fell into their hands in November 1918 they were ill prepared for the role forced upon them in the years of the republic. Finally, the bourgeois parties had essentially remained aggregations of notables rather than evolving into organizations capable of mobilizing mass support.[11]

The revolution of 1918, or rather the reasons for its failure, occupies a prominent place in the historiography of modern Germany.[12] Most interpretations of the political changes that shook Germany at the end of 1918 fall into two categories. There is the older school, begun by Karl Dietrich Erdmann, which argues that the revolution forged a union of moderate and traditional political forces in Germany that alone was able to prevent bolshevism from seizing power in the country.[13] In contrast, the so-called critical school denies the validity of this interpretation and holds instead that it was precisely the alliance of reformers and authoritarians that prevented a radical (and needed) restructuring of German society, enabling the old ruling classes to continue their successful efforts to prevent political modernization and democratization of the Reich. The critical school goes back to a seminal work by Arthur Rosenberg, although his thesis did not receive solid evidentiary support until the 1950s and 1960s.[14] The anti-Erdmann group has concentrated on exploring the possibility of the "third way." These historians postulate that the revolution provided Germany the opportunity for pursuing a genuine alternative between the stale and unproductive ideas of the right-wing Socialists and their bourgeois allies on the one hand, and the supporters of Leninism on the other. While the majority Socialists showed excessive concern for preserving lines of continuity between the empire and the republic,[15] and the Spartacists (later Communists) rigidly applied the Russian revolutionary model to quite different political conditions, there were, according to the proponents of the "third way," many in the Socialist parties who demanded both a radical break with Germany's authoritarian and militaristic past and the establishment of a genuine German—not Russian—form of socialism.

In recent years, the view that German history from 1871 to 1933 proceeded in a rather straight line from the Second—Wilhelminian—to the Third Reich has come under increasing criticism in a number of revisionist studies. Particularly the picture of imperial Germany as a protofascist society subject to the unquestioned domination of Prussian reactionaries has been called into question. Manfred Rauh has recently demonstrated that the political structures of Wilhelminian Germany were far less rigid than had previously been assumed. The Bismarckian constitution as the bedrock of reactionary rule was a "transitory phenomenon" which even before 1914 had been significantly eroded, especially at the Reich level, in favor of de facto parliamentarism.[16] Further developments in the course of the First World War only gave the system its *coup de grâce*.

The viability of the "third way" during the revolution of 1918–19 has also been questioned. Numerous documentary and analytical studies, mostly by scholars who set out to support the "third way" school of interpretation, have unwittingly disproved much of the original thesis. It is becoming increasingly clear that despite considerable popular appeal, the Independent Socialists, the primary support of the "third way," were an organizationally weak and ideologically divided party and thus a poor base on which to build a new political and social system in Germany.[17] Similarly, the Independents' institutional strength, the system of workers' and soldiers' councils, was not strong enough to serve as an alternative to the established institutions of government and legislation. This development should not have come as a complete surprise. Gerald Feldman has reminded us that the workers' and soldiers' council movement after World War I was a short-lived phenomenon in all areas of Europe with the exception of Soviet Russia.[18]

To date, revisionism has left the traditional picture of the Weimar Republic largely untouched. Interest in the Weimar Republic among historians continues to focus on its negative, "prefascistic" characteristics. The picture of the Weimar Republic as a "democracy without democrats" is still commonplace,[19] and research on the history of the German Republic remains dominated by the question of why it failed. Again, its shortcomings cannot be denied. A number of factors have been cited for the chronic difficulties faced by the republic. In addition to the long-term structural problems of German political life, there were problems with the constitution, particularly in the provisions for excessive proportional representation and the direct, popular election of the president. In addition, the republic never fulfilled its early promise of societal reforms. The interaction of economic difficulties and international complications (such as hyperinflation and the Treaty of Versailles) prevented the republic from taking credit for either economic prosperity or national successes.

There were also the inherent weaknesses in the German political party system.[20] Cooperation among the middle-of-the-road parties that supported parliamentary democracy (the SPD, the Center party, and the DDP, and, with reservations, the DVP) never became routine. Much of what had divided them before 1914 continued to drive them apart after the revolution. Among the bourgeois parties, which still did not evolve into true mass parties, a longing for a quasi-anthropomorphic political structure with a bourgeois head and a Social Democratic body prevented cooperation with the workers' party on the basis of genuine equality.[21] The SPD was not confronted with these difficulties, but it had other, no less serious, barriers to overcome. The right-wing Social Democrats did have a strong mass organization, enabling them to become the leading political party throughout most of the Weimar years, and they certainly did not long to return to the days of imperial Germany, but their strength was seldom optimally used. The SPD was a very cumbersome organization,[22] increasingly subject to what its critics derisively identified as *Verbonzung, Verkalkung, Verbürgerlichung* (bureaucratization, calcification, and bourgeoisification). Moreover, the party persisted in attempting to avoid political responsibility as a partner in coalition governments. The SPD's leadership always felt defensive about sending ministers into the Reich government, feeling that it had to justify such straying from the line of pure socialism to rank-and-file party members.[23] As a result, for much of the Weimar era the strongest party in the Reichstag refused to join the government and occupied the opposition benches instead.[24]

I will argue in the course of this study that our traditional picture of the Weimar era as a brief interlude in which democracy failed needs to be revised because most of the simplistic generalizations about Weimar Germany do not apply to the state of Prussia, which made up three-fifths of the country. Far more than their counterparts at the national level, the moderate parties in Prussia were able "to work together toward getting things done."[25] Pragmatists rather than ideologues dominated the state's political scene.[26] Prussian ministers for the most part had been leading members of the state legislature before assuming their executive posts; the Reich was often forced to select "nonpartisan" civil servants and businessmen as cabinet ministers because the national parliament could not come up with a majority for political appointees. The Reichstag was able to complete only one full legislative session; in all other legislative periods deadlocks forced early elections. The Prussian Landtag was never dissolved because it was unable to fulfill its parliamentary function. Coalitions encompassing the political spectrum from the SPD on the left to the DVP on the right held office for only a few months in the Reich, but in Prussia a grand coalition, as it was called, governed the state from November 1921 until the end of 1924, a period that included such momentous events as the Franco-Belgian occupation of the Ruhr region and Hitler's Beer Hall Putsch. The comparisons could be continued, but the conclusion seems clear: while parliamentary democracy may not have functioned well at the Reich level, the state that formed the greatest part of the Reich enjoyed consistent political stability under the same political system.[27] In fact, as will become apparent, to a large extent the viability of democracy in Prussia enabled the Weimar Republic as a whole to survive its first six turbulent years.

Our somewhat distorted view of the Weimar years derives, I believe, at least in part from a curious neglect of the role of Prussia in German political history after 1918. After being portrayed as the *deus ex machina* of German history before 1918, the state is largely ignored in accounts of political dynamics during the republican years. Typical is Golo Mann's assessment of Prussia's significance during the Weimar era: "a pale sequel to a sequel."[28] Only in recent years have a full-scale biography of the long-time prime minister of the state, Otto Braun, a study of the Center party's delegation in the Landtag, and an analysis of the state's territorial administration, righted the balance somewhat.[29] Nevertheless, to date there is still no overall analysis of the workings of the parliamentary system in Weimar Prussia.

This neglect of Weimar Prussia is unfortunate. The state demonstrated its resilience as early as the revolutionary upheavals of 1918–1919, when the question of Prussia's dissolution became a hotly debated political issue. There were no clear political divisions among Germany's new leaders on this question. Radical centralists, who demanded the immediate dissolution of Germany's largest state in order to strengthen the Reich's authority, could be found in all political camps. At the same time, the reverse was true as well. There were leaders in the various parties who hoped to use a strong Prussia as the foundation of the particular political system they advocated for Germany as a whole.

Uncertainties about the future of the state were not shared by Prussia's own leaders. Regardless of their political orientation, the Prussian spokespersons during the revolution immediately and vigorously pushed to retain the state's political and territorial integrity. The new rulers of the state did not share the conservative goals of their predecessors, but they too held fast to the idea of Prussia's paradigmatic mission. Only the political orientation had changed: for the state's republican leaders, Prussia was to serve as a model not of authoritarianism, but of the viability of parliamentary democracy in Germany.[30]

To a large extent, that decision was confirmed by the provisions of the Weimar constitution. Prussia remained by far the largest and most populous state in Germany. At the same time, the Weimar constitution decisively altered the balance of power in German federalism. The framers of the constitution substantially increased the powers of the Reich government. Taxation, economic policies, and foreign affairs were all largely decided at the Reich level, and the states' rights to influence their determination was reduced to indirect action through the *Reichsrat*, the second chamber of the national legislature composed of representatives appointed by the state governments. Adjusting to the new federal realities was particularly difficult for Prussia, which under the Bismarck constitution had dominated executive and legislative decisions in the Reich.

Still, the Weimar constitution stopped halfway in the "federalization" (in German bureaucratese, the term is *Verreichlichung*) of political power. It transferred a great deal of legislative power to the federal government, but very little administrative capacity. The Reich civil service, while growing rapidly in the Weimar years, remained small compared to the territorial administrations of the states, notably Prussia's. As a result, for those aspects of public life that in Germany have traditionally been regarded as the most political—party coalitions, cabinet formation, and the organization and composition of the territorial administrative apparatus—Prussia remained an important component in German political history.

Finally, although post–World War II developments are beyond the scope of this study, Weimar Prussia fulfilled an important function in establishing patterns of continuity from 1918 to the years after 1945. The Weimar era in

Prussia links the forces attempting to secure democracy in Germany after 1918 with their successors in the present-day Federal Republic of Germany. In this sense, it is indeed a mistake for today's Germans "to deny Prussia."[31] The state's history is an undeniable component of the German national identity, but, as this study will suggest, Prussia should be identified not only with the authoritarian state of the Junkers and Wilhelminian militarism, but also with successful parliamentarism and fruitful cooperation between the moderate bourgeois parties and Social Democracy.

The subtitle of this work is taken from a Social Democratic campaign pamphlet issued before the December 1924 Prussian state elections; it described Prussia as "the democratic . . . solid rock." (*Der Preussische Landtag 1921–1924,* ed. Paul Hirsch [Berlin, 1924], p. 13.)

PART ONE
1918–1921

CHAPTER 1

Political Parties in Prussia, 1914–1921

Prussia's political domination of the Reich from 1871 until the fall of the empire in 1918 led to a virtual identification of state and national politics. Ideologically and organizationally, parties developed largely along parallel lines in the state and the Reich.[1] All major German parties functioned under the same names in the Reich and in Prussia, and there were no political groups that restricted their activities to the state, as was true of such regional political groups as the Bavarian People's party (BVP) in Bavaria. Since both the national and state legislatures (the Reichstag and the Landtag) met in Berlin, many political leaders served as delegates in both bodies. Similarly, during the years of the empire most Reich cabinet ministers served as Prussian ministers as well.

As we shall see, the situation changed in the course of World War I and especially after the Weimar Republic was established in 1918. Prussian parties and politics became increasingly self-contained; the state's political leaders no longer dominated the national parties. To take but one example, in the SPD, the largest German party, only three of the twelve functionaries elected to the executive committee at the party's 1919 national congress were closely associated with Prussian politics, and none of the ten members of the party's Central Commission played a leading role in the state.

When the Prussian party leaders lost their grip on the levers of national decision making, the consequences were not without benefits for the evolution of pluralist politics in Germany's largest state. Since it was unlikely, especially after 1918, that a seat in the Prussian parliament would serve as a launching pad for a Reich-level career, politicians with national ambitions were seldom attracted to state politics. As a result there were fewer abrasive personalities in the state parliament (Landtag), and the representatives were generally more willing than their colleagues in the Reichstag to follow party discipline. More harmonious intraparty relations in turn helped reduce tensions between the executive and the party caucuses in the legislature.[2]

Until 1918 Prussian politics and parties were governed by the constitution of 1851. This document, drafted by the victorious counterrevolutionary forces after the revolutionary upheavals of 1848–49, was designed to make the state a bulwark of political authoritarianism and prevent the rise of parliamentary democracy. The constitution mandated the infamous three-class system of

13

voting that became the cornerstone of Conservative preeminence in Prussia. By the beginning of the twentieth century, the three-class system effectively condemned 82 percent of the eligible voters of the largest German state to political impotence. The severe distortion of the parties' popular vote strength and their parliamentary representation is evident from the figures for the last prewar state election, held in June 1913. (See table 1.)

Table 1. State Election, June 1913

Party	Popular Vote	% of Total	Seats	% of Total
Conservatives	402,988	14.8	147	33.2
Free Conservatives	54,583	2.0	54	12.2
National Liberals	370,575	13.56	73	16.5
Progressives	183,452	6.7	38	8.6
Center party	451,511	16.5	103	23.3
National minorities	215,506	7.9	12	2.8
Social Democrats	775,171	28.4	10	2.3

Source: Statistisches Jahrbuch für den preussischen Staat, ed. Königl. Statistisches Landesamt (Berlin, 1915), 12:632, 638.

The most reactionary of the Conservative groups, the German Conservatives, received only 14.8 percent of the popular votes cast, but 33 percent of the seats in the legislature. Their slightly more enlightened colleagues, the Free Conservatives, obtained 2 percent of the votes and 12 percent of the seats, the National Liberals 13.56 percent of the popular vote and 16 percent of the seats, and the left-wing Liberals (Progressives, or FVP) 6.7 percent of the votes and 8.6 percent of the seats. The Catholic Center party, too, benefited from the electoral rules. In contrast, the Social Democrats, with 28.4 percent of the popular vote but 2.3 percent of the parliamentary seats, were glaringly underrepresented.

Long before the First World War, the Social Democrats, the Progressives, and the national minorities (Poles and Danes) had made reform of the three-class system a perennial campaign issue.[3] The National Liberals and the Center party, however, remained firmly wedded to cooperation with the Conservatives, and rejected any meaningful changes either in the Prussian governmental system or the mode of electing the legislature.[4] The efforts of the groups demanding the complete abolition of the three-class system and the transformation of the authoritarian Prussian state into a modern democracy remained unsuccessful. Lacking influence in the legislature, they had neither a common plan of action nor any interest in forming a long-term alliance to achieve their aims.[5]

The situation changed dramatically with the outbreak of World War I in 1914, when the question of the electoral franchise became a component of the

Reich government's "intramural peace" *(Burgfrieden)* policy and Chancellor Bethmann Hollweg's "politics of the diagonal."[6] The policy of "intramural peace," which meant essentially that all political parties would agree to cease airing domestic controversies for the duration of the war and unite in face of the Reich's foreign enemies, had entirely different political implications in Prussia and the Reich. In the Reich, freezing the domestic political *status quo* satisfied, at least for a time, both the government and those advocating further reforms, since for some years before 1914 the power of the national parliament had been growing and Bethmann Hollweg's wartime policies continued this trend. The chancellor attempted to hold the divergent wings of his coalition together by the "politics of the diagonal," that is, simultaneous concessions to those at opposite ends of the political spectrum: he agreed to far-reaching territorial annexation demands made by the Conservatives, but also seemed to support some domestic reforms advocated by the Liberals and Social Democrats. Unfortunately, Bethmann Hollweg's *Burgfrieden* policy in the state resulted in exactly the reverse of what the chancellor sought to achieve. As long as the three-class electoral system remained in effect in Prussia, the chancellor's concessions at the Reich level had little impact on the political rights of the larger part of the German population. By 1917 domestic tensions had stretched the diagonal alliance too far; deserted and mistrusted by Conservatives and reformers alike, the chancellor was dismissed in August.

Many factors contributed to Bethmann Hollweg's—and eventually the empire's—fall, but there is no doubt that the Prussian electoral system had become a focal point of controversy in the debate over Germany's and Prussia's political future. It was the one Prussian issue that polarized the nation. For the Conservatives and the military leaders of the Supreme Army Command *(Oberste Heeresleitung, OHL)* Prussia with its three-class electoral system was the bulwark that would prevail against the "international democratic flood."[7] The Prussian National Liberals agreed, but that party's Reichstag leader, Gustav Stresemann, favored reforms.[8] For the Social Democrats, as we shall see, disagreements over the best tactical approach to reform politics in Prussia was the crucible that helped to divide reformists from revolutionaries.[9] But in 1918 all of these questions had become moot. The advent of mass politics forced all of the Prussian parties to make fundamental organizational and programmatic changes.

The Right: From Conservatives to the German National People's Party (DNVP)

Two conservative parties, the German Conservative party (DKP) and the Free Conservative party (FKP), dominated prewar Prussia.[10] Like all bourgeois parties, the prewar Conservatives were not mass parties in the modern sense of the term, but groupings of notables. It is true, however, that the parties' close ties to mass-membership interest groups such as the Agrarian League (Bund der Landwirte) and the Naval League (Flottenverein) gave the Conservatives a larger popular base than was true of other non-Marxist parties. Before 1918, of course, a mass base was not necessary to maintain political power in Prussia. The three-class electoral system guaranteed these parties numerical control of the lower house of parliament and the close meshing of personnel between party functionaries and the ruling elites in economic and social life, public administration, the military, and the Protestant church further buttressed the base of Conservative rule in Prussia.

With the outbreak of the revolution, the Conservative parties lost not only their power base, but also their *raison d'être* as electoral machines and parliamentary pillars of the existing governmental system. They were forced to pursue their political goals under radically altered conditions. Consequently, a genuinely modern mass party, the German National People's party (DNVP) appeared in place of the old elitist associations.[11] The DNVP was a "symbiotic association" of the old Conservatives and various groups supporting the new or revolutionary conservatism.[12] Indeed, supporters of racist *(völkisch)* ideas and the Pan-German Association (Alldeutscher Verband, ADV) became increasingly influential in the DNVP.

The conflict between old and new Conservatives was reflected in the membership, voter configuration, and continuous disputes over political goals and tactics within the party. The majority of the party's members and voters were now drawn from the middle classes, workers in cottage industries, and women. These social strata replaced the large landowners and high-ranking civil servants, who had dominated the prewar conservative parties. As a result of the realignment, the Prussian and especially the East Elbian influence in the party was reduced. At the same time the party's ties to the German National Union of Retail Clerks (Deutschnationaler Handlungsgehilfenverband [DHV]) significantly strengthened the white-collar workers' element in the DNVP.[13]

The first public announcement of the new party was a "Founding Proclamation" *(Gründungsaufruf)* which appeared in the November 24, 1918, issue of the *Kreuzzeitung*.[14] The authors of the proclamation were obviously still influenced by the shock of the revolution. The party presented itself as a moderate group that was willing to cooperate in bringing about necessary changes in Germany's political and economic structures. The DNVP endorsed the parliamentary form of government, stressed the importance of civil liberties, and called for the protection of private property. At the same time, it indicated support of some land reforms, expansion of welfare programs, and the right of workers to form and join labor unions. The only part of the program that specifically concerned Prussia was a demand for the preservation of the state's territorial and political integrity in any future Reich.[15]

The initial program, however, had little effect on the party's future development. Beginning with the second national congress in October 1920, the DNVP adopted a political platform that stressed its opposition to democracy, the republic, and parliamentary government, demanding instead the return of an authoritarian monarchy under the Hohenzollerns. The party now also rejected any economic or land reforms. The only remnant of the 1918 program was the DNVP's stand on the Prussian question: the vast majority of DNVP members supported a strong Prussia as the nucleus of a resurrected monarchy.

The reorganization of the conservative camp enabled a number of newcomers to enter Prussian political life. There were only fourteen members of the old Landtag (ten Conservatives, three Free Conservatives, and one *völkisch* representative) among the forty-nine members of the caucus elected to the Prussian Constitutional Convention (Verfassungsgebende Preussische Landesversammlung) on January 26, 1919. The social structure of the parliamentary group showed the reduced influence of the old agrarian bloc. The majority of representatives were civil servants; twenty-seven members listed their occupations as bureaucrat, minister, teacher, or professor—all occupational groups that in Prussia belonged to the civil service—while only four considered themselves farmers.[16] The party's leadership, however, remained in the hands of prewar Conservatives. The state and provincial leaders came for the most part from the ranks of the large landowners. The caucus chairman was Oscar Hergt, a former minister of finance in Prussia who had been close to the Free Conservatives' position before the war.[17]

Lacking a unified party program and hampered by organizational problems, the DNVP faced an uncertain future in Prussia. The traditional leaders were increasingly challenged by those in the party who rejected even the concept of cooperation with other middle-class parties.[18] It was clear from the results of the first postwar elections (see table 2) that without the aid of the three-class system the DNVP would not be able to dominate the state legislature, but needed to cooperate with other parliamentary groups to retain its influence in the state;[19] yet the party's leadership was subjected to constant pressure from those who wanted to use their parliamentary position purely for demagogic attacks on democracy and the republic. Hergt was forced, often against his wishes and better judgment, to play the role of a hot-blooded rabble rouser, or to see his rudimentary steps toward cooperation disavowed.[20]

The ideological and tactical controversies within the DNVP led the party to pursue an erratic and unpredictable course in 1919 and 1920. Party publicists used the national debate over the Treaty of Versailles to give full vent to

Table 2. Election for the Prussian Constitutional Convention,
January 1919

Party	% of Popular Vote	No. of Representatives
Social Democrats (SPD)	36.4	145
Center party (Z)	22.3	94
German Democrats (DDP)	16.2	66
People's party (DVP)	5.7	21
German Nationalists (DNVP)	11.2	50
Independent Socialists (USPD)	7.4	23

Source: Statistisches Jahrbuch für den Freistaat Preussen (Berlin, 1920), 16:422–23.

"stab-in-the-back" and anti-Semitic demagoguery.[21] But in September 1919 Hergt seemed to offer a hand of cooperation to the moderate bourgeois parties, notably the Center. His "program of order" contained a series of reform proposals, which as the Center party representative Brust pointed out, largely paralleled the proposals of the Weimar coalition parties.[22] The potential partners remained suspicious (as one Center party representative put it, "I hear the message, but I can't believe it"),[23] but Hergt's initiative was in any case effectively undermined by members of his own party. The acts of violence by groups sympathetic to the DNVP demonstrated support for the hard-liners who rejected all collaboration with moderate forces.[24]

The DNVP's efforts to seize power in the Reich and Prussia by violent, extraparliamentary means reached a climax in the spring of 1920 with the party's role in the preparation and execution of the Kapp Putsch.[25] There is no doubt that among the political parties the DNVP was most deeply involved in planning the putsch. Prominent DNVP leaders maintained close contact with the military leaders of the rebellion, and even participated in drawing up Kapp's political program. Similar patterns of cooperation developed between the conspirators and several of the DNVP's provincial organizations and their affiliated pressure groups.[26] When the mutinous troops occupied Berlin, the DNVP's leaders issued a public statement that heaped criticism upon the old, constitutional cabinet while accepting the "Kapp government" as a fait accompli. The official DNVP pronouncement avoided specific recognition of Kapp's regime, but the German Nationalists were obviously prepared to allow the insurgents to rule until they saw fit to call new elections.[27] In addition, during the few days of Kapp's control in the capital, the DNVP's leaders worked to make Kapp and Lüttwitz acceptable to the bourgeois parties in order to facilitate the establishment of Reich and Prussian bourgeois cabinets that were closely allied with the rebellious military.[28]

The collapse of the Kapp Putsch demonstrated that violent coup attempts had no chance of success. Recognizing this political fact of life, the German

Nationalist leaders after March 1920 concentrated on mobilizing mass support at the ballot box. They were quite successful in both the Reichstag elections (June 1920) and the Prussian Landtag elections of February 1921. (see table 3.)

Table 3. State Constitutional Convention Election, January 1919, Reichstag Election, June 1920, and Landtag Election, February 1921

Party	State Constitutional Convention (January 26, 1919)		Reichstag Election (June 5, 1920)		Landtag Election (February 20, 1921)	
	% of Popular Vote	No. of Delegates	% of Popular Vote	No. of Delegates	% of Popular Vote	No. of Delegates
SPD	36.4	145	21.7	102	26.3	114
Z	22.3	94	13.6	64	17.2	84
DDP	16.2	66	8.3	39	6.2	26
DVP	5.7	21	13.9	65	14.2	58
DNVP	11.2	50	15.1	71	18.1	75
USPD	7.4	23	17.9	84	6.6	28

Source: Statistisches Jahrbuch für den Freistaat Preussen (Berlin, 1920, 1921), 16:422–23, 17:430–33; Statistisches Jahrbuch für das Deutsche Reich (Berlin, 1921), vol. 41.

The DNVP's appeal for opposition to the Weimar Republic clearly struck a responsive chord among many voters. The party did spectacularly well in both the Reichstag elections and the Prussian Landtag contest held in February 1921. Campaigning on a platform of subsidies for agriculture and small business, demands for a return to the principles of "Christian and patriotic education," and an "undivided and undiminished Prussia" as well as stressing antidemocratic, anti-Semitic, and anti-Catholic themes, the DNVP became one of the big winners of both contests.[29]

The satisfaction over the party's good showing at the polls could not, however, hide the DNVP's dilemma as to what use the German Nationalists would make of their new parliamentary strength, particularly in Prussia. The moderates continued to work for simultaneous *Bürgerblock* cabinets (coalitions among the middle-class parties) in the state and the Reich,[30] but their influence was increasingly eroded by the growing strength of the Pan-German and *völkisch* elements within the DNVP. To be sure, a few responsible party leaders, such as Siegfried von Kardoff, then a member of the Prussian Constitutional Convention, and Victor Bredt, the future head of the Economics party (WiP), resigned from the DNVP when the leadership refused to repudiate the raucous racist and radical anti-Semitic groups within the party's ranks.[31] But such individual protests had little effect upon the growing radicalization of the rank and file.[32]

The political and tactical program of the *völkisch* and Pan-German groups within the DNVP was vague and contradictory. Their propagandistic appeal was to "purely negative anti-Semitism," while tactically they put more faith in weapons, acts of violence, and conspiracies than in the ballot box.[33] The radicals were also far less interested in Prussia than were the DNVP's traditional leaders. Because of the ascendancy of the *völkisch* elements in the party, the Conservatives became increasingly "de-Prussianized."[34] Their percentage of votes in Prussia sank from 25.6 percent (1912) to 14.1 percent (1920), while their strength outside the state increased. Indeed, after the Kapp Putsch, the radicals looked with considerable interest to developments in Bavaria to further their Prussian and national aims. The Escherich Organization (Organisation Escherich, or Orgesch), a brainchild of the Bavarian forestry official Escherich, posed as a strictly civilian instrument of law and order, but it was in reality a successor organization to the Ehrhardt Brigade which had been the primary military unit involved in the putsch. The Orgesch supported the authoritarian Kahr regime in Bavaria and maintained conspiratorial contacts throughout Europe. A number of prominent DNVP figures and many among the rank and file were joint members of both the party and the Orgesch.[35] The radicals hoped that in cooperation with the Bavarian far right they would enhance the chances of a "law-and-order state" in Prussia, which would then apply a "vice grip" to the Reich in partnership with the rightist Bavarian government.[36] (There was a glaring difficulty here, since all elements in the DNVP also favored restoration of Prussia's dominant position in the Reich, a demand rejected by every Bavarian Conservative.)

By the end of 1921, the Prussian DNVP faced an unhappy paradox. The strength of the radicals within the party was gaining, but their plans for a violent seizure of power had no realistic hope of success. At the same time, the party's chances for joining a parliamentary coalition with the middle-of-the-road parties was greater than at any time since November 1918. In April 1921, for the first time since the revolution, a bourgeois cabinet without participation by the SPD governed Prussia. (This will be discussed later.) The new prime minister, Adam Stegerwald, a member of the Center party, needed the parliamentary support of the DNVP to remain in power. In addition, the DNVP-affiliated Union of Retail Clerks, whose leaders represented the majority of workers in the DNVP, was a corporate member of the non-Marxist German Labor Union (Deutscher Gewerkschaftsbund, DGB), chaired by Stegerwald.

That the moderate bourgeois parties, and especially the Center party, nevertheless rejected a coalition with the DNVP was in no small measure the result of their distrust of the growing influence of the *völkisch* and Pan-

German elements in the DNVP. By the fall of the year, at least a few of the extremists in the DNVP had added individual terror to their arsenal of destabilizing tactics. A series of political murders reached a climax in August with the assassination of the former Reich finance minister (and prominent leader of the Center party) Matthias Erzberger. Such political murders widened the gap between the DNVP and potential political partners still further and even the head of the Pan-Germans, Heinrich Class, denounced individual acts of terror as politically senseless and counterproductive.[37] Still, the DNVP's third national convention, which met in Munich at the beginning of September, 1921, defeated a resolution expelling the virulent *völkisch* groups from the party. When the fourth party congress (at the end of October, 1922, in Görlitz) finally divested the party of them, the opportunity to join a bourgeois government and thus regain part of the Conservatives' position of power in Prussia had passed.

The Center Party

Among the major Prussian parties, the Center party went through the most profound political metamorphosis as measured against its prerevolutionary stance. Before 1918 the party saw itself as a bulwark against liberalism and socialism.[38] Until a few months before the end of the war, it rejected meaningful reforms of the three-class electoral system in favor of cooperation with the Conservatives in the Prussian legislature.[39] In contrast, during the Weimar years, the Center party became a solid pillar of support for the left-of-center coalitions in the state.

There was a pattern of consistency underlying these seemingly opportunistic turns of political orientation. The common denominator remained securing Catholic influence in cultural and particularly educational affairs. Prussian Catholics, a minority of the population in a state whose pre-1918 elite was proudly and aggressively Protestant, had always felt excluded from their rightful share of political power and influence. Since the end of the *Kulturkampf*, however, the Center party as the political arm of Prussian Catholicism had cooperated with the ruling elite in the state in order to safeguard and defend Catholic rights and institutions. It was, to be sure, a defensive alliance of unequals. The pattern of cooperation also meant that until 1918 the Center party in Prussia was dominated by its right wing. During the war, locals of the extreme right-wing Fatherland party (Vaterlandspartei) in Catholic areas were often founded by members of the Center party.[40]

With the introduction of universal suffrage and the establishment of the parliamentary form of government, further reliance on the tactics of the past would have meant political suicide.[41] Power and influence now rested upon success at the polls, and in this area the Center party had fallen short of its goal. There remained a substantial pool of potential voters that the Center party was not able to tap; typically the party received 50 percent of the eligible Catholic votes. It was also clear that most of these potential supporters were Catholic blue-collar workers, especially in the Rhenish-Westphalian industrial region, that is, voting blocs who sympathized more with the position of the SPD than the DNVP.[42]

After the revolution the Prussian Center party reversed political direction, opening the party to left-of-center coalitions with the Social Democrats and left Liberals. Remarkably, the shift was accomplished with a seemingly high degree of continuity in personnel; the old party leaders nominally remained in office after 1918. The Center caucus in the Prussian Constitutional Convention was headed by Felix Porsch (age 66), and Carl Herold (71), both of whom had seen long years of service in the prewar Prussian legislature.[43] The actual party leadership, however, increasingly fell to two younger men, Joseph Hess (41) and Adam Stegerwald (45). In this duo, Hess, who was by profession a schoolteacher, was largely responsible for cultural and educational affairs, while Stegerwald acted as spokesman on social policies. Stegerwald dropped out of the Prussian political limelight in 1921, but Hess during his long years of parliamentary service in Prussia (he died in 1930) developed a smoothly functioning partnership with his counterpart in the Social Democratic caucus, Ernst Heilmann. Hess's task was also facilitated by the fact that most delegates in the Constitutional Convention were political newcomers. Few of the party members who had opposed the reform of the suffrage laws in the Landtag of 1913 managed to remain politically alive in Weimar Germany.[44]

Nevertheless, the socially heterogeneous composition of the Prussian Center party made it difficult at times for Hess and the other leaders to maintain the party on its new left-of-center course. The party's agricultural wing (with which the nominal head of the party, Herold, identified himself) and the Catholic clergy remained suspicious of cooperation with the Socialists and favored exploring the possibilities of a partnership with the Conservatives instead.[45] The Center party accommodated such pressures through its political propaganda. In its campaign rhetoric of 1919 and 1921, the Center party made no distinction between left- and right-wing socialists and blamed "the Social Democrats" for the revolution and its educational policies.[46] Yet following the election, as will be discussed later, the party did not hesitate to enter into coalition negotiations with the SPD.

The Reichstag elections of June 1920 (see table 3) demonstrated the rapid polarization of German politics that had profound implications for the future of parliamentary democracy. Above all, the election results underscored the key position occupied by the Center party. For the next twelve years it would become impossible to form a government without Center party participation in the Reich or Prussia.[47] Consequently, the Center party faced the necessity of deciding whether it should use its influence to establish a right-of-center or a left-of-center coalition. The national party organization turned increasingly to the right, but the Prussian party did not follow the lead of the national party. A key factor strengthening the Prussians' resolve to reject a turn to the right was the Kapp Putsch, since for many Prussian Catholics Kapp and his followers personified the anti-Catholic conservatism of prewar Prussia.[48]

A curious and potentially dangerous challenge to the Prussians' center-left course emerged in the fall of 1920 when Adam Stegerwald proposed the formation of a new national party. At the October 1920 national congress of the Catholic union movement (DGB), Stegerwald made an impassioned plea for the establishment of a new "comprehensive middle-of-the-road party," that is, a mass party using the DGB and the Center party as its political and organizational basis. The plan, which actually originated with Stegerwald's assistant, Heinrich Brüning, was designed to establish a "strong political center" in Germany, but from the beginning the efforts were entangled in contradictions. For all his avowed interest in creating a centrist party, Stegerwald tended to emphasize only the dangers from the left. He regarded Marxism as a pernicious force among the German working classes, and consequently saw the SPD, the largest Marxist party, as the primary obstacle to his long-range plans. The Catholic labor leaders' relationship to right-of-center groups was considerably more cordial; Stegerwald wanted to be remembered as the political leader who brought the middle-of-the-road and the rightist parties together.[49]

The response to Stegerwald's speech from all sides was disappointing. The left-wing parties rejected the initiative out of hand, but the rightist parties were also skeptical. The DVP ignored the effort, and even the labor wing of the DNVP, which had close affiliations with the DGB, voiced apprehensions that the new party might be dominated by Catholics.[50] Precisely the opposite fears contributed to the cool response from within the Center party. While Prussia and Prussian politics had no major part in the development of Stegerwald's plans, the Prussian wing of the Center party did play a decisive role in their demise. The left wing of the Center's Prussian parliamentary group argued that the key to political stability lay in cooperation with the SPD and the maintenance of the Weimar coalition. The members of the clerical-conservative wing disliked cooperation with the Socialists, but here memories of the *Kulturkampf* remained strong. The *Kulturkampf* convinced particularly the clerics in the Center party that only if the party remained an exclusively Catholic interest group could it serve as a real bulwark protecting the Catholic minority against Protestant excesses.[51]

The reaction of the Center party's leadership indicated where German political Catholicism did not want to go, but its leaders remained deeply divided over the future of the unreconstructed party.[52] From mid-1920 to the summer of 1921, the party remained divided despite the conciliatory efforts of its new national chairman, an inoffensive Rhenish judge, Wilhelm Marx.[53] Only the tragic murder of Matthias Erzberger in August 1921 brought a clarification of sorts. The assassins were allied with the *völkisch* wing of the DNVP, and their deed completely discredited any efforts to move the party toward intensified cooperation with the German Nationalists.[54] In Prussia the Center party in November 1921 agreed to a grand coalition that included the SPD, but excluded the German Nationalists.

The formation of the grand coalition completed the political reorientation of the Center party in Prussia. Starting as silent partners of the Conservatives before the war, the party became an uneasy associate of the Social Democrats after the revolution. Until the end of 1921, the Prussian Catholics went through a period of deep internal strife, but then the actions of radical-right terrorists pursuaded the party to take its place permanently in a left-of-center coalition.

The National Liberals and the German People's Party

The right-wing liberal party, the National Liberals, was not a major political factor in prewar Prussia. True, they held almost a fifth of the seats in the legislature (16.5 percent in 1913), but the National Liberals were regarded as loyal confederates of the Conservatives without a real profile of their own. The party's role became crucial, however, during the war. With the failure of Bethmann Hollweg's "politics of the diagonal" and his successor's inability to stabilize the domestic situation, the leader of the National Liberals in Prussia became a key element in the development of de facto parliamentarism. When Georg Michaelis, who followed Bethmann Hollweg as Reich chancellor and Prussian prime minister, proved incompetent after only a few months, his successor, Georg Hertling, left the task of governing Prussia to others. As a man of advanced age who had spent his entire public career outside of Prussia, he had neither the qualifications nor the time seriously to concern himself with Prussian affairs. Instead, Hertling agreed to the selection of the National Liberal leader in Prussia, Robert Friedberg, as his deputy and de facto prime minister of Prussia.

Except for his ethnic background, Friedberg was in many ways a typical representative of Wilhelminian right-wing liberalism.[55] After his conversion from Judaism to Christianity in 1884, he pursued an academic career teaching political science at the University in Leipzig. He was elected to the lower house of the Prussian parliament in 1893, and named chairman of the National Liberal delegation in 1913. His liberalism primarily took the form of anti-clericalism; in other aspects of political life, his opinions tended to be quite conservative.[56] Friedberg distrusted the Social Democrats; in the spring of

1914, he still looked upon them as a "rabid cancerous growth in the German body politic."[57] For most of the war years he remained a reactionary chauvinist. As late as July 1917, he threatened to resign all of his party offices if the National Liberal Reichstag delegation voted for Erzberger's peace resolution, and Friedberg did not support any reform of the Prussian electoral system until just before he assumed his executive post.[58] Despite all this, Friedberg was not an uncompromising and dogmatic fanatic, but a politician of considerable tactical skill. And like the national leader of the right-wing Liberals, Stresemann, he had a much more realistic eye for the deteriorating domestic situation than for Germany's military weaknesses. Friedberg still expected a military victory in the summer of 1918.

Electoral reforms became the crucible of Friedberg's future political career. In accepting the post of deputy prime minister, Friedberg had in effect agreed to support speedy enactment of meaningful reforms. In the case of the Progressives, an atmosphere of trust was quickly established, but Friedberg's relationship to the Center party and even more so to the SPD remained strained.[59] More significantly, the deputy prime minister also faced serious opposition within his own party: one-third of the National Liberal lawmakers voted with Conservatives and Center against any significant reform of the electoral laws, blocking the enactment of electoral reform legislation until the end of the war.[60]

The opposition within his own party undoubtedly made it easier for Friedberg to turn his back on his colleagues when the liberal parties were reorganized after the empire's collapse in November 1918. Stresemann and Friedberg had originally sought to preserve the National Liberal party organization as a rallying point for right and left Liberals, but by mid-December 1918, Friedberg, in contrast to Stresemann, regarded this attempt as futile; he saw no further place for a National Liberal party in republican Germany.[61] Instead he joined the successor organization to the Progressives, the German Democratic party (DDP).

At first, political developments seemed to support Friedberg's assessment of the situation. Stresemann was able to create a successor organization to the National Liberal party, the German People's party, but it appeared that the new party had been politically stillborn. It could not even run a full slate of candidates in the Prussian elections of January 26, 1919, and the election results reflected the right Liberals' organizational and political weakness. The DVP received only 5.7 percent of the vote and twenty-one parliamentary seats (5.2 percent). (In 1913, it will be recalled, the National Liberals had received seventy-three seats, or 16.5 percent.) Moreover, the Prussian DVP suffered from leadership problems after 1918. The small parliamentary delegation was composed mostly of holdovers from the prewar Landtag under the nominal leadership of a man, von Krause, whose passion was hunting rather than political work. The actual leader was Ernst von Richter, but he suffered from a role conflict, which, some of his colleagues felt, lessened his effectiveness as an opposition leader. In addition to his legislative position, Richter served as provincial governor of Hanover. In the latter position he was a Prussian civil servant and as such was subordinate to the Prussian secretary of the interior. After the revolution the minister was a Social Democrat, so that Richter in his role as governor was a civil servant in an administration which he opposed as parliamentary leader of the DVP.[62]

In the first year of its existence, a majority of the Prussian DVP not only opposed the administration, but also regarded parliamentary democracy itself as an unsuitable form of government for state and Reich.[63] Some tactical agreements between the DVP and the parties of the Weimar coalition— Center party, the DDP, and the SPD—were possible on the question of Prussia's future role in the Reich and on educational issues,[64] but in general in the first year of its existence the DVP's attitudes and policies gave the impression that the National Liberals were merely continuing their role as junior partners of the Conservatives. Indeed, negotiations regarding a possible fusion of the two parties took place intermittently after February 1919. They proved to be unsuccessful largely because negotiators for the two parties started from incompatible points of departure. The DNVP wanted more or less to absorb the smaller party, while the DVP (and especially Stresemann) sought a relationship of equals. An agreement worked out by representatives of both groups in June 1919 was rejected by Stresemann and the Prussian delegation, and shortly afterward the two parties gave up the merger attempt.[65]

The DVP did not merge with the DNVP, but that decision still left it with an identity problem. Primarily for this reason during the first year and a half of its existence, the party seemed more concerned with its relationship to its left-Liberal rival than with establishing a positive, issue-oriented image of its own. The attitude was understandable since the battle of the two Liberal parties was one of political life and death. Without the protection of the three-class system of voting, both parties had to appeal to the same strata of voters. The left Liberals had received the support of the vast majority of these potential allies in the election of 1919 (the DDP had three times as many delegates in the Prussian Constitutional Convention as the DVP), so that the DVP could survive and grow only at the expense of the DDP.[66] In addition, particularly in Prussia personality clashes increased the bitterness between the two parties.[67]

The Kapp-Lüttwitz Putsch marked a real watershed in the DVP's evolution. To put it in somewhat oversimplified terms, the DVP cut the bonds that had tied it firmly to the Conservative camp and moved toward the middle of the road.[68] The development was somewhat surprising, since the involvement in the preparation of the enterprise and the initial reaction to the coup by DVP leaders seemed to parallel closely the activities of the DNVP. A number of DVP party leaders met with Lüttwitz several times before the putsch.[69] After the putschists had gained control of Berlin in the early morning hours of March 13, 1920, the party's right wing demanded a clear recognition of the Kapp government, though some party leaders condemned the putsch. In the end, the party compromised on a proclamation which, as one Prussian DVP leader, Eugen Leidig, put it, "declared the neutrality of the party, but still expressed a certain benevolence toward the men forming the new government."[70]

This stand, moderately favorable toward the putsch, went too far for Gustav Stresemann. The DVP's leader felt that the actions by the conspirators might well escalate into a full-scale civil war. (The consequences of their actions will be discussed later.) In the face of that danger, Stresemann was convinced the DVP had to pull back from its purely oppositional stance, even if it meant a break with the Conservatives. In Stresemann's view, the People's party now had to be willing to play a positive role in the political life of the republic as a leader of the liberal camp. The proposed shift to the left was not endorsed by all sections of the party. Particularly some older members favored a continuation of the old antirepublican stance in partnership with the DNVP, and for a time after the putsch they still dominated the Prussian DVP.[71]

Paradoxically, the party's success in the Reichstag election in June 1920 only intensified the internal party debate. The DVP's success at the polls enabled a large number of younger party members to move into the national parliament, and they were willing to follow Stresemann's lead in agreeing to become one of the coalition parties making up the Reich cabinet headed by Fehrenbach of the Center party. The Prussian delegation, however, received no infusion of new members, since there was no state election between January 1919 and February 1921. As a result, the Prussian and Reich DVP seemed to pursue opposite courses of action.[72] While Stresemann pushed for cooperation with the SPD in the form of a grand coalition at the Reich level, the eloquent Prussian party leader, Ernst von Richter (who was dismissed from his post as governor of Hanover in the wake of the Kapp Putsch), rejected any cooperation with the Social Democrats.[73] Still, the shift in Prussia was only delayed. Complaining that "extreme elements were gaining dominance in the DNVP," the DVP during the summer and fall of 1920 increasingly went its separate way.[74] Symptomatic was the party's decision in October to vote for the Prussian republican constitution, while the DNVP delegates unanimously rejected it.

The DVP welcomed the elections of February 1921, fully expecting them to provide a decisive breakthrough for the right Liberals. The party sought to benefit from a double image. Having joined a moderate coalition government in the Reich, and having voted for the new Prussian constitution, the DVP had proved its ability to act responsibly, while at the same time its opposition to the Weimar coalition in Prussia showed that it held firm to the ideals of the political right. The DVP campaigned with the promise that it would add its voice to those wishing to form moderate cabinets in the Reich and in Prussia that were free of Socialist influence, a promise that its left-Liberal rival could clearly not make.[75]

The election results demonstrated both the benefits and dangers of a two-faced campaign. The People's party gained popular votes and parliamentary seats at the expense of the DDP, but the DVP also lost a considerable number of its former voters to the DNVP, whose stand on the republic and the restoration of an authoritarian monarchy was unequivocal.[76] Still, since there were clearly few votes to be picked up on the right side of the political spectrum, the election results strengthened the hand of those within the party who endorsed a clear break with the DNVP and a simultaneous cooperation with the SPD in the Reich and in Prussia.[77] In the Reich cabinet the DVP increasingly refused to play the role of Trojan horse for monarchist restorationism which the DNVP had assigned to it.[78] The assassination of Erzberger and the SPD's Görlitz Program (to be discussed later), which represented a victory for the reform-minded right-wing Social Democrats, only widened the chasm between the right Liberals and the Conservatives. At a meeting of DVP Landtag and Reichstag delegations in Heidelberg, which took place at the same time as the Social Democratic party convention in Görlitz, a majority voted in favor of cooperation with the SPD.[79] The way was paved for a grand coalition in Prussia as well as in the Reich.

The Progressive People's Party and the German Democratic Party

The history of the left Liberals in the years 1914–1921 was almost the mirror image of that of their right-Liberal rivals. Without influence in prewar Prussia, the party briefly became a left-of-center mass party in 1919, but the left Liberals maintained their position at the pinnacle of political popularity for only about a year. The Reichstag elections of June 1920 brought a sharp decline, while the DVP surged ahead. The Prussian Landtag vote confirmed the reversal of political fortunes. Thereafter the left Liberals remained in the shadow of the resurgent People's party.

In the last prewar Landtag, the Progressives (FVP) held thirty-eight seats (8.6 percent), which meant that they wielded little political influence. The party was notable primarily because it was the only German bourgeois group favoring reforms of the Prussian electoral system. (Incidentally, their reformist zeal did not extend to local politics. Here the three-class system of voting gave distinct privileges to owners of real property and the Progressives traditionally represented urban landlords and homeowners.) The FVP was also the only bourgeois party willing to cooperate at least to some extent with the Social Democrats at the state level. The two parties concluded a series of tactical agreements in a number of runoff elections for the state legislature.

After the revolution the party renamed and reorganized itself. As the German Democratic party (DDP), the left Liberals hoped to become the successor organization to both the Progressives and the National Liberals. The resultant mass middle-class party would then lead the German progressive bourgeoisie into the Republican era in cooperation with the Social Democrats.[80] In the first postrevolutionary elections, large numbers of voters seemed to agree with the DDP's stand. However, even in these early months it was unclear whether the voters regarded the DDP as a link to the Social Democrats or as a bulwark against the "Marxists," especially since the DDP itself propagated "the prevention of a Social Democratic majority" as one of its goals, and fought its election campaign with some vehemently anti-Socialist slogans.[81]

The DDP delegation in the Landesversammlung was made up largely of parliamentary newcomers, although the leader of the delegation, Robert Friedberg, was certainly a veteran legislator. Only seven members of the DDP delegation were former National Liberals and sixteen former Progressives; forty-three had no previous parliamentary experience.[82] Despite its numerical strength, the party had a number of serious problems. In addition to political inexperience, the party lacked ideological consistency, and was beset by leadership problems.[83] Friedrich Naumann, the Progressives' long-time and universally venerated national leader, died in the summer of 1919. He was succeeded by Friedberg, but the Prussian leader, though a clever tactician, was no ideological mentor for the party. Several men sought to fill the vacuum.[84] The result was an increasingly bitter intraparty struggle over the future profile of the DDP as a left-of-center or right-of-center organization.

The debate over acceptance or rejection of the Treaty of Versailles began a process of disintegration that was accelerated by reaction to the Kapp Putsch.[85] Although the Prussian DDP firmly opposed both the Treaty of Versailles and the Kapp Putsch, the lack of unity within the Reichstag delegation during the treaty debates and the ambiguous role played by Vice-Chancellor Schiffer (DDP) during the putsch gave the party a chameleon like image.[86] In the June 1920 Reichstag elections, the DDP's strategy of portraying itself as the link between the liberal bourgoisie and the right wing of the Social Democratic party suffered an ignominious defeat. The DDP not only lost most of the voters who had turned to it for the first time in 1919, but also large numbers of those who had voted left Liberal in prewar years now found a new political home in the People's party. The hard-core DDP voters were seemingly reduced to some members of the old *Mittelstand* and parts of the bureaucracy and the teaching profession.[87]

The setbacks in the Reich certainly affected the Prussian DDP's morale as well, though the issues involved had no direct connection with the state.[88] Far more serious for the Prussian party was the unexpected death of its leader in June 1920, a few months before the Prussian Landtag elections.[89] In addition, during the Prussian campaign the DDP faced intense political competition from two sides. Just in time for the Landtag contest, the Economics party (WiP) entered the political arena competing for the votes of the traditionally left-Liberal homeowners, while the DVP renewed its efforts to capture the DDP's right wing.[90] The first Landtag elections did indeed prove to be a political disaster for the DDP. Only a small percentage of earlier left-Liberal voters honored the slogan "return to political moderation"; the majority moved further to the right along the political spectrum. The party sacrificed forty of its sixty-six parliamentary seats; the greater part to the DVP, a smaller number to the Economics party. The left Liberals faced a bleak future: they had lost the traditional middle-class vote and were unable to make inroads into the ranks of the new white-collar occupations.[91]

After the returns were in, the debate over the causes of the debacle began. "Reactionaries" blamed "radicals" and vice versa. The left wing of the Prussian delegation under the leadership of Otto Nuschke and Hugo Preuss pushed for a clear statement of intent to continue the Weimar coalition with the SPD, while the right wing under the leadership of Erich Koch-Weser and Alexander Dominicus sought to put as much political distance between the DDP and the SPD as possible.[92] The party leadership remained weak and undecided as to which course of action to follow. Friedberg's successor as party chairman, the mayor of Hamburg, Carl Petersen, refused to become involved in Prussian affairs. Here, too, only the assassination of Erzberger and the SPD's Görlitz Program brought a temporary clarification of sorts: the acute danger from the extreme right and the victory of the reformers in the SPD persuaded the Prussian DDP, as it had the Reichstag delegation earlier, that only a coalition stretching from the SPD to the DVP could stabilize the political situation.[93]

The Social Democrats

In one important respect the evolution of the Social Democratic parties paralleled that of the liberal groups. The Social Democrats, too, were more concerned with defeating their ideological rivals than with attracting new groups of voters. Perhaps even more than in the case of the liberals, the relationship between the three successor parties to the prewar Social Democrats was a sort of love-hate relationship, with the leaders more concerned with the differences, while the rank-and-file members emphasized the commonalities.[94] This resulted in chronic tensions not only between the parties, but also within them, between party leaders and rank-and-file members.

In prewar Prussia, the Social Democrats remained both by choice and necessity outside the political process. Self-isolation, political and social rejection by most bourgeois lawmakers, as well as the realization of their political impotence in the state, foreclosed any attempts to initiate legislation in conjunction with the other groups.[95] Instead, the Prussian SPD projected a particularly radical image as spokesman of the industrial proletariat and vanguard of the forces threatening Prussian authoritarianism. Its propaganda stressed sharp opposition to bourgeois values. While the party at the Reich level sought not to arouse religious controversies, one of the most prominent orators of the Prussian SPD was Adolph Hoffmann, a man known for his vehement attacks on organized religion.[96]

The crucial importance of the three-class system of voting in maintaining Prussia's prewar authoritarianism led the Prussian SPD to concentrate its campaigns almost exclusively on this issue. It was, as the SPD well knew, a futile exercise, and few ambitious national leaders ran for a seat in the Prussian legislature. As a result, until 1913 the necessarily small number of delegates to the Landtag consisted almost exclusively of members of the Berlin party organization. Of the seven SPD delegates who served in the lower house between 1910 and 1913, six (Hermann Borgmann, Hugo Heinemann, Paul Hirsch, Karl Liebknecht, Heinrich Ströbel, Adolph Hoffmann) were closely involved with party life in the capital. Hoffmann and Liebknecht were also Reichstag delegates. There was only one member from outside the capital, Robert Leinert, a union official from Hanover. The elections of 1913 brought two other prominent union leaders from the provinces to the Landtag, Otto Braun from East Prussia and Otto Hue from the Ruhr area, but the majority of the SPD delegates remained Berlin party functionaries. In the Reich and some other German states, lively debates centered on "negative integration" and whether it was possible for the party's state legislators to vote for a bourgeois budget, but in Germany's largest state the Social Democrats remained radical and isolated prior to 1914.[97]

The differences of opinion that caused the split of the Social Democratic party after the beginning of World War I were largely concerned with questions of national politics; Prussia and Prussian politics played only subordinate roles.[98] On the major Prussian issue, all elements in the party agreed that fundamental electoral reforms were absolutely essential. Nevertheless, the schism in the national party did affect the SPD in Prussia. For a time the paradoxical situation existed that the right-wing national majority formed only a minority in the Prussian legislature. The ten members of the Landtag delegation reflected the views of the three ideological wings in the party, but fully half (Liebknecht, Ströbel, Paul Hoffmann, Adolph Hoffmann, and Hofer) belonged to the left wing, which also dominated the Berlin party organization. Three delegates (Braun, Hue, Hirsch) represented the moderate approach, and two (Haenisch, Leinert) allied themselves with the party's right wing. The "Berlin Five" not only rejected the war credits from the beginning, but also took no part in the public displays of national unity, thereby rejecting the concept of the *Burgfrieden*.[99] Two of the leftist group, Liebknecht and Adolph Hoffmann, became actively involved in the conferences organized by Lenin in Zimmerwald, Switzerland.[100]

The three centrists included Paul Hirsch, the head of the SPD caucus. A recognized expert on local government, Hirsch already had a well-deserved reputation as an intraparty mediator. He tried for a long time—too long, as he later admitted—to preserve the unity of the delegation.[101] Otto Braun, too, straddled the ideological fence. He counted right-wing Socialists such as Hermann Müller and Otto Wels among his friends, but he also enjoyed the confidence of the left-radical Berlin workers, who elected him to the strike committee during the January 1918 strike of the metalworkers.[102]

A number of right-wing Social Democrats who would play leading roles in postwar Prussia were prominent in establishing the patriotic unity front that characterized the early years of the *Burgfrieden* era. Men like Albert Südekum, the future finance minister; Wolfgang Heine, after 1918 minister of justice and later minister of the interior; and Carl Severing, Heine's successor as minister of the interior in 1920, began to form or renew relationships with bourgeois parties and politicians, including the chancellor.[103] For Heine, in many ways the most outspoken and clear-headed among the rightists, the future of the SPD lay in outgrowing its proletarian base. He regarded the party as the embodiment "of the union of the politically independent parts of the German bourgeoisie with the ascending workers."[104] Ernst Heilmann, after 1918 for many years the undisputed leader of the SPD's delegation in the Prussian state legislature, had not yet moved to the front rank of the party's leadership, although his patriotic and chauvinistic writings were coming to the attention of the party's leaders.[105]

At the beginning of 1916, the Prussian delegation dropped the pretense of unity. Hirsch, the leader of the centrists and the head of the delegation, joined the left-wing majority in Prussia.[106] But the paradox of a left-wing majority in Prussia and a right-wing preponderance in the Reich was not of long duration. New initiatives within the context of the "politics of the diagonal" in 1916 and 1917, brought with it a realignment of the ideological fronts in the Prussian party. Bethmann Hollweg's seeming success in persuading the emperor to promise reforms of the Prussian electoral system—the imperial Easter message of 1916 was the pinnacle of this thrust—reopened the debate within the SPD on the question of the party's cooperation in forming Socialist-bourgeois coalitions. (At this time it could not be foreseen that the Conservatives and National Liberals would join forces to defeat Bethmann Hollweg's initiatives.) The party's right and center wings had no difficulty in advocating the SPD's participation in coalition governments with bourgeois parties— Heine wrote, "The goal is and remains a parliamentary democracy *(Volksstaat)*"—while the left rejected any cooperation with bourgeois parties.[107] Hirsch sided with the moderates on this issue, and since in 1916 the SPD's delegation in the Landtag had been reduced to nine members when Karl Liebknecht was forced to give up his seat after being convicted of treason, Hirsch's switch made the former minority the majority.[108] The remaining four delegates of the left wing then formed their own parliamentary group.

Looking back, it is evident that—aside from immediate war-related issues such as the war credits and Erzberger's peace resolution—the question of ministerial responsibility in coalitions with bourgeois parties was the issue that most clearly divided the right, center, and left wings of the Social Democratic party.[109] After the formal split of the national SPD, the Würzburg conference in August 1917 committed the party leadership of the majority Socialists to the concept of parliamentary democracy, though even that decision did not end the debate.[110] A little more than a year after the Würzburg conference, the deteriorating military and domestic situation confronted the SPD with the dilemma of cooperating with the old forces or seeing the Reich sink into chaos. Interestingly, in September 1918 Otto Braun, later prime minister of Prussia, was particularly vehement in opposing cooperation with the bourgeois parties. Pointing to the lack of domestic reforms in Prussia since the Easter Message, he insisted that the bourgeois parties had no intention of establishing a loyal working relationship with the Social Democrats.[111] The majority of the party's leaders, however, did not share his pessimism. They voted to accepted the moderate bourgeois parties' offer of a coalition Reich government, though as preconditions they insisted upon immediate reform of the Prussian electoral system and the establishment of a cabinet in Germany's largest state that reflected the actual strength of the political parties in Prussia.[112]

Following the revolution, the renewed cooperation with the left-wing Socialists in both the Reich and Prussia seemed to push the question of cooperating with bourgeois parties into the background. But the appearance was deceptive. The party leadership never shared the romantic enthusiasm of the rank-and-file membership for the reunification of the estranged brothers, and all of the SPD's ministers in Prussia during the revolutionary weeks regarded the coalition with the USPD as a purely tactical mariage de convenance; they harbored no illusions regarding any long-range cooperation with the USPD.[113] This was particularly true of the SPD's strong man in Prussia at this time, Wolfgang Heine, who became minister of justice late in

November 1918 and served as minister of the interior after the USPD left the coalition. Heine pushed the SPD to follow a clear and unambiguous political program for Germany and Prussia after the revolution: he regarded a strong Prussia as the key to German unity after 1918 as it had been before the war, and he wanted the right-wing Social Democrats to turn away from the USPD and instead cooperate closely with the left and middle-of-the-road bourgeois parties.[114] The minister had an almost pathological hatred for the USPD. He labeled the Independent Socialists the force behind the Communists; the USPD was a "pimp, who pockets the proceeds" and the KPD "the girls, who work for him."[115]

The dichotomy between the view of the SPD's leadership that in the long run the party would have to cooperate with the moderate middle-class parties to assure governmental stability in the Reich and in Prussia, and the romantic, largely irrational longing on the part of the party's rank and file for socialist unity forced the party leadership to give itself a very Janus-like image during the 1919 election campaign.[116] While cooperating with the middle-class interests at the executive level, the party's propagandists also emphasized the SPD's sharp differences with all bourgeois parties.[117] In one sense, the strategy was a complete success. The SPD was now the strongest party in the state, holding 145 seats (36 percent of the total) in the Prussian Constitutional Convention, while the erstwhile proud Conservatives were reduced to a pitiful minority. The SPD had clearly made significant inroads into new voting groups. The party retained a large part of its traditional blue-collar electorate, but it also succeeded in gaining votes among skilled independent craftsmen, small farmers in the west, and farm laborers in the eastern provinces.[118]

As it turned out, the SPD's electoral breakthrough to the status of a genuine integrative party was short-lived, but even in 1919 the euphoria over the SPD's success at the polls could not hide the fact that the Social Democrats were no nearer to solving their programmatic and ideological problems than they had been in 1914. In fact, some new ones, such as the problem of *ministerialisme* and its implications for party-state relations had been added. For Otto Wels, who headed the SPD after Friedrich Ebert became Reich president, and who never held a government post, "The [SPD's] central committee was superior to the [party's] ministers serving in the Reich government"—a view that was both politically and constitutionally untenable, but which was shared by a large number of party functionaries.[119]

The Prussian SPD faced many of the same problems as the party organization in the Reich, but in one important area, that of relations between the parliamentary group and the government ministers, it was in a more fortunate position. The Prussian Social Democrats quickly found a very talented caucus leader and parliamentary tactician in Ernst Heilmann. A series of lucky coincidences smoothed the path to political eminence for this parliamentary newcomer.[120] Since Heilmann had not been a member of the prewar parliament, he was not in line for a ministerial appointment in 1918, while the post of parliamentary leader fell vacant when almost all members of the prewar delegation did join the cabinet. (Heilmann himself even in subsequent years never aspired to ministerial status.) To be sure, Heilmann did not formally become head of the SPD delegation until November 1921, but even in 1919 he was the most effective spokesman for the party, since the two nominal heads of the party caucus in the Prussian Constitutional Convention, Richard Hauschildt (Kassel) and Wilhelm Siering (Potsdam) were neither good speakers nor clever parliamentarians. Ideologically, Heilmann belonged to the party's right wing in 1919. Landsberg, Noske, and Kuttner were his friends, and along with Haenisch he belonged to the inner circle around Parvus-Helphand, the influential editor of the journal *Die Glocke*.[121] His relations to the USPD and the Communists were correspondingly bad.[122]

Unlike some of his political associates, Heilmann honestly regarded parliamentary democracy as the best form of government. While many of his colleagues seemed uneasy about "bourgeois" or "formal" democracy and hoped for its speedy replacement by "socialism," the SPD's parliamentary leader saw parliamentary democracy at the center of a Social Democratic program that merged nationalism, socialism, and parliamentarism into a political unity. In his maiden speech to the Constitutional Convention, Heilmann expressed a hope for fruitful exchange between the majority government coalition and the views of the loyal minority opposition.[123] The opposition would severely disappoint Heilmann's expectations, but his early enthusiasm for the new form of government in Prussia undoubtedly facilitated the cooperation of the SPD with its bourgeois coalition partners, and helped smooth the SPD's initial acceptance of ministerial responsibility in Prussia.

The rapid polarization of political life in 1919 quickly destroyed Heilmann's hopes for fruitful interaction with the rightist opposition. In the face of counterrevolutionary excesses by the right, the SPD's rank and file and its middle- and lower-level provincial functionaries increasingly rejected alignment with the bourgeois parties, and favored cooperation with the USPD instead.[124] Rank-and-file pressure was particularly acute in the Reichstag delegation, but in Prussia, too, the leftward drift of party opinion forced the right-wing leadership into at least verbal gestures of appeasement. No doubt much against his convictions, even Heine felt obliged to deliver a sharp attack against the counterrevolutionary efforts of the rightist parties; unlike most of his remarks, this speech received the enthusiastic approval of the parliamentary delegation. Heilmann, for his part, joined in the chorus of those advocating cooperation and reunification with the USPD.[125]

The Kapp Putsch understandably accelerated the leftward trend in the SPD.[126] In the immediate aftermath of the coup, the Prussian party again came to be dominated by party leaders in Berlin, notably the head of the capital district's executive committee, Franz Krüger. Krüger and his allies demanded that both the Reich and the Prussian governments he placed under the joint control of the two socialist parties and the labor unions.[127] And even when the Independent Socialists refused the proposal, Krüger continued his efforts to have the labor unions exercise "decisive influence" over the Reich and Prussian governments.[128] It seemed for a time as if Krüger would be able to accomplish his goals, but, as will be seen in a later chapter, he was finally repulsed by a combination of the regrouped right wing in the SPD and the Reich president.

The SPD's poor showing in the June 1920 elections gave added impetus to the leftist tendencies in the party,[129] but it should be noted that the right wing was never completely eclipsed; it retained important positions of influence particularly in the state governments and legislatures.[130] In these circles the question of the SPD's participation in a so-called grand coalition government—that is, a cabinet in which all parties, from the SPD on the left to the DVP on the right, would be represented—was discussed most dispassionately. While in the Reich the SPD under the influence of its left wing continued to reject a grand coalition, and the party's 1920 national congress actually passed a specific resolution instructing the Reichstag delegation not to support such a government, in Prussia leading politicians began considering the idea as early as the second half of 1920.[131] In addition, some of those in the SPD, like the national chairman, Otto Wels, who opposed the grand coalition at the Reich level, stressed that the resolution against a coalition with the DVP did not automatically apply to coalitions in the states.[132]

Still, for a time after the June 1920 and February 1921 elections, the right wing seemed to be losing ground in Prussia as well. As had been true for the two liberal parties, the assassination of Erzberger was the catalyst that brought a turnaround. The political murder demonstrated to many in the Prussian SPD how dangerous it was for the party not to have "its hands on the source of power."[133] One month after Erzberger's death the 1921 party congress in Görlitz adopted a new party program that gave ideological sanction to the party's move away from a purely oppositional stance. The Görlitz Program, as it came to be known, has always had a rather tarnished reputation among the party's programs. Contemporary commentators as well as later historians derided it as a spur-of-the-moment document, designed to give an ideological vaneer to purely tactical decisions.[134] The fact that the Görlitz Program was the official party platform for only four years before it was replaced by the Heidelberg Program in 1925 heightened the impression.[135] Actually, such a view is one-sided. The Görlitz Program was not merely a response to the political crisis of August 1921. Under its chairman, Eduard Bernstein, the "father" of socialist revisionism, the program committee worked for over a year in order to create a party platform that addressed the party's future in the age of late capitalism. The Görlitz Program is noteworthy particularly for its redefinition of the proletariat to include white-collar workers, its ethical concerns, and its claim that socialism could be advanced in the context of parliamentary democracy.[136] Incidentally, the program was almost completely silent on Prussian political issues. The only direct influence of the Prussian SPD on the discussions was negative: at the express request of the Prussian SPD, the program said nothing about provincial autonomy.[137]

To be sure, the discussion of ideological issues could not be separated from the immediate tactical question of the SPD's stand on the formation of grand coalitions. As a result, the party leadership had expected violent resistance to the draft program from the left wing.[138] The opposition was indeed bitter and vociferous, but not nearly as strong as had been feared. The leftists relied largely on emotional arguments that accused the new program of breaking with the Marxist foundations of Social Democracy: the concept of class struggle, the unity of the working class, and the ideal of reuniting the USPD and the SPD.[139]

The arguments of the party leadership and the majority were skillfully delivered by the formerly leftist head of the Berlin district, Franz Krüger. Addressing the coalition issue, the Berlin leader stressed that the defense of democracy in Germany was more important than theoretical consistency. The potential dangers of forming a government coalition with the People's party were insignificant in light of the acute provocations by terrorists from the extreme right. Krüger argued that the previous distinction between cooperating with the "acceptable" DDP and the "unacceptable" DVP had become meaningless after the elections of June 1920: the DDP was becoming an "insignificant party" that was being rapidly absorbed by the DVP.[140] The leaders of the Prussian SPD supported the strongly "emotional idealization of democracy" contained in the Görlitz Program and its tactical implications.[141] Both Otto Braun and Carl Severing saw the new party program as a turning point in SPD history. Braun noted that the SPD had transformed itself from "a party emphasizing political agitation" to one that had "the will to assume power." Severing added that the party had demonstrated "the courage to assume governmental responsibility."[142] When the party congress passed an enabling resolution (containing the basic conditions under which the SPD would form a coalition with the DVP) by 290 to 67 votes, not a single member of the Prussian parliamentary delegation voted against it.[143]

While the SPD by the end of 1921 was moving into the mainstream of parliamentary and moderate politics, its left-wing rival, the Independent Social Democratic Party of Germany (USPD) had been all but absorbed by the fiercely antiparliamentary and antidemocratic Communists. As noted above, the final split of the old Social Democratic party and the establishment of the

USPD in 1917 was primarily the result of sharp divisions over the Socialists' attitude toward the German war effort. On the Prussian issue, the Social Democrats' left and right wings differed only on tactics. Both sides were in complete agreement on the abolition of the three-class system of voting, but the USPD argued that supporting the present government in the hope of obtaining gradual liberalization of the Prussian electoral system was counterproductive. The left wing was convinced that a policy advocating gradual reform was doomed to failure, since it merely helped to support the present anti-Socialist and antidemocratic regime in Prussia.

The left-wing opposition first appeared in public in June 1915, when it issued a manifesto against war credits and the *Burgfrieden,* arguing that the right-wing Socialists, who continued to support the imperial government, had "planted a cross on the grave of the class struggle."[144] Both at that time and when the SPD formally split some two years later, the major centers of Independent strength lay outside of Prussia. Only two electoral districts dominated by the USPD were in the state—Berlin and Frankfurt. In the areas east of the Elbe, the Independents had no significant organization, and in the western industrial regions they dominated only in part of the Lower Rhenish district.[145]

The lack of organizational strength was paralleled by the new party's lack of interest in Prussian developments. This proved to be a clear disadvantage in November 1918 when the party agreed to govern Prussia jointly with the SPD and to fill a number of ministerial posts. In effect, the positions were filled by default. This was true even of such an important position as the head of the Ministry of the Interior. While the SPD sent its prime minister to head Interior, the USPD chose Dr. Rudolf Breitscheid more or less because it did not know what else to do.[146] Breitscheid was an elegant man, an effective, almost demagogic speaker, but not a politician given to making decisions and even less a good administrator.[147] A radical democrat more than a Marxist, Breitscheid regarded the left-Liberal Theodor Barth, not Karl Marx, as his political mentor. Moreover, Breitscheid would have preferred to become Reich foreign minister rather than being named to the Prussian Ministry of the Interior.[148] The other USPD ministers did have what might be considered previous acquaintance with the issues they would face in their new positions. Kurt Rosenfeld (Justice), one of the few leading Social Democrats with a law degree, was known to the public principally as the defense attorney for Karl Liebknecht, and Adolph Hoffmann (Education) had made a name for himself as a fierce opponent of the royal government's educational and religious policies. The co-minister of finance, Hugo Simon, left the limelight to his SPD colleague, Südekum, although as a banker, Simon was a specialist in the field. In the Ministry of Agriculture the Independent appointee, Hofer, was similarly eclipsed by his SPD colleague, Otto Braun.[149] As a group, the

USPD ministers of the Prussian cabinet were certainly not proto-Bolsheviks. It is symptomatic that all of them later returned to the SPD when the USPD itself split in 1920. (Only Adolph Hoffman joined the Communists for a time before returning to the SPD.)

At the beginning of 1919, the USPD seemed to take extraordinary interest in Prussian politics. After the failure of the Spartacus uprising and the Independents' disappointing showing in the national elections, Prussia appeared to be an important bulwark to prevent the flooding of Germany with bourgeois–Social Democratic coalitions. The USPD had previously demanded the dissolution of the state, but now the destruction of Prussia was no longer under discussion; the largest state of the Reich should become a bridgehead for the USPD's triumphal march through Germany. But the interest quickly faded when the USPD did only little better on January 26, 1919, than it had in the national elections a week earlier. This was ironic, since in the course of 1919 it became increasingly apparent that the January results had little relation to the actual and growing strength of the party. Thousands of working-class voters, disappointed with the lack of government action in the areas of socialization and democratization, turned their backs on the SPD and became USPD supporters. But the Independents were unable to weld the masses of voters and members into a unified political power base. The political history of the left-wing Socialists in 1919 and 1920 was in a sense the mirror image of the difficulties the DNVP experienced at the same time. The USPD was beset by internal contradictions, just as the DNVP was, and it, too, tried to mask these through demands for new elections and uncontrolled verbal radicalism. Continuing ideological and organizational dissensions, of which the most important was the controversy over whether or not the USPD should affiliate itself with the Moscow-dominated Communist International, increasingly paralyzed the party.[150] The high-level ideological debates pushed Prussian affairs into the background; the USPD's role in state politics was limited to incessant and demagogic attacks on the government.[151]

In pursuing its object of toppling the government, the Prussian USPD followed two parallel tactical lines. On the one hand, it presented the bourgeois-Social Democratic coalition as an act of treason against the working class, concentrating its venom particularly on the cooperation between the SPD and the Center party, an arrangement that the Independents knew was unpopular among many of the rank and file of the SPD.[152] This tactic was aimed at drawing working-class support away from the SPD. At the same time the USPD attempted to split the SPD's Prussian leadership. Concentrating their attacks on Heilmann, Haenisch, and, of course, Heine, the Independents held out hopes that once the SPD had disavowed these "unacceptables," the USPD might cooperate in forming a Socialist unity government.[153]

The USPD's call for Socialist unity was not as unrealistic in 1919 as it might appear. The assassination of the party's national leader, Hugo Haase, in September 1919 was not politically motivated (the murderer was a disgruntled officeseeker), but the death of this universally respected Socialist leader led to an outpouring of sympathy toward the USPD by all members of the Social Democratic movement. The increasingly brazen acts of right-wing counter-revolutionaries also brought the two parties closer together, reaching a climax in their joint reaction to the Kapp Putsch, when both parties supported and actively organized the general strike that was a major factor in the defeat of Kapp and his right-wing vigilantes.[154]

The cooperation of the two estranged Socialist parties did not continue beyond Kapp's defeat, largely because by that time the Independents were already divided among themselves. The majority of USPD activists had decided to join the Communist International, while the party's national leaders tried desperately to follow a more moderate approach. The result was a series of contradictory stands taken by the party leadership during the crucial weeks after the putsch. On March 25, the leaders declared that only a government by "socialist workers of all persuasions" could save the revolution, but two days later, *Die Freiheit,* the USPD's central party organ (which was dominated by the forces of the party's right wing) seemed to represent the more moderate line.[155] The paper denied that the USPD could only join a socialist coalition; it announced that a final decision on this matter had not been made.[156] But three weeks later still, one of the party's reputed moderators, Arthur Crispien, again demanded a "socialist government" that would inaugurate "the epoch of the dictatorship of the proletariat."[157]

Ironically, while the party was politically paralyzed, it was also receiving the largest influx of new members and voters in its history. In the months between the end of the Kapp Putsch and the party's national congress in October 1920, the Independents became a major force on the political left, giving the USPD the deceptive bloom of a party suffering from political consumption.[158] Briefly it even appeared that the party might use its political strength constructively in Prussia. At the Reich level the USPD was opposed to all coalition governments; but in the states the party seemed to pursue a more flexible line. Wilhelm Dittman stressed in a semiofficial declaration that coalitions in the states would have to be decided on a case-by-case basis.[159] At the same time, the Prussian SPD's shift in leadership from Hirsch and Heine to Braun and Severing, along with favorable comments on the later two in the pages of the USPD press, seemed to hold out hope that Prussia might be one arena in which the Independents would accept governmental responsibility.[160]

The hope proved futile. Before the USPD's leadership could come to any positive decision, the party split and disintegrated. A special party congress in Halle in October 1920 voted to join the Communist International, a decision that most of the national leadership opposed. The left wing of the party's leadership, along with the bulk of the party's members, eventually joined the KPD.[161] What remained of the USPD was clearly not in a favorable position to campaign for the first regular state elections in February 1921. The party concentrated its attacks on the SPD, although the rump USPD also anticipated future cooperation with the right-wing Socialists, particularly in the form of extraparliamentary responses to what the USPD expected to be a new right-wing putsch attempt in the latter half of 1920.[162]

The Halle Congress marked the death knell of the USPD, but it was the beginning of the Communists' rise to political influence both in the Reich and in Prussia. The party had not run any candidates in the election for the Prussian Constitutional Convention, and its inconsistent policies during the Kapp Putsch further alienated potential supporters and voters. In retrospect, all observers agreed that the KPD's stance during the Kapp Putsch was a serious political mistake.[163] The party had enjoyed particularly strong support among the Berlin workers, so that it was in a key position to lead the resistance in the capital against the putsch forces.[164] However, the party's leadership was unable to rise to the occasion. It wavered between supporting a common front of SPD, USPD, and KPD on the one hand, and organizing preparations for an armed countercoup that would lead to the establishment of the dictatorship of the proletariat on the other. Initially, the party's leadership refused to support the call for a general strike, only to change its mind a few hours later. Yet, while the party's support of the general strike committed it to support nonviolent opposition to the putsch, the KPD also continued to sponsor armed vigilante groups in Berlin.[165]

There is no doubt that the KPD's vacillating course severely damaged its standing among German workers. The party was rescued from a descent into political oblivion by the ineptitudes of the reconstituted governments of the Reich and Prussia (to be discussed later) and the vote of a majority of the USPD to align itself with the Communist International. In the February 1921 state elections, the USPD lost about two-thirds of the votes it had gained in June 1920. Some went to the SPD, but by far the larger number of old USPD voters cast their ballots for the Communist party. In the first Weimar Landtag, the Communists formed the fifth largest parliamentary group.

The history of the major political groups in Prussia in the years 1914–1921 represented a decisive break with developments before the war. The dominant forces of authoritarianism, the Conservatives and National Liberals, were reduced to minority status and had little influence in the postrevolutionary parliaments, while the politically impotent prewar Social Democrats became the leading party in the state.

At the same time, the reversed power relationships did not endanger political stability in the state under the new governmental form of parliamentary democracy. The tentative, prewar cooperation of the SPD and the left Liberals developed, at least briefly, into the full-fledged coalition of two major mass parties. They were joined by the Prussian Center party, which for reasons of its own, turned to the left after the revolution. The new opposition parties at the left and right extremes of the political spectrum remained weak. The DNVP, successor to the Conservatives, was paralyzed by major internal divisions over tactics, while its support of Prussia's territorial integrity turned it into a de facto ally of the Weimar coalition on this crucial issue. The extreme left (the USPD and the KPD) was if anything even more divided and, in addition, tended to ignore Prussian politics for the most part.

The state elections of February 1921, in which the antidemocratic forces certainly gained votes and delegates, while the parties of the Weimar coalition suffered severe losses, had a less significant political impact in Prussia than was the case in the Reich six months earlier. While no fundamental differences divided the parties of the Weimar coalition, the opposition was paralyzed by division. The end of the prewar alliance of Conservatives and National Liberals destroyed any hope of a united right, and on the left side of the political spectrum the Communists had little interest in state affairs.

CHAPTER 2

Cabinets and Coalitions, 1914–1921

The process of political decision making under the rules of parliamentary democracy was a completely new experience for Prussia. The constitution of 1851 contained no provisions for ministerial responsibility, and, in any case, the three-class system of voting precluded the election of a truly representative legislature. To make parliamentary democracy viable, coalitions, compromises, and close cooperation between legislature and cabinet would have to replace parliamentary passivity and autonomous royal control of the executive, the salient features of Prussia's authoritarian political system before 1918.

War and revolution, of course, also brought democracy to the Reich, although it could be argued that at the national level the systemic changes were less radical than at the state level. After all, the Reichstag had been democratically elected since 1871, and after 1890 the national parliament played an increasingly important role in German political life. In contrast to the state, where before 1918 the reformist groups were completely excluded from political power, the parties that would become the dominant forces in the Weimar years—Social Democrats, Liberals, and Catholics—had had at least some experience with wielding power at the Reich level.

For this reason, the divergent experience with coalition politics in Prussia and the Reich during the early republican years is all the more remarkable. Both in the Reich and in Prussia the first parliamentary governments were coalitions of parity,[1] that is, they involved parties of approximately equal parliamentary strength. The national coalition collapsed in 1919, and thereafter the Reich was for the most part governed by minority cabinets that remained in office only as long as the parliamentary opposition did not combine forces to topple them. In sharp contrast, the Prussian coalition not only survived its first year in office, but as a rule it was the opposition, rather than the government, that suffered from political paralysis.

The paradox of parliamentary democracy's failure at the national level and its success in Prussia has puzzled both contemporaries and later historians. Explanations, as we shall see, range from the idea that Prussian stability succeeded by sheer luck to the thesis that it was achieved at the expense of the Reich—that is, democracy at the national level failed because the problem of Reich-Prussian relations was not solved.[2] Few analysts, however, have

43

pointed to the significance of the striking continuity in the consciousness of the political leaders of prewar Prussia and their successors after the revolution. Like their royal predecessors, the new democratic leadership regarded Prussia's territorial integrity and political stability as the cornerstone of German national unity and the viability of its political system. The old leaders saw Prussia as an authoritarian bulwark of the empire; for their republican successors, Prussia was the indispensable guardian of democracy against attempts to restore authoritarian monarchism to Germany. Parliamentary democracy in Prussia worked after 1918 because, as far as the state's new leaders were concerned, without it the state could not fulfill its paradigmatic role in the new Germany. That realization would prove to be a powerful incentive in making coalition politics a success in Prussia.

The Prussian Government during World War I

Before the outbreak of the war, the men who governed Prussia constituted a socially and politically homogeneous group. Not only members of the cabinet but also most high-ranking civil servants were recruited from the landholding class. In 1913 all twelve of the provincial governors were members of the nobility. Politically, these men were closely associated with the conservative parties, though the regulations of the Prussian civil service prohibited formal membership in a political party. While the Prussian constitution contained no provisions for parliamentary responsibility, in a sense the executive was responsive to the wishes of the majority of parliament as well: in most cases the views of leading executives and the dominant parties in the Landtag coincided.[3]

The war years shattered the illusion of political stability as the *Burgfrieden* forced the national and Prussian governments to address the question of electoral reform. Both wings of the diagonal saw the fate of the Prussian electoral system as symptomatic for the political future of the Reich as a whole. Although similar restrictions on the right to vote existed in other German states, electoral changes in Prussia would, given the size and significance of the state, lead to constitutional changes in the lesser *Länder* and accelerate the process of democratization at the national level as well. On the other hand, as long as the domestic political structure in Prussia was not democratized, the right wing of the diagonal could hope to continue to dominate both the state and nation. Closely related, though generally left unsaid, were the issues of parliamentarization and ministerial responsibility in the state and Prussia's relationship to the Reich.[4]

As long as the Prussian parliament was unresponsive to public opinion in the state, the question of parliamentary control of the executive remained a moot issue for both the Reich and Prussia. Even if the emperor were to agree to have the chancellor responsible to the Reichstag, such a constitutional change would be relatively meaningless as long as the same official in his capacity as Prussian prime minister confronted a state parliament elected by the three-class system of voting. Meaningful democratic reforms depended upon the election of a Landtag genuinely responsive to public opinion in the state, or fundamental changes in the structure of German federalism so that Prussia's administration would come under the control of a democratized Reich government.

The First World War led to far-reaching changes in the distribution of power between the Reich and the states. As more functions relating to the war economy were concentrated in the hands of the military and the offices of the Reich civilian government, the *Länder* suffered a corresponding decline in their economic and political autonomy. For most of the smaller states, this development was a blow to particularist pride, but in Prussia the shift of power toward the national government involved a diminution of the state's dominance over the Reich. Each transfer of power from Prussia to the Reich reduced the Prussian conservatives' political hold over Germany.[5] The state's executive leaders were fully aware of the shifting trend, but despite intense efforts were not able to prevent the transfer of crucial competencies, particularly to the military. The Supreme Command of the Armed Forces (Oberste Heeresleitung, OHL) and the heads of the military districts in Germany (the so-called deputy commanders) increasingly took a hand in the administration of virtually all aspects of public affairs.[6] Although at first glance it might appear that the shift of power to the military involved transfers of political influence between members of the same Prussian-dominated interest group (the German military leaders for the most part were members of the Prussian officer corps), the development nevertheless accelerated the trend toward "de-Prussification." Under the influence of the "politics of the diagonal," the first and second OHL virtually ignored not only the Prussian civil authorities, but the Prussian Ministry of War as well.[7] The policy was not reversed until Hindenburg and Ludendorff were named to head the third OHL in mid-1916 and General von Stein, a protegé of Ludendorff's, was appointed as new Prussian minister of war a year later. By that time, however, it was too late for the Prussian authorities to regain the influence they had lost.

Ironically, the stubborn resistance to change by the Prussian executive and the majority in the legislature also aided in the transfer of power to the Reich. The Prussian ruling class, like the Bourbons, had "learned nothing and forgotten nothing."[8] To be sure, there were differences of opinion among the members of the cabinet, but they concerned only questions of tactics, not matters of principle.[9] The only significant reform bill voted by both houses of the legislature prior to November 1917 provided for changes in the law on local home rule, making it possible for some Social Democrats to serve in municipal administrations.[10] More far-reaching proposals, such as the admission of parliamentary leaders into the cabinet, came only late in the war and were clearly desperate reactions to military setbacks or news of revolutionary activities in Russia.[11]

Especially in opening up lines of communication between the executive and the opposition parties, Prussia lagged far behind the Reich. At the national level, Bethmann Hollweg early in the war began inviting the leaders of all Reichstag parties to informal briefings,[12] but this practice did not include members of the Landtag. At best, the Social Democrats, pariahs in the prewar Landtag, noticed a more amiable and less hostile attitude on the part of their colleagues.[13] Some of the SPD leaders established or resumed personal and social connections with former friends and associates.[14] Still, the two "most important achievements of the war: the creation of a democracy that will become the foundation of a true German nation," and the coalition of right-wing Social Democrats and the moderate middle-class parties, a "German left in the best sense of the word," certainly did not come into being in Prussia.[15] It emerged instead at the communal level and in the Reich among the advisors of the various war boards, in the cooperation of the majority parties in the Reichstag, and in a variety of institutionalized social settings.[16]

While the sociopatriotic societies became forums for contacts among high-ranking leaders in Berlin, the economic side of the war effort enabled less prominent working-class and union leaders to rise to decision-making positions.[17] At the communal level, the exigencies of the war effort forced day-to-day contact and cooperation between the municipal administrations and the *Arbeitersekretäre* (workers' secretaries), a network of union ombudsmen.[18] At the national level, the membership of the Advisory Board of the War Food Office consisted of a numbers of imperial bureaucrats and the Socialist union leaders Robert Schmidt and Gustav Bauer.

The partial integration of significant numbers of Social Democratic functionaries into a variety of quasi-executive positions reached a climax of sorts with the Auxiliary Service Law of 1916. The primary aim of this legislation, passed by the Reichstag with the support of the Social Democrats, was the systematic mobilization and registration of the civilian work force. The provisions severely restricted the free movement of labor, but the law also marked a triumph for the union movement and particularly the head of the Socialist unions, Carl Legien.[19] The Auxiliary Service Law granted organized labor a legal role in running the war economy and simultaneously guaranteed the unions a considerable increase in membership.[20] At the same time, the legislation also demonstrated the limits of political change in prerevolutionary Prussia. The influence of the Social Democrats in drafting the legislation in the Reichstag contrasted vividly with the opposition's impotence in the Prussian legislature.

Despite the notable changes at the Reich and communal levels, the key to any real structural change in the largest part of Germany remained meaningful reform of the Prussian electoral system. Bethmann Hollweg recognized this quite soon after the outbreak of the war. Theoretically, changes in the Prussian electoral system could come in two ways: either through the legislative process in Prussia itself, or through initiatives at the Reich level whereby the emperor and the Reichstag would force reforms upon the state. The first manner was clearly preferable if the German federal system were to be maintained. Forcing changes in Prussia through Reich action would in effect destroy the essence of the Bismarck constitution, although until the fall of 1918 neither the government nor the reform parties fully recognized this effect.

It is not necessary here to repeat the long story of Bethmann Hollweg's agonizing failure to pursuade the Prussian ruling classes to accept electoral reforms.[21] Suffice it to say that electoral reforms was one of the issues that stretched the "politics of the diagonal" to the breaking point. Unable to stem the accelerating polarization of German politics, Bethmann Hollweg was caught between the extremists on the right and the pressures of the reformers on the left.[22] As a result, the chancellor lost the confidence of the parliamentary majority in the Reich, the emperor, and the OHL, and in August 1917 he resigned both as Reich chancellor and as Prussian prime minister.

The electoral reform was certainly not the only factor in the chancellor's dismissal, but it was crucial to the cabinet crisis that his resignation occasioned in the state. Along with the prime minister, four cabinet ministers in Prussia voluntarily left office, significantly not because they sympathized with Bethmann Hollweg's policies, but because they refused to be associated with any government that called for major reforms in the Prussian electoral system. In a sense the self-inflicted purge of the cabinet initially smoothed the path of Bethmann Hollweg's successor, Georg Michaelis. Like his predecessor, Michaelis came from the ranks of the Prussian civil service. During the war he became well known for his effective work in managing the food economy, and also for his close association with the extreme right-wing Pan-Germans and the OHL, notably Ludendorff himself. He was clearly the military's choice for chancellor,[23] but the new chancellor and prime minister was aware of at least some of the complexities of the domestic political situation, and even tried, albeit in a very awkward and counterproductive manner, to continue the "policies of the diagonal." By this Michaelis meant that he was willing to make an effort to obtain some major reforms in the Prussian electoral system, though for him that did not imply that a parliament politically more responsive to public opinion should control executive decisions or personnel. Indeed, Michaelis made no secret of his hope that the reform bill would halt the "radical flood" of demands for increased parliamentary control over the executive. From the prime minister's point of view electoral reform in Prussia would not initiate parliamentarism, but on the contrary, would prevent it.[24]

For the moment, however, the reform issue dominated discussions, and here Michaelis seemed to be pursuing a positive course of action. As successors to the four ministers who had resigned, he selected "moderate" Conservatives "who were willing to work actively for the passing of the [reform] bill."[25] The new minister of war, von Stein, was a close friend of Ludendorff and a staunch military annexationist, but he was not completely opposed to domestic reforms.[26] His colleague in the Ministry of Education, Friedrich Schmidt-Ott, was even considered a liberal by the standards applied to the incumbents of this ministry. He was a protegé of the long-time Prussian minister of education and reformer, Friedrich Althoff, and enjoyed the special confidence of the emperor. Schmidt-Ott's political views were described as "semi-rigid."[27] The appointment of Peter Spahn as minister of justice set both a constitutional and a religious precedent. Politically, Spahn was close to the Conservatives' position, but because he was a Catholic, a member of the Center party, and a delegate in the Landtag, his appointment caused a minor sensation. No Catholic had been named to the cabinet in many years, and Spahn's appointment clearly represented the government's attempt to broaden its political base. At the same time, the selection of a member of Parliament to head a ministry was highly unusual in the Prussian system, and represented at least indirectly a step toward parliamentarization in the state. The break with past practice was all the more glaring as Spahn retained his seat in the legislature and remained active in the parliamentary affairs of his party. Michaelis himself was well aware that Spahn's appointment would inaugurate a new era in the relationship between legislature and executive. The prime minister regarded the entry of an active legislator into the cabinet as the most far-reaching concession to parliamentarism that he was willing to entertain.[28] Finally, to head the Ministry of the Interior, the office responsible for drafting electoral reform legislation, Michaelis selected Bill Drews, a veteran civil servant, whose particular expertise was administrative reform.[29] Politically, Drews was the most "left" of the new appointees; in Conservative circles he was regarded as "red."[30] Stresemann regarded him as a closet National Liberal (like all civil servants in Prussia, Drews could not, of course, actually belong to a political party), and even in the SPD Drews enjoyed considerable respect.[31]

Drews lost no time in submitting an electoral reform proposal that would have "essentially" replaced the anachronistic three-class system with the universal manhood suffrage plan used in national elections.[32] However, his bill, while receiving cabinet endorsement, was tabled as the Reich and Prussia faced a new government crisis in the fall of 1917. After only a few months in office, Michaelis had failed completely in securing the confidence of the reformist majority parties in the Reichstag. At the same time, the Conservatives and particularly the military, whose creature Michaelis was, were unhappy with his inept handling of the growing polarization in the German political system. However, the search for a successor to Michaelis also brought into sharp focus the difficulties of finding a single individual who as chancellor headed the semiparliamentary system in the Reich, while in his capacity as Prussian prime minister he presided over the state's still rigidly authoritarian governmental system.

Michaelis's forced resignation made it possible to elect a Reich chancellor who had the clear confidence of the majority parties in the Reichstag. The eventual choice as Reich chancellor was a Bavarian, Count Hertling, who had been prime minister of Bavaria and who was acceptable to the Reichstag majority. But Hertling presented major difficulties as potential Prussian prime minister. As a southerner and a Catholic thoroughly unfamiliar with Prussian affairs, he was hardly an ideal choice to head the state's cabinet. In addition, precisely because Hertling enjoyed the confidence of the moderate groups in the Reichstag, the powerful Conservative parties in the Prussian legislature remained suspicious. For this reason both they and the king considered breaking with the tradition of combining the two offices in the hands of one official. A conservative, nonparliamentary prime minister in Prussia should act as a counterweight to the quasi-parliamentary chancellor.[33]

Needless to say, the significance of such a change was not lost on the reformers. For them a chancellor who was not also prime minister was unacceptable, since it would have meant a decrease in the influence that the Reichstag majority could exert through the chancellor on Prussian affairs. The National Liberals held a key position in the tug of war. In the Reichstag the party increasingly sided with the reformist forces on domestic and constitutional issues, but in the Prussian legislature that had so far maintained their firm alliance with the Conservatives. Clearly, then, the National Liberals in the Reichstag had to be persuaded to exercise pressure on their Prussian colleagues to free themselves from the political embrace of the Conservatives if reforms, and particularly electoral reforms, were to make headway in the state.[34]

At the same time, the majority parties in the Reichstag were not blind to the fact that Hertling had neither the desire not the requisite experience to govern Prussia effectively. A possible solution to the dilemma was put forward by the driving force of the Center party in the Reichstag, Matthias Erzberger.[35] Erzberger suggested that Hertling should formally accept the position of Prussian prime minister, but that the actual leadership of the state be left to a vice–prime minister. For this position Erzberger proposed Robert Friedberg, the leader of the National Liberals in the Prussian legislature. In addition, in order to further the links between the reformist parties and the Prussian executive, a member of the Progressive party would be appointed as Prussian minister of commerce. The political advantages of Erzberger's solution were readily apparent: it would have meant binding the National Liberals to the reform policy without risking an overt constitutional crisis. Stresemann and the National Liberals in the Reichstag assented enthusiastically; it appeared that the road to peaceful reform of the Prussian electoral system was now clear. Friedberg's appointment would transform the Prussian National Liberals into a virtual government party, and all but isolate the Conservatives.[36]

The plan was almost too perfect. Hertling, unenthusiastic at best over the prospect of sharing power with a vice–prime minister, balked at the corollary to Friedberg's appointment, the selection of a Progressive as a member of the Prussian cabinet,[37] and it required additional intervention by Erzberger and Stresemann to bring the affair to a satisfactory conclusion.[38] There is no doubt that Friedberg's appointment in November 1917 represented a major constitutional precedent in Prussia: for the first time since 1849 an active parliamentary leader became de facto head of the Prussian government.[39]

Friedberg himself fulfilled the expectations placed in him by the reformist forces; the cabinet did move quickly on the issue of electoral reform. Drews, who remained minister of the interior, submitted a slightly altered version of the bill drafted in August to the cabinet and the legislature. The cabinet passed it without difficulty, but in the Landtag Erzberger's carefully constructed scenario proved to be thoroughly unworkable. The National Liberals refused to desert their Conservative allies. About two-thirds of the National Liberal representatives joined with the Conservatives in voting down the bill placed before the house by the National Liberal leader. The intransigence of the Landtag majority hastened the political eclipse of Prussian authoritarianism. The appeals of the Conservatives and their allies in the OHL "to think Prussian," that is, to employ the remaining powers of the state in order to prevent the further erosion of the Bismarckian constitution in the direction of democratization and parliamentarization, had no effect.[40] Instead Prussia and its political system became increasingly isolated in the sweep of German political opinion to the left. Germany's largest state, the foundation of the Bismarckian and Wilhelminian Reich, now personified not the glory of Germany, but the immovable obstacle to peace and progress. In southern Germany a widely held view stated, "If Prussia is not destroyed, Germany will be destroyed by Prussia."[41]

The Reich's deteriorating domestic and military situation throughout 1918 made it imperative that there be visible reforms of the Prussian political system, but with the refusal of the House of Representatives to agree to meaningful reforms, the state in effect forfeited the right to determine its own political destiny. Realistically, change could now come only through pressure from the Reichstag on the chancellor and emperor.[42]

Toward the end of 1918, as the prospect of a democratically elected state legislature came closer, the question of ministerial responsibility also became acute, and on this issue serious divisions among the reformers emerged. With the appointment of Otto Fischbeck as Prussian minister of commerce, all three of the moderate bourgeois parties were represented in the cabinet. Yet formally Prussia had undergone no constitutional changes. More seriously, it was apparent that the members of the Prussian cabinet and significant forces in the bourgeois parties had no intention of advocating major constitutional changes beyond electoral reform. For many of the bourgeois political leaders, the essence of the Prussian constitutional system was not the electoral system, on which they were willing to compromise, but the question of parliamentarization, that is, the establishment of a constitutional system in which the government was formally responsible to a parliament elected on the basis of universal manhood suffrage.

For the SPD the same issue posed a different dilemma. The party asked whether in view of the passing of the Bismarckian order Prussia itself still had a raison d'être in the coming Reich.[43] And, if the answer to that question was yes, should the Social Democrats assume part of the responsibility for governing the state? In view of the rapidly accelerating radicalization of the German working classes, the leadership of the majority Socialists was under tremendous pressure both from its own membership and from the USPD to join the ranks of those seeking to destroy Prussia rather than attempt to stabilize and reform the state. On the other hand, the right wing of the SPD pointed to the obvious anomaly that for decades the party had demanded a representative legislature in Prussia, whereas now, when this goal seemed within reach, the party hesitated to take the next logical step and lead in the formation of a parliamentary coalition government.[44] As a leading spokesman of the right wing, Wolfgang Heine, proclaimed with some pathos, "Universal manhood suffrage [was] the prelude . . . to the parliamentary form of government."[45] Konrad Haenisch added that parliamentary government provided the means with which "we Socialists with the strength of our character and willpower shall inscribe our handwriting on the blank pages of Germany's political future and . . . transform the military defeat into a massive political victory."[46]

For a few short weeks in the early fall of 1918, it appeared that Haenisch's prediction would come true: Reich and Prussia would make a successful and peaceful transition from authoritarianism to parliamentarism. After the collapse of the summer offensive on the Western front and Ludendorff's subsequent panic at the beginning of October, Count Hertling was replaced by Prince Max von Baden as Reich chancellor. The prince, a southwest German liberal with close ties to the leadership of the Progressives, in turn established a parliamentary Reich cabinet that had the full confidence of the majority parties in the Reichstag. The de facto parliamentarization of the Reich was soon followed by a series of formal constitutional changes, ratified by the emperor, which transformed Germany into a constitutional monarchy. On the surface, the "October reforms" also seemed to complete the federalization of Prussia. Before his confirmation as chancellor, Baden (and the emperor) agreed to change the Prussian electoral system—overriding, if necessary, the objections of the Landtag majority.[47]

The October reforms certainly satisfied the reformist elements among both the moderate bourgeois parties and the Majority Socialists.[48] It was expected that the parliamentarization would not be limited to the Reich government. There were plans to appoint Social Democrats to the Prussian cabinet as well. The vice–prime minister, Friedberg, reflected after the war that he "had almost reached the culmination of his difficult work."[49] The euphoria was of short duration, largely because even at this eleventh hour the Prussian Conservatives refused to permit the parliamentarization of the state.[50] To be sure, the incumbent minister of war, General von Stein, a man particularly disliked by the SPD, was dismissed. His successor, General von Scheüch, could boast of good contacts with a number of union and parliamentary leaders, but he, too, was hardly a man of liberal views.[51] Like most military leaders, he remained a fanatical opponent of subordinating the military to parliamentary control.[52]

The opposition of the Conservatives and the military to changes in the Prussian constitution was not unexpected. Surprising, and in the end decisive for the failure of the October reforms in Prussia, was William II's sabotage as king of Prussia of the reforms he had approved as German emperor.[53] Not only did he refuse to put pressure on the Conservatives, but also in the final days before the revolution he clung with particular tenacity to the Prussian throne. Efforts by moderate members of the Prussian cabinet to persuade him to abdicate in the last days of October failed.[54] Instead, the monarch entertained "wild plans for a putsch" to recapture Prussia and "his capital," illusions of grandeur that had no effect on the course of events in Germany.[55]

The Revolutionary Cabinet in Prussia, 1918–1919

The revolutionary upheavals in Prussia began in the northern provinces and fanned out from there to the west and south.[56] It was not until the very end of the chain of events that the disturbances spread to the capital. Virtually everywhere the transfer of power took place without bloodshed. In the initial phase of the revolution, clashes between the workers' and soldiers' councils and the incumbent administrative forces were rare. In most instances the old administrators, lacking instructions from their superiors, were content to cooperate with the revolutionaries.[57] Nowhere in Prussia was there an organized attempt at counterrevolution in the first days after the fall of the empire. At the same time, instances of radicalism were noticeably absent among the revolutionaries.[58] Isolated attempts by local leaders to effect radical administrative changes on the basis of their presumed revolutionary authority were quickly halted by the intervention of leaders from either or both of the two Socialist parties.[59]

The Prussian cabinet, still under the de facto leadership of Robert Friedberg, made no attempt to gain control of the situation at the state level until November 8. It was only then that Friedberg suggested the transfer of power in the provinces be retroactively legitimized by the formal parliamentarization of the Prussian cabinet. The vice–prime minister proposed that all of the ministerial posts (except for that of defense minister) be assigned to members of the Landtag and that in addition to the present party representation, members of the SPD (but not the USPD) should join the cabinet. In line with this proposal, all members of the cabinet who were not members of the legislature resigned. The parliamentarians, Friedberg (who intended to continue as leader in Prussia),[60] Spahn, and Fischbeck, as well as Scheüch, stayed in office. Friedberg hoped to fill the six vacancies with two ministers each from the SPD, the Progressives, and the Center party.[61]

Friedberg's initiative was welcomed by the right wing of the SPD,[62] but when the revolutionary disturbances reached Berlin on November 9, it became clear that these political leaders had little influence among the masses in the streets of the capital. The hope of the SPD's right wing that the abdication of William II would provide a breathing space in which the moderate socialist and bourgeois parties could arrange for an orderly transformation of the government structure, was totally unrealistic. Not only did the king refuse to yield the throne, but also the workers of Berlin wanted immediate and dramatic evidence that the old era had come to an end. In contrast, while the right-wing Socialists had a political concept with few supporters, the USPD boasted large numbers of supporters but had no concrete plans for the future. There is no doubt that the Independents' strength in the capital enabled them potentially to exercise decisive influence over "the process of creating political will *(Willensbildungsprozess)*" in Berlin.[63] However, before November 9, no leader within the USPD had seriously considered that the party might soon have to exercise governmental power.[64]

The events of Saturday, November 9, in Berlin began with a strike call issued by the USPD and the leaders of the so-called Revolutionary Shop Steward's Movement. Both the SPD and the union hierarchy were caught by surprise, and could only belatedly attempt to influence the turn of events by delegating a number of top officials to the strike organizing committee. Yet, while the Independents took the lead in organizing activity on the street, the right-wing Socialists seized the initiative in the political negotiations. The SPD formally proposed to its sister party that the two groups assume responsibility for governing the Reich. Remarkably, the offer concerned only the Reich government. Although it is certain that one and perhaps two Prussian SPD leaders[65] were part of the negotiating team that approached Prince Max von Baden and the USPD, questions about handling the Prussian administration in the transitional period do not seem to have come up.[66]

The reason for the silence on Prussia was not that the new national political leaders had forgotten about the state. Rather, they seemed to assume that in the future Prussia's administration should be merged with that of the Reich.[67] For example, after their agreement to form a provisional Reich cabinet, the Council of People's Plenipotentiaries (CCP; in German, Rat der Volksbeauftragten), with three members from the SPD and three from the USPD, appointed an "overseer" *(Beigeordneter)* for the Prussian Defense Ministry, although this was clearly a state agency.[68]

The transfer of power in Berlin is of particular interest. Here again the new Reich authorities contacted the municipal offices in the capital directly, bypassing the Prussian territorial administration. The CPP named the head of the SPD delegation in the Landtag, Paul Hirsch, as the Reich cabinet's liaison with the Berlin Police Department and other municipal administrators.[69] But municipal affairs in Berlin soon developed a political dynamic of their own. On Saturday evening, Johann Sassenbach, a Berlin labor leader and SPD member of the city council, organized a "People's Committee for the Protection of Communal Institutions in Greater Berlin," consisting of members of both Socialist parties, representatives from organized labor, delegates from the workers' and soldiers' councils, and members from the Berlin municipal administration.[70] The committee, without consulting either the CPP or the Prussian Ministry of the Interior, began organizing a security force and issued a public appeal for trained personnel to volunteer to maintain vital services in the capital, presumably as a precaution against acts of sabotage by right- or left-wing radicals.[71]

The expectation that Prussia could be more or less quietly administered as a branch office of the Reich quickly proved to be an illusion. Before the revolution, the Prussian state administration had quite literally provided most government services for three-fifths of Germany. The Reich administration had virtually no infrastructure, and the revolutionary upheavals had not changed that situation. The revolutionary Reich government had no means of exercising day-to-day control of the far-flung Prussian territorial administration even under the best of circumstances. In the early days of November, with various autonomy and separatist movements (to be discussed below) making their appearance in the Prussian provinces, the need to fill the vacuum at the top of the Prussian government was readily apparent.

The establishment of the state's revolutionary cabinet was a peaceful and almost dignified affair. On the morning of November 12, Hirsch, Heinrich Ströbel, Ernst, Adolph Hoffmann, and Otto Braun appeared in Friedberg's office and informed the vice–prime minister that they had been authorized to take over the administration of the state. Friedberg in turn recognized that "factual authority" now lay in the hands of the revolutionary institutions, and yielded his office. A short time later, Hirsch returned to ask the civil servants working in the prime minister's office to stay on the job.[72] In a parallel action, Konrad Haenisch and Adolph Hoffmann appeared at the Ministry of Education, where the incumbent minister, Schmidt-Ott, also recognized that "factual power" lay in the hands of the men standing before him.[73]

The formation of the Prussian revolutionary government was deliberately patterned after the organization of the CPP in the Reich. Not only was the principle of equal power for SPD and USPD kept, but Prussia, too, created a six-member "Political Cabinet" consisting of three members from each of the two Socialist parties to oversee the administration of the state as a whole. As in the case of the Reich, the Political Cabinet did not have responsibility for administering specific policy areas. Rather, it was to issue overall policy directives and guidelines. In a departure from the CPP practice, however, the two Socialist parties also agreed that the incumbent ministers should not stay in office; instead, most would be replaced by Socialist cabinet members. In addition, the principle of parity was to extend to the individual portfolios as well, so that each ministry would be headed jointly by an Independent and a right-wing Socialist minister. Since the two parties had few leaders with state-level experience, the adoption of these principles meant that not only would almost all Socialist members of the old legislature become ministers, but also that virtually every member of the Political Cabinet would head one of the specific ministries as well.

The six members of the Political Cabinet were Ströbel, Hoffmann, and Kurt Rosenfeld for the USPD; Hirsch, Braun, and Ernst for the SPD. Hirsch and Ströbel served as co-chairmen. Of this group, only Ernst did not share responsibility for heading a specific ministry; he had to wait until the USPD withdrew from the government before moving to the Ministry of the Interior. In addition, a number of leaders who were not members of the Political Cabinet headed individual ministries. These included Rudolf Breitscheid, Hugo Simon, and Adolph Hofer from the USPD; Albert Südekum, and Haenisch from the SPD. The ministerial list was completed by Wilhelm Hoff, who had no party affiliation, and three holdovers from the prerevolutionary ministries, Scheüch, Fischbeck, and Spahn. Finally, to confuse matters even further, a number of "overseers" representing both the SPD and USPD were assigned to the ministries where non-Socialist ministers remained in office, although in practice none of these officials achieved lasting political influence.

The delineation of authority among the Political Cabinet, the government as a whole, and the individual ministers proved difficult. For the USPD, the unequivocal authority of the Political Cabinet as final arbiter of the decision-making process in Prussia had been a sine qua non of its agreement to join the Prussian revolutionary government. The Independents insisted that the Political Cabinet was the guarantee of socialist rule in Prussia. Without it the revolution would have been limited to bringing about a bourgeois- Socialist coalition in the state. On paper the right-wing Socialists yielded to the USPD on this issue, and on November 27, the cabinet formally assigned the members of the Political Cabinet a higher status than was given to holders of individual portfolios.[74] In practice, the distinction was much less clearly defined, if for no other reason than that the members of the organizationally distinct groups were for the most part the same persons. Moreover, the divisions of power ran counter to another accepted maxim, the equality of all Socialist ministers.[75] That principle became important when, as was the case in the Ministry of Education, the dual ministers, Haenisch (SPD) and Hoffmann (USPD), developed sharp disagreements over the policies of their ministry. In theory, the decision of November 27 gave Hoffmann the upper hand, since he was a member of the Political Cabinet while Haenisch was not. Understandably, Hoffmann sought to assign basic educational policy decisions to the agenda of the Political Cabinet, while Haenisch felt these were matters to be discussed by all ministers.[76]

The Political Cabinet never achieved the decisive role in Prussia that its counterpart in the Reich exercised. In fact, the Prussian institution played a decisive role only once: in determining the dates for the election of the Prussian constitutional convention. The Political Cabinet's first proclamation, issued by the new government on November 13, included a promise to summon a "Prussian National Convention,"[77] but no date was set for any elections. Within the Political Cabinet the SPD members predictably pleaded for the earliest possible election date, while the Independents argued for delay.[78] The Political Cabinet postponed a decision until mid-December, but the increasing support for separatist and autonomist movements in Catholic border areas (fueled in part by opposition to Hoffmann's pronounced anticlerical policies) forced the cabinet to take a clear stand on the future of the Prussian constitution.[79] When the leading opponent of early elections, Adolph Hoffmann, was absent because of an illness that kept him bedridden for a month, the Political Cabinet voted three to two to schedule elections for the state's constitutional convention two weeks after the contest for a national constitutional convention. The group also rejected a motion by the two remaining USPD members that the decision should be subject to final review by the workers' and soldiers' councils.[80] Contemporary observers found the members of the Prussian revolutionary leadership, as a group, unimpressive. Count Kessler's judgment, "an assembly of small town counsellors, informal *(salopp)* and without drive," revealed the author as a snob, but he was not far off the mark.[81] As noted before, Paul Hirsch and Heinrich Ströbel were co-chairmen of the Political Cabinet. Hirsch was "in the best sense of the word a Prussian Jew—conscientious, reliable," but he was also an indecisive man with little flair for political leadership.[82] He felt out of place in the political limelight.[83] Ströbel, too, was not naturally drawn to the rough-and-tumble of active politics. He inclined toward aesthetics, and had made a name for himself as a music critic. The debate over the issue of war credits led him to join the USPD when the SPD split in 1917, but he remained a moderate. Ströbel rejected the concept of the dictatorship of the proletariat, and favored early elections of the constitutional conventions.[84]

The remaining SPD members in the Political Cabinet, Otto Braun and Eugen Ernst, later went on to have very different political careers. In January 1919, Braun stood at the beginning of what was to be a long and distinguished ministerial career, while for Ernst his membership in the revolutionary Prussian government was both the climax and the virtual end of his public service. To be sure, at this time Braun was by no means the strong man and "red czar" of Prussia that he would become,[85] although a number of the personal characteristics that would later distinguish him were already apparent. The future prime minister was a pragmatist with a well-developed sense of what was politically possible and necessary, although like most East Prussians he had a romantic and almost chauvinistic concern for the problems and prospects of Prussia's and Germany's eastern areas. Braun's polonophobia could match that of any Junker.[86] In contrast, Eugen Ernst was undoubtedly the weakest member of the Political Cabinet. His contemporaries described him as a "typical functionary—satiated and sound," less agitator than organizer.[87] Ernst owed his membership in the Political Cabinet to his friendship with Paul Hirsch and to a political accident. The SPD had intended that Ernst should become the new police chief of Berlin, but by the afternoon of November 9 that post had been preempted by the USPD. Ernst's appointment to the Political Cabinet constituted something of a consolation prize.[88]

The Independent members Adolph Hoffmann and Kurt Rosenfeld at first glance appeared to be typical representatives of German left-wing radicalism. Hoffmann in particular personified passionate opposition to all things bourgeois, while Rosenfeld was known to the wider public primarily as Karl Liebknecht's defense attorney. Actually, Hoffmann talked more radically than he acted, and Rosenfeld's tenure in office demonstrated his concern that the political transformation of Prussia not be marred by legal abuses and administrative arbitrariness.[89] Like Ströbel, he too later voted against the USPD's affiliation with the Communist International and returned to the fold of the SPD.[90]

While the members of the Prussian cabinet were settling uneasily into their unfamiliar roles, the leaders of the provisional Reich government were finding it increasingly difficult to agree on basic policies. The relationship of the two socialist parties in the CPP was never free of tension, but the difficulties increased markedly during the second half of December. Frustrated by its inability to influence decisively the deliberations of the National Congress of Workers' and Soldiers' Councils and critical of the SPD's handling of the Christmas disturbances in Berlin, the USPD at the end of December resigned from the CPP.[91] The decision by their colleagues in the Reich left the Prussian USPD ministers in something of a quandary. As far as the state was concerned, there were at this time no major specific policy differences between the two parties,[92] so that at first the USPD's leaders saw no compelling reason to withdraw the party's representatives from the Prussian cabinet.[93] The Prussian Independents eventually joined their colleagues in the Reich as a demonstration of party solidarity, but it proved difficult to find a plausible reason to justify this step. On January 2 the USPD discovered that its continued presence in the Prussian administration was made impossible by the right-wing Socialists' disregard for Prussia's rights as a state. Specifically at issue was the fact that, according to the USPD, a new minister of defense, Colonel Walter Reinhardt, had been appointed by the Reich CPP without fully consulting the Prussian government. It was a "threadbare argument" at best.[94] After all, both the USPD and the SPD had long agreed that matters pertaining to the armed forces should be handled by the Reich and not the states, and the USPD's position seemed to favor a resurgence of Prussian particularism in an especially unsuitable area. Both the SPD members of the Political Cabinet and the Central Council of the Workers' and Soldiers' Councils (the executive committee elected by the national congress) rejected the USPD's argument, and the Independents submitted their resignation.[95] Perhaps to assuage their bad consciences, the USPD ministers showed themselves particularly cooperative in the final hours of sharing responsibility for Prussia's political affairs. They did not withdraw their signatures on an appeal by the Political Cabinet to workers against exaggerated strike activities, and Kurt Rosenberg even agreed to remain in office as a caretaker minister until a successor had been appointed.[96]

After the resignation of the USPD members, the remaining SPD members of the Political Cabinet agreed on a number of organizational changes. Most important, the division between the Political Cabinet and the ministry as a whole was abolished, in effect transforming the cabinet from a group formally dominated by the Socialist parties to an SPD-bourgeois coalition.[97] In addition, the Prussian cabinet was also streamlined so that a single minister headed each of the cabinet offices; for all practical purposes, then, the Political Cabinet ceased to exist. Hirsch retained only his position as prime minister, and Eugen Ernst moved to the Ministry of the Interior. At the end of January the cabinet also restored the traditional Prussian principle of ministerial collegiality. The cabinet members agreed that the ministry as a whole would stand behind all decisions voted by a majority of the group. A minister who opposed the majority opinion thus had only the choice of submitting to the majority or resigning and possibly creating a government crisis.[98]

The political viability of the new, de facto coalition in the state was challenged almost immediately by the events associated with the so-called second wave of the revolution, that is, the Spartacus uprising and its bloody defeat in the first week of January 1919. When the USPD ministers resigned their cabinet posts, the police chief in the capital, Emil Eichhorn, decided not to follow the example of his party colleagues and instead remained in office. As a result, he was now the only major Independent official in the Prussian state administration. He was also a challenge to the new minister of the interior, Eugen Ernst. The latter, who was legally the administrative superior of the Berlin police chief, regarded Eichhorn as politically suspect and professionally incompetent. There was certainly some truth in the latter charge. In the course of demonstrations on January 1 against the radical educational policies of Adolph Hoffmann, some of the rioters attempted to force their way into Hoffmann's official residence, and the police seemed completely unable to master the situation.[99]

The specific circumstances surrounding Eichhorn's dismissal and the subsequent uprising by left-wing radicals were later subject to considerable dispute. According to the official version put out by the Prussian government, the minister of the interior on January 3 charged Eichhorn with a number of failings in his exercise of the office of police chief. Eichhorn agreed to answer the charges in writing, but he refused to recognize the Prussian minister of the interior as his administrative superior, claiming that he was responsible only to the workers' and soldiers' councils, that it, to the Executive Committee (Vollzugsrat) of the Workers' and Soldiers' Council of Greater Berlin.[100] Not surprisingly, Ernst disagreed and on January 4 dismissed the police chief for incompetence and insubordination.[101] (Incidentally, the executive bodies of the national and the Berlin workers' and soldiers' councils concurred in Ernst's decision.)[102] Ernst himself assumed the responsibility for administering the police department.

The ministry's version of the confrontation contained a number of omissions, not to say distortions. The basic issue in the conflict was neither incompetence nor insubordination, but political power. It was no secret that Emil Eichhorn, the most popular figure in Berlin's left-wing Socialist circles, was growing increasingly disappointed with the pace and direction of revolutionary change in Germany, and was drawing closer to the Spartacus position.[103] It is also understandable that the Prussian government, knowing of Eichhorn's increasingly left-radical views, was anxious to remove him from the pivotal position of police chief in Berlin. The original initiative seems to have come not from Ernst, but from the defense minister and especially the head of the police desk in the ministry, Doyé.[104] This official, who was to become deeply involved in the Kapp Putsch, attempted to persuade the CPP, the Berlin city attorney general's office, and leading members of the Berlin Workers' and Soldiers' Council to move against Eichhorn.[105] All refused to preempt a decision by the Prussian ministry, but Doyé's intrigues clearly showed the political motivation of the ministry's move against the police chief.

Political motives were equally prevalent among the far left. The USPD leadership in Berlin, Spartacus, and the shop stewards' movement recognized Eichhorn's dismissal as a welcome focal point around which to rally their supporters against the right-wing Socialist governments in the Reich and Prussia. In this context the demand for the reinstatement of Eichhorn was as much of a pretext as his dismissal for incompetence. Neither Eichhorn nor his supporters took the demand very seriously.[106] The real issue in the struggle was the control of Germany's future and not the intra-Prussian altercation between the Berlin police chief and his superior ministry.

The First Cabinet of the Weimar Coalition

The elections for the Prussian Constitutional Convention took place as scheduled on January 26, 1919, without incident,[107] but the actual convening of the assembly presented more difficulties. To begin with, there was controversy over the meeting time. Friedrich Ebert, Robert Leinert (the chairman of the Central Council of the Workers' and Soldiers' Councils), Haenisch, and Hugo Preuss, the "father" of the future Weimar constitution, argued that the national constitutional convention should complete work on the Reich constitution first, since that document would determine the parameters of the states' rights. A number of Prussian ministers, among them Hirsch, Heine, and Südekum, but also the new Reich chancellor, Philip Scheidemann, advocated an entirely different approach. They felt that only parallel sessions of both the national and state conventions could counteract the centrifugal forces that were threatening the territorial integrity of Reich and state.[108] The latter point of view eventually prevailed, and the opening session of the convention was scheduled for February. However, transport and security considerations delayed the first plenary session until mid-March.[109]

Once convened, the Prussian Constitutional Convention moved quickly to establish the machinery of parliamentary democracy in the state. Within two days the convention had passed an interim constitution to replace the now inoperative document of 1851. The adoption of the interim constitution in turn formally ended the work of the revolutionary government. On March 20, the cabinet resigned, though it stayed on as a caretaker government until the convention could elect a successor. The interregnum lasted only five days; on March 25 Prussia was presented its first constitutional government, a cabinet of the parties of the Weimar coalition. The new ministry consisted of ten members: five Social Democrats, two each from the DDP and the Center party, and the nonpartisan minister of defense. A majority of the ministers, six in all, had already served in the revolutionary cabinet.

This first parliamentary coalition of the "strong center"[110] was to be characteristic of most Prussian governments during the Weimar era, but the picture of a smoothly functioning parliamentary system right from the beginning of the republican years is somewhat deceptive. In 1919 all of the coalition partners expressed serious reservations about their cooperation. Each justified the coalition by the extreme emergency conditions that required tactical cooperation, while insisting that their working together should not be misinterpreted as ideological compatibility. Particularly the two major supports of the coalition, the SPD and the Center party, seemed anxious to underscore that theirs was an alliance born purely of tactical considerations. In the SPD, a number of delegates in the Constitutional Convention were very reluctant to endorse a coalition with bourgeois parties, favoring instead another attempt to form a union with the USPD. The SPD delegation even voted to send its co-chairman Richard Hauschildt to Weimar in order to persuade the SPD delegation in the national constitutional convention that it should support Prussian overtures to the Independents along these lines.[111]

In practice, a coalition of the two socialist parties at this time was completely unrealistic. To begin with, the parliamentary arithmetic did not work out. The combined SPD and USPD votes in the state convention fell far short of a majority; the two parties controlled 169 out of 402 votes. Since it would have been political suicide for a bourgeois party to join a cabinet that included the USPD, any Socialist government would have remained a minority cabinet. In addition, the SPD and the USPD were ideologically further apart than had been true when they joined forces in November 1918. The Independents were coming under the increasing domination of left-wing radicals, and this was reflected in the conditions put forth by the party's leadership as a basis for cooperating with the SPD. The USPD demanded the dissolution of all Reichswehr and Freikorps units, the distribution of arms to class-conscious proletarians, wide-ranging economic nationalization measures, and an end to all policies that favored the continuation of capitalism in Germany. Recognizing that Prussia had little control over most of these policy areas, the USPD added as a final point, that if the Reich government refused to go along with the Independents' program, the Prussian cabinet was to do everything in its power to oppose and obstruct the national government.[112]

In the Center party, too, feelings ran high against a coalition with the "atheistic" Socialists, and the party of "Socialist dictatorship."[113] The negative sentiments within the party were so strong that the supporters of the Weimar coalition were reduced to primarily defensive arguments. They pointed out that not forming a government with the SPD would isolate the right-wing Socialists even more and drive additional workers into the arms of the USPD and the Communists.[114] The coalition supporters also attempted to silence their critics by emphasizing that in a Weimar coalition the bourgeois parties could not be outvoted by the SPD ministers. The latter consideration led the Center party to insist upon the inclusion of the DDP in the Prussian coalition. The Catholics threatened to bring down the Reich government if their demands were not met.[115]

Among the three Weimar coalition parties, only the DDP was unabashedly enthusiastic about forming a government with the Social Democrats and the Center party. Collaboration between the left Liberals and the right wing of the Social Democrats fulfilled an old dream of the left Liberals' venerated leader, Naumann.[116] In fact, the party's leaders had to overcome a certain amount of distrust of the Center party in the ranks of the Prussian DDP. Among the Democrats in the Prussian Constitutional Convention were a number of liberal Protestant theologians, who resented the clerical influence in the Catholic party and particularly the Catholics' desire for continued clerical control of public elementary schools.[117]

The actual negotiations on the formation of the coalition took place between March 20 and March 23. The result was virtually a foregone conclusion, though for form's sake the SPD did not break off talks with the USPD until the last minute.[118] In the negotiations Hirsch and Heine represented the SPD, Friedberg and Fischbeck led the DDP's team, and Porsch, Hess, and Stegerwald spoke for the Center party. As was expected, disagreements over educational policies were a major stumbling block in the negotiations, though the distribution of the ministerial seats also proved difficult. The DDP had at first demanded the Ministry of the Interior, the Ministry of Commerce, and the Ministry of Agriculture for itself. Modesty was not characteristic of the Social Democrats either: they also demanded Agriculture and Interior, but added the posts of minister of finance and prime minister.[119] Only the Center party restrained itself on personnel matters, concentrating instead on programmatic demands. The final compromise was probably most satisfactory for the Catholic party. It won its coalition partners' agreement to continue the educational status quo in Prussia, which meant the maintenance of confessionally segregated, public elementary schools.[120] The Center party was content with two relatively minor ministerial posts, Justice and Social Services *(Volks-wohlfahrt)*, while the DDP and SPD divided the remaining cabinet seats among themselves. The Socialists clearly had the upper hand, placing their supporters in the offices of prime minister, and in the Ministries of Agriculture, Finance, Interior, and Education. The Democrats had to be content with Commerce and Public Works. (The latter included responsibility for running the railroads).[121]

As noted above, the first parliamentary cabinet in Prussia contained few new faces. In fact, only two of the incumbents in the revolutionary cabinet (except for the USPD members) were missing. Eugen Ernst resigned as minister of the interior and restricted his activities to his second post as police chief of Berlin. The nonpartisan minister of public works, Hoff, went into retirement. As minister of the interior Ernst was succeeded by Wolfgang Heine, who vacated the Justice Ministry in favor of the Center party member Hugo am Zehnhoff. The latter now began what was to be one of the longest ministerial tenures in republican Prussia (he did not resign until 1927), but he remained an obscure official with little political influence.[122] Hoff's successor was Rudolf Oeser, a veteran left Liberal.[123] Stegerwald joined the cabinet as minister for social services. Politically, Albert Südekum, the minister of finance, stood closest to Heine, although as a person Südekum was much less abrasive. He moved easily in bourgeois and educated circles and was regarded as the "most polished of the Social Democrats." Südekum's passion was to provide for smooth continuity between empire and republic.[124]

The cabinet agreed to continue to function as a collegial government, and, in contrast to the practice in the Reich, it moved quickly to create an institution that would facilitate the day-to-day cooperation between cabinet and legislature.[125] These were the parliamentary undersecretaries. On March 26 the ministers formally adopted Wolfgang Heine's proposals for parliamentary undersecretaries as special "mediators and arbitrators."[126] The minister of the interior envisioned a role for the undersecretaries that combined some of the functions of the "overseers" in the revolutionary era and those of the parliamentary undersecretaries familiar from British administrative practice. (Indeed, the name was obviously borrowed from Great Britain.) As was true of their English counterparts, the Prussian officials served as links between parliament and executive. Each of the coalition parties was entitled to appoint one of its parliamentary delegates as parliamentary undersecretary for those ministries in which an incumbent of that party did not serve as minister. The minister for his part had the right to approve the nomination. The parliamentary undersecretaries had no administrative duties and received no salary other than their compensation as members of the legislature. Their sole task was to "secure the unity of the cabinet," that is, they were to alert the minister to possible items of friction between him and the coalition caucuses in the

Constitutional Convention.[127] At first the new institution was looked upon with some suspicion, particularly since the functions of the new officials were not always clear (including to the officeholders themselves),[128] but in the course of the next few months the parliamentary undersecretaries became increasingly accepted as major factors assuring the success of Prussia's youthful parliamentary democracy.

The first major test of the coalition's cohesion was the cabinet's stand on the Versailles Treaty. To be sure, the decision to accept or reject lay with the national government and the Reich Constitutional Convention, but this did not mean that Prussia could avoid the political impact of the decision. In the Reich the conflict over acceptance or rejection of the Allied terms eventually led to the fall of the Weimar coalition. Since the same parties made up the Prussian cabinet, it was expected that the state government could well suffer a similar fate. Surprisingly, the treaty debate caused no government crisis in Prussia. Even before the Allied terms became known, the Constitutional Convention by an overwhelming vote instructed the government to accede only to a genuine peace of understanding.[129] The legislature reiterated its stand after the draft treaty was made public.[130] The cabinet was equally unwavering in its rejection of the treaty imposed on Germany by the Allies.[131]

Paradoxically, the solid front of Prussian opposition was based upon a false premise. Legislators and ministers were convinced that the terms of the Versailles Treaty were deliberately designed to destroy Prussia as the foundation of the Reich's existence. The prospective territorial losses in the east made a particularly strong impression upon the ministers,[132] who feared that these territorial changes would unleash centrifugal forces in Prussia so that the state would no longer be the rivet holding the Reich together.[133] The cabinet also adduced economic arguments against the treaty. It feared that as a result of the territorial losses in the eastern regions of Prussia Germany's food production would collapse, "leading inevitably to widespread death by starvation among the German population."[134] The Prussian opposition was no mere public relations exercise by politicians who, in the end, would not have to bear the responsibility for their actions. The Prussian cabinet expected the Reich ministry to reject the treaty "as a matter of course," and the state government made preparations for declaring a state of siege and issuing instructions to its civil servants in case the state were invaded by Allied troops.[135]

The Reich government eventually and wisely decided to accept the Allies' ultimatum, but not before the Weimar coalition had fallen apart. In contrast, the Prussian cabinet was strengthened by the debate on the treaty. Already united in their stand against the Versailles Treaty, the parties of the Weimar coalition were brought together still further by what turned out to have been a serious tactical error by the USPD. On June 20, 1919, the Prussian Constitutional Convention adjourned for five days, so that it was not in session while the drama of accepting or rejecting the Treaty of Versailles was being played out in the National Constitutional Convention. When the national SPD delegation in the National Constitutional Convention voted to accept the treaty, the Independents apparently became convinced that the majority Socialists in Prussia would follow suit, thereby disavowing the rejectionist stand of the state cabinet. Anticipating this scenario, the USPD decided to introduce a formal motion of no confidence against the government when the Prussian Constitutional Convention reassembled on June 25.[136] If the SPD supported the resolution, the government would fall as had the Reich cabinet a few days earlier.[137]

Perhaps to alert its supporters to the anticipated crisis in Prussia, the USPD announced its parliamentary maneuver in the June 23 edition of the party's newspaper *Die Freiheit*.[138] That decision, however, also gave the coalition at least two days in which to prepare a united response.[139] Since the fate of the treaty itself was no longer an issue, the Prussian government decided that the resignation of the cabinet and the interregnum that would follow would serve no useful purpose, but only further the destabilizing efforts of the left-wing Socialists.[140] The Weimar coalition parties countered the USPD's motion of no confidence with a resolution of confidence. The latter explicitly approved the policies of the government, including its rejection of the Treaty of Versailles.[141] In a roll-call vote, the USPD's motion lost heavily, with the Weimar parties voting solidly for the motion of confidence.[142]

Although the Prussian cabinet had passed its first test of parliamentary support with flying colors, it was inevitable that politics in Prussia would feel repercussions from the changes within the Reich coalition. The Scheidemann cabinet of the Weimar coalition was replaced by a Reich cabinet composed only of the Center party and the SPD. For its willingness to accept the political liability of joining a government with the SPD that bore the burden of enforcing the hated treaty, the Center party demanded a price: the so-called second Weimar school compromise, essentially an agreement that the future federal constitution would prohibit legislation by the states that altered the status quo system of confessionally segregated public elementary schools. Instead, the entire matter would be left in abeyance until the passage of a Reich education law—a feat the Reichstag never managed to achieve.[143] The Prussian Social Democrats and German Democrats vigorously opposed the new educational pact in the Reich. Indeed, the Center party later complained that the Prussian Social Democrats were primarily responsible for weakening the absolute prohibition against any educational laws by the states that had been the Center party's original goal.[144] At the same time, the parties to the left and right of the Weimar coalition understandably hoped to take advantage of the tensions within the Prussian government coalition in order to drive a wedge between the Social Democrats and their moderate bourgeois partners.

Still, the Prussian coalition held. Once again, the primary reasons were factors unique to the political constellation in Prussia. Despite the undoubted differences on educational policies between the SPD and its bourgeois partners, few Social Democratic leaders wanted a new association with the USPD, which would have meant unleashing Adolf Hoffmann for a second time. The DDP and Center party, too, had no real alternative to cooperating with the SPD. For the Catholics, the relative accommodation of the Social Democrats contrasted vividly with the traditional anti-Catholicism of the Prussian authoritarian Right. As for the Democrats, they recognized that particularly in terms of political patronage they were far more influential in a government with the Center party and SPD than in a cabinet dominated by the People's party and the German Nationalists.[145]

In the second half of the year, the political climate worsened appreciably. Polarization and unrest became endemic. These were the weeks, it will be recalled, in which a Reichstag Committee of Inquiry held hearings into the reasons for the collapse of Germany in the fall of 1918, sessions which included Hindenburg's and Ludendorff's efforts to give respectability to the stab-in-the-back legend. At the same time, the Reichstag was debating economic legislation (the *Reichsbetriebsrätegesetz*) that pitted both Socialist parties against all of the bourgeois groups. Tensions among the government parties in Prussia increased as well, reaching a climax late in the year with what became known as the autumn malaise. The beginnings of the fall crisis go back to the debate on the Treaty of Versailles, but the intracoalition acrimony became public and visible particularly after the Constitutional Convention returned from its summer vacation in September. The autumn malaise was lingering and cumulative rather than explosive, so that it was difficult for the crisis management device of the parliamentary undersecretaries to go into action.

Evidence of centrifugal forces at work was not hard to find. Particularly on questions of economic and social policies the SPD and USPD seemed to draw closer together.[146] At the same time, both the DNVP and DVP sought to translate the bourgeois cooperation on economic matters into a more general "Christian majority," which would have the effect of creating a *Bürgerblock* in both the Reich and Prussia.[147] And there was widespread feeling among the SPD that these efforts by the Right might well succeed. The national chairman of the SPD, Otto Wels, was in a "blue *(Katzenjammer)*" mood,[148] a member of the Constitutional Convention expected a bourgeois coalition very soon,[149] and even the usually optimistic Ernst Heilmann saw the spectre of the blue-black bloc, that is, a DNVP–Center party coalition, on the horizon.[150]

To the surprise of most political observers, the Prussian coalition survived the malaise intact. To be sure, the press tended to overly dramatize tensions within the coalition. Heine also exaggerated when he remarked, "You wouldn't believe how well we [ministers] work together in Prussia," but it was true that collegiality within the cabinet continued to function well.[151] One major reason was the Prussian state ministers' complete misjudgment of the overall political situation at the end of 1919. All of the cabinet members felt that the major danger to the stability of the state came from the extreme left, that is, the USPD and the Communists. That assessment would soon be proved wrong, but subjective conviction of an acute danger from this quarter led the coalition parties—including the SPD—to emphasize the points of agreement between them, rather than stress issues on which they differed.[152] In fact, by mid-December Heine expressed the hope that the coalition parties would continue their cooperation during the upcoming election campaign.[153]

That hope was futile, since only three months after Heine's optimistic assessment the Prussian government and the Reich cabinet were both swept away by the Kapp Putsch and its aftermath. Still, until counterrevolutionary violence destroyed its credibility, the balance sheet of the first postrevolutionary cabinet was not unimpressive.[154] In contrast to the experience in the Reich, Prussian parliamentarism had functioned well. Throughout its term of office from March 1919 to March 1920, the Prussian cabinet could count upon strong parliamentary support. To be sure, the votes did not always come from the same quarters, but changed according to the topics under discussion. On educational issues the SPD, DDP, and USPD often voted as a bloc, as did the Center party, DNVP, and DVP on the opposing side. When economic questions were on the agenda, the Center party frequently sided with the Social Democrats, while the DDP as the spokesman for property owners joined with the Conservatives and right-wing Liberals. On issues of provincial autonomy, the Center party found itself isolated as the entire political spectrum except for the Catholics tended to favor a more centralized administration. Above all, however, the Weimar coalition was unintentionally supported by the intransigence of the opposition. The USPD, DNVP, and to a lesser extent the DVP again and again insisted that the price of their cooperation with one or more of the Weimar coalition parties was the destruction of the parliamentary system itself. Under these circumstances, the Weimar parties had no viable alternative except to cooperate with each other and continue the coalition established in March 1919.

The Second Weimar Coalition Cabinet, 1920–1921

The Kapp Putsch began what would be a twelve-year span of democratic and parliamentary stability in Prussia. This was hardly the intent of the conspirators, but there was nevertheless a causal relationship between the two developments. The frenetic atmosphere in Berlin during the brief occupation by Kapp's forces and the constant danger that civil war might break out in the capital led the moderate bourgeois parties to reject a *Bürgerblock* dominated by the DNVP, while the right-wing Social Democrats eventually opposed a variety of schemes designed to achieve extraparliamentary control of the executive by the unions.

The coup by Kapp and Lüttwitz was directed primarily against the Reich government, but it certainly affected Prussia as well. In the early hours of March 13, 1920, when reports of the Ehrhardt Brigade's march on the capital reached the highest government offices, the Prussian and Reich cabinets met under the chairmanship of the Reich president. A majority of the Reich ministers rejected armed action against the rebels, and instead recommended that the ministers leave Berlin. Only Vice-Chancellor Schiffer would remain behind as an unofficial observer.[155] Among the Prussian state ministers, Hirsch and Heine pleaded eloquently for remaining in Berlin. They felt that any other course of action would be interpreted as flight by the supporters of the government.[156] Their arguments failed to convince the Reich ministers, but they did sway their Prussian colleagues. Only Otto Braun reluctantly left the capital, since his life had been threatened previously by the very forces that were now marching into the city.[157] The Prussian ministers' presence in the capital meant that for the next six days the state's political leaders were in close touch not only with the Kapp forces, but also with the leaders of the labor unions. This factor in turn gave to the negotiations in Berlin a fluidity and flexibility that contrasted markedly with the rigid, ultimative demands with which the Reich leaders attempted to defeat Kapp.

The Prussian cabinet in Berlin was not in physical danger. After being briefly placed under house arrest, by the afternoon of March 13 the ministers were once again free to move about the city.[158] Kapp's seeming generosity was a tactical maneuver designed to persuade at least some members of the Prussian cabinet to cooperate with the new "government." Immediately after his appointment as Kapp's minister of the interior, Gottlieb von Jagow approached Oeser, asking him to participate in the insurgents' cabinet. A short time later, Lüttwitz summoned all of the old Prussian ministers to meet with him in the Reich chancellery. None of the republican ministers agreed to cooperate with the insurgents.

The putsch also affected the work of the Prussian legislature. One of Kapp's first decrees as self-appointed prime minister dissolved the state Constitutional Convention. All parties, including the DNVP, protested against this arbitrary administrative act, though the rightist parties, true to their ambivalent relationship to the putsch, refused to defy Kapp openly. They were willing to continue informal meetings of the convention's Rules Committee (Ältestenausschuss), but refused to hold formal sessions in defiance of Kapp's decree.[159]

In the days that followed the seizure of the capital, Prussian executive and legislative leaders were prominently involved in effecting the defeat of Kapp and the withdrawal of the insurgent forces from Berlin. The multilevel negotiations that took place between March 13 and March 26 can be divided into three chronological segments, though they overlapped to some extent. During the first period, from March 13 to March 15, the primary objective was to prevent acts of violence either by undisciplined elements among the rebels or by radicals from the extreme left. It was feared that such activity by either side would unleash a civil war. The second segment, roughly from March 15 through March 18, was primarily devoted to working out the modalities of Kapp's capitulation. Finally, in the days after March 18 the focus shifted to the reorganization of the Reich and Prussian governments. The primary issues now were the relationship between the executive and extraparliamentary pressure groups, notably the unions. Throughout the interregnum a fundamental cleavage existed between the attitude of the Reich government, temporarily exiled in Stuttgart, and the Prussian political leadership which remained in Berlin. While the Reich government insisted on unconditional surrender by Kapp and his allies even if this meant tolerating Kapp's control of the capital a few days longer, the Prussian negotiators were primarily concerned about the danger of civil war or uncontrolled violence. For this reason they were anxious to defuse the volatile situation in Berlin as rapidly as possible by achieving the physical withdrawal of the insurgents. To this end they were willing to agree to terms that fell short of abject surrender by the putschists. The basic thread running through the negotiations in Berlin was the simultaneous aim to have the Kapp forces withdraw and to reestablish constitutional law and order without alienating the forces on the left whose support of the general strike was primarily responsible for the defeat of the putsch.

The discussions about the post-Kapp future of Reich and state took place in a variety of settings, from formal meetings of the Reichsrat (Kapp had not dissolved this body, presumably because it had been a kingpin of Prussian influence before 1918) to numerous informal contacts between individual politicians, high-ranking civil servants, and business and union leaders.[160] The Reich government in Stuttgart was unaware of most of what was happening in Berlin; in fact, it was fully informed only about Schiffer's ongoing negotiations with the rebels.[161]

In contrast to Schiffer's semipublic talks, negotiations conducted by a number of Prussian political leaders were kept out of the limelight. Undoubtedly, the most important were various discussions led by the Prussian Social Democratic parliamentary leaders. The majority of the party's national leadership had left for Stuttgart and some cabinet ministers, like Hirsch and Heine, had been discredited by the outbreak of the Kapp Putsch, but the party's Prussian parliamentary leaders retained the confidence of rank-and-file workers. In particular Kapp's coup laid the foundation for the rise of Ernst Heilmann, later the long-term head of the SPD's delegation in the Landtag, to a position of *eminence grise* in the state.[162] Heilmann was the focal point of a dramatic if abortive attempt to draw the DNVP away from its stand of de facto support for Kapp and his forces. Essentially, Heilmann saw the DNVP's relationship to the Prussian republic and the Weimar coalition government as analogous to the relationship between the SPD and Bethmann Hollweg in the early years of World War I.[163] He was convinced that the Conservatives, too, could have no interest in destroying the parliamentary system since "you [the DNVP] can be sure of one thing: Kornilov will be followed by Lenin."[164]

Heilmann's concern for the survival of the Prussian parliamentary system led him to contact personally Oskar Hergt, the leader of the German Nationalists. On March 13, the SPD's parliamentary leader, after consulting leaders of his own party and others in the coalition,[165] went to Hergt's private residence in Berlin in order to persuade the Conservative leader to join with the Weimar parties in foiling the designs of the antiparliamentary forces of the extreme left and right. Both men kept the substance of the conversation confidential until the end of May. It was only when, in the course of the 1920 Reichstag election campaign, the DNVP attempted to deny its basically supportive attitude toward the Kapp Putsch,[166] that Heilmann published a detailed account of his talks with Hergt, which, the SPD leader noted, had actually been written immediately after the meeting. Hergt published his own version four days later.

The main thrust of Heilmann's argument to the Conservative leader was to forge a tactical alliance between all of the forces that Heilmann felt had an interest in preserving parliamentary government in Prussia. Such a political phalanx would then isolate and render powerless both the Kapp forces and any potential Communist counterforce. Hergt's response, however, was a severe disappointment to Heilmann. The leader of the DNVP refused the mission urged on him by the SPD leader, arguing that in the first place he had little influence over Kapp and Lüttwitz. The Conservative also doubted the effectiveness of the general strike. Instead of the immediate withdrawal and resignation of the putschists, Hergt proposed that the new "government" remain in office until national elections could be held, though he felt that the present group of "ministers" appointed by Kapp should be augmented by representatives from other parties, including the SPD after it had dissociated itself from the general strike. Heilmann of course rejected these "totally unrealistic suggestions" and expressed his disappointment in Hergt's unwillingness to denounce the putschists. The SPD leader left the talk in an extremely pessimistic frame of mind: civil war seemed to him inevitable.[167]

Prussia's Social Democrats also established contacts with the second party on the right, the DVP. Information on these talks is much less detailed, though in the long run the political consequences were more significant. Formal contacts between the DVP and the SPD were not established until March 17, that is, when the defeat of Kapp was already a fait accompli. The DVP took the initiative. Eugen Leidig, a leading member of the DVP delegation in the Constitutional Convention, phoned Heilmann to offer his party's cooperation in forming both a Reich and Prussian government. He emphasized that he spoke both for himself and for Stresemann, the DVP's national leader. At the time, the SPD ignored the proposal, but it did so with a "sense of inner satisfaction"; Heilmann did not close the door on the possibility of a future coalition.[168]

While Heilmann worked to enlist the right-wing parties in the defense of parliamentarism, other members of the SPD attempted to establish contacts with the USPD in order to prevent the Independents from joining forces with the KPD and staging a possible counterputsch from the left. Kapp's coup had undoubtedly brought the two parties closer together. There was widespread agreement that a number of personnel changes were necessary; Heine and Noske in particular had to be dismissed.[169] More significantly, the rightists' violent counterrevolution also convinced a wide spectrum of leaders as well as the rank and file in both the SPD and the USPD that any cabinet established after the defeat of Kapp should be a workers' or socialist government.

However, these two terms, *socialist government* and *workers' government,* while sounding very similar, expressed rather different plans for the future of left-wing control in Germany. A Socialist government was in essence the antithesis of the *Bürgerblock,* that is, it involved a government coalition composed solely of Socialist parties that could, at least in theory, include the KPD. A workers' government, on the other hand, might mean simply enlarging the Weimar coalition by the addition of the USPD. A workers' government did not imply excluding the moderate bourgeois parties, since organized labor had ties to the DDP and the Center party as well as to the SPD and the USPD. On the other hand, the Communists would have been excluded since the KPD endorsed the concept of the dictatorship of the proletariat, a goal that all wings of organized labor rejected.[170] From the point of view of the SPD, then, a workers' government was an enlarged Weimar coalition that included the USPD, but isolated the KPD.[171]

Negotiations between the left- and right-wing Socialists took place simultaneously on two levels. There were quasi-formal talks between SPD and USPD members of the constitutional convention. In these talks the SPD was

represented by Heinrich Limbertz and Eduard Gräf, the USPD by Kurt Rosenfeld and Heinrich Ströbel. More informal were contacts between members of
both parties mediated by representatives of the Amsterdam Socialist (that is,
non-Communist) International who happened to be in Berlin during the Kapp
Putsch.[172] In the quasi-formal talks, the SPD proposed its concept of a workers' government to end the crisis and invited the USPD to join such a cabinet.
The Independents refused and countered instead with a plan for a Socialist
government in both the Reich and Prussia, which would dissolve the two
constitutional conventions and govern without legislative support (or control)
for at least five months.[173] The SPD in turn rejected this proposal as a thinly
disguised dictatorship of the proletariat. The informal contacts began much
more auspiciously, though they too soon failed. The talks began almost
euphorically with the participants all but forgetting their political differences
in the face of the prospect of renewed Socialist unity, but once the acute
danger from Kapp had passed, the old divisions quickly reasserted themselves. On Friday (19 March), the USPD broke off all further contact with the
right-wing Socialists.[174]

It is true that the various discussions among Prussia's political leaders
failed to provide an immediate solution to the crisis facing the state, but the
indirect and long-term effects of the contacts were nonetheless significant.
They weakened the ties of cooperation between the DNVP and the DVP on
the right and the USPD and the KPD on the left. In this sense the various
discussions strengthened the parliamentary form of government in Prussia by
reducing the potential cohesion of the extraparliamentary forces arrayed
against it.

On Thursday, March 18, the focal point of political discussions in Berlin
shifted from the parties to the unions, or more precisely to the discussions
between leaders of the Weimar parties and organized labor. On the party side,
the discussions were led by the Socialist ministers in Prussia and the leaders of
the SPD's district organization in Berlin. The key spokesman for organized
labor was the chairman of the executive committee of the socialist unions,
the General German Association of Unions (Allgemeiner Deutscher
Gewerkschaftsbund, or ADGB), Carl Legien, a man whose real aims in these
crucial days have remained enigmatic and controversial.[175] After Kapp's
defeat was a foregone conclusion and the withdrawal of the mutinous forces
only a matter of time, Legien apparently considered at least briefly that the
time was ripe for a major shift in the political balance of power. "Very
suddenly" he invited representatives of the USPD and proposed what
amounted to a form of workers' government after Kapp's forces had with-
drawn from the capital. The labor leader apparently envisioned executive
leaderships in Germany and Prussia composed solely of representatives from
the various wings of organized labor, excluding a formal role by the political

parties. Legien's plan never reached the stage of practical consideration since the representatives from the USPD immediately rejected it and called instead for the establishment of the dictatorship of the proletariat.[176] Consequently, the union leaders had no choice but to turn to the parties of the Weimar coalition and persuade them to accept at least some of the demands of organized labor.[177]

Legien's failure to persuade the USPD to join forces with the unions strengthened the hand of the supporters of parliamentary government. Particularly the right wing of the Prussian Socialists now began to reassert itself, with Finance Minister Albert Südekum taking a leading part in the negotiations with the labor unions. Südekum was convinced that only a compromise between the demands of organized labor and the parties of the Weimar coalition would bring a permanent end to the crisis.[178] In the "very dramatic" negotiations that eventually led to the formulation of the Eight-Point Program on March 20 and the formation of new Reich and Prussian cabinets, Hirsch, Südekum, and Stegerwald represented the Prussian political parties.[179] Actually, for the most part, the future of Prussia was not the focal point of the discussions. Among the eight points, only two affected the state directly: the unions demanded the removal of the two ministers who "looked particularly bad" (Heine and Oeser),[180] and the accelerated democratization of the Prussian civil service and police. In fact, the removal of the ministers provided no difficulties. Hirsch announced that he had already "definitely decided" to resign when the putsch broke out.[181] Heine had also submitted his resignation before the unions demanded his dismissal. Eugen Ernst followed his friend into political exile.[182] Albert Südekum himself also recognized he had become persona non grata among many of his party colleagues. He was rejected not only because of his rightist leanings, but also because he alone among the socialist ministers had aroused Otto Braun's personal animosity. The minister of agriculture was particularly incensed by what he considered to be Südekum's overly generous proposals for compensation agreements with the House of Hohenzollern.[183] These personnel changes decimated the Prussian cabinet. Of the ten ministers only five remained in office after the putsch, and of the five Social Democratic members of the old cabinet, only two, Braun and Haenisch, survived the upheaval as members of the cabinet.

The reorganization of the government took place in two fairly distinct phases: the first might be called the Berlin or union segment, the second was a statewide or parliamentary phase. Initially the leaders of the SPD's left-wing organizations in Berlin and Frankfurt seemed to dominate the negotiations. Under consideration for major positions in the new cabinet were the two district chairmen, Franz Krüger (Berlin) and Eduard Gräf (Frankfurt). The Berlin regional spokesman had close ties to some unions, notably the Union of Technical Workers, whose Berlin business agent, Hermann Lüdemann, was also in line for a ministerial post.[184] For a time the SPD's delegation in the Constitutional Convention, too, seemed to support the left-wing leaders. A list of ministers leaked to the press on March 25 showed Krüger as prime minister–designate, but after "additional consultations" the SPD delegation was reported to have "definitely" decided to nominate Gräf as prime minister and Krüger as minister of the interior.[185]

Despite what appeared to be a final decision by the SPD's delegation, the "Berlin concept" for the composition of the Prussian cabinet failed for a variety of reasons. To begin with, it rested on a very shaky base of parliamentary support. It was obvious that the DDP and the Center party would be unenthusiastic over the appointment of two decidedly left-wing Social Democratic leaders. The leftists in the SPD apparently hoped to compensate for the lack of support from the moderate bourgeois parties with benevolent neutrality on the part of the USPD, but that expectation was based upon what turned out to be a misleading precedent. To be sure, left- and right-wing Socialists in the city council and executive offices of the City of Berlin had worked well together on many issues, but it soon became apparent that it would be difficult to transfer this informal local working agreement to the state level.[186] In addition, there were personnel problems. The USPD refused to accept Krüger as prime minister because of his association with Reich president Ebert. (Krüger was the president's administrative assistant.)[187] The Independents did not object to Gräf, and Krüger was willing to accept the post of minister of the interior,[188] but now the national union leaders intervened. Both Legien and Hue (the president of the mine workers' union), had already determined that Carl Severing was their man for the interior position.[189] Finally, there was a linkage problem with the Reich. Ebert objected to a left-oriented cabinet in Prussia, apparently fearing difficulties with the Weimar coalition in the Reich if the Prussian government were dominated by leftists. (Incidentally, disagreements with Ebert on this score led Krüger to resign his post in the president's office.)[190]

On March 27, after the newspaper *Vorwärts* had reported "that difficulties still remained" before a new Prussian government could be formed, the name of Otto Braun as prime minister–designate suddenly surfaced. This development was unexpected and, as the USPD was quick to point out, had not received the prior consent of the union negotiators.[191] Braun himself was not a controversial choice for ministerial office. He had a reputation as a spokesman for the left in the old cabinet,[192] and his name had appeared as minister of agriculture on all of the lists leaked to the press. However, so far his name had not been mentioned as a possible choice for prime minister. Indeed, there had been some discussion of his moving to the Reich cabinet as successor to Noske in the position of Reich defense minister.[193] Still, in retrospect it is easy to see why Otto Braun might be a suitable compromise candidate as Prussian prime minister. As a "leftist" he would appease the rebellious mood among the SPD's rank and file. At the same time, he was a firm supporter of the parliamentary form of government and the Weimar coalition. He could be expected to reject any claims to extraparliamentary influence by the unions or other pressure groups.[194] Within the SPD delegation in the Constitutional Convention, Braun's major supporter seems to have been Heilmann, while some other members were initially rather lukewarm.[195]

The Braun cabinet consisted of familiar bourgeois figures (Hugo am Zehnoff, Otto Fischbeck, and Adam Stegerwald all remained in office),[196] but among the Social Democrats, aside from the prime minister, only Konrad Haenisch stayed on as minister of education. If the support of the SPD delegation for Braun was lukewarm, it was little short of chilly for Haenisch. His former colleague and longtime adversary, Adolf Hoffmann, whose information about internal affairs of the SPD was usually quite reliable, claimed that the delegation had given Haenisch only the narrowest of approval; the vote for Haenisch was forty-three to forty-two.[197] Essentially, Haenisch stayed in office because no other Social Democrat was willing to take on the thankless task of being minister of education.

Of the two new Social Democrats in the cabinet, Severing was initially regarded as the spokesman for the national leadership of the ADGB, while Hermann Lüdemann, who succeeded Südekum in the Ministry of Finance, was an obvious concession to the SPD's left wing. Severing personified the concept of a workers' government in its constitutional and parliamentary form; he pointed with particular pride to his good relations with all wings of the labor movement, Catholic and liberal no less than Socialist.[198] Lüdemann, "a nice decent fellow" who would remain in office for less than a year, belonged to the team of SPD leaders in the capital city, though even here his personality and his position as head of a white-collar union distinguished him from some of the more radical, blue collar–oriented socialist leaders.[199]

What one delegate in the Constitutional Convention called "the Kapp foolishness," for all its farcical aspects, also had a profound impact on future political attitudes of the Prussian bourgeois parties. In particular the state's Center party moved perceptibly to the left as a result of the putsch. In delivering the Center party's response to Otto Braun's first state of the state address after the putsch, the parliamentary undersecretary in the Ministry of Education, Monsignor Rudolf Wildermann, emphasized his party's support for the continuation of the coalition: "The coalition . . . has proved itself and must remain." At the same time, Wildermann pledged the Center's allegiance to parliamentary democracy and even defended his party's support of the general strike as weapon to defeat Kapp and his forces. As for cooperation with the right, the Center party spokesman explicitly rejected a *Bürgerblock* cabinet for Prussia. He attacked the DNVP not only for its involvement in the putsch, but reminded that party of all of its past anti-Catholic sins.[200]

The Kapp Putsch began the meteoric rise to prominence of two Social Democratic politicians who would dominate Weimar Prussia until its demise in 1932. They were Ernst Heilmann and Otto Braun. Before the putsch, Heilmann had been an obscure back-bencher in the Social Democratic delegation (he was listed in sixth place on the SPD's statewide ballot and barely managed to get elected in 1919), but within months after the defeat of Kapp he had become, in the words of the SPD's national chairman Otto Wels, "indispensable."[201] The "uncrowned king of Prussia" was never a popular or beloved politician, but that did not diminish his effectiveness as a parliamentary leader.[202] Over the years the Prussian ministers came to value not only Heilmann's tactical skill in the halls of parliament, but also the fact that he never showed the slightest interest in becoming a member of the cabinet himself.[203] Braun, too, was not yet a household word in Prussia.[204] Like Heilmann, he enjoyed more respect than love or adulation. His political success was due primarily to a variety of tactical skills and was much less the result of either a wealth of ideas or a particular industriousness.[205] Otto Braun was, however, a master of consensus politics. Even more than his predecessor he led the government as a group of collegial equals. During his terms as prime minister the cabinet seldom took formal votes on various issues. Rather, Braun generally guided the discussion so that a common policy line would emerge to which all of the cabinet members could subscribe without formal divisions. The prime minister was similarly skillful in his relations with the parliamentary delegations of the coalition.[206]

The members of the Braun cabinet had hardly taken their seats when the national elections of June 1920 decisively changed the political makeup of Germany. To be sure, the Reichstag elections did not alter the composition of the state's legislature, but it was naive to believe that the profound shifts in the Reich as a whole would be without repercussions in Germany's largest state. There was no denying that whatever mandate the parties of the Weimar coalition had received in January 1919, it was lost a year and a half later. The primary beneficiaries of the shift in the voters' allegiance, the DNVP and DVP, demanded that parallel bourgeois governments in the Reich and Prussia be formed to reflect the wishes of the voters.[207] But a *Bürgerblock*, while enjoying a parliamentary majority in the new Reichstag, would have been a minority government in Prussia. On the other hand a coalition spanning the parties from the SPD to the DVP (the so-called grand coalition), seemed to provide all the answers. It would reflect the voters' mandate since the DVP was the largest winner in the June 1920 elections, yet not violate the rules of parliamentary government. A grand coalition would enjoy massive parliamentary support both in the new Reichstag and in the present Prussian Constitutional Convention.

But there were insurmountable difficulties. As far as the Reich was concerned, there was little doubt that at least for the immediate future most Social Democrats firmly rejected any coalition with the DVP.[208] A primary reason was concern over the future of the Social Democrats in light of the imminent collapse and dissolution of the USPD. The SPD hoped that it would inherit most of the fallout from the Independents and thus lay the foundation for a reunited workers' party. It seemed obvious to many Social Democrats that if the SPD joined a coalition with the DVP, traditionally the party of heavy industry, many of the former USPD members would be unwilling to rejoin the old party.[209] A second and more controversial reason was a desire to escape the burdens of governmental responsibility. In this area, Prussian SPD leaders were sharply critical of their colleagues in the Reich. Severing and Braun, for example, strongly rejected the majority's wish to escape executive responsibility at all costs.[210] Heilmann went one step further. He emphasized that a mass party, no matter how impressive its membership, that did not aim at executive power, was unable to represent the interests of its voters.[211] The views of the Prussians fell on particularly fruitful ground since all factions of the SPD were determined to retain a share of governmental power in the state. Moreover, there was a clear connection between remaining in the Prussian cabinet and leaving the Reich government. The SPD needed to maintain its position in the state simply to prevent a bourgeois Reich government from dominating the Reichsrat.[212] As the newspaper *Vorwärts* noted with polemical sharpness, "Prussia with its Social Democratic ministers and provincial governors represents the last obstacle against the reactionary flood."[213] But such tough talk did not solve another dilemma for the SPD: how could the Weimar coalition in Prussia remain in office if the bourgeois partners were determined to break up the coalition?

The Stegerwald Cabinet of 1921

The Social Democrats were spared a confrontation with this question for several months. There was general agreement among the Weimar parties that it would be impractical either to change the government or to hold state elections before the legislature had finished its work on the constitution. Haggling over setting the date for new state elections began almost immediately after the results of the June 1920 Reichstag elections were known. Understandably, the opposition parties insisted that new elections be held as early as possible, while the government coalition hoped to delay a new contest.[214] Eventually the parties compromised on February 20, 1921, as the date for new state elections.[215] The campaign for the first democratic Landtag did not succeed in arousing a great deal of voter interest.[216] No specifically Prussian campaign themes emerged, so that the issues for the state elections were little more than a rerun of the Reichstag campaign seven months earlier.

In view of the outcome of that contest, it is not surprising that the parties of the coalition were apprehensive about the state elections. Particularly the SPD was fearful of the outcome and sought safety in pre-election deals with its partners. Party leaders attempted, rather awkwardly, to persuade the Democrats and the Center party to commit themselves during the campaign to a continuation of the coalition.[217] The bourgeois partners rejected the suggestion, so that the Weimar coalition in Prussia formally ended with the dissolution of the Constitutional Convention.[218]

As expected, the Landtag elections of February 1921 confirmed the trend already apparent in the national elections a half year earlier (already discussed), with heavy losses for the government parties and corresponding gains for the opposition. In view of the election outcome, the formation of a new government promised to be both "not uninteresting" and "unspeakably difficult."[219] The initial result of the lengthy negotiations was a short-lived minority cabinet that, as Otto Braun put it, "could not live and had difficulty dying."[220]

It is ironic that the whole tragicomedy in Prussia could have been avoided if the various political groups had not committed themselves beforehand to positions that were both contradictory and incompatible.[221] Chief among these was the continued commitment to the Reich-Prussian linkage. Although a number of prudent voices in the Weimar coalition parties—among them Trimborn, Bernhard Falk (the future head of the DDP Landtag caucus), Severing, Braun, Haenisch, and the later Prussian minister of the interior, Albert Grzesinski—urged their respective parties to enter coalition negotiations without preconditions,[222] the party leaders decided on issuing public statements that allowed for little flexibility. The Center party and the DDP had gone on record before the election demanding grand coalitions at both the federal and state levels.[223] Even more unrealistic was the proposal by the DVP to insist upon national and Prussian cabinets that included the SPD and DNVP.[224] At the other end of the political spectrum, the SPD publicly rejected any cooperation with the DVP or the DNVP and insisted upon the return of the Weimar coalition.[225]

In a sense, the clearest path to a viable compromise was an agreement in principle by the SPD to join its former coalition partners in a quest for a grand coalition in the Reich and Prussia. This would have placed the onus for refusing on the DVP, rather than on the Social Democrats. Precisely such a scenario was proposed by the former Reich minister of defense, Gustav Noske (now the governor of the province of Hanover). On March 1 the left-Liberal Berlin newspaper *8-Uhr Morgenblatt* published an op-ed piece by Noske under the title "The government of Prussia." In it the former defense minister urged his colleagues to agree to grand coalitions in the Reich and in Prussia and, incidentally, to cease their excessive concern over the future fate of the USPD.

In retrospect it is doubtful that Noske's contribution served either the party or the course of action he advocated. The immediate reaction within the SPD was a storm of indignation. Noske was formally reprimanded by the national executive, ostensibly because he had violated a party rule against publishing in bourgeois publications.[226] More important, the SPD delegation in the new Landtag, at least in part responding to the outcry among rank-and-file members against Noske's suggestion, closed the door to the grand coalition on March 8. The Landtag delegation voted overwhelmingly for a return of the Weimar coalition, and for good measure, published a list of cabinet posts which the SPD would insist on filling with its nominees in the new cabinet.[227] The reaction of the bourgeois parties was predictably negative and blunt.[228]

When it became clear at the end of the first week of March that neither the grand coalition nor the Weimar coalition had a realistic chance of success in Prussia, the DNVP attempted to fill the political vacuum. One day after the SPD rejected the grand coalition, Oskar Hergt wrote identical letters to the DDP, the Center party, and the DVP, asserting that only a *Bürgerblock* was a realistic alternative for Prussia. However, Hergt's initiative was no more successful than other plans; the DDP immediately opposed any coalition that did not include both the DVP and the SPD.[229] By mid-March, almost a month after the elections, Germany's largest state still did not have a government.

At the beginning of April, recognizing the potential danger of a prolonged power vacuum in Prussia, the Reich president entered into the negotiations. He asked the chairmen of the DDP, the SPD, and the Center party Landtag delegations to meet with him to explore the possibility of forming a cabinet of the grand coalition. It is an indication of the changing atmosphere that all of those present, including the chairman of the SPD delegation, Siering, now stated that they were not in principle opposed to such a government.[230] A meeting of the SPD delegation, held a day later, seemed to confirm that the party had shifted from its obstructionist ground; Heilmann, for example, insisted only upon concessions from the People's party in specific policy areas, notably on the question of the financial settlement with the former royal house.[231] But the hopeful atmosphere was soon doomed when the SPD's national executive intervened to sabotage the seemingly accommodating stance by the Prussian SPD and, indirectly, the initiatives of the Reich president. Instead of face-to-face negotiations with the DVP, the SPD's national executive asked for indirect negotiations through the good offices of the head of the Center party's delegation, Carl Herold. On April 7 Siering wrote Herold that the SPD was willing to consider a coalition with the DVP, provided that the People's party agreed to accelerate the democratization of the civil service and allot the SPD three ministerial positions, those of prime minister, minister of the interior, and minister of agriculture.[232] In response, a majority of the DVP delegation demanded that the prime minister should under no circumstances come from the ranks of either the SPD or the DDP. In addition, the DVP seriously damaged the prospects for future negotiations by leaking Siering's letter to the press without his knowledge and permission. As a result, two days before the Landtag met for its first session, all meaningful contacts between the SPD and the DVP had been broken off.[233]

When the legislature assembled, no agreement had been reached either on the person of the prime minister or the political composition of the cabinet. Under the provisions of the new Prussian constitution (to be discussed later), the prime minister was elected by the legislature. He in turn selected the members of the government and presented them to the Landtag for confirmation. The legislature thus had not one but six chances (the number of cabinet members in 1921) to withdraw its confidence from the newly elected prime minister. Under normal circumstances, of course, the election of a prime minister would be preceded by agreement on the entire cabinet among the coalition parties, but in the absence of such an accord a prime minister nominated by the rightist parties might well receive the necessary plurality of votes to be elected. To retain some control of the situation, the SPD, DDP, and Center party agreed to support a candidate from the Center party as prime minister, although their agreement implied no commitment to support any government formed by him.[234] In fact, the consensus to elect a prime minister was largely devoid of political substance. When the three parties agreed to this maneuver, they had no specific individual in mind to head the government. In addition, the parties, as though to emphasize their lack of confidence in the arrangement, abolished the institution of parliamentary undersecretaries, an institution that had been a major factor in the stability of the old coalition.[235]

To the surprise of most observers, the Center party nominated the head of the Christian labor unions, Adam Stegerwald, as its candidate for prime minister. Stegerwald did not seem an obvious choice. He was not a member of the new Landtag, and had taken no part in the discussions that led to his selection.[236] The minister for social services had recently annoyed a large number of Social Democrats by his rallying cry against the dangers of Marxism at the October 1920 congress of the Christian Trade Union movement. Still, as a labor leader he retained some popularity among the leftist parties, while his recent remarks would endear him to the DNVP. Indeed, the Conservatives had informed the Center party that they would be willing to support a cabinet headed by Stegerwald, provided "it was free of Socialists."[237]

At first glance, Stegerwald did appear to be the man for all parties. He received more votes than any other Prussian cabinet leader; every group in the legislature except the extreme left (KPD and USPD) supported him. Difficulties began when the new prime minister started to assemble his cabinet. Stegerwald was apparently not informed that part of the price for his election was to grant the SPD and the DDP veto power over his ministerial selections.[238] Instead, the prime minister naively assumed that his broad parliamentary support provided him with a virtually free hand in selecting his ministers.[239] He expected to be able to select a cabinet from the entire spectrum of parties from the SPD to the DNVP, and to link the Prussian and Reich cabinets as well. For example, the prime minister suggested that Otto Braun should serve as Prussian liaison minister to the Reich.[240] Such ideas were totally unrealistic, Braun had no intention of giving up his pivotal position as minister of agriculture in order to serve as letter carrier to the Reich government.[241]

Stegerwald's efforts soon came to naught, but in the meantime Prussia continued to be without an effective executive. It was not until April 19 that a temporary solution, which really satisfied no one, was found. It came in the form of a bourgeois minority government headed by Stegerwald with ministers drawn from the DDP, the Center party, and the ranks of the senior civil service.[242] The cabinet received a vote of confidence in the Landtag with the ballots of all of the bourgeois parties, while the KPD, USPD, and SPD voted against a motion of confidence. As head of a rump cabinet, Stegerwald was then completely dependent upon the good will of the DNVP; without the approval of this party, Stegerwald's cabinet could not have survived the Landtag vote.

The members of Stegerwald's minority cabinet were a group of second-rate political leaders and weak personalities.[243] The government contained only three active politicians; the other ministers were senior civil servants. Stegerwald himself continued to function as minister for social services in addition to occupying the post of prime minister. Alexander Dominicus (DDP) became minister of the interior and am Zehnhoff remained at the Justice Ministry. All three belonged to the right wing of their parties; left-wing members of the two government parties had declined to serve.[244] Dominicus in particular had the reputation of a red-baiter.[245]

Stegerwald and his allies looked upon the minority cabinet as a transition government while they continued to work for simultaneous grand coalition cabinets in the Reich and Prussia. That expectation did not seem unreasonable since by this time all of the moderate parties were committed to such a course of action. However, the new ministers had hardly taken their oath of office when a foreign policy crisis created an entirely new political situation. In the Treaty of Versailles the Reich had accepted responsibility for paying reparations, but the actual amount had been left open. Now, on May 5, 1921, the

Allies informed Germany that the total amount of reparations would be 132 billion *Goldmark*. Most Germans regarded the figure as exorbitant and unacceptable, and the question of whether to accept or reject the Allied dictum deeply divided the coalition in the Reich. The national government fell when a majority of the DVP's Reichstag delegates voted to reject the Allied note, despite the pleas of the party's national leader, Gustav Stresemann, that rejection was an empty gesture that would have no practical effect.[246]

With the resignation of the Reich cabinet, the "chancellor carousel" began to turn again, but the hopes of forming a grand coalition receded as the DVP once again joined the ranks of the opposition. That meant the Reich government would again be a Weimar coalition, headed by a chancellor from the Center party. However, it was by no means clear whether the chancellor would be a left-wing or right-wing Catholic. Under discussion were both Joseph Wirth, a spokesman for left-wing Catholicism, and Konrad Adenauer, a leader of the Center party's conservative wing. Stegerwald favored Adenauer,[247] while Wirth was among his archenemies in the Center party. The eventual appointment of Joseph Wirth to head a left-of-center Weimar coalition thus left Stegerwald's bourgeois minority government in Prussia out of step with developments in the Reich, and after May, "The main activity of Stegerwald's cabinet consisted of negotiations to change the composition of the government."[248] Now it was the SPD's turn to raise the linkage issue. In view of the new developments in the Reich, the Socialists demanded parallel Weimar coalitions at the national and state levels.[249]

Discussions about the reorganization of the Prussian cabinet dragged on without visible success until the beginning of July. At that point the SPD employed a new tactic: it decided to apply pressure not on the Center party, but on the DDP. The July 2 issue of the *Frankfurter Zeitung* carried an article (under the byline, "by a well-informed politician") that contained a quite candid and detailed analysis of the current political situation in Prussia. The unnamed author, who was actually Hans Goslar,[250] the former press secretary in the Braun cabinet, contended that the Center party had really lost its freedom of action since it was completely dependent upon the good will of the DVP and the Conservatives to keep Stegerwald in office. The key to a way out of the political paralysis therefore lay in the hands of the Democrats. The DDP had to decide whether it would become little more than an appendage of the DVP or whether it would remain as an independent spokesman for the pro-Republican and liberal parts of the bourgeoisie. If the DDP chose the latter course, it would have to draw the consequences and cut its ties to the blue-black coalition.

Neither the article in the *Frankfurter Zeitung* nor the far more profound shock of the assassination of Matthias Erzberger led to the immediate fall of the Stegerwald government, although both developments set the stage for a change. Still, for some weeks the bourgeois parties and Stegerwald himself continued to insist on simultaneous grand coalitions in the Reich and in Prussia, while the SPD held fast to Weimar coalitions and the resignation of Stegerwald as prime minister. The difficulties were compounded by Stegerwald's stubborn attempt to have a reorganization in the Reich precede events in Prussia. On September 10, 1921, the latest round of negotiations broke off.[251]

At the beginning of October the Prussian parties seemed to recognize at last that the difficulties of attempting to form simultaneous and parallel coalitions in the Reich and Prussia were, for the moment at least, insurmountable. When representatives from the Landtag delegations of the grand coalition parties met, they quickly discovered that they could readily agree on the basic outlines of a program for Prussia.[252] In the Reich, on the other hand, negotiations by the same groups again demonstrated that unbridgeable differences remained between the Social Democrats and the DVP on a number of issues. The most acute among these was the German reaction to the Allied decision on Upper Silesia. (In the meantime, Germany had perforce acceded to the reparations sum.) The plebiscite provided for in the Treaty of Versailles had produced a victory for Germany in the popular vote in the area, but on October 13 the Allies for a variety of strategic and economic reasons divided the territory in question to the distinct benefit of Poland rather than Germany. The reaction of most German political parties was yet another patriotic outcry of indignation, though more sober voices (which again included Gustav Stresemann) realized that Germany could do little to alter the Allied decision except to issue paper protests. A majority of the DVP Reichstag delegation, however, joined the DNVP in a resolution demanding that the Reich formally reject the Allied dictum regardless of the consequences. In view of the fierce opposition among major parts of the bourgeois parties against a policy of yielding to the Allies, the Reich cabinet felt that it could not remain in office and, against the votes of the Social Democratic ministers, offered its resignation on October 22, 1921.[253]

The Reich was now faced with its second cabinet crisis of the year, one that came at a time when the Prussian negotiations were at a particularly delicate stage. Talk of polarization and apocalypse was in the air.[254] Fortunately, there still remained voices of reason that worked for a compromise among the moderate parties. Immediately after the resignation of the Wirth cabinet, the SPD again declared its readiness in principle to cooperate in a government that included political groups to the right of the Weimar parties, that is, the DVP.[255] Simultaneously, the DVP leadership also cut itself loose from the ideological bonds that periodically tied it to the DNVP. In a statement that expressed his sense of foreboding, Stresemann wrote in October 1921, "The next days will decide if we can still make independent decisions or if we have sunk to the level of being little more than a branch of the German Nationalists."[256] Indeed, it appeared briefly in late October that the time had come for a simultaneous establishment of grand coalition governments in the Reich and in Prussia. By October 24 all major obstacles to such a solution seemed to have been removed; Otto Braun's name was already mentioned as the new Reich minister of the interior.[257]

A short time later, action by the DVP again dashed these hopes. The party's Reichstag delegation addressed a letter to the SPD ostensibly to clarify some aspects of the ongoing negotiations over coalition arrangements in the Reich, but actually to raise public doubts about the SPD's commitment to the national cause.[258] In response, the SPD once again broke off all further negotiations.[259] The crisis in the Reich was then temporarily settled by the election of a second Wirth cabinet, this time a bourgeois minority government consisting of the Center party, the DDP, and the DVP.[260]

The second Wirth cabinet effectively precluded a grand coalition in the Reich, but paradoxically it paved the way for the formation of such a government in Prussia. Even Stegerwald now admitted that Prussia would have to go its own way and could not wait for the Reich.[261] The Gordian knot was finally cut by the Social Democrats. On October 26 or 28—both dates are mentioned by contemporaries—Severing informed Stegerwald and Oeser that beginning on November 3, that is, the date on which the Landtag would reassemble after its fall recess, the SPD would insist on being included in the cabinet with at least two ministers, including the minister of the interior. If the bourgeois parties did not agree, the Social Democrats would assume a position of uncompromising opposition to the government. Unofficially, Severing apparently went even further and talked not only in terms of parliamentary opposition, but also mentioned the word "obstruction," a term that could include extraparliamentary action in the form of street demonstrations and political strikes.[262] The ultimatum brought the Stegerwald cabinet to its timely end.

On November 1, the DDP decided to withdraw its ministers from the cabinet, thereby forcing the government's resignation.[263] The general political situation was now little short of explosive. In the Reich a minority government officiated; in Germany's largest state a caretaker cabinet held office. For the benefit of their rank-and-file members, the Prussian parties reiterated their maximal demands one more time. The moderate bourgeois parties (with the support of the Reich president) demanded a grand coalition, the SPD a Weimar coalition, and the German Nationalists, stressing the Reich-Prussian linkage, called for Stegerwald's reelection as prime minister coupled with the simultaneous resignation of the "Catholic Socialist Dr. Wirth."[264]

It fell to the SPD, as the largest party in the Landtag, to break the deadlock. In order to force his party's hand, Severing again took the initiative. On October 30 in a much-publicized address in Breslau, he expressed his personal opinion that the time for the grand coalition in Prussia had come. He noted that reactionary elements were by no means confined to the DVP, but could be found in the Center party and the DDP as well. Indeed, on one major issue, that of administrative reforms, the DVP's position was certainly closer to that of the SPD than was true of the Center party.[265] The SPD delegation's initial reaction to Severing's remarks was "unanimous" rejection,[266] but on November 4, the delegation met again to reconsider its decision. To be sure, the group was still not at full strength (twenty-seven members had not yet arrived in Berlin), but the significance of the second meeting was underscored by the presence of the national party's co-chairman, Hermann Müller. Richard Hauschildt cautioned his colleagues that the Social Democrats' resignation from governmental responsibility would allow Prussia to become a "second Bavaria,"[267] in other words, would yield the state to the extreme right. In addition, the supporters of the grand coalition could point to far-reaching accommodations by the DVP to the SPD's programmatic demands. In the course of previous negotiations the DVP had already accepted the principle that civil servants needed to be active supporters of the republic rather than passive loyalists.[268] The right Liberals and the Social Democrats also agreed on the necessity for administrative reforms and on revisions of the tax structure. Finally, the DVP limited its ministerial demands to three, Agriculture, Interior, and Commerce, while the DDP was content with one cabinet member.[269] In fact, about the only substantive issue on which the parties could not reach agreement were the terms of the financial settlement with the former ruling house. True, there were still many in the SPD who countered the pragmatic arguments in favor of the grand coalition with emotional appeals not to endanger the imminent reunification of the SPD and the USPD.[270] The final victory of the pragmatists was hardly impressive. The vote for the grand coalition was forty-six to forty-one, an outcome that could easily have been reversed if some of the twenty-seven absent members had been able to vote.[271]

Still, the SPD had now agreed to a grand coalition in Prussia on terms not dissimilar from those Stegerwald had offered the party some months earlier, and which at that time the Social Democrats had indignantly rejected. This led a number of contemporary commentators as well as later historians to criticize the party's earlier obstruction as a symptom of the SPD's irresponsibility and narrow-mindedness.[272] Both factors undoubtedly played a role in the Social Democrats' unedifying wavering between acceptance and rejection of the grand coalition, but it is also true that much had changed between the spring and the fall of 1921. Not only had the SPD itself undergone a process of political soul-searching, but it must also be remembered that in the fall there was no longer any question of Stegerwald's remaining as prime minister.[273] Then, too, the DVP had gone along way toward cutting its ties with the German Nationalists. Finally, and perhaps most important, the Reich-Prussian linkage had been dropped.

After the parties had agreed on the basic programmatic issues of the coalition, all that remained to be settled was the distribution of the ministerial posts. The negotiators for the coalition parties had originally envisioned a cabinet with Oeser (DDP) as prime minister, and Otto Braun continuing as minister of agriculture,[274] but at the last moment the new cabinet almost faltered on the question of whether Otto Braun would return to the Ministry of Agriculture. A number of right-wing delegates in the DVP agreed with the DNVP that a Socialist was intolerable at the agriculture post. On November 5, 1921, after yet more hours of intensive negotiations, Leinert, the chairman of the intracoalition negotiating committee, presented two ministerial lists for a final vote:

Position	Appointees	
Prime minister	Oeser (DDP)	Braun (SPD)
Interior	Severing (SPD)	Severing (SPD)
Agriculture	Braun (SPD)	Wendorff (DDP)
Commerce	Siering (SPD)	Siering (SPD)
Education	Boelitz (DVP)	Boelitz (DVP)
Treasury	von Richter (DVP)	von Richter (DVP)
Justice	am Zehnhoff (Z)	am Zehnhoff (Z)
Welfare	Stegerwald (?)(Z)*	Stegerwald (?)(Z)*

*The question marks after Stegerwald's name appear on the original list.

The decision rested with the DVP; the other coalition parties would accept either of the two arrangements. This was also clear to Gustav Stresemann, who intervened personally in order to prevent last-minute sabotage of the grand coalition by members of his own party.[275] The chairman of the DVP finally convinced his colleagues that having Braun occupy the "more decorative" post of prime minister was politically preferable to having him return to the Ministry of Agriculture.[276]

Although the grand coalition had been under discussion for almost a year, the final agreement in Prussia surprised most political observers.[277] In retrospect, it is clear that success was easier in Prussia than in the Reich because of a series of decisions and factors specifically related to the dynamics of Prussian politics. Contrary to its action in the Reich, the DVP delegation in Prussia did not insist upon politically impossible terms. Without question the final agreement was also facilitated by Adam Stegerwald's decision to remove himself from Prussian politics.[278] With Stegerwald absent from the cabinet, an unpredictable and mercurial factor was eliminated as potential source of disequilibrium in Prussian politics. If the former prime minister had stayed in the cabinet, he would have remained an important link between the right wing of the Center party and the DNVP. The SPD, too, had taken several steps in the direction of political realism. After months of chasing the phantom of reunification with the USPD, a majority—albeit a small one—of the Prussian Social Democrats recognized that the USPD represented not a factor of potential strength for the party, but a political dead weight. Yet despite all of these considerations, the most important factor in bringing about the grand coalition was cutting the presumed linkage between the Reich and Prussia. After the negotiations for the grand coalition failed in the Reich, the republican parties in Prussia, including the SPD and DVP, reached the decision that it was counterproductive to involve Prussia each time the Reich went through another crisis. Instead there was, at least for the time being, a consensus that "in the future, it would appear advisable for Prussia to go its own way."[279] The Prussian political leaders were not aware of it at the time, but it was this decision that would make possible the state's remarkable political stability in the coming years and its successful function as the rivet of the republic.

CHAPTER 3

Reich and State after 1918: New Constitutions and New Relationships

Although the revolution of 1918–19 was in many ways a half-hearted affair that left much unchanged in German society, it did alter the course of the country's political history in two important ways. As we saw in the previous chapter, a coalition of political parties supporting parliamentary democracy became the dominant political force in Prussia, replacing the alliance of Conservatives and right Liberals that had controlled the state since the middle of the nineteenth century. The other major change that resulted from the upheavals of 1918–19 concerned the structure of German federalism, specifically the relationship of the Reich and Prussia. After 1918 Prussia's political leaders no longer dominated the decision-making processes of the federal government. In the spring and summer of 1919, then, the state's new rulers faced a dual challenge: to create a new state constitution that institutionalized parliamentary democracy as Prussia's new system of government, and to maintain the state's political viability in the context of a new federal structure that fundamentally altered the Reich-state relationship. The remarkable success of the Weimar party leaders in Prussia in coping with this dual challenge does much to explain Prussia's ability to act as the pillar of democracy in Weimar Germany as a whole.

The German Empire of 1871 was a creation of Prussia, and the state's primacy within the Reich remained largely unbroken until the First World War.[1] The federal constitution, tailor-made to Bismarck's specifications, institutionalized Prussia's dominant influence over the affairs of the Reich. It provided for the permanent personal union of the Prussian king and the German emperor, and assured Prussia a majority of votes in the Bundesrat (the second chamber of the national legislature, whose members were not elected, but appointed by the state governments). Under the constitution of 1871, Prussia dominated the national government, while federal authorities had little influence in the state. The major characteristic of Bismarck's constitution was an extensive reservoir of states' rights. The national government had virtually no original or exclusive jurisdictions. It was almost a decade after the founding of the Reich before a federal judiciary and the Reich Ministry of the Interior began their work. The states maintained autonomous

89

armies, with Prussia's military establishment clearly the most important. Only in time of war were the states' armies federalized and put under a unified national command. Not even in foreign affairs did the federal government have exclusive powers. The states were empowered to maintain foreign embassies, and in most capitals the Reich and Prussian ambassadors were the same person. The German *Länder* were also financially independent of the Reich. Before 1918 the states, not the federal government, controlled the income from direct taxes. Prussia's financial position was particularly secure since the state government operated the state-owned Prussian-Hessian Railway System, the most important transportation network in Germany and a major revenue producer for the *Land*.

In spite of the overwhelming one-sidedness in the relationship between the federal government and the state, Prussia felt its position in the Reich threatened even before 1914. The state's politically dominant forces were concerned that the as yet weak and hesitant efforts toward democratization and greater parliamentary influence in the Reich, which became increasingly apparent after 1908, would spill over into Prussia and threaten the narrow political base that had prevailed in the state since 1851.[2] Equally significant, the dynamics of a rapidly growing industrial society and the escalating arms race in the years before World War I brought with them the de facto transfer of jurisdiction in defense allocation and social legislation from the states— and that meant primarily Prussia—to the Reich.[3]

As we saw earlier, the process of federalization accelerated rapidly during the First World War. By the end of the conflict, much of Prussia's (and the other *Länder*'s) autonomy had disappeared. Indeed, a number of political observers, especially among the Social Democrats,[4] felt that Prussia was an anachronism in the new Germany: the state was so intimately associated with the authoritarian past that with the collapse of Wilhelminian Germany, Prussia, too, should now be dissolved into its component parts.

Prussia still had its supporters, however. They included the revolutionary leaders of the state and, paradoxically, the new Reich government which discovered rather quickly that dissolving Prussia also endangered the authority of the Council of People's Plenipotentiaries (CPP). The state's administrative apparatus was needed to maintain government services and functions in much of Germany. But the issues involved ranged far beyond momentary concern for law and order. War and revolution had aggravated already existing anti-Prussian sentiments in southern Germany. The Bavarians in particular envisioned that the revolution would lead to a shift of power from Berlin and northern Germany to the south.[5] The larger states bordering Prussia also expected substantial territorial gains at the expense of Prussia.[6] All of these developments would indeed have destroyed Prussia's domination of the Reich, but the process would also have begun a territorial rearrangement of the Reich at the uncontrolled initiative of the states, rather than in response to plans developed by the Reich government. This explains, for example, the opposition of the USPD members on the CPP to territorial changes in Prussia, although the Independent Socialists in principle favored a centralized, rather than federal, construction of the Reich. Hugo Haase opposed the secession of Silesia from Prussia because "If we start with separatism in the southeast corner of our [sic] Prussian state, the others will soon follow suit." Breitscheid added. "Then we'll become a Marquis of Brandenburg and the surrounding countryside." [7]

In addition to the Reich, the numerous small states that bordered on the larger *Länder,* or were surrounded by them, also favored the continued existence of Prussia. Especially in the week prior to the Reich Conference of November 25, 1918, there was a strong possibility that the revolutionary fervor for territorial and political changes might sweep away the numerous midget states.[8] An intact Prussia as the largest state guaranteed the territorial status quo and provided a barrier that protected the smaller states from the encroachments of medium-sized *Länder,* such as Bavaria or Saxony.[9]

There was less consensus, however, about Prussia's long-term future—or, for that matter, who should decide such questions. Initially there was strong sentiment among the CPP members and the leaders of the workers' and soldiers' councils that the entire restructuring of the Reich should be placed in the hands of national authorities—that is, the council movement or the National Constitutional Convention—rather than left to the decisions of the states.[10] On the opposite side, not surprisingly, ranged the Prussian government and the revolutionary cabinets of the other states. The combined influence of the latter was strong enough to prevent the "nationalization" of the *Reichsreform.* By the time the National Constitutional Convention assembled in February 1919, the issue of large-scale territorial changes was all but academic.[11]

An important step in preserving the territorial status quo was the so-called Federal Conference (Reichskonferenz), an assembly of delegates from the various *Länder* who met in Berlin on November 25, 1918. To begin with, the conference itself was eloquent testimony to the vitality of the German federal tradition: only two weeks after the fall of the old rulers, all of the German states had recognized and functional cabinets.[12] Prussia took the Reichskonferenz very seriously. The state was represented by a seven-member delegation, which included no fewer than five ministers (Ernst, Hirsch, Rosenfeld, Ströbel, and Südekum). In addition, Wolfgang Heine, who formally represented the small state of Anhalt at the conference, passionately advocated the Prussian cause as well. During the discussions the Prussian delegates stressed over and over again that while the new republican Prussia agreed that a centralized structure for the Reich should be the common aim for the future,

Prussia was not willing to give up its sovereignty only to be divided among its neighbors. As long as the unitary structure could not be applied to all parts of the Reich, Prussia would oppose "with all [its] might" any efforts by its neighboring states to annex parts of the *Land*.[13]

The motivations of the Prussian and other Socialist state governments at the Federal Conference were complex. In part, traditional particularist sentiments prevailed among the revolutionaries no less strongly than in the ranks of their conservative predecessors. The political dynamics of the two Socialist parties were an additional factor. The USPD regime in Bavaria distrusted the increasing rightward drift of the CPP in Berlin. In contrast, right-wing Socialists remained suspicious of the workers' and soldiers councils, which often opposed the continued existence of the *Länder*.[14]

The Reichskonferenz precluded major territorial changes as part of the immediate revolutionary upheavals, but the issue of Prussia's size and political influence remained acute. The man whom the CPP chose to draft the new Reich constitution, Hugo Preuss, had very firm ideas on the subject. Preuss regarded the existence of an oversized Prussia as detrimental to the Reich's future development. Instead he proposed that the state be limited to its territory east of the Elbe. In the west, Schleswig-Holstein, Hanover, and the Rhineland would become (or become again) independent states, while the Hanseatic cities (Hamburg, Bremen, and Lübeck) would be permitted to annex additional lands from the surrounding Prussian areas.[15]

The state government was vehemently opposed to the territorial provisions of Preuss's draft constitution. In its opinion, dissolving Prussia would divide Germany into a series of "insolvent *(leistungsunfähige)* states."[16] And Prussia did not yield on this fundamental question. The cabinet even delayed its approval of the formation of the state of Greater Thuringia (an uncontroversial union of seven former ministates in central Germany, which turned out to be the only significant territorial reform to be enacted during the Weimar Republic) until the state was certain that Prussia's territorial integrity was no longer in danger. Prussia did not object to the transfer of a few insignificant square miles of Prussian territory to Greater Thuringia. Rather, it feared the precedent of yielding Prussian territory to other jurisdictions.[17] In the end, the state remained victorious on the territorial issue. The Weimar constitution contained provisions leaving the status quo intact for two years (later extended to three) after the adoption of the Reich constitution, and by that time (1921) the movement for breaking up Prussia had lost much of its momentum.[18]

Blocking major territorial changes did not, however, address the equally important question of the future political relationship between the Reich and its largest state. The revolutionary leaders were agreed that the prewar relationship of a dominant Prussia and a largely subservient Reich should not be continued after the revolution. Indeed, initially the CPP seemed to envision a simple reversal, that is, the council would be in a position to give instructions to the Prussian government.[19] The state's new political leaders were not willing to go that far, although they did acknowledge far-reaching obligations to inform the Reich government of their intentions and to coordinate policy decisions with the federal authorities.[20] Throughout most of 1919 the relationship of Reich and state saw the Prussians in the role of junior partner. During the crucial days of January 1919, all efforts to preserve law and order in the face of riots and putsch attempts by the extreme left originated with the People's Council of Plenipotentiaries.[21] The Prussian government merely countersigned and implemented decisions that were made in the office of the Reich defense minister. Similarly, the negotiations that led to the first parliamentary Prussian government took place in Weimar, the meeting place of the National Constitutional Convention, not in Berlin, the site of the Prussian Constitutional Convention.

The new Reich constitution seemed to hasten Prussia's political eclipse. Two provisions in particular signaled major changes. Article 15 of the draft reported out of committee (it became article 18 in the final document) permitted plebiscites on territorial changes within Prussia even if the state government opposed such a vote. And article 21 (eventually article 63 of the Weimar constitution) eliminated Prussia's prewar hegemony in the Bundesrat (now renamed the Reichsrat) by restricting the number of votes the Prussian government could control. The Prussian cabinet was able to cast only half of the votes to which the state was entitled by virtue of size and population. The other half of Prussia's votes in the Reichsrat were to be cast by delegates sent to the Reichsrat by the diets of the Prussian provinces.[22] While article 18 did not endanger Prussia's territorial integrity during the republican years, article 63, after becoming law in 1921, had a major, if unintended, effect upon the federal balance of power. Its originators hoped to further the course of democratic self-government in Prussia by granting greater autonomy to the elected provincial authorities. In practice, article 63 at times enabled antirepublican forces to sabotage the efforts of the democratic government of Prussia to strengthen democracy in the Reich as a whole. The rightist parties were able to dominate a number of the provincial diets and their appointees to the Reichsrat did not hesitate to vote against the Prussian government in a number of crucial cases. When the votes of the provincial delegates were combined with those of rightist members from other *Länder,* it was quite possible to defeat proposals backed by the Prussian and Reich governments.

Interestingly, these attempts to reduce Prussia's influence in the Reich produced a vehement reaction among the state's political leaders that eventually did much to strengthen the hand of the government in dealing with the national legislature and executive.[23] The government, including the ministers representing the Center party, the political group whose leaders in the

National Constitutional Convention spearheaded adoption of the two anti-Prussian articles, approved a sharp resolution against the language of the proposed articles 15 and 21.[24] Within the Prussian parliament a broad coalition backed the government's stand.[25] The vast majority of the delegates to the Prussian Constitutional Convention supported the republican government in its opposition against attempts to reduce the state's standing among the *Länder*.[26]

The key to the resurgence of Prussia's authority was the willingness of the parliament in Prussia to function as a support group for the government on these fundamental questions, or more precisely, the stability and forcefulness of the Prussian parliament contrasted with the weakness and instability of the national legislature. Preuss and his successor as Reich minister of the interior, Erich Koch-Weser, vigorously pursued plans to dissolve Prussia or at least reduce its political autonomy, but the parties of the Weimar coalition in the Reich gave them only incipient support. In the National Convention the Center party delegates supported Preuss's proposals without reservations, but the Social Democrats and the DDP were split on the question. In contrast, the Prussian government received strong backing for its efforts to preserve the independence of the state against the encroachments of the Reich government not only from the coalition parties, but from the right-wing opposition as well. On this question, government parties and the opposition formed a "reluctant coalition" that was a union of very unequal partners. Dyed-in-the-wool Prussian monarchists in the DNVP stood next to Social Democrats. The latter supported a centralized construction of the Reich in principle, but, in contrast to some of their colleagues in the National Convention, the Prussian Social Democrats were convinced that the premature dissolution of Prussia would hinder rather than further the formation of a centralized Reich.

True, the Prussian Center party delegates were somewhat uneasy in the ranks of the "reluctant coaltion," although the Prussian wing of the party never pursued the dissolution of Prussia with the same enthusiasm as did some of the party leaders in the National Convention. Moreover, the Center party in Prussia quickly discovered that on the question of Prussia's "to be or not to be," it was politically dangerous to stand alone. From March 21 through 24, the Prussian Constitutional Convention debated the future of the Rhineland.[27] In the course of the discussion, the Center party, whose speakers had advocated various degrees of autonomy for the region, found itself completely isolated.[28] At the conclusion of the discussion, the legislature overwhelmingly adopted a resolution that strongly opposed any autonomy or separation from Prussia for the Rhineland; the Center party abstained from voting on the resolution.[29] A few days later political Catholicism even became tainted with the suspicion of treason. Two members of the Center party's Prussian parliamentary delegation, Kastert and Kuckhoff, had engaged in private discussions on the Rhineland question with the commander of the French occupation forces in Germany, General Mangin.[30] The two representatives had not informed either the party's leadership or the Prussian government about their talks with a representative of a foreign power. After their initiative became public, the Center party promptly disavowed any part in the proceedings and the two delegates resigned from the parliamentary delegation.[31] Although no one seriously doubted that Kastert and Kuckhoff had acted entirely on their own, the Center party as a whole became the target of a vituperative attack by the "reluctant coalition." The Center party's isolation indirectly strengthened the Weimar coalition as well. The question of the future of Prussia divided the government parties, but since the Center party had no potential allies on this issue, there were no alternative coalition partners for the Catholics. The result was not only solid parliamentary backing for the government's position in its relations with the Reich, but also impressive evidence of the smooth functioning of the parliamentary and democratic system in the young Prussian republic.

By the end of 1919 Prussia had regained some of the initiative in Reich-state relations. When the Reich government decided to lift a state of siege in the city of Berlin in early December without consulting the Prussian government, the state's cabinet was outraged "to a degree that had not been previously experienced, nor would it in the future."[32] That controversy marked the low point of Prussian prestige and influence. A short time later the Prussian parliament seized the initiative completely (and created a political sensation) with the adoption of a "Resolution on the Centralized State" *(Einheitsstaatresolution)*. On December 15, the Constitutional Convention passed legislation putting the Prussian legislature on record as favoring the transformation of the Reich from a federal to a centralized state. Provided the other states agreed to follow suit, Prussia was willing to give up its state sovereignty and transfer its powers to the Reich government. The state's cabinet was asked to communicate the resolution to the Reich and the other *Länder,* and to take the lead in inaugurating the transformation process.[33]

The "Resolution on the Centralized State" was attached as a rider to the state budget. The idea for the resolution seems to have originated with the legislative leaders of the Prussian coalition parties; the action came as a complete surprise both to the cabinet and the parties' national leaders.[34] The decision to attach the rider was also made on very short notice; the list of speakers for December 15 had already been determined and all of them were fiscal rather than constitutional experts.[35] The circumstances surrounding the resolution prompted a guessing game about the objectives of the sponsors, and some of the uncertainty still persists. In retrospect it appears that the resolution was a prophylactic and tactical effort on the part of the parliamentary leadership of the coalition parties to cement their alliance and seize the initiative for Prussia in the continuing discussion over the reform of the Reich. Three concrete aims are apparent. First, the resolution enabled Prussia to take the lead in discussion of the *Reichsreform,* and curb the ambitions of the Reich minister of the interior Erich Koch-Weser. Second, the solid parliamentary backing for the resolution enabled the Prussian Center party to clarify the difficulty of its position just prior to the convening of the party's national congress in January 1920.[36] Finally, the move confronted the DVP with a difficult choice. The People's party either had to vote for the resolution and give up its strictly oppositional stance, or oppose the initiative and thus deny a major part of its liberal heritage.[37] Traditionally, the National Liberals had favored a strong and centralized Reich.

The resolution was a political if not a constitutional success. A roll call revealed a large number of unexcused absences and abstentions, but also sharp rifts among the opposition parties, while the coalition parties formed a solid phalanx in support.[38] Within the Center party the resolution strengthened the position of the Prussian delegation. The resolution led to a storm of protest in southern Germany, and the Bavarian section of the Center party used the Prussian move to make a final organizational break with the national Center party; it reconstituted itself as a separate political group under the name of Bavarian People's party (BVP). With this development, the Prussian Center became the largest unit in what remained of the national Center party. The resolution did indeed weaken the position of the Reich minister of the interior. By calling forth fierce opposition from Bavaria and Hessen, Koch-Weser felt, the Prussian resolution focused public attention upon the whole subject at a time when such interest was premature and prejudicial to his own plans.[39]

The actual constitutional consequences of the resolution were meager. A joint meeting of the Reich and Prussian cabinet members did take place on January 30, 1920, but the discussions brought no concrete results. The Prussian delegates emphasized that they favored a centralized state in principle, but rejected any move that would mean the unilateral dissolution of the state as a first step toward realization of this goal. The two governments agreed to form an ad hoc committee consisting of three cabinet ministers from each government, but this, too, was an empty gesture. Neither side showed much interest in further discussion.

Less than four months after Prussia's dramatic initiative, the Kapp Putsch and its aftermath seemingly reversed the Reich-state-relationship again. In one sense, Kapp and Lüttwitz were typical prewar-Prussian Conservatives who hoped to reestablish Prussia's predominant position in the Reich. As it turned out, the putsch, at least for a time, had almost the opposite result. After Kapp and Lüttwitz had fled the capital, Prussia's internal affairs were all but nationalized. Until the end of March, Prussia's central authorities were essentially excluded from real decisions affecting the maintainance of law and order in the state. For example, the Bielefeld Agreement, which applied the Berlin Agreement on ending the general strike to the industrial areas of the west, was negotiated by the Reich and state commisioner for the Ruhr, Carl Severing, without instructions from the Prussian government.[40] The situation did not change until Prussia once again had a cabinet that was backed by a strong parliamentary majority. At the end of March the new Braun government moved forcefully to reestablish its authority in the provinces and in its dealings with the Reich. On March 29, Severing, now Prussian minister of the interior, dismantled the emergency powers of his own office as Reich and state commissioner and returned authority to the civil offices.[41] And when the Reichswehr sent troops into the western Ruhr area on April 1, the decision was discussed beforehand with the Prussian government; the state cabinet gave its full approval.[42]

In analyzing the vagaries of the relationship between Reich and state in the early years of the Weimar era, it is tempting to see an excessive degree of continuity in the attitudes of the post–1918 Prussian leaders and their prewar predecessors.[43] Both sought to preserve the state's territorial and political integrity, but their motivations were completely different. The republican leaders did not wish to dominate the Reich. Rather, they thought Germany's largest state had to be preserved as an economic and administrative macro-unit that would serve as the foundation for the restructuring of the Reich as a whole.[44] Reich and Prussian leaders professed to share the same goal, a centralized Reich, but their methods diverged. The Braun government, like the state's revolutionary leaders, pushed for the simultaneous dissolution of all the German states in order to form a centralized Reich, while the Reich minister of the interior intended to reach this goal through the intermediate step of permitting the Prussian provinces to exist for a time as states in their own right.[45] Prussia rejected this scenario as a return to the political and economic impotence of Germany during the nineteenth century.[46] The impasse convinced the Prussians to hold fast to the status quo; Heilmann spoke of "a few decades" as the time span during which Prussia would retain its position as Germany's largest territorial unit.[47]

In spite of provisions in the Reich constitution that hindered rather than supported Prussia's claim to a special position among the German states in its dealings with the Reich, the state's republican leaders effectively pressed their point. They knew that virtually all political camps in Prussia shared the conviction that by maintaining its territorial integrity and administrative unity, Prussia was serving as a model for the Reich as a whole.[48]

Pressure for redrawing the Prussian boundaries came not only from the framers of the Reich constitution. Potentially far more dangerous for the territorial integrity of the state were simultaneous separatist and autonomist movements that sprung up in some of the Prussian provinces. The strongest internal challenge to the new order and the old boundaries came in the Rhineland.[49] The largely Catholic population had long resented the discriminatory practices of the old regime, and after the revolution these grievances were added to the seeming attractiveness of rumored French plans for a new Confederation of the Rhine, and opposition to the early anticlerical policies of the revolutionary government. The result was a movement calling for separating the Rhineland from Prussia that for a time aroused considerable concern among the state's revolutionary leaders. Significant support for the separatist and autonomist tendencies came from the upper middle class on the left bank of the Rhine, and, in more rural areas, from parts of the Catholic clergy.[50] The movement was centered in Cologne, particularly among the banking and industrial community in the city. Media support came from a number of journalists, especially the editor of the *Kölnische Volkszeitung,* Josef Froberger.[51] Among political leaders for a time at least, some prominent figures in the Rhenish Center party supported the drive for a separate Rhenish *Land,* with no ties to Prussia. They included the party's national chairman, Karl Trimborn, and the lord mayor of Cologne, Konrad Adenauer. The latter, especially, played a role that appeared to some observers to be both unclear and contradictory. It must be stressed, however, that other prominent politicians in the Center party, such as Wilhelm Marx (the party's future national chairman), Erzberger, and Stegerwald stayed clear of the movement.

The drive for a Rhenish republic began and in a sense reached its zenith with a mass meeting on December 4, 1918, the day before British occupation troops moved into Cologne. Froberger and others had organized the meeting in the city which was attended by more than five thousand persons. The rally unanimously adopted a resolution proposed by the organizers demanding a new independent Rhenish-Westphalian *Land* separate from Prussia. The resolution, as well as some of the speakers at the Cologne meeting, were vague on the important question as to whether the proposed new entity was to be merely autonomous of Prussia or independent of the Reich as well. To assuage the fears that they were attempting to reestablish the Confederation of the Rhine, Froberger and his associates did announce that the Rhenish republic should remain part of the Reich; they merely demanded a plebiscite on separation from Prussia. Even so, doubts about the *Reichstreue* of the movement remained. All of the non-Catholic parties in the area, but also the Westphalian district organization of the Center party rejected the Cologne initiative.[52] In the ranks of the wider Center party, considerable doubts arose as to the political wisdom of the planned Rhenish republic. To be sure, such an entity would be dominated by political Catholicism, but it was equally true that the price of Center party domination in this area was the political impotence of Catholics in the Prussian diaspora.[53]

For a time, unsure of the strength of the Rhenish movement and concerned about the ambiguous attitude of the Reich government, the revolutionary regime in Prussia reacted cautiously to developments in the Rhineland.[54] The cabinet did reject out of hand the viewpoint that only separation from Prussia could guarantee the Rhineland's remaining within the Reich, but the government, in an effort to stall for time, indicated its willingness to discuss other issues with local leaders.[55] One week after the Cologne rally, a sizable and distinquished delegation of Prussian officials under the leadership of Rudolf Breitscheid met with a number of Rhenish and Westphalian political and business leaders in Elberfeld.[56] (Elberfeld is now part of the city of Wuppertal.) Trimborn and Froberger rather weakly defended the initiative in Cologne, while Breitscheid argued convincingly that only the National Constitutional Convention should determine the future territorial and political makeup of the Reich. The minister's stand, by simultaneously emphasizing the need for a democratic decision-making process, while not closing the door completely on territorial changes in the west, apparently succeeded in weakening still further the Rhenish initiative.[57] Only one day after the Elberfeld meeting, the cabinet decided, on the strength of new reports from the governor of the Rhine Province, that the subject of the Rhenish republic was no longer a live issue among the population of the area.[58]

In retrospect it is clear that the drive for a Rhenish republic at no time seriously endangered the continued existence of Prussia, and became all but insignificant after the Center party joined the coalition state government in the spring of 1919.[59] The cabinet then quickly dropped its earlier appeasement policies. Instead, it issued repeated proclamations linking national unity to the Reich's and Prussia's territorial integrity. At the same time, however, the government took steps to fulfill some long-standing demands made by the people of the Rhineland. An important public relations gesture was the establishment of the University of Cologne as a third major Catholic university in the Rhineland. The government also promised to appoint more Catholics to civil service positions in the Rhenish areas, and held out hope that the question of increased provincial autonomy would be solved as part of an overall administrative reform program for all of the Prussian provinces.[60]

The motives for the indigenous separatist movements in Prussia's eastern frontier areas paralleled at least in part those in the west. Fears for the economic future of the area were widespread, and Hoffmann's educational policies aroused well-organized opposition among the largely Catholic population of Silesia. Other factors complicated the situation still further. As the new Polish state struggled into existence in the weeks after the war, ethnic conflicts between Poles and Germans escalated in the eastern border provinces of Posen, East Prussia, and West Prussia. Even personal factors played a role. The governor and Reich and state commissioner in East Prussia, August

Winnig (SPD), pursued an ambitious and ambiguous political program that even included maintaining direct contacts between members of his provincial council and representatives of the Russian Soviet government until the Prussian administration energetically protested against an independent foreign policy by a provincial governor.[61]

In the provinces bordering on what was to become the Polish Corridor, the political organizations representing the German population pursued aims and tactics that were in effect diametrically opposed to the officially proclaimed policy of the Prussian revolutionary government. The so-called People's Councils *(Volksräte)* hoped to prevent the loss of these Prussian territories to Poland through force of arms, while the government in Berlin put its faith in negotiations. In the weeks immediately following the revolution, the USPD minister of the interior, Breitscheid, was largely responsible for the cabinet's Polish policy. He in turn left the day-to-day execution to his undersecretary and confidant, Hellmuth von Gerlach. The latter was convinced that Germany and Prussia had to accept the loss of the eastern border areas with a predominantly Polish population, and that a solution to the nationality problem lay in negotiations between the two governments concerned, not strong-arm tactics.[62] Gerlach's views met with widespread rejection among the Germans of the east, but even within the cabinet his conciliatory policies were not undisputed. A number of Social Democratic ministers (Hirsch, Ernst, Heine, Braun) had a highly emotional and personal relationship to the German east and its significance for the future of the Reich as a whole.[63] Hirsch, Südekum, Ernst, and Reinhardt (as well as Landsberg and Ebert in the Reich government) were lukewarm in their support of negotiations, since they remained convinced that armed conflict between Poles and Germans was "bound to develop."[64] Their nationalistic feelings were shared by the bourgeois ministers in the cabinet and the leading members of the professional civil service. As a result, the majority of government leaders in the revolutionary cabinet and administration pursued policy aims in the east that seemed little different from those of the old Conservative governments before the war.

The conciliatory and hard-line approaches remained more or less in balance until the USPD left the revolutionary government. Gerlach initiated negotiations with Polish authorities, but his efforts merely led to a rapid deterioration in the relations between the government and the German *Volksräte;* from the later came a series of quixotic schemes for an independent East State.[65] After the USPD ministers resigned, the hard-liners quickly gained control of Prussia's Polish policy. Gerlach remained in office until March 1919, but stripped of Breitscheid's support he was isolated and without influence. Only two days after the Independent Socialists left the coalition, the cabinet decided that further negotiations with the Poles should be "carried on in a dilatory manner."[66] Aside from repealing a law from the 1880s providing state subsidies to Germans buying land from Poles, both the revolutionary government and the parliamentary cabinets that followed essentially held fast to a hard line that placed primary confidence in the effectiveness of military resistance.[67]

It is doubtful whether a tactically less rigid policy would have been more successful in the eastern provinces. The Poles were no more willing to be accommodating than the Prussians. In any case, at the end of May the Prussians had to admit that the disputed border areas were lost to Germany and Prussia.[68] The final territorial divisions in East Central Europe were the result of negotiations among the Allies, who were little interested in Prussian wishes or tactics. Worse, despite a major public relations effort,[69] the German population of the eastern provinces by and large felt little gratitude for the efforts of the revolutionary government, and saw only that the new regime had not prevented the severance of large areas from the Reich. The area became a fertile recruiting ground for the Kapp putschists and remained a stronghold of the DNVP.

The potentially most explosive situation emerged in Silesia. Here economic unrest, Catholic resentments against Protestant domination, and ethnic conflicts all fanned dissatisfactions. The revolutionary government was guilty of sins of both commission and omission. Until 1919 it left in office major symbols of prewar authoritarianism, notably the two district directors in the province, von Miquel (Oppeln) and von Jagow (Breslau).[70] Both were virulent Protestants and Conservatives. At the same time, the cabinet did not address major economic difficulties, while Hoffmann's anticlerical policies encouraged unrest among both German and Polish Catholics.[71]

The result was a series of movements demanding either greater autonomy for the entire province, the separation of Upper and Lower Silesia, with Upper Silesia becoming a new *Land,* or even the annexation of Silesia to the future (and mythical) *Oststaat.* In one form or other, the movements had the support of virtually all portions of the population, although some of their aims were contradictory. The lower- and middle-class Catholic population was primarily interested in gaining control of schools and cultural institutions in the province. Leaders of the upper and politically more conservative classes had more far-reaching ambitions. The military, some members of the Catholic nobility, and a number of coal and steel magnates saw the separatist and autonomy movements as effective vehicles for severing Silesia from its association with a democratic Prussia and Reich.[72] Still others pursued quite narrow economic interests. One of the representatives of the Silesian farmer's organization felt that the desires of his interest group could be fulfilled either by the establishment of an independent federal state of Silesia—or by the dismissal of Otto Braun as Prussian minister of agriculture.[73]

Silesia repeatedly presented the Prussian government with a delicate situation until, as we shall see, the question was finally settled by a plebiscite in the fall of 1921. To begin with, some leaders of the Reich government supported the establishment of a separate *Land,* Upper Silesia. They included the powerful Reich minister of finance, Matthias Erzberger, who was also a leader of the Center party.[74] Friedrich Ebert, too, favored a separate state of Upper Silesia, as did the Reich and Prussian commissioner in the province, Otto Hörsing (SPD).[75] But support for separating all or part of Silesia from Prussia was by no means unanimous. Ebert's co-chairman in the Council of People's Plenipotentiaries, Hugo Haase, wanted Silesia to remain part of Prussia. Haase's view was shared by all Prussian cabinets after the revolution. The state government consistently maintained that "[creating a separate *Land*] . . . Upper Silesia . . . is the stone that will initiate the avalanche of dissolution in Prussia."[76]

Still, the widespread support for various separation and autonomy movements in Silesia forced the Prussian government to grant some concessions. At the end of December 1918, Hirsch made a series of promises to the People's Committee (Volksrat) for Silesia that laid the basis for the eventual division of Silesia into two provinces, although both were to remain part of Prussia.[77] At the end of May 1919, partly in response to a series of crippling strikes in Upper Silesia, Hörsing publicly supported separate provincial diets for the two districts. The government, however, temporarily retreated from its earlier position. Fearful that the just-announced Versailles Treaty would set in motion a process of dissolution in all of Prussia, the cabinet reverted to its earlier support of an intact single province of Silesia as the southeastern rivet holding the entire state together.[78]

Germany's eventual acceptance of the peace treaty created a new situation in the province. The Versailles Treaty provided for a plebiscite in Upper Silesia to determine whether the population wanted to remain in Germany or join Poland. Consequently, for the Reich and Prussian governments the primary question after June 1919 became which policies were most likely to result in a favorable vote for Germany. Both the Reich government and the Center party delegation in the Reichstag remained convinced that only the separation of Upper Silesia from Prussia and its establishment as a new federal state would be sufficient incentive for the voters to decide to remain with Germany.[79] Prussia, for its part, was convinced that there was no need for such radical revisions of the map. It did, however, largely in response to pressure from the Reich government, agree to fulfill its earlier promises.[80] In October 1919, Upper Silesia was created as a separate province. It remained part of Prussia, and was put on equal footing with all other provinces.[81]

Although the establishment of the new province of Upper Silesia did much to pacify the population of the area, as the date for the plebiscite on the fate of Upper Silesia grew nearer, the Reich cabinet continued to press for the establishment of an independent federal state of Upper Silesia.[82] The Stegerwald cabinet, as had its predecessors, remained firm, and in a sense the voters proved it right. A majority of the population opted for Germany, although there had been no promise to establish a new *Land* called Upper Silesia. The subsequent division of Silesia by the Allies, awarding the bulk of Upper Silesia to Poland, largely rendered the question of the future status of the German part of the province moot. The small territory remaining in the Reich clearly was not viable as a federal state. In a new plebiscite, held in the fall of 1921, to determine Upper Silesia's future within the German Reich, the overwhelming majority of voters decided to remain with Prussia.[83] (This will be discussed later.)

Prussia lost large tracts of territory as a result of the Treaty of Versailles, but the state boundaries did not change in consequence of indigenous separatist movements. The new Prussian leaders proved remarkably convincing in their arguments that all separatist movements in the Prussian border provinces automatically involved discussion of the Reich's external boundaries and that, in any case, a territorial reorganization of Prussia as the foundation of the Reich would necessarily bring unpredictable consequences for the nation as a whole. Prussia placed little faith in the avowed motives of the groups ostensibly wishing to remain in the Reich while seeking separation from Prussia. The republican leaders saw such movements as purely destructive elements whose attacks upon the territorial integrity of the state merely camouflaged their real desire to destroy the Reich and the republican form of government.[84]

Prussia's position and influence in the new republican Reich depended only in part upon the territorial size of the state. Equally important were changes in the division of substantive responsibility for policymaking and administration between the two levels of government. These were questions that had to be addressed by the national and state constitutional conventions as they formulated new basic instruments of governance for their respective jurisdictions.

The basic tendency of Hugo Preuss's draft for the Reich constitution was to increase the power of the national authority at the expense of state and local entities. One area in which the reversal of the balance of power in favor of the Reich affected Reich-Prussian relations specifically was a traditional feature of Bismarckian federalism, the so-called personal unions in the executive offices of the Reich and of Prussia. Before 1918 Reich and Prussian cabinet portfolios had generally been held by the same person. While the state dominated the Reich, the arrangement was clearly to Prussia's advantage, but after the revolution Prussia feared for its autonomy and became increasingly wary of personal unions. Proposals to appoint Otto Landsberg, a member of the Reich Council of People's Plenipotentiaries, as Prussian minister without portfolio, or, somewhat later, the suggestion that Matthias Erzberger combine the posts of minister of finance for both the Reich and Prussia, were rejected by the Prussian political leaders.[85] Prussia remained equally skeptical of proposals, repeatedly advanced by the Reich minister of the interior, Erich Koch-Weser, that the Reich ministers should be alloted seats in the Prussian cabinet.[86] The state also rejected what might have been considered a logical continuation, under changed circumstances, of the prewar personal union of German emperor and Prussian king: giving the Reich president the title and functions of the Prussian head of state.[87]

The state was even dubious about more informal and temporary personal unions. During the weeks and months following the revolution, when the Reich administration was still in a very embryonic state, the national cabinet repeatedly appointed Reich commissioners *(Reichskommissare)* in order to deal with the recurring incidents of public unrest. Endowed with extraordinary authority, the Reich commissioners (who were for the most part leading figures of the Weimar coalition parties) generally reported directly to the chancellor or the Reich cabinet as a whole. Since the geographic area of authorization for the commissioners almost invariably involved Prussian territory, the state routinely accorded them the title "state commissioner," but Prussia severely curtailed their political authority. As state commissioners, they remained under the administrative jurisdiction of the minister of the interior, and the cabinet as a whole kept tight reigns on their activities within the state.[88]

In fact, the evolution of the state's own republican constitution shows a remarkable reluctance to give up the public symbols of sovereignty. An early draft of the new state constitution, which the Ministry of the Interior presented to the cabinet in January 1919, provided for the election of a state president as a sort of substitute king.[89] It required considerable pressure from the Reich government, which stressed the potential for conflict of two elected chiefs of state residing side by side in Berlin, before the Prussians dropped the office of state president from their original draft constitution.[90] Even so, subsequent drafts contained vestiges of the earlier proposals. Departing from the traditional Prussian practice of equality among the members of the cabinet, the draft of the "temporary constitution" submitted to the state Constitutional Convention by the cabinet in March 1919, provided that the prime minister would be nominated by the speaker of the Landtag and elected by the full house. The prime minister in turn would select members of the cabinet who would then be presented to parliament for confirmation. The proposed constitution also put considerable emergency powers—analogous to article 48 of the later Reich constitution—at the disposal of the chief executive.[91]

In contrast to Prussia's disinclination to continue the personal unions, the state at least in principle readily acceded to the transfer of decision-making authority in specific policy areas from Prussia (and the other *Länder*) to the Reich.[92] Specifically involved were three major areas of concern: control over the armed forces, allocation of the powers of taxation between the Reich and *Land*, and the administration of the railroads and the intra- and interstate waterways. Under the Bismarck constitution, these items of public administration had been assigned to the states, but by the end of World War I that division of power was seen as increasingly unworkable.

Perhaps least controversial was the question of national defense. Military authorities and political leaders from all parties agreed that state control of the armed forces had outlived its time, so that the formation of the Reichswehr to take the place both of the Prussian army and the other states' armed forces presented no major difficulty.[93] In fact, it was a foregone conclusion. The Reich and the Prussian revolutionary governments agreed to treat Prussian military affairs as de facto falling within the province of the Reich; the Prussian minister of war regarded his post as a receivership, winding down the affairs of his office.[94] In effect, then, the constitutional provisions creating the Reich's monopoly of authority over the armed forces were merely a formal ratification of a process that had been well under way since the revolution.

The problems that remained were primarily political rather than organizational. They concerned the degree to which the national armed forces would reflect the revolutionary transfer of power in terms of their command structure and the civil and political rights accorded the soldiers. Here the rump Prussian minister of war did play an active role, as he was in charge of the day-to-day operation of the armed forces during the transition period to Reich control. The first National Congress of Workers' and Soldiers' Councils had placed immediate and thoroughgoing democratization of the armed forces at the head of its priorities.[95] The congress adopted the so-called Hamburg Seven Points, which called for a variety of symbolic and actual changes in the armed services, ranging from the abolition of epaulettes for officers to permission for enlisted men not to salute officers unless both were on duty.

After the Congress adjourned, the Central Council (Zentralrat), the executive committee elected by the National Congress, pressed the Prussian government to translate the decision of the congress into concrete directives for the armed forces. The incumbent Prussian minister of defense, General Scheüch, an old-line conservative Prussian officer, was hardly the man to carry out reforms in the spirit of the Hamburg Seven Points. His retirement was welcomed by all, including Scheüch himself. His successor was a relatively junior staff officer in the army of the state of Württemberg, Colonel Walther Reinhardt.

For the moderate Social Democrats on the Central Council as well as the ministers in the Prussian revolutionary cabinet, Reinhardt represented a suitable bridge between old and new; he was a fully trained and capable staff officer who was willing to work within the framework of the changed political circumstances.[96] Some historians have seen Reinhardt less positively, but in a number of ways he was a "modern" defense minister.[97] He favored the parliamentarization of the army by reducing the power and autonomy of the general staff and increasing the role of the defense minister, that is, the man responsible to Parliament. Reinhardt was also quite willing to work with the Central Council in carrying out a number of symbolic changes embodied in the Hamburg Seven Points.[98]

The new Prussian minister of defense fulfilled the expectations that his supporters had placed in him. He capably facilitated the transfer of the Prussian armed forces to the Reich; in September 1919 the Prussian Ministry of War went out of existence. In fact, turning the reigns of command over to the Reich probably happened too fast. The democratization of the army was the particular responsibility of Reinhardt's parliamentary undersecretary, the left-wing Social Democrat Albert Grzesinski. Reinhardt put no obstacles in Grzesinski's path,[99] but by the time the energetic labor leader joined the ministry, the transfer to the Reich was all but accomplished, and warnings by Grzesinski and other political leaders about the dangers of leaving the old officers in control of the Reichswehr fell on deaf ears. The national Reichswehr minister, Gustav Noske, preferred to believe the protestations of loyalty from the old imperial officers under his command.[100]

Equally important, Reinhardt remained loyal to the republic during the Kapp Putsch. Unlike Reich President Ebert and the Chief of the General Staff General von Seeckt, the minister favored the use of force to put down the mutinous troops during the Kapp Putsch. His reasoning showed a keen appreciation of political realities. He argued that unless the government could demonstrate firmness against the putschists, it would soon lose the loyalty of the working classes. As we saw, a majority of the Reich cabinet rejected Reinhardt's counsel, but he continued to work against the putsch while Kapp and Lüttwitz were in control of Berlin. The minister of defense issued clear directives against any cooperation with the putschists, and formulated the Prussian cabinet's promulgation of March 17, which specifically praised the conduct of those Reichswehr units that had stayed loyal to the government.[101]

Few difficulties were foreseen in the transfer of the Prussian state railway and canal system to the Reich. The leaders of the Weimar coalition parties all favored a national transportation system. When the revolutionary cabinet was formed, Hirsch proposed the appointment of Hoff, a senior civil servant in the Ministry of Public Works, as the new minister precisely because Hoff favored a takeover of the Prussian railroads by the Reich.[102] His successor, Rudolf Oeser (DDP), similarly worked for the transfer of the transportation system to the Reich at the earliest possible date.[103]

The Prussian eagerness had constitutional, economic, and, by no means least, fiscal reasons. The Prussian railroad system, which before the war had been a profit-making enterprise and a major source of revenue, was by 1918 a highly deficitary operation and a "cancerous growth" in the state budget.[104] Understandably, the Prussian cabinet was eager to transfer the state's transportation system to the Reich's authority. It stipulated only that the Reich take over the Bavarian state railroads at the same time.[105] An agreement between the Reich and Prussia was ready in April 1920. Basically, it provided for the turnover of all Prussian railroad rolling stock and property as well as operational authority to the Reich. In return, Prussia was to receive annuities for the loss of its capital investment. In addition, the Reich agreed to pay the state the operational deficit covering the period January 1, 1919, to March 31, 1920.[106] A similar agreement covered the Prussian canals, though here Reich and state remained divided on the question of compensation for several years.

Not surprisingly, the delineation of fiscal and taxation authority between the Reich and the states proved considerably more difficult to resolve. The issue not only involved complicated questions of money allocation, but also concerned the heart of federalism, the degree of state autonomy under the new Reich constitution. All fiscal experts, including those from the rightist opposition, agreed that the prewar German system of taxation, which essentially assigned direct taxes to the states and localities and indirect revenue to the Reich, was inadequate to meet the needs of a modern, developed society. In the future, the national government should have control of the bulk of the revenues. In practice that meant assigning the Reich the income from personal and corporate income taxes, while the states would retain priority claim on some indirect taxes and the property levies.[107]

General agreement on the basic issue did not prevent sharp and acrimonious debates on the specifics of the future division of fiscal power. A primary reason lay in the person and program of Reich Minister of Finance Matthias Erzberger, architect of what came to be known as the Reich Finance Reform Act of 1919.[108] The minister did not hide the fact that he hoped to use the needed changes in the Reich-state fiscal relationship to accomplish far wider political goals. Erzberger's aim was to use the Reich's new financial hegemony to make the states fiscally dependent upon the Reich and consequently more amenable to territorial changes. It was no secret that among the latter Erzberger regarded the dissolution of Prussia as the most important first step on the road toward a new Reich federal structure.[109]

In view of its full knowledge of Erzberger's political goals, the Prussian government tried from the beginning to separate the technical fiscal questions from the larger political issues. Essentially the state, while accepting the need for federal fiscal hegemony, attempted to obtain the federal government's agreement to constitutional safeguards that would guarantee the states sufficient resources to carry out their specific obligations. This was particularly important for Prussia, which as a "mini-Reich" in many ways confronted the same tasks as the Reich as a whole.[110] Specifically, Südekum and his colleagues in the Hirsch cabinet insisted upon contractually fixed percentages from the direct tax income of the Reich which would be earmarked for Prussia and the other states. In addition, Prussia wanted written into the law that certain specific revenues, such as property levies, would be reserved entirely for use by the states and the municipalities.[111]

Erzberger at first refused the Prussian demands, but in this case the Prussians had greater political leverage. Secure in their knowledge that the entire Prussian Constitutional Convention "from Hergt to Adolf Hoffmann" supported the cabinet's point of view, the ministers did not hesitate to attack Erzberger's proposals. The conflict quickly became a bitter battle between prominent political leaders in the Reich and in Prussia. On the Prussian side Hirsch, Heine, and Friedberg were particularly vociferous in their opposition to Erzberger's Reich reform plans, while Erzberger found strong support for his views within the Reich Ministry of the Interior.[112] At first the combatants had attacked each other indirectly through allusions and hidden references in editorials and speeches, but the battle burst into full public view at the beginning of November 1919. Heine delivered a speech in Dessau that was sharply critical of Erzberger personally and of the anti-Prussian tendencies of the Reich constitution generally.[113] Erzberger replied with equal vehemence. Addressing the National Constitutional Convention, he attacked the prewar ruling circles of Prussia, and seemed to imply that the republican leaders of the state shared the hegemonial ambitions of their predecessors.[114] The Prussian cabinet reacted with unusual force and publicity. While eight of the ten ministers sat on the government bench in parliament, Hirsch delivered a forceful speech to the Prussian Constitutional Convention in which he strongly rejected both Erzberger's attacks upon the new republican Prussia and his plans for reorganization of the Reich.[115]

In the end neither side could be very happy with the outcome of the conflict. On paper the state was victorious. For the most part Prussia was successful in obtaining the desired assurances after protracted negotiations.[116] In practice, however, the guarantees proved ineffective; the fiscal realities of runaway inflation in the next years increasingly forced the states to become financial wards of the Reich. Still, Erzberger did not realize his political ambitions, and it was not until Heinrich Brüning became chancellor ten years later that a Reich government would again attempt to use its fiscal lever to achieve a full scale *Reichsreform*.

The evolution of the Reich-state relationship after 1918 revealed a clearcut pattern: the republican leaders of Prussia made no attempt to retain the state's hegemonial position in the Reich constitution, but Prussia was equally unwilling to be prematurely federalized, that is, to accept the Reich's hegemony in state affairs. Seemingly running counter to this overall trend, however, were instances in which either the Prussian cabinet or the coalition parties for reasons of narrow political interest turned authority over to the Reich without a cogent reason.

There were a number of such cases of clear political opportunism. The Prussian cabinet repeatedly did not challenge the Reich's authority in order to avoid responsibility for unpopular decisions. This was particularly true in the area of economics. The Prussian state government left it to the Reich to deal with the increasing clamor for wage increases and structural changes in the economy.[117] There were also occasions when a coalition party used the Reich lever to carry its point of view against a hostile majority in the state Constitutional Convention. The SPD was the first to seek refuge in this device. When the party's parliamentary delegation in the state Constitutional Convention recognized that its views on indemnifying the former royal family for its lost property would not prevail against the opposing arguments of the Prussian finance minister and the bourgeois majority in the state convention, it suggested turning the entire matter over to the National Constitutional Convention.[118] Similarly, the Center party turned to the Reich for help regarding a controversial item of educational policy. The SPD and the two liberal parties in the Prussian Constitutional Convention submitted a bill that would have eliminated the prewar practice of according parish pastors and priests ex officio membership on local school boards. Instead, the clergy would have to be elected like all other eligible citizens. The Center party, fearing defeat, sought a ruling from the Reich Ministry of the Interior that the planned law violated the new Reich constitution's provision prohibiting state education laws before the planned national education bill was passed.[119]

In these and a number of similar instances, the Reich cabinet eagerly took advantage of the opportunity to enhance its authority vis-à-vis Prussia. The pattern held true regardless of the subject matter and political groups involved. In the school issue, for example, the Reich minister of the interior, Erich Koch-Weser, a member of the DDP, did not hesitate to support the Center party's position, although this meant opposing a measure introduced by his own party in Prussia.[120] The Prussian SPD and DDP protested vigorously, but the Reich's position prevailed; the Reich president, too, supported the stand of the national cabinet.[121]

At the same time that Reich and state were developing their new relationship, the Prussian Constitutional Convention was drafting and debating the state's new constitution. But the two developments were connected by far more than chronological coincidence. In a very real sense Prussia's ability to draft a viable constitution would determine its success in reestablishing its position as partner of and paradigm for the Reich. The members of the state's

Constitutional Convention faced a difficult task. The far right and left rejected parliamentary democracy as a matter of principle, but writing the constitution would also strain the cooperation of the government coalition. The parties of the Weimar coalition held widely differing views on such fundamental issues as the nature and powers of the legislature, the relationship of executive and parliament, and the rights of self-government for the provinces and municipalities. The Social Democrats, for example, traditionally favored a centralized form of government and a unicameral legislature, while the bourgeois parties preferred a bicameral parliament and greater rights of autonomy for the provinces and local governmental bodies.

As minister of the interior, Wolfgang Heine was responsible for guiding the draft document through the cabinet and the convention, and he was determined to prevent public debates "which dragged on for months and might endanger the coalition through bickering and wheeling and dealing."[122] Instead, the draft constitution was to be worked out in behind-the-scenes negotiations among the Weimar coalition parties so that the final draft submitted to the legislature would be a document that all three parties could vigorously support. The consultations continued throughout 1919. On January 21, 1920, the cabinet unanimously approved the document, and after some further consultation with the leaders of the coalition parties, the government sent a draft constitution to the Constitutional Convention on February 25, 1920. The convention adjourned between March 3 and 16, and planned to begin the first reading of the document when it returned from its spring recess.

The original draft was modeled on the temporary constitution which the convention had passed on March 19, 1919. It provided for a collegial executive responsible to a parliament elected on the basis of the "widest possible suffrage." The only really novel feature of Heine's draft was the provision for a second chamber of the bicameral legislature. Pressed by its bourgeois coalition partners, the SPD agreed upon an institution called the Budget Council (Finanzrat). Unlike the Landtag, whose members were directly elected by the people, the members of the Budget Council were to be elected by the provincial legislatures. The primary power of the council would have been in the area of budget formation: the draft constitution provided that both houses of the legislature needed to assent to the budget before it became law. On all other items of legislation, the powers of the Budget Council, much like those of the British House of Lords, were limited to delaying votes that could be overruled by the Landtag.[123]

Needless to say, the legislature did not begin its deliberations on March 16; on that day Berlin was still occupied by the Kapp insurgents. More important, even after the republican forces had regained control of the Reich and Prussian governments, the putsch left as its legacy a changed political climate that jeopardized the laboriously constructed compromise on the draft constitution. With the evidence in hand that much of Kapp's support had come from political notables in the Prussian provinces, the SPD would have nothing further to do with the Budget Council, a "smaller version of the [prewar] House of Lords," dominated by provincial delegates and exercising "almost more power than the Landtag."[124] Prominent Social Democratic leaders now demanded a complete rewriting of the draft constitution.[125]

In effect, the new Braun cabinet agreed. Severing, Heine's successor as minister of the interior, decided to leave the fate of the Constitution in the hands of the legislature itself. He resubmitted the original draft to the convention at the end of April, noting expressly that it was his "inheritance [not his] brainchild."[126] That also meant, however, the collapse of Heine's carefully constructed compromise among the coalition parties. The government parties were no longer committed to support the draft submitted by the government, and the final version of the constitution would be the result of the compromises and deals directly worked out by the convention, or, more specifically, the Landesversammlung's Constitutional Committee. The committee debated the constitution from June until October 1920. Unlike much of the work in the Weimar parliaments, the discussions were characterized by a businesslike atmosphere with little personal animosity or acrimony. A primary reason lay in the fact that all parties, including the opposition groups that rejected parliamentary democracy as a suitable form of government for Prussia and Germany, were interested in concluding the constitution-writing process so that either new elections could be held or, alternatively, they could gain time to cement the cooperation of the coalition. Since everyone recognized that adopting a constitution was a prerequisite for adjourning the Constitutional Convention, there was little attempt to filibuster during the drafting process.[127]

Personal factors also facilitated the work. All of the major parties sent their best minds to the committee. Preuss (DDP), Heilmann (SPD), Leidig (DVP), Porsch (Center party), Kries, and Hoetzsch (both DNVP) were all leading members of the convention and respected spokesmen for their political parties. The government was usually represented by a well-known constitutional lawyer, the permanent undersecretary in the Ministry of the Interior, Friedrich Freund; Interior Minister Severing was involved in reparations and disarmament negotiations and therefore absent from Berlin throughout most of the summer.

Finally, the results of the June 1920 Reichstag elections indirectly aided the work of the convention. Until then all four Prussian opposition parties (DNVP, DVP, USPD, and KPD) rejected, for differing reasons, a parliamentary and democratic constitution for Prussia.[128] A significant change occurred in the attitude of the DVP, however, after the party joined the bourgeois coalition in the Reich.[129] The DVP became increasingly less vociferous in its denunciation of a democratic constitution for Prussia, and on October 20 the DVP delegate in the Constitutional Committee created a minor sensation when he cast his vote for the draft constitution along with the representatives of the DDP, the SPD, and the Center party.[130]

The controversial parts of the constitution included both symbolic and substantive items. Among the former were the designation of Prussia as a "republic" (the actual term used was the German *Freistaat*). The committee voted for this SPD proposal by only the narrowest of margins: twelve to eleven. The bourgeois majority on the committee succeeded in retaining the state colors of black and white (these had been, of course, the family colors of the House of Hohenzollern as well) against the opposition of the Social Democrats.[131]

Among the substantive issues, by far the largest amount of time in the committee's deliberations was occupied by the question of the role and power of a second legislative chamber. The SPD now categorically rejected the earlier proposal for a budget council and demanded a simple unicameral legislature. The bourgeois parties were equally adamant that a second chamber in some form was necessary to guard against the dangers of parliamentary absolutism and centralism.[132] The delegates compromised on the creation of a State Council (Staatsrat). The Social Democrats still had "considerable misgivings" about a second chamber in any form, but from their point of view the State Council certainly represented an improvement over the Budget Council.[133] While Heine's earlier proposal affected the Landtag's power of the purse, the Staatsrat had few specific budgetary powers. Instead, it was intended to assure the Prussian provinces an advisory voice—but only that— in all bills submitted to the Landtag. Of the Budget Council's financial veto rights a single vestige remained: the State Council could hold up money bills passed by the Landtag if the allocations involved were in excess of amounts proposed in the state budget submitted by the cabinet. On all other legislative action, negative votes by the Staatsrat could be overridden by the Landtag with a two-thirds majority (article 42).[134]

Only slightly less controversial was the relationship between the executive and legislative branches of government, including the manner of selecting the prime minister. Heine's draft had taken over the provision embodied in the temporary constitution: the prime minister was to be selected by the speaker of the Landtag and the chief executive officer in turn would choose the members of his cabinet. In the Constitutional Committee the Center party proposed a major change in that the prime minister would be nominated by the president of the State Council and then confirmed by the Landtag. Such a provision would have given the president of the Staatsrat a position analogous to that of the Reich president. It would also have removed the selection of the chief executive officer from the direct control of the Landtag, thus diluting the democratic and parliamentary nature of the Prussian government. The Center party's proposal received little support from its coalition partners or the opposition. On the contrary, the permanent constitution involved Parliament more directly than had been the case under the temporary document. The mode of selection provided that the Landtag itself elect the prime minister on the basis of a secret ballot without debate from nominations submitted by members of Parliament. To prevent deadlocks, the constitution provided that after the first ballot a plurality of votes sufficed for election. The prime minister, once elected, selected the members of his cabinet and submitted them for a vote of confidence to the Landtag.[135]

It is ironic that the Social Democrats, who were the later beneficiaries of the strong executive powers written into the constitution, still held fast to their long-term fears of a powerful executive during the deliberations of the Constitutional Committee.[136] In the constitutional debates the bourgeois parties (with the exception of the Center party) argued for a strong executive, while the SPD sought to enlarge the authority of the Landtag. In general, the constitutional views of the bourgeois parties prevailed. The powers of the prime minister (articles 45–47) were considerably more extensive than those of the Reich chancellor in the national constitution. In addition, the document contained an effective emergency powers clause (article 55), analogous to article 48 of the Reich constitution, that could be invoked by the prime minister and the cabinet, although paradoxically the stable parliamentary conditions in Prussia meant that the state government did not need to use these powers until shortly before the demise of the republic.[137]

The Constitutional Committee finished its first reading of the draft on July 11 and sent the document to the party caucuses for further discussion. In the course of the next three months, various differences among the coalition parties were ironed out and by the end of September it was clear that a constitution would pass at least with the votes of the Weimar parties—though there remained some doubt as to how firm even their commitment was.[138] Actually, in the final roll-call vote of the convention the constitution passed very comfortably with the votes of the SPD, DDP, Center party, and DVP. The tally was 280 for and 60 against. The opposition was represented by the votes of the USPD, KPD, and DNVP.[139]

The Constitutional Convention concluded its sessions shortly before Christmas 1920, having finished, as its speaker noted in a self-congratulatory vein, "a workload as probably no other Parliament before it." Other observers were considerably more critical of its performance, but it is true that the convention created a constitution that turned out to be remarkably successful.[140] This is all the more surprising as the state convention seems to have made few attempts to learn from the experience of the Reich constitution. (The Prussian document, it will be recalled, did not go into effect until more than a year after the Reich constitution.) Thus, the constitutional articles that bolstered the powers of the executive were not the result of the ineffectiveness of the executive in the Reich, but a continuation of the Prussian tradition of strong governments. The various political groupings had different motives for wishing to continue this tradition, but they certainly shared the feeling that a strong state executive was an important vehicle for maintaining Prussia's status and influence in Germany both in its relations with other states and the Reich government. If the convention learned from any historical experience, it was the Kapp Putsch. The coup doomed the originally proposed Budget Council, since the uncertain attitude of a number of provinces persuaded even a majority of the delegates from the bourgeois parties that the degree of provincial autonomy in the constitution had to be circumscribed.

The effectiveness of the constitution as a framework of parliamentary government in Prussia mitigated the adverse effect of the severe losses of state sovereignty to the Reich that had been incorporated earlier in the Reich constitution. The Prussian constitution went into effect in 1921, and the three years since the revolution had seen a steady increase in the powers of the federal government. The largest German state no longer dominated the Reich as a whole. Erzberger's financial reforms largely stripped the state of its fiscal autonomy. The changes in the voting rules for the Reichsrat erected a constitutional barrier against Prussian hegemony in that body. Yet, while Prussia lost much of its de jure authority, the *Land* managed to retain a considerable amount of de facto power. Of paramount importance in this regard was the fact that contrary to the plans of Hugo Preuss and the early Reich ministers of the interior, Prussia was never in real danger of dissolution and therefore by the very nature of its size retained a significance that outstripped that of any other state within the Reich. Prussia could not dominate the Reich, but neither could the Reich control Prussia. The state successfully resisted proposals to join federal and state offices initiated by the Reich and thwarted any plans to accord Reich ministers the status of members of the Prussian cabinet. Moreover, in the course of 1919 and 1920 Prussia regained much of the political status it had lost earlier. The parliamentary strength of the Weimar coalition in Prussia contrasted with the weak position of the Reich government in its relations with the Reichstag. While the national government was subject to frequent crises, the phenomenon of the reluctant coalition in the Prussian Constitutional Convention and later in the Landtag assured the Prussian cabinet of strong backing as it sought to safeguard the state against encroachments from the federal authorities.

CHAPTER 4

Personnel Policies and Administrative Reforms, 1918–1921

In addition to the political structures embodied in the state constitution of 1851 and Bismarck's Reich constitution of 1871, political control in Prussia traditionally depended upon a third factor: the state's efficient, tightly knit, and politically conservative corps of civil servants. Prussia's physical size and population, as well as the virtual absence of a federal civil service before 1914, meant that in a real sense Prussia administered most of Germany. The organization and political makeup of this corps of administrators was therefore crucial not only for the political direction of the state, but also for the Reich as a whole.

The loyalty and effectiveness of the corps of administrators had been a major factor of strength for prewar Prussian authoritarianism; "democratizing" the bureaucracy, taking steps to assure that it was organized and staffed in such a way that the corps of administrators would support rather than sabotage the democratic system, should have been high on the agenda of the revolutionary and early parliamentary cabinets. As we shall see, the ministries' failure to act decisively in this area seriously undermined the viability of the new form of government in the first year of its existence. Conversely, when the new rulers did undertake energetic reforms after the Kapp Putsch had exposed their earlier mistakes, the Prussian civil service helped the state to become the democratic bulwark that it was to be during the crisis-ridden years of the 1920s.

The Prussian administration was traditionally divided into three parts, although transfers between the divisions, especially at the higher levels, were not uncommon: the territorial administration, the technical services (which included public school teachers), and the police forces. At least in the short run, the territorial administrators and the police were the politically most important components of the triad.

On paper, the organization of the state's territorial administration was a model of rationality and efficiency. Prussia was divided into twelve provinces, each headed by a governor *(Oberpräsident)*. The provinces in turn consisted of thirty-two districts *(Regierungsbezirke)*, presided over by district directors *(Regierungspräsidenten)*. The districts were further subdivided into

115

some 450 counties *(Kreise)*, headed by county commissioners *(Landräte)*. A unique and anachronistic feature of the county organization were the so-called estate-townships *(Gutsbezirke)*. Located in East Elbia, about 200 county sub-divisions had administrative boundaries coterminous with privately owned latifundia so that they constituted administrative units that were in effect private property. The administrative personnel for the entire system, some 550 individuals who constituted the political administration (the term also covered major officials in the central administrations in Berlin and the munici-pal police chiefs), were appointed by the Prussian cabinet after nomination by the relevant ministers, primarily the minister of the interior. The only group of administrators exempt from direct control by the cabinet were in the larger cities. Here the city councils elected the municipal administrators and mayors, but even in the case of these officials the minister of the interior had to give his approval before they could serve their terms of office.

As a group, the prewar Prussian political administrators formed a body of civil servants that was hard-working and virtually free of corruption, but also recruited from an exceedingly narrow political and social base. All of the provincial governors serving in 1913 came from the nobility, and aristocratic titles predominated among the district directors as well. Particularly in East Elbia, close personal relations between the political administrators and the Junker landowners were common. In the lower and middle-level ranks of the civil service, retired noncommissioned officers often found a second career. The political administrators were also overwhelmingly Protestant. Even in heavily Catholic areas, the cabinet tended to appoint Lutherans or Calvinists. In terms of their political identification, the territorial administrators over-whelmingly supported the Conservative parties; it was not until 1916, for example, that an avowed National Liberal became district director.

In spite of its surface rationality and efficiency, experts in public admin-istration recognized long before the collapse of the empire that the Prussian system of territorial administration was badly in need of reform. To be sure, for the most part the criticism did not focus on what was clearly the most glaring fault of the entire system, the narrow political and social strata from which the administrators were drawn. Instead, before the First World War administrative experts concentrated on the need for organizational reforms in the territorial administration. There are widespread recognition that the state's present administrative structure, with its numerous differentiated systems of local self-rule, cumbersome overlapping jurisdictions between the governors and the district directors, enormous differences in the size and wealth of the provinces, and uneasy relationships of between the county executives and the state administration on the one hand and the county legislatures on the other, was neither an ideal nor an efficient system of administration.[1] Countless royal commissions and ministers of the interior worked out detailed reform plans, none of which were put into actual practice. Each time the subject was aired in Parliament or in the cabinet, administrative reform as a whole seemed too complicated to be realized in its entirety, and the individual aspects too interrelated for any one reform to be enacted in isolation.

After the revolution the new government inherited all of the old administrative problems, but the new rulers also had an unprecedented opportunity to effect rapid and far-reaching changes. In November 1918 the widely hailed and feared symbol of Prussian authoritarianism, the corps of conservative public administrators, had collapsed.[2] Unfortunately, the revolutionary ministers did not seize the opportunity. Their immediate priorities lay elsewhere. To begin with, for revolutionaries they exhibited an uncharacteristic fear of having their legitimacy questioned. The new ministers made deliberate (and slightly ludicrous) attempts to preserve the appearance of legal continuity and orderly transition from the old authorities to the new. The first major appointments by the revolutionary government were made public on November 14. The USPD co–prime minister, Ströbel, appointed his SPD colleague, Hirsch, in the name of the "Prussian government" as minister of the interior. That same government, this time over the signatures of Hirsch and Ströbel, named Breitscheid to the same ministry. An executive order dated November 11, which still carried the signature of the prerevolutionary minister of the interior, Drews, was ostentatiously published along with an order of the new government dated November 14.[3]

The claims to buttress the cabinet's legitimacy were designed at least in part to meet the challenge from another set of institutions which had no claim to authority except the revolution itself: the workers' and soldiers' councils. Their role during the fall and winter of 1918–19 has now been recognized as something of a historic tragedy. The German revolution "failed" in the sense that it did not produce fundamental social changes in Germany, in large part because the councils did not recognize their own strength until it was too late, and because the Reich and the Prussian revolutionary governments saw their relationship to the councils primarily in terms of confrontation and mutual antagonism.[4]

The council movement included a wide range of regional and occupational interest groups,[5] but essentially only the various workers' and soldiers' councils had the political potential to influence the decision-making process in personnel policies and administration. The political character of the Prussian workers' and soldiers' councils varied considerably from area to area. SPD and Socialist trade union leaders dominated the councils in the urban concentrations of the west. In smaller towns west of the Elbe, most of the councils were never true workers' assemblies at all, but cooperative ventures of labor and bourgeois interest groups. In contrast, a few councils in central Germany,—for example, in Magdeburg, Merseburg, and Halle—were dominated by quite radical syndicalist-anarchists elements.[6] In the eastern, agricultural provinces with their latifundia ruled by Junker landlords, the councils also reflected the prevailing class conflicts between landowners and agricultural labor.[7] As noted earlier, in the actual border areas of eastern Prussia, that is, the areas directly adjacent to the newly created Polish state, so-called People's Councils *(Volksräte)*, were dominated by conservative and chauvinistic elements.

In the first days of the revolution, the councils sprang up spontaneously with little effort at regional or national coordination, but within a relatively short time the Executive Committee (Vollzugsrat) of the Workers' and Soldiers' Council of Greater Berlin claimed authority as the "highest organ of the revolution." In this capacity it sought to supervise the activities of local councils, the Reich government, and the Prussian cabinet. For the state the executive committee at the beginning of December established a nine-member Prussian Commission.[8]

The Berlin executive committee was never a very effective control organ. For one thing, the "subordinate" local councils were by no means willing to acknowledge the superior position of the Berlin officials. The Berlin Executive Council, for example, was forced to enlist the aid of the Prussian Ministry of the Interior to prevent the local workers' and soldiers' council in Potsdam from organizing a "Reich Conference of Workers' and Soldiers' Councils" on its own authority.[9] Above all, however, the executive committee was its own worst enemy. It could never find a clear policy line or an effective form of organization. The group started enormous paper projects, but at the same time, it yielded rapidly to the demands of numerous Berlin pressure groups that managed to invade its chambers almost daily.[10] As a result, there was no continuity in either policy guidelines or membership and the committee quickly succumbed to organizational chaos. The group was no match for the Council of People's Plenipotentiaries in the Reich; as early as the beginning of December Ebert commented confidentially, "Actually, the executive committee has no real influence."[11] Often lacking a quorum, burdened with financial irregularities and frequent splits among its political factions, the Berlin executive committee continued to exist virtually in name only until October 1919, when the Prussian cabinet dissolved it.[12]

By that time, the Berlin group had long lost its monopoly position as the apex of the workers' and soldiers' councils. In December 1918 the First National Assembly of Workers' and Soldiers' Councils had been elected as an expression of "proletarian democracy."[13] The majority of seats were held by delegates who were either members of or leaned toward the SPD; the USPD was supported by a decided minority. Like the Berlin councils, the National Assembly elected an executive organ, the Central Council (Zentralrat), but in contrast to the executive committee in Berlin the Central Council had a politically homogeneous composition. The SPD proposed that the Central Council's membership should reflect the strength of the various parties in the assembly, but the USPD demanded parity, and when a vote of the full assembly rejected its proposal, the Independent Socialists in turn indicated they would boycott the Central Council. As a result, this body was made up solely of SPD and "soldier" members, with the latter faction also politically affiliated with the majority Socialists. The Central Council, too, claimed control powers over both the Reich and the Prussian governments. It also formed a special committee for Prussian affairs, which was headed by Albert Grzesinski, then the chairman of the workers' and soldiers' council in Kassel (Hessen).[14] In March 1919 the Central Council formally transferred its control functions to the Prussian Constitutional Convention.

Personnel Policies

Throughout the relatively brief time of their existence, the workers' and soldiers' councils at all levels—local no less than statewide—had a particular interest in the present and future composition of the political civil service. To be sure, for the most part the council members did not want to become officials themselves. The great majority of the workers' and soldiers councils initially limited their function to allowing the local and county officials to continue routine administrative work, albeit under the supervision of representatives from the councils. Looking somewhat further into the future, however, the councils perceived their role as midwives active in the birth of democracy in Germany, a process that included the "democratization" of the Prussian territorial administration.

Unfortunately, this catchword, democratization, was subject to rather different interpretations. On the one hand it meant opening the civil service to all qualified citizens regardless of political ideology, economic background, or religious affiliation. In this sense democratization did not preclude maintaining many of the old competency requirements, and especially the regulation requiring a university law degree for entrance into the higher ranks of the civil service.[15] However, democratization could also involve much more radical changes, such as the dismissal of all "reactionary" officials, and their replacement by civil servants who might not meet the formal educational requirements, but who were unquestionably loyal to the revolution and the republican form of government.[16]

At first, cooperation between the councils and the Prussian government seemed to make a good start. The cabinet issued a directive prohibiting local councils from dismissing officials without ministerial approval, but the Ministry of the Interior also directed its subordinate offices to recognize the supervisory role of the workers' and soldiers' councils, and to settle local disputes through negotiations with the councils.[17] The era of good feeling continued with the joint handling of the "Spahn affair" by the cabinet and executive committee of the Berlin workers' and soldiers' councils. In November 1918, the Catholic and conservative minister of justice, Martin Spahn, remained in office as a holdover from the prerevolutionary regime. Although certainly no friend of the revolution, he was quite willing to make far-reaching concessions to the new leaders in order to stay in office. Spahn was, however, particularly unpopular with the USPD and under pressure from its Independent members, the Political Cabinet asked the Berlin Executive Council to determine Spahn's future as a Prussian minister.[18] The Executive Council in turn voted unanimously to dismiss Spahn, or more precisely, not to confirm him in office. He was replaced by two socialist ministers, Wolfgang Heine (SPD) and Kurt Rosenfeld (USPD).[19]

The period of cooperation was brief. Cabinet and councils clashed when the councils interpreted democratization of the territorial administration as instituting personnel decisions of their own. The workers' and soldiers' councils were particularly suspicious of the county commissioners, the largest category of officials in the territorial administration and the backbone of Prussian authoritarianism before 1918. After order had been restored in the Prussian countryside, local workers' and soldiers' councils in various counties moved against "uncooperative county commissioners" either by preventing them from carrying out their duties or summarily dismissing them. The Berlin Executive Committee admitted that the local councils were not always very discriminating, but agreed that it was better to err on the side of excess. The Berlin group authorized local workers' and soldiers' councils "to dismiss all county executives and other civil servants . . . who carry out their duties according to the old system or who support . . . counterrevolutionary activities.[20]

The cabinet took a dim view of such independent action by the councils. As noted above, the ministers almost immediately after taking office prohibited the councils from making personnel decisions on their own. They also attempted to draft guidelines delineating the jurisdiction of the councils, in order "to prevent them from encroaching on the competencies of the state authorities."[21] Unlike the councils, whose primary concern was the elimination of politically unreliable officials in the territorial administration, the government was more concerned with potential administrative chaos if two parallel lines of authority—the councils and the administrative structure headed by the cabinet—attempted to lead Prussia into the republican era.[22] This conviction was held as firmly by the Independent ministers as by their majority Socialist colleagues. Breitscheid's comment, "In many areas the presence of the councils raises problems," is typical.[23] Similarly, all members of the Reich Council of People's Plenipotentiaries supported the point of view of their Prussian colleagues. After November 16, the Prussian cabinet moved vigorously to limit the councils' authority in making personnel appointments, and by the end of the year the councils' authority was restricted to making informal suggestions and registering complaints.

Beset by internal problems, faced with widespread apathy among their initial supporters, and confronted with a cabinet that increasingly identified them with left-wing radicalism, the Prussian workers' and soldiers' councils within a few weeks of their creation retained little political authority.[24] Attempts by the Central Council (Zentralrat), the executive committee elected by the National Assembly of Workers' and Soldiers' Councils in December 1918, to regain lost ground met with little success. The council insisted that it had the right to participate in drafting personnel guidelines and it wanted to retain a voice in the appointment and supervision especially of the county commissioners,[25] but the group was in a weak position to enforce its writ. After the democratic election of local, provincial, and state legislative bodies, it was certainly difficult to justify the existence of an extraparliamentary control organ within the Prussian parliamentary system of government.[26] By the spring of 1919 the cabinet, and specifically the Ministry of the Interior, was the sole determinant of personnel policies and appointments in Prussia; the councils had to recognize their lack of real power.[27]

Between 1918 and 1921, four men served as Prussian minister of the interior: Paul Hirsch (SPD), Wolfgang Heine (SPD), Carl Severing (SPD), and Alexander Dominicus (DDP). Among this group, Heine and Severing were by far the most important. Wolfgang Heine's position was pivotal. As the first republican minister of the interior, Heine could make decisive policy regarding the transformation of Prussian administrators from handmaidens of authoritarianism into servants of the republic. The minister did not come from a working-class background. His family belonged to the upper middle class and he first became politically active as a member of an anti-Semitic fraternity and the Christian Socialist movement of Paul Stöcker.[28] (The latter hoped to attract workers away from Marxism by propagandizing social reform within a Christian but also anti-Semitic context.) Heine soon turned his back on these bourgeois fringe groups and joined the SPD, although he was affiliated with the extreme right wing of the party and remained a staunch German and Prussian nationalist.[29] Heine was also feared for his abrasive and egocentric personality. Adolph Hoffmann's verdict that Heine never outgrew being "the snotty anti-Semite" was clearly colored by the sharp political differences between them, but Eduard David, who shared Heine's political views and recognized his talents, also commented on the minister's "need for personal praise" and his "astonishing lack of control." A leading member of the DDP, the prime minister of Baden, Willy Hellpach, described Heine as "almost like a Prussian officer . . . self-confident and a bit domineering."[30] Even Hirsch, whose political mentor Heine was in many respects, on occasion mocked his colleague.[31]

In contrast to Heine, his successor, Carl Severing, was one of the most popular figures in the SPD. Heine's bourgeois background always kept him somewhat isolated in the predominantly working-class SPD. Severing, however, came from a proletarian family, had been apprenticed as a locksmith, was self-taught, and had worked himself up in the ranks of the union movement.[32] In time, Severing became an effective mass orator and one of the party's favorite speakers.

Alexander Dominicus differed in yet another way from the other two. He again came from a bourgeois background, and had been active in local politics and municipal affairs before the revolution. In this sense he had a career that paralleled that of Paul Hirsch in many ways. By 1918 Dominicus had become a fixture as long-term mayor of the city of Charlottenburg, then an independent residential city just outside of Berlin. He retained this position after the revolution until the fall of 1920 when Charlottenburg was incorporated into the capital city. Politically, Dominicus was affiliated with the right wing of the DDP.

All four of the ministers were convinced that thoroughgoing administrative and personnel reforms had been needed for some time; they differed among themselves (and with the councils as long as these existed) over questions of tactics, priorities, and timing. Undoubtedly, Hirsch and Heine confronted the most difficult task. They not only had to deal with the immediate pressures occasioned by the revolutionary upheavals, but also had to assure the continuity of public services.[33] In their personnel policies, the ministers tried to square the circle—that is to say, they wanted to find a mechanism that would rejuvenate and enlarge the reservoir of civil service candidates, while at the same time sacrificing neither the traditional educational and other skill prerequisites nor the continuity in office of most of the civil service corps.[34] Unlike the workers' and soldiers' councils, the cabinet placed priority on institutional, rather than immediate personnel changes to democratize the Prussian territorial administration. Especially Heine wanted to establish a system of equal employment opportunity, not affirmative action. As far as the minister of the interior was concerned, the Prussian civil service would be democratized primarily by eliminating from consideration for employment and promotion all written or unwritten advantages and disadvantages that accrued from membership in certain classes or religious groups.[35]

Like many of his contemporaries, Heine believed in what Wolfgang Elben has called the "ideology of experts."[36] Under this doctrine, administrators, even most of those holding political appointments, were regarded as essentially apolitical technocrats whose political beliefs were largely irrelevant, at least in comparison to the importance of their technical skills. In practice,

applying this principle was largely counterproductive, particularly in the crucial first months immediately after the revolution. The doctrine of apolitical
experts failed to recognize that the pre–1918 civil service, for all its
undoubted professional competence, had not been politically neutral, but was
in fact a staunch pillar of support for conservatism and authoritarianism. In
the short run only a massive influx of loyal republican "outsiders," that is,
men who had made their mark outside the civil service pecking order, could
make the old civil service politically and socially more heterogeneous. But
Heine had little faith in outsiders. "I cannot govern Prussia with union leaders
and Jewish lawyers," was his deprecating conclusion.[37]

The folly of Heine's personnel policies became glaringly apparent when
the cabinet addressed the question of changing the composition of the corps of
county commissioners. Immediately after the revolution the ministers had
replaced all of the state's provincial governors and many of the district directors with politically reliable officials (here the cabinet did select some "outsiders"), but few county commissioners had been replaced.[38] As noted
before, many of the workers' and soldiers' councils were particularly vociferous in their demands that a number of county commissioners be immediately dismissed because of their close association with the Conservatives.
Heine and the cabinet agreed that the key to any meaningful democratization
of the territorial administration was the staffing of the county commissioners'
offices, but the minister continued to argue that institutional changes were
sufficient to bring about the desired results.[39] In this area, in addition to
opening the position to all qualified applicants, Heine was convinced that the
basic change needed was what came to be called the "communalization" of
the county commissioners, that is, the election of the county commissioners
by the elected county legislatures rather than their appointment by the central
government. With this reform the problem of personnel selection could be
solved as a matter of course.[40] For Heine, then, the key to the "democratization" of the county commissioners was not the appointment of new officials,
but the establishment of rules for truly democratic elections at the local level.
As a result, the government made no major personnel appointments in the
counties in the first half of 1919, wanting to wait instead until the county
legislatures had been elected according to the new rules. This gave the old-
guard county commissioners several months not only to administer their counties, but to use their influence during the election campaign as well.[41] The
election results in turn demonstrated clearly that the communalization concept
was not workable. Particularly in the eastern provinces, the DNVP emerged
as the leading party in a significant number of counties. Under these circumstances the communalization of the county commissioners would have meant
handing administrative authority in a number of counties over to the German
Nationalists. Even Heine was not willing to go that far. By the end of 1919 he

warned that Prussia threatened to disintegrate into a series of "county republics," and reaffirmed that the state would maintain supervisory authority over the county commissioners.[42] But by then it was already too late. The old *Landräte* had had more than a year in which to further the activities of various groups that would eventually stage the Kapp Putsch.

The cabinet's failure to make meaningful changes in the personnel makeup of the corps of political administrators was all the more regrettable, since for some months after the revolution the government had the legal authority to act on its own to "clean up" the administrative apparatus. A decree of February 26, 1919, authorized the cabinet to remove political appointees who had not reached the customary retirement age of sixty-eight, and permitted officials in this category to apply for early retirement themselves if they felt that remaining in office would create a conflict of conscience for them.[43] In practice, the decree remained a blunt sword. It constituted an elective procedure *(Kannvorschrift)* for both sides and was seldom used. In the weeks between the revolution and the first meeting of the state Constitutional Convention, the minister of the interior and the cabinet rarely initiated mandatory retirement proceedings against politically suspect individuals. And even when an official started the process on his own, the burden of proof in demonstrating a conflict of conscience was on him. The cabinet intended to demand a thorough and convincing presentation of the conflict of conscience, precisely in order to reduce the number of applications. No wonder the minister of finance confidently predicted that the number of applicants, especially among the younger members of the political civil service, would be negligible.[44] In addition, the original decree did not apply to judges and judicial personnel, because Heine and the majority of the cabinet felt that including them would endanger the nonpolitical character of the judicial system. This was certainly correct in a formal sense, but the Prussian judges were also among the most powerful opponents of the new democratic state. Judicial personnel was not included within the meaning of the act until a year later— after the Kapp Putsch.

Aside from appointing new men to political positions in the state, the cabinet had two other possibilities open to it to speed the democratization process within the Prussian administration. One was the appointment of supervisors *(Beigeordnete)*. These were "outsiders" attached to various offices to oversee the routine work of the civil service. The other involved the appointment of commissioners who served as temporary officials with extraordinary powers to override the decisions of the regular civil service in a particular geographic area or a specific field of administration.

The supervisors were an outgrowth of the activities of the workers' and soldiers' councils.[45] In the early days immediately following the collapse of the old regime, most of the councils delegated supervisors to the various levels of the Prussian administration from county commissioners to the ministries. For a variety of reasons, the new institution had little effect at the upper administrative levels, although some quite distinguished political leaders held appointments. The supervisor of the Prussian Ministry of Finance, for example, was the long-time Socialist leader Eduard Bernstein. He had a professional background in banking, but in his capacity as supervisor he restricted his role to assuring that the routine work of the Finance Ministry went on uninterrupted.[46] In addition, Bernstein's appointment exemplified a peculiar redundancy in some of the supervisor appointments: it was not clear what there was to supervise in a ministry already headed by two Socialist ministers. A similar situation prevailed in the Ministry of Agriculture. The supervisor here, Emmanuel Wurm (USPD), was also a well-known Socialist leader. Wurm was a highly respected expert in agricultural and consumer affairs, but he viewed his position as supervisor simply as an appendage to his primary post as Reich and Prussian commissioner for food distribution.[47] Moreover, there were no discernible policy differences between him and Otto Braun, the SPD minister of agriculture. In contrast, the Ministry of Defense did represent a fruitful object for the work of a supervisor, but here neither the SPD nor the USPD was able to make an effective choice during the months when it would have been possible to produce major changes. The USPD never sent a supervisor to the ministry at all. The Independent co-chairman of the Executive Committee of the Berlin Workers' and Soldiers' Council, Ernst Däumig, was selected by his party, but he refused to accept the appointment, and the Independents could not find an alternate choice.[48] The SPD did appoint a supervisor, but its selection, a former pastor by the name of Paul Göhre, was totally unsuited to the post. His primary interest was in educational policy, and he had neither experience nor qualifications for dealing with the military. Moreover, the experience of the First World War had driven Göhre to the far right of the SPD where he remained in awe of the German military. As a result, he became little more than a "signature machine" in the hands of the old officer corps.[49] His successor, Albert Grzesinski, was cut from an entirely different cloth, but as we have seen, by the time he became supervisor in the Defense Ministry in the spring of 1919 the optimal time for fundamental reforms of the military had passed.

The ineffectiveness of the supervisors was less pronounced at the local and county levels. Here they often recognized the shortcomings of the old-line civil servants, and attempted to effect real changes.[50] At the same time, they too exemplified the limits of the German revolutionary mentality. For the most part, they quickly succumbed to feelings of departmental particularism: once appointed, all supervisors protected "their" offices against unwelcome encroachments by the workers' and soldiers' councils and supervisors of higher offices viewed themselves as the superiors of those attached to subordinate offices.[51] As a rule, they were also "good Prussians" who were particularly adamant in countering any attempts by non-Prussian forces to extend control over parts of the Prussian administration or Prussian territory.[52]

In contrast to the Reich, where the "commissioners" became a favorite form of crisis management, Prussia made little use of state commissioners as a catalytic element in personnel reform. The state had an encompassing and smoothly functioning civil service, and the individual ministries understandably resented outside interference in the form of commissioners.[53] The extraordinary authority of these officials tended to reduce the autonomous position of the ministries at least for the duration of their appointment.[54] For this reason Prussia appointed only one state commissioner on its own,[55] although the state cabinet did routinely give the title of state commissioner retroactively to various Reich commissioners. Such appointments were, however, primarily courtesy gestures, particularly since in several cases Prussia did not approve of the individual chosen by the Reich authorities.[56] In assigning the commissioners areas of competence, Prussia tended to limit the Reich and state commissioners to tasks that were clearly outside the usual framework of routine administrative work, such as organizing the plebiscites specified in the Treaty of Versailles or attempting to settle major strikes.

The slow pace of meaningful reforms did not change markedly after the formation of the first parliamentary coalition government. Despite increasingly vociferous criticism from the ranks of all coalition parties, the cabinet tightened the burden of proof necessary for early retirement.[57] In the face of mounting evidence of antirepublican activities by a number of county commissioners, the Ministry of the Interior held fast to the principle of "communalization" of the county commissioners as the key to personnel reforms.[58] In fact, in the course of the year Heine grew progressively more arrogant in his handling of personnel policies, wanting to consult neither the parliamentary leaders of the coalition parties (including his own), nor his colleagues in the cabinet.[59] Instead, he placed full confidence in the personnel officer of his ministry, Baron Magnus von Braun, an old-line civil servant who later proudly remembered that he had deliberately sabotaged even the weak democratization attempt that the minister advocated.[60]

Until the Kapp Putsch, Heine's ill-conceived personnel policies met with little public opposition. Otto Braun, the minister of agriculture, saw the dangers inherent in Heine's path, but as a fellow Social Democrat he was prevented from vigorous attacks upon his colleague by the rules of party discipline. The same applied to a somewhat lesser degree to the Social Democratic party's parliamentary delegation. It, too, was reluctant formally to oppose a minister from its own ranks, and dissatisfaction among the backbenchers was usually aired only in the form of heckling and the drafting of angry but confidential memoranda.[61] In addition, all of the coalition parties were more interested in a fairer distribution of political patronage than in addressing the character of the political administration as such. The SPD, the DDP, and the Center party had been excluded from the ranks of the higher civil service in prewar Prussia, and they understandably clamored for the rewards of political patronage. But there were some initial difficulties. The Center party and especially the SPD had a few candidates who were fully qualified under the rules of the professional civil service, while the DDP possessed a large reservoir of members with degrees in administrative law.[62] The coalition did find an equitable manner of distributing the relatively few new appointments that were made. The DDP was awarded the bulk of the available director posts, since these required considerable amounts of routine administrative work. The Center party was especially well represented among the provincial governors, as many of the volatile border provinces of Prussia had a largely Catholic population. Finally, the Social Democrats provided a large number of new police chiefs; this was a post for which an administrative law degree had not traditionally been a prerequisite. The cabinet made virtually no appointments to the corps of county commissioners in the first year after the revolution.

Heine had intended that personnel appointments should be handled essentially as internal matters in his ministry, with the cabinet merely ratifying his recommendations after the ministers had had an opportunity to submit written evaluations of the candidates suggested by the Ministry of the Interior. Such methods of indirect consultation went too far for the cabinet. In June 1919 the ministers agreed to a proposal by the minister of commerce, Fischbeck, that all major political appointments be discussed in full plenary sessions by all ministers.[63] In actual practice, candidates for major political positions were also reviewed by the parliamentary undersecretaries and the legislative leaders of the coalition parties before the full cabinet made a final decision.[64]

The provincial governors stood at the apex of the territorial administration so that they were visible of the political appointees.[65] Consequently it may be useful to illustrate the interaction of forces in the appointment process during the early months of the Prussian republic by focusing on the selection of one particularly controversial new appointment, that of Otto Hörsing as governor of the province of Prussian Saxony in the spring of 1919. Hörsing was a typical "outsider." He had no college diploma, much less a degree in administrative law. Instead, Hörsing was a labor leader whose abrasive personality and "rough life style" had already aroused controversy.[66] Heine nominated the labor leader to be the new governor of Hörsing's native province after the minister's first choice—the right-wing Social Democrat August Müller, a former editor of the *Magdeburger Zeitung* and now an official in the Reich Department of Commerce—was vehemently opposed by the SPD's district organization in the province. Heine for his part refused the candidate put forth by the local party activists, the former head of the workers' and soldiers' councils in Saxony, Ernst Wittmack.[67] In launching a trial balloon for Hörsing, Heine praised his "unquestioned loyalty to Prussia" and noted that he was "one of the few people who have a natural instinct for political matters and effects." To overcome the residual opposition to his candidate, Heine appealed to party solidarity among his SPD colleagues, and to the benefits of executive logrolling in the ranks of the DDP. In the end Hörsing was appointed governor, while a DDP nominee went to Magdeburg (a city in the same province) as district director.[68]

When the Kapp Putsch had put an end to the ministerial careers of Heine and the first Weimar cabinet, they could look back upon their accomplishments in personnel policy with little pride. Hirsch's claim that the government had made full use of its powers to democratize the civil service during its term of office revealed little more than political naiveté.[69] At the level of the central administration, only in the Ministry of Education, had there been a considerable influx of younger officials, but even in this bastion of Prussian authoritarianism nothing like a wholesale turnover of officials ever took place. In the territorial administration change was the exception rather than the rule. By the end of 1919 a significant changeover had taken place only among the provincial governors. None of the prewar incumbents remained in office, and all of the new appointees had close ties to the coalition parties. In addition, most of the police chiefs of the major Prussian cites were regarded as reliable supporters of democracy. In contrast, a majority of district directors and most county commissioners were still men who had been appointed by the prewar regime.

The lack of turnover in the territorial administration can be illustrated by the number of Social Democrats who held office at the end of 1919. That figure is also a good indicator of the degree to which "outsiders" had been able to penetrate the political appointments; the Social Democrats had the fewest number of candidates who had the traditional qualifications. When Kapp's troops marched into Berlin, four of the provincial governors, ten of twenty-five police chiefs, but only three of twenty-one district directors and twenty-four of four hundred and fifty county executives were regarded as Social Democrats.[70] Finally, the record was worst among the ranks of the judicial personnel, a category that even Heine regarded as his "most difficult problem child." Here almost none of the without exception politically conservative judges and judicial administrators had been replaced.[71]

The putschists did not have the time to develop any coherent personnel policies during their five-day control of Berlin and parts of Prussia, but from the conspirators' few appointments and the differentiated reaction of the incumbent administrators to the putsch, it is possible to discern both Kapp's aims and the fervor of antirepublican sentiment in the Prussian civil service.

Kapp's minister of the interior–designate, Traugott von Jagow, was a personi-fied political statement: as the prewar police chief of Berlin he had gained a reputation for being a particularly vociferous opponent of Social Democracy and democratic reforms in general.[72] Jagow lost no time in taking control of his office in the early hours of March 13, 1920. As his state secretary he chose Doyé, Eichhorn's nemesis, who had headed the police desk in the Interior Ministry under Heine.[73] Jagow set to work purging the republican appointees among the political members of the civil service. He dismissed four provincial governors, those of Pomerania, Silesia, Saxony, and Schleswig-Holstein. All but one of these were in provinces east of the Elbe. A similar pattern prevailed in the retirement of district directors: of the eight fired officials (the directors of Potsdam, Frankfurt-on-Oder, Köslin, Stralsund, Breslau, Liegnitz, Mag-deburg, and Arnsberg) only one headed a district west of the Elbe (Arnsberg). Politically, all of the officials dismissed were affiliated with either the SPD or the DDP.[74]

As replacements, Jagow chose old-line Conservatives or men from the extreme right. The designated governor of Schleswig-Holstein was a Conser-vative and former mayor of the city of Kiel, Lindemann; for the governor of Silesia, he chose a DNVP member of the Prussian Constitutional Convention, von Kessel. The commissioner *(Regierungskommissar)* for the Greater Ham-burg area, Alfred Jacobsen, belonged to the Pan-German Association and had been active as an organizer of the "Bund," a secret group within the racist and right-extremist Deutschvölkischer Schutz- und Trutzbund.[75] The appoint-ments clearly revealed the pattern of Kapp's and Jagow's future intentions with regard to personnel policy: an immediate end to the weak democratiza-tion measures of the republican government, restoration of conservative, authoritarian rule, particularly in the areas east of the Elbe, and steps to deal with autonomist tendencies in the northern and western border provinces by a return to the rigid centralism of prewar Prussia.

Kapp was never able to control effectively even the central government, much less the provinces, during his five days in office, but the response of high-level officials in the ministries and the territorial administration to the putschists says much about the failure of the personnel policies of earlier cabinets. To be sure, a few high-level civil servants, such as Freund and Meister in the Ministry of the Interior (both, incidentally, prewar appointees) attempted to use their influence to keep their subordinates loyal to the toppled parliamentary government, but the majority of higher civil servants were probably at least sympathetic toward the aims of the Putschists.[76] It was symptomatic that the Prussian state secretaries waited until a day after their Reich colleagues announced that they would not work for the Kapp govern-ment before associating themselves with this step.[77]

The response of the political administrators in the provinces varied greatly. As would be expected, Kapp received the most active support from officials in the rural heartland of Prussia east of the Elbe, while many western areas remained loyal to the republican government. Especially in the west and north of the state, potential sympathizers with the insurgents also had to deal with a revitalized council movement. In many industrial cities workers' councils were spontaneously reestablished through the cooperation of the Socialist parties and union leaders of all persuasions.[78]

The degree of cooperation between the putschists and the regular territorial administration was most pronounced in Kapp's home province of East Prussia. Here strong traditions of allegiance to political Conservatism both among the population and the civil service were reinforced by fears about the uncertain political and economic future of the province. In addition, the Social Democratic provincial governor, August Winnig, seemed to sympathize with some of the antigovernment sentiments.[79] No democratization of any significance had taken place in East Prussia before March 1920, and when the putsch broke out, the province stood quite solidly behind Kapp. Both the Reichswehr and the civil authorities (including Winnig) immediately recognized the new force as exercising de facto executive powers.[80]

A somewhat similar situation prevailed in the southeastern and northern border areas. The governor of the (still undivided) province of Silesia, Ernst Philipp (DDP) and the police chief of the capital, Breslau, Friedrich Voigt (SPD), had failed to discourage the anitrepublican activities of the Conservative forces, in the vain hope that these groups would join in a common German front against the aims and activities of the Poles. Their efforts did not prevent Jagow from dismissing them, but unwittingly they facilitated the planning activities and success of the putschists in Silesia. In the province of Schleswig-Holstein the situation on the eve of the putsch was particularly delicate.[81] The coup broke out one day before a scheduled plebiscite that was to determine whether a portion of Schleswig would remain German or become part of Denmark. Under these circumstances Kapp's efforts to turn the clock back and reestablish the old Prussian authoritarian rule only intensified political tensions in the province. As in many provinces of the east, the Reichswehr officer corps in Schleswig-Holstein declared its support for the putsch.[82] The city commandant of Kiel ordered the arrest of the republican provincial governor, Kürbis (SPD), even before Jagow dismissed Kürbis.[83] The picture was not markedly different among the top civilian administrators. Only a few of the senior civil servants refused to work for the new regime. The district director of Schleswig found what to him seemed to be a Solomonic solution, in that he claimed that he could serve both the republican and the putschist governments simultaneously.[84] However, the lower echelons of the civil service and the noncommissioned officers and enlisted men in the Reichswehr stationed in Schleswig-Holstein for the most part remained loyal to the legally constituted government.[85] At the county level a number of commissioners, often as a result of pressure exerted by rejuvenated workers' and soldiers' councils, prevented the Reichswehr officers in their areas from joining Kapp and his forces.

Among the western provinces Hanover presented a rather special case. To begin with, its provincial governor was the only one in the west to sympathize openly with Kapp.[86] Another complicating factor was the presence of the Guelph movement and its influence among the citizens' militia units in the province. (This will be discussed later.) The Guelph party was as opposed to the republic as Kapp and Lütwitz were, but while the latter sought a Hohenzollern restoration, the Guelphs hoped for a return of an independent state of Hanover under a restored monarch from the family that had been dethroned by Prussia in 1866.[87]

The putsch undoubtedly had its most far-reaching results in the industrial heartland of Prussia and Germany, the Ruhr area. Here latent and deep-seated tensions between labor and management had created an atmosphere of class antagonism that the Kapp Putsch fired up into open warfare.[88] To be sure, the civil authorities were almost universally loyal to the republican government, but in the eyes of the workers this did not adequately counterbalance the opportunistic wait-and-see attitude on the part of the regular troops and the Freikorps units operating in the area.[89]

Despite its swift collapse, the putsch underscored the failure of republican Prussia's early personnel policies. By bringing into the open the unreliability of large parts of the political civil service, the coup also demonstrated the incompetence and naiveté of Minister of the Interior Wolfgang Heine. After the defeat of the putsch, it was clearly imperative to make significant progress in the direction of democratization of the civil service. The new minister of the interior, Carl Severing, saw his task clearly before him: "We will clean up one province after the other, until we have a civil service corps that is prepared to work with the Prussian government to make Prussia into a democracy and the Prussians into democrats." At the same time, the new interior minister did not want a return to the confusion that had sometimes marked the early days of the revolution. Severing warned against political witch hunts and emphasized that only specific evidence warranted disciplinary action against suspected civil servants.[90]

As an initial step, the reconstituted republican government a few days after the putsch asked the governors to supply the names of civil servants who had openly and blatantly sided with the putschists.[91] At the beginning of April the cabinet issued formal guidelines for the political cleanup: the provincial governors were ordered to appoint commissioners to investigate the statements and activities of the territorial civil service during the putsch days.[92] In addition, in at least a few provinces the revolutionary institution of supervisor was resurrected, especially to oversee the activities of the county commissioners and mayors.[93]

After the shock of Kapp's coup, the Weimar coalition parties were agreed on the need to eliminate politically unreliable officials from the Prussian civil service. The other side of the democratization process, the "positive" steps leading to future appointments that would create a civil service loyal to the parliamentary form of government, was more complex and controversial. This issue had to confront the proper balance between technical competence, as demonstrated by traditional educational qualifications, and the positive political leaven that "outsiders" would bring to the corps of administrators. The DDP remained the primary spokesman for retaining the traditional requirements, although in light of the Kapp Putsch even they were willing to permit the "lay element" among the civil servants a somewhat larger share of civil service positions.[94] The Center party and the SPD wanted to accommodate more "outsiders," but they remained divided on the specific candidates who should be chosen.[95]

Disagreements among the coalition parties did not erupt into the open largely because the negative aspects of the personnel policies took up most of the few months that remained before the first Braun cabinet came to an end. The driving force of the purge was the minister of the interior. Like his predecessors, Severing rejected radical solutions to the problem. He refused to abolish the concept of tenure for civil servants, or to enlarge the number of patronage appointments. Similarly, he opposed the appointment of permanent commissioners to supervise the civil service.[96] The new minister also did not look with favor upon the institutionalization of extraparliamentary influences in the appointment and dismissal process; neither the professional organizations of the civil servants themselves nor the labor unions were able to realize their ambitions for routine consultation on personnel appointments.[97] In fact, the major difference between Severing's methods and those of Heine and Hirsch came not in the area of policy, but of personnel. While Heine unsuccessfully endeavored to depoliticize as much of the civil service as possible, Severing left no doubt that he insisted upon conscious, active support of the democratic form of government from political appointees. He also made it clear that the degree of political engagement he expected varied proportionally with the level of the appointment. In addition, unlike Heine, Severing did not hesitate to involve representative groups of the coalition parties in the selection and appointment of major civil servants. Severing readily consulted not only his colleagues in the cabinet but also the parliamentary leaders and provincial organizations of the coalition parties.[98] At the same time the professionals in the Ministry of the Interior were given far less influence than had been the case under Heine.[99]

Although Severing insisted upon loyalty to republican Prussia, the vociferous complaints from the Conservatives about the "Severing system" as a machine to benefit the Social Democratic party were unjustified. Severing's reform of the civil service was never a one-party affair.[100] This can be illustrated by the process of selecting county commissioners to replace those dismissed in the wake of the putsch. It involved receiving recommendations from the district organizations of the coalition parties, which in turn reflected consultations among their county organizations.[101] The nominations were then forwarded to the provincial governor, who sent them on to the cabinet along with his comments. At this point they were scrutinized within the Ministry of the Interior by the head of the personnel desk and the two parliamentary undersecretaries—Oskar Meyer (DDP) and Wilhelm Linz (Center party)—before being presented to the minister for his decision.[102]

The multipartisan political consultation process was particularly important in the appointment of provincial administrators. More than any other category among the political administrators, these officials had to enjoy the confidence of all the coalition parties. To be sure, the need for compromise also resulted in sending to the provinces a group of self-conscious and sometimes abrasive prima donnas who were not always easy subordinates for the minister of the interior. However, once appointed, these men became effective supporters of the coalition as a whole and, given the stability of the Prussian parliamentary coalitions, the governors and district directors as a group provided a great deal of administrative continuity at the apex of the territorial civil service.

The manner in which the new governor and the two district directors in Hanover were chosen can serve as an example of the "Severing system" in action. The incumbent governor, Ernst von Richter (whose appointment in 1917 ironically represented a concession to the left on the part of the old regime, since Richter was a National Liberal and not a Conservative) was dismissed because of his pro-Kapp stand during the putsch. At the same time, two of three district directorships in the province also became vacant. In dividing the three posts, the coalition parties agreed that the provincial governor should be a Social Democrat, while the director of the district of Hanover (one of the three districts of the province of Hanover) would come from the ranks of the DDP and his colleague in the largely Catholic district of Hildesheim from the Center party. For the post of provincial governor Otto Braun had suggested Gustav Noske, the former Reich defense minister. Braun (supported behind the scenes by Reich President Ebert) argued that Noske had unfairly become the scapegoat for the conditions that had led to the Kapp Putsch and that his undoubted services to the party and the republic should be rewarded in some suitable manner.[103] Severing was less enthusiastic: in the spring of 1920 Noske was very unpopular among all factions of Social Democracy, and his gruff manner found few sympathizers in the other coalition parties.[104] The minister of the interior favored the former Prussian minister of finance, Südekum, who had also been forced to resign in the wake of the Kapp Putsch instead. Politically, there was little difference between the two men—both belonged to the extreme right wing of the SPD—but Südekum enjoyed the support of the minister of education in the cabinet and of the speaker of the Prussian Constitutional Convention, Robert Leinert, in the legislature. The latter's support was particularly important, since he was also the head of the SPD's district organization in Hanover.[105] But Südekum, too, was not without enemies. These included the new prime minister, who did not forgive Südekum his political blunders in the question of the financial settlement with the former royal family and Eduard Gräf, an influential member of the SPD's left wing in the legislature. In the end the prime minister prevailed. The cabinet nominated Noske as provincial governor of Hanover.[106] Noske's opponents did not give up. Only after Robert Leinert switched sides was Noske confirmed, five months after his nomination.[107]

For all the German Nationalists' ranting against a spoils system that was appointing "party secretaries . . . factory laborers, and metal workers" to government positions, the concrete results of Severing's "little purge" of the Prussian civil service were limited,[108] and Severing did not saturate the political administration with "outsiders."[109] The ministerial level was quantitatively least affected. Only two prominent officials were immediately dismissed: Gottlob von Berger, whose formal title was State Commissioner for the Supervision of Public Order, and Doyé, the head of the police desk in the Interior Ministry. Understandably, turnovers in the territorial administration were more numerous. By July 1920 three governors, an equal number of district directors, two chiefs of police, and sixteen county commissioners had lost their positions as a result of their political stance during the Kapp Putsch. In the following six months, another seventy-two county commissioners were dismissed. Geographically the areas most affected were the eastern provinces. In East Prussia the governor (Winnig), a district director, and the chief of police in Königsberg were removed from office; in Silesia, the provincial governor (Philipp) and the police chief of Breslau were dismissed.[110] In the west, Richter was the only governor to be dismissed, and the number of forcibly retired county commissioners was also far fewer than in the eastern areas. In quantitative terms, the purge that followed the most serious challenge to the republican form of government in Prussia involved less than 20 percent of the state's corps of political administrators.[111] Moreover, all of those affected represented blatant cases of disloyalty or incompetence. The cabinet generally did not inaugurate disciplinary proceedings in more doubtful cases, but decided instead on the more general step of reducing the mandatory retirement age for the civil service. It was lowered from sixty-eight to sixty-five for political and administrative appointments, and from seventy to sixty-eight for judicial personnel. Needless to say, whatever the merit in the long run, the change in retirement age had little immediate impact upon the composition of the corps of political administrators.[112]

Severing left office after a little more than a year, and while his successor, Alexander Dominicus, did not serve long enough to have left a lasting impression on the development of Prussian personnel policy, the general tendencies of his policies became evident even in the few decisions that he did make.[113] Dominicus, like Heine, believed in the "ideology of experts"; he too remained a strong advocate of the traditional professional civil service. He saw as his primary task "to persuade the old civil servants to accept the new state."[114] In practice this meant abandoning Severing's insistence on active identification with the republic, and tolerating a considerable degree of antirepublican sentiments among the civil servants—as long as the officials' identification was with the rightist rather than the leftist opposition. Dominicus promoted a number of officials who had been censured by Severing, and a decree that became a cause célèbre, specifically prohibited the confirmation of members of the Communist party as municipal officials, but was silent on the appointment of members of the extreme right.[115]

On the eve of the inauguration of the cabinet of the grand coalition, the democratization of Prussia's political administrators had made only moderate headway. In retrospect it was clearly unfortunate that the workers' and soldiers' councils and the cabinet worked at what were essentially cross purposes during the crucial, early months after the revolution. The councils' instinctive suspicions of the old-line territorial administrators (and particularly the county commissioners) were in many cases fully justified, but it is equally true that the councils in their totality were too unsystematically structured and too inconsistent in pursuing their reformist goals to provide a realistic alternative to the guidelines laid down by the government.[116]

While the workers' and soldiers' councils were, perhaps, overly concerned with the political character of individual civil servants, the early republican cabinets erred in the opposite direction. Especially the first parliamentary minister of the interior, Wolfgang Heine, the key figure in bringing about administrative and personnel policy from 1918 to 1920, saw these policies as a series of extremely complicated organizational and institutional problems that defied short-term solutions but in which personnel appointments played a relatively minor role. The result of this attitude was a fruitless search for global structural solutions that had little effect on the composition of the corps of the Prussian civil service. Only after the Kapp Putsch did the new minister, Carl Severing, introduce fundamental appointment changes. They were in turn quickly shelved (and partially reversed) by his successor, Alexander Dominicus.

Administrative Reforms

As noted above, structural reforms of the state's administration had been the subject of lively discussions in political and professional circles long before 1914. The topics ranged from reorganization of the Interior Ministry and redrawing provincial boundaries to increasing the rights of self-government for the municipalities and counties.

Among various reform projects, improving local government had absolute priority for the new Social Democratic prime minister, Paul Hirsch, whose scholarly and professional background was in local administration. He was convinced that the key to creating democracy in Prussia lay in the selection of local executives—that is, town magistrates and county commissioners—by democratically elected city and county legislative bodies.[117] The idea was not new; Drews, the last royal minister of the interior, had made a similar proposal.[118] Hirsch agreed with Drews's arguments, but he also had parochial political reasons for advocating municipal self-rule after 1918. Until 1918 urban property owners—for the most part, supporters of the Progressives—had dominated Prussia's cities,[119] while the three-class system of voting effectively kept the Socialists out of positions of influence. With the institution of universal suffrage it was likely that, especially in the major cities, the dominant political force would be the Socialist parties, the SPD, the USPD, or the Communists. While in the west universal manhood suffrage would result in a series of town councils and county legislatures with Socialist or moderate bourgeois majorities,[120] the result in the eastern provinces might well be a strengthening of the political power of the conservative, anti-republican forces.

The revolutionary Political Cabinet decided to risk these consequences. Its program for local administrative reforms, which Hirsch somewhat grandiosely described as the culmination of the Stein-Hardenberg reforms that had made possible Prussia's rebirth after the Napoleonic Wars, called for the abolition of the three-class system of voting in municipal and county elections, the democratization of city charters, the election of county commissioners by the county legislative bodies, and the dissolution of the *Gutsbezirke*.[121]

The various parts of this ambitious reform program were realized to very unequal degrees. The cabinet did move quickly to abolish the three-class system of voting in local elections, but agreement on the next steps proved to be more difficult.[122] Among the ministers Braun, Ströbel, and Rosenfeld argued for immediate reforms by decree of local election laws so that new assemblies could be elected while the revolutionary experience was still fresh in the voters' minds. Most local workers' councils and the Central Council agreed.[123] Hirsch, Heine, and Breitscheid, on the other hand, favored a more encompassing approach. They preferred to wait until the National and Prussian Constitutional Conventions had been elected in order to then present these bodies with a thoroughgoing municipal reform act that would not only incorporate new electoral laws, but also deal with a variety of other questions involving local self-government.[124] The disagreements were resolved by what turned out to be a not very workable compromise. The cabinet dealt with the electoral laws as a separate issue, but it hesitated until January 24 to issue the requisite decrees for municipal elections, while the regulations for county elections did not appear until mid-February.[125] And the first postwar elections were not held until April. By that time the counterrevolutionary wave was already in full swing and acts of administrative sabotage against democratic reforms were common among the county commissioners.[126]

The first parliamentary government in Prussia, then, inherited a highly unrealized reform program. In principle, the government of the Weimar coalition favored the continuation of the reform efforts inaugurated by its revolutionary predecessor.[127] In practice, the realization was far more difficult for a parliamentary government than it had been for a revolutionary one; the latter could at least theoretrically issue decrees with the force of law, the former had to rely on parliamentary compromises. It soon became apparent that major differences of opinion among the coalition parties doomed any prospect of presenting an overall municipal reform act.[128] In addition, given the growing political polarization in the course of the year 1919, there were increasing doubts as to whether enlarging the scope of local home rule really served the cause of parliamentary democracy. For example, the USPD now saw local reform as an ideal opportunity to accomplish within the municipalities what the revolution had left undone at the state and national levels. The Independents were particularly interested in removing local police forces from the state's supervisory authority and to have the municipalities gain control of the operation of utility companies as a first step toward "socialization" of the economy.

In view of the obvious difficulties, the cabinet decided not to draft legislation for an overall municipal reform act, but to limit its initial efforts to two specific projects. One was a law authorizing the city of Berlin to incorporate a number of its suburbs, and the other established a regional planning board for the densely populated Ruhr area. Both of these projects had been widely discussed before to the war and in a sense the postwar atmosphere merely provided the needed catalyst to make them politically palatable. The Ruhr project established something akin to the Port Authority of New York and New Jersey in the heart of Germany's industrial region. The law permitted the cities and towns in the area to negotiate communal services on a regional basis without regard to city boundaries. It was not a controversial piece of legislation. In fact, the Ruhr bill became one of the few pieces of legislation passed unanimously by the Constitutional Convention.[129]

Such unanimity of views could not be attained in the case of the Greater Berlin Law. The government bill was ready for submission to parliament in June 1919; it was drafted in close cooperation with the mayor of the capital, Karl Wermuth.[130] By that time, however, it had become clear that the Independent Socialists were now the strongest political force in the city. In view of the lower population density in the more affluent suburbs surrounding Berlin, this meant that expanding local self-rule to a wider geographic area would place governmental power in the capital city of Prussia and the Reich in the hands of declared opponents of the present government and the system of parliamentary democracy. The cabinet decided to withhold presenting the bill to the Constitutional Convention until November 1919, and it did not come to a vote prior to the Kapp Putsch.[131]

During the days of Kapp's rule in Berlin, the two Socialist parties had cooperated in defeating the insurgents, and the afterglow of that brief era of good feeling helped the Greater Berlin Law to pass. With both the USPD and the SPD voting for the bill, the convention approved the legislation narrowly by a vote of 165 to 148 at the end of April. Among the bourgeois parties only the DDP supported the bill, and that was largely the result of personal lobbying by Alexander Dominicus, the mayor of Charlottenburg, the largest of the newly annexed towns. Like the Socialists, Dominicus argued that for reasons of administrative efficiency a city as large as Berlin could not be governed on a decentralized basis. The final version of the bill created a centralized municipal governmental structure for Berlin, placing most of the decision-making powers in the hand of the city council and the mayor. The districts, which now included the recently incorporated areas, had few rights of autonomy.[132]

In its original version, the Greater Berlin Law soon proved unworkable, largely because the USPD destroyed the anticipated basis of cooperation between the two Socialist parties. The left wing of the USPD, which was soon to split from the Independent Socialists and join the Communists, insisted on using its strength in the city council of Greater Berlin to further its intraparty aims. It refused, for example, to permit members of the bourgeois parties on municipal commissions, and arbitrarily sought to limit the number of right-wing Socialists who headed municipal departments. The Berlin district organization of the SPD was resentful, but felt that in the interest of Socialist unity it should not break with the USPD.[133] At the state level, however, the Social Democrats were unwilling to appease the left-wing radicals. The straw that broke the camel's back was the USPD's insistence that Emil Eichhorn receive a major appointment to the police commission and that Kurt Löwenstein be made a member of the board of education. Eichhorn was a provocation for both the bourgeois parties and all right-wing Socialists because of his activities in January 1919, and Löwenstein, a Jewish radical educational reformer and bitter opponent of both Christian churches, aroused the hatred especially of the Center party and clerical interests. The governor of the province of Brandenburg in his capacity as state supervisory agency for the city of Berlin intervened and formally refused to confirm Eichhorn's and Löwenstein's appointments. In the Prussian coalition the two bourgeois parties went a step further and demanded a revision of the Greater Berlin Law to reduce the powers of the city council and decentralize the municipal administration. By this time—late summer 1920—the USPD was in an advanced state of disintegration, and the SPD recognized that there was little hope of future cooperation with the Independents. For this reason, the Social Democratic leaders in the legislature joined their coalition partners in voting for a revision of the law.[134] Politically, that decision assured continued cooperation among the Weimar coalition parties both at the state and the municipal level. When Lord Mayor Wermuth had to resign at the end of 1920 because he had allied himself too closely with the USPD, his successor, Gustav Böss, was elected with the combined votes of the SPD and the moderate bourgeois parties in the city council; both the USPD and the DNVP remained isolated and without influence.[135]

Neither the revolutionary government nor the first Weimar coalition had done much to advance the cause of administrative reforms in the counties. On the contrary, as expected, county elections in the spring of 1919 gave the DNVP a dominant position in a number of counties east of the Elbe, and under the mantle of fulfilling the democratically expressed wishes of the electorate, political forces in the east were busy planning for the overthrow of democracy and the republic; the Kapp Putsch was a temporary fulfillment of their ambitions. Severing had no hesitation in abandoning Heine's proposed "communalization" of the county commissioners "as long as the young democracy remained endangered by reactionary forces."[136] The commissioners remained centrally appointed state officials. The dissolution of the East Elbian administrative latifundia (Gutsbezirke), however, made no more progress under Severing than under Heine; "narrow . . . fiscal objections" of the Finance and Agriculture Ministries stymied the project.[137]

Long before the revolution experts had agreed that extensive reforms of the Prussian provincial administration were overdue. The revolutionary cabinet, however, assigned provincial reforms a low priority, and the decisions it made were largely negative in character. In its haste to schedule statewide elections for a constitutional convention, the government agreed to leave the Prussian electoral districts unchanged which meant, since these traditionally followed provincial boundary lines, that the borders of the old provinces were in effect sanctioned by the new revolutionary leaders.[138] In consequence, these boundaries, which were largely the result of historical, genealogical, and diplomatic happenstance, but which often had little regard for the requirements of economic and administrative rationality, remained in force despite the government's promise of efficient administration.

The first parliamentary cabinet sent a provincial reform bill to the Constitutional Convention in the summer of 1919. The proposed law reflected the pivotal position of the Center party in the Reich and the state in mid-1919.[139] It provided for a far-reaching decentralization of Prussia's territorial administration, giving the provincial legislatures extensive powers in making education and personnel policy.[140] The government's draft did not address the question of delineating more clearly the areas of jurisdiction between the provincial governors and the district directors, nor, as many experts advocated, did it eliminate one or the other of these offices. Neither the SPD nor the DDP shared the Center party's enthusiasm for decentralization, although both muted their objections within the cabinet in order not to endanger the coalition.[141]

When the bill came up for debate on the floor of the Constitutional Convention, however, it was sharply attacked by a broad coalition of forces, and the Center party soon found itself isolated. As a result, the cabinet withdrew the draft legislation, and no meaningful reforms passed the legislature prior to the Kapp Putsch. The opposition, which included members of all parties from the USPD to the DNVP, objected particularly to leaving educational policy in the hands of elected provincial officials and to the provision in the bill which provided that the state government had to choose candidates for the offices of governors, district directors, and police chiefs from among lists of three presented to the cabinet by the provincial legislatures.[142]

The rate of progress for administrative reforms was not markedly improved after the second Weimar coalition government took office. As Severing later admitted, he underestimated the technical complexity and political sensitivity of the issues involved.[143] Everyone paid lip service to the idea that the provinces should have a greater voice in the administration of their affairs, but the political parties held widely divergent views on what this meant in practice. Proponents of provincial autonomy claimed that decentralizing the Prussian administration would serve to defuse the centrifugal tendencies in the provinces and thereby stabilize the unity of Prussia as a whole. Critics of such proposals pointed out that provincial separatism would be encouraged by overly large grants of self-rule, and that the consequences would be the dissolution of Prussia and the Reich. Equally controversial was the future of the two major territorial officials, the governors and district directors. In June 1920 a number of provincial governors and *Landeshauptmänner* (the latter officials were titular heads of the provinces elected by the provincial legislatures; they had no real power) presented the minister of the interior a joint memorandum demanding the abolition of the office of district director as superfluous.[144] Naturally enough, the district directors were vehemently opposed to such a change, and they in turn received support from the county commissioners. Both argued that the provincial governors were archaic vestiges of the office of royal viceroys of premodern times, and not needed in a modern state administration. Finally, the question of national minorities played a major, if not always explicit, part in rejecting or accepting the concept of greater provincial self-rule. The opponents of the scheme argued that granting the provinces greater rights especially in the field of educational policy would unduly strengthen the position of the Polish minority, which was a major population element in several of the eastern provinces that bordered on Poland.[145]

Among the major political parties, the SPD, the USPD, and the DNVP were "centralists" in principle; they had serious reservations about increasing provincial autonomy.[146] The middle-of-the-road bourgeois parties—the DVP, the DDP, and the Center party—were more favorably inclined toward decentralization, with the last the most outspoken proponent of this point of view.[147] In practice, the division between proponents and opponents of centralization did not run so neatly along party lines. The DNVP, for example, was officially a strong adherent of the traditional Prussian administrative centralism, but its provincial party leaders made ample use of the provinces' right to cast votes in the Reichsrat in order to sabotage the efforts of the democratic central government.

Since the coalition included proponents of both centralization and decentralization, the cabinet sought refuge in the opinion of experts. It designated the former minister of the interior, Bill Drews, as the cabinet's consultant on administrative reforms. Drews in turn proposed (or rather resurrected, since he had already published similar proposals before the war) a scheme that favored increased self-rule in the provinces and abolished the office of district director, leaving only the governors and county commissioners as centrally appointed territorial administrators.[148] The expert's plan failed in the face of political reality. Not only were the provincial governors and district directors the backbone of the embryonic Republican civil service in Prussia, but also staffing these offices formed part of the patronage system which was one of the cohesive elements in the coalition. The SPD and Center party had a primary interest in the post of provincial governor, while the DDP (and later the DVP) were hopeful of placing their members in district director positions.

The result was a deadlock and no major reform effort was launched before the end of 1921. Provincial administrative reforms were limited to a few tactical adjustments, such as the division of Silesia into two new provinces, Upper and Lower Silesia (which will be discussed later), and the establishment of a new province in the east, the Grenzmark. The latter was formed from the small territory that remained part of Prussia after the province of Posen had been divided between Germany and Poland. The creation of the Grenzmark was motivated solely by political and particularly foreign policy considerations, and ran counter to all principles of rational administration. (For this reason, the cabinet opposed its establishment.) The new province was too small to form a viable administrative unit and economically too poor to stand on its own feet. Its sole purpose was to serve as evidence of Germany's and Prussia's determination to uphold German interests against the "Polish tide." [149] Neither the creation of the Grenzmark nor the division of Silesia contributed significantly to solving the problem of Prussian provincial reform or, for that matter, to altering the disappointing record of the first republican cabinets in effecting administrative reforms.

Police and Militia Reforms

It is a truism that reliable police and other internal security forces are of utmost importance for the maintenance of public law and order, particularly in uncertain times. The surprisingly rapid collapse of the Prussian authoritarian state in November 1918, and especially the fall of the central government, came because the police in the city of Berlin, until then a particularly visible pillar of Prussian authoritarianism and the pride of a number of reactionary chiefs of police, proved to be unreliable, leaderless, and hated by the population which it had cowed for so long.

If the new republican Prussia wanted to avoid the fate of its predecessor, it had to establish units of internal order that were reliable and loyal to the new regime. At the same time, it was clear that this task required a high degree of psychological and political finesse. Police forces are by their very nature authoritarian organizations with a paramilitary mindset, and in prewar Prussia both officers and men in the various police units identified closely with Prussian militarism. As a result, groups who were the political opponents of the authoritarian state also had the most abiding negative view of police forces. In other words, the democratization of the internal security forces would require a high level of engagement by political leaders who heretofore had had no positive relationship with the police. Moreover, the work of rebuilding and reforming the police had to proceed in an atmosphere of almost constant instability, and at a time when a number of political forces were already actively at work attempting to overthrow the new regime.

The police in prewar Prussia were divided into two groups. In the municipalities, so-called blue police units (the name derived from the color of their uniforms) served as regular street patrols; they were subject to the control of the municipal authorities. In the rural areas gendarmes were under the control of the county commissioners and, at the provincial level, the governors. In addition, regular army units could be placed at the disposal of the territorial authorities in case of severe disturbances or emergencies.

In retrospect, the protective measures which the government took in the face of the rapidly spreading revolutionary upheavals look almost ludicrous. It was not until the first days of November that the minister of the interior established a special office to collect reports of unrest in the various provinces. As late as November 7 the commander of the Berlin military district, General von Linsingen, sought to stop the revolution with an order simply prohibiting the formation of workers' councils. He also commanded the use of force in countering any disturbance, but this decision was quickly countermanded by the Reich authorities.[150]

The collapse of the authoritarian state left a vacuum among the forces of public safety that a variety of more or less officially sanctioned units attempted to fill. Immediately after the revolution, a series of self-proclaimed security forces, with widely divergent political orientations and numerous leaders, emerged. As we shall see in a later section, among these "police forces," the citizens' militias and the ad hoc organs of public safety created by the various workers' councils were most important. In addition, the operations of the Freikorps in the border areas of Prussia and within the state itself had a profound influence upon the domestic security of Prussia, although these units remained under the control of the Reich Ministry of Defense.

A widely accepted thesis holds that control of the armed forces and the police units in the capital city of a country subject to revolutionary upheaval is decisive for the eventual fate of a revolution, and events in Berlin certainly confirmed the rule. As a result, a bitter power struggle for political and administrative control of the forces of internal security began with the overthrow of the royal government on November 9, 1918; it did not end until the police reforms that followed the Kapp Putsch in the second half of 1920.[151] For some time after the fall of the royal government, the revolutionary cabinet really had no reliable force of coersion at its disposal. True, when the unrest reached the capital city on November 9, the bulk of the Berlin garrison troops sympathized with the right wing of the Social Democrats rather than the Independents or Spartacists. (It was characteristic that a soldiers' council formed in the Ministry of War on Saturday morning, November 9, issued black, red, and gold armbands rather than red insignia to its members.) This development was largely the result of the effective organizational activities of the SPD's district leader for Berlin, Otto Wels. On November 10, Wels was named municipal commandant, a position that made the Marxist party leader a nominal subordinate of the Junker Prussian minister of defense, General von Scheüch.[152] But the Berlin garrison was by no means the only group of armed men in the capital. Also much in evidence on the streets of Berlin during the revolution was the People's Naval Division, a completely unauthorized unit composed mostly of former sailors, who had deserted from their units and drifted to the capital. It contained some very radical elements, but was generally too undisciplined to be a reliable source of power for either the government or its opponents.[153]

Both Socialist parties attempted to gain control of the Berlin municipal police force on November 9.[154] The USPD won the race. The Independent party leader in Berlin, Emil Eichhorn, led a demonstration to police headquarters and demanded that he be placed in control of the police. After lengthy negotiations Eichhorn assumed the duties of police chief on the evening of November 9.[155] At this point he acted solely by "right of revolution." Neither his demands nor his negotiations had been authorized by the workers' and soldiers' councils or the Council of People's Plenipotentiaries. Still, both soon accepted Eichhorn's fait accompli, especially since the new police chief initially did seem to work hard to reestablish law and order in the city.[156] Within a week after the overthrow of the royal government, public safety in the capital city appeared assured. Richard Müller, the USPD co-chairman of the Executive Council of the Berlin Workers' and Soldiers' Council, praised Wels and Eichhorn equally for the effective work they were doing.[157]

The spirit of cooperation was short-lived. It was generally agreed that preserving law and order in the tense times of November 1918 was beyond the capabilities of the regular municipal police forces, and that the revolutionary authorities needed to create additional, loyal forces to safeguard the revolution. Ernst Däumig, a spokesman for the Revolutionary Shop Steward movement in Berlin, Eichhorn, and Otto Wels all presented plans for ad hoc security forces drawn from the unions, the Socialist parties, or the returning veterans.[158] None of these myriad creations was effective. During the Christmas disturbances in Berlin, Wels's Republican Militia (Republikanische Soldatenwehr) was able neither to control the rebellious sailors, nor to prevent the capture of its commander by units of the People's Naval Division. Eichhorn's Security Force (Sicherheitswehr) on the other hand, was plagued by criminal elements in its ranks and by the fact that it made common cause with the rebellious sailors.[159] The pattern repeated itself during the Spartacist uprising; the Berlin police forces were again completely useless in protecting law and order. Eichhorn's successor as Berlin police chief, Eugen Ernst, was equally incapable of molding the municipal police into a unit loyal to the republic. During the Kapp Putsch these forces of law and order again proved to be unreliable, and it was not until after the Kapp Putsch that a new chief of police, Richter, was able to effect fundamental changes.

Before Richter's appointment, the Spartacus revolt and particularly the Kapp Putsch not only had shown the inadequacy of the police forces in the capital, but also had made it clear that the security situation in the provinces was equally fragile. On the eve of the revolution the government had urged local authorities to establish citizens' militias *(Einwohnerwehren),* with the ostensible purpose of preventing looting and sabotage in the rural areas. The initiative for the citizens' militias came from the Agrarian League (Schutz-bund der deutschen Landwirtschaft), a powerful lobbying group representing farmers and estate owners. The league was closely allied with the conservative parties and consequently saw a danger to law and order only in the activities of left-wing organizations. Nor surprisingly, the citizens' militias, whose membership was originally restricted to landed property owners, had little enthusiasm for the revolution when it came.[160] In fact, friction between the citizens' militias and the new workers' and soldiers' councils was common throughout Prussia.[161]

In view of the origins and composition of the citizens' militias, the attitude of the revolutionary government toward these vigilante groups was, to say the least, naive. In a decree of November 15, 1918, the Prussian government merely reaffirmed the need for the militias, but made no attempt to change their composition.[162] Even when the Agrarian League published a set of guidelines that all but excluded workers from membership in the citizens' militias in March 1919, the Ministry of the Interior at first voiced no objection.[163] It was not until a storm of protest arose from the workers' and soldiers' councils that the ministry insisted upon a revision of the guidelines. In a series of additional decrees issued in April, September, and December 1919, the government required that the militias recruit a representative cross-section of the local population. In addition, to emphasize the civilian purposes of the units, they were transferred from the operational control of the Ministry of Defense to that of the Reich and Prussian Ministries of the Interior.[164]

The effect of these measures was minimal. Throughout the months of their existence, the citizens militias contained virtually no working-class members. Despite official encouragement, few workers wanted to join, and when they did, the county commissioners often sabotaged such efforts.[165] The officials in the Reich and Prussian ministries responsible for the militias did little to alter the situation. Within the Prussian Ministry of the Interior, the man in charge of the militias was the notorious Doyé, the head of the police desk, who cooperated with the Kapp putschists. In addition, it proved impossible to sever the link between the militias and the armed forces. The Reichwehr commander in Silesia wrote that the decrees issued by the Interior Ministry "in general follow along the lines intended by the army command [in Breslau]."[166] Particularly the regional and national leaders of the militias saw their units not so much as a civilian force to assure law and order as a reserve force for the Reichswehr to be used in a war of revenge. At the county level, the militia commanders, while technically civilian employees of the Prussian state, were almost invariably former army officers who conducted themselves as though they were in command of a reserve unit.

The government's naive policy had disastrous consequences during the Kapp Putsch. Especially in the eastern provinces, the civilian authorities, including the Ministry of the Interior, had lost virtually all control over the militias.[167] The insurgents counted upon the militias' support during the putsch, and they were fully justified in their expectations: a majority of the citizens' militias went over to the putschists.[168] The national office of the militias issued a statement on Saturday, March 13, 1920, only hours after the Ehrhardt Brigade had occupied Berlin, that affirmed support of the new "government of work" *(Regierung der Arbeit)* which had "taken the affairs of Germany in hand for the time being after the flight of the Reich government."[169]

The third area of concern for the revolutionary and early parliamentary governments was domestic intelligence gathering. For this purpose the cabinet established the office of the State Commissioner for the Supervision of Public Order *(Staatskommissar für die Überwachung der öffentlichen Ordnung)*. The establishment of such an agency was a natural response to the prevailing political instability during the postrevolutionary months. Particularly after the Spartacus uprising had revealed how little the government knew about coup plans and preparations by left and right extremists, it seemed necessary to create a central agency that would gather information about the activities of enemies of the republic. The Prussian cabinet formally established the office on July 21, 1919.[170] By the end of the year, the State Commissioner for the Supervision of Public Order was the funnel through which all information on extremists' activities had to pass before they reached the cabinet.[171]

In view of the sensitivity of this post, it was more than unfortunate that Heine failed the republic here as well. His choice for state commissioner, Gottlob von Berger, was in political terms thoroughly unreliable. Moreover, Berger's political sympathies, which lay with the rightist antidemocratic forces, were well-known; both Breitscheid and even the Reich minister of the interior, Erich Koch-Weser, had warned Heine and Hirsch against this devious figure.[172] Berger was in office for some seven months. During this time he was completely "blind in his right eye," seeing only dangers from leftist extremists; his closest associates were involved in the preparations for the Kapp Putsch.[173] The commissioner counseled consistently against taking actions to prevent the outbreak of violence among the right-wing extremists. As late as five days before the Kapp Putsch, Berger reported dangers from this quarter as nonexistent, while reiterating his fear of violence from Communists and Independent Socialists.[174] Heine trusted his subordinate to the very end: the minister's last major public address a few days before the Kapp Putsch was a vehement attack upon the high treason practiced by the USPD.[175]

The pattern of failures in security policy before the Kapp Putsch was so blatant that there was no disagreement among the members of the Braun cabinet about the need for immediate and energetic changes. The new government turned first to the continued existence of politicized paramilitary units, like the citizens' militias, with their large cachees of arms. It should be stressed that this was not a one-sided political decision. Braun and Severing opposed private armies in any form; they were no more in favor of arming workers' batallions than rightist militias.[176] Still, in the spring and summer of 1920 the major danger clearly came from the extreme right. To undercut the expected outburst of indignation from the parliamentary opposition about the dissolution of indispensable forces of law and order, Severing took advantage of an order by the Allied Control Commission demanding the seizure of arms still in private hands and the dissolution of all militias. Ostensibly in response to Allied pressure, the Prussian government in August ordered the end of authorized and unauthorized militias in Prussia.[177]

There was one exception to the minister's blanket condemnation of the militias. Even Severing decided not to dissolve these units in the eastern border areas facing Poland. Since the revolution, the eastern militias, operating under the name People's Militias (*Volkswehren*), had always had primarily military functions. The cabinet regarded them essentially as border security forces, but some Reichswehr commanders hoped that with the militias' help Germany's prewar territories could be won back from Poland.[178] During the putsch the eastern militias were no more loyal to the parliamentary form of government than were other units; on the contrary, they were among the most enthusiastic backers of Kapp's coup.

Despite their dismal record, the August decree exempted the *Volkswehren* from the dissolution order, though the government attempted to gain greater control over the border patrol organizations by attaching new commissioners to them. These were politicians from the government parties who had been dismissed from office in the wake of the putsch, but who enjoyed a good reputation in rightist circles. The former police chief of Berlin, Ernst, for example, was named special commissioner for border security in Silesia.[179] The Braun cabinet did not formally dissolve the border militias until November,[180] and the Stegerwald government informally tolerated the operation of various private armies especially in Silesia even later. Particularly Dominicus and am Zehnhoff were convinced that the militias were a defense against the possibility of a Communist coup attempt supported by Poland.[181]

It was, of course, naive to believe that a simple dissolution decree would rid Prussia of its private armies. Quite aside from the fact that a number of paramilitary groups simply went underground and pursued their activities in a clandestine manner, the problem of paramilitary groups in Weimar Germany could not be contained by the boundaries of a single state, even Prussia.[182] Bavaria, Germany's second largest state, pursued a radically different policy in dealing with rightist militias. Even after the Kapp Putsch and the formal dissolution of the citizens' militias, it permitted the state's territory to be used as the nerve center of what was in fact an extensive international rightist conspiracy.[183] The most important of the numerous paramilitary organizations in Bavaria was the Organisation Escherich (Orgesch), named after its leader and founder, the Bavarian state forestry official Georg Escherich. The Orgesch claimed to be a politically neutral force protecting law and order; in reality it served as an important focus for right-radical, counterrevolutionary activity, and, not incidentally, as the new organizational home for many fugitives from Kapp's major military unit, the Ehrhardt Brigade.[184] Escherich expanded his organizational net to include Prussia as well. A number of figures in the bourgeois parties, especially the DNVP, were members of the Orgesch. Even within the cabinet, Minister of Justice am Zehnhoff argued that in some areas the organization represented a needed supplement to the as yet weak police forces.[185]

Confronted with evidence of the organization's antigovernment activities, Severing proved less gullible. In August he ordered the governors in Prussia (again with the significant exception of Upper Silesia and East Prussia) to dissolve whatever Orgesch units existed within their administrative territories.[186] The decree had little effect outside of Prussia. The Bavarian government did not follow suit, and the Reich cabinet waited until May 1921 before moving against the Orgesch.

In a sense the Prussian attempt to rid the state of the militias was the equivalent in the security field of Severing's purge of unreliable elements among the political administrators. In both cases a potential or immediate danger to the republic was eliminated. Both actions—even assuming they had been effective and encompassing enough—left behind a vacuum that had to be filled by democratic administrators and loyal regular police forces. We have already seen that the government made little headway in restructuring the corps of political administrators, relying instead on an organic rejuvenation of the civil service as retirements opened up places for junior, and presumably more progressive, officials. Regarding security, the cabinet did not have the luxury of time. An effective police force was needed immediately to carry out the negative part of the security reforms: it had to move against the militias, since charging the Reichswehr with disarming the rightist units would have little practical effect.[187]

Both the need to neutralize the statewide militia organizations (actually they were often nationwide, but that is another story) and the simultaneous requirement of maintaining internal security necessitated an effective state police system. The local police forces, no matter how politically reliable, did not have the organizational resources necessary for the task, nor could the territorial administration control their deployment outside the municipalities.

The cornerstone of an effective statewide police force was to be a reorganized and revitalized Security Police (Sicherheitspolizei).[188] This was not a new organization; the Security Police traced its origins to one of the many attempts to create a loyal militia during the revolution, in this case something called the Republican Soldiers' Force (Republikanische Soldatenwehr), a unit created at the initiative of Otto Wels. Originally confined to Berlin, the Security Police was later intended to be stationed in company and batallion-sized units in barracks located strategically around the state. Its deployment was to be determined by the governors and district directors, and it was anticipated that the Security Police would see action particularly in times of political unrest.[189]

Like the other militias, the original Security Police proved to a severe disappointment to its founders. In the course of the year 1919 the force lost its original republican orientation and came under extreme rightist influence. Through the diligent efforts of Major Pabst, a close and energetic associate of Erich Ludendorff and Wolfgang Kapp, the Security Police in Berlin was riddled with sympathizers of the putschists. Even General von Seeckt, the Reichswehr's chief of staff, expressed concern that the attitude of the force's officers was "highly uncertain."[190] When the Kapp Putsch broke out, the leadership of the Security Police in Berlin cooperated with the "government" of Kapp and Lüttwitz, and after the collapse of the coup, members of the police force helped Wolfgang Kapp escape to Sweden.[191] A few bright spots, such as Essen and Dortmund, where men loyal to the parliamentary government dominated the Security Police,[192] could not erase the Security Police's generally dismal record.[193]

In reorganizing the state police apparatus, Severing and the cabinet relied primarily upon personnel changes, while preserving the organizational format and command structure of the Security Police. The state police was to remain a well-armed, garrisoned force with an emphasis on mobility and rapid deployment. It was specifically intended for cases of civil unrest. Severing rejected a decentralized command structure; the Security Police was placed under the authority of the governors. Under the original reform plans, the local police forces would have been closely associated with the Security Police. In fact, the DDP's parliamentary delegation proposed that the local police "should become a part of the state security forces if possible."[194]

As it turned out, the reorganization plan was almost turned on its head. The Allied Central Commission remained fearful that the garrisoned Security Police had the potential of becoming an embryonic supplement to the regular army, thus enabling Germany to violate the limitations on the size of the Reichswehr laid down in the Versailles Treaty. They prohibited the creation of the Security Police, insisting instead that its personnel be integrated into the local police forces.[195]

The dictum became a blessing in disguise, since it prevented the saturation of the local police with politically unreliable elements. That danger was real. While the cabinet concentrated on reforms of the Security Police, members of the now dissolved citizens' militias found refuge in the local police forces.[196] The personnel changes in the Security Police which the cabinet had inaugurated meant that the, now integrated, local police forces would reflect the decidedly prorepublican character of the state police. As a first step, Severing replaced Heine's confidant, von Berger, as State Commissioner for the Supervision of Public Order, with Robert Weismann, a Berlin district attorney who had close ties to the right wing of the SPD.[197] Next, the minister established a loyal corps of officers and men in the Security Police. Here the unions claimed a decisive voice immediately after the putsch. For example, the district council of the Socialist labor unions in Berlin demanded the right to have exclusive control over the nomination of police officers serving in the capital. The SPD and USPD organizations in the city seconded the request for extragovernmental control over the security forces. Not surprisingly, the minister of the interior and the cabinet rejected the labor organizations' demand, but they did permit officers and men to join unions.[198] As a result, the Prussian police force became an organ of government that had direct and close links to extraparliamentary interest groups that openly supported the republic and democracy. In effect, the Prussian police, in sharp contrast to the police units it some other states, gained an increasing reputation as an actively prorepublican force.[199]

When the first Braun cabinet left office, the positive accomplishments of the early republican governments in personnel policy and administrative reform were not impressive. They were essentially limited to the beginnings of prorepublican activism in the police forces, and the fact that all of the governors and most of the district directors were warm supporters of parliamentary democracy. For the rest of the corps of political administrators, and that meant primarily the large number of county commissioners, the results were limited to negative rather than positive effects. Active and outspoken opponents of the republic were no longer tolerated in the civil service, but particularly in the ranks of the *Landräte* a substantial number continued to wish, albeit quietly, for the return of king and authoritarianism.

Even more disappointing was the record of administrative reforms. The only significant pieces of reform legislation were the democratic elections of local, county, and provincial legislatures, and the law creating the municipality of Greater Berlin. In the provinces little changed. It is true that two new provinces were established in response to acute political pressure, but the functions of governors and district directors continued to overlap, there were no changes in the territorial boundaries of most provinces, and the state retained the anachronism of private latifundia that were coterminous with governmental administrative units.

The major reason for the weak record in these pivotal areas was a combination of political blindness and unfortunate circumstances. It is certainly true that for most of the time span under discussion, the cabinet was beset by a series of strikes, political unrest, and putsch attempts by various groups, all of which required day-to-day crisis management and left little time for working out comprehensive reform plans. But the cabinets also demonstrated great political naivete: In effect, the ministers, including the members of the Political Cabinet during the revolution, failed to appreciate the significance of the link between the authoritarian political superstructure and the administrative infrastructure of pre-1918 Prussia. Relying upon changes in the electoral process, the establishment of equal opportunity laws, and the "ideology of experts," they rejected the demands for immediate democratization of the corps of political administrators, and permitted the authoritarian infrastructure to retain its cohesion in the face of formal political changes. Only after the Kapp Putsch did the cabinet move vigorously to purge the territorial administration of its most blatant supporters of authoritarianism, although even then the promise of positive administrative reform remained unfulfilled.

PART TWO
1921–1925

CHAPTER 5

Parties and Prussia, 1922–1925

In retrospect, the history of German parties during the first three years of the Weimar Republic seems almost straightforward in comparison to the complexities of the next four years. At the Reich level political life after 1921 war characterized by instability and lack of systemic consensus. Two large political blocs confronted each other across a seemingly unbridgeable ideological chasm. On the one hand there were the parties of the Weimar coalition, somewhat hesitatingly joined by the DVP after the Kapp Putsch, and on the opposite side ranged the groups of the extremist right and left, united only by their desire to destroy parliamentary democracy in Germany. There were fewer coup attempts than in the early years, but the absence of putsches did not mean that popular support for the antidemocratic parties had dissipated; on the contrary, after abandoning their coup tactics, the groups actually increased their popularity. Communists, the DNVP, and the *Völkische* (the amalgam of groups whose primary appeal was hypernationalism, anti-Marxism, and anti-Semitism) all increased their voting strength.

The situation was further complicated by the appearance of a new type of political force in this second phase of the Weimar Republic, the so-called single-interest parties. These groups sought to exploit politically the economic difficulties of specific and often quite narrow economic and social interest groups. The most successful among them was the Wirtschaftspartei (Economics party, WiP). It gave itself the subtitle "Reich party of the German Mittelstand," although it was originally little more than the political action group of the German Association of Urban Landlords. The Economics party's and other groups' specific appeals to various components of the *Mittelstand* posed a threat to all moderate bourgeois parties, but particularly to the two major liberal groups, the DDP and the DVP, which had traditionally represented the bulk of German middle-class voters.

The strength of the extremists and the narrow-interest parties (the two groups were not, of course, mutually exclusive) increased markedly in 1923 and 1924, the period of hyperinflation and subsequent currency stabilization. The political attractiveness of republicanism reached a nadir in the Reichstag elections of May 1924. (See table 4.)

The results of the May elections confirmed some of the worst fears among the prorepublican forces. With only moderate voter participation by German

Table 4. Reichstag Election, May 1924

Party	Popular Vote (in millions)	% of Vote	Delegate Strength
Völkische	1.9	6.5	32
DNVP	5.7	19.5	95
DVP	2.7	9.2	45
Center party	3.9	13.4	65
WiP	0.4	—	—
DDP	1.7	5.7	28
SPD	6.0	20.5	100
KPD	3.7	12.6	62

Source: Statistisches Jahrbuch für das Deutsche Reich 1924/25 (Berlin, 1925), 44:390–91.

standards (a drop of 2.1 percent in comparison to 1920), the extremist groups on the left and the right did well, while the moderate parties suffered severe losses. Particularly the two major pillars of support for the Weimar political system, the SPD and the DDP, lost ground at the polls; the term "fiasco" for the SPD's showing was not inappropriate.[1] The DDP was reduced to little more than a splinter party (in May 1924, 5.7 percent; in 1920, 8.3 percent). Among the other moderate parties, the DVP also declined. The share of the popular vote for the right Liberals dropped from 13.9 percent in June 1920 to 9.2 percent. In fact, among the moderate bourgeois parties only the Center party was able to keep and even expand its share of the vote. As always in times of crisis, the "Center tower" stood firm.

The opposition groups could generally be satisfied with the election results. The DNVP achieved 19.5 percent of the popular vote, a figure that placed the German Nationalists only one percentage point behind the Social Democrats. In conjunction with several splinter groups, the DNVP formed the largest parliamentary caucus in the Reichstag. The Communists, too, were not hurt by their record of opportunism and frequent putsch attempts. They received 12.6 percent of the vote, an increase of 115 percent over their showing four years earlier. Finally, perhaps most depressing from the republicans' point of view, was the success of the völkische parties. The Hitler putsch clearly did not hurt the Nazis and their allies; in fact, it seemed to have enhanced their stature.

The weakness of the moderate center meant that the formation of Reich governments would be difficult. Since the opposition groups were unable to form a coalition, the number of realistic cabinet combinations was limited. The Weimar coalition (SPD, DDP, and Center party) with 39.4 percent of the delegate strength in the new Reichstag fell far short of a parliamentary majority. But the Bürgerblock, too, could not provide a stable parliamentary base; the DNVP, DDP, Center party, and DVP together commanded only 47.8

percent of the Reichstag delegates. The most favorable coalition, at least in mathematical terms, was the grand coalition (DDP, DVP, SPD, and Center party); it controlled 48.8 percent of the delegates.

At best, then, Germany faced the prospect of another series of short-lived minority Reich cabinets. An even worse prospect was the possibility of a complete political deadlock, a *Verfassungsnotstand,* and the collapse of the republic. To avoid the latter, the moderate groups in the center sought to harness and neutralize the volatility of the groups to the left and the right of the center by saddling them with governmental responsibility at either the state or national level. The quest led to seemingly incompatible proposals. The DVP, a coalition partner of the SPD in Prussia throughout these years, was constantly trying to bring the DNVP into the Reich government, although the German Nationalists insisted that a sine qua non of their willingness to join any cabinet would be the exclusion of the SPD from such a government. Similarly, the Social Democrats after March 1923 formed a coalition with the Communists in Saxony and Thuringia, while the SPD minister of the interior in Prussia combated the Communists as enemies of the republic and his own party. The moderates' concern with the competition on the fringes also made it increasingly difficult for them to cooperate with each other. The forces in the center could not even agree on where to draw the line between groups that supported the constitutional system and those that were an undeniable danger to it. Even the *Völkische,* whose avowed aim was to destroy the republic created "by Jews and November criminals," were courted by the government of Reich Chancellor Cuno in an effort to create the illusion of national unity during the Ruhr crisis.

Ironically, although the years 1922–1925 were punctuated by a seemingly endless series of foreign and domestic policy crises, the republic proved considerably more viable than its opponents assumed. It was hardly universally liked, but the chances of overthrowing the parliamentary form of government by force were becoming increasingly less promising. There were a number of reasons for the paradoxical resilience of republicanism. Many of the extremist parties had short political half-lives and fickle voting support. The Reichstag elected in May 1924 sat for only a few months, but even the short time between spring and December, when new national elections were held, brought important shifts in the national political balance. Generally speaking, the moderate parties, and particularly the SPD, made good many of their earlier losses, while the left and right radicals lost a significant number of the votes cast for them in May. (See table 5.)

In December, a Weimar coalition in the Reich still fell short of a majority (45.9 percent) but both a *Bürgerblock* cabinet (50.5 percent) and especially a grand coalition (56.0 percent) could have had solid backing in the Reichstag. Moreover, some of the extremist groupings increasingly recognized that they

Table 5. Reichstag Election, December 1924

Party	Popular Vote (in millions)	% of Vote	Delegate Strength
Völkische	0.9	3.0	14
DNVP	6.2	20.5	84
DVP	3.0	10.1	33
Center party	4.1	13.6	54
WiP	1.0	3.3	4
DDP	1.9	6.3	12
SPD	7.9	26.0	115
KPD	2.7	9.0	28

Source: Statistisches Jahrbuch für das Deutsche Reich (Berlin, 1926), 45:448–49.

would have to work within the parliamentary system to further their aims or forego any chance of gaining a share of political power. As a result there were some significant shifts in political alignments that reached across the antagonisms between republican and antirepublican groups, although they also created coalitions and tactical arrangements that were much less stable than those characteristic of the period before 1922.

Another important and often overlooked factor was the strength of republicanism in Prussia. This was true both of voter support for the moderate parties in the state and in terms of those parties' willingness to cooperate with each other in order to make parliamentary democracy work in Prussia.

There were no Landtag elections in May 1924, but a survey of the results of the Reichstag election showed that the swing of the Prussian political pendulum covered a far narrower field than was true for the Reich as a whole. On balance, the political center remained considerably stronger in Prussia than in other parts of Germany.[2] The pattern held true for the Landtag elections of December 1924. (See table 6.) This was the first statewide contest since 1921, and it coincided with the Reichstag campaign held at the same time. As was always true when a state campaign was held simultaneously with the national contest, national issues overshadowed questions of state politics. This factor distorted the results somewhat, since many voters gave their ballot in the Landtag contest automatically to the same party they had favored in the Reichstag election. (In Weimar elections there were, of course, no single-member districts and the candidates' individual personalities were not a major factor.) Even so, there were again some noteworthy differences.

In comparison to the 1921 elections, the Weimar coalition parties lost ground, but the political center in Prussia remained remarkably stable. True, in absolute terms the clear winner was the DNVP. The German Nationalists recovered from their poor showing of 1921 and captured a sizable portion of the vote that had earlier gone to the liberal parties. However, the Center party

Table 6. Landtag Election, December 1924

Party	Popular Vote (in millions)	% of Vote	Delegate Strength
Völkische	0.45	2.5	—
DNVP	4.40	23.7	109
DVP	1.80	9.8	45
Center party	3.20	17.6	81
WiP	0.45	2.5	11
DDP	1.10	5.9	27
SPD	4.60	24.9	114
KPD	1.80	9.6	40

Source: Handbuch für den Preussischen Landtag 1925 (Berlin, 1925), table 11.

did much better in Prussia than in the Reich; the state's voters clearly approved the party's left-of-center line in Prussia.[3] The Völkische did far less well in Prussia than in the Reich, receiving almost 25 percent fewer votes than in the national contest. On the left, the KPD could point to a marginally better showing. In terms of forming a coalition, a cabinet of the Weimar parties fell short of a parliamentary majority (48.4 percent). It could command a stable base of support only if the Economics part succumbed to the siren calls of the moderate parties. Both a Bürgerblock (57.0 percent) and a cabinet of the grand coalition (58.2 percent) were, however, realistic possibilities.

The history of the German and Prussian parties in the years 1922 to 1925, then, is full of paradoxes. The original republican center, the parties of the Weimar coalition, had been weakened, but less so in Prussia than in the Reich as a whole. In addition, the republican parties in the state had been strengthened by the DVP's addition to the coalition. The moderate parties also received increasing competition from single-issue parties and there remained impressive support for a variety of antidemocratic forces, but this, too, was less of a problem in Prussia than elsewhere. In addition, much of the support for the extremists was "soft": the voters' commitment to the splinter parties and the radicals was likely to dissipate as quickly as it was given.

Right-Wing Extremists

On a nationwide scale, the most significant development among the völkische groups was a tactical and organizational shift of their activities. Instead of trying to overthrow the constitutional government with a small-scale military force, the rightist extremists now attempted to mobilize mass popular support in order to destabilize the operations of parliamentary democracy. To be sure, the switch was hardly the result of rampant pacifism among the extreme right; their continuing love of uniforms, military demeanor, and weekend field exercises was clear evidence to the contrary. Rather, the failure of the Kapp Putsch had demonstrated that the chances of success for further coups d'état by armed bands were slim, and the public outcries after the assassinations of Matthias Erzberger (August 1921) and Foreign Minister Walther Rathenau (June 1922) convinced right-wing leaders that continuing acts of individual terror were equally counterproductive.

At the same time the political climate was ripe for political, as opposed to military, extremist groups. Rapidly accelerating inflation, uncertain economic times, and chauvinistic sentiments created a reservoir of antidemocratic, antirepublican, and anti-Semitic voters that the established parties, including the DNVP, were unable to assimilate. Into the breach stepped organizations of revolutionary conservatives, "untainted" by association with traditional politics. Typical among them was the Deutschvölkischer Schutz- und Trutzbund. (The organization's name can perhaps be best translated as the "German *völkisch* Protection and Revenge League.") The Bund was founded in early 1919 as an umbrella organization for all anti-Semitic groups that were not formally affiliated with any of the established parties. Actually, the group was organized by and always remained a front for the Pan-German Association, which also continued to supply the bulk of its financial support. Under its secretary-general, Alfred Roth, the Bund launched a massive program of virulently anti-Semitic and antirepublican propaganda activities. The response was explosive; by 1922 the organization boasted a membership of between 160,000 and 180,000.[4]

The Schutz- und Trutzbund saw itself as an agitation vehicle that would indirectly influence the political atmosphere, but two other extremist groups constituted themselves formally as political parties—though like all rightist extremists, they too rejected the parliamentary system of government. These were the National Socialist German Workers party (NSDAP, or Nazis) and the German *völkisch* Freedom party (DVFP). The Nazis, whose early history is too well known to need repeating here, concentrated their activities in Bavaria before 1925.[5] There were a number of sectarian groups in northern Germany that had more or less regular contact with Nazi headquarters in Munich, but the party's first locals in Prussia were not established until 1922. Most of the early Prussian cells were located in the Ruhr. Ideologically the early Nazis had no distinguishing characteristics. The founder of the NSDAP once described the program of his party as "essentially the same as that of the Schutz- und Trutzbund." The Prussian Nazis languished until the summer of 1922 when significant numbers of Schutz- und Trutzbund members joined Hitler's organization after the Prussian government dissolved the Bund as an organization that was actively involved in trying to undermine the constitutional form of government.

The early Nazis had little political impact in Prussia, but the DVFP was for a time a significant political force. In contrast to Hitler's group, the DVFP was primarily a North German organization. The Freedom party was organized in late 1922 by two former German Nationalist Reichstag members, von Graefe-Goldebee and Wulle. Both had been expelled from the DNVP for their extremist views.[6] The DVFP's program was as anti-Semitic and anti-democratic as those of the Bund and the Nazis, but at least for a time the Freedom party seemed to steer a tactical course toward the political center. During the first months of the Ruhr crisis, the DVFP's leaders offered to support Chancellor Cuno's obstructionist course against the French, provided that the Reich government used its influence to topple the grand coalition in Prussia and remove Severing from office as Prussian minister of the interior.[7] The party also underscored, however, that its offer of cooperation included an implied threat. The DVFP made it clear that if Cuno was not willing to do its bidding, it would move against the "domestic traitors" on its own, that is, attempt to unleash a civil war.[8]

While the membership and voting support of the rightist extremists was impressive for a time, the numbers could not hide the groups' internal and external difficulties. The Schutz- und Trutzbund, for example, like other self-professed "unity" organizations, was never free of sectarianism and internal leadership intrigues. There were also chronic money shortages and questions about the degree to which the Pan-Germans should interfere directly in the Bund's activities. An additional handicap for the political future of the radical right was their self-isolation from the traditional Conservatives. Especially after the assassination of Walther Rathenau, a growing segment within the DNVP saw the rightist extremists as an albatross for the political future of the German Nationalists. As a result, the DNVP's 1922 national congress, held in Görlitz in October, adopted a resolution expelling a number of *Völkische,* including the two members of the German Nationalists' Reichstag delegation who then proceeded to establish their own party, the DVFP.

Above all, popular success for the radical right also called forth effective countermeasures by the republican authorities, especially in Prussia. Until Hitler's and Ludendorff's abortive Beer Hall Putsch in November 1923, Bavaria remained hospitable ground for the radical right, while the Reich cabinets oscillated between repression and equivocation.[9] Prussia, however, consistently moved vigorously against rightist extremist groups. After clear links between the Bund and the murderers of Rathenau had been exposed, the Reich and state authorities ordered the dissolution of the organization on July 1, 1922, using the authority of the newly passed Law for the Protection of the Republic. The Bund attempted to continue its operations through a number of clandestine successor organizations, but its role as a mass movement on the German extreme right was clearly over.[10] A few months later, on November 18, the Nazi party was prohibited in Prussia. Thereafter the Hitler movement, at least until its reestablishment in 1925, survived only in the form of a few underground locals grouped around some regional leaders such as a *völkisch* member of the Landtag, Heinz Haake, and the Nazi chief in Cologne, Joseph Grohé.[11]

Finally, to the consternation of the Reich government, the state government dissolved the DVFP in August 1923. Like the Bund, the Freedom party did not recover from this blow. In 1924 the remnants joined with a splinter group of the Nazis to form a new entity, the National Socialist Freedom party (NSFP). This organization was led by Erich Ludendorff and a Nazi, Gregor Strasser. When Hitler was released from jail in early 1925 he reestablished the NSDAP and prohibited all Nazis from holding membership in any other political organization. As a result, the NSFP dissolved itself and some of its members attempted to resurrect the DVFP. They were largely unsuccessful, however, and after 1925 the North German *Völkische* increasingly operated in the form of various sectarian groups overshadowed by the growing Nazi party.

In summary, the right radicals were never able to achieve the status of a major political force in Prussia in the years between 1921 and 1925. The reason lay partly in sectarianism and a lack of charismatic leaders, but a far more important cause of their failure was the vigilance of the Prussian authorities. In contrast to their experience in Bavaria, right-wing extremist groups were not tolerated in Prussia. They remained short-lived organisms that were dissolved as soon as they became a threat to parliamentary democracy in the state.

The German National People's Party

As Richard Hamilton has recently shown, the line between the supporters of right radicalism and traditional Conservatism was fluid rather than rigid.[12] Voters casting ballots for the DNVP did not necessarily reject the radical right groups for their extremism, but for their ineffectiveness. In the years 1921 to 1925 the DNVP seemed to be at the height of its power; other political groups found it increasingly difficult to ignore the DNVP when contemplating various government coalitions. But success did not lessen the intraparty conflict that had characterized the DNVP since its establishment. In fact, as the likelihood of sharing executive power increased, so did the intraparty wrangling over the best tactics for persuading potential coalition partners to include the DNVP in the cabinet and over what use the German Nationalists should make of their share of power.

One wing of the DNVP, led by such men as Admiral von Tirpitz, the former chief of the imperial navy, Ernst von Schlange-Schöningen, a Pomeranian Junker and member of the Prussian Landtag, and (until their expulsion) the right-wing Reichstag members Wulle and von Graefe-Goldebee argued that if the DNVP were to join in any government, that development would have to signal the end of parliamentarism and democracy. In making this demand, the radicals were seemingly oblivious of the fact that it was precisely an ultimatum of this sort that would lead the moderate bourgeois parties to reject any coalition with the DNVP. Without coalition partners, however, the party was effectively excluded from a Reich or Prussian cabinet, since even the German Nationalists' spectacular electoral successes did not enable them to form a government without the help of other parties.

The moderates in the party seemed to appreciate the dilemma. Their principal spokesmen, Oskar Hergt and Count Westarp, recognized that the party needed the cooperation of moderate bourgeois groups to effect the move from the opposition to the ministerial benches. For this reason, they let it be known that the DNVP was willing to abide by the parliamentary rules in its drive for power. In effect, the DNVP would become a parliamentary political force, though in return for this "concession" the German Nationalists demanded an agreement from its potential coalition partners to form simultaneous *Bürderblock* cabinets in the Reich and Prussia.

Moderates and radicals were sharply divided over the road to power, but their views tended to converge when it came to the question of what would happen after the DNVP ministers had taken their seats in the cabinet. The radicals now envisioned the destruction of the parliamentary system de jure and de facto. The moderates were willing to tolerate it de jure, but emphasized that with executive power in the hands of the DNVP, the parliamentary form of government would quickly become inoperative in practice since forces of the left and particularly the Social Democrats would be excluded from political power as effectively as they had been before 1914.[13]

For much of 1922 it appeared that the moderates were gaining the upper hand within the party. As noted above, the feud between the *völkisch* wing and the moderate party leadership came to a head in the fall of 1922. Reinhold Wulle, one of the leaders of the *völkisch* group, used his position as editor of the extreme right-wing journal *Deutsche Zeitung* to accuse the DNVP's national leadership of opportunism and lack of political backbone. He criticized the leaders' courting of the moderate bourgeois parties, and urged the DNVP instead to ally itself more closely with extraparliamentary radical groups and to obtain additional popular support by stressing anti-Semitic themes in the party's propaganda. After Wulle was expelled from the party at the DNVP's 1922 national congress, he and his followers organized the DVFP. They continued to attack the DNVP's national leaders for "sliding to the left" and "scheming to join a coalition at any price."[14]

The *Völkische* were certainly correct in their assumption that the leadership of the DNVP was anxious to become part of a government coalition.

The DNVP formally offered to join a *Bürgerblock* cabinet in the Reich in September 1922, and the party repeated its offer several times during the next two years.[15] After the DNVP had given parliamentary support to Cuno's national unity front at the time of the Ruhr crisis, the moderate wing of the DNVP felt in 1924 that the time had finally come for it to lead a *Bürgerblock* cabinet in the Reich. Hergt and Westarp indicated that the German Nationalists were willing to make meaningful concessions to reach their goal. These included voting for the Dawes Plan (which involved indirectly recognizing the Treaty of Versailles) and formally acknowledging the legitimacy of the republican constitution. As a quid pro quo, the DNVP insisted that the DVP and the Center party break off their coalition ties to the SPD in Prussia.[16]

In order to persuade the DVP and the Center party to cooperate with the DNVP, the German Nationalists used a combination carrot and stick approach. On the one hand, the DNVP raised the spectre of a split within the ranks of the DVP, with the right wing joining the DNVP in protest against the right Liberals' continued association with the Social Democrats. In September 1923, when grand coalitions held office in the Reich and Prussia, the German Nationalist press gave prominent space to a lengthy article that purported to reflect feelings of deep alienation within the ranks of the People's party. The author, described as a leading member of the DVP, sharply attacked the Prussian DVP ministers Boelitz and von Richter, demanding their immediate resignation since their presence in the cabinet was causing widespread disaffection within the DVP.[17] Similarly, the DNVP threatened the Center party with the loss of conservative Catholic votes if it continued its alliance with antheistic Socialism.[18] At the same time, the German Nationalists painted a picture of cooperation between the moderate bourgeois parties and the Conservatives. The DNVP praised the majority of the DVP members as conservative and nationalistic, and offered the Center party cooperation "on the basis of Christian principles."[19]

The DNVP felt it was in a strong position to make its influence felt during the tenure of the Cuno cabinet. The party played two trump cards. It recognized that the chancellor's goal of national unity against the French could be realized only with the support of the German nationalists. For this reason the DNVP's national chairman pointedly assured Chancellor Cuno of the German Nationalists' support for strong measures in the war of nerves with France.[20] In addition, the Conservatives offered to help Cuno in domestic affairs. They argued that strains between the national cabinet and the state government of Bavaria would be markedly reduced if the DNVP were part of the national coalition.[21] In return for these contributions to Cuno's cause, the DNVP demanded again the end of the grand coalition in Prussia and the reestablishment of the Reich-Prussia linkage under Conservative auspices.[22] The fall of the Prussian cabinet was essential; the state's "dovish attitude" weakened the national resolve in the struggle with France.[23]

While the DNVP moderates, who tended to dominate the Reichstag delegation in the years under discussion here, used what they felt were persuasive arguments to forge parliamentary alliances with the bourgeois parties, the radicals urged a sledgehammer approach instead. One of the extreme right-wingers who had remained in the party after October 1922 was Ernst von Schlange-Schöningen, an influential member of the Landtag delegation, head of the party's Pomeranian organization, and a man once described by a colleague in the Landtag as "the most radical politician the German Nationalists had to offer."[24]

The Pomeranian leader was not particularly interested in how the DNVP came to power; his concern was with the time after German Nationalist ministers had received their appointment papers.[25] From that time on, Schlange-Schöningen insisted, the DNVP had to govern by dictatorial methods, permitting no other political group to share in the exercise of real power. Parliamentarism should "be destroyed." Schlange-Schöningen warned particularly against concessions to the Center party or to the leader of the DVP, Stresemann. The latter, he felt, was under the influence of the "Jewish press." The Prussian DNVP leader even had a foreign policy program in readiness. Once the DNVP had dictatorial control of the Reich and Prussian governments, the party should not hesitate "cold-bloodedly" to abandon the occupied areas on the Rhine and the Ruhr to the French. The government would then consolidate the rest of the Reich and prepare for the future recapture of the temporarily lost territories by armed force. None of this, Schlange-Schöningen argued, could be achieved without the reestablishment of the Reich-Prussian linkage; specifically the Reich Ministry of Defense and the Prussian Ministry of the Interior had to be in the hands of the DNVP.

While the two wings of the DNVP agreed on ultimate aims, their disagreements on tactics paralyzed the party as a whole. In practice, the two factions of the DNVP tended to block each other and thus hinder the political success of the party as a whole. On a number of occasions the radicals effectively sabotaged the efforts of the Hergt forces to lure the moderate bourgeois parties into cooperation. Each time that the DNVP's appeals for cooperation seemed to evoke a positive response from the DVP, for example, the radicals and their allies in the Pan-German Association would be sure to attack the DVP and its leader Stresemann as part of the "international" (the term was a synonym for "Jewish") phalanx that included the SPD, the DDP, and the Center party.[26] The pattern was particularly apparent on Prussian issues, where even the DNVP's moderates were reluctant to make any meaningful concessions to the other bourgeois parties of a potential *Bürgerblock* cabinet. Westarp, for example, turned a deaf ear to urgings that the DNVP yield to the Center party on some educational issues (much as the SPD had done in 1919) in order to hasten the fall of the Weimar and grand coalitions that had governed Prussia since 1919.[27]

The moderates' tactical efforts reached a climax of sorts on August 29, 1924, when exactly half of the DNVP's Reichstag delegates voted for various pieces of legislation putting the Dawes Plan into effect.[28] The vote saved the Reich cabinet, indirectly helped to stabilize the republic, and lent credibility to Germany's international negotiations. In return, the national leadership of the DNVP expected a call from the other bourgeois parties asking the Conservatives to join a new Reich government.

The invitation did come, but not before the Dawes vote had laid bare the conflict within the DNVP and brought the party to the brink of disintegration.[29] The final vote of the Reichstag delegation came as a complete shock to the party's rank and file; virtually until the moment the ballots were cast, the leaders had left the impression that the delegation as a whole would reject the government's proposals.[30] After the balloting, the radicals, who included a majority of the party's provincial leaders, indignantly attacked what they saw as the national leadership's betrayal of Conservative principles. They demanded that, in return for the DNVP's desertion of its essential principles, the party at the very least had to be rewarded with important cabinet seats in the Reich and Prussian governments.

That, of course, raised the linkage issue, a question the moderate bourgeois parties had not been willing to address in the past, and rejected again now. In effect, the strength of the radicals in the DNVP nullified the expected benefits of the moderates' strategy. The radicals did achieve another, albeit equally counterproductive triumph: they managed to force the resignation of the party's moderate national chairman, Oskar Hergt, though characteristically they were not able to impose a successor from their own ranks upon the party.[31] (Incidentally, the radicals, and especially their Prussian faction, had problems of their own at this time. A leading member of the DNVP's Landtag delegation, Paul Lüdicke, had been implicated in some questionable business practices conducted by the Prussian Bank for Agricultural Cooperatives; Lüdicke was a member of the bank's board of directors.)[32]

In the end the radicals could only watch impotently as the DNVP's new national chairman, Friedrich Winckler, all but ignored the linkage between the Reich and Prussia and restricted his negotiations with the moderate bourgeois parties to the modalities of the DNVP's joining the Reich coalition.[33] By the end of 1924 the radical Schlange-Schöningen course had been unsuccessful in gaining executive power in Prussia. Yet the moderates too had failed, at least as far as Prussia was concerned. German Nationalist ministers would join the Reich cabinet at the beginning of 1925, but the road to executive power in Prussia was no less blocked by staying within the parliamentary rules than by demanding dictatorial authority.

The German People's Party

In sharp contrast to the experience of the DNVP, its neighbor to the left on the German political spectrum was spectacularly successful in gaining a share of executive power between 1921 and 1924. Members of the party served in almost every Reich cabinet; the DVP's national leader, Gustav Stresemann, was Reich chancellor for a brief time and, beginning in 1923, was foreign minister for more than six years. Moreover, in contrast to the DNVP, the People's party succeeded in becoming part of the Prussian coalition. For more than three years it was a partner of the Weimar coalition parties in the grand coalition that governed German's largest state.

Still, political triumphs did not preclude intraparty feuds and tensions. In the spring of 1924, right-wing members of the DVP established a National Liberal Caucus to lobby for cooperation with the German Nationalists and against the coalition with the Social Democrats in Prussia. The right wing dominated the Reichstag delegation, and while its influence in Prussia was considerably smaller, there is no doubt that some Landtag members were also anxious to substitute a *Bürgerblock* with the DNVP for the grand coalition with the SPD.[34]

A number of DVP leaders supported an opening to the right, but they did not speak with one voice. On the contrary, the various factions advocated their courses of action for rather contradictory reasons and for different government jurisdictions. Stresemann himself, for example, was primarily concerned with establishing a viable parliamentary base for his foreign policy. By cooperating with the DNVP at the Reich level he hoped to neutralize the German Nationalists' vehement opposition to his goal of gradual reconciliation with German's former enemies. Consequently, Stresemann approached the DNVP only in terms of a Reich coalition.[35] He had no interest in breaking up the Prussian grand coalition, and he used his considerable personal influence to discourage independent initiatives by autonomous factions in the party.[36]

Other leaders in the party were less concerned with foreign policy issues than with the DNVP as the People's party's primary rival for the same reservoir of middle-class voters. Particularly after the Reichstag elections of May 1924 had demonstrated the "momentum" of the DNVP, a number of right Liberals feared that, unencumbered by governmental responsibility, the German Nationalists would continue to take votes away from the DVP.[37] This group argued that once the DNVP had joined a government coalition and recognized the republican constitution, the resulting tensions among the German Nationalists would lead to a split of the DNVP, enabling the DVP to inherit the moderate wing of the German Nationalists.[38]

Most of these game plans, too, concerned the Reich, and the role of the Prussian coalition in them was not always clear. Certainly many of the party's rank and file remained uneasy about the DVP's cooperation with the "Marxists," and even the relative absence of friction among the coalition partners did not entirely eliminate negative sentiments in the party.[39] Still, the Prussian DVP leaders continued their support of the grand coalition. The party's leadership recognized that on a number of issues it could work with either the SPD or the DNVP, but it insisted that the politically uncertain times from 1921 to 1924 called for cooperation and integration with the SPD and the forces of labor rather than confrontation, as the Prussian DNVP advocated. The strategy of an opening to the left was particularly persuasive during the crisis year 1923 when a stable government in Prussia was all that prevented political disintegration and national dissolution in Germany. In July 1923, at the height of the Ruhr crisis, the Central Committee of the DVP issued a public vote of confidence for the grand coalition in the state.[40]

The political situation changed significantly with the end of the acute Ruhr crisis and the Reichstag election of May 1924. The DVP's Reichstag delegation now committed itself firmly to forming a cabinet with the DNVP and to rejecting any coalition that included the SPD.[41] The German Nationalists hoped that the resolution would also apply to Prussia, and a group of DVP Landtag delegates did call for the formation of a parallel *Bürgerblock* in Prussia, but the party's leaders in the state were in no hurry either to break up the coalition or, alternatively, to join in the call for new Landtag elections.[42] A major stumbling block was the radical character of the Prussian DNVP. While a coalition with the German Nationalists in the Reich meant cooperating with men like Hergt, Winckler, and Westarp, any *Bürgerblock* in Prussia would have involved dealing with Schlange-Schöningen and his supporters.

The DVP's Prussian leadership did not waver in its position throughout 1924. It is incorrect to conclude, as some analysts have done, that the decision of the DVP in the Reichstag also sealed the fate of the grand coalition in Prussia.[43] As will be shown later, the DVP's decision to withdraw from the grand coalition was a consequence of a series of developments that followed the Landtag elections of December 1924, and even then the decision remained controversial within the Prussian DVP literally until the last minute.

German Democratic Party

The DDP and DVP stood in an almost reciprocal relationship to each other during these years. While the DVP reached the zenith of its political influence, the left Liberals were reduced to a mere shadow of their former eminence. The Party was shaken by bitter debates over its future. In Mecklenburg a number of disgruntled left Liberals quit the DDP because they felt that the Democrats were leaning too far to the right. They founded a new group, the Republican party. At the other end of the spectrum a National Liberal caucus within the DDP advocated ending the coalition with the SPD and restricting the DDP's political partners to the bourgeois parties. Pressure from the right wing increased after the May elections. A number of DDP leaders, including Westermann, Dominicus, and Schiffer, felt the party had to clear the air and proclaim itself in favor of a *Bürgerblock*. When a majority of the—much reduced—Reichstag delegation rejected their ultimatum, the group resigned from the party.[44] The polarization of the party affected the DDP's Landtag delegation less than its Reichstag caucus. The reason was partly that there were fewer controversial Prussian issues, but also that the DDP's left wing maintained control of the party in the state.[45] In addition, both the state and the national legislative delegations favored the continuation of the grand coalition in Prussia.[46]

The Landtag elections of December 1924 brought severe losses for the DDP, but to some extent the party was able to substitute quality for quantity. The new head of the Landtag delegation, the Rhinelander Bernhard Falk, was a sincere republican who resolutely kept the DDP on a left-of-center course. In addition, two members of the delegation, Schreiber and Höpker-Aschoff, later became effective members of the Prussian cabinet, where the DDP continued to have representation far in excess of its parliamentary strength.

Hermann Höpker-Aschoff was in the forefront of the DDP's quest for the political grail in the years between 1921 and 1930: the search for a reunited Liberal party or, alternatively, the creation of a new moderate bourgeois party.[47] Clearly the most immediate answer to the DDP's declining fortunes was unification (or, perhaps more accurately, reunification) with the right Liberals. In fact, discussions on this topic, in one form or other, run like a red thread throughout the entire period, and, according to Falk's testimony, at one point negotiations between him and three Prussian DVP leaders, von Krause, von Campe, and von Richter, had almost reached a successful conclusion.[48] In the final analysis, however, all fusion plans failed because the negotiators started from incompatible premises. A number of prominent DVP members were convinced that the DDP was no longer a politically viable entity, so that the People's party needed only to wait to inherit the right wing of the left Liberals.[49] The DDP, for its part, insisted on complicating the discussions by attempting to involve the Economics party in any merger plans.

The Economics Party

The left Liberals recognized that their own rapid decline toward political oblivion was in no small part a result of competition from the Reich party of the German Mittelstand (Economics party). As noted before, the Economics party derived most of its support from elements of the old *Mittelstand* that had traditionally backed left-wing liberalism: professionals, small businessmen, and, above all, urban real estate owners. Founded by Victor Bredt, an eminent jurist and former DNVP Reichstag member, the WiP attempted to carve out a political niche halfway between the DVP and the German Nationalists.[50] The WiP rejected the right Liberals' close relationship to big business, and, like the DNVP, unequivocally demanded a restoration of the monarchy. At the same time, the Economics party opposed the *völkisch* extremism in the ranks of the German Nationalists.

The WiP's founder may have envisioned a broadly cross-segmental, ideologically differentiated party, but the group's dependency on the financial and organizational support of urban landlords and small businessmen forced the Economics party to remain a special interest group—albeit a very successful one. In the post-1923 era, the WiP grew rapidly into a major voice promoting the interest of the old *Mittelstand*.[51] The WiP's impact was greatest in the years immediately after the currency stabilization, when the question of compensation for assets lost to inflation was a major campaign issue in all elections.

By the end of 1924, the WiP had largely replaced the DDP as the political representative for many among the petty bourgeoisie; at the national level the Economics party was able to increase its vote from 441,000 in May 1924 to more than a million in December of the same year. In Prussia its rise was similarly meteoric: the WiP delegation in the Landtag numbered four in February 1921 and eleven in December 1924.

In view of the often precarious balance of power in the Weimar parliaments, a party like the WiP had frequent opportunities to tip the scales one way or the other, so that its stand on coalition possibilities became crucial. Here the party proved a severe disappointment to the moderate forces. In the Reich the Economics party rejected any government but a *Bürgerblock*,[52] and in Prussia the Economics party stood even further to the right. In fact, in state politics the WiP was virtually indistinguishable from the DNVP. The party's Prussian leader was Carl Ladendorff, the president of the Prussian and Berlin Association of Urban Landlords. Ladendorff was a particularly demagogic and narrow-minded spokesman for his special interest group. Under his leadership the Prussian WiP directed a steady stream of venomous attacks against the Prussian tax on income from real property, against the minister of social services, Heinrich Hirtsiefer (who administered the state's rent control laws), and against the cabinet and parliamentary democracy in general.[53]

The Center Party

Of the major parties in the Weimar Republic, the Center party was seemingly least burdened by intraparty tensions. The Catholic party had by now rejected all plans for restructuring itself so as to appeal to both Catholics and Protestants, and instead settled for remaining the primary political spokesman for German Catholics. Nevertheless, while there were no debates within the party about the confessional orientation of the group, there remained important differences on nonreligious issues. As was true of other moderate groups among the bourgeois parties, generally speaking, the party's political center of gravity in the Reichstag moved steadily to the right, while in Prussia it remained left of center.

The drift toward the right of the Center party's Reichstag delegation began in July 1922 with the creation of a so-called Bourgeois Working Group (Bürgerliche Arbeitsgemeinshaft), composed of the DDP, DVP, and Center party. The process culminated in the formation of the *Bürgerblock* cabinet that included the DNVP in early 1925.[54] The initiative for creating an institutional channel for contacts among the bourgeois parties came from the right wing of the Center party, specifically two businessmen, von Guérard and ten Hompel, and the head of the Catholic trade unions, Adam Stegerwald. The three intended to persuade the moderate bourgeois parties to reduce their political ties to the Social Democrats, while increasing the channels of communication to the DNVP.[55] For Stegerwald the Bourgeois Working Group was a step toward realizing his Essen Program. He remained convinced that the ideas of Social Democracy were detrimental to Germany's future, while in his view the DNVP contained positive forces that should be harnessed to help govern the Reich.[56] Within the Reichstag delegation the arguments of Stegerwald and his associates met with a positive echo. When Wilhelm Marx, the chairman of the national party and the head of its Reichstag delegation (he had been elected to both posts in 1920), took an informal poll of his colleagues in mid-November 1923, he was surprised by the large number of delegates who favored the establishment of a Reich government that included the DNVP, but not the SPD.[57]

But Prussia was not the Reich. The Center party's Landtag delegation held fast to its left-of-center position. In fact, the coalition between the Catholic party and the SPD in the state was accepted as a given by most leaders of the party;[58] in the course of the debates during its national congress in January 1922 the issue was not mentioned. The coalition also received important and consistent media support, notably from the daily *Germania,* published in Berlin. True, there were members of the Landtag delegation who joined their colleagues in the Reichstag in hoping that the DNVP would join the cabinet, but few advocated substituting the German Nationalists for the Social Democrats. Instead, the right wing of the Prussian Center party (and the national chairman, Wilhelm Marx) favored a coalition that included the present members of the grand coalition as well as the German Nationalists.[59]

The intransigence of the radicals in the DNVP, who dominated the Prussian wing of the German Nationalists, undoubtedly helped to maintain the Center party on its left-of-center course in Prussia.[60] The Prussian Catholics repeatedly accused Schlange-Schöningen and his group of wanting to renew the *Kulturkampf.*[61] At the same time Wilhelm Marx was persona non grata among the DNVP because of his active membership in the largest pro-republican paraparliamentary organization, the Reichsbanner Schwarz-Rot-Gold.[62] It did not even prove difficult to persuade the party's Reichstag delegation that the party's left-of-center course in Prussia actually brought the national Center party closer to its goals. Any move toward the DNVP in the Reich, so the argument ran, had to be balanced by a corresponding stance toward the left in Prussia if the Center party was to remain true to its self-chosen function as the hinge of German politics.[63]

Still, all was not harmonious in the Prussian Center party. One vexing regional difficulty was the continuing agitation for the creation of an independent *Land* in Upper Silesia.[64] As noted above, all Prussian cabinets since 1918 had opposed the separation of Upper Silesia from Prussia, although they had grudgingly agreed to the establishment of a new province of Upper Silesia. The Prussian Center party was caught in the middle of the dispute. The Catholic members of the cabinet and the party's Landtag leaders opposed the creation of a new federal *Land.* The leadership feared that the Center party would pay a severe price for a new state of Upper Silesia. While it was likely that the Center party would become the dominant force in the new state, the party would lose much of its influence in what remained of Prussia. The party's statisticians projected that the Center party would have its strength in the Landtag reduced from eighty-four to fifty-seven.[65] At the same time the party's leaders hesitated to disavow the campaign directly since it was spearheaded by the party's charismatic regional leader, Father Carl Ulitzka.[66]

Actually, the campaign was something of a tempest in a teapot. A provincial plebiscite on the question of separatism from Prussia held in November 1921 demonstrated that Ulitzka and the Prussian cabinet had vastly overestimated the cleric's support. Some 90 percent of Upper Silesia's voting population preferred to remain a part of Prussia, albeit in the form of a separate province.

A more serious source of intraparty tension was dissatisfaction among the

Center party's agrarian supporters. As was true of their Protestant colleagues, Catholic farmers were quick to blame the revolution and the "Marxist" governments that had led Prussia since 1918 for the economic and structural problems that confronted postwar German agriculture. The agrarian wing of the Center party was always uneasy about the Center party's coalition with the SPD, and after 1922 the effects of hyperinflation and the beginnings of the worldwide drop in the price of agricultural commodities intensified the calls for a break with the Social Democrats. Instead, spokesmen for Catholic farm organizations urged cooperation with the German Nationalists as the leading political voice of Protestant farmers.[67]

The intraparty frictions smoldered under the surface for some years, but in the course of the Prussian government crisis at the beginning of 1925 (to be discussed) the dissatisfactions of the agrarian wing erupted into open revolt. In February two of the Center party's Landtag delegates, Franz von Papen and Friedrich Loenartz, publicly broke party discipline by refusing to cast affirmative ballots on a vote of confidence for the new prime minister–designate (and national chairman of the Center party), Wilhelm Marx.[68] Their move caused a sensation since, given the Weimar coalition's extremely narrow voting edge in the Landtag of 1925, the defection of the two delegates meant that the Marx government lost the vote of confidence.

Both Papen and Loenartz were recognized as representatives of the extreme right wing of the Center party as well as leading spokesmen for the interests of Westphalian agriculture.[69] (Incidentally, Loenartz's disaffection was a particularly open affront to the republican forces. He was a political civil servant, having served as county commissioner of Bitburg in western Germany since 1920.) Papen's aim was to move the Center party closer to the DNVP. In a letter of February 6, 1925, to the head of the Center party's Landtag delegation, Porsch, Papen announced that he would support a Prussian cabinet that included both DNVP and SPD ministers, but that he categorically rejected a revival of the Weimar coalition in Prussia.[70] Thus he had supported Marx's candidacy as prime minister when the chairman of the Center party announced his intention of forming a National Community Cabinet, that is, a government that included both the SPD and the German Nationalists. When the creation of such a government proved impossible, and Marx fell back upon the Weimar coalition as an alternative, Papen refused to give the leader of his party a vote of confidence.

The fronde of the two Center party delegates had the immediate effect of prolonging the then current Prussian government crisis for a few weeks, but in the long run it served to anchor the Prussian Center party more securely to its left-of-center position. Papen's and Loenartz's defiance of the party leadership sent shock waves throughout political Catholicism. The spectre of "cracks in the Center tower" called forth immediate and passionate reaction among all sectors of the party.[71] In the Landtag delegation a resolution was introduced to expel Papen and Loenartz for breach of discipline, and a number of provincial organizations passed similar resolutions condemning the two delegates' actions.[72] Strong support for both men in their regional organization prevented their formal expulsion, but the majority of the Prussian Center party left no doubt about its sentiments. In the future Papen and Loenartz remained isolated and without influence in the Prussian party.[73]

The Social Democratic Party

The SPD remained something of a paradox among German political groups. At the national level the Reich's largest party exhibited a persistent tendency to flee from governmental responsibility. The trend had been apparent since June 1920, but it was considerably strengthened by the reunification of the SPD with what remained of the USPD in September 1922. The reunited party, which briefly styled itself United Social Democratic party (Vereinigte Sozialdemokratische Partei, VSPD) was returned as the strongest party in every Reichstag and Prussian Landtag from May 1924 to the spring of 1932, yet only in the period May 1928 to March 1930 was the SPD part of the government coalition in the Reich. In Prussia the party remained the mainstay of the cabinet, but even here the leadership felt constantly obliged to justify what was for many among the rank and file an unpopular decision. Severing, an enthusiastic supporter and major architect of the grand coalition, defended cooperation with the moderate bourgeois parties in largely negative terms. It was a "political necessity" and the only possible alternative to a return of "semiautocratic conditions" in Prussia.[74] Richard Hauschildt, a prominent leader of the right wing of the Landtag delegation, added that the grand coalition was really the party's second choice; in November 1921 it would have preferred to form a government with the USPD.[75]

Actually such apologia were in the nature of denying the obvious. It had been clear to competent observers for a number of years even before World War I that the SPD was not really a revolutionary socialist party whose main goal was to organize class-conscious proletarians for the coming overthrow of capitalism. Instead, German Social Democracy was developing into a modern, popular mass party with members and supporters that clearly reached beyond the traditional blue-collar clientele. The process was accelerated after the revolution and reached a climax with the adoption of the party's Görlitz Program in 1921. The trend toward "positive integration" into German society enjoyed considerable support both from the leadership and the rank and file, although there remained powerful and residual opposition as well.[76]

The reunification of SPD and the rump-USPD had been expected ever since the Independents lost the bulk of their members to the Communists in the fall of 1920, but until early 1922 all moves toward unification had been thwarted by internal dissensions in what remained of the USPD. In the spring and summer of that year, however, developments within the USPD and in Germany as a whole accelerated the reunion of the two sister parties. The Independents faced considerable financial difficulties and suffered a rapid loss of members and supporters. In March the entire editorial board of the party's national newspaper *Freiheit* resigned because the members felt they could no longer support the USPD's hard-line opposition to the prorepublican Wirth government.[77] The final catalyst was the assassination of Reich Foreign Minister Walther Rathenau, which demonstrated both the strength and the danger of rightist extremism in Germany. Rudolf Breitscheid wrote, "In one fell swoop what had been almost impossible, became easy."[78] Within a few weeks after the assassination, the two Reichstag delegations formed a working group *(Arbeitsgemeinschaft),* and in September a joint party congress formalized the reunification of the two Socialist parties.[79]

Throughout the party the news of reunification was greeted with boundless if unrealistic euphoria.[80] There were very few SPD leaders (Noske among them)[81] who felt the union would hurt rather than help the future of Social Democracy. Actually, there is a little doubt that the fusion strengthened the party's left wing and that this development contributed to the SPD's self-paralysis in the crucial middle years of the Weimar era. The differences between the left and right wings in the reunited SPD pitted pragmatists and ideologues against each other, and it was precisely for this reason that it was difficult for the two groups to compromise their differences. The left wing argued that the majority Socialists had begun to forsake Social Democracy's Marxist heritage when it voted for war credits in August 1914 and the trend toward *ministerialisme* since 1918 had compounded the unfortunate shift away from the line of Marxist ideological orthodoxy and class consciousness.[82] The former Independents were particularly adamant in rejecting the Görlitz Program and its implications for the future development of the party. Instead, the former USPD leaders urged the united party to return "to the policies of the prewar days, . . . not to suppress the healthy revolutionary element in our party," and to keep in mind, "We can't trust the bourgeoisie!"[83]

After the unification, the influence of the left wing was disproportionately strong in the Reichstag delegation.[84] The last national elections prior to reunification were held in June 1920, that is, when the USPD was at the peak of its electoral success. About 55 of the 178 delegates in the VSPD's Reichstag delegation in September 1922 belonged to the left wing. They opposed *ministerialisme* in any form, but particularly in the form of a grand coalition.[85] Their strength largely paralyzed the party's Reichstag delegation as the leadership, anxious to preserve party unity, pursued a zig-zag course giving in to the tactical demands of one side or the other.[86] Fatalism and a lack of realistic appreciation of its own strength became characteristic hall-marks of the party's behavior in national politics.[87]

While the SPD's Reichstag delegation appeased the left-wing purists, men with a more pronounced view for political realities continued to lead the Prussian Social Democrats. The delegation was still effectively led by its de facto chairman Ernst Heilmann. In fact, Heilmann's position had been strengthened. The elections of February 1921 had brought a number of his close political friends into the Landtag, among them Friedrich Stampfer, the editor of the SPD's national newspaper, *Vorwärts*. Reunification with the USPD did not markedly increase the influence of the party's left wing in the Landtag delegation. The last Landtag had been elected in February 1921, when the USPD had already passed its organizational and electoral peak. That did not mean, of course, that Prussian Social Democracy was not affected by develop-ments at the Reich level. The state leaders certainly resented that while they worked hard to make parliamentary democracy work, some of their colleagues in the Reichstag, as Otto Braun put it, "saw the essence of parliamentarism in introducing votes of no confidence and engineering the fall of ministers."[88]

For a variety of reasons, the SPD staggered from disaster to disaster at the polls in the first half of 1924. The party clearly suffered from political burn-out; it lacked "fire and the desire to fight."[89] In Prussia several prominent Social Democrats were involved in a series of highly publicized corruption cases. The speaker of the Landtag, Robert Leinert, was forced to resign his post as mayor of Hanover over pension irregularities. Both the police chief of Berlin, Richter, and Ernst Heilmann were tainted by their connection with a scandal-ridden financier, Julius Barmat. Richter, too, had to resign under public pressure. For other SPD leaders the years of continuous service brought on serious health problems.[90]

The election setbacks began with the Lübeck municipal elections of Feb-ruary 1924,[91] and continued unabated until the Reichstag elections of May. In the latter contest the reunited Social Democrats received little more than half of the votes which the USPD and SPD had obtained separately in June 1920 (1920: 11.1 million, or 39.6 percent; May 1924: 6 million, or 20.5 percent). To be sure, the SPD remained the single strongest political party in the Reichstag, but understandably the mood within the party was "very bleak."[92]

It goes almost without saying that the left and right wings of the party blamed each other for the debacles at the polls. Both sides used the forum of the July 1924 national party congress to air their mutual recriminations. (The 1923 national congress had been canceled because of the Ruhr crisis, and the party leadership deliberately scheduled the 1924 meeting after the national elections in order to avoid publicizing the intraparty tensions during the cam-paign.) The left wing had a clear if simplistic answer to the party's dilemma: the SPD needed to return to the tried program of a proletarian party that refused to cooperate with bourgeois parties and institutions. It emphasized that there was no essential difference between any of the bourgeois groupings; restoring a healthy party life depended upon, among other things, "ripping the Center party apart."[93] In contrast, the right wing emphasized the viability of the republic and parliamentary democracy rather than the ideological purity of the SPD. It demanded the establishment of closer ties between the SPD and the moderate bourgeois parties in order to contain the antidemocratic forces of left- and right-wing extremists.[94] Although the left-wing position had only minority support at the party's 1924 national congress, the SPD's national leadership decided on a lame Solomonic compromise that treated the two wings as virtually equal in strength.[95] The leaders yielded to the demands of the left wing at the national level and permitted the SPD in the Reichstag to play a largely oppositional role, but they encouraged the party's cooperation in coalition governments at the state and local level.[96]

The compromise may have relieved internal party pressures, but it was more difficult to make it plausible to the voters. This was particularly true when national and state elections were held at the same time, as was the case in December 1924. In fact, the Reichstag contest completely overshadowed the Prussian state elections,[97] so that the sharply confrontational, anti-bourgeois stance of the SPD in the Reichstag carried over into the Landtag campaign. The SPD spoke of DVP and DNVP as two manifestations of the same bourgeois-reactionary enemy, and this attitude was hardly conducive to continuing the coalition with the People's party in Prussia.[98] To be sure, the Prussian SPD leaders attempted to soften the strident tone of their Reichstag colleagues, and spoke only of the need to reduce the DVP's influence in the Prussian coalition,[99] but the basic impression of the growing gap between the two parties remained.

The results of the December 1924 national and state campaigns were a pyrrhic victory for the party. At the national level the SPD regained some of the strength it had lost in the May elections, but in Prussia, where the relevant comparison was the state election of February 1921, the results were a relative setback (February 1921: 26.3 percent; December 1924: 24.9 percent). The political effect, then, was to strengthen the oppositional forces in the Reichstag, while weakening the Prussian SPD which favored a course of cooperation with the moderate bourgeois parties.

The Communist Party

Any account of the relationship between Prussia and the German Communist party can be brief. That is not to say that the KPD was an unimportant political factor in the state. On the contrary, the political strength of the KPD grew in proportion to the USPD's decline. As the dissolution process among the Independents spread, a number of that party's largest and politically most active organizations went over to the KPD. In parts of the Ruhr, the Lower Rhine district, Berlin, and the Prussian province of Saxony the Communists scored spectacular gains among working-class voters, in some cases overtaking the SPD. However, like the USPD, the KPD never developed a specific Prussian strategy.

The Communists did have a national policy, or, more precisely, a succession of strategies that corresponded to the equally rapid changes in the KPD's leadership personnel. These were the years during which various factors, some intra-German and others related to developments in the Soviet Union, gave the KPD a chameleonlike image and completely inconsistent political strategies. The KPD suffered from the consequences of its own errors in assessing the chances of revolution in Germany, and from having to fulfill the equally unrealistic demands of the Soviet Comintern leaders. The results were rapid shifts in strategy and personnel as the Communists moved the party line pendulum from "left-wing infantilism" to "right-wing opportunism" and back again.[100]

Prussian politics were most directly affected by the KPD's rightist or popular front phase, which characterized the party line for most of 1922 and 1923. In this period the Communists pursued tactics that were particularly attractive to the left wing of the reunited SPD, while the Prussian Social Democrats rejected the Communist overtures. The ultraleft leaders of the KPD, who had led the party into the disastrous putsch attempt in central Germany in the spring of 1921, were subsequently purged.[101] Their successors did an abrupt tactical about-face; they seemed anxious for good relations with the Social Democrats and non-Communists unions. In 1921–1922 there was even talk that the Communists might tolerate (though not join) a Reich cabinet composed of SPD and USPD ministers.[102]

In 1923 Communists and Socialists did form a government in the states of Saxony and Thuringia, but the coalitions remained tactical mariages de convenance with which neither partner felt comfortable. The SPD distrusted the KPD's commitment to working within the parliamentary system, and the KPD accused the Social Democrats in Saxony "of diverting the attention of the working classes from the revolutionary class conflict with pseudo-radical slogans."[103] Neither partner was unhappy to see the cooperation end.

The Prussian SPD leaders opposed the "proletarian coalitions" in the Central German states, but they were particularly distrustful of any form of extraparliamentary political mobilization that included the Communists. After the assassination of Walther Rathenau, left-wing paramilitary groups were formed in several German cities and in at least some areas (including Berlin) their membership included Communists.[104] In addition, the socialists unions became politically active again and a few of their leaders welcomed Communist participation as well. Thus, the purpose of a demonstration planned in Berlin on July 4, 1922 was (according to one Socialist union leader) not merely to express support of the Weimar constitution, but "finally to achieve what we failed to do in [March] 1920."[105] During the Ruhr occupation, some KPD regional organizations attempted to organize political strikes and in a few areas so-called "proletarian hundreds," or KPD-sponsored paramilitary groups, were established.[106]

The Communist tactics had two—contradictory—aims. One was to destabilize the Social Democrat–bourgeois coalitions by stirring up fear among the bourgeois parties that the Socialists were deserting their coalition partners in favor of proletarian unity.[107] Simultaneously, left-wing forces in the KPD were using the party's modest successes in forging extraparliamentary cooperation schemes to prepare for yet another attempt at a Bolshevik-style revolution in Germany. The KPD's 1923 national congress, which took place shortly after French and Belgian troops moved into the Ruhr, gave increased control functions to the central leadership, thus facilitating centralized planning for any future "action."[108] It eventually came in the form of an abortive and very amateurish attempt at an insurrection in the port city of Hamburg in October 1923. Led by Ernst Thälmann, then the leader of the KPD's Hamburg district and later national chairman of the party, the putsch attempt had no support from other regions and collapsed almost immediately.[109]

Paradoxically, despite the KPD's contradictory and vacillating party line, the rapidly worsening economic crisis in Germany persuaded a large number of voters to cast their ballots for the Communists.[110] The KPD increased its votes by 600 percent in the Reichstag election of May 1924 in comparison to that of June 1920 (1920: 2.1 percent; May 1924: 12.6 percent). Its Prussian gains were less spectacular, but still significant (1921: 7.4 percent; 1924: 9.6 percent). By December 1924, the KPD had become the second strongest opposition party in the Landtag. But to a large extent these were empty numbers. In Prussia the KPD still had no consistent political strategy, and in any case it was already clear that a large percentage of the party's supporters felt no profound commitment to the party, but cast their ballots in momentary desperation. Between May and December 1924, the KPD lost a million votes.

Conclusion

During the years from 1922 to 1925, significant changes took place among Prussia's and Germany's political parties. Essentially, the bipolarity of politics was transformed into something akin to tripolarity. One group of parties supported parliamentary democracy and the republic. This category was composed of the parties of the Weimar coalition and the DVP, although important elements in the latter were always uneasy about their association with the Majority Socialists, while the left wing of the SPD had similar reservations about associating with bourgeois interest groups. A second group was formed by those parties absolutely and irrevocably opposed to parliamentary democracy. Politically the most important organizations here were the Communists and the *Völkische*. Between those two poles stood the German Nationalists and the various economic interest parties. They were certainly not ideologically committed to the republic. On the contrary, they professed their longing for a restoration of the monarchy. At the same time they were not willing to dissipate their strength by joining the *Völkische* in total obstruction of parliamentary government. Indeed, important forces among them recognized that in order to further the cause of their supporters most effectively, they would have to join parliamentary coalitions. In the final analysis, the third group always remained Janus-faced: in the Reich they eventually joined coalitions with the moderate bourgeois parties, in Prussia they remained vehemently in opposition.

Politically the time span can be divided into the crisis-ridden years of 1922 and 1923 and the campaign-saturated year 1924. After the republic had survived the aftermath of the assassination of the Reich's Foreign Minister Walther Rathenau and the Franco-Belgian occupation of the Ruhr, Prussia and Germany were subjected to almost nonstop campaigning between May 1924 and May 1925. In these twelve months there were two Reichstag elections, a Landtag election, and two contests to elect a new Reich president. At the end of the series of elections, the political fulcrum in the Reich had shifted perceptibly toward the right. Symbolic of this development were DNVP ministers in the Reich cabinet led by Hans Luther, and the election of a former imperial field marshal, Paul von Hindenburg, as Reich president.

Throughout, seemingly undaunted, the parties of the grand coalition held office in Prussia. This came as a surprise not only to historians, but to contemporary politicians as well. When the cabinet of the grand coalition assumed office in the state, neither the coalition partners nor the opposition felt it was destined for a long life.[111] The coalition partners originally saw the new government in essentially negative terms. The SPD was convinced that only the grand coalition had prevented the transplantation of the Kahr regime in Bavaria to Prussia.[112] The bourgeois parties argued that their participation in the government prevented the Marxists from exercising a power monopoly in Germany's largest state.[113] In retrospect it became clear that the decided lack of enthusiasm with which the coalition partners greeted their cooperation obscured substantial underlying agreement on the nature and future of political interaction in Prussia.[114] At the end of 1921 (and for the next three years) the four coalition parties were dominated by what might be termed "republican Prussian *étatistes*."

Otto Braun's acceptance of the state as a "structure supported by the rule of law" was certainly not a typically Marxist view, but it was one that could be readily subscribed to by such old-line civil servants as the new minister of finance, Ernst von Richter.[115] More significantly still, this view of the relationship between government and society contrasted sharply with the avowed dictatorial ambitions by the extremist groups on the left and right, and the Prussian radicals in the DNVP. In political practice Prussian *étatisme* meant that the coalition partners accepted a view of the state that merged Prussia's territorial integrity and its present republican form of government into an entity that was to serve as a foundation for Prussia's and Germany's viability. In comparison to realizing this overriding goal, the undoubted differences among the coalition partners on substantive questions of day-to-day policy receded into the background. Moreover, the cooperation among the coalition parties was reinforced in the course of the next three years as a series of crises threatened the specific *étatiste* concept of Prussia's political and territorial function. As a result, the crises actually strengthened the bonds among the coalition partners instead of serving to loosen them.

Additional factors aided in establishing a climate of cooperation in the Prussian coalition. Somewhat to their surprise, both the members of the cabinet and the parliamentary leaders of the coalition parties discovered that they were able to work well together not only on a political, but also on a personal level. The good relationship between the de facto parliamentary leaders of the two largest parties, Ernst Heilmann (SPD) and Joseph Hess (Center party) had already been established, and it was not affected by the enlarged coalition. Both Hess and Heilmann continued to work together inside and outside of the established institutional channels—undaunted by criticism from friends and foes alike.[116] Hess and Heilmann did not have particularly good contacts with the leaders of the DVP, but as it turned out, this was not a serious drawback. The lack of established relationships here was compensated for by good contacts between the minister of the interior, Carl Severing, and a number of leading right Liberals, including the chairman of the party's Landtag delegation, von Krause.[117]

CHAPTER **6**

Crises and Coalitions, 1922–1925

The cabinet of the grand coalition held office in Prussia during what were undoubtedly some of the most difficult of the Weimar years. Interlocking foreign policy and domestic factors led to successive crises culminating in the Franco-Belgian occupation of the Ruhr and the collapse and stabilization of the German currency in 1923 and 1924.

At the heart of the problem lay a monumental failure on the part of many Germans and their political leaders to acknowledge that following the Reich's defeat in World War I it would not be possible to return to life as it had been in the summer of 1914. Rather, the sacrifices of war would be followed by further years of hardship as the country adjusted to new realities. The extreme right, of course, refused to admit even the truth of military defeat; these groups pretended that the changing tides of war were a domestic political problem: democracy had led the Reich to defeat; overthrowing democracy would reverse the process.

But even those who acknowledged military defeat—and they certainly included the leaders and supporters of the republican parties—had difficulty accepting the economic and social consequences. The attempt to evade this aspect of postwar reality crystallized in what has become known as the "reparations issue." [1] Successive Reich (and Prussian) cabinets insisted that Germany was unable to pay the financial obligations imposed by the Allies. To attempt to do so, they argued, would inevitably lead to economic ruin and the disintegration of German society. In contrast, the Allies, whose appreciation of Germany's economic resources was considerably better than their eye for the political dynamics in the Reich, remained convinced that far from being unable to pay, Germany was trying to evade the economic consequences of its defeat.

For four long years the Allies and the Germans played a tragic game of charades. The Reich repeatedly declared its inability to fulfill its obligations. In response, the Allied Reparations Commission imposed "productive sanctions" upon Germany, usually in the form of the temporary occupation of some German cities. Unable to put up effective resistance, the Reich cabinet of the moment tended to resign as a gesture of protest, throwing the country into another political crisis, and reducing still further confidence in Germany's already badly inflated currency. As a result the mark took one precipitous fall after another on the international currency markets. The new German government that would eventually be formed then predictably argued that it was now less than ever in a position to resume payment of the reparations, and the spiral began anew.

By the time the grand coalition took office in Prussia, all moderate political groups in Germany acknowledged not only that the cycle of sanctions, political crises, and economic decline had to end, but that essentially there was only one way out of the morass. It was what Reich Foreign Minister Walther Rathenau called the "policy of fulfillment." [2] To be sure, the term had a rather specific and unusual meaning for the Germans. The fulfillment policy, even for its sincerest supporters, was never a policy of appeasement, designed to give in to the Allies' demands. [3] The Germans' ultimate aim was not to pay the reparations in full, but to demonstrate to the victorious powers that even with the best of intentions on the part of the Reich, the reparations imposed exceeded Germany's capacity to pay. In the final analysis, then, as far as Germany was concerned, the "policy of fulfillment" was intended to lead to new negotiations and an inevitable downscaling of the reparations bill.

In addition to agreeing on the ultimate aims of the policy of fulfillment, the groups supporting the tactic were also united in their belief that to be creditable in the eyes of the Allies, the policy of fulfillment needed a broad base of domestic political support. As a result, the leitmotif of German politics during these years of acute crises became the search for a "coalition of national unity."

Unfortunately, here the unanimity ended. The parties, various Reich governments, and the Prussian cabinets had widely differing and rather contradictory ideas on how to establish a national unity coalition and which groups should be included under such an umbrella designation. In addition, an integral part of the controversy was the question whether the achievement of a national unity coalition was more important than the preservation of Germany's parliamentary democracy. It was Prussia's firm and consistent opposition to separating the two aims that enabled parliamentary democracy in Reich and state to survive its severest test.

The Prussians insisted that to make the policy of fulfillment credible in the eyes of the Allies, it was important to demonstrate that the Reich cabinets would seek the support only of the republican forces and not of those political groups that sought to destroy democracy in Germany. [4] In fact, throughout its term of office the grand coalition in Prussia stressed that the Prussian model, that is, cooperation of the moderate bourgeois parties and the Social Democrats, should serve as a paradigm of responsible national unity. The most severe of the reparations crises, the Franco-Belgian occupation of the Ruhr, strengthened the Prussians' belief that Germany had to continue linking its commitment to fulfillment with the preservation of parliamentary democracy.

The cabinet stressed the political unity of the moderate parties that made up the coalition and their commitment to democracy.[5] The Prussian government ordered the "elimination of all monarchical symbols . . . in a manner that leaves no doubt [about the democratic status of the state]."[6] At the height of the Ruhr crisis, in August 1923, all state offices down to the level of county commissioner were instructed to organize official celebrations commemorating the anniversary of the adoption of the Weimar constitution.[7] In addition, the parties of the grand coalition emphasized that once again in the face of foreign danger the cohesion of the Reich as a whole depended upon the territorial integrity and political stability of the state.

Among the Reich governments, only the short-lived grand coalition under Stresemann and Wirth's second cabinet came close to sharing Prussia's view of national unity.[8] The other cabinets, and particularly the Cuno ministry, which was in office during most of the Ruhr occupation, pursued a radically different concept. Cuno's goals was a *Volksgemeinschaft* (national community) that included the cooperation of all political groups from the extreme right to the moderate left. In pursuit of his aim, Cuno worked tirelessly, albeit unsuccessfully, to integrate the antidemocratic groups on the right, including the DNVP and the *Völkische,* into the German resistance front. In order to make the concept of the *Volksgemeinschaft* palatable for the forces of the extreme right, the Reich cabinet emphasized its commitment to *Volk,* Reich, and nation, while terms like republic, parliamentarism, and democracy were rare in the Reich's public pronouncements.

Personnel and Organization of the Grand Coalition

As noted above, political observers held out little hope for a long life of the new Prussian cabinet.[9] Actually, not only did this ministry hold office longer than any of its predecessors since the revolution, but the cohesion of the coalition grew as the ministers continued in office. By the time of the May 1924 Reichstag elections, all of the coalition parties agreed that the Prussian cabinet would remain in office regardless of the outcome of the national contest. Severing and Richter were so confident of this that prior to the national elections they scheduled joint appearances in the campaign against the Guelph movement in Hanover for the weeks following the Reichstag elections.[10]

A key reason for the grand coalition's longevity was the decision by the SPD's bourgeois partners to reject the DNVP's repeated calls for a *Bürgerblock.* Such a government, the Conservatives promised, would permeate public and private life in the state with "Christian spirit," increase subsidies to the established churches, reject the Marxist doctrine of class conflict, and provide "solicitous treatment of all legally constituted nationalist groupings."[11] The DNVP's coalition offers were addressed to all bourgeois parties, but there could be no doubt that the repeated references to "Christian politics" were meant specifically to entice the Center party into cooperation. The Catholics remained wary. They recalled that the Conservatives' concept of the "Christian spirit" had always contained a good portion of anti-Catholicism, and that the demand for "solicitous treatment" of the nationalist forces in practice meant giving the rightist paramilitary organizations a free hand for their activities.

There were many factors responsible for the unexpected growth of good will among the coalition partners, but the harmonious personal relations among the ministers was undoubtedly one of the more important ones. In November 1921 the degree of accord (or its absence) was an open question. Four members of the new cabinet had never held ministerial office before, and only one, Minister of Justice Hugo am Zehnhoff, could look back on an uninterrupted career as cabinet official since the spring of 1920. At first glance the ministerial groups seemed a study in political and personality contrasts. Among the three Social Democrats, two, Otto Braun and Carl Severing, were well-known public figures and avowed enemies of Prussia's prewar authoritarianism. The third, Minister of Commerce Wilhelm Siering, was a fairly colorless union functionary. In contrast, the DVP contingent consisted of a jovial, rotund former high school teacher, Otto Boelitz, as minister of education, and a thin-lipped, ascetic archetype of the old-style Prussian civil servant, Ernst von Richter, as minister of finance. The DDP undoubtedly had the weakest representative in the cabinet. The new minister of agriculture, Hugo Wendorff, was formally trained in the field, but he was not a well-known political figure; his previous post as prime minister in the small northeast German state of Mecklenburg-Schwerin did not put him in the limelight. Among the Center party cabinet members, the minister of social services, Heinrich Hirtsiefer, turned out to be a surprise. This position had originally been left vacant in the expectation that Adam Stegerwald would return to his old post. The head of the Catholic trade unions, however, decided to turn his back on Prussian affairs. His successor was also a Catholic trade union functionary, but, in contrast to Stegerwald, he sympathized with the left wing of the Center party.

The Prussian cabinet was dominated by Braun, Severing, Boelitz, and Richter. Indeed, some contemporary accounts pictured Richter as the "actual political motor" of the government, probably because as one fiscal crisis followed another in 1923–1924, it was he who represented the cabinet most frequently in public.[12] This view is undoubtedly an exaggeration; historians have left no doubt about the effectiveness of Otto Braun's leadership in the prime minister's office. Braun worked hard to maintain and even augment the powers of his office. He was able to expand the role of his personal staff, delegating many routine tasks to his chief of staff and personal confidant, Robert Weismann.[13] He also gained the approval of his colleagues for a formal codification of the powers of the prime minister.[14] At the same time Braun, by recognizing the limitations of his authority, was instrumental in forging a spirit of trust and cooperation within the cabinet. When the DVP rejected his proposal that the prime minister receive weighted voting rights within the cabinet, he accepted the defeat without rancor and did not raise the question again.[15]

Good personal relations among the cabinet members were an asset for the coalition, but they alone could certainly not assure the success of the venture. Coalitions are cooperative agreements among parties, not individuals, and in the final analysis, success or failure of a coalition in the context of parliamentary democracy depends as much upon well-functioning legislative processes as upon a smoothly operating executive branch. It has already been pointed out that the original reservoir of mutual trust among the four coalition parties was not large. For this reason the two smaller coalition partners, the DVP and the DDP, had insisted upon a number of institutional safeguards to ensure that the legislative leaders of the parties were able to monitor and control the coalition. The DVP demanded the reestablishment of the system of parliamentary state secretaries, which had fallen into disuse after the resignation of its initiator, Wolfgang Heine.[16] In addition, at the urging of Alexander Dominicus, until his resignation from the party one of the DDP's parliamentary leaders, the coalition partners had also agreed to the establishment of a formal multipartisan committee in the Landtag, modeled upon a similar body in the Reichstag.[17] The latter group's ostensible function was to provide a forum in which the coalition parties could negotiate compromises among themselves before differences of opinion emerged into the open. Specifically, the partners agreed that any hostile interpolation directed at a cabinet minister by a member of one of the coalition parties had to be submitted to the multipartisan committee prior to its placement on the agenda of the Landtag.[18] In addition, the initiators of the multipartisan committee at least implicitly hoped that the body would permit the parliamentary delegates a greater role in the formulation and execution of governmental policy.[19]

As originally envisioned by its proponents, the multipartisan committee had the potential for changing the balance of power between legislature and executive in Prussia; in the Reichstag the institution all but paralyzed the cabinet's powers of initiative. But in Prussia this did not occur; the parties of the grand coalition accepted the continuation of the division of power that had been successfully established since early 1919. The legislature did not interfere in the cabinet's right to initiate and administer policies, while the government recognized the Landtag's control functions. Leaders of the two government branches, for the most part, did not attempt to challenge each other's sphere of authority.

All of the ministers were members of their parties' Landtag delegations, but the prime minister, to take but one example, rarely attended meetings of the SPD's caucus. At the same time, the ministers, including the newly appointed DVP cabinet members, were quick to reject what they saw as unwarranted interference by their colleagues in the legislature in the functioning of the cabinet.[20] One test of will came quite early in the life of the coalition. The Landtag caucus of the People's party demanded that the cabinet submit drafts of the government's inaugural policy declaration to the parliamentary caucuses of the coalition parties for their approval before it was delivered as part of the prime minister's "State of the State" address to the full Landtag. The DVP minister gave only pro forma support to the demand of their own parliamentary caucus, and when Braun curtly rejected the demand altogether, the DVP quickly withdrew its request.[21]

As a result of the routine day-to-day cooperation within the cabinet and the skillful parliamentary management on the part of the leaders of coalition parties, the formal safeguards for intracoalition cooperation quickly fell into disuse. The multipartisan committee was never called into session to deal with a coalition crisis.[22] In fact, it seldom met in formal session. Instead, weekly informal meetings by representatives of the coalition parties took the place of formal gatherings by the multipartisan committee. The informal sessions also served as a forum "for working out a common reaction to current political questions," but they lacked the drama and publicity of formal meetings.[23] These mechanisms served their purpose very well, notably reducing, for example, the number of interpolations from the ranks of the coalition parties.[24]

Linkage and Reich-Prussian Relations

While the establishment of the grand coalition in Prussia had been made possible by severing the linkage of Reich and state coalitions, this was clearly not an issue that would remain dormant for long. In view of the precarious parliamentary balance in the national parliament, the parties in the Reichstag were frequently tempted to use the linkage issue in order to put pressure on present or potential coalition partners at the federal level. In addition, there was a pragmatic and practical side of the question. Whatever their ideological and political differences, the Reich and Prussian cabinets recognized that in times of acute crisis cooperation between them was of vital importance.

As an issue of partisan politics the linkage question was first raised by the DVP and the Center party. Shortly after the DVP ministers took their places in the Prussian cabinet, the People's party demanded that it be permitted to join the Reich cabinet.[25] At this time the national cabinet was a Weimar coalition, headed by a left-leaning Center party chancellor, Josef Wirth. With the addition of the DVP, Reich and state would have been governed by parallel grand coalitions. The DVP emphasized then and in the months to come that its demand was not intended to signal dissatisfaction with the Prussian coalition. On the contrary, Prussian leaders of the People's party doubted the feasability of cooperating with the DNVP,[26] and even after the reunification of the USPD and the SPD, the DVP publicly denied reports that it would now leave the coalition in Prussia because the Social Democrats had moved too far to the left.[27]

For different reasons, influential leaders in the Center party also wanted to include the DVP in the Reich cabinet. Stegerwald and the right wing of the Center party strongly favored increased cooperation with the DVP in order to locate the fulcrum of the Catholic party further toward the right of the political spectrum.[28] In contrast, Wirth and the left-wing forces in the Center party hoped to involve the DVP to broaden the coalition in support of the policy of fulfillment. They were particularly anxious to associate the powerful industrial and financial interests that had close ties to the DVP with a grand coalition in the Reich in order to solve what by late 1921 was becoming an increasingly unmanageable financial crisis.[29]

Despite good intentions on all sides, during the term of office of Wirth's second cabinet (26 Oct. 1921–22 Nov. 1922), parallel grand coalitions remained an elusive and unrealized goal. The difficulties lay primarily with the SPD. Some influential voices among the Social Democrats did endorse the linkage concept, particularly as the success of the Prussian coalition demonstrated the feasibility of working with the DVP, but the majority of the SPD delegation in the Reichstag refused to accept the burden of governmental responsibility.[30]

Still, at the level of practical cooperation, Reich-state relations were relatively good during the tenure of the Wirth cabinet, far better than under Wirth's successor Cuno. There were a number of reasons for the era of good feeling. Leaders in both governments shared a commitment to the threatened republic; Wirth was a *Herzensrepublikaner,* not a *Vernunftrepublikaner.* The relationship was also improved after Prussia's old nemesis, Erich Koch-Weser, no longer headed the Reich Ministry of the Interior. His successors did not attempt to resurrect the earlier plans for dissolving Prussia.[31]

This did not mean, however, that all points of friction had been eliminated. In addition to personal antagonisms among some Reich and Prussian ministers,[32] the two jurisdictions supported differing concepts of post-1918 German federalism. The state regarded itself as primus inter pares among the *Länder.* The grand coalition protested no less vehemently than its predecessors against Reich policies it saw as slights to Prussia's eminence among the states. The cabinet and the coalition parties jointly issued a "protest in the strongest terms" when it appeared that the Reich favored Bavarian representation over Prussia's membership of the board of directors of the Reichsbank.[33] Similarly, the Prussian government requested that the Reich permit Braun to participate in the London negotiations that would eventually lead to the agreement on the Dawes plan. In contrast, the Reich government felt it had to escape Prussian tutelage if the federalism envisioned in the Weimar constitution were not to atrophy. Although Prussia regarded it as an unnecessary duplication of effort and staff,[34] the Reich insisted that to avoid being dependent on Prussian personnel in administering Reich legislation, the federal government had to expand its territorial administrative offices in the areas of finance, justice, and transportation. The Reich also curtailed the long-standing practice of having a Prussian official present as observer at Reich cabinet meetings, and the Reich denied Prussia's request for representation in London as an infringement upon its constitutionally guaranteed prerogative in foreign policy.[35]

Wirth's second Reich cabinet resigned in November 1922 after the SPD rejected the chancellor's formal proposal to include the DVP in the Reich government.[36] The fall of the Reich government involved Prussia only very indirectly, since all of the coalition parties, including the various factions of the SPD, supported the continuation of the grand coalition in the state.[37] Reich-state relations, however, took a decided turn for the worse under Wilhelm Cuno, Wirth's successor.

The new chancellor was a prominent businessman with good international connections and a personal favorite of Reich President Ebert.[38] Cuno moved well in society, a quality that would presumably facilitate diplomatic negotiations with Germany's former enemies.[39] The chancellor had no formal ties to any particular party, but he was neither apolitical nor nonpartisan. A Catholic, he stood somewhere between the right wing of the Center party and the DVP, and at the time of his appointment he seemed most comfortable with the views of the Papen faction in the Center party or the positions of the Bavarian People's party.[40]

Cuno's sympathies for the right encouraged some elements in the Center party as well as the DNVP to raise the linkage issue in a new form. These opponents of the Social Democrats' strong position in Prussia were waiting for an opportunity to use the "Prussian lever" in order to force the SPD out of the Prussian cabinet and to reduce what they saw as left-wing dominance in the Prussian Center party.[41] Members of the Center party and the Catholic caucus of the DNVP initiated behind-the-scenes intrigues against Heinrich Hirtsiefer, the minister of social services, as a leading exponent of the center party's left-of-center course in the Prussian cabinet.[42] The German Nationalists were also untiring in pointing out that while the DNVP supported Cuno's concept of national unity, the Prussian government (and particularly Severing as minister of the interior), combated forces on the right side of the political spectrum that both Cuno and the DNVP considered legitimate members of the national unity front. Once the SPD had been eliminated from Prussia, the DNVP suggested, parallel bourgeois coalitions with a strong rightist focus in the Reich, in Bavaria, and in Prussia would cooperate to confound Germany's external enemies.

Seductive calls from the right did not deter the Prussian Center party from its course, but they were not entirely without effect of the DVP. When the DNVP announced plans to introduce a vote of confidence against Severing at the end of April 1923, the head of the DVP's Landtag delegation, von Campe, wrote to the minister of the interior to express his fear that the attitude of the SPD in the Reich made it difficult for the DVP in Prussia to reject the DNVP's proposal out of hand.[43] But the supporters of the grand coalition skillfully countered the rightists' moves. Deliberate leaks to the press exposed the attacks upon the welfare minister.[44] Severing reacted to von Campe's admonitions by denying for the record that his colleagues in the Reichstag pursued excessively leftist policies. He added that in any case the Prussian Social Democrats were not responsible for the actions of the Reichstag delegation. Above all, however, he reminded the DVP that linkage cut both ways. A vote for the DNVP's motion of no confidence would provoke a government and political crisis in Prussia, but any attempt to topple the Prussian government would also call forth sharp Social Democratic opposition to the Cuno government and undoubtedly force its resignation.[45] The moderate bourgeois parties were not willing to risk the consequences of a new crisis and the resulting polarization in the midst of the most dramatic foreign policy crisis since the debate over the acceptance of the Treaty of Versailles. In a roll-call vote on the DNVP's motion of no confidence on May 4, 1923, only the German Nationalists and the Economics party voted for the resolution; the DVP delegation cast its ballots unanimously against the resolution and for Severing.[46]

The power of the linkage issue in the hands of a determined Prussian coalition was demonstrated a few months later when the state government set in motion a series of developments that unseated the Cuno government. By the summer, the Reich government had lost virtually all credibility in the occupied Ruhr area. (This will be discussed later.) The mood of the urban proletariat grew worse from day to day as the Reich authorities increasingly ignored the local Committees for the Resistance *(Abwehrausschüsse)* which had been organized to keep passive resistance from growing violent, while seemingly casting a blind eye on the acts of sabotage and putsch preparations of the radical right.[47] The result was a rapidly accelerating polarization in the Ruhr. As right-wing radicals seized the initiative, union leaders found it increasingly difficult to prevent left-wing radicals from gaining support among their rank-and-file members.[48] Even State Secretary Hamm, Cuno's personal assistant, admitted that "if the radicals on the right make the slightest attempt to stage a coup, the resistance front on the Ruhr would be in utmost danger of collapse."[49]

This was the situation when the Prussian government in July 1923 decided to express its "extreme concern," and requested a joint meeting of the Reich and Prussian cabinets to work out clear guidelines for the further conduct of Germany's Ruhr policy.[50] Cuno argued that German resistance might well have to continue through the winter and into the following spring, but he held out no hope that even then the German policies would be successful in persuading the French to withdraw.[51] During the meeting the most vociferous critic of the Reich's policies was not a Social Democrat, but a member of the Center party, Heinrich Hirtsiefer.[52] It thus came as no surprise that on the day following the joint cabinet session, the Berlin organ of the Center party, *Germania,* began to publish a series of articles attacking the Reich government's handling of the Ruhr crisis.[53] The lead article contained no byline or author, and the Center party issued an official denial that the piece expressed either the party's official position or that it was inspired by the party, but the statement was given little credence.[54] Additional remarks by spokesmen for the bourgeois parties in the Cuno coalition undermined the chancellor's position even further, and in August the Cuno cabinet resigned.[55] Since the Prussian government had initiated the attacks on the Cuno government, the fall of the Reich cabinet had no repercussions for the state. Indeed, the cabinet ministers did not even have to be called back from their vacations.[56]

The hapless Cuno experiment was followed by a grand coalition under the chancellorship of Gustav Stresemann. For a few months the political Reich-Prussian linkage was actually reestablished. It became possible largely because of the parties' good experience in working together as part of the grand coalition in Prussia.[57] Stresemann had come to see the Social Democrats in a different light on the basis of the Prussian experience; he now praised Otto Braun and Carl Severing for their unswerving support of Germany's national cause.[58] Eugen Leidig, a leading member of the DVP's Landtag delegation, asked Severing to act as midwife in the formation of the grand coalition in the Reich, but the minister of the interior later reported that he did not even need Leidig's request; he "would have volunteered his services anyway."[59]

The Reich-Prussian linkage was not of long duration. The Stresemann cabinet was able to end the passive resistance in the Ruhr, but it floundered soon afterward in dealing with the domestic difficulties that followed in the wake of the decision to end the conflict with France. At the end of October a majority of the government approved the takeover by the Reich of the state administrations in the *Länder* of Saxony and Thuringia.[60] The two states had been governed by "unity front" coalitions, that is, governments composed of both SPD and KPD ministers. The bourgeois parties saw these as a threat to the internal security of the Reich and approved—with varying degrees of enthusiasm—the use of Reichswehr troops in order to federalize the state administrations. The Social Democrats opposed this decision, or more precisely, demanded that at least similar measures be adopted against the equally antirepublican, but radical right regime in Bavaria. When the bourgeois ministers refused to move against Bavaria, the Social Democrats resigned from the Reich coalition, and on November 3, 1923, the Stresemann government fell.[61]

With the SPD back in self-imposed isolation, the time seemed ripe in the fall of 1923 for another attempt at linkage with a right-of-center focus—in other words, *Bürgerblöcke*, in the Reich and in Prussia.[62] Bourgeois political leaders from Stresemann to Stegerwald argued that the time had come to share governmental responsibility with the German Nationalists.[63] The DNVP agreed, but the party felt the time was also ripe for far-reaching changes in the political and constitutional fabric of Germany. The German Nationalists demanded membership in a national cabinet that was free of parliamentary control by the Reichstag, the dismissal of Stresemann as chancellor, and the establishment of a *Bürgerblock* cabinet in Prussia that would embark on a full-scale purge of the civil service as its first item of business.[64] The DNVP did not insist upon heading the two cabinets; the German Nationalists were willing to join a Reich government headed by Stegerwald, provided the DNVP were represented in the Reich and the Prussian cabinets "in numbers commensurate with its strength."[65] On the evening of November 28, the DNVP issued its demands in the form of a public ultimatum to the other bourgeois parties: the latter had to decide within twelve hours if they were prepared to form *Bürgerblock* cabinets with the DNVP in both the Reich and in Prussia.[66]

The time did not seem inauspicious for the DNVP's ambitions. In the Reichstag, all members of the DVP and a majority of the Center party were anxious to burden the DNVP with a share of governmental responsibilities. The left-wing minority in the Reich Center party would be unlikely to reject a *Bürgerblock* coalition if Stegerwald headed it. Stresemann had already indicated that he would be willing to continue as foreign minister in a Stegerwald cabinet.[67] In Prussia rumors abounded that the DVP delegation in the Landtag, as well as members of the Center party, were tiring of the grand coalition and anxious to break their ties to the Social Democrats.[68]

But the scheme failed again. The Democrats and Social Democrats in the Reichstag simply rejected the DNVP's ultimatum.[69] The DVP and Center party were somewhat more diplomatic, but in the final analysis equally unaccommodating. The stumbling block was the Reich-Prussian linkage, precisely the aspect of the DNVP's proposal that was of primary importance to the

German Nationalists. The bourgeois parties were willing to accept the DNVP's participation in the Reich government, but they were not prepared to "add a crisis in Prussia to that already existing in the Reich." Essentially, the DNVP paid the price of the radicalism of its Prussian wing. The DVP emphasized that during the Ruhr conflict the DNVP had consistently sided with the Communists in the Prussian Landtag, rather than support the government's effort to stabilize the situation during the long crisis.[70] The Center party, too, denied the efficacy of the linkage argument. The head of the Center party's caucus in the Landtag, Porsch, noted with seeming naïveté that a right-of-center cabinet in the Reich under Stegerwald would be an excellent complement to the grand coalition in Prussia. Both reflected the voters' sentiments in the two jurisdictions. In contrast, a right-of-center *Bürgerblock* cabinet in Prussia would only serve to drive the SPD into the arms of the Communists and the working masses onto the streets. For these reasons, it was incumbent upon the Center party to reject the Prussian aspects of the DNVP's demands.[71]

The DNVP-sponsored linkage scheme failed in the fall of 1923, but a few months later the Reichstag elections of May 1924 brought new contours to the German political landscape. In view of the SPD's tendency to remain on the sidelines of government and the German Nationalists' success at the polls, it was clearly difficult to exclude the DNVP from any national coalition. Indeed, all of the moderate bourgeois parties now welcomed the participation of the DNVP in the Reich government. On May 15, 1924, they formally invited the DNVP to enter into discussions on the formation of a new Reich cabinet, stipulating only that the Conservatives would have to recognize the Weimar constitution and accept the London Accords—that is, the economic and financial settlement of the reparations issue embodied in the Dawes Plan. The offer was conspicuously silent on the future of Prussia. This was no accidental omission. The DDP, DVP, and the Center party all continued to reject the demand for immediate and full-scale linkage. Even the right Liberals, who found the DNVP's desire to join the Prussian government "thoroughly understandable," rejected a simultaneous reshuffling of the two cabinets.[72]

The DNVP responded to the moderates' proposal with a set of maximal counterdemands. The German Nationalists insisted upon the immediate resignation of Marx (the current Reich chancellor) and of Stresemann, the election of former Grand Admiral Tirpitz as Reich chancellor, renegotiation of the London Accords, and an immediate reorganization of the Prussian cabinet.[73] The set of conditions clearly reflected the view of the party's radicals, like Ernst von Schlange-Schöningen, who urged the party leaders to make no compromises in their drive for power.[74] But the DNVP's national leaders soon demonstrated flexibility in their negotiating stance. When the Center party and the DVP insisted that Marx and Stresemann had to remain in the cabinet, and rejected any consideration of Tirpitz as Reich chancellor, the DNVP quickly offered Hergt instead of the imperial admiral.[75] The party also seemed to recognize that a renegotiation of the London Accords was not a realistic goal.

The German Nationalists remained adamant, however, on the Prussian linkage question. And on this issue the negotiations deadlocked. The DNVP insisted upon the simultaneous reorganization of the Reich and Prussian governments, while the moderate bourgeois parties were equally insistent that, as the Prussian DDP leader Otto Nuschke put it, "Prussia has nothing to do with [the negotiations.]"[76] After two weeks, the German Nationalists broke off the discussions, citing as the reason for the failure of the negotiations the unwillingness of the moderate parties to agree to fundamental changes in Germany's foreign and domestic policies and, "particularly" their lack of cooperation in Prussia.[77]

Why did the moderate bourgeois parties prove, from the DNVP's point of view, to be so singularly uncooperative? To a large extent the answer lies in the pervasiveness of the concept of Prussian *étatisme* among the leaders of the moderate bourgeois parties in the state. They feared that simultaneous, DNVP-led *Bürgerblöcke* in the Reich and in Prussia would polarize political opinion in Germany's heartland to the point where a complete breakdown of law and order and the possibility of civil war could not be dismissed. The Reichstag elections had resulted in massive gains not only for the German Nationalists, but also for the Communists. Yielding to the Prussian demands of the DNVP, and as far as the state was concerned that meant increasing the influence of the extremist forces led by men like Schlange-Schöningen, could only exacerbate an already tense situation. Schlange-Schöningen himself had long sought this sort of confrontation in order to "cleanse" the domestic situation, but the moderate bourgeois parties were not willing to follow him down this road.

The May negotiations failed, but as long as the DNVP and its allies remained the strongest bloc in the Reichstag, efforts by the German Nationalists to participate in *Bürgerblock* cabinets at the federal and especially the state level would continue.[78] The German Nationalists were determined to control Prussia. The former crown prince, who had excellent connections with the radicals in the DNVP but who was not given to subtleties of expression, urged the Conservatives to demand "above all a Prussian government without Severing."[79] Throughout the summer and fall the German Nationalists seemed to edge closer to their goals. Reports of tensions in the Prussian grand coalition—some of them true—circulated, especially during the summer months when there was the traditional lull in newsworthy items.[80] Since the Prussian cabinet did indeed fall a few months later, both some contemporary participants and later historians were persuaded that the primary cause of the eventual crisis in the winter of 1925 should be sought in the DNVP's summer initiatives.[81] That argument is not persuasive. It is noteworthy, for example, that on the eve of the dramatic vote in the Reichstag on the implementation of the Dawes Plan, there was no corresponding crisis atmosphere in Prussia. Indeed, it proved difficult to assemble a quorum of Prussian ministers for a cabinet meeting during the tension-filled days of mid-August.[82]

Nevertheless, it was obvious that the DNVP would renew its quest for cabinet status when it became clear that only the German Nationalists could provide the votes needed for the acceptance of the Dawes Plan.[83] This time the DNVP concentrated its approaches on the Center party. A team from the Conservatives headed by Hergt began discussions with von Guérard and Lammers, two leading members of the Center party's right wing, who had been designated as spokesmen by that party's Reichstag delegation. (It should be noted that the national chairman of the Center party, Reich Chancellor Marx, was not directly involved in the negotiations, and did not know the details of the offer made by his party's negotiating team.)[84] The negotiators for the Center party and the DNVP had widely differing recollections of the proposals made by each party after the talks had ended and failed, but it appears that Guérard and Lammers essentially offered to form a Reich government with the DNVP and agreed to support the protective agricultural tariffs demanded by the German Nationalists, if the DNVP supplied the votes needed to pass the enabling legislation necessitated by the London Agreements.[85] Both sides agreed that they were far apart on the Prussian issue: the DNVP insisted on linkage, the Center party rejected it.[86]

Although the Conservatives were rebuffed in what was clearly their primary goal, the DNVP promptly fulfilled its end of the bargain. On August 29, 1924, the "impossible" happened;[87] exactly half of the members of the DNVP delegation voted for the enabling legislation. However, the resulting furor among the rank and file forced the party's national leadership to return to a set of maximum demands in order to appease the dissatisfied elements in the party.[88] The DNVP now demanded the immediate resignation of Reich Chancellor Marx, a formal note to the Allies stating that the Reich had not been responsible for the outbreak of World War I, and, once again, the simultaneous creation of *Bürgerblock* governments in the Reich and in Prussia. The moderate bourgeois parties again rejected the package. The Center party could hardly disavow its own national leader as chancellor, the note on war guilt would have negated much of the Versailles Treaty, and the linkage of Prussia and the Reich was no more acceptable in August than it had been in May.[89]

When negotiations resumed in October, the German Nationalists had a new national chairman, Winckler. He seemed to have learned something from the failure of the previous negotiations as well as from his own observations in the Landtag. Recent developments in Prussia had demonstrated that it was unrealistic to insist upon immediate changes in the state. When the DNVP introduced a motion of no confidence against Severing in the Landtag at the beginning of September as a sort of trial balloon, Joseph Hess's unwavering support of the minister of the interior convinced even the most optimistic German Nationalist that there was no real chance of an imminent rift between the Center party and the SPD in Prussia.[90] As a result, the DNVP now quietly dropped its demand for linkage and concentrated on the Reich alone.[91]

The Prussian issue did not return to the limelight until the results of the December elections were in. They confirmed the DNVP's pivotal position in the Reichstag, and attested to the party's significant strength in the Landtag. On the basis of numbers alone, then, the DNVP was fully justified in renewing its demand for a major share of executive power in both the Reich and state. Moreover, the German Nationalists fully expected that they would join a Prussian *Bürgerblock*. According to press reports, the DNVP demanded at least four ministerial posts in Prussia (including that of prime minister and minister of the interior). Among the specific names floated were Hergt as prime minister and Count von Westarp as minister of the interior.[92]

But coalitions are partnerships, and despite the conclusions of some historians, the evidence that in December the DNVP's potential partners were enthusiastic about a Prussian *Bürgerblock* is not very convincing.[93] To be sure, the DVP Reichstag delegation on December 10 voted to commit itself to bringing the Conservatives into the Reich government.[94] A number of the DVP's Landtag delegates were present for the discussion, and according to one observer, the Prussian delegates recognized the need for simultaneous *Bürgerblock* cabinets in the Reich and Prussia.[95] But the testimony of this observer, Eduard Dingeldey, is suspect: the future national chairman of the party (who succeeded to the post after Stresemann's death in 1929) was a member of the extreme right wing of the People's party and enthusiastically favored working together with the German Nationalists. Other political leaders noted in contrast that the resolution of the DVP's Reichstag delegation pointedly contained no reference to Prussia.[96] Clearly, if the DVP would not spearhead the drive for linkage, the other moderate bourgeois parties would be even more hesitant. The omission was not lost on the DNVP's leadership, which, contrary to the demands of the radicals, decided not to press for simultaneous linkage at this time.[97] Instead, the DNVP's leadership was content to provide three ministers in the Reich "cabinet of personalities," which took office in January 1925. It was headed by Hans Luther, a former mayor of Essen with no formal party affiliation.

By the end of 1924, the DNVP's linkage strategy of using the Reich lever to force its way into the Prussian cabinet had clearly failed. True, a Prussian government crisis developed in the winter and spring of 1925, but it had indigenous causes that deserve a separate section in this chapter.

The Grand Coalition and the Ruhr Crisis of 1923

During the grand coalition's terms of office, Reich and state were confronted with the most serious challenge to the viability of the republican institutions since the Kapp Putsch, the so-called Ruhr crisis. The state's handling of the challenge provides useful insights for the evolution of Reich-state relations, the functioning of Prussian parliamentary democracy in times of stress, and, perhaps most interesting, the application of the grand coalition's concept of Prussian *étatisme*.

Like most German politicians, Prussia's leaders were convinced that the French (and the Belgians, but they were regarded as France's junior partners with no aims of their own) decided to occupy the Ruhr for primarily political rather than financial reasons. In the Prussian view, France was attempting to sever the occupied areas (almost all of which were within the boundaries of Prussia) from the state. The truncated state, according to the Prussian interpretation of French motives, would then have disintegrated, preventing it from functioning as *Reichsklammer*. The final result would have been the fulfillment of France's long-term ambition, the destruction of German unity.[98]

The interpretation of France's motives as directed above all against Prussia's territorial integrity and political stability in turn led to serious differences between the Reich and state on the value and forms of German resistance. The Reich cabinet and especially Chancellor Cuno himself regarded the Ruhr crisis primarily as a test of wills between Germany and France in which a German "victory" was predicated upon demonstrating high morale on the "home front."[99] From this perspective, it was essential to show that regardless of French pressure Germany would not yield to the foreign enemy. As noted earlier, to impress France with Germany's will to resist, the Reich government was anxious to enroll as many segments of German political opinion as possible in the national unity front. These included the organizations of the far right. From Cuno's point of view, the major political danger lay not in the potential infiltration of the resistance front by the forces of the nationalist, antirepublican radical right, but in the consequences that would follow if France detected cracks in the support for the government's policy. If the nation remained united, Poincaré, the French prime minister, realizing that he could not destroy Germany's will to resist, would eventually be forced to negotiate an acceptable compromise with the Reich.[100]

Prussia (and the leaders of some of the other *Länder*) saw some grave dangers in this scenario. To begin with, the Prussian cabinet insisted that the advantages of heroic resistance had to be weighed against the dangers of economic chaos and disintegration that would enable left and right extremists to overthrow the republic and cast Germany into the throes of civil war. Equally important, Cuno's willingness to integrate the radical right into his unity front was counterproductive from the Prussian point of view. The state's leaders repeatedly pointed out that in view of the numerous clandestine ties between these organizations and the Reichswehr,[101] giving a free hand to the rightist paramilitary organizations might easily involve the Reich in military adventurism.[102]

The state was particularly concerned about what it regarded as the Reich's irresponsible policies in the east. It was obvious to all but a handful of fanatics that any military actions in the west were foolhardy, but there were some who argued that moves against Poland as France's major ally might have a better chance of success and indirectly weaken the French position. Prussia was not reassured when the Reich government refused to give categorical assurances that this might not happen.[103] The Prussian government felt that military adventurism brought with it not only the potential danger of losing further (Prussian) territory in the east, but much more significantly, that such mobilization might be used by the antirepublican forces to stage a putsch and overthrow the constitutional government. It was no secret that a number of paramilitary groups were as anxious to turn their weapons against the republican government in Prussia as they were to use force against Poland. For this reason the state, beginning in the middle of March 1923, pressured the Reich government to modify its policy of resistance and to enter instead into serious negotiations with France.[104] The Cuno government refused, so that for the moment Prussia could do little but to give its resistance efforts forms that were consistent with Prussian *étatisme*. That meant primarily identifying state, nation, and republic. The Prussian ministers worked hard to forge a unity front that included all prorepublican forces, from the Social Democratic to moderate bourgeois groups, but excluded the extremist forces on both the right and left.[105] Prussia portrayed itself as the "rock on which the republic stands."[106]

The fundamental differences over the nature of the emergency also led to some serious jurisdictional disputes between the Reich and Prussia. The Reich, contending that this was a foreign policy matter, demanded total control over the coordination of all aspects of the resistance effort.[107] Prussia, on the other hand, insisted that the state government be fully consulted before any decisions were taken, since the *Länder* had the primary constitutional responsibility for preserving internal security.[108]

As the Franco-German deadlock continued, cooperation between the two levels of government became increasingly difficult.[109] A serious conflict arose in March 1923 over the question of whether action should be taken against the German *Völkische* Freedom party (Deutschvölkische Freiheitspartei, or DVFP), already discussed. The Prussian Ministry of the Interior regarded the DVFP as part of a conspiratorial network that was plotting a rightist putsch against the republic, and on March 27 Severing prohibited the DVFP throughout Prussia.[110] However, Prussia's attempts to coordinate the state's moves against the party with the Reich government were unsuccessful. The Prussian government twice asked for an opportunity to present its case against the DVFP to a joint meeting of the two cabinets, but the Cuno government was not interested.[111] In fact, when Prussia moved on its own, the Reich government registered procedural and political objections.[112] The Reich cabinet was concerned about the political repercussions from the dissolution of the DVFP, which it regarded as a legitimate part of the national unity front. Knowing this, the party attempted to mobilize support in order to prevent the Prussian dissolution order from taking effect. Graefe, the head of the DVFP's national organization, reminded Cuno that Severing's "excesses" were in reality a "declaration of war" against the chancellor's unity program; Prussia had sabotaged the Reich government's efforts.[113] In addition, Graefe pointedly reminded Cuno of the close ties between his party and the Reichswehr, an argument that unwittingly lent additional justification to the Prussian moves against the DVFP.[114]

Eventually, of course, the Prussian point of view on the Ruhr crisis prevailed. The Cuno government fell in August and its successor, the grand coalition cabinet headed by Gustav Stresemann, moved quickly to abandon passive resistance. By that time, however, the danger signs of social disintegration, of which the Prussian leaders had warned all along, had become so advanced that immediate and drastic action was required. As a first priority Germany had to restore confidence in its currency. Passive resistance had been financed through the printing press, as the Reichsbank issued a flood of unsecured paper currency. The resulting hyperinflation not only brought the country to the brink of economic collapse, but also developed a dynamic of its own, so that a simple official announcement that the printing presses would be stopped was in no way sufficient to reassure the market forces. The German government had neither credit nor credibility among either the international banking community or its own people. Currency stabilization was predicated upon balanced Reich and state budgets and visible credit lines. The first required massive cutbacks in government outlays, the second was obtained— in return for massive concessions—from German private industry and later international loans.[115]

Even then a major problem remained. Since the Germans remained convinced that France had primarily political aims, both the Reich and state cabinets were fearful that the French would attempt to undermine any efforts to stabilize the mark by manipulating the reparation and occupation costs charged to Germany. In part this could be accomplished by requiring immediate payment of the reparations due for 1923.[116] Far more dangerous, in German eyes, was the assessment of uncontrollable occupation costs. To prevent the "hole in the west" from sucking out and undermining the new, stable *Mark,* the Reich and Prussian governments as well as local leaders in the Rhine-Ruhr area for a time in the fall of 1923 seriously considered a bizarre and dramatic course of action that later became known as "the policy of abandonment" *(Versackungspolitik).*

The policy of abandonment was never put into effect and, in looking back on the events, all concerned came to the realization that it would have been an unwise move.[117] But such retrospective rethinking should not obscure the historical record that for a time the *Versackungspolitik* had widespread support from a diverse group of national, state, and local political and business leaders.[118] To be sure, the advocates included men with completely contradictory motivations. On the one hand ranged some Reichswehr officers who wanted to abandon the Ruhr area as a prelude to a new war with France. At the other extreme were the handful of separatists who hoped to sever the Rhineland from Germany and transform it into a French protectorate.

But most of those who supported the policy of abandonment did so for the economic and administrative benefits it promised to bring. Concretely, the policy of abandonment meant that the new, stable currency would be issued only in the unoccupied parts of Germany, thereby presumably saddling France and Belgium with the responsibility for maintaining the economy of inflation in the occupied areas. Otto Braun summarized the reasons as follows: "The important thing now is to keep the unoccupied areas viable, so that in the future the occupied parts will be able to lean on a healthy, unoccupied segment of the Reich."[119] The high point of support for the policy of abandonment probably came during a high-level conference in Hagen on October 5, 1923.[120] The meeting was attended by leaders of the Reich and Prussian government as well as prominent politicians, industrialists, and bankers from the Rhineland and Westphalia. The lord mayor of Duisburg, Karl Jarres, chaired the session. In Hagen all participants acknowledged that Ruhr and Reich faced a politically hopeless and economically disastrous future if a way could not be found out of the present catastrophe. Reich Chancellor Stresemann conceded in the course of lengthy remarks that the Reich government regarded the occupied areas as at least economically lost to Germany for the time being, which meant that the Rhineland and Westphalia would have to look to the occupying powers for short-term support. At the same time, Stresemann restricted the policy of abandonment to economic measures. The Reich chancellor specifically refused to authorize any group or individual in the occupied areas to conduct political negotiations with Allied military or political authorities. Throughout the discussions at the Hagen conference, the

Prussian representatives were conspicuous by their reticence. Prime Minister Braun delivered only brief remarks to the effect that the Prussian cabinet agreed with Stresemann's assessment of the situation.

There was no united response from the representatives of the occupied areas to the gloomy message from the nation's and the state's leaders. Interestingly, the delegates from the heavily industrial Westphalian region rejected all parts of the abandonment policy, but the lord mayor of Cologne, Konrad Adenauer, and other spokesmen for Rhenish interests argued that while Stresemann's analysis was realistic, the conclusions he drew were not. They pointed out that if the territories were to be left to their own devices economically, they would also have to be free to consider changes in their political status. In the words of one prominent banker, "Whoever tampers with the currency question also raises political issues, and had better have the courage to do so."[121] Adenauer and the Cologne banker Louis Hagen had already submitted a plan to Stresemann in September that envisaged the creation of a separate Rhenish state with authority to issue its own currency.[122] The Rhenish representatives insisted that the Reich and Prussia should give official (albeit secret) authorization to regional representatives to begin negotiations with officials of the occupying powers.

As a result of the sharp differences of opinion among the participants at the Hagen conference, the decisions on a future course of action were a compromise. The participants designated a Committee of Fifteen (Fünfzehnerausschuss), whose members represented the major political parties and economic interest groups in the Rhine-Ruhr area. The committee was specifically authorized to conduct negotiations with Allied representatives on economic questions, but its powers to discuss political issues remained deliberately vague.[123] The Prussian government approved both the composition and the terms of authorization of the Committee of Fifteen, a decision that was tantamount to endorsement of the policy of economic abandonment.[124]

The decisions at Hagen were based upon the illusion that it was possible to draw a clear distinction between economic and political abandonment. It did not take the Prussian cabinet long to conclude that this distinction had no basis in political reality. Konrad Haenisch, the former minister of education who now served as district director of Wiesbaden (a district in the occupied area), hastened to warn the cabinet that once the Ruhr had been economically severed from the rest of the Reich, it would be permanently lost to Germany.[125] A few weeks later, Ernst Mehlich, one of the union leaders in the region and a close personal friend of Interior Minister Severing, issued an equally stern warning. He, too, noted that if the policy of economic abandonment were put into effect, the occupied area would also be politically lost both to the Reich and to Prussia.[126]

The negotiations of the Committee of Fifteen also developed a dynamic of their own. Within the group, representatives supporting—or at least leaning toward—the Adenauer line formed a majority, so that the committee's negotiations with the chairman of the Interallied Control Commission, Tirard, soon involved discussing a new administrative structure for the occupied areas, as well as the pressing economic issues.[127] The group was perhaps inadvertently encouraged on this path since the new Reich cabinet under Wilhelm Marx (the Center party leader had succeeded Stresemann as chancellor in November 1923) seemed less insistent upon maintaining the distinction between political and economic negotiations than had its predecessor. Paul Moldenhauer (DVP), the minister of finance in the Marx cabinet, had been a member of the Committee of Fifteen, and he was the author of a proposal to create an independent administrative structure for the Rhineland with its own taxing authority and an autonomous budget. "It appeared" that Moldenhauer's plan enjoyed Marx's support.[128]

Fearful that the policy of abandonment would lead to the political disintegration of Prussia and consequently the Reich, the state in early December unequivocally renounced both economic and political abandonment.[129] In the cabinet meeting of December 3, the ministers adopted a resolution stating:

a. Prussia will neither explicitly nor implicitly agree to any changes in the legal status [of the occupied areas] that violate the Constitution; rather, the state will oppose in the sharpest form possible all efforts in this direction;

b. Prussia rejects as a matter of principle any treatment of the occupied areas that is different from that of the unoccupied areas.[130]

The cabinet's renunciation of the abandonment policy had the effect of uniting virtually all political groups in the state behind the government, much as the cabinet's rejection of the Versailles Treaty had done in 1919. Most Landtag delegations drafted formal statements in support of the renunciation, and the majority of the population in the occupied area, too, felt a sense of relief that the cabinet's resolution had cleared the air.[131]

In view of the division of power between the Reich and the states, Prussia's decision to oppose the *Versackungspolitik* had a largely symbolic value. Only the Reich government had the authority to translate sentiment into policy directives, and despite Prussian urging, the Reich government was slow to follow the state's example of reversing its policy in the occupied areas.[132] Until the end of the year, the Reich currency commissioner proceeded on the tacit assumption that a Rhenish Bank of Issue would be established.[133] The Reich was also reluctant to remove itself from the day-to-day administration of the occupied areas.[134] Not until early February did the federal cabinet agree that questions affecting the Ruhr and the Rhine areas should be treated only in consultation with Prussia and that "under no conditions [would the Reich agree to solutions to the Rhineland problem] which would touch upon the sovereignty of Prussia and the Reich."[135] The Rhenish supporters of the policy of abandonment were even more reluctant to desert the cause. As late as January 1924, the Prussian undersecretary in the Minister of the Interior, Freund, felt obliged to address a sharp reprimand to Adenauer because the lord mayor of Cologne was continuing his discussions with Tirard.[136]

A stable new currency, the *Rentenmark,* which was issued throughout the Reich in mid-November, eventually put an end to any discussion of the *Versackungspolitik,* but the existence of the financial vacuum in the fall of 1923 seemed to encourage a new wave of proposals for territorial and political *Reichsreform.* Two significant contributions to the debate were submitted separately by the lord mayor of Königsberg, Lohmeyer, at the beginning of September 1923 and by the minister of defense, Otto Gessler, in February of the following year.[137] The two officials differed in their political outlook and their specific recommendations, but, like the framers of the 1919 Weimar constitution, they regarded change in the relationship of the Reich and Prussia as the key to any meaningful federal reform.

Lohmeyer emphasized the constitutional anomaly in which one level of government, the Reich, had the constitutional authority to determine the parameters and content of legislation, while one state, Prussia, had virtually exclusive jurisdiction over administering these laws in three-fifths of the country. When the two cabinets were of a different political composition, as had been the case for most of the time since 1918, friction was inevitable. To eliminate this chronic problem, Lohmeyer proposed major alterations in the constitutional and administrative structure of Prussia. He urged strengthening the Prussian administration at the provincial and county levels, while minimizing the authority of the state's cabinet. Under Lohmeyer's plan, the Reich chancellor, as had been true for much of the time before 1918, would serve as Prussian prime minister. Most decision-making authority would be concentrated in his hands, while the power of the Prussian ministers was to be limited to administrative supervision of the territorial administration.

Gessler went even further in urging a reduction of Prussia's autonomy. The Reich minister of defense began his reform proposals with the assumption that the "emergency structure embodied in the Weimar constitution" was not working and that an entirely new document was needed. It should provide for the personal union of all Reich and Prussian ministers, and the abolition of the Prussian Landtag. The latter's place would be taken by the Prussian delegates to the Reichstag. Since under these terms "Prussia" would in reality be controlled by the federal government, Gessler proposed that the "state" should annex the smaller north and central German states in order to make the structure of German federalism more rational. "Under ideal conditions," the defense minister argued, only Bavaria, Würtemberg, Baden, Hessen, and the three Hanseatic cities would retain the status of genuine *Länder* under the restructured constitution. These states could then be granted quite extensive rights of home rule without endangering the authority of the now predominant Reich-Prussia.

Neither the mayor nor the defense minister submitted his proposal solely as a contribution to abstract debates on constitutional questions; both pursued specific political goals. Lohmeyer, who had close connections to right-wing political circles, wanted to reduce the power of a state cabinet that since 1918 had been dominated by the Social Democrats.[138] Interestingly, Lohmeyer sent one copy of his memorandum to the chief of staff of the Reichswehr, General von Seeckt. It was no secret that the general was well disposed toward plans that "were primarily [directed] against the red bulwark that was Prussia."[139] Gessler, on the other hand, belonged to the right wing of the DDP. He regarded his proposals as a defense against the possible consequences of a Prussian government dominated by the DNVP, a development he felt would occur "in the foreseeable future." Prussia's absorption by the Reich was a way of forestalling the Conservatives' penetration of the Prussian civil service.

Lohmeyer's and Gessler's plans remained position papers without concrete consequences, since the political prerequisites for their realization were completely lacking. The Reich government was too weak to initiate major territorial or constitutional reforms, and Prussia vehemently opposed changes in the status quo. Among the cabinet members Braun and von Richter were particularly opposed to any consideration of major structural changes, but even the Center party, traditionally the most vociferous advocate of reducing Prussia's power, was content to continue working within the present federal context.[140] In addition, the states that could expect to benefit from a restructured Reich were reluctant to raise the constitutional question. Even Bavaria had no wish to stir up a new constitutional crisis while Hitler's Beer Hall Putsch was still a fresh memory.

The Cabinet Crisis and the Election of the Reich President, 1924—25

The cabinet of the grand coalition governed the state for three crisis-ridden years. Ironically, it fell on the threshold of what came to be known as Weimar's golden era, the years of relative political stability and economic recovery that began with the currency stabilization and ended with the Great Depression. It is appropriate to begin the analysis of the government crisis with the December 1924 Landtag elections, although they did not directly cause the long interregnum that followed. The Prussian parties agreed to hold state elections simultaneously with the Reichstag contest for tactical and financial reasons.[141] Landtag elections had to be scheduled no later than February 1925 in any case, holding them in December 1924 saved the parties the additional expense of a separate campaign two months later. There was also a feeling that elections might clear the air. Acrimony and tensions among the coalition partners had certainly increased in the wake of the budget cuts (to be discussed below) necessitated by the currency stabilization.[142]

The Prussian parties entered the election campaign without prior coalition commitments. But it is equally true that there is no evidence that any of the parties of the grand coalition had irrevocably decided to abandon the combination. On the contrary, a man who was certainly close to the inner circles of the cabinet, Braun's personal assistant Robert Weismann, thought the coalition would return to office after the election, albeit with changed personnel.[143] Legislative leaders similarly anticipated the continuation of the coalition.[144] In addition, the cabinet's first actions after the contest seemed to confirm this impression. The ministers gave a unanimous vote of support to Reich President Ebert, who was at the time the object of particularly vicious attacks from the DNVP and the radical right.[145]

In purely mathematical terms, the Landtag election results permitted a number of parliamentary coalitions while precluding others. The Weimar parties (the SPD, DDP, and Center party) and the opposition were almost equal in strength (223 to 222). In comparison, a grand coalition could expect a solid vote of confidence; the four parties together had 268 delegates. On paper, a *Bürgerblock* could also obtain a parliamentary majority.

But coalitions, of course, are political as well as arithmetic combinations. A *Bürgerblock* required the cooperation of the Center party and the DDP. The latter, for one, was not willing to go this route. Immediately after the election, the party announced that it continued to support the grand coalition, although it hoped to augment the cabinet's parliamentary strength by the addition of the Economics party.[146] That hope proved illusory. The WiP would only consider joining a *Bürgerblock,* and even then wanted to exclude the DDP from the coalition.[147] The Center party, too, continued to have doubts about the wisdom of entering into an unequal relationship with the DNVP. Quite aside from the very real policy differences that existed between the two groups in Prussia, the Center party had to consider its self-chosen role as the pivot of German politics. It was already a member of a *Bürgerblock* in the Reich; to keep the symmetry of its political profile, the Center party needed to balance its membership in the right-of-center Reich cabinet with a left-of-center Prussian government. Finally, a "government of national unity" which both the SPD and the DNVP would join, was politically no more realistic after the December elections than before.

Formally, the cabinet crisis of 1925 began with the decision of the DVP's delegation in the new Landtag to withdraw the party's ministers from the grand coalition. That decision was reached after four hours of debate on January 4, 1925. During the meeting, whose importance was underscored by the attendance of the party's national leader Gustav Stresemann, the two DVP ministers argued strenuously against withdrawing from the government.[148] But a majority of their colleagues decided, as the *Vorwärts* put it, to sacrifice specific Prussian interests to the party's national strategy, that is, to seek parallel bourgeois cabinets in the Reich and in Prussia.[149]

The DVP's action came as a surprise to its coalition partners.[150] Moreover, while it was certainly possible for the DVP to demand the establishment of linked *Bürgerblöcke,* it was quite outside the party's power to bring them about without the cooperation of the Center party and the DDP. The new chairman of the DVP's Landtag delegation, Rudolf von Campe, who was not particularly well like by the DNVP, certainly knew the difficulties involved.[151] Why, then, did he agree to abandon the grand coalition at a time when the prospects for a *Bürgerblock* were at best uncertain?

In retrospect, it appears that at least von Campe did not really intend to destroy the grand coalition. Rather, he set out upon some very complicated maneuvers whose intricacies and goals were misunderstood by most of his contemporaries. There are indications that von Campe, aided by von Richter, was pursuing a two-step scenario after the decision of January 4. After it became clear that a majority of the Landtag delegation opposed continuing the grand coalition, von Campe set out to prove that there was no realistic alternative to the combination that had governed since 1921. To expose the faulty political reasoning of his colleagues, he proposed a government that was a thinly veiled cabinet of national unity.[152] If the DNVP, as expected, refused to join such a coalition, the DVP could then with a clear conscience return to the grand coalition, though the cabinet might officiate under a different name.[153] In effect, von Campe was confident that the already apparent resentment against the decision to link the DVP's political fate with that of the Conservatives would increase as the DNVP's Prussian radicals made their demands public.[154]

The multipartisan committee representing the parties of the grand coalition met on January 5 to consider the new political situation. The group consisted of Grzesinski and Hirsch from the SPD, Schreiber and Höpker-Aschoff from the DDP, Porsch and Herold from the Center party, and von Campe, Stendel, and Schwarzhaupt from the DVP. The prime minister also attended the session. The DVP delegates argued that the cabinet should resign and afford the new Landtag an opportunity to form another government, rather than await a formal vote of no confidence from the legislature. Representatives from the other coalition parties disagreed strongly. They rejected the suggestion out of hand, noting that the resignation of the cabinet was neither constitutionally or politically mandated. The DVP's partners took such a hard line because by this time they were convinced that the People's party was not concerned about the constitution, but was determined to bring down the grand coalition at any cost.[155] The scene was repeated in a cabinet meeting on the following day. Boelitz and Richter presented the DVP's case; the other ministers opposed it. The prime minister, contrary to his usual practice, then called for a formal vote. Boelitz and von Richter remained in the minority, and consequently had no choice but to make good their threat to resign from the government.[156]

Up to this point the DVP's scenario had been followed, but now an unexpected development occurred. Contrary to what von Campe had expected, Boelitz's and von Richter's resignation did not lead to the fall of the entire cabinet. Instead, the other ministers remained in office with Braun temporarily taking over the administration of the Ministries of Finance and Education. Braun and his colleagues from the Weimar parties were convinced that their decision, "We will continue to govern," foiled what they saw as the DVP's deliberate attempt to create a power vacuum and government crisis in Prussia.[157]

In retrospect, the villains and heroes seem less clearly drawn. It is possible that Braun's quick and perhaps rash action did not so much solve the crisis as provoke it. With the benefit of hindsight, it is doubtful that von Campe actually expected either a "national unity" or a *Bürgerblock* coalition to emerge from the crisis. Instead, it appears more likely that von Campe, after forcing a pro forma resignation of the coalition, expected the government would return to office politically unchanged, but with a few new faces on the ministerial bench.[158] A change was especially likely at the Ministry of the Interior. Severing's resignation would appease the right wing of the DVP, and it was well known at this time that Severing himself was anxious to give up his burdensome office for reasons of health.[159]

After the Weimar parties had interpreted the DVP's initiative as a declaration of political confrontation, such subtleties became moot; Prussia was about to enter its second interregnum. It will be recalled that the Prussian constitution of 1920 facilitated the election of the prime minister, but made it rather difficult for the designated leader of the government to form a cabinet. Article 45 provided that the Landtag select the prime minister by secret ballot without debate. This meant that each election involved a positive decision on an individual candidate, precluding, for example, the possibility that the DNVP and the KPD would cast their votes for the same man. This was not the case, however, when the prime minister–designate presented his cabinet to the legislature for a vote of confidence. The parties in the Landtag were now able to exercise a negative decision. Consequently, in the following weeks and months the Landtag elected a number of prime ministers, but repeatedly refused them votes of confidence when they presented their cabinets.

On January 14, the rump Braun cabinet asked the Landtag for a formal vote of confidence, while the opposition proposed a series of resolutions of no confidence.[160] A Communist resolution which asked for a motion of no confidence because the government had ruled against the interests of the proletariat, was voted on first. The result was a tie ballot, 221 to 221, which meant that under the Landtag's parliamentary procedures the motion had been rejected.[161] Voting in favor were the KPD, the DNVP, the DVP, the *Völkische,* and the Economics party; the Weimar coalition parties, to the surprise of some of its members voted solidly for the government.[162] At the same time, the government recognized that the outcome of the balloting was a pyrrhic victory, since it obviously did not command a majority in the legislature. At the urging of the Center party, the ministers now formally resigned, though they stayed in office as a caretaker cabinet until the legislature could select a successor.[163]

There now began a feverish search for a solution to the impasse. The parties looked for new allies and new combinations. The DDP still hoped to win the support of the Economics party for the Weimar coalition, the DNVP indicated its willingness to join a coalition headed by the venerable leader of the Center party, Porsch, and the SPD was torn between reminding its potential partners of the dangers of political polarization and mobilizing its supporters in the streets in order to demonstrate that such a polarization had taken place.[164]

On January 30, Braun was reelected as prime minister–designate. From the distribution of the votes it became clear that six members of the DVP delegation had cast blank ballots. This raised hopes that the DVP might "tolerate" a government of the Weimar coalition headed by Braun.[165] Although the SPD was willing to make far-reaching concessions to the DVP, and Braun and Severing labored almost to the point of physical exhaustion to gain the DVP's good will, the effort failed.[166] On February 5 Braun returned his mandate to the legislature.

In the course of the negotiations with the DVP, it appeared that one of the stumbling blocks to bringing the People's party back into the coalition was the presence of a Social Democratic prime minister at the head of the cabinet. As a way out of the impasse, the SPD agreed to yield the post of prime minister to the Center party.[167] After reluctantly dropping from consideration their first choice, the speaker of the provincial legislature in the Rhine province, Horion, because of his lack of political experience at the state level, Hess and the Center party approached the former Reich chancellor and head of the center party, Wilhelm Marx.[168] On the surface Marx did, indeed, seem an ideal compromise candidate to obtain the confidence of the DVP and possibly even the DNVP.[169] He had worked with the People's party in the Reich government, and was known to favor a coalition of "national unity" stretching from the SPD to the DNVP. His election seemed to confirm the early hopes. He received 233 votes in a runoff election against von Richter—more than the votes of the Weimar coalition parties.

Marx entered into intensive negotiations with all potential members of a government of "national unity." The SPD did not seem to reject such a combination out of hand.[170] In the face of considerable opposition within the Landtag delegation, the SPD leaders even reduced their demand for ministerial posts to a minimum. They insisted only on the Ministry of the Interior, and even here the Social Democrats were willing to accept a nonparty minister if Marx found it necessary to camouflage the political color of his government by the appointment of various civil servants.[171] In contrast, the Conservatives remained adament. They rejected any cabinet over which Social Democrats exercised influence.[172] Under these circumstances, Marx quickly abandoned his efforts to form a government of "national unity."[173]

Foiled in his attempt to form an all-encompassing coalition, Marx fell back upon a cabinet of the Weimar parties with minimal SPD representation and a conservatively worded policy declaration. Like Braun he hoped that Stresemann would be able to induce the DVP to "tolerate" the new ministry, or at least to cast blank ballots on a motion of confidence.[174] Despite much optimistic anticipation, it was all in vain.[175] By a vote of 221 to 217, the Landtag failed to give the Marx government a vote of confidence, in part because (as already described) two members of the Center party delegation refused to vote for their party's chairman. Marx was not discouraged, however. He set out on a new round of discussions, and intended to submit his cabinet for a new vote of confidence on March 3.

Before the new vote was scheduled, the unexpected death of Reich President Friedrich Ebert, and the need to elect a successor, gave an entirely new dimension to the Reich-Prussian linkage question.[176] To be precise, the composition of the Prussian coalition became one of the bargaining chips as the party leaders scrambled to find candidates who could appeal to a broad coalition of forces and voters.

The nomination process had actually begun ever earlier. On February 12, some two weeks before Ebert's illness and death, a number of delegates from the bourgeois parties and various nationalist extraparliamentary groups met to consider the possibility of running a common candidate for the office of Reich president. The coordinating efforts were spearheaded by the wartime Prussian minister of the interior, von Loebell. The February 12 meeting resulted in an agreement among the participants to support a common right-of-center candidate, though no specific names were mentioned.[177]

The negotiations among the rightist and moderate groups intensified after

Ebert's death on February 28. As usual, the Center party occupied a key position; any joint bourgeois candidate who was not supported by the Catholic party would lack credibility. In fact, various Center party candidates were aired, but so was the Prussian price the Catholics would have to pay for obtaining the other groups' support of a Center party candidate. There were press reports that the DVP and the DNVP were willing to support either Stegerwald or Marx for Reich president, if the Center party were willing to abandon its cooperation with the Social Democrats in Prussia.[178] The DNVP added for good measure that the Center party would have to accept the support of the *Völkische* as part of the bargain.[179] Conversely, the Center party could retain Prussia, so to speak, if it supported a Protestant as the joint bourgeois candidate for Reich president.[180]

In the end the Loebell committee produced no joint candidate. Instead, most of the bourgeois parties ran their own candidates. The Democrats fielded Willy Hellpach, the prime minister of Baden; Marx was the nominee of the Center party.[181] General Ludendorff ran a very inept campaign for the *Völkische*. Only the DVP and DNVP agreed to support a joint candidate, Mayor Jarres of Duisburg.[182]

In contrast to the initially high hopes for cooperation in the bourgeois camp, there was never any serious consideration of a joint candidate by the SPD and KPD. The Communists nominated their chairman, Ernst Thälmann, and the SPD put up Otto Braun. The former Prussian prime minister, who had urged the three Weimar parties to support a joint republican candidate, had no illusions about his own chances of winning.[183]

The campaign was marked by polarization and a great deal of mudslinging.[184] Wounds that had barely healed, such as the controversy over the *Versackungspolitik* in the Ruhr, were torn open again. Under the provisions of the Weimar constitution, a candidate had to win a majority of the votes cast in the first round of balloting in order to be elected. Predictably, none of the candidates did. In fact, each received pretty much the same number of votes that his party had obtained in the last Reichstag elections.[185]

Without a majority winner on the first ballot, the election of the Reich president required a second round two weeks later. This time a plurality of votes sufficed for victory, but under the Reich constitution's hyperdemocratic election provisions the parties were not restricted in any way in the second round of balloting: candidates could drop out in favor of joint nominations, but it was also possible to nominate entirely new candidates who had not run in the first round.

The results of the first election demonstrated the precarious balance between supporters of the republic and its opponents in Germany. In the second round of balloting either a joint candidate representing all the bourgeois parties or a candidate supported by the Weimar coalition had good statistical prospects of winning not only a plurality, but a majority. In fact, in Prussia the candidates of the Weimar coalition had actually outpolled the opposition in the first round. (See table 7.)

Table 7. Prussian Results of Balloting for President, March 1925

	Party	Candidate	Popular Vote (in thousands)
Weimar coalition	SPD	Braum	5,063
	Center party	Marx	3,074
	DDP	Hellpach	918
	Total		9,055
Opposition parties	DNVP & DVP	Jarres	6,644
	BVP	Held	122
	Völkische	Ludendorff	146
	KPD	Thälmann	1,896
	Total		8,808

Source: Compiled from Vorwärts, no. 152 (31 Mar. 1925).

The nomination of a joint candidate of the Weimar parties had profound implications for the still unresolved cabinet crisis in Prussia. Any agreement by the Center party and the SPD on a common candidate would have meant a sharp break between the Catholics and the Conservatives in Prussia, and all but precluded the possibility of forming a coalition between the latter, while considerably increasing the likelihood that a coalition of Weimar parties would return to govern the state.[186] (Incidentally, it was noted even during the first campaign that the Weimar parties continued to work closely together in the steering committee of the Landtag.)[187] Moreover, a decision on the presidential candidate had repercussions for the political color of the Prussian prime minister. The only candidate with good chances for widespread support among all of the Weimar parties was Wilhelm Marx.[188] He was popular among SPD voters, while a Social Democratic candidate would have alienated a large number of middle-class voters and the DDP was too small an organization to carry out a full-scale presidential campaign. However, the DDP and SPD insisted that the highest offices in the Reich and Prussia should not be held by members of the same party. The election of Marx, then, would have precluded a prime minister from the Center party.[189]

All of these calculations applied equally forcefully to the groups on the right—the self-styled nationalist camp. Unlike their rivals among the Weimar parties, however, they had no suitable candidate to unite their ranks. There was general agreement that in the second round of balloting Jarres stood little chance of winning against a candidate supported by all of the Weimar parties.[190] For this reason they searched for a new and more charismatic candidate. Among the names for whom trial balloons were started, that of the retired Field Marshal Paul von Hindenburg figured prominently. Hindenburg's candidacy was supported vigorously by leaders of the Prussian DNVP such as Winckler and von Schlange-Schöningen. At the same time, it had to be recognized that the nomination of the World War I hero would seriously alienate especially the left wing of the Center party and drive it into the arms of the SPD. As a Protestant, Junker, monarchist, and career officer, the former field marshal personified the old authoritarian Prussia. To a lesser extent, a bandwagon for Hindenburg placed the DVP in a difficult position. The right Liberals would find themselves in the dubious company of the *Völkische* and unreconstructed reactionaries. The party decided to support the general, but a significant number of the DVP's rank and file remained uneasy about the decision.[191]

The second campaign between the eventual nominees, Marx, Hindenburg, and Thälmann (whom the KPD had nominated again), was no less bitter than the first. Particularly the confrontation between the former Prussian field marshal, who was supported (among others) by a variety of organizations on the extreme right, and the Catholic judge and parliamentary leader whose entire political career had taken place since the revolution, could not avoid being a plebiscite on political and socioeconomic developments since 1918.[192] At the same time, the vicious attacks on Marx as a Catholic and republican had the effect of drawing the parties of the Weimar coalition closer together.[193] Hindenburg won the national contest, but in the Prussian electoral districts Marx gained a plurality—albeit a meager one—of 86,677 votes, attesting to the continued popularity of the Weimar parties in Germany's largest state.[194] (See table 8.)

Understandably, during the two campaigns little progress had been made in finding a solution to the Prussian cabinet crisis. Marx was relected prime

Table 8. Reich and Prussian Results of Balloting for President, April 1925

Candidate	Popular Vote	
	Reich	Prussia
Hindenburg	14,655,641	9,206,153
Marx	13,751,605	9,292,830
Thälmann	1,931,151	1,244,817

Source: Statistisches Jahrbuch für das Deutsche Reich 1926 (Berlin, 1926), p. 451; *Mitteilungsblatt der SPD* 2 (May 1925).

minister–designate on March 10, and his goal remained a government of "national unity," but after he had been selected as the joint presidential candidate of the Weimar parties, both the DVP and DNVP broke off further negotiations with him on Prussia.[195] Marx resigned as prime minister on March 18, blaming the Conservatives for his failure to form a government. In what was for him an unusual outburst of emotion, he later wrote:

> I assure you that nothing has upset me so much in a long time as the developments in Prussia. It became increasingly evident that the rightist parties were playing with the welfare of the Prussian state in an extremely irresponsible manner. They wanted to force the Center party to follow a path that it neither wanted nor could follow.[196]

Two weeks later, on March 31, a development occurred that contemporary observers later described either as a parliamentary farce or as an unfortunate misunderstanding: the election of the DDP's Landtag delegate Hermann Höpker-Aschoff as Prussian prime minister.[197] In reality, the thought of electing a Democrat to the post was not all that farfetched. Since neither the Center party nor the Social Democrats had been able to nominate candidates that could successfully form a government, it seemed reasonable to let the Democrats try their hand. Höpker-Aschoff was popular among some Center party leaders, and since at this time the Catholics insisted they would "under no circumstances" support Braun's reelection, the SPD, too, had to be content with a DDP candidate.[198] Moreover, Höpker-Aschoff was not disliked among the SPD members, and he had the reputation of having good contacts to the Economics party and the Hanoverian (Guelph) party, both of whom would add important numerical strength to the government's position in the Landtag.[199]

Like his predecessors, Höpker-Aschoff at the time of his election had of course no cabinet to present and no assurance of a vote of confidence for his government. He hoped to form a cabinet composed of ministers from the Weimar parties that would be "tolerated" by the Economics party and the Hanoverians, but both rejected his overtures.[200] When the SPD, after hesitating for a few days, also rejected Höpker-Aschoff's political base as too weak to support a government, the Democrat returned his mandate three days after he was elected.[201]

In the meantime, it will be recalled, discussions were proceeding among the Weimar parties to find a joint presidential candidate. As its price for supporting Marx, the SPD demanded that the Center party accept Otto Braun's reelection as Prussian prime minister. Despite its earlier resolution, the Catholic party agreed. On April 3 Otto Braun was once again elected to the post of prime minister.[202] On the same day, Marx received the final approval of the Weimar parties as their joint candidate for the presidential office. The linkage between the two political decisions was thus an honest compromise, though in retrospect it was of greater benefit to the SPD than to the Center party.[203] At the beginning of April it could not be foreseen that Marx would lose the election; on the contrary, at the time of his nomination, it appeared likely that the rightists would turn to the colorless Jarres for a second time, thus all but assuring Marx's success.[204]

After Marx had lost the presidential contest, criticism arose against the Center party's "giveaway" in Prussia. In a private letter, Marx assured one of the critics that the Center party had merely promised its votes for the election of Braun as prime minister, much as it had supported Höpker-Aschoff. Any question of a subsequent vote of confidence for the entire government was still open.[205] The argument was a bit disingenuous. In terms of political realities, after Marx and Höpker-Aschoff had failed to form a government in Prussia, and in view of the decision by the Weimar parties to support Marx as joint candidate for president, the only possible solution to the Prussian government crisis was the renewal of the Weimar coalition under the leadership of the SPD.[206]

Still, there was no cabinet (serious negotiations on the distribution of ministerial posts was delayed until after the Reich presidential contest) and the balance of power in the Landtag remained precarious. The Weimar parties considered new state elections. They had done well in the state during the presidential balloting, and it was probable that the Weimar parties would do even better if the right had to campaign without Hindenburg's coattails. On the other hand, there was the fear that the voters would resent a major new campaign, and that the resulting alienation would benefit antiparliamentary candidates of the left and right. On balance, the Weimar parties decided to delay a decision on new elections and agreed to await the outcome of a vote of confidence on the new Braun cabinet.[207]

Both the prime minister and the parliamentary leaders of the coalition parties proceeded with utmost tact in forming the new cabinet. Representatives of the Center party asked for the cooperation of the DNVP one last time, while Braun appealed to the DVP to reestablish the grand coalition.[208] The German Nationalists flatly refused,[209] and the DVP, too, would not join the government. Braun also took great care not to alienate any factions of the Weimar parties. The cabinet that Braun introduced to the Landtag on April 28 was, with the exception of the prime minister, identical to Marx's group of ministers. In addition, the new government accepted in full the policy declaration of its predecessor.[210]

Still, a vote of confidence in the Landtag remained in doubt. As a first tactical maneuver, the coalition parties decided to await a resolution of no confidence by the opposition parties, rather than initiate a positive vote of their own. They imposed strict party discipline to prevent defection from their own ranks.[211] In addition, the Weimar parties empowered the prime minister to announce before the vote in the Landtag that if the government lost the vote of confidence, the legislature would be dissolved and new elections scheduled.[212] Ballotting took place on May 8. A motion of no confidence was handily defeated, and subsequently a resolution of confidence passed by a vote of 222 to 216. There were no defections from the coalition's ranks, but a small number of opposition delegates abstained.[213]

Conclusion

When the third Braun cabinet took its seats on the ministerial bench, many a Landtag delegate not only must have had a sense of déjà vu, but also must have asked if the long interregnum had been necessary at all. It all seemed more of the same. The new cabinet was another Weimar coalition; three of the six ministers had been in office since 1920.

In retrospect, one must conclude that the cabinet crisis of 1925 could not have been avoided. The cabinet of the grand coalition worked effectively during the years of immediate crisis because there was consensus on the parameters of Prussian *étatisme,* on the need to safeguard the state's political and territorial integrity. Throughout 1922–1924, the Prussian DVP resisted the DNVP's siren call for linking Prussia and the Reich in a resurgence of authoritarianism. With the abatement of the acute domestic and foreign threat to Prussia, *étatisme* lost some of its strength and traditional political differences among the coalition parties reasserted themselves. The state elections of December and the premature resignation of the DVP ministers created a political deadlock in Prussia that paralyzed the parliamentary system which had worked so well until then. Political maneuverings by the Prussian parties failed to resolve the impasse; only unforeseen events outside of Prussia brought movement to the rigid political fronts.

The Reich presidential election had the effect of restoring the viability of Prussia's parliamentary democracy and returning the Weimar coalition to power in the state. The decision by the DVP and the DNVP to run a common candidate on the first ballot pushed the Center party toward greater cooperation with the DDP and SPD. The polarization was reinforced by the second balloting for president. Hindenburg's unexpected nomination as the candidate of the right and the viscious antidemocratic and anti-Catholic campaign that his supporters waged, forced the Weimar parties to rally around the republican candidate Wilhelm Marx. After Hindenburg's election, the incentives for cooperation were even greater. A Weimar coalition cabinet in Prussia was more than ever necessary as a counterweight to what was expected to be the dominance of the right in the president's office.

CHAPTER 7

Personnel, Security, and Administrative Policies, 1922–1925

As a venture in political cooperation, the survival of the grand coalition was dependent upon a shared commitment to a sense of Prussian *étatisme* by the members of the cabinet and their parties in the Landtag. A key to the long-term viability of the parliamentary democracy as a system of government in Prussia, however, was the cabinet's ability to effect concrete decisions in the area of what in German bureaucratic parlance is termed "domestic politics" *(Innenpolitik)*. These concerns included, it will be recalled, appointments to the corps of "political civil servants," high-level police officials, and the vast thicket of structural administrative reforms. The record of the Weimar coalition that governed Prussia from 1919 to the end of 1921 had not been impressive in this area.

At first glance it seemed unlikely that the grand coalition would do much better. On the contrary, the addition of the DVP to the cabinet increased the group's political diversity and the chances for conflict. At the same time the government could not ignore *innenpolitische* decisions. During the first two years of its existence, as the unending series of domestic and foreign policy crises from the assassination of Rathenau to the occupation of the Ruhr shook the foundations of Reich and state, survival of Germany as a republic quite literally depended upon Prussia's choices for political administrators and police chiefs. A different, but politically no less precarious situation developed in the fall of 1923 and throughout 1924. Massive budget cuts at all levels of government were necessary if Germany was to prevent the value of its new currency, the *Rentenmark*, from being eroded by a new wave of inflation induced by uncontrolled government spending. A prime target of the budget slashes at the state level were personnel and administrative outlays. Traditionally, these items constituted the major cost factor in the *Länder* budgets, and there was general agreement that these line items had exploded beyond all reason since the war. But the budget cuts had political as well as financial dimensions. On the one hand, the need to cut positions and streamline the administration provided the state with a powerful incentive to put into effect long-standing plans for structural administrative reforms, but on the other the necessary reductions in the number of civil servants and other state employees could unleash fierce battles among the coalition partners as to who should be dismissed for what reasons. The cabinet's ability to work out acceptable compromises in this volatile field was additional if surprising evidence of the resilience of Prussia's young democracy and the commitment of her new rulers to preserve the state as the foundation of the Reich's political stability.

Personnel Policies and Appointments

Initially many observers predicted that friction over personnel policies and appointments would be a major point of conflict among the coalition partners and a contributing factor in what was expected to be a short life for the grand coalition. The pundits based their judgment in large part upon the sharply contrasting personalities and ideologies of the two ministers primarily responsible for personnel decisions. On the one hand there was Carl Severing, as minister of the interior the man charged with maintaining domestic security and nominating personnel appointments to the cabinet. In addition, his ministry was responsible for drafting any proposed legislation on structural administration reforms. In the previous government Severing had personified what the opposition called the "Severing system," that is, the deliberate policy of placing officials with decidedly prorepublican leanings in key positions throughout the Prussian civil service. Among those who had personal reasons for resenting the "Severing system" was Ernst von Richter, now Severing's colleague in the cabinet as the new Minister of Finance. As noted before, the minister of the interior had dismissed Richter as governor of Hanover in the wake of the Kapp Putsch. Not surprisingly, the fired official, who served as de facto head of the DVP delegation in the Landtag, had directed bitter attacks against Severing and his personnel policies.[1] It was thus a pleasant surprise to both men that as members of the same cabinet they worked well together. Indeed, their cooperation surpassed Severing's "boldest expectations."[2]

The unexpected era of good feeling came about largely because the two men, despite their political differences, by now shared a commitment to the republican concept of Prussian *étatisme*. Severing and Richter agreed that in the post—World War I era Prussia had to fulfill its national mission in the form of a parliamentary democracy. In other words, maintaining the republican form of government in Prussia was a prerequisite for the state's ability to function as the rivet that held the Reich together. For this reason, Richter and Severing did not hesitate to cooperate in thwarting the numerous challenges to the republican form of government in state and Reich that arose during their joint tenure in office.

In terms of specific personnel policies, the cabinet early on reached a compromise that essentially continued the pattern of appointments established when the first Braun government had assumed office after the Kapp Putsch in

March 1920. The systematic, "organic," but undramatic democratization of the Prussian civil service continued, and since political positions were traditionally allocated more or less according to the parlimentary strength of the coalition parties, Severing raised no objections to granting the DVP its share of sympathizers among the appointees. Except for the top posts, democratization continue to involve minimal commitment to the republic and the parliamentary form of government; the compromise certainly was not a bar to candidates whose commitment to the republic was less than heartfelt, a category of officials that included a particularly large percentage of DVP supporters. In return, the People's party raised no objection to the dismissal (or nonconsideration for appointment) of avowed monarchists and Conservative agitators.[3]

These principles assured stability and consistency in the area of personnel appointments during most of the cabinet's term of office.[4] Severing quickly rescinded the decidedly right-wing course of his immediate predecessor Dominicus, but, despite a recent court decision affirming the government's right to change the retirement age, there was no wholesale purge of the Prussian civil service.[5] Perhaps as a *quid pro quo* for Severing's moderation, the DVP, after some initial delaying tactics, agreed to retain in office the major officials in the Ministry of the Interior who had been primarily responsible for the personnel policies in the Weimar coalition cabinet.[6] They included the decidedly prorepublican state secretary, Friedrich Freund. The DVP's accommodating stance was particularly remarkable since at the time the terms of the grand coalition were being negotiated, a DNVP insider claimed to know that Freund's dismissal had been a *sine qua non* demand of the DVP before it would agree to join the cabinet.[7]

In the first few months, then, the new government moved cautiously. The ministers not only recognized the lack of a parliamentary mandate for radical changes,[8] but they felt there was no particular need for dramatic measures. Time seemed to favor gradualism. There was some evidence that the domestic political situation was stabilizing, and that the republican form of government was gaining increasing acceptance among the state's voters and civil servants. Newspapers friendly to the government noted with approval the rising tide of activism among youth organizations in the democratic parties, and observers of the official Prussian celebrations marking Constitution Day (August 11) remarked upon the genuine enthusiasm that characterized these occasions in contrast to the lackluster events staged by the Reich government.[9]

Still, not all factions in the coalition parties were content to wait patiently as political administrators genuinely committed to parliamentary democracy oozed into the system. To prevent a recurrence of the cabinet's failures prior to the Kapp Putsch, the Social Democratic party organization was determined to play a larger role in selecting appointments to the Prussian civil service.

The party's Görlitz party congress (September 1921) adopted a resolution ordering the SPD's national leadership to creat a Liaison Office for Civil Servants. It was to be a part of an already existing Coordinating Office for the Political Education of Civil Servants. The new party office was given the task of bringing to the attention of Social Democratic ministers in the Reich and state governments qualified candidates who "held firm Socialist convictions." When the Görlitz congress met, there were no Social Democrats in the Prussian ministry, but the return of Severing to the Ministry of the Interior gave the resolution immediate and practical significance.[10] The SPD's initiative potentially affected relations between the coalition partners, and it raised constitutional issues as well. Ministers from all parties had on previous occasions rejected efforts by their party organizations to dictate personnel choices as unwarranted interference in the decision-making autonomy of the executive. In addition, nominating (not to mention appointing) civil servants who were specifically certified as ideologically reliable by an organ of the Social Democratic party would inevitably lead to similar efforts among the other coalition parties, and thus reduce the ministers' freedom of action to reach compromises in the cabinet discussions.[11] For these reasons the ministers, including Severing, rejected interference from party organizations in personnel policy decisions, pointing to the growth of prorepublican sentiment in the civil service as evidence that there was no need for radical initiatives from the outside.[12]

The cabinet's complacency was shattered by the assassination of Walther Rathenau by right-wing terrorists in June 1922.[13] The foreign minister was a man who had been almost universally respected for his lofty character and force of personality. Even politically conservative civil servants in Prussia were deeply touched by this latest in a series of political murders.[14] But the assassination was doubly shocking because it took place at a time of supposed growing domestic stabilization. As a result, the Rathenau murder had a popular (as opposed to political) impact quite unlike that felt after the death of Erzberger a year earlier. The supporters of the republic formed a solid and vocal front inside and outside the halls of parliament demanding immediate measures to counteract the clear danger from the extreme right.

The Prussian cabinet responded positively and decisively. It issued decrees severely curtaining the freedom of political action and expression for antirepubilcan elements, and, more important, ordered a new review of the personnel in the political civil service.[15] It is indicative of the pervasive influence of republican *étatisme* in the grand coalition that the necessary directives passed the cabinet with the unanimous consent of all ministers.[16] The purge concentrated on the provincial governors and district directors. By the end of August one provincial governor and nine district directors had been suspended; by the end of the year two more governors and three additional district directors were forced to retire. There was never any doubt that these changes in the top ranks of the political civil service had purely political and short-term aims. Their purpose was to appease the anger of the prorepublican political forces,[17] and to assure that the top positions of the territorial civil service were staffed with reliable men at a time of domestic turmoil. The republican leaders of Prussia set out to demonstrate that, unlike other *Länder*, Germany's largest state "had learned something from Rathenau's assassination."[18]

In place of the dismissed officials the cabinet appointed men who were affiliated with or at least close to one of the coalition parties. The specific political assignments were made in accordance with a previously agreed upon distribution key for major political appointments. The selection process involved full-scale consultations among the ministers and the coalition party leaders in the *Landtag*. This ensured that the compromise candidates eventually appointed to sensitive positions were political moderates who acted as effective spokesmen for the coalition rather than as ideologues of their individual party.[19]

The tendency was reinforced by the participation of the provinces in the appointment process. Under the terms of the Prussian constitution, the provincial diets had a consultative voice in the appointment of political civil servants in their provinces. The distribution of political power in the provincial legislatures was often quite different from the parliamentary strength of the parties in the Landtag, with the right-wing parties exercising considerably more influence than in the cabinet and the Landtag. In addition, the coalition patterns were dissimilar. Instead of cooperation among the Weimar parties and the DVP, working arrangements among the bourgeois parties—often including the DNVP as well—that left the SPD (and sometimes the DDP) isolated, predominated in the provinces. All of this meant that while the dynamics of provincial politics did not change the political affiliation of the nominations— the cabinet made sure that only supporters of the parties of the grand coalition were proposed—it did mean that candidates who were well known as party partisans had difficulty obtaining the necessary approbation. Hans Krüger, for example, encountered serious difficulties when the cabinet nominated him to be district director of Hildesheim in the province of Hanover. Krüger, it will be recalled had been a major spokesman for the SPD's left wing after the Kapp Putsch, and the bourgeois parties in the provincial diet refused to confirm his appointment of the grounds that he was too "political." It required considerable exertion on the part of Severing before the provincial diet yielded and agreed to Krüger's installation.[20]

The purge after the Kapp Putsch had left the judiciary largely untouched, but the experience of the last two years had clearly demonstrated that changes in the personnel of this branch of government were overdue. Under the benevolent gaze of Heine and am Zehnhoff as ministers of justice, almost all of the royal judges inherited from prewar times had remained in office, while the few prorepublican additions felt isolated and demoralized.[21] There was no lack of reform proposals—everything from the wholesale purge of judicial personnel and the popular election of criminal judges to thoroughgoing reforms of the system of legal education were suggested—but until 1922 the Ministry of Justice had sidetracked all concrete measures either by ignoring the demands, or by encouraging endless theoretical discussions and conferences which buried the proposals in mountains of paper.[22] Here, too, the murder of the Reich foreign minister spurred the cabinet to action. As a first step, the ministers issued a decree instructing all judges to abstain by either word or deed from activities hostile to the republican form of government. Subsequently, the Landtag passed a law that limited candidates for leading judicial positions in Prussia to reliable supporters of the republican constitution, while the cabinet expanded the scope of applicability of the February 1919 decree permitting early retirement of judges and prosecutors.[23]

As was true of the purge two years earlier, the 1922 changes in the composition of the corps of political administrators was symbolically and qualitatively more important than in terms of its quantitative results. In fact, the actual numbers of civil servants involved in the second purge was small. Even in a region as politically sensitive as Hanover the cabinet changed only three (out of eleven) county commissioners during its three-year term of office. It is true, however, that the dismissals and new appointments which came in the wake of the Rathenau assassination sent signals throughout the civil service.[24] In this sense the turnovers had a long-term effect that continued well beyond its immediate numerical impact.

The momentum generated by the 1922 measures became particularly important during the months of the Ruhr occupation when the cabinet virtually halted any systematic effort to advance the democratization of the political administration.[25] Instead, the cabinet emphasized the need for all segments of the state administration to rally against the foreign enemy.[26] Since Prussia's territorial administration formed a living link between the occupied and unoccupied parts of the Reich, and the cabinet adopted a number of procedures in order to maintain Prussia's effectiveness as national administrative rivet. To prevent long-term vacancies in the occupied areas, the Ministry of the Interior adopted the practice of appointing adjuncts to serve as understudies for the county commissioners in the Ruhr. These aides were then in a position to replace incumbent county commissioners when, as frequently happened, the French or Belgian military authorities expelled the latter for violating directives by the military authorities.[27] In order to promote understanding among officials in the East for the difficulties in the West, the government also routinely assigned officials from regions east of the Elbe to serve in the occupied area.

It must be emphasized, however, that in their efforts to forge a sense of political unity among the administrative civil service, the state's leaders never ignored Prussia's status as a republic and parliamentary democracy. A directive issued by the cabinet in February 1923 reminded all personnel offices that only civil servants "who were . . . professionally well qualified, but who were also absolutely reliable supporters of the Republican constitution" should be proposed for appointment or promotion.[28] In July, at the height of the Ruhr crisis, the ministers reemphasized the importance of political considerations in the appointment of administrative personnel. In a decree ostensibly clarifying the necessary qualifications of county commissioners, the cabinet determined that while applicants should in principle be qualified for entry into the higher civil service (that is, should possess a law degree, which would exclude most Social Democrats), in practice the principle could be breached for valid political reasons.[29]

The coalition's choices as county commissioners in the state's frontier areas during the Ruhr crisis were especially important. Political reliability among county commissioners in the areas bordering the Reich's national frontiers was crucial because of the often unclear relationships between the Reichswehr and various right-wing paramilitary groups in the border regions. County commissioners who turned a blind eye or even encouraged such cooperation were indirectly contributing to the downfall of the republic. Here again the cabinet set clear republican signals.[30] To underscore his concern in this area, Severing with the full backing of his colleagues, dismissed two popular county commissioners in East Prussia who had been particularly active in Conservative and antirepublican circles. They were replaced by Ferdinand Friedensburg, a left Liberal who, according to the governor of the province, became "one of the most capable county commissioners."[31] At the same time, contrary to the claims of its Conservative opponents, the cabinet also kept a watchful eye on the extreme left. The ministers insisted that heads of municipal departments who were members of the Communist party (there were no Communists among the governors, district directors, and county commissioners) could remain in office only if they signed a declaration to the effect that in carrying out their official duties they would not be bound by instructions from their party.[32]

Such balanced policies enabled the Prussian civil service to administer the state during the crisis-ridden year of 1923 with a minimum of tension, but the era of currency stabilization and budget cuts that followed created an entirely different set of problems. As noted above, there was general agreement that a balanced state budget (and Prussia's budget had not been free of deficits since

1914) required sharp cutbacks in personnel costs; the cabinet envisioned a 25 percent drop in the total number of state employees.[33] Under these circumstances, instead of debates over the pace of democratizing the civil service, the focus was shifted to protecting the prorepublican elements among the Prussian administrators while cutting back severely on the total number of civil servants.

Equally important, the new budgetary situation brought with it a significant shift of authority for personnel decisions within the cabinet. Prussia's attempts to cut spending involved a cutback in both programs and personnel costs, but in practice the efforts to save money quickly reduced themselves to "who" rather than "what"; virtually no new programs had been authorized since the beginning of 1923.[34] It was understandable that the prorepublican forces feared the personnel reductions would become a one-sided vendetta against democratic elements in the civil service. Particularly vulnerable were the so-called *Aussenseiter*, officials who had been appointed to major posts after 1918, although, for the most part, they did not possess the traditional qualifications for entry into higher ranks of the Prussian civil service. Not only did the *Aussenseiter* have low seniority status, but also since most of them were either members or supporters of the SPD, many career bureaucrats who had come up the seniority ladder resented these "outsiders" as an alien and unwanted element in the civil service.[35]

Until now the minister of the interior had initiated most decisions in this policy area, but it was obvious that if the foremost priority was to cut the budget, the minister of finance would have to play a key role in the decision-making process. The Reich government, which faced essentially the same problems, provided a model for the finance minister's increased authority. At the beginning of October 1923 the national cabinet had voted to give the Reich minister of finance extensive powers to determine the expenditure levels for both operating and personnel outlays for all parts of the Reich administration. His decisions could not be vetoed by the cabinet colleague directly affected, but could only be overruled by a vote of a majority of the entire cabinet.[36] A few weeks later, the Prussian ministry voted to give Ernst von Richter analogous powers. Indeed, the Prussian ministers went further: the finance minister's decisions could be overruled only if the majority of the cabinet voting against him included the prime minister.[37] To implement the reduction in force at the ministerial level, teams of officials from the ministry of finance met with administrators from each of the other ministries to work out acceptable plans for reducing the number of employees in each office.[38] At the subcabinet level, the district directors played a key role in the personnel reduction program, a factor that underscored the significance of the purge which the cabinet had carried out among these officials after the Rathenau assassination.[39] For the most part the cabinet approved the regional officials' recommendations. The ministers merely made sure that the dismissals did not overly disrupt the relative strength of each coalition party's supporters in the political civil service.[40]

As a result of the acute fiscal crisis, then, the minister of finance obtained a position in the cabinet that far exceeded anything envisioned two years earlier when the government was formed. Potentially, the changed circumstances could severely destabilize the coalition; they certainly provided a major test of the functional viability of parliamentary democracy in Prussia. The coalition, the parliamentary system, and the prorepublican forces in the civil service all survived the challenge remarkably well. A key element in the successful operation was the close cooperation between the Ministry of Finance and an eleven-member Select Committee of the Landtag which was set up to oversee the implementation of personnel reductions. The parliamentary committee was headed by two strong and influential leaders of the coalition parties, Rudolf von Campe (DVP) and Albert Grzesinski (SPD). Under their joint direction the group became a model instrument for constructive parliamentary control of executive decisions.[41]

To their credit, Richter and his colleagues acted vigorously to preclude one-sided attacks upon any particular group of civil servants. The cabinet not only rejected giving the traditional civil servants' organizations an institutionalized role in determining whose position would be eliminated, but also issued guidelines emphasizing that in carrying out the layoffs, the "introduction of organic reforms of the internal administration should be speeded up," that is, the reductions should be used to further the government's long-range political goals.[42] The minister of finance reminded all personnel offices in the state that political beliefs or religious affiliations could not be cited as factors in dismissal decisions.[43] Finally, the cabinet used the occasion of the appointment as county commissioner of a prominent Social Democratic member of the Landtag, Richard Hauschildt, to underscore "that the reductions in personnel should not be applied in such a manner that future appointments of *Aussenseiter* to positions of political significance would become impossible.[44] Hauschildt's appointment was particularly significant, since he was taking the place of a retiring career civil servant.

Decrees and guidelines are evidence of policy intent, but they tell little about the actual results of the formal decisions. What effect did the 1923–24 personnel reduction program have on the size and composition of the Prussian civil service? To begin with, as the government intended, in purely quantitative terms most of the burden fell on employees and laborers who were not permanent members of the civil service.[45] Still, a total of 15,001 permanent civil servants *(Beamten)* were dismissed or laid off. The number of high-ranking officials working in the central ministries who lost their posts was small; only 213 positions were eliminated at this level. Most of the 15,000 cancelled positions were in the territorial administration and among Prussia's public school teachers. The territorial administration lost 3340 (22.27 percent) of its civil service force, and in the state's educational system 5873 were laid off.[46] The latter figure included about 10 percent of Prussia's public schoolteachers.[47]

More important, perhaps, than the raw numbers were the qualitative results, that is, the changes in the political composition of the civil service. Critics later charged that the dismissals had seriously set back the democratization process and "eliminated the last republican civil servant."[48] After the fall of the grand coalition, Severing recalled that he had fought a lonely battle for democratization against his reactionary colleagues in the bourgeois parties.[49] Such blanket criticisms are unwarranted. True, some of those dismissed were *Aussenseiter,* but there is no evidence of a systematic campaign against this, or any other, category of officials. Rather, it seems that consistent efforts were made at each level of the review process to weed out the least effective officials within the civil service.[50]

Two other criticisms also fell short of the mark. It was charged that in an effort to match the parallel program in the Reich, the Prussian cabinet had to, cut too deeply into the state's administrative flesh. In contrast to the artificially inflated ranks in the Reich, argued these critics, Prussia had far fewer excess civil servants.[51] True, the Reich's administrative apparatus had expanded very rapidly since 1919, but so had the scope of federal jurisdictions under the Weimar constitution, and in any case Prussia's postwar hiring had also proceeded at an accelerated pace. Another criticism concerned the *ad hoc* and *ad hominem* nature of the curtailment program. Here critics complained that proceeding on a case-by-case basis not only required immense amounts of paperwork, but also gave superiors an opportunity to dismiss able subordinates with whom they did not get along. It would have been preferable, according to these complaints, to have used an across-the-board method, such as reducing the retirement age to 60 or 55 years of age. This process would not only have had the virtue of administrative simplicity, but have provided indirect political benefits as well: there was clearly a general correlation between age and political conservatism in the ranks of the civil service.[52] Unfortunately, such a proposal also ignored political reality. Lowering the retirement age would have restricted the reduction program disproportionately to supporters of the bourgeois coalition parties, and thus have been unacceptable to the SPD's coalition partners.

When the emergency budget slashing formally ended in July 1924, it left behind mixed results and major implications for the future.[53] Some observers professed to find cause for pessimism in the balance sheet. After the fall of the coalition in January 1925, Josef Hess, the parliamentary leader of the Center party, estimated that the total of Prussian civil servants who were members of any of the three Weimar parties was around 10 percent. He also noted that since the revolution only 177 *Aussenseiter* had been accepted into the civil service and given permanent appointments.[54] Hess's point, of course, was to underscore what he regarded as a continuing underrepresentation of the supporters of the Weimar coalition in the ranks of the civil service, but such number games did not fully reflect the qualitative changes that the grand coalition had effected. To begin with, the overwhelming number of Prussian civil servants did not belong to any party, so that Hess's percentage of party members was somewhat misleading. More important, raw statistics were inadequate to express what was perhaps the most profound result of the DVP's entry into the coalition: the republican form of government in Prussia became identified with Prussia itself for many of the more tradition-oriented civil servants. As early as December 1921 the Association of Prussian County Commissioners, the successor organization to the Association of *Republican* County Commissioners, a group originally established to coordinate activities among sympathizers of the Weimar coalition parties, reported a membership of 300, representing about 75 percent of all county commissioners in the state.[55] In effect, then, within a short time after the establishment of the grand coalition a large majority of these pivotal political administrators no longer hesitated to be associated with a professional organization that openly supported the republic. This early trend was reinforced in the next three years. The DVP's participation in the Prussian cabinet had led to a significant increase among the number of *Vernunftrepublikaner* in the ranks of the civil service, so that even after the personnel cutbacks in 1923 and 1924 loyalty to the republican form of government among most of Prussia's civil servants remained assured.[56]

This did not mean, of course, that the budget slashes had no adverse effects on the process of democratizing the state's administrative personnel. The number of *Aussenseiter* likely to be appointed, small in the best of times, would be further reduced as the total number of positions shrank. In addition, rejuvenation of the civil service would be slowed in the future, again partly because of the smaller number of available positions, but also because the expulsion of many civil servants from the occupied Ruhr area by the Allied authorities left a large pool of qualified applicants with seniority status "waiting" (the Prussian technical designation was literally *im Wartestand*) for reappointment.[57] At the end of 1924 the basic agreement among the coalition parties on maintaining the civil service as a pillar of support for Prusso-Republican *étatisme* remained in force,[58] but those advocating a speedier pace of democratization were clearly on the defensive. It was symptomatic that during the negotiations on the formation of a new coalition in 1925, the SPD no longer demanded new initiatives for further democratization of the civil service, but limited its request to protection for those republican officials who remained in office.[59]

Security Matters and the Police Force

No one in the Reich cabinet or the Prussian government doubted that the state had to deploy a reliable and well-trained police force in these years of constant domestic turmoil.[60] The need for such forces was obviously particularly acute during and immediately after the Ruhr conflict, but political disturbances did not end with the abandonment of passive resistance. Only one week after the Reichstag elections of May 1924 came the so-called Bloody Sunday of Halle. A riot broke out when a ceremony staged by rightists to rededicate a statue of a former Prussian chief of the general staff, Hellmuth von Moltke, went out of control. Wild fighting between right-wing extremists and Communists resulted in a number of injuries. The events in Halle (and similar incidents in other localities) not only demonstrated the continuing need for an effective police force to prevent and control urban riots, but they also pointed up a second major security problem in Prussia: the existence of the numerous politicized paramilitary units that plagued political life throughout the Weimar years.[61]

The grand coalition was not particularly concerned about restructuring the state's police forces. The Prussian police was by now regarded as a reliable, if not always sufficiently powerful, support of the republic and the coalition. Instead, the cabinet turned its attention almost immediately to the problem of the paramilitary units. In dealing with this issue, the grand coalition broke sharply with some practices of its predecessor. The Stegerwald government, in cooperation with Reich authorities, had adopted an attitude of benevolent neutrality toward many of the paramilitary groups, especially in border regions. The Prussian minister of the interior, Alexander Dominicus, was unconcerned as Reich and Prussian officials cooperated at least indirectly with a variety of paramilitary outfits in some Silesian districts,[62] And, following the example of his minister, the Prussian plebiscite commissioner in Silesia, Eugen Ernst, was notorious for his lack of purposefulness in confiscating weapons illegally held by various paramilitary groups.[63]

With the support of the new cabinet, Severing reversed these policies; he set out to achieve the complete disarmament of all political paramilitary groups. Even in times of acute domestic danger, as for example during the Ruhr conflict, the government tolerated prorepublican vigilante groups only if they were willing to subordinate themselves completely to the orders of the civil authorities and the regular police.[64]

Contrary to the chorus of complaints from the German Nationalists and their *völkisch* allies, the cabinet was as concerned about left-wing paramilitary groups as it was about the extreme right. For example, in August 1923 the Prussian government formally dissolved the "hundreds" (*Hundertschaften*) set up by the KPD and confiscated their weapons arsenals.[65] Nevertheless, it is true that the cabinet concentrated most of its attention on the groups of the radical right.[66] There were a number of reasons for this. The numerical strength of the rightist paramilitary units was always for greater than that of their Communist rivals. The prevalence of leaders with professional military experience among the extreme right groups made them dangerous as organizers of potential coups. But the cabinet was primarily concerned about the frequently close relationships between extreme right paramilitary groups and the Reichswehr. The problem was endemic throughout the Weimar years, but it became particularly acute during times of heightened domestic or international tension, that is, whenever the radical right and some of their friends in the Reichswehr saw a chance for staging a military putsch to overthrow the republic.

Stegerwald and Dominicus had largely abandoned earlier efforts by the first Braun cabinet to curtail cooperation between the Reichswehr and paramilitary groups, and the Reich Ministry of Defense and the regional military commanders were quite surprised when the new Prussian government, soon after assuming office, presented the Reichswehr with a set of "nonnegotiable" demands designed to force the army to cut its ties with rightist paramilitary groups. In addition, Prussia specifically asked that the Reichswehr cease organizing volunteer units *(Zeitfreiwilligenverbände)* since it was an open secret that most of the volunteers had been and would continue to be members of the rightist paramilitary units. In presenting the Reich government with their demands, the Prussians stressed the doubtful political loyalty of the rightist formations, and consequently the inherent dangers in the Reichswehr's policies.[67] The Reich government rejected Prussia's accusations, and for much of the life of the grand coalition relations between the Prussian government and the Reich minister of defense were acrimonious. Prime Minister Braun complained to the Reich president that "it was difficult . . . to take the Reich minister of defense seriously"; the minister, Otto Gessler, formally protested against Prussian interference in the internal matters of his ministry.[68]

Still, on the concrete issue of relations between Reichswehr and paramilitary groups, Prussia appeared at least for a time to have won its case, largely because the state received support from an unexpected source. General von Seeckt, the Reichswehr's chief of staff, did not share Severing's opposition to the rightists' political views, but he was fearful of the extremists for another reason. Seeckt, who had little faith in the military effectiveness of the paramilitary units, regarded their cooperation with local Reichswehr commanders as a potential threat to his own lines of command.[69] The general discovered that individual Reichswehr district commanders had in the past entered into a variety of agreements with rightwing paramilitary leaders without obtaining either Seeckt's prior permission or even informing him of such pacts. Consequently, Seeckt and Severing—for quite different reasons—agreed in late January 1923 that the Reichswehr would end all forms of cooperation between the army and paramilitary groups by March 31, 1923. Implementation of the agreement was to be overseen jointly by the regional military commanders and the Prussian governors.[70]

In principle the Prussian government had won its point, but in practice the agreement of January 1923 turned out to be a dead letter. With the onset of the Ruhr crisis the Reich authorities increasingly ignored the terms of the pact. Fearful of domestic disturbances from the radical Left and further military action by France or Poland, the Reich cabinet looked upon the rightwing paramilitary groups as potential allies in its quest to strengthen the lines of national defense.[71] Under the excessively benevolent eye of the Reich minister of defense, a number of Reichswehr district commanders continued their cooperation with right-wing paramilitary groups in ostensible preparation for a possible conflict with foreign troops or to suppress a Communist coup. The forms of cooperation ranged from support for sabotage units in the west to the establishment of secret reserve units in the east.[72]

In contrast to the Reich government, the Prussian cabinet felt that the security problem during the Ruhr crisis lay primarily in the danger that the antidemocratic forces would take advantage of the deteriorating economic and social conditions to undermine domestic political stability in Reich and state. It was well known that many groups on the extreme right saw the Ruhr crisis as a signal for the overthrow of democracy, while in the ranks of the republic's supporters fatalism swelled. Civil war, military dictatorship, a new war with France and Poland, and consequent dissolution of the Reich were among the scenarios discussed.[73] Under the circumstances it was clearly not reassuring to Severing and his colleagues to know that particularly in such traditional political bellwether provinces as Schleswig-Holstein, Silesia, Pomerania and East Prussia, large amounts of weapons were under the control of regional military commanders who often maintained close relations with right-wing vigilante groups.[74]

The contrasting views on the relationship of the Reichswehr and politics led to almost constant friction between the Reich and Prussia during the Ruhr conflict. In the opinion of the Prussian cabinet, the Weimar constitution assigned responsibility for maintaining internal security to the states. This meant that the Prussian cabinet and the provincial governors, relying on units of the by now well-organized and politically loyal *Sicherheitspolizei*, were in charge of implementing security policy. For extreme and unforeseen situations, Severing had authorized the "liaison commissioner" in the Ruhr, his close associate Ernst Mehlich, to create an auxiliary police force made up of members of the coalition parties. It was to serve as an adjunct to the regular police in case of putsch attempts by left or right extremists.[75] As for the Reichswehr, the Prussian cabinet insisted not only on consultation with the Prussian civilian authorities, but also on their active participation whenever the Reichswehr undertook domestic operations, such as distributing rifles and ammunition from its weapons depots to paramilitary units or establishing secret reserve units.[76] In sharp contrast, the Reichswehr contended, "National security is a matter of Reich concern," that is, the Reich cabinet and the national armed forces had a constitutional monopoly in deciding questions of national security, whether they involved foreign or domestic enemies.[77]

The debate over constitutional principles was politically less important than conflicts over concrete actions by the military authorities.[78] To facilitate contacts with paramilitary groups, a number of the district commanders added the office of "military provincial representative" *(Militärischer Provinz-ialleiter)* to their staff organizations. The ostensible purpose was to coordinate border defenses and to maintain internal security, but, as Severing was quick to point out, some army commanders had difficulty distinguishing between maintaining law and order and staging a putsch. Recruitment efforts to form auxiliary units seemed to be limited to members of various right-wing "patriotic associations."[79] During the Ruhr conflict, Prussia conceded the need for some temporary auxiliary units to supplement the Reichswehr's border troops,[80] but with this regional exception the cabinet continued to demand effective control of the vigilante groups and a complete severance of relations between them and the army. When repeated requests to the Reich government for concrete measures met with little success, the state decided to take action on its own. Backed by a unanimous decision of the cabinet, the minister of the Interior ordered the dissolution of the largest political organization among the radical right, the Deutschvölkische Freiheitspartei (DVFP).[81] (As has been shown the politically insignificant Nazi party had already been prohibited in 1922.) Severing also ordered the compilation of lists of known right-wing radical leaders who were to be arrested in times of acute unrest.[82]

An even more dramatic and controversial move was Prussia's dissolution of what was widely regarded as the paramilitary counterpart of the DVFP, the Rossbach Organization. Under the leadership of a former army officer, Lieutenant Gerhard Rossbach, this group had been an active component of virtually every rightist conspiracy since 1919.[83] Rossbach's political goals were simplistic: overthrow democracy at home, stage a new war with France abroad. By the spring of 1923, Severing had gathered sufficient evidence to show that under the cover of renewed hostilities with France (which Rossbach expected in mid-April 1923), the Rossbach Organization was planning a putsch in the near future. While some units of the organization would rush to the front, the rest of Rossbach's units were to be active behind the front preventing "another stab in the back by the Socialists." There was also undeniable evidence of close ties between the Rossbach Organization and the DVFP. The Freedom party was Rossbach's major source of financial support. The leaders of the two groups were in frequent personal contact, and the two groups exchanged lists of code names and the location of hidden weapons depots.[84]

With the evidence of a conspiracy before it, the cabinet did not hesitate to dissolve the lieutenant's group.[85] Rossbach appealed to Cuno and the Reich government to prevent Severing from acting, claiming that his organization had acted in accordance with the Reich cabinet's policies. This was an exaggeration, to say the least, and in any case Prussia's revelations about Rossbach's organization finally persuaded the Reich government to take a new look at the paramilitary organizations.[86] At the beginning of April, the Reich and Prussian ministers met again to discuss future relations between the Reichswehr and the paramilitary units. This time the Reich cabinet agreed that the armed forces should indeed keep their distance from all political groupings. A statement issued jointly by Gessler and Severing emphasized the ministers' agreement that the best guarantee for maintaining the Reich's unity was "energetic and impartial measures against left and right-wing agitators."[87] More important was Gessler's willingness to accord the state's provincial governors the right to participate in all decisions by the army's regional commanders that affected matters of domestic security.[88] For Prussia this was a key concession from the Reichswehr, since it assured that the state's civilian officials would be able to retain a modicum of control over the army even when the Reich government declared a formal state of emergency or martial law.

Such an occasion arose only a few months later. Simultaneously with its decision to end passive resistance in the Ruhr, the federal government proclaimed a state of emergency for the entire territory of the Reich. The suspension of civil liberties under the state of emergency continued from September 1923 to March 1, 1924.[89] The primary purpose of the decree was to preclude violence by political extremists; it was an open secret that numerous groups, especially on the *völkische* right, intended to use the end of passive resistance as a signal for a new putsch to overthrow the republic. (The justification would be that the government in giving up passive resistance had betrayed the nation.) Under the provisions of the decree, the Reichswehr was assigned a major role in maintaining domestic law and order and without some civilian control mechanisms the army's plenipotentiary powers could easily have become the road to military dictatorship. This unfortunate development was avoided largely because of the influence and authority of the territorial administration in Prussia. In announcing the state of emergency, the Reich cabinet also put into effect the terms of the Reich-Prussian agreement of April 1923, which meant that in Prussia the state of emergency would to a large extent be administered by the regular civil administration.[90] The Prussian civil service was in constant touch with the Reichswehr, and the army agreed that the state's provincial governors would serve as the executive organs of the Reichswehr district commanders.[91] The cooperation between Prussia and the Reich during the state of emergency not only thwarted the plans of the antirepublican forces, while restraining the political ambitions of the Reichswehr, it also contrasted vividly with the frictions and open conflict that characterized relations between the national government and some other state cabinets.

The two major confrontations between the Reich and non-Prussian state authorities, the conflict between the Reich, Saxony, and Thuringia in October and Ludendorff's and Hitler's so-called Beer Hall Putsch less than a month later threatened neither the internal security in Prussia nor the cohesion of the grand coalition. The Reich's decision to remove the "united front" governments of Saxony and Thuringia from office was made by the national cabinet entirely on its own; Prussia was neither consulted beforehand nor asked to assist the Reich in any form. While the federal government took the initiative in central Germany, the Bavarian revolt, which at first appeared to be supported by regular Reichswehr units, constituted a direct threat to the democratic system of government in all of Germany. This time the Reich asked for Prussia's support. The two cabinets met in joint emergency session on the night of the putsch in Munich (November 9, 1923), and the state's ministers fully supported the Reich government's firm stand. Prussia also mobilized its police forces, since, as Severing proudly pointed out, in contrast to the days of the Kapp Putsch, Prussia now had at its disposal a dependable force of coercion.[92] It was almost a case of overkill. Nazi activities in Prussia during the putsch days were limited to sporadic anti-Semitic vandalism in a few localities.[93]

The calm that prevailed in Prussia during Hitler's putsch was symptomatic of the state's successful efforts to maintain public order in very difficult times. The security policies of the grand coalition were among its most impressive accomplishments. The primary cause of the cabinet's success was the remarkable unanimity of *étatiste* views among its members. In agreeing that the republican form of government in Prussia was interdependent with the state's continued existence, the ministers were determined to support measures that would effectively preserve the state in its present political form. In addition, the Prussians' self-image as the foundation of national unity and guarantor of democracy in all of the Reich meant that Prussia's security policies were frequently used to stiffen the resolve of the often indecisive and shaky Reich authorities rather than being employed, as was true in Bavaria, to exploit the Reich's weakness and increase the state's powers at the expense of federal authority.[94]

Administrative Reforms

It was not quite true that, as one exasperated observer wrote, prior to November 1921 Prussia had not made the "slightest beginning toward systematic [administrative] reforms," but progress had certainly not been spectacular.[95] All of the long-standing problems that had plagued the state before the war and after the revolution remained unresolved. Like its predecessors, the cabinet of the grand coalition recognized the need for a comprehensive administrative reform package that would deal with such varied, but interrelated, issues as the overlapping jurisdictions of the governors and district directors and the rights of municipal corporations. Again like earlier governments, however, it quickly recognized the political pitfalls of a comprehensive approach and opted instead for a series of specific reform bills to relieve the most pressing and acute problems.

The cabinet directed its attention first to the long overdue reforms of municipal self-government, although even here it took almost three years for the deliberations to reach the stage of draft legislation. The major difficulty was to find a compromise between the municipalities' understandable desire for as much autonomy in conducting their affairs as possible, and the state's wish to retain some control powers, particularly in the areas of personnel appointments and fiscal affairs. Following long discussions with the interested parties—and they included virtually every city and town in the state—the ministers, shortly before leaving office as it turned out, submitted a bill to the Landtag which they felt provided the municipalities with sufficient, but not irresponsible rights of autonomy.[96]

The municipal reform bill was a failure. It was defeated by an odd and incongruous coalition of municipal leaders from the bourgeois parties and some left-wing Socialists. Spokesmen from the bourgeois parties complained that the bill provided for excessive supervisory authority by the state's territorial administrators, but decisive for the fate of the legislation was a successful effort by left-wing Social Democrats to link the municipal reform bill to what was really a problem of local government in rural areas. They complained that neither this bill nor any other proposed legislation dealt with the problem of the so-called *Gutsbezirke*. (These, it will be recalled, were estates owned by a individual proprietor, which because of their size also constituted a unit of local government, something equivalent to a U.S. township.) In 1923 there remained some 12,000 *Gutsbezirke* in existence. The estate owners, for the most part Junkers in the more backward stretches of East Elbia, held positions as virtual dictators, at least as far as their powers as local administrators were concerned. The cabinet did consider abolishing the *Gutsbezirke*, but the ministers soon faced massive problems. Aside from the political opposition of the Conservatives, the counties surrounding the latifundia-townships balked at the additional expense of providing services to the now annexed *Gutsbezirke*.[97] Under these circumstances the cabinet decided to hold off legislation on the *Gutsbezirke,* but the price was the defeat of the municipal reform bill. It remained bottled up in committee deliberations and never reached the floor of the Landtag.[98]

Reform proposals for county *(Kreis)* government were similarly stillborn. In May 1923, not, to be sure, a propitious time for rational deliberation of technically complicated administrative reforms proposals, the cabinet submitted draft legislation for a reorganization of Prussia's county government. The bill contained provisions for codifying the rights of self-government for the counties, as well as proposed boundary changes to rationalize the crazy-quilt pattern of the more than 400 counties.[99] The bill also represented the final chapter in the long controversy over the "communalization" of the county commissioners. Wolfgang Heine's misguided plans for grassroots democracy were laid to rest. The bill drafted by the grand coalition accorded the county legislatures *(Kreistage)* a voice in selecting county commissioners, but the powers of appointment, overall supervision and control were vested in the cabinet. Despite the political passions that the issue of "communalizing" the *Landrat* had aroused in earlier years, the cabinet's proposals on this question were not the Achilles' heel of the bill. Rather, it failed because of the plans for territorial reforms, that is, the redrawing of county boundaries. These produced such a storm of protest from various local interest groups that debate on the bill soon became deadlocked.[100]

The overriding issue for administrative reforms at the provincial level continued to be the question of which set of officials, the provincial governors or the district directors, were superfluous. Severing, who regarded the office of provincial governor as an anachronism left over from feudal times, had earlier proposed that the district directors serve as the sole territorial representatives of the central government in the provinces,[101] but at the time the grand coalition assumed office, his proposals had not advanced beyond the stage of draft discussions. Moreover, the experience of the years 1922–1925 seemed to make a good case for retaining the office of provincial governor. The incumbent governors themselves argued vigorously that in times of domestic instability the central government needed a single point of reference in each province both to gather information and deploy the Security Police if necessary.[102] Also related to the security issue was the role the provincial governors played in the relations between Prussia and the Reichswehr. The Prussian provincial boundaries in some cases corresponded to the army's territorial divisions *(Wehrkreise),* so that provincial governors and the military district commanders shared jurisdiction over the same territory. As noted above, when a state of emergency was declared the parallel jurisdictions facilitated both implementation and control of the measures ordered by the Reichswehr.

On the other hand, strong governors and vigorous provinces were not without political problems. By 1922 the provinces had developed a sense of identity as constitutionally sanctioned entities, an evolution that had implications both for Reich-state relations and for the political balance of power in Prussia itself. As noted earlier, under the terms of the Weimar constitution the Prussian provinces were entitled to cast half of the state's votes in the Reichsrat. In the past some of the provincial delegates had at times voted against proposals supported by the Prussian government, thereby reducing the political weight of the state as a whole in the Federal Council.[103] To correct this imbalance, three of the four parties in the grand coalition—the SPD, DDP, and DVP—supported legislation to reduce the powers of the provincial representatives in the Reichsrat; abolishing the office of provincial governor would have been a step in the same direction. The proposal was stillborn, however, because coalition dynamics intervened. The Center party, traditionally the guardian of provincial autonomy, rejected all efforts to re-centralize the state's administration, including proposals to reduce the power of the provinces in the Reichsrat.[104]

The Catholic party was also at the center of the controversy over the role of the Staatsrat. This body, of course, was specifically created to permit the provinces to exercise some influence over the state's budgetary and legislative processes. Under its long-time president, the influential right-wing Center party leader and lord mayor of Cologne, Konrad Adenauer, the Prussian state council developed into an organ that jealously guarded the rights of provincial autonomy against what it saw as the constant danger of creeping centralism.[105] It was already suspicious of the cabinet's intentions with regard to the future of the provinces; thus any attempt to reduce the visibility of the provinces would have called forth vigorous protests from the *Staatsrat* and its energetic president.[106]

Political considerations also superseded whatever rational arguments could be adduced for changing the boundaries of the Prussian provinces in order to reduce some of the discrepancies in territorial size between them and thus streamline their administration. Aside from the expected protests of the larger provinces that might lose some territory to their smaller neighbors, the state's leaders continued to fear the linkage between intrastate territorial reform and the danger of separatism.[107] On this issue too, the grand coalition continued the policies of its predecessors. Equating any change in Prussia's territorial structure with a threat to the Reich's unity as a whole,[108] Prussia remained suspicious of attempts by its smaller neighbors to improve the viability of their *Länder* at the expense of the Prussian superstate. Although Carl Severing and the prime minister of Thuringia were personal friends, Prussia blocked Thuringia's efforts to annex the neighboring Prussian region of Waldeck.[109] Similarly, the state recognized the economic and administrative benefits that would result from the establishment of a Port Authority for Greater Hamburg, but feared the political repercussions from such an agreement in the neighboring province of Hanover, where the Guelph movement continued to agitate for the province's separation from Prussia.[110] As a result, even a less than comprehensive agreement for the Hamburg region was not reached until 1929.

Actually, the cabinet vastly overestimated the political strength of the various provincial separatist and autonomy movements. In the Rhineland the Rheinischer Volksbund (Rhenish Popular Association) still wanted to free the Rhineland from what it called the Prusso-German yoke, but it had become an insignificant fringe group among the region's voters.[111] The Guelphs' quest, too, met with little support among the province's voters. By heavy majorities the Hanoverian voters rejected the Guelphs' proposal for a referendum on the question of Hanover's separation from Prussia.[112] In effect, the Hanoverians gave Prussia a vote of confidence.[113]

Even the autonomy movement in Upper Silesia, which Prussia's leaders regarded as the politically most dangerous challenge to the state's territorial integrity, came to an anticlimactic conclusion. The Prussian government, of course, consistently opposed separating Upper Silesia from Prussia for both political and economic reasons, but concerns for the coalition and Reich-Prussian relations, had led previous cabinets to mute their public opposition to the Silesian agitation.[114] By the time the grand coalition came into office, however, the political balance had shifted in favor of the government's position. The last of the plebiscites mandated by the Treaty of Versailles had been held and the final division of the disputed territory between the Reich and Poland determined, so that foreign policy reasons could no longer be legitimately adduced to delay a settlement of Upper Silesia's future. The addition of the DVP to the cabinet strengthened the opponents of separatism among the coalition.[115] In addition, the leadership of the Prussian Center party increasingly disassociated itself from the aims of the party's provincial leader, while in the province itself there were indications that support for the autonomy movement was declining.[116] Finally, the Reich government of Chancellor Wirth agreed to cooperate with the Prussians in attempting to arrange a truce among the political parties in the province.[117]

The truce was not of long duration, and in the spring of 1922 the cabinet took to the offensive. The Prussian prime minister, with the full knowledge and approval of the cabinet, decided to make public the government's opposition to the province's secession and at the same time attempt to focus the debate on "more rational economic issues." [118] On the occasion of a major trade fair in Breslau, the capital city of Upper Silesia, Otto Braun delivered a carefully worded speech on March 19, 1922. In his remarks the prime minister stressed the economic disadvantages that would follow from separating Upper Silesia from Prussia. He also put the issue into a considerably broader context and characterized attempts to change the territorial boundaries of Prussia "as downright disastrous." Braun opposed the establishment of what he called "barely viable governmental entities" which would emerge when small areas seceded from larger states. A host of medium-sized states like Upper Silesia would lead not to increased cohesion of the Reich as the proponents claimed, but give unwanted support to centrifugal forces that would eventually aid the overall strategic aims of Germany's enemies, most notably France. [119]

The prime minister's address created a sensation, less because of what he said—the ideas were hardly new—than for the forum in which he chose to say it. Braun's speech signaled that the Prussian government was no longer content to argue against Upper Silesian separatism behind the scenes, but instead would combat the autonomy movement in the open. Initial reaction to Braun's remarks was overwhelmingly and somewhat surprisingly negative. As expected, the Center party press in the province reacted with fury and scorn, but even the opponents of separation regarded the prime minister's remarks as tactically unwise, since they would drive additional supporters into the ranks of the separatists. [120]

Actually, the prime minister had gauged opinion far more accurately than the pundits. By clarifying and publicly identifying the issues in the conflict, Braun's words had the effect of exposing the weakness of Ulitzka's support, while aligning those who favored retaining Upper Silesia as a province of Prussia behind the prime minister. Whatever disunity there had been in the SPD disappeared immediately; after the Breslau speech the regional party organization solidly supported Braun and the cabinet. [121] The German Nationalists once again formed part of the reluctant coalition. The conservative *Kreuzzeitung* had warm words of praise for Braun's speech, and gave editorial support "without reservation" to the government's position on Upper Silesia. [122] In the end it required relatively few concessions by the Prussian government in order to deflate the autonomy movement completely. The cabinet replaced four incumbent Protestant county commissioners with Catholic appointees, and in July 1922 the Landtag agreed to legislation giving the Upper Silesian provincial diet increased consultative rights for political appointments in the province and greater autonomy in educational matters. [123] The plebiscite that Ulitzka had been demanding since 1918 proved to be an anticlimax: 91 percent of those voting favored the province's remaining a part of Prussia.

In at least one case the cabinet's fear of losing control of the situation in the border provinces led it to decisions that in retrospect clearly did not benefit the democratic system as a whole. This was true for a province with severe and perennial problems, East Prussia. Here was an area whose economic structure—chronically depressed even before the war—was especially adversely affected by the territorial provisions of the Treaty of Versailles.[124] Partly as a result of these massive economic problems, the province became a stronghold of the DNVP and various extreme right movements. In May, 1922 a trip to the province by former Field Marshal von Hinderburg (subsequently Reich president) was quickly transformed into a triumphant procession of militarists and monarchists.[125] In the face of clear evidence that the province was politically seething, the government's reaction was decidedly weak. The cabinet removed some of the more outspoken Conservative county commissioners from office, and increased some economic subsidies, but it refused to authorize any substantive structural or administrative changes.[126] A persuasive argument by the provincial governor, Ernst Siehr (DDP), to grant his office extensive powers to coordinate provincewide economic matters, was rejected by Severing, ostensibly because such a decision would prejudice future consideration of the role of the governors and district directors in any comprehensive administrative reform.[127]

Conclusion

When the grand coalition left office at the beginning of 1925, its record of accomplishments in the areas of personnel and administrative reforms was, at least from a long-range perspective, not impressive. It inherited massive problems which for the most part it bequeathed to its successors. Neither a municipal reform act nor major changes in the provincial administration had become law; and there was no program of aggressive democratization for the civil service.

But was this a fair judgment? The cabinet and the coalition parties viewed their achievements in a different light. They pointed with pride to the fact that by maintaining the state's internal administration during these years of chronic crises, Prussia had safeguarded the republican form of government in both the state and the Reich. Typical was the self-congratulatory conclusion by the Prussian SPD that "the waves of the Hitler putsch would have engulfed Germany, had not the democratic, republican Prussia provided a solid rock to which the weak Reich government could cling."[128] Hyperbole aside, there was some truth to the metaphor. At the beginning of 1925 the state's domestic political situation could be described as stabilized.[129] Prussia had reliable police forces, and the corps of civil servants had acquired the reputation of being loyal if not always enthusiastic supporters of the parliamentary form of government. The autonomy agitation had all but vanished; increasingly, demonstrations of "faithful loyalty to Prussia" replaced sentiments of separatism and autonomy.[130]

The Prussia that commanded loyalty, it must be recalled, was a republic and a democracy. In the long run (if there was to be a long run for Weimar) this development, the internalization and identification of republic and "Prussia consciousness," was undoubtedly of major significance in maintaining domestic stability in Germany as a whole. In comparison with this achievement the obvious failures of the grand coalition in the area of personnel and administrative policies appear less serious. They were defects that could be remedied with time, while the fall of the parliamentary form of government in Prussia would probably have involved the end of the Weimar Republic as well.

CHAPTER 8

Conclusion

In the spring of 1925 both Prussia and the Reich inaugurated new leaders: Otto Braun returned to power at the head of a cabinet composed of members of the Weimar parties; a retired field marshal, Paul von Hindenburg, was inaugurated as Reich president. In their contrasting personalities, backgrounds, and political ideologies, the two men epitomized the very different paths of politics in the Reich and its largest state during the first six years of the Weimar Republic. Paradoxically, the president of the republic was now a Prussian Junker officer, who "in his heart had remained a monarchist," while the prime minister of Prussia was a Social Democrat and the son of a Königsberg cobbler.

But the contrasts between the two levels of government were political as well as personal. At the national level parliamentary democracy did not function well. Rather, the years 1918–1925 were characterized by political instability and polarization, with the center of political gravity moving steadily to the right. As national elections produced Reichstags unable to establish firm parliamentary alliances in support of stable coalitions, a series of minority cabinets composed mostly of coalitions among the bourgeois parties followed in quick succession. Distrust of the party system at the federal level was epitomized by Reich Chancellor Luther's description of himself as a "politician without a party."[1] Prussia, on the other hand, had neither followed the Reich's lead toward the political right, nor abandoned the processes of parliamentary democracy. Rather, the "parallelogram of political power," established in 1918 and 1919, that is to say, the cooperation of the Liberals, Social Democrats, and Catholics, remained in force, producing, except for the short-lived Marx and Stegerwald cabinets, stable parliamentary coalitions.[2] The continuing vitality of the "coalitions of a strong center" in turn assured the Prussian cabinets much longer terms of office. In contrast to the eleven Reich cabinets and eight chancellors, only six ministries and four prime ministers had served in the state during the seven-year time span. And even these figures are misleading, since both the Stegerwald and Marx cabinets were transition governments that held office for only a few months or weeks. Seemingly, then, the accepted picture of the Weimar Republic as representing the "failure" of parliamentarism in Germany does not apply to Prussia.[3] On the contrary, Germany's largest state presented a picture of democratic and parliamentary stability.

At first glance, the divergence in the political evolution of the Reich and

243

Prussia is surprising, to say the least. It cannot be readily explained by the fortuitous circumstances of regionalism. Both before and after World War I Prussia by virtue of its territorial size and population was something of a mini-Reich. The state made up roughly three-fifths of Germany and contained a similar proportion of the Reich's population. Since the Thirty Years' War the political histories of Germany and Prussia had been inextricably interdependent. Unlike some of the southern German states, Prussia in modern times had no tradition of particularism. All of the major parties that contested elections at the national level also attempted to gain seats in the Prussian Landtag. In addition, Prussia's history seemed a poor foundation on which to build a successful parliamentary democracy: before 1918 Germany's antidemocratic and authoritarian traditions were closely associated with the name and history of Prussia. Weimar Prussia, then, presents a paradox that raises a number of questions about the larger history of Weimar Germany. With parliamentary democracy alive and well in three-fifths of the Reich, perhaps the accepted thesis that this form of government was unwanted and unwelcomed in Germany needs to be reexamined.

This political history of Prussia in the first half of the Weimar era has focused on answers to two basic questions: first, why did parliamentary democracy function far better at the state level than for the Reich as a whole, even though both jurisdictions were subject to many of the same pressures; and second, how did the state's republican leaders see the relationship between parliamentary democracy and the evolution of modern social structures in the greater part of Germany? What, in other words, were their political and administrative reform goals?

These questions are not new, although in recent years they have not been in the forefront of interest among historians of modern Germany. The answers of earlier researchers—grossly oversimplified, to be sure—can be divided into two basic categories. The first holds that specific developments in Prussia had little to do with the state's stability; instead, the success of parliamentary democracy in Prussia was the result of a number of fortuitous accidents.[4] In a variation of the famous aphorism about the good luck of the Hapsburgs, here was a case of *felix Borussia*. Supporters of this thesis point out that disputes over the conduct of foreign policy, which traditionally were a major cause of the downfall of Reich governments, were not a factor in Prussian coalition politics (nor, for that matter, in the other states), since the Weimar constitution assigned the Reich a monopoly position in this jurisdictional area. Similarly, the Weimar constitution relieved the states of primary responsibility in another major area of controversy, tax and fiscal policy. The Reich Finance Reform Act of 1919 had transferred most tax revenues and fiscal responsibility to the federal level, so that the state's were severely constrained in their decision making, thereby reducing the opportunity for conflict and crises.

Supporters of the accident theory also note that Prussian state elections were held at times that happened to be favorable to the cause of the republican parties. Thus there were no Landtag elections in either June 1920 or May 1924, that is, when the antiparliamentary and antidemocratic parties made particularly spectacular gains in national contests. Even the tragic and unexpected death of Reich President Ebert apparently contributed to the return of stability to Prussia. At the time of his death the state was in the midst of a major government crisis, and no ready solution seemed in sight. Ebert's passing and the need for a presidential election made it possible to renew the Weimar coalition in Prussia as part of a quid pro quo agreement under which Wilhelm Marx became the presidential candidate of the three Weimar parties, while Otto Braun resumed his position as the state's prime minister.

A second widely accepted thesis might be called, somewhat facetiously, the parasite school of Prussian historiography. Its supporters contend that a reciprocal relationship existed between the Reich's crises and Prussia's stability. In effect, the state's constitutional, territorial, and political uniqueness in the context of the German federal structure hindered the development of national institutions and political life. Concretely, as long as Prussia remained in existence as a state covering three-fifths of the national territory, the Reich was doomed to impotence and instability. The only possible remedy was a thoroughgoing constitutional and territorial reform package—the elusive *Reichsreform*—that would correct the imbalance in the German federal structure and either dissolve Prussia or reduce it to the level of a "normal" state.[5] Since Prussia was a major factor blocking the *Reichsreform*, proponents of this thesis see the state in a very real sense as a cause of the Reich's political weakness.

The Reich-Prussia dualism in this view also had political consequences that worked against the creation of stable coalitions in the Reich. The two largest republican parties, the SPD and the Center party, were not ideologically homogenous. Rather, under the organizational umbrella of a single party, left- and right-wing factions held sharply antagonistic views on many policy issues. To facilitate party unity, both the Center party and the SPD balanced their positions in the Reich with opposite leanings in Prussia. In the SPD the left wing was accorded disproportionate strength in the Reichstag, while the right wing dominated the party in Prussia.[6] The reverse was true in the Center party.[7] As a result, the right wing of the SPD and the left wing of the Center party were able to form coalitions in Prussia, while the Reichstag delegations of the same parties increasingly pulled in opposite directions. Consequently, the SPD and the Center party seldom supported the same policies in the Reich, but in Prussia their cooperation formed the basis of virtually every cabinet coalition.

A closer look at Prussia's political history in the early Weimar years reveals that the traditional reasons adduced for the success of parliamentary democracy in the state are neither sufficient nor convincing. True, Prussia was not able to determine Germany's foreign policy, but the state's political leaders certainly did not avoid taking stands on foreign policy. Beginning with the Treaty of Versailles and extending to the Ruhr crisis of 1923, Prussian politicians not only debated the issues vigorously in the state's legislative and executive institutions, but also attempted to persuade the Reich to accept the state's point of view. In contrast to the Reich, the discussions in Prussia did not cause government crises for the state because there was widespread agreement among the overwhelming majority of political forces in the state on the course of action to be pursued. In the same vein, Prussia did not avoid tax issues. Fierce battles raged over the nature and level of the tax on rental property, the *Hauszinssteuer*, but despite sharp disagreements among the coalition partners, in the end the moderate political forces found compromises acceptable to all parties in this group. Parliamentary democracy in Prussia remained viable not because the legislative and executive avoided politically difficult issues, but because they dealt with them successfully.

Other aspects of the *felix Borussia* thesis present similar difficulties. Again, it is true that state elections were held far less frequently than national contests, but the reason had little to do with luck. Instead, governmental stability eliminated the need for frequent recourse to the ballot box. As for the specific case of the Reich presidential election of 1925, our analysis has demonstrated that while there was certainly a connection between the two offices at the level of personalities, that is, the linkage of Marx as republican presidential candidate and Braun as prime minister of Prussia, the substantive decision of the Weimar parties to resume their coalition agreement had been reached before the question of supporting a joint candidate for Reich president became acute.

The linkage between a weak Reich and a strong Prussia also needs reexamination. To be sure, the size of Prussia presented something of a rarity among historical cases of federation, but there is no evidence that Prussia's political success contributed to weakness of the executive or the failure of parliamentarism in the Reich. In fact, the foreign policy and tax argument can be turned upon its head here. After all, precisely because there were areas in which the Reich had a constitutionally assigned preeminence in the decision-making process, the failure of the coalition partners in the Reich to reach acceptable compromises demonstrated that the problem lay in the dynamics of Reich politics themselves.

There is little evidence that Prussia's stability adversely affected the outcome of the frequent cabinet crises in the Reich. On the contrary, while leaders of the Reichstag parties repeatedly attempted to solve coalition crises at the national level by involving Prussia as part of the political power balancing act, it is difficult to see how compounded crises would have benefited Weimar democracy as a whole. Certainly the instances of parallel coalition crises, the interregna of 1921 and 1924–1925, demonstrated that dual difficulties merely prolonged the lack of firm leadership at each level of government.

Finally, the thesis that cooperation among the republican parties at the state level had the effect of precluding their working together in the Reich is unconvincing. Again, it is true that the Center party and the SPD tended to diverge in the Reich and converge in Prussia, but the reasons do not lie in a deterministic reciprocal orientation of the two parties. Rather, the phenomenon was a result of conscious decisions by the Prussian leadership of the two parties to cooperate at the state level.

The traditional explanations of Prussia's political success as a parliamentary democracy, then, are inadequate, largely because most historians have approached the question of Prussia's political success from a rather too narrow perspective. Attention has focused on the "prefascistic" contours of Prussia's political evolution. The primary historiographic effort, in other words, was directed toward explaining the state's history as a factor in permitting the Nazis to come to power.[8] Weimar Prussia's success as a parliamentary democracy was either ignored or dismissed because it appeared to be the result of incidental causes.

Unfortunately, this fascination with the Nazis' coming to power has had the effect of seriously distorting our view of Prussia's role in the political dynamics of modern and especially Weimar Germany. The state's success as a parliamentary democracy after 1918 appears less surprising if this aspect of Prussia's political evolution is seen as part of a considerably longer pattern of continuity: the confict over Prussia's role in the process of modernization and national unification of Germany. That debate began in earnest not with the revolution of 1918, but with the earlier upheavals in 1848–1849.

In 1848 German and Prussian reformers had attempted to set the stage for the country's national unification and sociopolitical modernization on the basis of political liberalism and a rough balance of power among Germany's federal states. It proved to be a task of squaring the circle. The reformers achieved neither their political nor their national goals. Instead, neoconservative forces regained power in the counterrevolution of 1850–51. But there was an important change. In the second half of the century, Prussian Conservatives led the quest for national unification, albeit at the price of creating a united Reich that was dominated by a Prussia that continued to be the political domain of Conservative authoritarianism. The reformist tradition in Prussia did not die, but until 1918 it was effectively excluded from political power in the state. At the same time the reformers came to accept the first part of the conservatives' scenario: the sense of Prussian consciousness, the peculiar form of Prussian *étatisme*. In effect, then, the political antagonists in the state agreed that the continued existence of Prussia, whatever its specific form of government, was both the foundation of national unity and provided the paradigm for the Reich's political system.

Until 1918 the Prussian constitution narrowly limited the powers of parliament, while a restrictive suffrage system made even the weak legislature unrepresentative of the relative strength of political forces in the state. The focus of political power rested with the king, the military, and the East Elbian landowners. Specifically excluded from political power were Catholics, both left and right Liberals, and later Social Democrats. It is important to keep in mind that before 1918 civil service restrictions in Prussia extended far beyond the infamous example of the Social Democrat whose political beliefs barred him from appointment as night watchman in a state office building. Even leaders of the national Liberals were denied high office in the executive branch until well into World War I when growing domestic tensions forced the Prussian Conservatives grudgingly to accede to a widening of the political base in the state.[9] The Reich constitution of 1871 in turn assured that Prussian authoritarianism would dominate Germany as a whole. Specific avenues of power transmittal from state to Reich were the "personal union" of emperor and king, Prussia's ability to control more than half of the votes in the Bundesrat, and the preponderant position of the Prussian army.

The rule of the Prussian Conservatives came to an end with the revolution of 1918. Historians are still debating whether the events of 1918 deserve to be labeled a "revolution"; the upheavals certainly did not result in a complete restructuring of Prussian and German society. There is no doubt, however, that the events of 1918–1919 resulted in a profound shift in the political balance of power within Prussia. At the same time, while the state's control over Reich affairs was severely curtailed by the Weimar constitution, the state's new political leaders accepted Prussia's peculiar sense of *étatisme* virtually unchanged. As their Conservative-authoritarian predecessors had done, the new rulers of the state insisted on the linkage between Reich and state: Prussia's political system would provide the model for the Reich as a whole, while the state's territorial integrity provided a guarantee of national unity. The only difference was that while the Conservatives saw an authoritarian Prussia as the major barrier against Western democracy and liberalism, the new Prussian leaders worked to ensure that a functional parliamentary democracy in the state would provide the foundation for the same governmental system in all of Germany. The "German mission" of Prussia remained constant. The state was still the rivet that held the Reich together and the guarantee of its political stability.

In the winter of 1918 the forces that had been systematically excluded from participating in the political decision-making process before then assumed responsibility for the political fate of Prussia; they retained control until almost the end of the republican years. That Catholics, Liberals, and Social Democrats found it far easier to cooperate in Prussia than in the Reich had a great deal to do with their role as political outcasts in the state during the past half-century. In the prerevolutionary era the Prussian Conservatives had grouped all three ideologies and their corresponding organizations together, not just as political opponents, but as threats to the authoritarian system of government in the state. Even the National Liberals, who in the prewar legislature tended to act as junior partners of the Conservatives, were never accepted as equals. After the revolution of 1918, the old rulers did not change their point of view. The German Nationalists (as well as the *Völkische* and the Communists) were determined to destroy parliamentary democracy. Their intransigence in turn facilitated cooperation among the Weimar parties and later the DVP.

The German Nationalists, successors to the prewar Conservatives, were now powerless to form governments on their own, but since the majority of the Prussian DNVP never accepted parliamentarism, the party could not function either in the positive role of a loyal opposition or as a coalition partner of the moderate bourgeois parties.[10] Instead, the party spent useless energies in active support of the Kapp Putsch and drawing up von Schlange-Schöningen's plans for a right-wing dictatorship. The Conservatives' unwillingness to compromise and their parochial Prussian restorationist aims isolated them in the Reich and weakened their position in the state. It is true that the German Nationalists in Prussia talked constantly about taking the Reich into a vice grip of restorationist regimes in Prussia and Bavaria, but the price for such cooperation between the Prussian and Bavarian right, as far as the Prussian Conservatives were concerned, was the restoration of Hohenzollern rule and the reestablishment of Prussian hegemony in the Reich. The Bavarian monarchists, needless to say, had no interest in furthering such plans. Finally, the Conservatives labored under a self-imposed handicap in their relentless attacks on the system of parliamentary democracy in the state. They agreed with the new democratic leaders of Prussia that there was a linkage between a strong Prussia and a unified Reich. As a result, the DNVP repeatedly rallied behind the democratic rulers in defending the state's "national mission," particularly in the first years of the republic, when that "mission" was repeatedly called into question by the Reich authorities. The consequent "reluctant coalition" had the effect of not only strengthening the Prussian government's hand in dealing with the Reich, but also of aiding the viability of Prussia's young parliamentarism.

The Weimar and grand coalitions were held together not merely by negative factors of self-preservation. Equally, if not more, important was their shared belief in Prussian *étatisme*. The *leitmotif* that underlay all major decision making in the state during the first seven years of the republican era was the conviction held by virtually all Prussian leaders that the state's territorial integrity and political stability were the major factors holding the Reich together. It provides the key for interpreting Prussia's stands on the series of domestic crises from 1918 to 1925. The leitmotif became apparent in a most dramatic way in the course of the debate over the acceptance or rejection of the Treaty of Versailles. In the Reich passionate disagreements among the SPD, DDP, and Center party led to the fall of the Scheidemann cabinet when the Weimar coalition parties could not agree on a common stand. In Prussia the leadership of the same three parties both in the Landesversammlung and the cabinet never wavered in their rejection of the treaty. They were convinced the terms of the treaty were specifically intended by the Allies to destroy the viability of Prussia and consequently dissolve Germany as a nation. The Prussian leaders were wrong, but their misguided belief had the positive effect of strengthening the political stability in the state and also preventing parallel government crises in Prussia and the Reich.

The democratic rulers adopted equally consistent attitudes when faced with domestic challenges to the authority of the state. The net effect of the Kapp Putsch was not to restore authoritarian rule, but to solidify support for parliamentarism and democracy in Prussia. The coup was a major factor in the DVP's decision to turn its back on the intransigence of the DNVP. It fell to the cabinet of the grand coalition to defend Prussia's self-chosen German mission under particularly difficult circumstances. The combination of two major crises, the murder of Walther Rathenau and the Franco-Belgian occupation of the Ruhr, severely threatened the republic's domestic stability. The cabinet of the grand coalition was equal to the challenge. The Prussian government left no doubt that it regarded threats to the republic and parliamentary democracy as identical with dangers for the political viability and territorial integrity of the Reich. The Prussian ministers vigorously enforced the provisions in the Law for the Protection of the Republic. During the Ruhr crisis the state strenuously opposed the Cuno cabinet's flirtation with various rightist paramilitary groups, while moving decisively on its own to combat these self-proclaimed protectors of German unity.

The only seeming disparity in this pattern was Prussia's short-lived support of the policy of temporarily abandoning the Ruhr area financially, the *Versackungspolitik*. This must be seen as a sort of Versailles decision in reverse. In view of the economic ravages caused by the occupation and passive resistance, it appeared to the Prussian leaders that the state could fulfill its mission for the unoccupied part of Germany only if it temporarily abandoned the occupied areas. The policy of abandonment was similar to a decision that the cabinet considered in the summer of 1919: if war broke out again, to give up the Western areas of Prussia and retreat to the state's Eastern "heartland." It is significant that Prussia dropped its support of the *Ver-*

sackungspolitik immediately once it became obvious that the policy had the effect of destroying the state's unity rather than solidifying it.

The absence of an external crisis at the end of 1924 forging the Republican parties together in defense of Prussia's self-proclaimed German mission undoubtedly contributed to the length of the second interregnum. The original cause of the government crisis lay outside the state. It came about because the DVP leaders in the national legislature insisted on bringing the DNVP into the national coalition, and the German Nationalists in turn insisted that they be part of the Prussian cabinet as well. A substantial minority of the DVP's Landtag delegation and particularly the two DVP ministers had strong reservations about resuming the Reich-Prussian linkage in this form, while the majority of the DDP and Center party Landtag delegations rejected a *Bürgerblock* cabinet in Prussia altogether. Especially the Catholic party, which held the balance of power in the Reich and the state, preferred a left-of-center coalition in Prussia to balance its participation in the series of right-of-center combinations in the Reich. In addition, while there was evidence that the DNVP in the Reichstag was willing to make some concessions in order to become an acceptable coalition partner for the moderate bourgeois parties, the German Nationalists in Prussia remained intransigent in their antidemocratic stand.

If there had been any doubt about the attitude of the Prussian DNVP, the party's activities during the Reich presidential campaign quickly disspelled them. Among the political leaders who suggested Hindenburg as the candidate of the nationalist Right was Ernst von Schlange-Schöningen, then the most radical of the state's DNVP leaders. For the Pomeranian Junker the election of the former field marshal was part of a long-range plan to alter fundamentally the political balance of power in Germany and Prussia. Schlange-Schöningen envisioned a three-point alliance between the new Reich president, the Reichswehr, and the Prussian DNVP that could act decisively and permanently to destroy parliamentary democracy in state and Reich and restore the rule of Prussian authoritarianism over all of Germany. Knowledge of these plans in turn contributed to the failure of the *Bürgerblock* in Prussia; neither the Center party nor the DDP was willing to acquiesce in restoring the pre-1914 power constellation in Prussia. And if that had not been sufficient to deter the Center party from embracing the German Nationalists as coalition partners, the Conservatives' style of campaign in the spring of 1925 sealed the issue. Wilhelm Marx, head of the Center party and joint presidential candidate of the republican parties, felt very strongly that the Conservatives had acted deliberately to stir up anti-Catholic feelings among their Protestant constituencies.

Despite the continuity of coalitions, the record of concrete reform accomplishment by the republican governments is not very impressive. Here the narrow ideological limits of Prussia's republican *étatisme* became quickly apparent. The Revolutionary Cabinet brought democracy in the formal sense to the state, but it failed to enact any major reforms of the Prussian administrative and personnel structure. The errors were only partially and belatedly remedied by the succeeding governments. In the course of the next five years Prussia did create both a police force and a civilian administrative corps that successfully weathered a number of major crises, and repulsed efforts from the extreme right and the extreme left to destabilize the state, but all of the republican governments neglected to make structural administrative reforms. Except for the creation of the provinces of Upper Silesia and Grenzmark, both of which were the result of foreign policy considerations or pressure by the Reich, neither the Weimar nor the grand coalitions were able to enact any significant territorial reform legislation. The size of the provinces and districts was still determined primarily by the accidents of their feudal heritage rather than being the product of rational planning. Individual reform acts, such as the Greater Berlin Law and the Ruhr Regional Planning Act *(Ruhrsiedlungsverband)* covered relatively limited areas and at any rate remained exceptions that proved the rule. Provincial governors and district directors continued to exist side-by-side as they had since the beginning of the nineteenth century, although every royal and republican commission on administrative reforms argued that one or the other was superfluous in a modern state. In what was perhaps their most glaring failing, the cabinets could not even agree to abolish the anachronistic latifundia governmental units *(Gutsbezirke)*.

The record on personnel policy was somewhat more positive, at least in part because the governments set themselves decidedly modest goals. Beginning with the Revolutionary Cabinet, the Prussian governments rejected the demands for wholesale dismissals of "reactionary" civil servants; they contented themselves with creating a civil service that was "loyal" to the republic. Concretely, this meant that for the most part Prussian bureaucrats were expected to conform at least outwardly to the new form of government and to refrain from active or passive sabotage of the governments' writ. Except for the top echelons of political appointments, republican Prussia did not mandate enthusiastic support for the new form of government.

This decision meant, of course, that the majority of the old royal civil servants remained in office, though it does not follow that Prussia was riddled with closet monarchists who worked actively to bring the king back to his throne. To be sure, there were some who fell into this category, but with time their numbers decreased. Most members of the civil service corps were loyal to the republican Prussia because, like the cabinet members, they accepted the concept of Prussian *étatisme*. Especially during the years of the grand coalition acceptance of the republic in Prussia in this sense was quite high among the civil service. In addition, the corps of political officials (provincial governors, district directors, and county executives), whose members were expected to be ideologically committed to parliamentary democracy, was characterized by a high degree of political homogeneity and continuity in office. Since the basic personnel policy lines of the Prussian cabinets did not substantially change, the makeup of the group of political appointments remained remarkably stable from 1918 to 1925.

Generally speaking, then, political reforms worthy of the name were enacted only when the coalition parties saw the parliamentary system itself threatened. With the benefit of hindsight, it is not difficult to see that this cautious approach toward major reforms, that characterized all of the republican governments, in the long run undermined the democratic system itself. Moreover, by 1925 even contemporary observers asked if a smoothly functioning parliamentary system as such was not a sterile accomplishment in the absence of meaningful changes in the structure of society? This was particularly true in view of the pressures on the Center party to move further to the right, and the lack of a vertical substructure to support the coalition patterns at the state level.[11] In the provincial diets and county legislatures, Social Democrats and the moderate bourgeois parties tended to be on opposite sides of the aisle, with the bourgeois side often including the DNVP in a working relationship.[12]

Another glaring omission from the palette of reforms was the absence of fundamental changes in the relationship between the Reich and Prussia. Despite the state's support in principle of the elusive *Reichsreform*, Prussia— supported by the other German *Länder*—prevented a thoroughgoing revision of the German federal structure. The state's "success" in this area forced the Reich to build up its own administrative structure, in many cases duplicating Prussian offices and leading to constant if minor friction between Prussia and the Reich.

We should not ignore, however, the circumstances and aims—some of them admittedly misguided—that affected the decisions of the state's republican leaders. True, to an extent the Prussians were less moderate than timid. It was in some ways easier to ignore the problems, particularly in the face of perennial crises that required instant if short-range solutions. But more important here again were the dual factors of political rationalism and Prussian *étatisme*. Along with the political ideologies of the second half of the nineteenth century, the republican leaders inherited the nationalist and positivist optimism of that era. They were sincerely convinced that parliamentary democracy would be accepted by the state's administrative substructure because it was a better, that is, a more rational system of governing a modern society. The state's civil servants would recognize it as such because as technical and rational experts they would be convinced by empirical evidence.

In this sense Prussia could square the circle: the state could experience gradual change without having to endure the experiences of forced dismissals and personal bitterness.

Overshadowing all other considerations, however, was the consciousness of Prussia's "German mission." The republican leaders were not willing to undertake any initiatives that might endanger Prussia's political stability and territorital integrity since they were convinced Prussia's role as *Reichsklammer* was indispensable to the continuation of Germany's national unity. Here lay a major reason for the state's reluctance to move vigorously in making reforms. Forcing the pace of change, as the disastrous attempts by Adolph Hoffmann in the Ministry of Education had demonstrated, endangered the existence of the state and Prussia's German mission itself.

The first seven years of Prussia's republican history, then, showed notable accomplishments and posed significant questions for the future. The new political leadership after 1918 succeeded in establishing and maintaining Prussia as a democratic and parliamentary state; Prussia undoubtedly enabled Weimar Germany to survive as long as it did. Yet, in the long run the impressive facade of the "democratic rock that was Prussia" could not hide a certain lack of substance.[13] Until now, for the most part, parliamentary and cabinet stability had remained ends in themselves, rather than serving as means to transform the structure of Prussian society.

NOTES

GLOSSARY

BIBLIOGRAPHY

INDEX

Abbreviations Used in Notes

Ak/Rk Cuno	*Akten der Reichskanzlei: Das Kabinett Cuno 22. November 1922 bis 12. August 1923,* ed. Karl-Heinz Harbeck (Boppard a.Rh., 1968)
Ak/Rk Marx	*Akten der Reichskanzlei: Die Kabinette Marx I und II,* ed. Günter Abranovski (Boppard a.Rh., 1973)
Ak/Rk Scheidemann	*Akten der Reichskanzlei: Das Kabinett Scheidemann,* ed. Hagen Schulze (Boppard a.Rh., 1971)
Ak/Rk Stresemann	*Akten der Reichskanzlei: Die Kabinette Stresemann I und II.,* ed. Martin Vogt (Boppard a.Rh., 1978)
Ak/Rk Wirth	*Akten der Reichskanzlei: Die Kabinette Wirth I und II,* ed. Ingrid Schulze-Bidlingmaier (Boppard a.Rh., 1973)
Arch.HiKo	Archiv der Historischen Kommission, Berlin
Arch.SD	Archiv der sozialen Demokratie, Bonn – Bad Godesberg
AVB	*Aufrufe, Verordnungen und Beschlüsse des Vollzugsrates des Arbeiter- und Soldatenrates Gross-Berlins* (Berlin, 1918)
BA	Bundesarchiv, Koblenz
BA/Kl.Erw.	BA/Kleine Erwerbungen
"DDP-Fr.Prot."	"Fraktionsprotokolle der DDP-Landtagsfraktion 1919–1932," BA 45/III
DNVP-Bericht Okt. 1924	*Regierungskrise und Reichstagsauflösung* (Berlin, 1924)
DNVP-Parteitag	Unpublished protocols of the DNVP national congresses, Forst.Hbg./7533 (DNVP)
Dok.Arb.Bew.	*Dokumente und Materialien zur Geschichte der deutschen Arbeiterbewegung* (Berlin: Institut für Marxismus-Leninismus beim ZK der SED, 1958)
DrSVPrLV	*Sammlung der Drucksachen der verfassungsgebenden Preussischen Landesversammlung 1919/21* (Berlin, 1921)
Forst.Hbg.	Forschungsstelle für die Geschichte des Nationalsozialismus, Hamburg

"Giebel-Aufz.Rtagsfr."

"Aufzeichnungen über die Reichstagsfraktionssitzung [13.6.1920]," Giebel papers/ 210-15 (Arch. SD)

GK

Generalkommission der Gewerkschaften Deutschlands

Hap.Arch.

Hapag-Archiv, Hamburg

IFA

Der Interfraktionelle Ausschuss, ed. Erich Matthias and Rudolf Morsey (Düsseldorf, 1959)

IISG

International Institute for Social History, Amsterdam

"Januar-Unruhen"

"Bericht des Untersuchungsausschusses über die Januar-Unruhen 1919 in Berlin," *DrSVPrLV,* doc. 4121, pp. 8066–8175

"Kampf"

Albert Grzesinski, "Im Kampf um die deutsche Republik," manuscript, Grzesinski papers/ 2457 (IISG)

LASH

Landesarchiv Schleswig-Holstein, Schleswig

LBI

Leo Baeck Institute, New York

NaVV

Bestand Nationale und Völkische Verbände/ Forst.Hbg.

NSStaG

Niedersächsisches Staatsarchiv, Göttingen

NSStAH

Niedersächsisches Staatsarchiv, Hanover

PK

Parteikorrespondenz (SPD publication)

Pr.GS

Preussische Gesetzsammlung

PrGStAB

Preussisches Geheimes Staatsarchiv, Berlin

"Prot.A-Rat Berlin 19.11.1918"

"Protokoll der Berliner Arbeiterräte am 19. November 1918 im Zirkus Busch," ed. Horst Neumann and Günter Vebel, *Beiträge zur Geschichte der deutschen Arbeiterbewegung* 10, no. 6 (1968)

Prot.d.Sitz.d.NV

Stenographische Berichte der Verhandlungen der Deutschen Nationalversammlung (Berlin, 1919)

"Prot.VZR.16.11.1918"

"Protokolle der Sitzungen des Vollzugsrates des Arbeiter- und Soldatenrates Gross-Berlins . . . vom 16., 17. und 19. November 1918," ed. Horst Neumann and Günter Vebel, *Beiträge zur Geschichte der deutschen Arbeiterbewegung* 10 (Sonderheft, 1968)

II. Rätekongress

Referate auf dem II. Kongress der Arbeiter-, Bauern-, und Soldatenräte Deutschlands am 8. bis 14. April 1919 (Berlin, 1919)

Reichskonferenz 5.5.1920

Protokoll über die Verhandlungen der Reichskonferenz der Sozialdemokratischen Partei

	Deutschlands . . . Berlin . . . 5. und 6. Mai 1920 (Berlin, 1920)
"Reichskonferenz 25.Nov.1918"	Protocol of the federal conference, *RVB-Protokolle* Vol. 1, doc. 30, pp. 149–215.
RheinZ-Parteitag	*Bericht über die Verhandlungen des Parteitages der Rheinischen Zentrumspartei . . . Köln 15.–18. September 1919,* ed. Rhenish Center Party (Cologne, 1919)
RK	Reichskanzlei papers, BA
RVB-Protokolle	*Die Regierung der Volksbeauftragten 1918/19,* ed. Susanne Miller and Heinrich Potthoff (Düsseldorf, 1969)
"RVB u.VZR-Sitz.18.11.1918"	"Sitzung des Rates der Volksbeauftragten und des Vollzugsrates," 18. Nov. 1918, *RVB-Protokolle*
SBPrLT 1921–24	*Sitzungsberichte des Preussischen Landtages 1921–1924* (Berlin, 1924)
SBPrLT 1925–28	*Sitzungsberichte des Preussischen Landtages 1925–1928* (Berlin, 1928)
SBVPrLV	*Sitzungsberichte der verfassungsgebenden preussischen Landesversammlung* (Berlin, 1921)
"Sitz.d.Pr.Reg.u.d.ZR"	"Sitzung der Preussischen Regierung und des Zentralrates," *ZR-Protokolle*
"Sitz.d.RVB"	"Sitzung des Rates der Volksbeauftragten," *RVB-Protokolle*
"Sitz.PrStMin."	"Protokoll der Sitzung der Preussischen Staatsregierung (Staatsministerium)"
"Sitz.ReiReg."	"Protokoll der Sitzung der Reichsregierung"
"Sitz.Z-Rtagsfr."	"Sitzung der Zentrum-Reichstags-Fraktion," 23 Feb. 1921, ten Hompel papers/15, BA
SPD 1898–1918	*Die Reichstagsfraktion der deutschen Sozialdemokratie 1898–1918,* ed. Erich Matthias and Eberhard Pikart (Düsseldorf, 1966)
SPD-Parteikonferenz 22.3.1919	*Protokoll der Parteikonferenz in Weimar am 22. und 23. März 1919* (Berlin, 1919)
SPD-Parteitag 1919	*Protokoll über die Verhandlungen des Parteitages der Sozialdemokratischen Partei Deutschlands . . . Weimar 10. bis 15. Juni 1919* (Berlin, 1919)
SPD-Parteitag 1920	*Protokoll über die Verhandlungen des Parteitages der Sozialdemokratischen Partei Deutschlands . . . Kassel 10. bis 16. Oktober 1920* (Berlin, 1920)

SPD-Parteitag 1921

Protokoll über die Verhandlungen des Parteitages der Sozialdemokratischen Partei Deutschlands . . . Görlitz . . . 18. bis 24. September 1921 (Berlin, 1921)

Staatsarch.Hbg.

Staatsarchiv, Hamburg

Stadtarch.Cologne

Stadtarchiv, Cologne

"Unruhen in Mitteldeutschland"

"Bericht des Untersuchungsausschusses über die Unruhen in Mitteldeutschland von November 1918 bis zum 19. März 1919," *DrSVPrLV*, vol. 10, doc. 3227, pp. 5574–84

"Verf.-Ausschuss"

"12. (Verfassungs-) Ausschuss—wörtliche Niederschrift, 16. Juni–8. Okt. 1920," *DrSVPrLV*, doc. 3120B, pp. 5224–5382

"Weimar MS"

Otto Braun, "Von Weimar zu Hitler," corrected typescript of O. Braun's memoirs, Braun papers/B/A/68, PrGStAB

Z-Parteitag Jan.1920

Erster Reichsparteitag des Zentrums—Offizieller Bericht . . . 19. bis 22. Januar 1919 (Berlin [1920])

ZR-Arch.

Archiv des Zentralrates, IISG

ZR-Protokolle

Der Zentralrat der Deutschen Sozialistischen Republik 19.12.1918–3.4.1919, ed. Eberhard Kolb and Reinhard Rürup (Leiden, 1968)

"ZR-Sitzung 21.12.1918"

"Sitzung des Zentralrates," 21 Dec. 1918. *ZR-Protokolle*

Notes

Introduction

1. Felix Gilbert, "Prussia: Attempt at a Balance," *New York Review of Books,* 18 March 1982, pp. 48–50.

2. *Amtsblatt des Allierten Kontrollrates,* 25 Feb. 1947, p. 262.

3. A small sample: Sebastian Haffner, *Preussen ohne Legende* (Hamburg, 1980): *Preussen in der deutschen Geschichte,* ed. Dirk Blasius (Königstein/Ts., 1980); Volker Hentschel, *Das war Preussen* (Düsseldorf, 1980); Bernt Engelmann, *Preussen—Land der unbegrenzten Möglichkeiten* (Munich, 1979); Kurt Forstreuter, *Wirkungen des Preussenlandes* (Cologne, 1982); Kurt Birrenbach, ed., *Preussen—Seine Wirkungen auf die deutsche Geschichte* (Stuttgart, 1982); and the 1980 special volume of the periodical *Geschichte und Gesellschaft,* devoted to "Preussen im Rückblick."

4. For a review of the exhibition, see Gilbert, "Prussia," pp. 48–50.

5. For the historiography and conceptualization of the term, see Hartmut Kaelble et al., *Probleme der Modernisierung in Deutschland* (Opladen, 1978), pp. 6–10; for the ideological conflict between the conservative-agrarian and industrial-social forces in Germany, see Gerhard Schulz, *Aufstieg des Nationalsozialismus—Krise und Revolution in Deutschland* (Frankfurt a.M., 1975), esp. ch. 2.

6. The significance of interregional differences has been particularly stressed in the writings of Arnold Brecht. See *Federalism and Regionalism in Germany* (New York, 1945), p. 34; and *Mit der Kraft des Geistes—Lebenserinnerungen* (Stuttgart, 1967), p. 265.

7. For example, Enno Eimers, *Das Verhältnis von Preussen und Reich in den ersten Jahren der Weimarer Republik* (Berlin, 1969); and Hans Peter Ehni, *Bollwerk Preussen—Regierung, Reich-Länderproblem und Sozialdemokratie* (Bonn–Bad Godesberg, 1975).

8. See Manfred Rauh, *Die Parlamentarisierung des Deutschen Reiches* (Düsseldorf, 1977), pp. 7–14 for a detailed and critical analysis of the literature and methods of this historiography.

9. The phrase is used with reference to the Weimar Republic by Karl-Dietrich Bracher, "Auflösung einer Demokratie," in *Faktoren der Machtbildung,* ed. A. R. Gurland (Berlin, 1952), p. 40.

10. Dieter Grosser, *Vom monarchischen Parlamentarismus zur parlamentarischen Demokratie* (The Hague, 1970), p. 18; and Susanne Miller, *Das Problem der Freiheit im Sozialismus,* 2d ed. (Frankfurt a.M., 1964), pp. 277–78.

11. This point is emphasized by Gerhard A. Ritter, "Kontinuität and Umformung des deutschen Parteiensystems 1918–1920," in *Entstehung und Wandel der modernen Gesellschaft—Festschrift für Hans Rosenberg,* ed. Gerhard A. Ritter (Berlin, 1970), pp. 342–76.

12. See Reinhard Rürup, *Probleme der Revolution in Deutschland 1918/19* (Wiesbaden, 1968); and Dietrich Orlow, "1918/19: A German Revolution," *German Studies Review* 5 (May 1982), 187–203.

13. Karl Dietrich Erdmann, "Die Geschichte der Weimarer Republik als Problem der Wissenschaft," *Vierteljahreshefte für Zeitgeschichte* 3 (Jan. 1955), 1–19.

14. Arthur Rosenberg, *Geschichte der deutschen Republik* (Karlsbad, 1935). For examples of later work on the subject, see, for instance, Eberhard Kolb, *Die Arbeiterräte in der deutschen*

Innenpolitik 1918–1919 (Düsseldorf, 1962); and Reinhard Rürup, "Entstehung und Grundlagen der Weimarer Verfassung," in *Vom Kaiserreich zur Weimarer Republik*, ed. E. Kolb (Cologne, 1972), pp. 218–43.

15. Such efforts were praised, among others, by Wally Zepler, "Zur deutschen Nationalversammlung," *Sozialistische Monatshefte* 52 (Feb. 10, 1919), 65–74; Georg Kotowski, "Preussen und die Weimarer Republik," *Preussen, Epochen and Probleme seiner Geschichte*, ed. Reinhard Dietrich (Berlin, 1964), p. 159; Ritter, "Kontinuität"; Ritter, *Die Reichstagsfraktion der deutschen Sozialdemokratie 1898–1918*, ed. Erich Matthias and Eberhard Pikart (Düsseldorf, 1966), p. lxxxviii. On the other hand, Harry Graf Kessler, *Tagebücher 1918–1937*, ed. Wolfgang Pfeiffer-Belli (Frankfurt a.M., 1961), p. 643 (Nov. 2, 1930), treats them with sarcasm and disdain.

16. Rauh, *Parlamentarisierung*, p. 14.

17. For a "revision of the revisionists," see Susanne Miller, *Burgfrieden und Klassenkampf—die Sozialdemokratie im Ersten Weltkrieg* (Düsseldorf, 1974); and David W. Morgan, *The Socialist Left and the German Revolution* (Ithaca, N.Y., 1975).

18. Gerald Feldman, "Wirtschafts- und sozialpolitische Probleme der deutschen Demobilmachung," in *Industrielles System und politische Entwicklung in der Weimarer Republik*, ed. Hans Mommsen et al., (Düsseldorf, 1974), pp. 618–19.

19. Paul Löbe, *Der Weg war lang*, 3d ed. (Berlin, 1954), p. 95.

20. This point of view is emphasized by Ritter, "Kontinuität"; Grosser, *Konstitutionalismus*, p. 210; and Walter Tormin, *Geschichte der deutschen Parteien seit 1848* (Stuttgart, 1968), p. 130. Cf. also the bibliography in Schulz, *Aufstieg*, pp. 783–84, n. 79.

21. Gerhard Schulz, *Zwischen Demokratie und Diktatur* (Berlin, 1963), p. 22; Werner Becker, *Demokratie des sozialen Rechts* (Göttingen, 1971), pp. 273–74; and Hartmut Schustereit, *Linksliberalismus und Sozialdemokratie in der Weimarer Republik* (Düsseldorf, 1975), p. 197.

22. Richard N. Hunt, *German Social Democracy 1918–1923* (New Haven, Conn.: 1964), p. 241.

23. The SPD's national chairman, Hermann Müller, was almost perversely proud of the fact that the party joined the Reich coalition only when reasons of foreign policy made such a decision absolutely unavoidable. See *Protokoll des Sozialdemokratischen Parteitages 1924* (Berlin, 1924), p. 83.

24. Alfred Kastning, *Die deutsche Sozialdemokratie zwischen Koalition und Opposition 1919–1923* (Paderborn, 1970), p. 7.

25. Otto Braun, *Von Weimar zu Hitler*, 2d ed. (Hamburg, 1949), pp. 84, 94. See also Grosser, *Konstitutionalismus*, p. 211, for a discussion of the relationship between party strength and successful coalitions.

26. See Grzesinski, "Kampf," p. 137.

27. Horst Möller, "Parlamentarisierung und Demokratisierung im Preussen der Weimarer Republik," *Gesellschaft, Parlament und Regierung*, ed. by Gerhard A. Ritter (Düsseldorf, 1974), p. 379; Hans Peter Ehni, "Zum Parteienverhältnis in Preussen 1918–1932," *Archiv für Sozialgeschichte* 11 (1971), 276.

28. Golo Mann, "Das Ende Preussens," *Preussen—Portrait einer politischen Kultur*, ed. Hans-Joachim Netzer (Munich, 1968), p. 160. See also Kotowski, "Preussen," pp. 152–53.

29. Hagen Schulze, *Otto Braun oder Preussens demokratische Sendung* (Berlin, 1978); Herbert Hömig, *Das preussische Zentrum in der Weimarer Republik* (Mainz, 1979); Horst Möller, *Parlamentarismus im Preussen der Weimarer Republik* (Berlin, 1978).

30. Grzesinski, "Kampf," p. 203. See also Helga Grebing, *Geschichte der deutschen Arbeiterbewegung* (Munich, 1966), p. 171; Golo Mann, *Geschichte und Geschichten* (Frankfurt

a.M., 1961), p. 50; Erich Kuttner, *Otto Braun* (Berlin, 1932), pp. 5–6; and Ernst Portner, *Die Verfassungspolitik der Liberalen 1919* (Bonn, 1973), pp. 13–14.

31. Heinrich Albertz, cited in *Süddeutsche Zeitung,* 23–24 Aug. 1980.

Chapter 1. Political Parties in Prussia, 1914—1921

1. Gerhard A. Ritter, "Kontinuität und Umformung des deutschen Parteiensystems 1918–1920," in *Entstehung und Wandel der modernen Gesellschaft* ed. Gerhard A. Ritter, (Berlin, 1970), p. 345.

2. Interview with Dr. Ernest Hamburger (member of the *Landtag,* 1925–1932), 6 August 1976.

3. See the detailed discussion in Reinhard Patemann, *Der Kampf um die preussische Wahlreform im Ersten Weltkrieg* (Düsseldorf, 1964).

4. Wolfgang Hartenstein, *Die Anfänge der Deutschen Volkspartei 1918–1920* (Düsseldorf, 1962), p. 9; Rudolf Morsey, *Die Deutsche Zentrumspartei 1917–1923* (Düsseldorf, 1966), p. 58; Gerhard Senger, *Die Politik der Deutschen Zentrumspartei zur Frage Reich und Länder von 1918–1932* (Hamburg, 1932), p. 11; Patemann, *Kampf,* pp. 186–87.

5. Dieter Grosser, *Von monarchischen Konstitutionalismus zur parlamentarischen Demokratie* (The Hague, 1970), p. 86.

6. Susanne Miller, *Burgfrieden und Klassenkampf* (Düsseldorf, 1974), p. 41. On Bethmann Hollweg, see also Konrad Jarausch, *The Enigmatic Chancellor* (New Haven, Conn., 1967).

7. Report by Colonel Bauer, 4 Apr. 1918, in *Militär und Innenpolitik im Weltkrieg 1914–1918,* ed. Werner Deist, (Düsseldorf, 1970), vol. 1, no. 452, p. 1215.

8. Hartwig Thieme, *Nationaler Liberalismus in der Krise: Die nationalliberale Fraktion des Preussischen Abgeordnetenhauses 1914–1918* (Boppard a.Rh., 1963), pp. 100ff.; and *SPD 1898–1918* 2:289.

9. Eduard David, *Das Kriegstagebuch des Reichstagsabgeordneten Eduard David 1914–1918,* ed. Erich Matthias and Susanne Miller (Düsseldorf, 1966), p. 223 (8 Apr. 1917); and Miller, *Burgfrieden,* p. 287.

10. For a general discussion of the politics and organization of the conservative parties in prewar Prussia, see Hans-Jürgen Puhle, *Agrarische Interessenpolitik und preussischer Konservatismus* (Hanover, 1966), esp. pp. 213ff.; Hans-Jürgen Puhle, "Parlament, Parteien und Interessenverbände 1890–1914," in *Das Kaiserliche Deutschland,* ed. Michael Stürmer, (Düsseldorf, 1970), pp. 340–77; and Gottfried Mehnert, *Evangelische Kirche und Politik* (Düsseldorf, 1959), pp. 41–42, 73ff.

11. On the early history of the DNVP, see Jan Striesow, "Die Deutschnationale Volkspartei und die Völkisch-Radikalen" ["DNVP"], (Ph.D. diss., University of Hamburg, 1977). See also Anneliese Thimme, *Flucht in den Mythos* (Göttingen, 1969), p. 12; and Werner Liebe, *Die Deutschnationale Volkspartei 1918–1924 [DNVP]* (Düsseldorf, 1956), p. 12.

12. For a detailed discussion of this concept, see Gerhard Schulz, *Aufstieg des Nationalsozialismus—Krise und Revolution in Deutschland* (Frankfurt a.M., 1975), esp. ch. 2.

13. For the history and importance of the DHV, see Iris Hamel, *Völkischer Verband und Nationale Gewerkschaft* (Frankfurt a.M., 1967).

14. The DNVP party programs are printed in Liebe, *DNVP,* pp. 107–08.

15. *SBVPrLV,* 26 Mar. 1919, vol. 1, col. 735 (Kardorff). See also Thimme, *Flucht,* p. 22; Hoetzsch ["Denkschrift"], 5 Nov. 1918, Forst. Hbg./7533 (DNVP). vol. 1; Class to Gebsattel, 10 Jan. 1920, Forst. Hbg/412 (Alldeutscher Verband).

16. Walther Graef, "Der Werdegang der Deutschnationalen Volkspartei, 1918–1928," in *Der nationale Wille,* ed. Max Weiss (Berlin, 1928), p. 23. See the comparison of the professions of

the DNVP legislators in the Prussian Constitutional Convention and those in the National Constitutional Convention, in Liebe, *DNVP*, p. 18.

17. For a discussion of the leadership and Hergt's election as party chairman, see Striesow, "DNVP," pp. 37, 111. For a characterization of Hergt's administrative style, see Paul Moldenhauer, "Politische Erinnerungen," Moldenhauer Papers/1, p. 23 (BA); and von Kardorff to Neuhaus (executive secretary of the DNVP delegation), 19 Apr. 1920, Kardorff Papers/16 (BA).

18. See "Bericht über die Vertretertagung der Deutschnationalen Volkspartei am 7. und 8. Februar 1919 . . . " (n.d.), Forst.Hbg./7533 (DNVP), vol. 1; "Verhandlungsbericht über die Sitzung des geschäftsführenden Ausschusses des Alldeutschen Verbandes," 30 Aug. 1919, and 6 and 7 Dec. 1919, Forst.Hbg/412.

19. Hoetzsch, "Denkschrift."

20. See Hergt's fulsome praise for the performance of his Social Democratic successor, Albert Südekum, *SBVPrLV*, 27 Mar. 1919, vol. 1, col. 884. See also the character study in Heinrich Köhler, *Lebenserinnerungen*, ed. Josef Becker (Stuttgart, 1964), p. 208; and the thorough discussion in, Striesow, "DNVP," pp. 128ff., 141–42.

21. Compare *SBPrLV*, 25 June 1919, vol. 1, cols. 2530–32 (Kardorff) and 10 July 1919, vol. 3, cols. 3274–90 (Negenborn).

22. See Hergt's speech in *SBVPrLV*, 26 Sept. 1919, vol. 4, cols. 4408–09. Brust's commentary is in ibid., col. 4482. For the content of and the reaction to the party program, see Thimme, *Flucht*, p. 40. For additional contemporary and scholarly analyses of the Hergt initiative, see *SBVPrLV*, 15 Nov. 1919, cols. 6542, 6548 (Heilmann); Enno Eimers, *Das Verhältnis von Preussen und Reich in den ersten Jahren der Weimarer Republik (1918–1923)* (Berlin, 1969), pp. 257 and 257, n. 16; Paul Hirsch, *Der Weg der Sozialdemokratie zur Macht in Preussen* (Berlin, 1929), p. 159; Lewis Hertzman, *DNVP* (Lincoln, Neb., 1963), pp. 79–81; and Carl Severing, "Für die Grosse Koalition," *Sozialistische Monatshefte* 57 (5 Jan. 1925), 1.

23. *SBVPrLV*, 30 Sept. 1919, vol. 4, col. 4482,

24. Acts of violence increased in frequency during the fall of 1919. See Striesow, "DNVP," pp. 147ff. Typical of the hard-liners' views is *DNVP-Parteitag*, col. 6060c (Traub). Cf. also Striesow, "DNVP," pp. 143–44, 161.

25. The best account of the antecedents and course of the Kapp Putsch is Johannes Erger, *Der Kapp-Lüttwitz Putsch* (Düsseldorf, 1967).

26. This was particularly true of the East Elbian synod of the Lutheran church, as well as the Agrarian League. See the announcement of the Pomeranian Agrarian League of 13 March 1920, in *Fünf Tage Militärdiktatur*, ed. Karl Brammer (Berlin, 1920), pp. 42–43. On the role of the DNVP in the preparations for the putsch, see also Striesow, "DNVP," pp. 185–91.

27. Hergt [?], "1. Entwurf 13.3," manuscript, Forst.Hbg./7533 (DNVP), vol. 1.

28. Cf. *SBVPrLV*, 30 Mar. 1920, vol. 8, cols. 10535–36 (Hergt); vol. 9, 10586–87 (Friedberg); and Westarp, "Der 18. März 1920," Westarp [?], "[Notiz]," n.d. and Hergt, "[Aufzeichnung]" n.d., Forst.Hbg./7533 (DNVP), vol. 1.

29. See the election platform of the DNVP published in the *Hamburger Fremdenblatt*, 18 Nov. 1920. For analyses, see Jochen Jacke, *Kirche zwischen Morarchie und Republik* (Hamburg, 1976), pp. 54, 72, 110–15; Mehnert, *Kirche*, p. 176.

30. Lüdicke to S. von Kardorff, 19 Sept. 1920, S. von Kardorff papers/11 (BA).

31. Kardorff became a member of the DVP and joined the Reichstag delegation of that party. On the controversy, see H. E. von Lindeiner-Wildau, *Wir und die Deutsche Volkspartei* (Berlin, 1921), pp. 18–19; S. Kardorff to Neuhaus, 19 Apr. 1920, and Kardorff to Lindeiner-Wildau, 30 Jan. 1921, S. von Kardorff papers/16 and 11 (BA). The 1921 letter is a specific reply to Lindeiner's pamphlet, *Wir und die Deutsche Volkspartei*. (The Economics party will be discussed later.) The leadership's refusal to purge its ranks of extremists is explained in *Deutsche Zeitung*, 21 Apr. 1920. See also Striesow, "DNVP," p. 234.

32. Cf. the reports and discussions at the DNVP's second national party congress.

33. Cf. Dr. Pfannkuche, "Reichseinheit and parlamentarisches System," *Deutsche Zeitung*, 6 Jan. 1921.

34. Hartenstein, *Aufänge*, p. 232.

35. Lüdicke to S. von Kardorff, 24 Dec. 1920, in ibid., p. 15. Cf. F. Werner, "Deutsch-völkisch—eine Fanfare," *Deutsche Zeitung*, 6 Jan. 1921.

36. Cf. Andreas Gildemeister, "[Unterredung mit dem Kronprinzen von Bayern]," 1 Sept. 1920, p. 1, Forst.Hbg/7533 (DNVP), vol. 1; Hergt, "Niederschrift zwischen dem Kronprinzen . . . Helfferich und . . . Hergt am 1 September 1920," in *ibid.*; Kurt Borsdorff, "[Unterredung mit Graf Bothmer]," 10 Sept. 1920, in *ibid.* See also Striesow, "DNVP," p. 310.

37. Cited in Wolfgang Ruge, "Deutschnationale Volkspartei," in *Die Bürgerlichen Parteien in Deutschland*, ed. Dieter Fricke et al. (Leipzig, 1968), 1:733.

38. Oswald Wachtling, *Joseph Joos* (Mainz, 1974), pp. 15-16.

39. Martin Spahn, "Julius Bachem," *Hochland* 15 (1917/18), 17-21; and John K. Zeender, "German Catholics and the Concept of an Interconfessional Party 1900-1922," *Journal of Central European Affairs* 23 (1964), 426. This also explains the deep hostility between Erzberger, Peter Spahn, and Spahn's son, Martin (Zeender, ibid., p. 430, n. 26). On Peter Spahn, cf. the short biography in *Zeitgeschichte in Lebensbildern*, ed. Rudolf Morsey (Mainz, 1973), pp. 65-80.

40. Wolfgang Stump, *Geschichte und Organisation der Zentrumspartei in Düsseldorf 1917-1933* (Düsseldorf, 1971), p. 18. Some of the diehards joined the DNVP in 1919-1920.

41. *RheinZ-Parteitag*, Sept. 1919, pp. 196-99.

42. Johannes Schauff, *Die deutschen Katholiken und die Zentrumspartei* (Cologne, 1928), pp. 108-15; *RheinZ-Parteitag*, pp. 211-14 (Kaiser). Cf. Erich Kosthorst et al., *Jakob Kaiser* (Stuttgart, 1967), 1:92.

43. For a short biography of Porsch, see *Zeitgeschichte in Lebensbildern*, pp. 113-28. Otto Braun characterized Herold as "my diehard antagonist" (Otto Braun, "Weimar MS," p. 189.)

44. "Prot.A-Rat Berlin 19.11.1918," p. 1034.

45. Cf. *SBVPrLV*, 25 Nov. 1920, vol. 11, col. 13968 (Dallmer); Graef, "Werdegang," Weiss, Wille, p. 36; and *Was wir deutschen Männern und Frauen vor dem 7. Dezember [1924] sagen müssen!* [Berlin, 1924], Deutschnationale Flugschrift no. 195, p. 12; and *Kreuzzeitung*, 2 Nov. 1921. *RheinZ-Parteitag*, p. 73 (Joos), p. 138 (Biermann); Alois Klöckner, *Die Zentrumsfraktion in der preussischen Landesversammlung* (Berlin, 1919), pp. 14, 48; Otto Braun, *Von Weimar zu Hitler*, 2d ed. (Hamburg, 1949), pp. 21-22; and G. Heller, ed., *Die Preussische Landesversammlung vom 13. März bis 12. Dezember 1919* ([Berlin, 1920]), pp. 42-43.

46. David, *Tagebuch*, p. 36, (entry for 6 Sept. 1914); and Wolfgang Elben, *Das Problem der Kontinuität in der deutschen Revolution* (Düsseldorf, 1965), p. 141.

47. Cf. the contemporary analyses from the viewpoint of the Center party in Alois Klöckner, *Der erste preussische Landtag* (Berlin, 1921), p. 34; and Friedrich Grebe, "Die Landtagswahlen in Preussen," *Allgemeine Rundschau* 18 (5 Mar. 1921), 109. See also Morsey, *Zentrumspartei*, p. 354, n. 13.

48. The Prussian Center party strongly condemned the Kapp Putsch and saw in it a renewal of anti-Catholic Prussian reactionary forces and the danger of another *Kulturkampf*. See Robert Jansen, *Der Berliner Militärputsch und seine politischen Folgen* (Berlin, 1920), pp. 36, 41; cf. the extraordinarily sharp statements by Wildermann (Center party delegate to the Prussian Constitutional Convention), *SBVPrLV*, 30 Mar. 1920, vol. 8, cols. 10512-24.

49. For an analysis of the composition and relative strength of the DGB, as well as Stegerwald's political motivation, see Larry Jones, "Adam Stegerwald," *Vierteljahrshefte für Zeitgeschichte* 27 (Mar. 1979), 1-29. Cf. also Zeender, "Catholics," pp. 434-36; Karl Buchheim, *Geschichte der christlichen Parteien in Deutschland* (Munich, 1953), p. 412. Morsey,

Zentrumspartei, pp. 397, 428. Heinrich Brüning later wrote that he had composed the speech (*Memoiren* [Stuttgart, 1970], p. 70). Incidentally, both contemporaries and historians agree that Stegerwald's ambitions considerably exceeded his abilities. See Helga Grebing, "Weimarer Portraits," *Politische Studien* 6 (Mar. 1956), 23; "Adam Stegerwald," *Zeitgeschichte in Lebensbildern,* pp. 206–19; Carl Severing, *Mein Lebensweg* (Cologne, 1950), 1:332; and Koch-Weser, diary entry, 17 June 1921, Koch-Weser papers (BA).

50. Jones, "Stegerwald," pp. 10–11, 15–17; on the DNVP's fears, see Ritter to Engerer Ausschuss der Staatspolitischen Arbeitsgemeinschaft, 14 Jan. 1921, Diller papers/11/D9 (Forst.Hbg.); and Stegerwald, "Mein Rücktritt," *Germania,* 8 Nov. 1921.

51. See meeting of the Center party Reichstag delegation, 29 Sept. 1921 (Joos), ten Hompel papers/15 (BA); and Brüning, *Memoiren,* p. 404.

52. Jones, "Stegerwald," p. 9.

53. During the summer, three of the Center party's prominent leaders died: Trimborn on 25 July, Hitze on 20 July, and Burlage on 19 August 1920. On Marx's efforts at conciliation, see S. Joos, "Die Verantwortung Stegerwalds," and Stegerwald's reply in *Germania,* 23 and 24 Sept. 1921; and Marx, diary entry, 26 Sept. 1921, Marx papers/1070/227/6 (Stadtarch. Cologne). Cf. the interesting analysis from the left-socialist point of view: Curt Geyer, "Zur inneren Politik," *Unser Weg 3* (1 July 1921), 137.

54. Morsey, *Zentrumspartei,* p. 405. Cf. the meeting of the Center party's Reichstag delegation, 27 Oct. 1921, ten Hompel papers/15 (BA); and Jones, "Stegerwald," p. 21.

55. See the quite critical evaluation in Ernest Hamburger, *Juden im öffentlichen Leben Deutschlands . . . 1848–1918* (Tübingen, 1968), p. 74.

56. Stresemann wrote that Friedberg's appointment was meant "to prevent the spread of the dominance of the Center party to the Prussian Landtag" (Stresemann to the Bavarian Reichsrat member Franz von Buhl, 5 Nov. 1917, in *IFA* 1:33). On Stresemann's conservatism, see the statements by Dr. Helles (secretary-general of the DVP), *Coblenzer Zeitung,* 21 Feb. 1920. Helles and Friedberg had been party colleagues until 1918; as we shall see, Friedberg joined the DDP after the revolution.

57. Friedberg to Stresemann, 11 July 1917, *IFA* 1:33.

58. Thieme, *Nationalliberale,* p. 189; Patemann, *Kampf,* pp. 58, 70. Cf. the sharp attack by Stendel (DVP delegate to the Prussian Constitutional Convention) against Friedberg, *SBVPrLV,* 17 Dec. 1919, vol. 7, col. 8313.

59. Haussmann to Payer, 4 Nov. 1917, *IFA* 1:393, 1:454.

60. Patemann, *Kampf,* p. 119.

61. Hartenstein, *Anfänge,* pp. 20–21; Werner Stephan, *Aufstieg und Verfall des Links-liberalismus 1919–1933* (Göttingen, 1973), p. 37; Ludwig Luckemeyer, "Die Deutsche Demokratische Partei," Ph.D. diss., Erlangen, 1975, pp. 55–56; Moldenhauer, "Erinnerungen," p. 24.

62. Moldenhauer, "Erinnerungen," pp. 17–18.

63. Ibid., p. 22; *SBVPrLV,* 15 Mar. 1919, vol. 1, cols. 825–30 (von Richter); Hartenstein, *Anfänge,* pp. 78–79; Hirsch, *Weg,* pp. 160–61.

64. *SBVPrLV,* 15 Mar. 1919, vol. 1, col. 171 (von Richter); report of the DVP caucus to the second party congress 18–20 Oct. 1919, *Nationalliberale Correspondenz* (special edition), Forst. Hbg/7523 [DVP], vol. 1.

65. See Hergt's statements, "Bericht über die Verbandsvertretertagung der Deutschnationalen Volkspartei am 7. und 8. Februar 1919 . . ." Forst.Hbg./7533 [DNVP], vol. 1; Henry Ashby Turner, *Stresemann and the Politics of the Weimar Republic* (Princeton, N.J., 1963), pp. 33–34; Hartenstein, *Anfänge,* pp. 134–35; Hergt's speech to the DNVP party congress, 7 Dec. 1919, p. 6060b, Forst.Hbg/7533 (DNVP), vol. 1.

66. Cf. *SBVPrLV,* 17 Nov. 1919, vol. 5, cols. 6645, 6651–52, 6658 (Leidig); 16 Dec. 1919, vol. 7, cols. 8173, 8185 (Garnich); 17 Dec. 1919, vol. 7, cols. 8311–15 (Stendel).

67. The DVP resented the fact that Friedberg agreed to head the DDP delegation in the Prussian Constitutional Convention. The situation was particularly awkward since two prominent DVP members at the convention, Lotte and Hugo Garnich, were Friedberg's daughter and son-in-law. See Fritz Rathenau, "1895–1935—Als Jude in Dienste von Reich und Staat," typescript, p. 100 (LBI).

68. Lothar Albertin, *Liberalismus und Demokratie am Anfang der Weimarer Republik* (Düsseldorf, 1971), p. 400; Hartenstein, *Anfänge*, p. 120.

69. See Stresemann's speech of 18 Mar. 1920, *Reden und Schriften 1897–1926*, ed. Rochus Freiherr von Rheinbaben (Dresden, 1926), 1:317ff. Cf. Hergt's deposition, Karl Brammer, *Der Jagow-Prozess* (Berlin, 1920), p. 20; and Jansen, *Militärputsch*, p. 5.

70. Hartenstein, *Anfänge*, pp. 152ff. In his justification of the DVP's attitude during the Kapp Putsch, Stresemann drew a historical parallel between the Ebert-Scheidemann government in November 1918 and the Kapp enterprise. Both came to power by nonparliamentary means, and in both cases the DVP cooperated with the new rulers to preserve law and order. Stresemann, *Reden*, pp. 322–23.

71. See Lüdicke to S. von Kardorff, 19 Sept. 1920, S. von Kardorff papers/11 (BA).

72. Cf. Stresemann, *Deutsche Stimmen* 37 (12 Sept. 1920); and *SBVPrLV*, 7 Oct. 1920, vol. 10, col. 12902 (Heilmann). Cf. *Vorwärts*, no. 458 (15 Sept. 1920).

73. *SBVPrLV*, 7 July 1920, vol. 9, cols. 11639–53.

74. Ernst von Richter, *Nationalliberale Correspondenz* 40 (11 Jan. 1921). See also Siegfried von Kardorff to Neuhaus, 19 Apr. 1920, S. von Kardorff papers/16 (BA). On the other hand, the DNVP criticized the lack of a thoroughly "German *völkisch* character" in the DVP. See Oskar Hergt, *Auf zum Preussenkampf!* (Berlin, 1921), p. 19.

75. See von Richter, *Nationalliberale Correspondenz* 40 (10, 11 Jan. 1921). See also Robert Jansen, *Die Regierungsbildung in Preussen* (Berlin [1921]), p. 4; and Klöckner, *Landtag*, p. 26.

76. Moldenhauer, "Erinnerungen," p. 64; Hermann Kranold, "Nach den preussischen Landtagswahlen 1921," *Sozialistische Monatshefte* 56 (18 Feb. 1921), 171. See also Ernst Laubach, *Die Politik der Kabinette Wirth* (Lübeck and Hamburg, 1968), p. 87; and Brant, "Politische Chronik," *Neue Rundschau* 32, no. 2 (1921).

77. Graef, "Werdegang," p. 41; Hagen Schulze, *Otto Braun* (Berlin, 1977), p. 342; and Katharina von Oheimb to Eymern, 27 August 1921, K. von Kardorff papers/18 (BA).

78. Cf. Trimborn's statements during the meeting of the Center party's Reichstag caucus ("Sitz.Z-Rtagsfr."), 23 Feb. 1921, ten Hompel papers/15 (BA).

79. Turner, *Stresemann*, p. 92.

80. *SBVPrLV*, 26 Sept. 1919, vol. 4, col. 4431 (Friedberg); and Stephan, *Aufstieg*, p. 77. The SPD, too, honestly regretted the death of Friedrich Naumann (cf. the obituary, *Vorwärts*, nos. 432, 433 (25 Aug. 1919). On the relationship of the SPD and the DDP during the Weimar Republic, see Hartmut Schustereit, *Linksliberalismus und Sozialdemokratie in der Weimarer Republik* (Düsseldorf, 1975). On the founding of the DDP, see Albertin, *Liberalismus*.

81. See the resolution of the DDP executive committee cited in Werner Becker, "Die Rolle der liberalen Presse," in *Deutsches Judentum in Krieg und Revolution*, ed. Werner E. Mosse (Tübingen, 1968), p. 122.

82. Hartenstein, *Anfänge*, p. 55; Thieme, *Liberalismus*, p. 199.

83. Albertin, *Liberalismus*, p. 306; Hedwig Wachenheim, *Vom Grossbürgertum zur Sozialdemokratie*, ed. Susanne Miller (Berlin, 1973), p. 100; Bruce B. Frye, "The German Democratic Party 1919–1930," *Western Political Quarterly* 16 (Mar. 1963), 167–79.

84. They included the Prussian minister of commerce, Otto Fischbeck, the Reich minister of the interior, Erich Koch-Weser, Theodor Wolff, editor of the distinguished *Berliner Tageblatt*, and the publicist Alfred Weber. See A. von Holtzendorff to Cuno, 21 May 1919, Hap.Arch./I and

II; Koch-Weser, diary entries 21 July 1919 and 13 Jan. 1920, Koch-Weser papers (BA); Ritter, "Kontinuität," p. 349; and Stephan, *Aufstieg,* p. 39.

85. See Max Weber to Carl Petersen, Peterson papers/L 53 (Staatsarch.Hbg); and Albertin, *Liberalismus,* p. 319.

86. See the detailed discussion in Erger, *Kapp-Putsch.*

87. Albertin, *Liberalismus,* p. 166.

88. See "DDP-Fr.Prot.," 6, 7, and 8 July 1920; Cf. Klöckner, *Landtag,* p. 27.

89. See *Dem. Parteikorrespondenz* 3 (21 June 1920); and Stephan, *Aufstieg,* p. 166.

90. For a description of the Economics party, see Martin Schumacher, *Mittelstandsfront und Republik* (Düsseldorf, 1972); Werner Fritsch, "Reichspartei des deutschen Mittelstandes (Wirtschaftspartei)," ed. Fricke, *Parteien* 2:541–54; and Johann Victor Bredt, *Erinnerungen und Dokumente,* ed. Martin Schumacher (Düsseldorf, 1970), p. 34.

91. See "DDP-Fr.Prot." 5 Apr. 1921.

92. See "DDP-Fr.Prot." 15 June 1921. Cf. Becker, "Rolle," p. 81, n. 77; and Koch-Weser, diary entry, 25 April 1921, Koch-Weser papers (BA). Koch's relationship even to the bourgeois left was very bad indeed; he called the Catholic Chancellor Wirth "a Catholic Independent Socialist" (see ibid., 10 May 1921). See also Koch to his wife, ibid., 16 June 1921.

93. See Petersen to Ebert, 22 Sept. 1921, in *Bürgermeister Carl Petersen,* ed. Erich Lüth and Hans-Dieter Loose (Hamburg, 1971), pp. 70–71.

94. Eberhard Kolb, *Die Arbeiterräte in der deutschen Innenpolitik 1918–1919* (Düsseldorf, 1962), p. 87. Heinrich Schäfer, *Tagebuchblätter eines rheinischen Sozialisten* (Bonn, 1919), p. 18; and Erich Wasa Rodig, diary entry for 14 Nov. 1918. (Rodig, who was mayor of the Prussian city of Wandsbek near Hamburg, kept a diary from 1915 to 31 Mar. 1923. The original is in the Forst.Hbg.) For a complete discussion of this subject, see Susanne Miller, *Die Bürde der Macht* (Düsseldorf, 1978).

95. The future prime minister of Prussia, Paul Hirsch, reported that the SPD delegates were treated like "untouchables" (see Hirsch, *Weg,* p. 28).

96. See Hoffmann's famous and infamous publication, *Die Zehn Gebote* (Berlin, 1891).

97. Dieter Groh, *Negative Integration und revolutionärer Attentismus* (Frankfurt a.M., 1973).

98. Eimers, *Verhältnis,* p. 25. See Miller, *Burgfrieden;* and David Morgan, *The Socialist Left and the German Revolution* (Ithaca, N.Y., 1975), ch. 1.

99. See Hermann Weber, ed., *Der Gründungsparteitag der KPD.—Protokolle und Materialien* (Frankfurt a.M., 1969), p. 12.

100. Miller, *Burgfrieden,* p. 115. Hirsch mistakenly regarded Ströbel as one of the most radical. See David, *Tagebuch,* p. 50 (Oct. 1914).

101. Hirsh *Weg,* p. 65 described his position as "for war credits but against enthusiasm." Much to David's disappointment, he tried to reach an agreement between the left wing and the Reichstag caucus majority as late as July 1916. See David, *Tagebuch,* p. 188 (21 July 1916).

102. Hans J. L. Adolph, *Otto Wels und die Politik der deutschen Sozialdemokratie 1894–1939* (Berlin, 1970), p. 52. On the other hand, David did not always agree with Braun. See David, *Tagebuch,* p. 135 (26 June 1915); and Morgan, *Socialist Left,* p. 89.

103. Cf. Konrad Haenisch, *Die deutsche Sozialdemokratie in und nach dem Weltkriege* (Berlin, 1916), pp. 33–38, 114–15, 145–47. See also David, *Tagebuch,* pp. 157–58 (4–5 Feb. 1916). See also Antrimck (SPD Reichstag delegate) to Karl Kautsky, 4 June 1915, Kautsky papers/DII/105 (IISG). Heine and Max Weber were the main speakers at a rally for a peace of reconciliation in 1915. See Wolfgang Mommsen, *Max Weber und die deutsche Politik 1890–1920,* 2d ed. (Tübingen, 1974), p. 289.

104. Heine to J. Braun, 24 Apr. 1931, H. and J. Braun papers (LBI).

105. See *SBVPrLV*, 14 Jan. 1921, vol. 12, col. 15949; and David, *Tagebuch*, p. 54 (24 Oct. 1914). Heilmann, like Haenisch, worked for the right-Socialist journal, *Die Glocke*.

106. David, *Tagebuch*, p. 153, n. 4 (14 Jan. 1916); and Haenisch, *Sozialdemokratie*, p. 52.

107. Wolfgang Heine, "Der Weg zur Demokratie," *Sozialistische Monatshefte* 50 (8 Jan. 1918), 7. Cf. Heine's contributions to the discussion, *SPD 1898—1918* (10 July 1917), 2:299ff. See also the volumes of the right-wing journal *Die Glocke* for 1917 and 1918.

108. Haenisch, *Sozialdemokratie*, p. 52.

109. Hirsch regarded the Reichstag peace resolution as an honest offer of peace; Hoffman, on the other hand, felt it was meant to hide the fact of the German war of conquest. See David, *Tagebuch*, pp. 219, 219, n. 3 (20 Jan. 1917); and Hirsch, *Weg*, p. 78.

110. See the caucus debate of 19 July 1917, *SPD 1898—1918*, p. 309; and Grosser, *Konstitutionalismus*, pp. 152—54;

111. *Vorwärts*, no. 69 (19 Mar. 1917). See also Scheidemann, *Der Zusammenbruch* (Berlin, 1921), pp. 40—44; Scheidemann, *Memoiren eines Sozialdemokraten* (Dresden, 1928), 1:395—97; and Paul Lensch, "Nun wohin," *Glocke*, 17 Mar. 1917, pp. 921—27.

112. For the reaction of the bourgeois forces, see "Sitz. Pr StMin., 17 Sept. 1918," *IFA* 2:704—07; cf. Turner, *Stresemann*, p. 11. The preconditions show that the SPD had no confidence in Friedberg. See Ebert in the IFA meeting of 5 Nov. 1917, *IFA* 2:565; Hirsch, *Weg*, pp. 100, 110; see also Patemann, *Kampf*, p. 118.

113. All of the SPD ministers came from Berlin or the eastern provinces of the state. The leading labor representatives in the western industrial cities, such as Robert Leinert in Hanover and Albert Grzesinski in Kassel, were forced to stay in their home areas during the revolution, because they headed their local workers' and soldiers' councils. Their Berlin days did not begin until the election of the Prussian Constitutional Convention.

114. At the beginning of the war, Heine had already established a relationship with Theodor Wolff and other left-Liberal newspaper people. See David, *Tagebuch*, p. 31 (2 Sept. 1914).

115. *SBVPrLV*, 14 Mar. 1919, vol. 1, col. 63. The antipathy was mutual (see *Freiheit*, 15 Mar. 1919), so that Heine's absence from the cabinet until late November undoubtedly fostered cooperation between the SPD and the USPD in the early days of the revolution.

116. As an illustration of the rank-and-file sentiment, the delegate of the Constitutional Convention from Breslau, Scholich, regarded it as a "misfortune" that the SPD was now forced to make compromises, because it had accepted governmental responsibility. See *SPD-Parteitag 1919*, p. 269.

117. See *Schlesische Bergwacht*, 8 Jan. 1919. For a general discussion of the relationship between the DDP and the SPD, see Schustereit, *Linksliberalismus*.

118. Cf. Heinrich August Winkler, *Mittelstand, Demokratie and National-sozialismus* (Cologne, 1972), p. 71; Koch-Weser, diary entry 22 Jan. 1919, Koch-Weser papers (BA); and *SPD-Parteitag 1919*, p. 162.

119. Adolph, *Wels*, p. 107; and *SPD Parteikonferenz 22.3.1919*, p. 23. For an opposing view, see Gustav Noske, *Erlebtes aus Aufstieg und Niedergang einer Demokratie* (Offenbach a.M., 1947), p. 294; and Ritter, "Kontinuität," p. 251.

120. He was elected to the Landesversammlung as the last name on the state list.

121. Heilmann had made Kuttner an editor at the *Chemnitzer Volksstimme*. See Kuttner's letters to his mother, 10 Oct. 1913, 21 Sept. and 20 Oct. 1914, Kuttner papers/67 (IISG). Heilmann published his fervent affirmation, "I'll hold fast to Hindenburg," in the *Chemnitzer Volksstimme*, 30 July 1915.

122. See the KPD leaflet published in mid-1919, in Dok.Arb.Bew., II/3, doc. 78, 174; and *Freiheit*, 16 Sept. 1919.

123. *SBVPrLV*, 15 Mar. 1919, vol. 1, col. 146.

124. Ibid., 18 July 1919, vol. 3, cols. 3937–38 (Cassel). Cf. the reports of cooperation between the two parties in Pomerania and Upper Silesia in *Freiheit*, 26 May 1920. The political squaring of the circle, i.e., cooperation between the DDP, SPD, Center party, USPD, and KPD occurred only in areas with acute border problems, such as Kiel and Breslau. See Reichszentrale für die Einwohnerwehren, "Nachrichten zur Lage," 20 Mar. 1920, Heine papers/344 (IISG); and the undated proclamation of the Vollzugsausschuss Kiel, LASH/301/5713.

125. *SBVPrLV*, 15 Nov. 1919, vol. 5, cols. 6535–40, 6568.

126. The party's executive committee even went so far as to advise districts not to hand over weapons to "reactionary" troops—even if ordered to do so by governmental authorities. See *Reichskonferenz 5.5.1920*, p. 32 (Enz [Barmen]).

127. *Vorwärts*, nos. 152, 154 [*sic*] (24 May 1920).

128. Ibid.; see also Erwin Könnemann, ed., "Protokolle Albert Südekums aus den Tagen nach dem Kapp-Putsch," in *Beiträge zur Geschichte der deutschen Arbeiterbewegung* 8 (1966), 265–66, 276. Krüger favored some modifications in the democratic form of government, but he was hardly a "Leninist." See his pamphlet, *Sozialdemokratie und Revolution—Leitfaden für Parteifunktionäre*.

129. *Reichskonferenz 5.5.1920*, p. 4 (Bartels).

130. Even Franz Krüger emphasized (ibid., p. 47) that the party had to wage its election campaign against both right and left and needed to highlight its positive principles. Cf. Wilhelm Blos, *Von der Monarchie zum Volksstaat* (Stuttgart, 1922), 2:141–42.

131. *SPD Parteitag 1920*, pp. 146–48; Severing, "Grosse Koalition," p. 1.

132. *SPD PA 8. u. 9.12.1920*, pp. 3–4; and *SPD Parteitag 1920*, p. 259 (H. Müller). The greater willingness on the part of the SPD to enter into coalitions with bourgeois parties at the state level was undoubtedly influenced by the not very successful experiment at forming a coalition with the USPD in Saxony.

133. See Franz Krüger's report of the party's executive committee at the 1921 SPD party congress. See *Protokoll über die Verhandlungen des Parteitages der Sozialdemokratischen Partei Deutschlands . . . Görlitz . . . 18. bis 24. September 1921* (Berlin, 1921), p. 139. Cf. Severing *Lebensweg* 1:332–33. Hermann Müller agreed: "Above all, we must join the Prussian government coalition (very good!) The way to do that must be found." See *SPD-Parteitag 1921*, p. 114.

134. See "Rundschau," *Sozialistische Monatshefte* 57 (19 Dec. 1921), 820; Paul Levi, "Parteitag in Görlitz," *Unser Weg* 3 (Oct. 1921), 294; Heinrich Ströbel, *Die deutsche Revolution* (Berlin, 1922), 2:221; Stefan Brant, "Politische Chronik," *Neue Rundschau* 32, no. 2 (1921), 1226.

135. Morsey, *Zentrumspartei*, p. 411, n. 12; Albertin, *Liberalismus*, pp. 421, 584; and Alfred Kastning, *Die deutsche Sozialdemokratie zwischen Koalition und Opposition 1919–1923* (Paderborn, 1970), pp. 69–70.

136. Cf. the commission's documentation and especially Max Quarck, "Bemerkungen zum Programmentwurf Kautsky," Bernstein papers/N1–N10 (IISG). See also Friedrich Stampfer, *Das Görlitzer Programm* (Berlin, 1922): and Eduard Bernstein, "Entstehungsgeschichte des Görlitzer Programms," unpublished, Bernstein papers/N8 (IISG).

137. Eimers, *Verhältnis*, p. 280.

138. Grzesinski to Scheidemann, 16 Sept. 1921, Grzesinski papers/304 (IISG).

139. See Marckwald's (Frankfurt a.M.), and Eckstein's (Berlin) contributions to the discussions, *SPD-Parteitag 1921*, pp. 160–63; and Ströbel, *Revolution*, p. 219. The USPD naturally took over these arguments. See *Mitteilungsblatt des Bezirksverbandes Berlin-Brandenburg der USPD* 5 (5 Oct. 1921). Even those who supported a grand coalition regarded a good relationship to the USPD as essential, especially when the political situation required extraparliamentary

actions on the part of the working classes. See *Correspondenzblatt der Generalkommission* 31 (24 Sept. 1921).

140. *SPD-Parteitag 1921*, pp. 7–8, 148, 180. The quotation is on p. 148.

141. Walter Tormin, *Geschichte der deutschen Parteien seit 1848*, 3d ed. (Stuttgart, 1948), p. 137.

142. *SPD-Parteitag 1921*, p. 193 (Braun), and p. 195 (Severing). Severing used the same words as Braun did, in "Ein Wort zum sozialdemokratischen Parteitag 1921," *Sozialistische Monatshefte* 57 (19 Sept. 1921), 788.

143. *SPD-Parteitag 1921*, pp. 207–08.

144. A copy of the pamphlet *An den Vorstand . . . 9.6.1915* is in the Otto Braun papers/22 (IISG). Cf. Ströbel to Kautsky, 2 June 1915, Kautsky papers/D/XXI/573 (IISG).

145. Morgan, *Socialist Left*, pp. 68, 75–76; and Jürgen Reulecke, "Der Erste Weltkrieg und die Arbeiterbewegung im rheinisch-westfälischen Industriegebiet," in *Arbeiterbewegung an Rhein und Ruhr*, ed. J. Reulecke (Wuppertal, 1974), pp. 205–39.

146. See Hellmut von Gerlach, *Meine Erlebnisse in der Preussischen Verwaltung* (Berlin, [1919]), pp. 77–78.

147. Wachheim, *Vom Grossbürgertum*, pp. 42–43.

148. Hermann Müller, *Die November-Revolution* (Berlin, 1928), p. 160.

149. On Hofer's views, see "Wer trägt die Schuld?" and "Sozialismus und Landwirtschaft," *Freiheit*, 24 Nov. 1918.

150. See Rudolf Hilferding, "Der Parteitag," *Freiheit*, 8 Dec. 1919. On the disintegration of the USPD, see Morgan, *Socialist Left*.

151. None of the members of the party's executive committee elected in March 1919 was a delegate to the Prussian Constitutional Convention. Its opposition to the government repeatedly forced the USPD in the course of the year into unwanted and embarrassing cooperation with the DNVP. See *SBVPrLV*, 26 Mar. 1919, vol. 1, cols. 763–89; 15 Dec. 1919, vol. 7, col. 8134 (Rosenfeld).

152. Cf. Rosenfeld's response to the government declaration, *SBVPrLV*, 26 Mar. 1919, vol. 1, cols. 763–89; and *Freiheit*, 25 Mar. 1919.

153. See *Freiheit*, 21 Oct. 1919; *SBVPrLV*, 26 Mar. 1919, vol. 1. col. 769 (Rosenfeld). As far as *Die Freiheit* was concerned, Heine was "the man, who lacked a sense of justice" (25 Mar. 1919), "a worthy successor to Puttkammer" and "a cultural disgrace" (27 Mar. 1919). Hirsch was the object of fewer personal attacks, because the USPD regarded him merely as Heine's mouthpiece. See *SBVPrLV*, 26 Mar. 1919, vol. 1, cols. 768–69 (Rosenfeld).

154. *Freiheit*, 13 Oct. 1920.

155. See, for instance, ibid., 25 and 31 Mar. 1920.

156. Ibid., 27 Mar. 1920.

157. See Arthur Crispien, "Zur politischen Situation," ibid., 18 Apr. 1920.

158. The best analysis of the inflation and the disintegration of the USPD is in Morgan, *Socialist Left*, pp. 34ff.

159. See the discussion of the formation of governments in the individual states in *Freiheit*, 11 June 1920.

160. Ibid., 8 July 1920.

161. Fourteen of the twenty-three USPD delegates to the Prussian Constitutional Convention remained with the USPD. See ibid., 20 Oct. 1920.

162. Ibid., 1, 14 Jan. 1921; 4 Dec. 1920; 12 Jan. 1921; 19 Feb. 1921; *Mitteilungsblatt des Bezirksverbandes Berlin-Brandenburg der USPD* 5 (4 Feb. 1921); and *Freiheit*, 19 Feb. 1921.

163. Cf. Karl Radek's severe criticism of the KPD executive committee's position, Commu-

nist International, *Protokoll des III. Kongresses, Moskau 22. Juni bis 12. Juli 1921* ([Moscow], 1921; rpt. Milan, 1967), p. 457.

164. *Illustrierte Geschichte der Deutschen Revolution* (Berlin, 1929), p. 473. The leftist tendencies of the Berlin workers were reflected in the composition of the Berlin city council. While the USPD won 14 seats and the SPD 145 seats in the Prussian constitutional convention election of 26 Jan. 1919, the USPD won 47 and the SPD 46 seats in the February 1919 Berlin city council elections. In June 1920 the number of USPD city councilors rose to 86 in comparison to the SPD's 39. At the end of October, 21 of the USPD council members reconstituted themselves into the KPD caucus. See Christian Engel, *Gustav Böss, Oberbürgermeister von Berlin 1921–1930* (Stuttgart, 1971), p. 85.

165. Erwin Könnemann and H. J. Krusch, *Der Kapp-Putsch und der Kampf der deutschen Arbeiterklasse*, ed. Institute for Marxism-Leninism of the Central Committee of the SED (Berlin [East], 1972), p. 188.

Chapter 2. Cabinets and Coalitions, 1914–1921

1. Alfred Kastning, *Die deutsche Sozialdemokratie zwischen Koalition und Opposition 1919–1933* (Paderborn, 1970), p. 45. See also Hans Peter Ehni, "Zum Parteienverhältnis in Preussen 1918–1932," *Archiv für Sozialgeschichte* 11 (1971), 279–80.

2. This thesis is advocated by Enno Eimers, *Das Verhältnis von Preussen und Reich in den ersten Jahren der Weimarer Republik (1918–1923)* (Berlin, 1969), pp. 156–57, 424.

3. See Hans-Jürgen Puhle, *Agrarische Interessenpolitik und preussischer Konservatismus* (Hanover, 1966), esp. pp. 213ff.; Hans-Jürgen Puhle, "Parlament, Parteien und Interessenverbände 1890–1914," in *Das kaiserliche Deutschland*, ed. Michael Stürmer, (Düsseldorf, 1970), pp. 340–77.

4. Dieter Grosser, *Vom monarchischen Konstitutionalismus zur parlamentarischen Demokratie* (The Hague, 1970).

5. Cf. Hans Luther, *Politiker ohne Partei* (Stuttgart, 1960), p. 63.

6. Eimers, *Verhältnis*, pp. 17–19.

7. See, the introduction in *Militär und Innenpolitik im Weltkrieg 1914–1918*, ed. Werner Deist, (Düsseldorf, 1970), vol. 1.

8. Eduard David, in *Das Kriegstagebuch des Reichstagsabgeordneten Eduard David 1914–1918*, ed. Erich Matthias and Susanne Miller (Düsseldorf, 1966), p. 206 (21 Oct. 1916).

9. See Gerald Feldman, *Army, Industry, Labor in Germany 1914–1918* (Princeton, N.J., 1966), pp. 104, 127.

10. Constantin Stein and Erwin Stein, eds., *Die deutschen Landkreise* (Berlin-Friedenau, 1926), 2:7; Paul Hirsch, *Der Weg der Sozialdemokratie zur Macht in Preussen* (Berlin, 1929), p. 60.

11. Hans Goldschmidt, *Das Reich und Preussen im Kampf um die Führung* (Berlin, 1931), p. 120; and Erich Kuttner, *Von Kiel bis Berlin* (Berlin [1918]), p. 7.

12. Konrad Jarausch, *The Enigmatic Chancellor* (New Haven, Conn., 1973).

13. Hirsch, *Weg*, p. 58.

14. Erich Matthias and Eberhard Pikart, eds., *Die Reichstagsfraktion der deutschen Sozialdemokratie 1898–1918* (Düsseldorf, 1966), pt. 2, p. 187, n. 4.

15. See Carl Petersen in his letters to Dr. Nic. Darboven, 26 April 1917, and Capt. Matthaei, 22 Oct. 1917, Petersen papers/L 53 (Staatsarch. Hbg.). Cf. Conrad Haussmann to his wife, 10 Mar. 1915, in Conrad Haussmann, *Schlaglichter: Reichstagsbriefe und Aufzeichnungen*, ed. Ulrich Zeller (Frankfurt a.M., 1924), pp. 30–31.

16. The latter included a number of quasi-political social clubs, such as the German Society of 1914, the Union of the New Fatherland, and the Society for Social Reform. See Gustav Mayer,

Erinnerungen (Zurich, 1949), p. 250; Eugen Schiffer, *Ein Leben für den Liberalismus* (Berlin, 1951), pp. 30–31. See also Udo Bermbach, *Vorformen parlamentarischer Kabinettsbildung in Deutschland* (Cologne, 1967), p. 167; and Hermann Heidegger, *Die deutsche Sozialdemokratie und der nationale Staat* (Göttingen, 1956), p. 91.

17. See the detailed analysis in Feldman, *Army*. See also Eduard Bernstein, *Die deutsche Revolution* (Berlin-Fichtenau, 1921), pp. 172–73; GK, *Rechenschaftsbericht vom 1. Juni 1914 bis 31. Mai 1919* (Berlin, 1919), pp. 107–14.

18. Cf. Adolf Wermuth, *Ein Beamtenleben* (Berlin, 1922), pp. 370–71; Albert C. Grzesinski, *Inside Germany,* trans. Alexander S. Lipschitz (New York, 1939), pp. 37–39.

19. Feldman, *Army,* p. 249.

20. GK, *Rechenschaftsbericht,* pp. 8–9; and Heinz Josef Varain, *Freie Gewerkschaften, Sozialdemokratie und Staat . . . (1890–1920)* (Düsseldorf, 1956), p. 90.

21. For details, see Jarausch, *Chancellor,* pp. 310ff. Kurt Riezler, *Tagebücher, Aufsätze, Dokumente,* ed. Karl Dietrich Erdmann (Göttingen, 1972); and Reinhard Patemann, *Der Kampf um die preussische Wahlreform im Ersten Weltkrieg* (Düsseldorf, 1964).

22. Saul Friedländer, "Die politischen Veränderungen der Kriegszeit und ihre Auswirkungen auf die Judenfrage," and Eva G. Reichmann, "Der Bewusstseinswandel der deutschen Juden," in *Deutsches Judentum in Krieg und Frieden 1916–1923,* ed. Werner E. Mosse (Tübingen, 1971), pp. 27–65, 511–612.

23. The provincial governor of East Prussia claimed that he had launched Michaelis's candidacy for chancellor. See Magnus Freiherr von Braun, *Von Ostpreussen bis Texas* (Stollhamm, Oldb., 1955), pp. 133–36 (entries for 10 and 13 July 1917). See also Feldman, *Army,* p. 366.

24. Georg Michaelis, *Für Staat und Volk,* 2d ed. (Berlin, 1922), pp. 365–70; and M. Braun, *Ostpreussen,* p. 145 (23 Sept. 1917). Cf. Heinrich Class's report on his meeting with Michaelis in "Sitzung des geschäftsführenden Ausschusses des Alldeutschen Verbandes . . . 8. und 9. Dezember 1917," Forst.Hbg., NaVV/412.

25. Michaelis, *Staat,* p. 365.

26. Cf. Rathenau's notes on his conversation with Ludendorff, in Walther Rathenau, *Tagebuch 1907–1922,* ed. Hartmut Pogge von Strandmann (Düsseldorf, 1967) p, 217, n, 38 (entry for 10 July 1917); and Patemann, *Kampf,* p. 92.

27. Erich Wende, *C. H. Becker* (Stuttgart, 1959), p. 58; Friedrich Schmidt-Ott, *Erlebtes und Erstrebtes* (Wiesbaden, 1952), pp. 152–53, 157. See also Haenisch, "Ein offener Brief an Prof. Saenger," *Neue Rundschau* 30, pt. 1 (1919), 18; and *Glocke* 4 (16 June 1918), 335–52.

28. Michaelis, *Staat,* p. 361; John K. Zeender, "German Catholics and the Concept of an Interconfessional Party 1900–1922," *Journal of Central European Affairs* 23 (1964), 430, n. 26. Cf. Rudolf Morsey, *Die Deutsche Zentrumspartei 1917–1923* (Düsseldorf, 1966), p. 68.

29. See *Fünf Grundzüge einer Verwaltungsreform* (Berlin, 1917). The continued relevance (and slow progress) of his suggestions is shown by the fact that this copy contains Braun's handwritten marginalia from the 1920s. See O. Braun papers/482 (IISG).

30. Heinrich Potthoff, ed., *Friedrich v. Berg als Chef des Geheimen Zivilkabinetts . . . Erinnerungen* (Düsseldorf, 1971), p. 100; and Eimers, *Verhältnis,* pp. 28–29.

31. Stresemann in the meeting of the IFA, 5 Nov. 1917, in *IFA* 1:467. Cf. Riezler, *Tagebücher,* p. 457 (11 Feb. 1918); Hirsch, *Weg,* p. 191.

32. See Erich Koch-Weser's diary, entry for 11 Oct. 1918, Koch-Weser papers (BA); and Patemann, *Kampf,* p. 103.

33. Bermbach, *Vorformen,* p. 191; Matthias Erzberger, *Erlebnisse im Weltkrieg* (Stuttgart, 1920), pp. 292–94; and IFA meetings of 31 Oct. and 3 Nov. 1917, *IFA* 1:397–98, 404, 438–39. Among the state candidates under discussion were Michaelis, von Loebell (Drews's predecessor as minister of the interior), and von Krause, a high-ranking official in the same ministry whose views were close to the extreme right wing of the National Liberals.

34. The question of the parliamentarization of Prussia was secondary. See David and Stresemann in the IFA meeting of 5 Nov. 1917, *IFA* 1:466-67.

35. Cf. Erzberger's notes on his conversation with Kühlmann, 30 Oct. 1917, *IFA* 1:383; and the summary statements on the chronology of the November Crisis by Erzberger and Stresemann in ibid., pp. 560-68, 578-83. Cf. Bermbach, *Vorformen*, p. 191; and Erzberger, *Erlebnisse*, pp. 294-95.

36. Cf. IFA meeting of 31 Oct. 1917, *IFA* 1:368-69, 397-98.

37. Cf. the excerpt from the transcript of the Crown Council session of 5 Nov. 1917 in ibid., p. 465, n. 34.

38. See Stresemann's and Erzberger's notes of 11 Nov. and 9 Nov. 1917, ibid., pp. 582-84, 568.

39. Hergt, who was minister of finance in 1917, later referred to Friedberg as "the prime minister, who was a party leader in Prussia." See *SBVPrLV*, 27 Mar. 1919, vol. 1, col. 878.

40. Berg to Under State Secretary Heinrichs, 16 Sept. 1918, cited in Potthoff, ed., *Chef*, p. 210.

41. Oscar Geck (SPD Reichstag delegate) during the joint meeting of the caucus and the party executive committee on 23 Sept. 1918, *SPD 1898-1918* 2:458.

42. The king refused to exert pressure on the Prussian Conservatives. See the meeting of the Prussian cabinet, 27 Sept. 1918, *IFA* 2:704-07. See also Henry A. Turner, *Stresemann and the Politics of the Weimar Republic* (Princeton, N.J., 1963), p. 11.

43. See Heinrich Cunow, "Preussen und das Reich," *Neue Zeit* 37 (18 Oct. 1918), 49-52. Cf. Gerhard Anschütz, "Gedanken über künftige Staatsreformen," in *Die Arbeiterschaft im neuen Deutschland,* ed. Friedrich Thimme and Carl Legien, (Leipzig, 1915), pp. 42-57.

44. Even the SPD's "action program" of 23 May 1918 made no mention of the consequences that the electoral reform would bring. See Eberhard Kolb, *Die Arbeiterräte in der deutschen Innenpolitik 1918-1919* (Düsseldorf, 1962), pp. 361, 361, n. 2.

45. Wolfgang Heine, "Preussiche Wahlreform," *Sozialistische Monatshefte* 51 (24 Sept. 1918), 871.

46. Haenisch, "In erstester Stunde," *Glocke* 4 (5 Oct. 1918), 843.

47. Prinz Max von Baden, *Erinnerungen und Dokumente,* ed. Golo Mann (Stuttgart, 1968), pp. 303ff.

48. Heinrich Cunow, "Ein historischer Wendepunkt," *Hamburger Echo,* 12 Oct. 1918; Ernst Müller-Meiningen, *Aus Bayerns schwersten Tagen* (Berlin, 1923), p. 261; Wilhelm Keil, *Erlebnisse eines Sozialdemokraten* (Stuttgart, 1947-48), 1:474. Hermann Müller, *Die November-Revolution* (Berlin, 1928), pp. 19-21; Wilhelm Groener, *Lebenserinnerungen* (Göttingen, 1957), p. 450; and Scheidemann's letter to the SPD Reichstag delegation, 19 Mar. 1920, Grzesinski papers/526 (IISG). Cf. Kolb, *Arbeiterräte,* pp. 78-79; *Hamburger Echo,* 27, 29 Oct. 1918.

49. Cited in Friedberg's obituary, *Demokratische Partei-Korrespondenz* 3 (21 June 1920).

50. Koch-Weser, diary entries for 6, 9 Oct. 1918, Koch-Weser papers (BA).

51. Friedrich Payer, *Von Bethmann Hollweg bis Ebert—Erinnerungen* (Frankfurt a.M., 1923), p. 118. Groener regarded him as Erzberger's favorite candidate. See Winfried Baumgart, ed., *Von Brest-Litovsk zur deutschen Novemberrevolution: Aus den Tagebüchern . . . von Paquet, Groener und Hopmann* (Göttingen, 1971), p. 445.

52. Wolfgang Sauer, "Das Scheitern der parlamentarischen Monarchie," in *Vom Kaiserreich zur Weimarer Republik,* ed. Eberhard Kolb (Cologne, 1972), pp. 78-79. See also Gustav Böhm, *Adjudant im preussischen Kriegsministerium,* ed. Heinz Hürten and Georg Meyer (Stuttgart, 1977).

53. Sauer, "Scheitern," pp. 77-93. Cf. David Morgan, *The Socialist Left and the German Revolution* (Ithaca, N.Y., 1975), p. 111.

54. Even Friedberg and Schëuch hoped that William would abdicate of his own free will (Payer, *Erinnerungen,* pp. 148–49). Cf. Gen. Albrecht von Thaer to his wife, 2 Nov. 1918, in *Generalstabsdienst an der Front und in der O.H.L.,* ed. K. G. Rönneforth and Siegfried Kaehler (Göttingen, 1958), p. 251; and Groener, *Erinnerungen,* p. 443.

55. Cited in Sauer, "Scheitern," p. 85.

56. Ulrich Kluge, *Soldatenräte und Revolution* (Göttingen, 1975), p. 124; and Erich Kuttner, "Der Untergang der deutschen Sozialdemokratie," in Kuttner papers/139b, p. 29. (IISG).

57. A request of the provincial governor of Schleswig-Holstein dated 7 Nov. for "immediate instructions . . . as to how I should conduct myself [toward the workers' and soldiers' council] and which instructions I should give the government officials," resulted in the answer "government officials should carry on their functions for the time being. [sic] Insofar as this is necessary for the maintainance of law and order." See Moltke to Ministry of the Interior, 9 Nov. 1918, LASH/310/2401. The Council of Ministers did not even establish a (completely useless) Central Office to Gather Riot Reports until 7 Nov. See *Vorwärts,* no. 309 (9 Nov. 1918).

58. Cf. the report by Richard Hauschildt (later a member of the Prussian Constitutional Convention and the Landtag) on the revolution in Kassel, "Der 9. November 1918 in Cassel [sic.]," *Kasseler Volksblatt,* 10 Nov. 1919. A copy of this article is in the Grzesinski papers/481 (IISG).

59. The workers' council of Kiel declared itself "the provisional government of the province [Schleswig-Holstein]" on 9 Nov., but the arrival of the Reichstag delegates Noske and Haase as well as the designation of the Schleswig-Holstein SPD leader, Heinrich Kürbis, as assistant to the provincial governor reestablished cooperation between the council movement and the old bureaucracy. The relevant exchange of letters is in "notes" of the provincial governor, 9 Nov. 1918, LASH/301/2401. Cf. Gustav Noske, *Erlebtes aus Aufstieg und Niedergang einer Demokratie* (Offenbach a.M., 1947), pp. 69–70.

60. Hirsch, *Weg,* p. 111; Schmidt-Ott, *Erlebtes,* pp. 162–63; and *Vorwärts,* no. 309 (9 Nov. 1918).

61. Cf. a leaflet issued by the SPD's central committee as cited in Ministry of the Interior to all provincial governors, 9 Nov. 1918, NStAH/122a/29.

62. *Vorwarts,* no. 308 (8 Nov. 1918); and *Vossische Zeitung,* 8 Nov. 1918, in *Revolutionsdokumente—Die deutsche Revolution in der Darstellung der zeitgenössischen Presse,* ed. Eberhard Buchner (Berlin, 1921), vol. 1, doc. 107a.

63. Kluge, *Soldatenräte,* p. 82.

64. Wilhelm Dittmann, "Wie alles kam . . ." (Manuscript, Mar. 1934), p. 98 Dittmann papers (Arch.SD); and Richard Müller, *Vom Kaiserreich zur Republik* (Berlin, 1924), 2:11. See the meeting of the SPD Reichstag delegation, 9 Nov. 1918, *SPD 1898–1918* 2:19.

65. The presence of Otto Braun is documented, but that of Paul Hirsch is not certain. See Otto Braun, "Weimar MS"; *RVB-Protokolle,* vol. 1, docs. 16, 9; Otto Braun's speech in Königsberg, 11 Aug. 1929, Braun papers/612 (IISG); Friedrich Stampfer, *Der 9. November* (Berlin, 1919), p. 24; and H. Müller, *November-Revolution,* p. 51.

66. See *RVB-Protokolle,* vol. 1, nos. 1a–1d, 3–18; Dittmann, "Wie," p. 106; Gerhard A. Ritter, "Kontinuität und Umformung des deutschen Parteiensystems 1918–1920," in *Entstehung und Wandel der modernen Gesellschaft,* ed. Gerhard A. Ritter (Berlin, 1970), p. 348; and H. Müller, *November-Revolution,* p. 59.

67. Karl Kautsky, the SPD's leading theoretician, favored a centralized Reich without "particularist plunder" and especially without Prussia, "that remnant of Hohenzollern dynastic politics." See "Die ersten Schritte der Revolution," *Sozialist* 4 (22 Nov. 1918), 2.

68. *RVB-Protokolle* 1:7, 12.

69. Hirsch, *Weg,* p. 111.

70. Wermuth, *Beamtenleben,* pp. 414–15.

71. *Vorwärts,* no. 310 (10 Nov. 1918). R. Müller, *Kaiserreich,* p. 42, describes this proclamation as a measure deliberately directed against the Spartacists.

72. A number of sources agree on the course of these events: Hirsch, *Weg,* p. 112; Otto Braun, *Von Weimar bis Hitler* (New York, 1940), p. 12; A. Hoffmann, in *SBVPrLV,* 4 Dec. 1919, vol. 6, col. 7183; Information Office of the Prussian Cabinet, ed., *Zwei Jahre Regierungsarbeit in Preussen* (Berlin, 1921), p. 7; and *Vorwärts,* no. 531 (12 Nov. 1931).

73. Hoffmann read the protocol in *SBVPrLV,* 4 Dec. 1919, vol. 6, col. 7184. Cf. Schmidt-Ott, *Erlebtes,* pp. 163–64. The transfer was preceded by a revealing attempt on Wolfgang Heines's part to persuade Schmidt-Ott to remain in office for the time being: "You [Schmidt-Ott] do not wish to turn your ministry . . . over to the Hoffmann and Haenisch, do you?" (ibid., p. 163).

74. See *Deutsche Allgemeine Zeitung,* 28 Nov. 1918; Buchner, *Revolutionsdokumente,* vol. 1, no. 449.

75. An unsigned account written at this time designates all of the ministers equals. See "Sitz.PrStMin.," 30 Nov. 1918, O. Braun papers/26 (IISG).

76. Haenisch to O. Braun, 29 Nov. 1918, O. Braun papers/105 (IISG). In general, Haenisch was successful not so much because his colleagues agreed with him on the principle of the division of ministerial responsibility, but rather because the other USPD ministers also had reservations about Hoffmann's iconoclastic educational policies. Cf. Breitscheid's statements in the meeting of the Reich cabinet, 28 Dec. 1919, *RVB-Protokolle* 2:60, 64.

77. Cf. the proclamation of the Prussian government in *Die deutsche Revolution 1918–1919—Dokumente,* ed. Gerhard A. Ritter and Susanne Miller (Frankfurt a.M., 1968), p. 104.

78. Hirsch, *Weg,* p. 117; *SBVPrLV,* 15 Mar. 1919, vol. 1, col. 798 (Hirsch); and Breitscheid, "Der 16 Februar," *Sozialist* 4 (5 Dec. 1918), 1–2.

79. See Hirsch and Breitscheid to provincial governor of Hanover, 8 Dec. 1918, NStAH/122a/VIII/2g; and the proclamation of 10 Dec. 1918, in Gerhard Schulz, *Zwischen Demokratie und Diktatur* (Berlin, 1963), 1:161, n. 98.

80. See meeting of the Prussian cabinet, 12 Dec. 1918, NStAH/27 (IISG). The "Zentralrat" mentioned in the protocol probably referred to the Berlin Vollzugsrat, since the Zentralrat was not yet in existence. Cf. Hagen Schulze, *Otto Braun* (Berlin, 1977), p. 236.

81. Harry Graf Kessler, *Tagebücher 1918–1937,* ed. Wolfgang Pfeiffer-Belli (Frankfurt a.M., 1961), p. 77 (21 Dec. 1918).

82. Hedwig Wachenheim, *Vom Grossbürgertum zur Sozialdemokratie,* ed. Susanne Miller (Berlin, 1973), p. 108.

83. See Hirsch's article in *Vorwärts,* no. 166 (31 Mar. 1919); and the characterization in *Die Glocke* 5 (27 Mar. 1920), 1603–04.

84. Cf. his speech at the Berlin USPD general assembly, 11 Nov. 1918, in *Freiheit,* 16 Dec. 1918; his article, "Die unabhängige Sozialdemokratie," *Freiheit,* 8 Dec. 1918; and *Vorwärts,* no. 345a (16 Dec. 1918).

85. Schulze, *Braun,* pp. 234–35, exaggerates Braun's role during the revolution.

86. See his speech to the SPD party congress in 1919, *SPD-Parteitag 1919,* pp. 252–54. Cf. the relevant titles in Braun's private library, O. Braun papers/B/A/9 (PrGStAB).

87. Kessler, *Tagebücher,* p. 139 (25 Feb. 1919); and U. Emil [i.e., Emil Unger], "Politische Köpfe," *Die Glocke* 5 (28 Feb. 1920), 1498.

88. See "Januar-Unruhen"; *DrSVPrLV* 15:7861–62.

89. See *Vorwärts,* no. 564 (16 Nov. 1920); and Braun to Heine, 4 Nov. 1926, O. Braun papers/H/11/B–2/76 (PrGStAB).

90. Morgan, *Socialist Left,* p. 372.

91. The decisive discussions can be found in "Sitz.d.RVB u.d.ZR," 31 Dec. 1918, *RVB-Protokolle* 2:167–68; and *ZR-Protokolle*, pp. 115–37.

92. See Kessler, *Tagebücher*, p. 84 (27 Dec. 1918); and *Freiheit*, 1 Jan. 1919. Cf. Siering (SPD), *SBVPrLV*, 17 Mar. 1919, vol. 1, col. 207.

93. Hermann Weber, ed. *Der Gründungsparteitag der KPD* (Frankfurt a.M., 1969), p. 60; and Saemisch, diary entry for 31 Dec. 1918, Saemisch papers/23 (BA).

94. The protocol of the meeting of 2 Jan. 1919 is in *ZR-Protokolle*, pp. 174–84.

95. See USPD ministers to ZR, 3 Jan. 1919, ZR/05–07. (The document is printed in *Revolutions-Dokumente*, ed. Ritter and Miller, pp. 162–63.) Cf. *Freiheit*, 3 Jan. 1919.

96. Hirsch, *Weg*, p. 121; *ZR-Protokolle*, p. 186, n. 8.

97. Heine, *Wer ist Schuld?* (Berlin, 1919), p. 31; and Adam Stegerwald ["Aus meinem Leben"], *25 Jahre christliche Gewerkschaftsbewegung 1899–1924* (Berlin, 1924), pp. 144, 146.

98. "Sitz.PrStMin.," 31 Jan. 1919, O. Braun papers/32 (IISG).

99. Kessler, *Tagebücher*, p. 90 (1 Jan. 1919); Schmidt-Ott, *Erlebtes*, p. 165; and Friedrich Thimme, "Das Verhältnis der revolutionären Gewalten zur Religion und den Kirchen," in *Revolution und Kirche*, ed. Friedrich Thimme and Ernst Rolffs (Berlin, 1919), p. 40.

100. *Freiheit*, 5 and 6 Jan. 1919.

101. "Januar-Unruhen," doc. 4121A, p. 7681. Ernst himself assumed the post after Eichhorn's dismissal.

102. Meeting of the ZR, 4 Jan. 1919, *ZR-Protokolle*, doc. 29, p. 217; *Republik*, 7 Jan. 1919, cited in "Januar-Unruhen," doc. 4121C, pp. 8126–27. Cf. ibid., doc. 4121B, pp. 775–76, 7708, 7867; and "Sitz.PrStMin.," 4 Jan. 1919, O. Braun papers/29 (IISG). The vote in the Berlin executive committee was twelve to two; only Richard Müller and Ernst Däuming voted against concurrence.

103. Eichhorn preceded Haase, the USPD's national chairman, on the candidate list for the National Constitutional Convention. See Morgan, *Socialist Left*, p. 210; and Ernst Heilmann, *Die Noskegarde* (Berlin [1919]), p. 13. Eichhorn's changing views are discussed in H. Müller, *November-Revolution*, p. 248; and Henning Köhler, "Ein französischer Agentenbericht aus dem revolutionären Berlin vom Dezember 1918," *Internationale Wissenschaftliche Korrespondenz*, no. 16 (Aug. 1972), p. 53. The agent describes Eichhorn as "entièrement devoué au parti bolcheviste." Cf. Anton Fischer, *Die Revolutionskommendantur Berlin* (Berlin [1919]), p. 15. For criticism of Eichhorn's move to the left from within the USPD, see Breitscheid, "Schuld und Sühne," *Sozialist* 5 (17 Jan. 1919), 1; and Heinrich Ströbel, "Die deutsche Revolution," *Klassenkampf* 2 (1 Nov. 1928), 652.

104. Scheüch wanted to dismiss Eichhorn in mid-December. See Gustav Böhm, *Adjudant im preussischen Kriegsministerium*, ed. Heinz Hürten and Georg Meyer (Stuttgart, 1977), p. 107. It is unclear if Doyé discussed his move with Ernst prior to the event; Hirsch was in Upper Silesia at the time.

105. See meeting of the RVB, 31 Dec. 1918, *RVB-Protokolle*, vol. 2, doc. 87, pp. 150–51; meeting of the ZR, 4 Jan. 1919, *ZR-Protokolle*, doc. 29, p. 217; "Januar-Unruhen," doc. 4121B, p. 7867; Fischer, *Revolutions-Kommandantur*, p. 54; and Molkenbuhr, diary entry for 5 Jan. 1919, Molkenbuhr papers (Arch.SD).

106. A proclamation issued by the KPD, USPD and the Revolutionary Shop Stewards movement on 5 Jan. 1919 demanded "Down with the Oppressive Rule of Ebert-Scheidemann-Hirsch and Ernst." See *Freiheit*, 5 Jan. 1919.

107. The *Düsseldorfer Tageblatt* commented, "Düsseldorf has never before experienced such a boring election day." Cited in Wolfgang Stump, *Geschichte und Organisation der Zentrumspartei in Düsseldorf 1917–1933* (Düsseldorf, 1971), p. 31.

108. DrS. 2000, *DrSVPrLV* 6:3005–09.

109. On the day the Prussian Constitutional Convention first met, the parliament building was

under heavy security to assure that "the Prussian Constitutional Convention would not meet the fate of the Bavarian Constitutional Convention." See *Vorwärts*, no. 134 (14 Mar. 1919).

110. Ernst Troeltsch, *Spektator-Briefe*, ed. Hans Baron (Tübingen, 1924), p. 43 (20 Mar. 1919); and Erich Wende, *C. H. Becker* (Stuttgart, 1959), p. 184.

111. See the report of the Prussian caucus, *Vorwärts*, no. 189 (12 Apr. 1919); and *SBVPrLV*, vol. 5, col. 6613 (Ludwig [USPD]).

112. This is confirmed by *Vorwärts*, no. 189 (12 Apr. 1919) and *Freiheit*, 25 Mar. 1919.

113. *SBVPrLV*, vol. 7, col. 8092 (Gronowski).

114. *RheinZ-Parteitag*, pp. 94–95.

115. *Vorwärts*, no. 105 (26 Feb. 1919). See also "DDP-Fr.Prot.," meeting of 20 Mar. 1919, R 45/III; Wachenheim, *Grossbürgertum*, p. 100.

116. Lothar Albertin, *Liberalismus und Demokratie am Anfang der Weimarer Republik* (Düsseldorf, 1971), p. 224.

117. Jürgen Jacke, *Kirche zwischen Monarchie und Republik* (Hamburg, 1976), p. 113; and Claus Motschmann, *Evangelische Kirche und preussischer Staat in den Anfängen der Weimarer Republik* (Lübeck and Hamburg, 1969), p. 55.

118. *Vorwärts*, no. 93 (20 Feb. 1919); and *SBVPrLV*, 26 Mar. 1919, vol. 1, cols. 590–91 (A. Hoffmann) and 716 (Porsch).

119. "DDP-Fr.Prot.," 12, 22 Mar. 1919.

120. Cf. *SBVPrLV*, 9 July 1919, vol. 3, cols. 3217–18, 3231–32 (Otto and Hess). For details on the complicated educational controversies, which involved the formation of the Reich governments as well, see Christoph Führ, *Zur Schulpolitik der Weimarer Republik* (Weinheim, 1970); and Hermann Giesecke, "Zur Schulpolitik der Sozialdemodraten in Preussen und im Reich," *Vierteljahrshefte für Zeitgeschichte* 13 (Apr. 1965), 162–77.

121. "DDP-Fr.Prot.," 24 Mar. 1919.

122. Ernest Hamburger, "Betrachtungen über Heinrich Brünings Memoiren," *Internationale Wissenschaftliche Korrespondenz* 15 (Apr. 1972), 33. Moldenhauer described am Zehnhoff as "old . . . smart, but completely burned out." (See Paul Moldenhauer, "Politische Erinnerungen," p. 22, Moldenhauer papers/1 [BA].) Brüning (*Memoiren* [Stuttgart, 1972]), p. 60, had high praise for the Catholic jurist.

123. Oeser (1858–1926), who served as a member of the Reichstag, 1907–1912, and as member of the Prussian Landtag, 1902–1924, was known before the war for his efforts to unite the liberals. After the Prussian railroads were nationalized, Oeser in 1923 was named director-general of the Reich Railroads.

124. Holtzendorff to Cuno, 27 Feb. 1919, Hap.Arch./I & II. Südekum's attitude earned him the nickname "confidant of the Hohenzollerns." See Walther Oehme, *Damals in der Reichskanzlei 1918/1919* (Berlin [East], 1958), p. 184; and *Freiheit*, 18 Nov. 1918.

125. "Sitz.PrStMin.," 27 Mar. 1919, O. Braun papers/37 (IISG). The Reich's practices are discussed in Bermbach, *Vorformen*, pp. 249–50; Ritter, "Kontinuität," p. 351; and Kastning, *Sozialdemokratie*, p. 33.

126. See "Grundsätze," O. Braun papers/55 (IISG); *SBVPrLV*, 15 Nov. 1919, vol. 5, col. 6572 (Heilmann); "Sitz.PrStMin.," 26 Mar. 1919, O. Braun papers/37 (IISG); and "DDP-Fr.Prot.," 24 Mar. 1919.

127. "Grundsätze," O. Braun papers/55 (IISG); *Die Preussische Landesversammlung— Tätigkeit der sozialdemokratischen Fraktion vom 13. März bis 18. Dezember 1919* [Berlin, 1920], p. 8; and "DDP-Fr.Prot.," 9 and 12 Apr. 1919.

128. Albert Grzesinski, "Polizei und Militär während der Revolution 1918," Grzesinski papers/2456 (IISG).

129. *SBVPrLV*, 3 Dec. 1918, vol. 7, cols. 7097–98, 7133 (Haenisch); 18 July 1919, vol. 3, col. 3845 (Meyer, parliamentary state secretary in the Ministry of the Interior); 7 Oct. 1919, vol.

4, col. 4792 (Schönwalder [SPD]); 15 Nov. 1919, vol. 5, col. 6572 (Heilmann); Grzesinski, "Polizei," p. 5.

130. *SBVPrLV*, 11 Apr. 1919, vol. 1, cols. 1185–89. Cf. *Vorwärts*, no. 188 (12 Apr. 1919). Even the DNVP emphasized it would support the government if it persisted in rejecting the treaty. See *SBVPrLV*, 13 May 1919, vol. 2, cols. 1513–20 (Hergt). Only the USPD refused to side with the majority, claiming the Allied terms were a logical consequence of the aborted German revolution. See *SBVPrLV*, 13 May 1919, vol. 2, cols. 1531–50 (A. Hoffmann). Heine repaid the debt in kind; he accused the left Socialists of "betraying us to our enemies," ibid., 25 June 1919, vol. 4, col. 2547. Incidentally, SPD members of the Prussian Constitutional Convention who were also representatives in the National Constitutional Convention (Heine, Braun, Quark, Thiele, Hue) explained later that they had voted for acceptance of the Versailles Treaty in the national parliament only because the rules of party discipline left them no choice. See, *Vorwärts*, nos. 312, 315 (21 and 23 June 1919). Cf. also Braun, *Weimar*, p. 25; and Eimers, *Verhältnis*, p. 103.

131. "Sitz.PrStMin.," 4 June 1919," O. Braun papers/46 (IISG); Heine's comments at the 19 June 1919 meeting of the Reich cabinet, *Ak/Rk Scheidemann*, doc. 114, p. 490; *SBVPrLV*, 25 June 1919, vol. 2, col. 2522 (Hirsch).

132. Ernst Hesterberg, *Alle Macht den A.—und S.—Räten* (Breslau, 1932), p. 233 (entry for 24 June 1919); and Fritz Rathenau, "1895–1935—als Jude im Dienste von Reich und Staat," typescript, LBI, p. 62ff.

133. See "Geheime Aufzeichnung des Reichsministers des Auswärtigen über die Kabinettssitzungen . . . am 18. und 19. Juni 1919," 2 July 1919, *Ak/Rk Scheidemann*, doc. 118, p. 507. See also Friedrich Tischbein, "Aus dem Reichsrat—Erinnerungen," typescript, Kl.Erw./25 (BA) p. 20; and *SBVPrLV*, 25 June 1919, vol. 2, cols. 2547–48 (Heine).

134. Ramm (undersecretary in the Prussian Ministry of Agriculture), "[Denkschrift betr. landwirtschaftliche Erzeugung in Deutschland]," 25 May 1919, O. Braun papers/77 (IISG).

135. The cabinet's opposition to the treaty is noted in Hirsch, *Weg*, pp. 171–72; preparations for a state of siege are found in "Sitz.PrStMin.," 7, 12 May 1919, O. Braun papers/41, 43 (IISG); and "Sitz.ReiReg.," 8 May 1919, *Ak/Rk Scheidemann*, doc. 66, pp. 303–04, 314; emergency instructions are given in Prussian Ministry of the Interior to all Reich and state offices, 10 June 1919, RK I/2127. The Reich government apparently prevented the publication of this decree. In addition, the Prussian cabinet expected that the Reich delegation at Versailles "include a Prussian delegate with a decisive voice" in matters effecting Prussia. The cabinet had in mind an independent representative, who would get his instructions from the state cabinet and who would be accompanied by a group of Prussian advisors. The Reich government immediately rejected this proposal. See *Ak/Rk Scheidemann*, doc. 44, pp. 182, 182, n. 15; p. 189, n. 2, and doc. 53, p. 225; and "Sitz.PrStMin.," 7 Apr. 1919," O. Braun papers/39 (IISG).

136. *SBVPrLV*, 25 June 1919, vol. 2, cols. 2501–02, 2506 (A. Hoffmann).

137. The sense of crisis was reinforced when the Prussian minister of defense resigned on June 23 to protest the acceptance of the treaty. See *Vorwärts*, no. 315 (23 June 1919).

138. *Freiheit*, 23 June 1919.

139. The DDP caucus discussed the resolution of the USPD one day later. See "DDP-Fr.Prot.," 24 June 1919.

140. *SBVPrLV*, 25 June 1919, vol. 2, col. 2522 (Hirsch).

141. *DrSVPrLV*, vol. 2, DrS. 490, 767–68.

142. *SBVPrLV*, 26 June 1919, vol. 2, cols. 2646–50.

143. An analysis of the difficult and complicated negotiations is provided by Günter Grünthal, *Reichsschulgesetz und Zentrumspartei in der Weimarer Republik* (Düsseldorf, 1968), pp. 54ff; and Giesecke, "Schulpolitik."

144. *RheinZ-Parteitag*, p. 151 (Hess).

145. Ibid., p. 149 (Wilhelm Marx). Hess reminded the delegates that the DNVP had voted against the Center party during the deliberations on clerical supervision of the schools (ibid., p. 128). *SBVPrLV*, 18 July 1919, vol. 3, cols. 3937–38 (Cassel).

146. See Bezirksverband Berlin-Brandenburg der USPD, ed., *Preussen unter der Koalitionsregierung* [Berlin, 1921], p. 5; and *SBVPrLV*, 13 Nov. 1919, vol. 5, col. 6389.

147. See *SBVPrLV*, 22, 23, 24 Oct. 1919, vol. 5, cols. 5513, 5539, 5638, 5701, 5742. See also *RheinZ-Parteitag*, pp. 89, 257.

148. Hans J. L. Adolph, *Otto Wels und die Politik der deutschen Sozialdemokratie 1894–1939* (Berlin, 1970), p. 151. Wels was not alone. Cf. Conrad Haussmann's pessimistic views on the future of German parliamentarism in Haussmann, *Schlaglichter*, p. 295 (21 Oct. 1919).

149. *Vorwärts*, no. 579 (12 Nov. 1919).

150. Heilmann, "Feiern," *Die Glocke* 5 (8 Nov. 1919), 994–95. A series of rightist pronouncements at the first Reich party congress of the Center party reinforced this impression. See for example, the statements by Kaas, ten Hompel, and Trimborn in *Z-Parteitag Jan. 1920*, pp. 56, 58, 120–26.

151. *SBVPrLV*, 15 Nov. 1919, vol. 5, col. 6537. Cf. Wels's complaint in this regard in *Sitzung des SPD-Parteiausschusses, 13 Dec. 1919* (Berlin [1920]), p. 7.

152. *SBVPrLV*, 17 Nov., 15 Dec., 16 Dec. 1919. vols. 5, 6, cols. 6599–6600 (Dominicus [DDP]), 8079–80 (Hauschildt), and 8253–54 (Lauscher [Z]). Cf. Kardorff's ironical remark in ibid., 16 Dec. 1919, vol. 7, col. 8216.

153. *SBVPrLV*, 17 Dec. 1919, vol. 5, col. 8234.

154. Cf. Willy Paetzel, "Ein Jahr Landesversammlung," *Vorwärts*, no. 50 (28 Jan. 1920).

155. The Reich minister for reconstruction and later minister of defense, Otto Gessler, accompanied the ministers because of a mixup. Ebert had forgotten that Gessler was supposed to aid Schiffer in Berlin. See Gessler, *Reichswehrpolitik in der Weimarer Zeit*, ed. Kurt Sendtner (Stuttgart, 1958), p. 123.

156. Johannes Erger, *Der Kapp-Lüttwitz-Putsch* (Düsseldorf, 1967), p. 148.

157. Erich Kuttner, *Otto Braun* (Berlin, 1932), p. 67; Hirsch, *Weg*, pp. 218–19; and Braun, *Weimar*, p. 30.

158. This description is based on a later statement by Mrs. Oeser to the Berlin journalist Ernst Feder; cf. Ernst Feder, *Heute sprach ich mit . . . Tagebücher*, ed. Cecile Lowenthal-Hensel and Arnold Paucker (Frankfurt a.M., 1971), pp. 127–28. Cf. Erger, *Kapp*, p. 156; Hirsch, *Weg*, p. 219, incorrectly gives the date of release as 14 March.

159. Cf. the quite humorous report of the USPD delegate, Adolph Hoffmann, *SBVPrLV*, 31 Mar. 1920, vol. 8, cols. 10660–61, 10664–65.

160. Details in Erger, *Kapp;* and Dietrich Orlow, "Preussen und der Kapp-Putsch," *Vierteljahrshefte für Zeitgeschichte* 26 (Apr. 1978), 192–236. See also "Der Kapp-Putsch," 16 Mar. 1920 in Rathenau, *Tagebuch*, pp. 232–34. Among the more bizarre episodes was an attempt by Undersecretary Ramm of the Prussian Ministry of Agriculture to get Ludendorff to ask Lüttwitz to resign; see Karl Brammer, ed., *Fünf Tage Militärdiktatur—Dokumente zur Gegenrevolution* (Berlin, 1920), p. 62. For a discussion of the relationship between industry and the Kapp putsch, see Gerald D. Feldman, "Big Business and the Kapp-Putsch," *Central European History* 4 (1971), 112.

161. Koch-Weser's diary contains only comments on Schiffer's negotiations. Schiffer's tightrope act cost him his political career. Once it became apparent that Kapp would be defeated, left-wing members of the SPD opposed Schiffer's policy of cosmetic concessions to the insurgents in order to hasten their withdrawal, and even within his own party a number of prominent members, including Koch-Weser, accused Schiffer of political cowardice in not standing up to the rebels. See Erger, *Kapp*, pp. 274–75. Cf. *Vorwärts*, no. 214 (27 Apr. 1929); A. von Holtzendorff to

Cuno, 31 Mar. 1920, (Hap.Arch.); and Koch-Weser, "Kapp-Putsch," 17 Mar. 1920, Koch-Weser papers (BA).

162. Noske, *Erlebtes*, p. 281.

163. *SBVPrLV*, 26 Sept. 1919, vol. 4, cols. 4412, 4419–20.

164. Ibid., 16 Dec. 1919, vol. 7, col. 8245.

165. *Vorwärts*, no. 263 (25 May 1920).

166. Ibid., nos. 263, 277 (25 May and 1 June 1920).

167. The contrasting versions of the meeting can be found in *Vorwärts*, no. 263 (25 May 1920); and *Hamburger Fremdenblatt*, 29 May 1920.

168. Cf. Heilmann's remarks in *SBVPrLV*, 29 Apr. 1920, vol. 9, col. 11297; and *Freiheit*, 2 June 1920.

169. Noske regarded himself as the sacrificial lamb of SPD-USPD cooperation (*Erlebtes*, p. 152).

170. The commitment to democracy was particularly pronounced among the members of the Prussian SPD delegation. Richard Hausschildt, the co-chairman of the delegation, for example, differentiated between "socialism, which he regarded as a means to further the material well-being of the masses, and "democracy, which we regard as an end in itself" (*SBVPrLV*, 26 Apr. 1920, vol. 9, col. 11010).

171. *Vorwärts*, no. 276 (1 June 1920).

172. Members of a delegation from the Amsterdam Socialist International, who arrived in Berlin on the eve of the general strike, decided to devote themselves to bringing the warring factions of the German Socialist movement together.

173. Cf. Limbertz's and Rosenfeld's reports in *SBVPrLV*, 30 and 31 Mar. 1920, vol. 7, cols. 10564, 10637–38. Cf. Koch-Weser, "Kapp-Putsch," 15 Mar. 1920, Koch-Weser papers (BA).

174. Cf. report of Friedrich Stampfer, "Bei den Internationalen," *Vorwärts*, no. 179 (8 Apr. 1920). A report of this episode from the viewpoint of the USPD does not seem to have survived.

175. The controversy involves the question if Legien's aim was to rescue Germany from disaster in March 1920, or did he hope to become the dictator of the Reich? See "Zum Gedächtnis Carl Legiens," *Sozialistische Monatshefte* 56 (17 Jan. 1921), 4; Robert Jansen, *Der Berliner Militärputsch und seine politischen Folgen* (Berlin, 1920), p. 46; and Giebel papers/Kasette II/Mappe 9 (Arch.SD).

176. Thus Legien demanded "government only by Social Democratic workers. . . . The workers must be included in military units. . . . Disarm and eliminate the mutinous troops. . . . Change the constitution. . . . Establish workers' militias to maintain law and order." See Erwin Könnemann, ed., "Protokolle Albert Südekums aus den Tagen nach dem Kapp-Putsch," *Beiträge zur Geschichte der deutschen Arbeiterbewegung* 8 (1966), 269–70. Cf. Erger, *Kapp*, doc. 58, pp. 350–52.

177. Wilhelm Koenen, "Zur Frage der Möglichkeit einer Arbeiterregierung nach dem Kapp-Putsch," *Beiträge zur Geschichte der deutschen Arbeiterbewegung* 4 (1962), 347–49.

178. "Niederschrift über die Sitzung des geschäftsführenden Vorstandes der Zentralarbeitsgemeinschaft am 17. März 1920 (Erwin Könneman, ed., "Dokumente zur Haltung der Monopolisten im Kapp-Putsch," ibid. 9 [1967], 1011).

179. The quoted words are from Friedrich Stampfer, *Die vierzehn Jahre der ersten deutschen Republik*, 3d ed. (Hamburg, 1953), p. 174. The final agreements are printed in *Dokumente und Materialien zur Geschichte der deutschen Arbeiterbewegung* 7 (1965), 223–24.

180. Cf. the comments of Kugler (representative of the German Civil Servants' Association) in "Südekum-Protokolle," p. 266. Oeser was rejected by organized labor because he had repeatedly opposed wage and benefit demands by the railroad workers.

181. Hirsch, *Weg*, p. 224.

182. Heine's letter of resignation of 18 Mar., O. Braun papers/151/1 (IISG). Heine discussed

the reasons for his resignation in detail in a telephone conversation on 20 Mar. 1920 with the speaker of the Prussian Constitutional Convention, Robert Leinert, Heine papers/339 (IISG). Pressure from the SPD's Berlin district organization forced Police Chief Ernst out of office. Heine wrote to Ernst, "The mood of the party is against you," and said that Ernst was a victim of the closer cooperation between the SPD and the USPD (Heine to Ernst, 27 Mar. 1920, Heine papers/337 (IISG).

183. Südekum to Severing, 7 June 1920, and Südekum to Leinert, 18 June 1920, Severing papers/Kassette I, nos. 105, 107 (Arch.SD).

184. Cf. Heine to Ernst, 27 March 1920, Heine papers/337 (IISG); and *Vorwärts*, no. 158 (26 Mar. 1920); Cf. Krüger, "Berliner Diktatur," *Vorwärts*, no. 158 (26 Mar. 1920); *SBVPrLV*, 31 Mar. 1920, vol. 8, col. 10627.

185. *Vorwärts*, nos. 158, 159 (26 Mar. 1920). The juxtaposition made political sense. As a member of the convention since 1919, Gräf had parliamentary experience, while Krüger had never been a member of the legislature.

186. *Sozialdemokratisches Handbuch für die preussischen Landtagswahlen* (Berlin, 1921), p. 114.

187. *Freiheit*, 22 Apr. 1920.

188. Ibid., 28 Mar. 1920; and *Vorwärts*, no. 159 (26 Mar. 1920).

189. *Vorwärts*, no. 157 (25 Mar. 1920).

190. Ibid., no. 158 (26 Mar. 1920).

191. Ibid., no. 161 (27 Mar. 1920); and *Freiheit*, 28 Mar. 1920.

192. *Vorwärts*, no. 166. (30 Mar. 1920) noted, "It is obvious that Otto Braun symbolized the *leftist tendencies* [*sic*] of the previous Prussian cabinet" under the headline, "Prime Minister Braun against the Right." Cf. Erich Kuttner, *Braun*, p. 69; *SBVPrLV*, 31 Mar. 1920, vol. 8, cols. 10629–30 (Rosenfeld [USPD]).

193. Braun, *Weimar*, p. 31.

194. Cf. *SPD-Parteitag*, June 1919, p. 135.

195. Cf. *SBVPrLV*, 14 Jan. 1921, vol. 12, cols. 15915–16 (Leidig [DVP]); 30 Mar. 1920, vol. 8, cols. 10563–64.

196. Stegerwald himself stated later that he had remained in office only at the insistence of the Center party delegation ("Aus meinem Leben," pp. 144–45). Oeser was technically still public works minister, but only to wind up the affairs of his ministry, before the Prussian railroads were transferred to the Reich.

197. *SBVPrLV*, 13 Jan. 1921, vol. 12, col. 15719. Obviously, sixty members of the delegation abstained.

198. *SBVPrLV*, 29 Apr. 1920, vol. 9, cols. 11285–86. Cf. Severing's opinion on the political role of labor unions in Carl Severing, *Mein Lebensweg* (Cologne, 1950), 1:423. See also *Vorwärts*, no. 157 (25 Mar. 1920).

199. Wachenheim, *Grossbürgertum*, p. 91.

200. *SBVPrLV*, 30 Mar. 1920, vol. 8, cols. 10512–24.

201. *Sitzung des Parteiausschusses [der SPD] am 8. Dezember 1920 . . . [Berlin 1920]*, p. 45.

202. The epithet is found in Abegg to Severing, 31 May 1947, Severing papers/60/12 (Arch.SD).

203. *SBVPrLV*, 22 Sept. 1920, vol. 10, col. 12357 (Heilmann).

204. Emil Unger's book, *Politische Köpfe des sozialistischen Deutschlands* (Leipzig, 1920), which was published after the Kapp Putsch, does not contain a separate article on either Braun or Severing.

205. Cf. Theodor Wolff, *Der Marsch durch zwei Jahrzehnte* (Amsterdam, 1936), p. 366; Willy Hellpach, *Wirken im Wirren 1914–1925* (Hamburg, 1949), 2:311; Rathenau, "Jude,"

pp. 51, 57–58, 62–63; and Helga Grebing, "Weimarer Portraits," *Politische Studien* 6 (Mar. 1956), 30. Ferdinand Friedensburg, *Lebenserinnerungen* (Frankfurt a.M., 1969), 1:208 comments that Braun was not very anxious to work.

206. Kuttner, *Braun,* pp. 75–76; and Schulze, *Braun,* pp. 392–93.

207. See Lüdicke to S. von Kardorff, 19 Sept. 1920, S. von Kardorff papers/11 (BA); and Albrecht Mareth (MdR) to Katherine von Oheimb, 18 Sept. 1920, ibid./19a.

208. See *Protokoll der Sitzung des Parteivorstandes, des Parteiausschusses und der Reichstagsfraktion, 13.6.1920* (Berlin, 1920), pp. 7, 21 (H. Müller and O. Hue); "Giebel-Aufz.Rtagsfr."; Heinrich Cunow, "Wohin geht die Fahrt," *Neue Zeit* 38 (18 June 1920), 265–69; and Kastning, *Sozialdemokratie,* p. 82.

209. According to Wachenheim, *Grossbürgertum,* p. 132, the SPD leadership already knew during the Kassel party congress, that the majority of USPD delegates in Halle would vote to join the Communist International. Cf. Curt Geyer, *Die revolutionäre Illusion,* ed. Wolfgang Benz (Stuttgart, 1976), p. 216; and *Vorwärts,* nos. 442, 471 (5 and 22 Sept. 1920).

210. "Giebel-Aufz.Rtagsfr."; and von Hanstein to Severing, 17 Sept. 1920, Severing papers 10/71–72 (Arch. SD). Cf. Paul Hahn, *Der rote Hahn* (Stuttgart, 1922), pp. 126–27.

211. Wachenheim, *Grossbürgertum,* p. 131.

212. *Protokoll der Sitzung des Parteivorstandes, 13.6.1920,* pp. 7–8 (H. Müller).

213. *Vorwärts,* no. 408 (17 Aug. 1920).

214. Among the suggestions advanced by the Weimar parties were to combine elections in Prussia with the next national contest or even to elect the Reich president and the members of the state legislature simultaneously. See, *SBVPrLV,* 3 Dec. 1920, vol. 11, col. 14472 (Severing); *Vorwärts,* no. 474 (24 Sept. 1924); and A. von Holtzendorff to Cuno, 6 Dec. 1920, Hap.Arch./ V, VI.

215. *SBVPrLV,* 28 Oct. 1920, vol. 10, col. 13244 (Hirsch); and "Sitz.PrStMin.," 26 Nov. 1920, O. Braun papers/162 (IISG). Since the Prussian electoral districts were the same as those used for Reichstag elections, voters in East Prussia and Schleswig-Holstein also voted for their national representatives. They did not vote in June 1920 as at that time the national boundaries in these border areas had not yet been determined.

216. Hermann Kranold, "Nach den preussischen Landtagswahlen 1921," *Sozialistische Monatshefte* 6 (28 Feb. 1921), 169.

217. It was not exactly helpful to press for enlarging the powers of the (Social Democratic) prime minister at the same time that the offer to extend the life of the coalition was made (see Eimers, *Verhältnis,* p. 372; Schulze, *Braun,* pp. 370–71). Calls to continue the coalition are found in Robert Jansen, *Die Regierungsbildung in Preussen* (Berlin, [1921]), p. 5; *SBVPrLV,* 14 Jan. 1921, vol. 12, cols. 15945–46 (Severing). See also the report on Braun's address in Königsberg in *Freiheit,* 6 Jan. 1921.

218. Jansen, *Regierungsbildung,* p. 5; Eimers, *Verhältnis,* p. 297; and Schulze, *Braun,* p. 325. A later report in *Sozialdemokratische Korrespondenz* 16 (15 May 1921), 37–38, that the coalition parties had reached an agreement was the product of wishful thinking.

219. Alois Klöckner, *Der erste preussische Landtag* (Berlin, 1921), p. 34; Troeltsch, *Spektator-Briefe,* p. 182 (16 Mar. 1921); and Jansen, *Regierungsbildung,* p. 3.

220. Braun, *Weimar,* pp. 39–40. The passage of the budget for the fiscal year 1921 illustrates the short tenure of this government: the budget had been prepared by the Braun cabinet, Stegerwald's ministry presented it to the Landtag, but the grand coalition guided the document through the parliamentary debates.

221. Schulze, *Braun,* p. 330; and *Vorwärts,* no. 89 (23 Feb. 1921).

222. Haenisch to H. Braun, 4 May 1921, Heinrich and Julie Braun-Vogelstein papers (LBI); Grzesinski to Scheidemann, 16 Sept. 1921, Grzesinski papers/304 (IISG); and Werner Stephan, *Aufstieg und Verfall des Linksliberalismus 1918–1933* (Göttingen, 1973), p. 191. See also

Trimborn's remarks at the meeting of the Reichstag caucus of the Center party on 23 Feb. 1921, ten Hompel papers/15 (BA). Precedents for a grand coalition at the state and local level existed in Mecklenburg and the city of Berlin, where the mayor had recently been elected with votes from the SPD, DDP, and DVP, against those of the KPD, USPD, and DNVP.

223. On the DDP, see Klöckner, *Landtag,* p. 37; Paul Saupe, "Die Bedeutung der Preussen-wahlen für die christlich-nationale Arbeiterschaft," *Deutsche Arbeit* 6 (1921), 124. See also Trimborn's statements at the meeting of the Center party's Reichstag delegation on 23 Feb. 1921, ten Hompel papers/15 (BA); and Stephan, *Aufstieg,* pp. 190–91.

224. See "Die Bemühungen der Deutschen Volkspartei um die Bildung einer nationalen Einheitsfront, 15.2.1921," Forst.Hbg/7523 (DVP); *Korrespondenz der Deutschnationalen Volkspartei* 4 (16 Feb. 1921); and Curtius to Dingeldey, 26 Feb. 1921, Dingeldey papers/ 13 (BA).

225. Paul Hirsch, "Der sozialdemokratische Landtagssieg," *Die Glocke* 6 (26 Feb. 1921), 1333; and Werner Peiser, "Die Wahlen in Preussen," ibid. 6 (12 Feb. 1921), 1245.

226. Wels to Noske, 23 Mar. 1921, Noske papers/20 (Arch.SD). Noske claimed that Social Democratic newspapers had refused to publish his contribution. See Gustav Noske, *Erlebtes,* pp. 199–200.

227. See Schulze, *Braun,* p. 332.

228. See Friedrich Grebe, "Stegerwald preussischer Ministerpräsident," *Allgemeine Rundschau* 18 (16 Apr. 1921), 193–94; Johannes Fischart, *Neue Köpfe,* 4th ed. (Berlin, 1921), p. 70; Jansen, *Regierungsbildung,* pp. 8, 11; and "DDP-Fr.Prot.," 8 and 10 Mar. 1921.

229. Jansen, *Regierungsbildung,* pp. 11–15.

230. See Dominicus's statements at the meeting of the DDP caucus on 5 Apr. 1921; and Jansen, *Regierungsbildung,* p. 16.

231. See "DDP-Fr.Prot.," 5 Apr., 1921.

232. The letter is reprinted in Schulze, *Braun,* pp. 335–36. See also Jansen, *Regierungs-bildung,* pp. 16–17.

233. "DDP-Fr.Prot.," 8 Apr. 1921; Jansen, *Regierungsbildung,* p. 20; and Grebe, "Steger-wald," p. 194.

234. See Hermann Molkenbuhr, diary entry for 16 Apr. 1921, Molkenbuhr papers/Kassette IV (Arch.SD); and the detailed article by Erich Dombrowski, *Berliner Tageblatt,* no. 166 (9 Apr. 1921).

235. Hans-Peter Ehni, *Bollwerk Preussen?* (Bonn–Bad Godesberg, 1975), p. 51.

236. Grebe, "Stegerwald," p. 194; and Fischart, *Köpfe,* p. 71. Several contemporaries suspected that he had been nominated for the post of prime minister on such short notice in order to strengthen his ties to the Center party. Cf. Jansen, *Regierungsbildung,* pp. 20–21; and Werner Conze, Erich Kosthorst, and Elfriede Nebgen, *Jakob Kaiser* (Stuttgart, 1967), 1:93.

237. Walther Graef, "Der Werdegang der Deutschnationalen Volkspartei 1918–1928," in *Der nationale Wille,* ed. Max Weiss (Berlin, 1928), p. 35. The party's Pan-German wing disagreed. See Gustav Roethe, "Preussen den Preussen," *Der Tag,* 22 Apr. 1921.

238. Stegerwald, "Leben," p. 145; and Josef Deutz, *Adam Stegerwald* (Cologne, 1952), pp. 92–93.

239. Jansen, *Regierungsbildung,* p. 26; Grebe, "Stegerwald," pp. 236–37; and Grebe, "Das Ministerium Stegerwald," *Allgemeine Rundschau* 18 (7 May 1921), 137. Schulze, *Braun,* p. 336, misjudges the connection: not Stegerwald, but rather Porsch and Gronowski made these concessions.

240. Jansen, *Regierungsbildung,* pp. 25–26.

241. Haenisch to Braun, 11 Apr. 1921, O. Braun papers/161 (IISG).

242. "DDP-Fr.Prot.," 19 Apr. 1921.

243. Stegerwald hoped to appoint Gustav Noske as his "nonpartisan" minister of the interior,

and Noske apparently did not reject the idea at the outset, but declined on Ebert's advice. See Ulrich Czisnik, *Gustav Noske* (Göttingen, 1969), pp. 96–97.

244. Stephan, *Aufstieg*, pp. 188, 191, 279.

245. See "DDP-Fr.Prot.," 5 Apr. 1921.

246. See Moldenhauer, "Erinnerungen," pp. 108–09; and Stresemann's notes dated 13 May 1921, in Gustav Stresemann, *Vermächtnis*, ed. Henry Berhard et al. (Berlin, 1932), 1:20–21. Stegerwald supported Stresemann's stand. The Prussian prime minister did not think that the ultimatum could be fulfilled, but felt that an occupation of the Ruhr area would have dire consequences. See Moldenhauer, "Erinnerungen," p. 109. In DDP councils, Fischbeck supported acceptance, Dominicus was opposed. See Koch-Weser, diary entries for 7 and 9 May 1921, Koch-Weser papers (BA).

247. Georg Schreiber, *Zwischen Demokratie und Diktatur* (Regensburg, 1949), p. 121; Ernst Laubach, *Die Politik der Kabinette Wirth* (Lübeck and Hamburg, 1968), p. 22; and Hugo Stehkämper, "Konrad Adenauer und das Reichskanzleramt," *Konrad Adenauer*, ed. Stehkämper (Cologne, 1976), pp. 407–09.

248. Stegerwald's efforts to change the government are described in Adolf Gottwald, *Ziele und Erfolge der Zentrumsfraktion des Preussischen Lantages 1921/24* [Berlin, 1924], p. 5. See also Robert Jansen, *Die Grosse Koalition in Preussen* (Berlin, [1921]), p. 14. The SPD was deeply divided over the question of joining the Wirth government. See "Aufz. über die Fraktionssitz., 20.5.1921," Giebel papers/216H (Arch.SD). At the end, the caucus voted 56 to 20, and the party committee voted 28 to 13 for joining the cabinet.

249. See Stegerwald, "Leben," p. 145; Jansen, *Grosse Koalition*, pp. 4–5; *Deutsche Allgemeine Zeitung*, 2 Oct. 1921; and *Sozialdemokratische Parteikorrespondenz* 16 (15 July 1921), 59–60.

250. According to a handwritten marginal note on the copy of the article in Otto Braun's newspaper clipping collection (O. Braun papers/264–65 [IISG]). Rathenau, "Jude," p. 58 is very critical of Goslar.

251. On the negotiations, see Krüger's report in *SPD Parteitag 1921*, p. 139; *Germania*, 3–10 Sept. 1921, and *Berliner Tageblatt*, no. 458 (2 Sept. 1921). See also Koch-Weser to his wife, 1 Sept. 1921, Koch-Weser papers (BA); and *Berliner Tageblatt*, no. 499 (23 Sept. 1921).

252. *Vorwärts*, no. 473 (7 Oct. 1921).

253. See the discussions of the Multi-Partisan Committee on 17, 18, and 20 Oct. 1921 and the cabinet meeting of 22 Oct. 1921, *Ak/Rk Wirth*, vol. 1, docs. 114, 115, 116, 119, 120, pp. 322–32, 339–41.

254. Sebastian Brant, "Politische Chronik," Neue Rundschau 32 (1921), 1002; and H. Mokenbuhr, diary entry for 23 Oct. 1921, Molkenbuhr papers/IV (Arch.SD).

255. "Meetings of the Multi-Partisan Committee, 22 Oct. 1921," Ak/Rk Wirth, vol. 1, doc. 118, p. 337.

256. "Notes," 22 Oct. 1921, in Stresemann, *Vermächtnis* 1:21.

257. See Wilhelm Marx's remarks at a meeting of the Center party's Düsseldorf-Ost district, *Volksstimme* (Duisburg), no. 293 (2 Nov. 1921); and Laubach, *Politik*, p. 104.

258. *Volksstimme* (Duisburg), no. 293 (2 Nov. 1921); and Laubach, *Politik*, p. 104.

259. Lothar Albertin, "Die Verantwortung der Liberalen Parteien für das Scheitern der Grossen Koalition im Herbst 1921," *Historische Zeitschrift* 205 (Dec. 1967), 566–627.

260. Jansen, *Grosse Koalition*, p. 11.

261. See the interview with WTB, *Deutsche Tageszeitung*, 3 Nov. 1921; and *Vorwärts*, no. 520 (3 Nov. 1921). Cf. "DDP-Fr.Prot.," 31 Oct. 1921 (Oeser).

262. Severing, *Lebensweg* 1:333–34; Jansen, *Grosse Koalition*, pp. 13–14. See also Stegerwald's WTB interview; and Schulze, *Braun*, p. 348.

263. See circular letter written by Minister of Education Becker to relatives, 10 Oct. 1921, p. 4, Becker papers (PrGStAB).

264. *Germania,* 4 Nov. 1921; and *Deutsche Tageszeitung,* 3 Nov. 1921; *Kreuzzeitung,* 3 Nov. 1921.

265. Graef, *Werdegang,* p. 41; and Schulze, *Braun,* p. 342.

266. *Die Zeit,* 26 Sept. 1922.

267. *PK* (SD), vol. 16 (15 Dec. 1921), 115; and [Paul Hirsch], ed., *Der Preussische Landtag 1921–1924* (Berlin [1924]), p. 12.

268. *Vorwärts,* no. 525 (6 Nov. 1921).

269. See Jansen, *Grosse Koalition,* p. 17.

270. *Vorwärts,* nos. 524, 544 (5 and 18 Nov. 1921).

271. See, Cunow to Tönnies, 7 Nov. 1921, Tönnies papers (University of Kiel archives); *Berliner Tageblatt,* no. 510 (5 Nov. 1921); *Vorwärts,* no. 523 (5 Nov. 1921). Friedrich Grebe, "Die grosse Koalition in Preussen," *Allgemeine Rundschau* 18 (19 Nov. 1921), 640.

272. See Grzesinski to Scheidemann, 16 Sept. 1921; Koch-Weser, diary entries for 12 and 22 Apr. 1921; and Schulze, *Braun,* p. 337.

273. As late as the end of November, Hergt again tried to entice the bourgeois parties with the siren call for a coalition "encompassing all nationalists, but not the Majority Socialists" under Stegerwald's leadership. See *Der Deutsche,* 25 Nov. 1921. Cf. *Deutsche Zeitung,* 6 Nov. 1921; *Berliner Tageblatt,* no. 510 (5 Nov. 1921); *Vossische Zeitung,* 6 Nov. 1921; Jansen, *Grosse Koalition,* p. 21; and Grebe, "Grosse Koalition," p. 641.

274. *Germania,* 5, 6 Nov. 1921; and Jansen, *Grosse Koalition,* pp. 19–20.

275. Jansen, *Grosse Koalition,* pp. 21–22.

276. *Der Tag,* 7 Nov. 1921.

277. *Germania,* 6 Nov. 1921, commented, "Signs and miracles still happen in domestic politics."

278. He decided not to occupy the post of welfare minister that had been kept open for him in the Braun cabinet, since the composition of the new government did not conform to "his basic political principles." See Stegerwald, "Mein Rücktritt," *Germania,* 8 Nov. 1921.

279. Grebe, "Grosse Koalition," p. 640.

Chapter 3. Reich and State after 1918: New Constitutions and New Relationships

1. On Prussia's prestige and image after 1871, see especially Otto von Stolberg-Wernigerode, *Die unentschiedene Generation* (Munich, 1968).

2. Jürgen Kocka, "The First World War and the Mittelstand,'" *Journal of Contemporary History* 8 (1973), 106; Heinrich August Winkler, *Mittelstand, Demokratie und National-sozialismus* (Cologne, 1972), p. 44.

3. See J. Alden Nichols, *Germany After Bismarck* (New York, 1968); Manfred Rauh, *Die Parlamentarisierung des Deutschen Reiches* (Düsseldorf, 1977); Dirk Stegman, *Bismarcks Erben* (Cologne, 1970); and J.G.G. Röhl, *Germany after Bismarck* (Berkeley, Calif., 1967) for details of the post-Bismarck era.

4. See for instance, *Vorwärts,* no. 334a (5 Dec. 1918); H. Molkenbuhr to Arthus M., 1 Nov. 1918, and Molkenbuhr, diary entry for 24 Nov. 1918, Molkenbuhr papers/II/81 and IV (Arch.SD).

5. See the letter of Gustav Landauer of 22, 23, 24 Nov. [*sic*] 1918 for details (Martin Buber, ed., *Neue Rundschau* 34, pt.2 [1923], 908). Cf. Francis L. Carsten, *Revolution in Central Europe 1918–1919* (Berkeley, Calif., 1972), p. 187. Kurt Eisner called the members of the CPP the "rulers in Berlin," without any differentiation on the basis of party membership. See Philipp Loewenfeld, "Erinnerungen," typescript p. 252 (LBI).

6. Enno Eimers, *Das Verhältnis von Preussen und Reich in den ersten Jahren der Weimarer Republik (1918–1923)* (Berlin, 1969), p. 332.

7. "Meeting of the RVB, 28 Dec. 1918," in *RVB-Protokolle*, vol. 2, doc. 76, pp. 59, 63. Cf. the report on Haase's speech in Gleiwitz on 22 Nov. 1918, in *Revolutions-Dokumente—Die deutsche Revolution in der Darstellung der zeitgenössischen Presse*, ed. Eberhard Buchner (Berlin, 1921), vol. 1, no. 397. Breitscheid remained conspicuously tough in questions involving Upper Silesia. See Eimers, *Verhältnis*, p. 59.

8. Max Cohen-Reuss was convinced that a centralized Reich could have come into being at this time. See *II. Rätekongress*, p. 160.

9. See Payer's statements in the meeting of the DDP caucus of the National Constitutional Convention, 9 Feb. 1919, Petersen papers/262 (Staatsarch.Hbg.). See also Wilhelm Blos, *Von der Monarchie zum Volksstaat* (Stuttgart, 1922–23), 2:10; Wolfgang Benz, *Süddeutschland in der Weimar Republik* (Berlin, 1970), p. 93; and Gerhard Senger, *Die Politik der Deutschen Zentrumspartei zur Frage Reich und Länder von 1918–1928* (Hamburg, 1932), p. 14.

10. Among the many voices supporting this point of view: Ebert and Leinert at the ZR and CPP meetings on 31 Dec. 1918, *RVB-Protokolle*, vol. 2, doc. 89, p. 166; A. von Holtzendorff to Cuno, 11 Dec. 1918, Hap.Arch.1/17/II; Max Cohen's speech, *II, Rätekongress*, p. 160; and Friedrich Meinecke, "Verfassung und Verwaltung der deutschen Republik," *Neue Rundschau 30*. pt. 1, (1919), 4–5. On the controversy, see also Ströbel's speech, "Reichskonferenz 25. Nov. 1918," p. 183; and ZR to NV, 5 Feb. 1919, in Albert Grzesinski, "Im Kampf um die Republik— Lebensweg eines Staatenlosen," typescript, Grzesinski papers/2457, p. 80 (IISG); and meeting of the RVB, 28 Dec. 1918, *RVB-Protokolle*, vol. 2, doc. 76, pp. 62–64.

11. Efforts on the part of the ZR chairman, Cohen-Reuss, to reopen the question of the territorial and political restructuring of Prussia in Feb. 1919 met with derisive laughter from his colleagues. See meeting of the Prussian cabinet and the ZR, 13 Feb. 1919, and meeting of the ZR, 15 Feb. 1919, in *ZR-Protokolle*, docs. 86, 88, pp. 641, 658.

12. Reinhard Rürup, "Entstehung und Grundlagen der Weimarer Verfassung," ed. Eberhard Kolb, *Vom Kaiserreich zur Weimarer Republik* (Cologne, 1972), pp. 227–29.

13. See Hirsch's comments, "Reichskonferenz 25.Nov.1918," p. 200. A good synopsis of the Prussian views on the organization of the Reich is in Willipalt Apelt, *Geschichte der Weimarer Verfassung*, 2d ed. (Munich, 1964), pp. 60–63.

14. Heine, in "Reichskonferenz 25.Nov.1918," pp. 165–66.

15. Preuss was so certain that Prussia would cease to exist in its present form that he did not even invite representatives of the new revolutionary Prussian government to take part in the early consultations on his draft constitution for the Reich. Cf. Carl Petersen's notes for Dec. 1918, Petersen papers/L 59 (Staatsarch.Hbg.). See also, "Besprechung d. Verfassungsentwurfs, 14.1.1919," *RVB-Protokolle*, vol. 1, doc. 104, p. 237. Incidentally, some members of the committee working on the constitution draft, including Undersecretary von Krause of the Reich Ministry of Justice and Max Weber, no longer believed at this time that Prussia would disintegrate or dissolve without resistance. See Petersen's notes and Wolfgang Mommsen, *Max Weber*, 2d ed. (Tübingen, 1974), p. 381. Cf. A. von Holtzendorff to Cuno, 15 Dec. 1918, Hap. Arch./I, II.

16. "Sitz.PrStMin.," 24 Jan. 1919, O. Braun papers/31 (IISG); and *SBVPrLV*, 15 Mar. 1919, vol. 1, col. 134 (Hirsch). Cf. *Vorwärts*, no. 44 (24 Jan. 1919).

17. August Maudert, "Ein Anfang deutscher Einheit," *Sozialistische Monatshefte 60* (24 Apr. 1923), 203–04. In the fall of 1919 the Prussian Constitutional Convention passed a resolution stating that the new Thuringian state should not be founded at the expense of Prussian territory. See *SBVPrLV*, 2 Oct., vol. 7, cols. 1616–17; 16 Dec. 1919, vol. 12, cols. 8189–90; and *DrSVPrLV*, DrS. 1918, 6:2771. The cabinet had earlier expressed its willingness to enter into

negotiations without any preconditions. See "Sitz. PrStMin.," 19 Apr. 1919, O. Braun papers/41 (IISG).

18. Ernst Rudolf Huber, ed., *Dokumente zur deutschen Verfassungsgeschichte* (Stuttgart, 1966), 3:154; See Carl Severing, "Provinzialautonomie?" *Neue Zeit* 40 (4 Nov. 1921), p. 122.

19. Ebert spoke of the Prussian finance minister as "an official installed by us." See *RVB-Protokolle*, vol. 2. doc. 68, p. 26.

20. See the joint meeting of the RVB and the Prussian cabinet, 14 Nov. 1918, *RVB-Protokolle*, vol. 1, doc. 10, p. 140. Cf. Eimers, *Verhältnis*, p. 66.

21. Eimers, *Verhältnis*, pp. 62–63.

22. Huber, ed., *Dokumente* 3:132, 138. Ernst Rudolf Huber, *Deutsche Verfassungsgeschichte seit 1789* (Stuttgart, 1981), 6:378–79.

23. Gerhard Anschütz, et al., "Föderalismus," in *Der deutsche Föderalismus*, ed. Anschütz (Berlin, 1924), pp. 31–32; and Wilhelm Keil, *Erlebnisse eines Sozialdemokraten* (Stuttgart, 1947–48), 2:176–77. Hagen Schulze, *Otto Braun* (Frankfurt a.M., 1977), p. 400, calculates that the Prussian government lost 54 votes (out of a total of 259 votes) because some of the provinces cast ballots against the cabinet.

24. See Eimers, *Verhältnis*, pp. 154–55; Koch-Weser, diary entry for 4 Dec. 1919, Koch-Weser papers (BA); and Heine to O. Braun, 1 Feb. 1920, O. Braun papers/51 (IISG).

25. "Sitz.PrStMin.," 4 June 1919, O. Braun papers/46 (IISG); see also *Ak/Rk Scheidemann*, doc. 101, pp. 421–22; and Eimers, *Verhältnis*, p. 291.

26. *SBVPrLV*, 15 July 1919, vol. 1, col. 3483 (von Kardorff [DVNP]); 15 Nov. 1919, vol. 5, col. 6569 (Heilmann); 17 Nov. 1919, vol. 5, col. 6656 (von Richter [DVP]). See also Heilmann, "Die Weimarer Verfassung," *Die Glocke* 5 (9 Aug. 1919), 582; Ernst Troeltsch, *Spektator-Briefe*, ed. Hans Baron (Tübingen, 1924), p. 101 (12 Jan. 1920); and Gerhard Schulz, *Zwischen Demokratie und Diktatur—Verfassungspolitik und Reichsreform in der Weimarer Republik* (Berlin, 1963), p. 235; and *Freiheit*, 23 Mar. 1919.

27. The Center did not wish to discuss the issue in plenary session, but the SPD and the DDP insisted. See "DDP-Fr.Prot.," 19 Mar. 1919.

28. *RheinZ-Parteitag*, p. 167 (Lauscher).

29. *SBVPrLV*, vol. 1, col. 617.

30. On these negotiations, see Karl Dietrich Erdmann, *Adenauer in der Rheinlandpolitik* (Stuttgart, 1966), p. 54; and Henning Köhler, *Autonomiebewegung oder Separatismus* (Berlin, 1974), pp. 83–86.

31. *SBVPrLV*, 27, 28 May 1919, vol. 2, cols. 1851, 1911–16 (Herold).

32. Eimers, *Verhältnis*, p. 155. The cabinet also complained that it was not consulted in working out the legislative proposals on the Temporary Reich Economic Council; it had learned of the decisions from the press. See *SBVPrLV*, 14 Nov. 1919, vol. 5, col. 6430.

33. *SBVPrLV*, 15 Dec. 1919, vol. 7, cols. 8126ff.

34. *SBVPrLV*, 15 Dec. 1919, col. 8126 (Hergt).

35. The rider was not discussed at a December 13 meeting of the SPD caucus.

36. See Trimborn's statements in *Z-Parteitag Jan. 1920*, p. 32. Cf. Jochen Hauss, *Die erste Volkswahl des deutschen Reichspräsidenten* (Kallmünz, Opf., 1965), p. 15.

37. "DDP-Fr.Prot.," 9 and 12 Dec. 1919.

38. *SBVPrLV*, 17 Dec. 1919, vol. 7, cols. 8281–82 (Friedberg) and col. 8320 (von Kries). This was a purely tactical decision. In the DDP caucus meeting of 17 Dec. Schnackenburg suggested that "the DDP call for a name-call vote if there were enough [favorable] members present." See "DDP-Fr.Prot.," 17 Dec. 1919. Party divisions are revealed by the fact that about half of the DNVP and DVP delegates did not vote. On the strength of the coalition parties, see *SBVPrLV*, vol. 7, cols. 8407–12.

39. The Hessian minister of justice, von Brentano, regarded the resolution as an attempt to

reestablish Prussian preeminence. See his statements in *Z-Parteitag Jan. 1920*, p. 21. See also Koch-Weser, diary entry for 19 Jan., 20 Feb. 1920, Koch-Weser papers/16 (BA); Koch-Weser's memo of Jan. 1920, RK 43 I/1872.

40. Carl Severing, *1919/1920 im Wetter-und Watterwinkel* (Bielefeld, 1920), pp. 173, 176, 181. The text of the Bielefeld Agreement is in ibid., pp. 177–80. Cf. Georg Eliasberg, "Der Ruhrkrieg 1920," *Archiv für Sozialgeschichte* 10 (1970), 343, also published in expanded form under the title *Der Ruhrkrieg von 1920* (Bonn–Bad Godesberg, 1974).

41. Severing, *1919/1920*, p. 236; and Ministry of the Interior to OPrä and RPrä, 29 Mar. 1920, LASH/301/216.

42. "Sitz.PrStMin.," 1 Apr. 1920, O. Braun papers/B/A/19a (Forst.Hbg.); Weismann to Braun, 2 Apr. 1920, RK 43 I/2305 (BA). Cf. Eliasberg, "Ruhrkrieg," pp. 363–65.

43. Such miscalculations led the Kapp conspirators to expect that some of the Republican ministers would continue to serve in the putschists' cabinet. Heine's name appeared on several ministerial lists prepared by the Putschists. See Erwin Könnemann, "Zwei Denkschriften der Kapp-Putschisten über ihr Verhältnis zur Sozialdemokratie," *Beiträge zur Geschichte der Arbeiterbewegung* 9 (1969), p. 490; and Johannes Erger, *Der Kapp-Lüttwitz-Putsch* (Düsseldorf, 1967), p. 22. In reality, there were no points of common interest. Kapp wanted to dispense with Parliament and parliamentarism and restore prewar authoritarianism.

44. See for example, "Sitz.d.Pr.Reg.u.d.ZR," 23 Jan. 1919, *ZR-Protokolle*, doc. 60, pp. 458–60; "Sitz. d. RVB, 28 Jan. 1919," RVB-Protokolle, vol. 2, doc. 123, p. 342; "Sitz. d. Berliner A.—u.S.—Räte [31 Jan. 1919]," *Vorwärts*, no. 58 (1 Feb. 1919); and *Freiheit*, 23 Jan. 1919. Cf. Heine's memo of 21 Mar. 1921, in Eimers, *Verhältnis*, p. 444ff. Max Cohen-Reuss represented the opposing point of view: he feared that retaining Prussia as a large economic unit would block the natural growth of a common German market. See Cohen's statements at the *II. Rätekongress*, p. 160.

45. Koch-Weser, diary entries for 31 May and 24 Nov. 1920, Koch-Weser papers (BA).

46. Eimers, *Verhältnis*, pp. 169, 320–21.

47. *SBVPrLV*, 5 Nov. 1920, vol. 10, col. 13553. Cf. Braun to cabinet, 20 May 1920, cited in Eimers, *Verhältnis*, p. 284.

48. Eimers, *Verhältnis*, pp. 69–70; "Beratung der Pr. Vorl. Verf., 14 Jan. 1919," *RVB-Protokolle*, doc. 60, pp. 461–62; and Dominicus's statements, "DDP-Fr.Prot.," 29 Sept. 1921.

49. Among the vast literature on the Rhenish movement, the following are representative of the various points of view: Rudolf Morsey, *Die deutsche Zentrumspartei 1917–1923* (Düsseldorf, 1966), pp. 117ff.; Erwin Bischof, *Rheinischer Separatismus 1918–1924* (Bern, 1969); Erdmann, *Adenauer;* Köhler, *Autonomiebewegung;* Fritz Brüggemann, *Die rheinische Republik* (Bonn, 1919); Senger, *Politik;* and Stephen A. Schuker, *The End of French Predominance in Europe* (Chapel Hill, N.C., 1976).

50. See Marx, "Erinnerungsbericht, Okt. 1936," *Der Nachlass des Reichskanzlers Wilhelm Marx*, ed. Hugo Stehkämper (Cologne, 1968), 1:288–89. Cf. Bischof, *Separatismus*, pp. 36, 36 n. 35; Erdmann, *Adenauer*, pp. 28ff.; and Köhler, *Autonomiebewegung*, pp. 27, 87ff.

51. Köhler, *Autonomiebewegung*, provides the most detailed account of Froberger's role and aims.

52. Bernhard Falk, "Aufzeichnungen," typescript, pp. 101–02, Kl.Erw./385 (BA); Senger, *Politik*, pp. 33–34; and Brüggemann, *Rheinische Republik*, pp. 22–24. Marie-Luise Becker claims that Adenauer supported the division of Prussia in order to cause England to reject the French plans for reorganizing the Rhenisch borders. See, "Adenauer und die englische Besatzungsmacht," *Konrad Adenauer*, ed. Hugo Stehkämper (Cologne, 1976), pp. 104–05. Cf. Erdmann, *Adenauer*, pp. 31, 43.

53. Brüggemann, *Rheinische Republik*, pp. 9–10, 19, 34, 47–49, 51–52, 64–66; Senger, *Politik*, p. 36; Falk, "Aufzeichnungen," pp. 111–12; Erich Kosthorst, Werner Conze, and

Elfriede Nebgen, *Jakob Kaiser* (Stuttgart, 1967), 1:85; and Hess, *SBVPrLV*, 24 Mar. 1919, vol. 1, cols. 558-59. See also Paul Moldenhauer, "Die Abtrennungsbestrebungen in Deutschland," in *Handbuch der Politik*, 3d ed., ed. Gerhard Anschütz (Berlin, 1920), pp. 285-90.

54. While the Reich government never specifically supported new *Länder* in the west, neither did it help Prussia to fend off such a movement in any significant way. The issue arose again in plans for the creation of a Greater Hessen state, which would have annexed considerable Prussian territory. See the protest of the Prussian cabinet, "Sitz.PrStMin.," 8 July 1919, O. Braun papers/B/A/19a (PrGStAB); and Heine's memorandum of 23 Mar. 1921 in Eimers, *Verhältnis*, pp. 450-51. See also Carl Ulrich, *Erinnerungen*, ed. Ludwig Bergsträsser (Offenbach, 1953), pp. 143-45; and *Prot.d.Sitz.d.NV*, Sitz. no. 63, cols. 1813-14C.

55. Bischof, *Separatismus*, p. 53.

56. See the list of participants and the minutes of the conference for 13. Dec. 1918, in *Die deutsche Revolution 1918-1919—Dokumente*, ed. Gerhard A. Ritter and Susanne Miller (Frankfurt a.M., 1968), pp. 351-56. Cf. Bischof, *Separatismus*, pp. 37-38; Morsey, *Zentrum*, pp. 126-27; Peter Klein, *Separatisten an Rhein und Ruhr* (Berlin, 1961), pp. 61-62; Senger, *Politik*, p. 36; and Schulz, *Demokratie*, pp. 161-62, and 162, n. 98.

57. The Rhenish separatists had demanded a referendum on the future of the western provinces even before the National Constitutional Convention and the Prussian Constitutional Convention met.

58. See *DrSVPrLV*, vol. 4, DrS. no. 1009, pp. 1495-97.

59. Helmut Metzmacher, "Der Novembersturz 1918 in der Rheinprovinz," *Annalen des Historischen Vereins für den Niederrhein*, nos. 168/169 (1967), pp. 135-37.

60. See *SBVPrLV*, 28 May 1919, vol. 2, col. 1907 (Hirsch); and Morsey, *Zentrum*, p. 261.

61. Rudolf Klatt, *Ostpreussen unter dem Reichskommissariat 1919/1920* (Heidelberg, 1958), pp. 39-42, 48-49; and Max Worgitzki, *Geschichte der Abstimmung in Ostpreussen* (Leipzig, 1921), pp. 28-29. See also Seemann's (SPD) address, *II.Rätekongress*, p. 90.

62. Hellmut von Gerlach, *Der Zusammenbruch der deutschen Polenpolitik* (Berlin, 1919), pp. 11-14. Breitscheid, "Bankrott der Polenpolitik," *Sozialist* 5 (22 Feb. 1919), 114-15; and Holtzendorff's "Notizen," of 21 May 1919, Hap.Arch./I, II.

63. This was reflected in their frequent travels to the area. In mid-December, Hirsch and Ernst visited Posen, Thorn, Allenstein, Insterburg, and Danzig (*RVB-Protokolle*, vol. 1, doc. 355, p. 373, n. 13); in the spring of 1919 Heine undertook a longer trip during which he visited Königsberg and other cities (*SBVPrLV*, 25 June 1919, vol. 4, cols. 2547-48). Braun also traveled through East Prussia (Worgitzki, *Ostpreussen*, p. 27).

64. Gerlach, *Polenpolitik*, p. 19. Cf. Albrecht von Thaer's praise of Hirsch in *Generalstabsdienst . . . Aus Briefen und Tagebuchaufzeichnungen 1915-1919*, ed. R. G. Rönnefarth and Siegfried Kaehler, (Göttingen, 1958), p. 24 (entry for 4 Feb. 1919).

65. On the often confusing developments in the east, see Wolfgang Schumann, *Oberschlesien 1918/19* (Berlin [East], 1961), pp. 76-77, 81-83; Georg Cleinow, *Der Verlust der Ostmark* (Berlin, 1934); and Hagen Schulze, "Der Oststaat-Plan 1919," *Vierteljahrshefte für Zeitgeschichte* 18 (Apr. 1970), 123-63.

66. "Sitz.PrStMin.," 4 Jan. 1919, O. Braun papers/29 (IISG).

67. Ulrich Kluge, *Soldatenräte und Revolution* (Göttingen, 1975), pp. 321, 325. On the general security situation on the frontier, see ibid., pp. 301-05; and Hagen Schulze, *Freikorps und Republik 1918-1920* (Boppard a.Rh., 1969).

68. "Sitz.PrStMin.," 27 May 1919, O. Braun papers/45 (IISG).

69. Hirsch and Heine visited Königsberg on May 19 (Klatt, *Ostpreussen*, p. 126). See also *II.Rätekongress*, p. 223; and *Vorwärts*, nos. 168, 256 (2 Apr. and 20 May 1919).

70. Breitscheid replied to Haase's complaints in this regard by stating that the Prussians were

not aware of complaints against Miquel and that no suitable substitute for Jagow was available. See "RVB-Sitz. v. 28.12.1918," *RVB-Protokolle*, vol. 2, doc. 76, pp. 61−62.

71. Ibid., pp. 57−58; Schumann, *Oberschlesien 1918/19*, pp. 70ff.; Eberhard Kolb, *Die Arbeiterräte in der deutschen Innenpolitik 1918−1919* (Düsseldorf, 1962), p. 111; and Ernst Hesterberg, *Alle Macht den A.—und S.—Räten—Kampf um Schlesien* (Breslau, 1932), pp. 13−14.

72. Schumann, *Oberschlesien*, pp. 165, 219. The chief of staff of the Sixth Army, Hesterberg, noted in his diary on 2 Dec. 1918: "The thought of separating ourselves from Berlin long enough for the red brothers of the old Social Democracy and the USPD to eat each other up, would not be a bad idea" (Hesterberg, *Macht*, p. 44). See also ibid., p. 64, (entry for 12 Dec. 1918).

73. Franz Krüger, "Die Autonomie Oberschlesiens," *Vorwärts*, no. 462 (17 Sept. 1920); and *SBVPrLV*, 14 Jan. 1921, vol. 12, col. 15878.

74. The Center Party Congress for Upper Silesia and the Silesian provincial committee continued to demand an independent federal state of Upper Silesia. See *Vorwärts*, no. 469 (13 Sept. 1919); and "Resolution des Schlesischen Provinzausschusses," 15 Sept. 1919, RK 43 I/1921 (BA). Cf. Heine's criticism in *Vorwärts*, no. 479 (19 Sept. 1919). Cf. Heine's statements in Hesterberg, *Macht*, pp. 197−98 (15 May 1919); and "Sitz.ReiReg.," 10 May 1919," *Ak/Rk Scheidemann*, doc. 68, p. 309; and Morsey, *Zentrum*, p. 206.

75. Heine to the Social Democratic ministers in Prussia, 1 Feb. 1920, O. Braun papers/51 (IISG). Cf. Friedrich Th. Körner, "Der Kampf um Oberschlesien," *Die Glocke* 5 (3 Jan. 1920), 1257; and Hesterberg, *Macht*, pp. 78−81.

76. Troeltsch, *Spektator-Briefe*, p. 75 (8 July 1919).

77. Paul Hirsch, *Der Weg der Sozialdemokratie zur Macht in Preussen* (Berlin, 1929), p. 140; Hesterberg, *Macht*, p. 75 (entry for 2 Jan. 1919): *RVB-Protokolle*, vol. 2, doc. 91, p. 174, n. 6; and Schumann, *Oberschlesien*, pp. 162−64, 166. See also "Sitz.PrStMin.," 4 Jan. 1919, O. Braun papers/29 (IISG).

78. "Sitz.PrStMin.," 10 June 1919, O. Braun papers/47 (IISG).

79. Cf. Trimborn's and Ulitzka's statements during the Center party's Reichstag caucus meeting of 19 Oct. 1920, ten Hompel papers/15 (BA); and A. von Holtzendorff to Cuno, 27 Oct. 1920, Hap.Arch./V, VI. See also Eimers, *Verhältnis*, pp. 325−26; and Schulze, *Braun*, pp. 321−22.

80. Heine's memorandum of 23 Mar. 1921 in Eimers, *Verhältnis*, pp. 454−55.

81. *DrSBVPrLV*, vol. 4, DrS. no. 1009, pp. 1495−97.

82. Eimers, *Verhältnis*, pp. 322−23; "Sitz.PrStMin.," 29 July 1921, O. Braun papers/267 (IISG); Hans Herschel, "Oberschlesien und Zentrum," *Allgemeine Rundschau* 18 (7 May 1921), p. 235; and the documentation in Severing papers/81/65 (Arch.SD).

83. In addition to the autonomy movements discussed here, there were similar efforts in Schleswig-Holstein and Hanover, but neither the drives in the north nor the perennial and noisy Guelph agitation in Hanover had enough support seriously to concern the Prussian government. On Schleswig-Holstein, see Adolf Köster, *Der Kampf um Schleswig* (Berlin, 1921); and Hans Dietrich Lehmann, *Der "Deutsche Ausschuss" und die Abstimmungen in Schleswig 1920* (Neumünster, 1969). For the Prussian policy toward Hanover, see Minister of the Interior to OPrä, 13 Dec. 1918, cited in Danneberg's statements (Dt. Hann. Partei), in *SBVPrLV*, 24 Mar. 1919, vol. 1, col. 600.

84. Hirsch, *Weg*, p. 201. See also von Stark (OPrä of the Rhine Province) to Freund, 20 Apr. 1919, cited in Klein, *Separatisten*, p. 46. Cf. Hirsch in *SBVPrLV*, 28 Oct. 1920, vol. 10, col. 13239; Brüggemann, *Rheinische Republik*, p. 79; *Freiheit*, 6 Dec. 1918; Breitscheid's comments in "RVB-Sitz. 23.12.1918," *RVB-Protokolle*, doc. 76, p. 71; and Eimers, *Verhältnis*, p. 355. Cf.

the polemic between a Social Democratic supporter of Greater Hessen (*Vorwärts*, no. 374 [24 July 1919]), and Wolfgang Heine, who was a passionate supporter of an undivided Prussia (ibid., no. 386 [31 July 1919]).

85. See the correspondence from Landsberg and Schiffer to Hans Goldschmidt, in Goldschmidt, *Das Reich und Preussen im Kampf um die Führung* (Berlin, 1931), p. 133.

86. Schulz, *Demokratie*, p. 257; Eimers, *Verhältnis*, p. 273; Koch-Weser, diary entry for 3 Jan. 1920, Koch-Weser papers (BA). Cf. the communication of Schiffer cited in Goldschmidt.

87. Südekum, cited in Eimers, *Verhältnis*, p. 172; and *SBVPrLV*, 15 Mar. 1919, vol. 1, col. 144 (Heilmann).

88. See "Sitz.PrStMin.," 30 June 1919, O. Braun papers/48 (IISG).

89. Eimers, *Verhältnis*, p. 86; and "Sitz.PrStMin.," 6 Mar. 1919, O. Braun papers/35 (IISG). Cf. "Sitz. d. RVB," 28 Jan. 1919, *RVB-Protokolle* vol. 2, doc. 121, p. 325; and cf. Heine's statements in *SBVPrLV*, 16 Dec. 1919, vol. 7, col. 8211.

90. "Sitz.d.PrStMin.u.d.ZR," 13 Feb. 1919, *ZR-Protokolle*, doc. 86, pp. 639–40, 639, n. 45, and pp. 141–42, n. 57. See also David, diary entry for 27 Jan. 1919, David papers/14 (BA); and *Freiheit*, 22 Feb. 1929.

91. "Sitz.PrStMin.," 6 Mar. 1919, O. Braun papers/35 (IISG); Fischbeck's statements at the meeting of the DDP executive board, 4 Feb. 1919, Petersen papers/L62; Erich Koch-Weser, diary entry for 1 Mar. 1919, Koch-Weser papers/16 (BA); and Valentiner (official in the prime minister's office), "Sitz.PrStMin.," 2 Mar. 1919, O. Braun papers/107 (IISG). The SPD caucus in the Landesversammlung also opposed the dominance of the Reich parliament. See *Protokoll der Parteikonferenz in Weimar am 22. und 23. März 1919* [Berlin, 1919], pp. 24–25; and Runge's statements, *SBVPrLV*, 21 Mar. 1919, vol. 1, col. 464. Incidentally, these steps in the direction of presidential government in Prussia went too far for the members of the Constitutional Convention. As reported out of a select committee, chaired by Felix Porsch (Center party) and Eduard Gräf (SPD), and adopted by the convention on 19 Mar. 1919, the temporary constitution specified that the speaker of the Constitutional Convention appoint the prime minister, while the legislature itself selected the other members of the cabinet. The final version also narrowed somewhat the emergency powers of the cabinet. See, *SBVPrLV*, 19 Mar. 1919, vol. 1, cols. 328–31, 366; ibid., 20 Mar. 1919, vol. 1, cols. 389, 395, 397 (am Zehnhoff and Rosenberg). See also *Vorwärts*, no. 143 (19 Mar. 1919); and Hirsch, *Weg*, p. 211.

92. For a discussion of the constitutional issues involved, see Ernst Rudolf Huber, *Deutsche Verfassungsgeschichte seit 1789* (Stuttgart, 1981), 6:59ff.

93. For the views of the Prussian military, see Gustav Böhm, *Adjudant im preussischen Kriegsministerium*, ed. Georg Meyer (Stuttgart, 1977).

94. "Sitz.d.RVB u.d.Rei.Reg.," 14 Nov. 1918, *RVB-Protokolle*, vol. 1, doc. 10, p. 40; and "Sitz.PrStMin.," 31 Jan. and 11 Feb. 1919, O. Braun papers/32, 33 (IISG).

95. Cf. the final report of the Central Council, ed. Gustav Heller, *Vom I. Rätekongress zur Nationalversammlung* (Berlin, 1919), [p. 5].

96. Gustav Noske, *Erlebtes aus Aufstieg und Niedergang einer Demokratie* (Offenbach a.M., 1947), pp. 177–79; *Vorwärts*, no. 5 (3 Jan. 1919); and Grzesinski, "Kampf," pp. 85, 87. It is indicative of the political leanings of the German military that Groener, Ludendorff's and Hindenburg's successor as head of the OHL, regarded Reinhardt as too radical. Groener favored General von Thaer, commander of the army corps in Silesia, who ironically saw Groener as "politically far to the left . . . not much different from the moderate Socialists [*sic*]" (Thaer to his wife, 16 Dec. 1918, in *Tagebuch*, pp. 281–82 [13 Dec. 1918]). Cf. Böhm, *Adjudant*, p. 166 (23 Dec. 1918). For a full account of the negotiations leading to Reinhardt's appointment, see Ulrich Kluge, *Soldatenräte und Revolution* (Göttingen, 1975), pp. 271ff.

97. Kluge, *Soldatenräte*, pp. 271–72.

98. See the notes written by Fleck, Reinhardt's chief of staff, ca. 1919, in "Aus dem Nachlass des Generals Walther Reinhardt," ed. Fritz Ernst, *Welt als Geschichte* 18 (1958), pp. 39ff; Wilhelm Groener, *Lebenserinnerungen,* ed. Friedrich Freiherr von Gaertringen (Göttingen, 1957; rpt. Osnabrück, 1972), p. 519; A. von Holtzendorff to Cuno. 9 Mar, 1919, Hap.Arch./Ber 1; and Thaer to his wife, in *Tagebuch,* pp. 283–84 (19 Dec. 1918).

99. Grzesinski, "Kampf," p. 82; "Die Liquidation der deutschen Kriegs-Armee," Grzesinski papers/2456, pp. 2–3 (IISG); and "Sitz.ReiReg.," 16 June 1919, *Ak/Rk Scheidemann,* doc. 112, pp. 468, and 468, n. 11.

100. Grzesinski, "Kampf," p. 105; Koch-Weser, diary entry for 28 Aug. 1919, Koch-Weser papers (BA); and Müller-Brandenburg to SPD and DDP caucuses of the Berlin Executive Committee, 15 Aug. 1919, ZR-Arch/B-48 (IISG). Müller-Brandenburg was a member of the Republican Leadership Corps *(Republikanischer Führerbund),* an association of pro-Republican officers.

101. Erger, *Kapp-Putsch,* pp. 141–42, 144, 146, 183 ff. Cf. Karl Brammer, ed., *Fünf Tage Militärdiktatur* (Berlin, 1920), p. 35; Fleck, ed., "Aus," pp. 101, 104, 107; and O. Braun to Rudolf Vogler, 28 Dec. 1921, O. Braun papers/114 (IISG).

102. Cf. the minutes of the joint meeting of the Prussian government and the Council of Plenipotentiaries, *RVB-Protokolle,* vol. 1, doc. 10, p. 40. Hoff had already submitted his letter of resignation at the beginning of March. See "Sitz. PrStMin.," 6 Mar. 1919, O. Braun papers/B/A/19a (Berlin).

103. Senger, *Politik,* p. 23.

104. This Südekum quotation is in *SBVPrLV,* 30 Sept. 1919, vol. 4, col. 4466. Cf. the discussion of the question of the railroads, 1 Apr. 1919, *Ak/Rk Scheidemann,* doc. 30, pp. 122–23; and "Niederschrift über die Sitzungen des Sachverständigenbeirates," 14 Nov., 29 Nov. 1919, 5 Feb. 1920, *DrSVPrLV,* vol. 6, 3177–90.

105. "Sitz.PrStMin.," 7 Apr. 1919, O. Braun papers /39 (IISG).

106. *SBVPrLV,* 21 Apr. 1920, cols. 10784–85.

107. *SBVPrLV,* 30 Sept. 1919, vol. 4, col. 4487 (Richter [DVP]).

108. For a comprehensive treatment of Erzberger's financial reforms, see Peter-Christian Witt, "Finanzpolitik und sozialer Wandel im Krieg und Inflation 1918–1924," *Industrielles System und politische Entwicklung in der Weimarer Republik,* ed. Wolfgang Mommsen et al. (Düsseldorf, 1974), pp. 395–426; Klaus Epstein, *Matthias Erzberger* (Princeton, N.J., 1959), pp. 334–48; and Franz Menges, *Reichsreform und Finanzpolitik* (Berlin, 1971), pp. 184–228. Erzberger describes the Reich's financial situation in April 1919 in *Ak/Rk Scheidemann,* doc. 54b, pp. 233–43.

109. Arnold Brecht, *Aus nächster Nähe* (Stuttgart, 1966), p. 284; and Schulz, *Demokratie,* pp. 217, 223.

110. "Sitz.d.RVB," 21 Nov. 1918, *RVB-Protokolle,* doc. 20, p. 116.

111. See "Sitz.PrStMin.," 22 Apr. 1919, in Braun papers/36 (IISG); "Vortrag . . . über Kapitalrentensteuergesetz" in Südekum papers/8 (BA); *SBVPrLV,* 3 Sept. 1919, vol. 5, cols. 4468–69 (Südekum); and *Ak/Rk Scheidemann,* p. 256, n. 10.

112. See the report on a meeting of the SPD party caucus, 28 Aug. 1919, *Vorwärts,* no. 440 (28 Aug. 1919).

113. Koch-Weser, diary entry for 10 Nov. 1919, Koch-Weser papers (BA); and *Vorwärts,* no. 578 (11 Nov. 1919).

114. *Prot.d.Sitz.d.NV,* 27 Nov. 1919, 120th session, pp. 3803, 3814–15.

115. *Vorwärts,* no. 610 (29 Nov. 1919).

116. Even Südekum's opponents acknowledged his successes at the bargaining table. See *SBVPrLV,* 26 Sept. 1919, vol. 4, col. 4396.

117. See ibid., 10 Nov. 1919, vol. 5, col. 6124 (Riedel [DDP]).
118. See *Vorwärts,* nos. 74, 106, 109 (10, 27 and 28 Feb. 1920). For a detailed history of this controversy, which was not settled until 1926, see Ulrich Schüren, *Der Volksentscheid zur Fürstenenteignung 1926* (Düsseldorf, 1978).
119. *SBVPrLV,* 18 July 1919, vol. 3, cols. 3782–83.
120. See the report of 31 Jan. 1920, DrSVPrLV, vol. 9, DrS, 2939, appendix A, p. 4681.
121. Eimers, *Verhältnis,* p. 608.
122. *SBVPrLV,* 15 Nov. 1919, vol. 5, col. 6539. See also his statements in ibid., 16 Dec. 1919, vol. 7, cols. 8210-11.
123. *Vorwärts,* nos. 9 and 106 (6 Jan. and 27 Feb. 1920); and *DrSVPrLV,* vol. 6, DrS. 2000, pp. 3005–09.
124. *SBVPrLV,* 26 Apr. 1920, vol. 9, col. 11013; *Vorwärts,* nos. 108, 315 (28 Feb. and 23 June 1920); and Heinrich Cunow, "Der preussische Verfassungsentwurf," *Neue Zeit* 38 (2 Apr. 1920), 3.
125. Cunow, "Verfassungsentwurf," pp. 1–2.
126. *SBVPrLV,* 26 Apr. 1920, vol. 9, col. 11005.
127. Walter Stoecker, "Die preussische Verfassung," *Freiheit,* 24 Apr. 1920; and *SBVPrLV,* 26 Apr. 1920, vol. 9, cols. 11024–28, 13988.
128. Cf. the position of the DVP delegate in *SBVPrLV,* 28 Apr. 1920, vol. 9, col. 11128 (Leidig); "Verf.-Ausschuss", *DrSVPrLV,* DrS. 3120B, pp. 5250–51. See also Wolfgang Hartenstein, *Die Anfänge der Deutschen Volkspartei* (Düsseldorf, 1962), pp. 117–18.
129. *SBVPrLV,* 26 Nov. 1920, vol. 9. col. 13977 (Meyer [DDP]); and Günter Arns, "Regierungsbildung und Koalitionspolitik in der Weimarer Republik 1919–1924," Ph.D. diss., University of Tübingen, 1971, pp. 118–19.
130. At this time Leidig explained that his vote for the draft was an expression of his personal views; the party had not yet announced its stand. See "Verf.-Ausschusses," p. 5382.
131. Ibid., p. 5226; and *SBVPrLV,* 29 Oct. 1920, vol. 10, col. 13294.
132. *Die Verfassung des Freistaates Preussen vom 30. November 1920,* intro. Paul Hirsch (Berlin, 1921), p. 13. Adolf Gottwald, *Ziele und Erfolge der Zentrumsfraktion des Preussischen Landtages 1921/1924* (Berlin, 1924), p. 15; Senger, *Politik,* p. 53; and *SBVPrLV,* 18 Oct. 1920, vol. 10, col. 13265 (Leidig).
133. [Paul Hirsch], *Der Preussische Landtag 1921–1924,* (Berlin [1924]), p. 83.
134. See the preliminary report of the Constitutional Committee, 21 June 1920, *DrSVPrLV,* vol. 8, p. 4198; "Verf.-Ausschuss," pp. 5227 ff., 5239; *SBVPrLV,* 28 Oct. 1920, vol. 10, cols. 13247–50 (v. Kries), and 26 Nov. 1920, vol. 11, cols. 13985–86 (Hauschildt). On the history of the Staatsrat in the Weimar years, see Adenauer, "Konrad Adenauer als Präsident des Preussischen Staatsrates," in *Konrad Adenauer,* ed. Hugo Stehkämper (Cologne, 1976), pp. 357–61.
135. *Verfassung,* pp. 20–21; and *Vorwärts,* no. 328 (1 July 1920).
136. *Vorwärts,* no. 328 (1 July 1920); *SBVPrLV,* 28 Apr. 1920, vol. 9, col. 11140; "Verf.-Auschuss," p. 5294 (Leidig).
137. Braun, *Weimar,* p. 73. Cf. Erich Kuttner, *Otto Braun* (Berlin [1932]), p. 74.
138. *Vorwärts,* nos. 464, 482 (18 and 29 Sept. 1920). Hugo Preuss implored his colleagues in the coalition not to undo any of the seams of the compromise, lest the whole construction become unraveled (*SBVPrLV,* 28 Oct. 1920, vol. 10, col. 13253).
139. *SBVPrLV,* 30 Nov. 1920, vol. 11, cols. 14319–24; and *Verfassung,* p. 26.
140. *SBVPrLV,* 14 Jan. 1921, vol. 12, col. 15988; and Hermann Kranold, "Zu den preussischen Landtagswahlen 1921," *Sozialistische Monatshefte* 60 (20 Dec. 1920), 1045.

Chapter 4. Personnel Policies and Administrative Reforms, 1918—1921

1. Bill Drews. "Deutscher Einheitsstaat und preussische Verwaltungsreform," 27 Jan. 1920; and Drews to provincial governors and *Landeshauptmänner*, 12 Oct. 1920, LASH/301/4951.

2. See, for example, F. H. [*sic*], "Reform der preussischen Verwaltung," *Die Hilfe*, 7 Nov. 1918; Eberhard Kolb, *Die Arbeiterräte in der deutschen Innenpolitik 1918—1919* (Düsseldorf, 1962), pp. 359—60; and Hedwig Wachenheim, *Vom Grossbürgertum zur Sozialdemokratie*, ed. Susanne Miller (Berlin, 1973), p. 104.

3. *Pr.GS*, no. 38 (1918), pp. 189—91; the directives of 14 Nov. 1918, NSStAH/122a/VIII/Zg; and LASH/301/216.

4. Kolb, *Arbeiterräte*, p. 86; Ulrich Kluge, *Soldatenräte und Revolution* (Göttingen, 1975), p. 121; and Susanne Miller, *Die Bürde der Macht* (Düsseldorf, 1978).

5. Of some interest are the citizens' councils *(Bürgerräte)* and peasants' councils *(Bauernräte)*. In many places the former were merely company unions under a different name (see Heinrich, chairman of the Bürgerrat in Lustnau near Tübingen, 1 Feb. 1919, ZR-Arch./B-24) or the first stages of a counterrevolutionary movement. Cf. a. e. [*sic*], "Die bolschevistische Gefahr," *Deutscher Bürger* (Feb. 1930), (Forst.Hbg./451 [Bügervereine]), but their goals were not exclusively negative. The bourgeois councils were often also the institutionalization of willingness on the part of the bourgeoisie to contribute to the establishment of a new, democratic Germany. Cf. Lothar Albertin, *Liberalismus und Demokratie am Anfang der Weimarer Republik* (Düsseldorf, 1971), pp. 33—35. For a description of the agricultural councils, see Heinrich Muth, "Die Entstehung der Bauern-und Landarbeiterräte im November 1918 und die Politik des Bundes der Landwirte," *Vierteljahrshefte für Zeitgeschichte* 21 (Jan. 1973), 1—38.

6. See the series of lectures, *Wege und Ziele der Sozialisierung*, ed. Hermann Beck (Berlin, 1919), pp. 7—9; "Unruhen in Mitteldeutschland," pp. 5574—79. Cf. David W. Morgan, *The Socialist Left and the German Revolution* (Ithaca, N.Y., 1975), pp. 168—76. Generally speaking, East German historians have criticized the councils for their lack of Leninist consciousness. See Marion Einhorn, "Zur Rolle der Räte im November und Dezember 1918," *Zeitschrift für Geschichtswissenschaft* 4 (1956), 545—59.

7. Cf. Provinzialkonferenz der Arbeiter-, Soldaten- und Bauernräte Pommerns, "Richtlinien für Arbeiter-, Soldaten- und Bauernräte der Provinz Pommern," 1 Feb. 1919. Grzesinski papers/406 (IISG).

8. Richard Müller, *Vom Kaiserreich zur Republik* (Berlin, 1924), 2:55; and R. Müller, *Was Arbeiterräte wollen und sollen* (Berlin, 1919), pp. 7—8; and VZR (Abt. Landbevölkerung), "Richtlinien für die Landbevölkerung," [Dec. 1918], O. Braun papers/92 (IISG); *AVB*, no. 33 (29 Nov. 1918), p. 39.

9. Workers' and Soldiers' Council of Potsdam to Provincial Governors of Hanover and Schleswig-Holstein, 24 Nov. 1918; Minister of the Interior (Breitscheid) to Provincial Governors of Hanover and Schleswig-Holstein, 26 Nov. 1918, NSStAH/122a/VIII/20; and LASH/301/2401.

10. See the plans for a "Propaganda Service of the Republic," Presse- und Propagandadienst VZR to ZR, 21 Dec. 1918, ZR-Arch./B-14. See also Hermann Müller, *Die November-Revolution* (Berlin, 1928), pp. 114—15; and Heinrich Schäfer, *Tagebuchblätter eines rheinischen Sozialisten* (Bonn, 1919), pp. 64—70. Cf. O. Braun to H. Müller, 6 Apr. 1929, H. Müller papers/I/135 (Arch.SD). The chaotic atmosphere of the meetings is also illustrated in the protocols of the plenary sessions that are still in existence (Levi papers/20A [Arch.SD]).

11. A. von Holtzendorff to Cuno, 4 Dec. 1918, Hap.Arch./Ber. 1).

12. *SBVPrLV*, 15 Nov. 1919, col. 6511 (Hirsch). According to Hagen Schulze, *Otto Braun* (Berlin, 1977), p. 249, Braun was the initiator of the action.

13. "Prot.A-Rat Berlin 19.11.1918," p. 1040.

14. "ZR-Sitzung 21.12.1918," *ZR-Protokolle*, doc. 6, pp. 50–51; "1. Sitzung des Internen Ausschusses am 27. Dezember 1918," 28 Dec. 1918, ZR-Arch./OS-4; and Albert Grzesinski, "Kampf," pp. 72–73.

15. See Hans-Karl Behrend, "Zur Personalpolitik des Preussischen Ministeriums des Innern," *Jahrbuch für die Geschichte Mittel- und Ostdeutschlands* 6 (1957).

16. Cf. meeting of the Central Council, 11 Feb. 1919, Grzesinski papers/445 (IISG).

17. *PrGS*, no. 38 (1918), pp. 189–91; see also the announcement of 16 Nov. 1918, ibid., pp. 191–92; and the "Erläuterung der Bekanntmachung v. 9.12.1918," *Minusterialblatt für die innere Verwaltung* 80 (1919), 2–3. Cf. Grzesinski's notes of Dec. 1918, Grzesinski papers/414–30 (IISG).

18. Enno Eimers, *Das Verhältnis von Preussen und Reich in den ersten Jahren der Weimarer Republik (1918–1923)* (Berlin, 1969), p. 61, n. 81; *SBVPrLV*, 26 Mar. 1919, vol. 1, col. 766 (Rosenfeld); Walter Oehme, *Damals in der Reichskanzlei* (Berlin [East], 1958), p. 52; and R. Müller, *Kaiserreich* 2:57–58, n. 1.

19. *Deutsche Zeitung*, 26 Nov. 1918, and *Berliner Tageblatt*, 26 Nov. 1918 cited in *Die deutsche Revolution in der zeitgenössischen Presse*, ed. Eberhard Buchner, (Berlin, 1921), vol. 1, docs. 426, 426a. The power of the executive committee in influencing personnel decisions at the ministerial level should not be exaggerated. Whenever a high SPD or USPD government official opposed the councils, the government tended to prevail. Thus the executive committee's demand "that things be put right" in the Ministry of Defense, while certainly justified, had no practical effect because the supervisor *(Beigeordneter)* of the ministry, Paul Göhre (SPD), brooked no interference from the councils in "his" ministry. See the joint meeting of the RVB and the VZR, 18 Nov. 1918, in *RVB-Protokolle*, vol. 1, doc. 15b, pp. 73–75.

20. R. Müller, *Arbeiterräte*, p. 7; *AVB*, no. 19 (16 Nov. 1913), p. 20.

21. See "Sitz.PrStMin.," 15 Nov. 1918, O. Braun papers/B/92/19a.

22. On the opposing points of view, see "RVB u.VZR-Sitz.18.11.1918," pp. 80–83, 93; *RVB-Protokolle*, nos. 19, 24, 28, 16 Nov. and 23 Nov. 1918, pp. 20, 25, 31–33; "Prot. VZR. 16. u. 17.11.1918", p. 145; "Protokoll Arbeiterrat Berlin 19.11.1918," p. 1041; Ministry of the Interior to all provincial governors and the police chief of Berlin, 17 Nov. 1918, LASH/301/216. See also *Die deutsche Revolution 1918–1919—Dokumente* ed. Gerhard A. Ritter and Susanne Miller (Frankfurt a.M., 1968), p. 104, 104, n. 1; and R. Müller, *Kaiserreich* 2:253.

23. Breitscheid, "Die Zunkunft der Arbeiterräte," *Sozialist* 5 (7 Feb. 1919), 81.

24. Heine to ZR, 7 June 1919, Grzesinski papers/442 (IISG); ZR to Workers' Council member Leer, 31 May 1919, ZR-Arch./B-12/2. See also *Vorwärts*, no. 337 (4 July 1919); and the cabinet's answer to Rosenfeld's parliamentary inquiry, *SBVPrLV*, 3 June 1919, vol. 2, col. 2176. Paul Hirsch (*Der Weg der Sozialdemokratie zur Macht in Preussen* [Berlin, 1929], p. 143) wrote later that the masses "fully understood" the government's policies. At the end of November 1919, the Prussian Constitutional Convention decided to stop supporting the workers' and soldiers' councils financially. On the decline of the councils at the local level, see Kolb, *Arbeiterräte*, p. 88; Francis L. Carsten, *Revolution in Central Europe, 1918–1919* (Berkeley, Calif., 1972), p. 49; Schäfer, *Tagebuch*, pp. 59–60; and Helmut Metzmacher, "Dez Novembersturz in der Rheinprovinz," *Annalen des Historischen Vereins für den Niederrhein* 168/169, (1967), p. 227.

25. See the notes on the joint meeting of the cabinet and the ZR, 23 Jan. 1919, and "Sitz. d. ZR," 25 Jan. and 28 Feb. 1919, in *ZR-Protokolle*, docs. 60, 64, 94, pp. 452–53, 480, 487, 734–37; "Sitz.ReiReg," 15 Jan. 1919, *RVB-Protokolle*, vol. 2, doc. 107, p. 272; ZR to Prussian Constitutional Convention, 12 Mar. 1919, *ZR-Protokolle*, doc. 100, pp. 784–85. Cf. the undated memo signed by Grzesinski and [Heinrich] Schäfer, Grzesinski papers/446 (IISG). See also Grzesinski to ZR, 29 Dec. 1919; Grzesinski to SPD caucus of the Prussian Constitutional Convention, 9 May 1919; and Hauschildt's plan, 24 June 1919, ibid./439, 441. The councils still in existence demanded the right to make personnel proposals for the various state government

offices. See "Volksrat f.d. Provinz Schleswig-Holstein," 1 Apr. 1919, LASH/301/4873.

26. It was also true that the Central Council tended to err on the other side of the question. Its demand that the government "place a large number of experienced and qualified, carefully selected [Socialist] party members as supervisors in as many offices as possible," was no more democratic than the prewar Conservative monopoly. See ZR to RVB and Prussian Ministry of the Interior, 29 Jan. 1919, Grzesinski papers/444 (IISG).

27. (Cramer) to Workers' Council Limburg, 1 Oct. 1919, ZR-Arch./B-12/4.

28. Gustav Noske, *Erlebtes aus Aufstieg und Niedergang einer Demokratie* (Offenbach a.M., 1947), p. 42; and Harry Graf Kessler, *Tagebücher 1918-1937*, ed. Wolfgang Pfeiffer-Belli (Frankfurt a.M., 1961), p. 140 (entry for 26 Feb. 1919).

29. Ernest Hamburger, *Juden im öffentlichen Leben Deutschlands . . . 1848-1918* (Tübingen, 1968), p. 409; Eimers, *Verhältnis*, pp. 116, 333; and Philipp Loewenfeld, "Erinnerungen," (manuscript in LBI), p. 175. (Loewenfeld was a right-wing Jewish functionary in the Prussian Ministry of the Interior.)

30. Eduard David, *Das Kriegstagebuch des Reichstagsabgeordneten Eduard David 1914-1918*, ed. Erich Matthias and Susanne Miller (Düsseldorf, 1966), p. 42 (entry for 24 Sept. 1914); and Willy Hellpach, *Wirken im Wirren* (Hamburg, 1949), 2:325.

31. *SBVPrLV*, 28 Mar. 1919, vol 1, col. 979; David, *Tagebuch*, pp. 51, 52, 134 (entries for 11-17 Oct. 1914 [sic], 17 Oct. 1914, and 22 June 1915).

32. Carl Severing, *Mein Lebensweg* (Cologne, 1950), vol. 1.

33. In addition to the daily and hourly crises with which the ministries had to deal, they were often beleaguered by the physical presence of all sorts of delegations in their offices. See Hellmut von Gerlach, *Meine Erlebnisse in der preussischen Verwaltung* (Berlin [1919]), pp. 80-89.

34. See Wolfgang Runge, *Politik und Beamtentum im Parteienstaat—Die Demokratisierung der politischen Beamten in Preussen zwischen 1918 und 1933* (Stuttgart, 1965), p. 157. The USPD ministers did not develop a systematic personnel policy before they left the cabinet.

35. See the decree of 18 Feb. 1919 in Behrend, "Personalpolitik." On the practical application of Heine's personnel policies see his testimony before the finance committee of the Prussian Constitutional Convention, *DrSVPrLV*, vol. 3, pp. 515, 845 ff.; and Heine to Wilhelm Sollmann, 21 Sept. 1919, Sollmann papers (Bryn Mawr, Pa.), as well as Behrend, *Personalpolitik*, pp. 173-214.

36. Wolfgang Elben, *Das Problem der Kontinuität in der deutschen Revolution* (Düsseldorf, 1965), pp. 31, 83.

37. The quotation is in Eugen Schiffer, *Ein Leben für den Liberalismus* (Berlin, 1951), p. 244. Cf. Heine to Robert Scholz, 10 Nov. 1929, Heine papers/580 (IISG); and Runge, *Politik*, p. 118.

38. "Sitz.PrStMin.," 19 Apr. 1919, O. Braun papers/41 (IISG); and *RheinZ-Parteitag*, pp. 199-200 (Hess).

39. See Provincial Governor of Schleswig-Holstein to Ministry of the Interior, 28 May 1919, and Beigeordneter to the RPrä Schleswig to Ministry of the Interior, 13 May 1919, LASH/301/4873.

40. *SBVPrLV*, 25 Mar. 1919, vol. 1, cols. 628-33.

41. An unnamed member of the convention's finance committee stated in July, that less than "half a dozen" appointments were involved; see *DrSVPrLV*, vol. 3, doc. 545, p. 856; Hirsch, *Weg*, pp. 165-66; Grzesinski to Heine, 31 Mar. 1919, ZR-Arch./B-49.

42. *SBVPrLV*, 16 Dec. 1919, vol. 7, col. 8224.

43. Decree of 26 Feb. 1919, *PrGS* (1919), p. 33. The decree was passed unanimously by the cabinet ("Sitz.PrStMin.," 26 Feb. 1919, O. Braun papers/B/A/19a [PrGStAB]). Cf. Hirsch's justification of the decree in *SBVPrLV*, 27 Mar. 1919, vol. 1, cols. 898-99.

44. "Sitz.PrStMin.," 6 Mar. 1919, O. Braun papers/55 (IISG).

45. Provincial governor of Schleswig-Holstein to Ministries of the Interior and Finance, 11 Jan. 1919, LASH/301/216.

46. Cf. Friedrich Saemisch, diary entries for 16 and 18 Nov. 1918, Saemisch papers/23 (BA).

47. *Vorwärts*, no. 1 (1 Jan. 1919); and Adolf Wermuth, *Ein Beamtenleben* (Berlin, 1922), p. 418.

48. Morgan, *Socialist Left*, pp. 143–44; and "Prot.A-Rat Berlin 19.11.1918," p. 1042.

49. David, *Tagebuch*, p. 36 (entry for 6 Sept. 1914); and Elben, *Problem*, p. 141.

50. See the extensive correspondence on the relationship between the Landrat von Meldorf (Schleswig-Holstein) and his supervisor Fröhlich, LASH/301/3169.

51. Provincial governor of Schleswig-Holstein to provincial governor of Saxony, 29 Dec. 1918, LASH/301/216; Provincial governor of Schleswig-Holstein to Ministry of the Interior, 28 May 1919, and supervisor of the district director of Schleswig to Ministry of the Interior, 13 and 24 May 1919, LASH/301/4873.

52. Cf. the documents in the reports of the district director of Schleswig to the provincial governor of Schleswig-Holstein, 22 and 26 Nov. 1918, LASH/301/216.

53. See Adolf Köster, *Der Kampf um Schleswig* (Berlin, 1921), pp. 142–43; and provincial governor of the Rhine Province to cabinet, 17 Apr. 1919, Severing papers/7/174.

54. Eimers, *Verhältnis*, pp. 219, 251.

55. This was the State Commissioner for the Supervision of Public Order and his task involved police work, not the democratization of the civil service.

56. Braun, for example, had considerable doubts about the wisdom of appointing Winnig as Reich and state commissioner in East Prussia. See Wilhelm Matull, ed., *Ostdeutschlands Arbeiterbewegung* (Würzburg, 1973), p. 86.

57. See, for example, H. Müller, in *SPD-Parteikonferenz 22.3.1919*, p. 26; and *SPD-Parteitag 1919*, pp. 183–85, 318. The decree was weakened further at the beginning of April ("Sitz.PrStMin.," 4 Apr. 1919, O. Braun papers/38 [IISG]; and Ministry of Finance, "Directive," 12 July 1919, LASH/301/3160).

58. *SBVPrLV*, 25 Mar. 1919, vol. 1, cols. 628–33.

59. Heine to Social Democratic ministers, 1 Feb. 1920, O. Braun papers/51 (IISG); "Sitz.PrStMin.," 10 Apr. 1919, O. Braun papers/40 (IISG); and the letter to the editor written by Scholich, a Social Democratic member of the Prussian Constitutional Convention, *Vorwärts*, no. 440 (28 Aug. 1919).

60. Magnus Freiherr von Braun, *Von Ostpreussen bis Texas* (Stollhamm [Oldenburg], 1955), p. 175. See also A. von Holtzendorff to Cuno, 7 June 1919, Hap.Arch./I, II; and Grzesinski to SPD caucus of the Prussian Constitutional Convention, 9 May 1919, Grzesinski papers/439 (IISG).

61. *SBVPrLV*, 27 June 1919, vol. 3, col. 2760.

62. Behrend, "Personalpolitik," pp. 176–77. See also Stegerwald's speech at the *RheinZ-Parteitag*, p. 92.

63. "Sitz.PrStMin.," 4 June 1919, O. Braun papers/46 (IISG).

64. See Heine to all ministers, 1 Feb. 1920; and "Sitz.PrStMin.," 13 May 1919, O. Braun papers/51 and 44 (IISG).

65. On the corps of provincial governors, see also Horst Möller, "Die preussischen Oberpräsidenten der Weimarer Republik," *Vierteljahrshefte für Zeitgeschichte* 30 (Jan. 1982), 1–26.

66. Heine to SPD ministers, 1 Feb. 1920, O. Braun papers/51 (IISG). See also *SBVPrLV*, 15 Nov. 1919, vol. 5, col. 6545 (Heilmann).

67. Heine to SPD ministers, 1 Feb. 1920. Wittmack was elected president of the Landtag in April 1932.

68. Eimers, *Verhältnis*, pp. 221–22, 522; and *Vorwärts*, no. 597 (22 Nov. 1919). Mag-- deburg was the capital of the province; the Prussian districts were named after the city in which the seat of administration was located.

69. Hirsch, *Weg*, p. 115. The prime minister was not the only one to engage in this kind of naiveté. Cf. *Vorwärts*, nos. 219/22 [*sic*] (30 Apr. and 1 May 1919).

70. Behrend, "Personalpolitik," pp. 200–05; *Sozialdemokratisches Handbuch für die preussischen Landtagswahlen* (Berlin [1920]), pp. 22–25. Cf. *SBVPrLV*, 20 Feb. 1920, vol. 7, cols. 9614–15 (Schubert); and Heine's remarks in *SBVPrLV*, 16 Dec. 1919, vol. 7, cols. 8111–12.

71. Wolfgang Heine, "Die Beamten der Republik," *Sozialistische Monatshefte* 63 (20 Sept. 1926), 612.

72. He should not be confused with his namesake, Gottlieb von Jagow, the Reich foreign minister during World War I.

73. Johannes Erger, *Der Kapp-Lüttwitz-Putsch* (Düsseldorf, 1967), pp. 42, 94.

74. Ibid., p. 170; Karl Brammer, ed., *Verfassungsgrundlagen und Hochverrat—Der Jagow-Prozess* (Berlin, 1922), p. 57.

75. Uwe Lohalm, *Völkisher Radikalismus* (Hamburg, 1970), p. 87.

76. Cf. the declarations of Freund and Meister in *Jagow*, ed. Brammer, pp. 56–58; Niegel to Reich chancellor, 24 Mar. 1920, RK 43 I/2720 (BA). Niegel was a union official employed in one of the army depots in Prussia.

77. Karl Brammer, *Fünf Tage Militärdiktatur* (Berlin, 1920), p. 53. However, the superior officers did not always provide the Prussian civil servants with clear orders or models of behavior although they may have had good intentions in not doing so. Minister of Railroads Oeser was asked by both Kapp and Lüttwitz as well as the railroad unions to remain in office. He rejected Kapp's offer, accepting that of the railroaders, but his step nevertheless represented a form of continuity between Kapp and the legitimate government. Eugen Ernst, the police chief of Berlin, also remained in office and "made no trouble for Kapp." See Robert Jansen, *Der Berliner Militärputsch und seine politischen Folgen* (Berlin, 1920), p. 61; Erger, *Kapp-Putsch*, pp. 124ff.; and a leaflet distributed by the putschists, a copy of which is in RK 43 I/2720 (BA).

78. Runge, *Politik*, pp. 130–31; and Erger, *Kapp-Putsch*, pp. 212–13.

79. On the East Prussian and Winnig problems, see Gerhard Schulz, *Zwischen Demokratie und Diktatur* (Berlin, 1963), 1:268–76; Eimers, *Verhältnis*, pp. 182–88; Wilhelm Ribhegge, *August Winnig—Eine historische Persönlichkeitsanalyse* (Bonn–Bad Godesberg, 1973). See *Freiheit*, 28 Dec. 1919; and Wilhelm Keil, *Erlebnisse eines Sozialdemokraten* (Stuttgart, 1947–48), 2:169, on Winnig's controversial position even within the SPD.

80. August Winnig, *Urkunden über mein Verhalten zur Gegenregierung* [Königsberg, 1920]. Cf. Braun, *Ostpreussen*, p. 182.

81. Köster, *Kampf*, p. 181.

82. It is indicative of Kapp's concern with the Reichswehr that of the five decisions that the new provincial governor had time to make in his brief stay in office, no less than two were concerned with the powers of the Reichswehr and the citizens' militias under the new regime. Cf. "Tagebucheintragung des Wandsbeker Bürgermeisters Erich Wasa Rodig v. 13.3.1920 und seinen Lebenslauf und Familienerinnerungen" [1938], Forst.Hbg., pp. 56–57. See also the notes of the investigating federal judge of 5 Apr. 1920, LASH/301/5712.

83. Cf. von Hammerstein (the Reichswehr commander in Schleswig) to Ministry of Justice, 3 June 1920, LASH/301/5713. Telegram of Ministry of the Interior to Kürbis, 15 Mar. 1920, and arrest order (signed by Loof, the city commandant of Kiel), LASH/301/5712–13. Heine reinstated Kürbis on 19 May, LASH/301/5712.

84. Cf. "Niederschrift über Einwände und Konferenz Lindemanns mit sechs sträubenden Beamten," 15 Mar. 1920; and his proclamation, LASH/301/5712.

85. Adler to Kürbis, 7 Apr. 1920, LASH/301/5713.

86. *DrSVPrLV*, vol. 10, p. 5739; and NSStAH/122a/XXXVII/156.

87. Regional Commander of the Citizens' Militia von Wolff, "Bericht über den Stand des Einwohnerwehrwesens," 27 Mar. 1920, NSStAH/122a/XXXVII/65.

88. On the postwar development of the Ruhr area, see Carl Severing, *1919/1920 im Wetter- und Watterwinkel* (Bielefeld, 1920); and George Eliasberg, "Der Ruhrkrieg 1920," *Archiv für Sozialgeschichte* 10 (1970), 291–377, expanded as *Der Ruhrkrieg von 1920* (Bonn–Bad Godesberg, 1974); and Erhard Lucas, *Märzrevolution im Ruhrgebiet, Vom Generalstreik gegen den Militärputsch zum bewaffneten Arbeiteraufstand, März–April 1920* (Frankfurt a.M., 1970).

89. Erger, *Kapp-Putsch*, p. 186; There were some praiseworthy exceptions here too. The security forces in Essen and Dortmund, for example, were clearly anti-Kapp. See Eliasberg, *Ruhrkrieg*, p. 320.

90. *SBVPrLV*, 29 Apr. 1920, vol. 9, cols. 11229–30, 11671 (Severing).

91. Rudolf Klatt, *Ostpreussen unter dem Reichskommissariat 1919/1920* (Heidelberg, 1958), p. 196. Cf. the order to arrest Kapp's governor of Schleswig-Holstein, Lindemann, and others, LASH/301/5713.

92. Eimers, *Verhältnis*, p. 227.

93. District director of Schleswig to provincial governor, 15 Apr. 1920, LASH/301/216.

94. Runge, *Politik*, p. 36.

95. Cf. "Sitz. der Z-Reichstagsfraktion," 25 and 26 June 1920, ten Hompel papers/15 (BA); *SBVPrLV*, 1 Dec. 1920, vol. 11, cols. 14377–79 (Meinecke). Cf. Brüning's sharp criticism of the appointment of "left-wing journalists" by the "Prussian camarilla" after the Kapp Putsch in *Memoiren* (Stuttgart, 1970), p. 67.

96. Haenisch was particularly active in pushing this project after the Putsch. See Haenisch, *Neue Bahnen der Kulturpolitik* (Stuttgart, 1921), p. 53. Cf. Severing, *1919/1920*, p. 57.

97. Runge, *Politik*, p. 81; and SPD local in Hanover to Severing, 30 June 1920, Severing papers/86/54 (Arch.SD). On the handling of an individual case, see the exchange of letters on the position of the police chief of the city of Hanover, 15 Aug. to 3 Oct. 1920, NSStAH/122a/IX/19.

98. See for example, Wels to Giebel, 10 Sept. 1920, Giebel papers I/II (Arch.SD); see also Heilmann's criticism of the minister of justice's personnel policies, *SBVPrLV*, 16 Nov. 1920, vol. 11, col. 13744.

99. See the complaints in Abegg to Severing, 31 May 1947, Severing papers 60/12 (Arch.SD); and Abegg papers. See also Runge, *Politik*, p. 154.

100. *SBVPrLV*, 4 Dec. 1920, vol. 11, col. 14580.

101. Cf. SPD district organization of Schleswig-Holstein to provincial governor, 4 June 1920, LASH/301/4875.

102. Severing, *Lebensweg* 1:283.

103. In subsequent years, Braun repeatedly considered naming Noske to a Prussian ministerial post.

104. See Heine to Braun, 16 Nov. 1935, Braun papers/652 (IISG); and Loewenfeld, "Erinnerungen," pp. 399–400. Dr. Weyl (USPD) exclaimed, "We'd rather have Mr. von Richter!" (*SBVPrLV*, 6 July 1920, vol. 9, col. 11609).

105. Südekum to Severing, 28 May and 7 June 1920, Severing papers 01/104, 105 (Arch.SD).

106. Südekum to Severing, 29 Apr., 7 June 1920, and Severing to SPD local in Hanover, 3 June 1920, Severing papers 01/103, 105, and 86/54 (Arch.SD). Severing's letter to the Hanover local originally contained a reference to Braun's opposition against Südekum, but it was struck out of the final text. The "purified" version is also in Severing, *Lebensweg* 1:308–09.

107. Noske, *Erlebtes*, p. 183; and Ministry of the Interior to Noske, 26 June and 25 Oct. 1920, NSStAH/122a/VIII/300/vol. 1.

108. *SBVPrLV,* 7 July 1920, vol. 9, col. 11595 (von der Osten). For a general review of the personnel purge, see Runge, *Politik,* pp. 121–34.

109. *DrSVPrLV,* vol. 7, pp. 3673ff., vol. 8, pp. 4015–85.

110. Matull, ed., *Arbeiterbewegung,* p. 88.

111. Runge, *Politik,* pp. 121–22, 134, 145.

112. Between 1920 and 1926 the Prussian government did appoint 229 new county commissioners.

113. Behrend, *Personalpolitik,* p. 181.

114. See "DDP-Fr.Prot.," 29 Sept. 1921. Cf. Runge, *Politik,* p. 73.

115. Noske to district director Aurich, 27 July 1921, NSStAH/122a/VIII/418; Minister of the Interior to provincial governors and district directors, 16 June 1921, NSStAH/122a/IX/zf. Municipal officials were selected by the city councils, but they could take office only after being confirmed by the governor of the province in which the municipality was located.

116. Runge, *Politik,* p. 109. As an example, see the protocol of a meeting between the district director of Schleswig and the Arbeiterrat, 11 and 12 Nov. 1918, LASH/301/2401.

117. Of the 37 edicts and decrees promulgated prior to the assembly of the Prussian Constitutional Convention, 10 concerned the democratization of local and district elections. For comparison, the number of decrees concerned with other topics were: day-to-day administration (7), personnel policies (5), Hohenzollern property (4), settlement policies (4), the councils (2), and social policies (2) ("Verzeichnis der von der Staatsregierung seit dem 9. November 1918 erlassenen und verkündeten Verordnungen," 18 Apr. 1919, *DrSVPrLV,* vol. 13, no. 234, pp. 384–86). One of the most detailed sections of the official government report, *2 Jahre,* pp. 99–106, deals with local reforms.

118. A. v. Holtzendorff to Cuno, 12 Nov. 1919, Hap.Arch./Ber 2.

119. See provincial DDP organization of Schleswig-Holstein and Lübeck to Ministry of the Interior, 31 Jan. 1919, LASH/301/4945; and the protests of various city councils and district committees, NSStAH/122a/XI/x. Cf. Walter Gagel, *Die Wahlrechtsfrage in der Geschichte der deutschen liberalen Parteien 1848–1918* (Düsseldorf, 1958), pp. 165–66.

120. Hirsch, "Gemeindeverfassung," *Die Arbeiterschaft im neuen Deutschland,* ed. Friedrich Thimme and Carl Legien (Leipzig, 1915), pp. 68–80.

121. *SPD-Parteitag 1919,* p. 223; and *Freiheit,* 17 Nov. 1918.

122. "Decree of 26 Nov. 1918," *Vorwärts,* no. 235 (26 Nov. 1918).

123. "Sitz.PrStMin." 14 Dec. 1918, O. Braun papers/28 (IISG); and "Sitz.d.Pr.Reg.u.d.ZR," 9 Jan. 1919, *ZR-Protokolle,* doc. 40. pp. 268–76. Cf. Karl Anlauf, *Die Revolution in Niedersachsen* (Hanover, 1919), pp. 146–47; and Zentralrat, *Vom I. Rätekongress zur Nationalversammlung,* ed. Gustav Haller (Berlin, 1919), pp. 25-26.

124. Eimers, *Verhältnis,* p. 97; Hirsch, *Weg,* p. 154; *Vom I. Rätekongress,* p. 25; *SPD-Parteitag 1919,* p. 224; and *SBVPrLV,* 22 Mar. and 21 Apr. 1919, vol. 1, cols. 480–87, 1192–96. Cf. "Sitz.PrStMin.," 31 Jan. 1919, O. Braun papers/32 (IISG).

125. *PrGS,* no. 6 (1919), pp. 13–14; ibid., no. 10 (1919), pp. 23–25. See "Sitz.PrStMin.," 18 Feb. 1919, O. Braun papers/34 (IISG); *Freiheit,* 17 Feb. 1919; and Hirsch to ZR, 4 Feb. 1919, ZR-Arch./B-12/1.

126. Eimers, *Verhältnis,* p. 97; Hellmut von Gerlach, *Meine Erlebnisse in der Preussischen Verwaltung* (Berlin, 1919), p. 83; and *SBVPrLV,* 11 Apr. 1919, vol. 1, cols. 1204–13.

127. *SBVPrLV,* 18 July 1919, vol. 3, col. 3859 (Heine); *DrSVPrLV,* vol. 3, doc. 545, pp. 345–46; Heine to Sollmann, 21 Sept. 1919, Sollmann papers; *RheinZ- Parteitag,* Sept. 1919, pp. 199–200 (Hess); and Runge, *Politik,* p. 31. Cf. the commentaries from the viewpoints of the conservative parties in Paul Lüdicke, *Die sozialdemokratische Misswirtschaft in Preussen* (Berlin, 1921), p. 12; and Georg Glatow, "Die Bedeutung der Kreistagswahlen," *Neue Zeit* 37 (18 Apr. 1919), 57.

128. *Vorwärts*, no. 341 (7 July 1919).

129. *SBVPrLV*, 3 Feb. 1920, vol. 7, cols. 9257–81.

130. Christian Engeli, *Gustav Böss* (Stuttgart, 1971), p. 33. See also Walther Oehme, "Das Problem Gross-Berlin." *Sozialistische Monatshefte* 52 (14 Apr. 1919), 323–24.

131. The government draft is in *DrSVPrLV*, vol. 4, doc. 1286, pp. 1691ff.

132. *SBVPrLV*, 23 Apr. 1920, vol. 9, col. 10871 (Dominicus). See also Ernst Reuter, "Reform der Berliner Verwaltung," *Sozialistische Monatshefte* 70 (14 Apr. 1930), 344–49.

133. Karl Wermuth, "Um den Berliner Magistrat," *Vorwärts*, no. 448 (9 Sept. 1920); "Bericht über die Berliner Parteifunktionärskonferenz," ibid., no. 488 (2 Oct. 1920); and Franz Krüger, "Die rote Gewaltherrschaft," ibid., no. 476 (25 Sept. 1920).

134. *Freiheit*, 8 Oct. 1920; when amendments to the Greater Berlin Law proposed by the bourgeois parties came to vote in October 1920, the SPD abstained (*SBVPrLV*, 7 Oct. 1920, vol. 10, cols. 12835, 12848, 12933–38).

135. Engeli, *Böss*, pp. 39–42. The Independents severely criticized the SPD's attitude. See *Freiheit*, 25 Nov. 1920; and *Mitteilungsblatt des Bezirksverbandes Berlin-Brandenburg der USPD* 15 (4 Feb. 1921).

136. *SBVPrLV*, 7 July 1920, vol. 9, col. 11672.

137. Gerlach, *Erlebnisse*, p. 83.

138. Decree of 21 Dec. 1918, *PrGS* (1918), p. 201. See also, *DrSVPrLV*, vol. 6, doc. 1747, p. 2684.

139. *SBVPrLV*, 16 June 1919, vol. 3, cols. 3356–57 (Limbertz [SPD]).

140. "Sitz.PrStMin.," 10 Apr. 1919, Südekum papers/8 (BA); and *SBVPrLV*, 26 June 1919, vol. 3, cols. 2635–36 (Meister).

141. See *2 Jahre*, pp. 16–17; *SBVPrLV*, 15 June, vol. 3, cols. 3522–25, 3545; 5 and 6 Nov. 1919, vol. 5, cols. 5873, 5889. Cf. the criticism in *Freiheit*, 12 Aug. 1919.

142. Cf. the debate in *SBVPrLV*, 5 and 6 Nov. 1919, vol. 5, cols. 5555, 5858–59, 5871, 5883, 5889, 5892–5900. Cf. Kardorff's statements at the *DNVP-Parteitag*, 12 July 1919, pp. 6060b–c, in Forst.Hbg/7573 (DNVP), vol. 1.

143. Severing, *Lebensweg* 1:279.

144. The memorandum was signed by the governors Maier, Noske, Lippmann, Würmeling and the Landeshauptmänner Renvers (Rheinprovinz), von Winterfeldt (Brandenburg), v.d. Wense (Hanover), von Thaer (Silesia), and Dieckmann (Westphalia). See LASH/301/4951. For an opposing view, see Kürbis to Ministry of the Interior, 17 June 1920, ibid.

145. Ferdinand Friedensburg, *Lebenserinnerungen* (Frankfurt a.M., 1969), p. 175.

146. Severing, "Preussen-Problem," *Neue Zeit* 39 (1 July 1921), 313–16; *SBVPrLV*, 5 Nov. 1920, vol. 10, cols. 13511 (Scholich [SPD]) and 13558 (Dallmer [DNVP]); and *Freiheit*, 31 Dec. 1920.

147. See Lauscher's statements in *Germania*, 13 Dec. 1920. There were differences even among Center Party leaders, however. Cf. Stegerwald's comments at the "Sitz d. Z-Reichstagsfraktion," 19 Oct. 1920, ten Hompel papers/15 (BA).

148. Drews, "Einheitsstaat."

149. Cf. the discussion in "Verf.-Ausschuss." The cabinet decided "firmly" against forming the new province. See "Sitz.PrStMin.," 18 Sept. 1920, O. Braun papers/B/A/19a (PrGStAB). See also *SBVPrLV*, 29 Oct. 1920, vol 10, cols. 13354, 13420–26.

150. *Vorwärts*, no. 309 (9 Nov. 1918). There is no doubt that the decision by the Reich cabinet saved Prussia the likelihood of bloody conflict and Linsingen a personal embarrassment, since it is virtually certain that by this time most of the troops under his command would have refused to fire upon striking workers or demonstrators.

151. On developments in Berlin in early November, see Kluge, *Soldatenräte*, pp. 82–94.

152. Walther Reinhardt, "Eindrücke v. 8, bis. 10. November 1918, Aus dem Nachlass des Generals Walther Reinhardt," ed. Fritz Ernst, *Welt als Geschichte* 18 (1958), 44–46; and Kluge, *Soldatenräte*, p. 85.

153. On its history and composition, see Hagen Schulze, *Freikorps und Republik 1918–1920* (Boppard a.Rh., 1969), pp. 17ff.

154. Hirsch, *Weg*, p. 131; and "Sitz.d.ZR," 4 Jan. 1919, *ZR-Protokolle*, doc. 29, pp. 214–15. For a general history of the Berlin police in the Weimar years, see Hsi-huey Liang, *The Berlin Police Force in the Weimar Republik* (Berkeley, Calif., 1970).

155. "Januar-Unruhen," pp. 7670, 7811, 7969, 7979, 7983. Emil Eichhorn's own report, *Eichhorn über die Januar-Ereignisse* (Berlin, 1919) is based on his testimony before the committee examining these events.

156. Cf. the positive evaluation of Eichhorn's activities, *Vorwärts*, nos. 328, 347a (29 Nov. and 18 Dec. 1918).

157. "Prot.A-Rat Berlin 19.11.1918," p. 1034.

158. *AVB*, no. 11 (13 Nov. 1918), p. 11. See also Kluge, *Soldatenräte*, pp. 171–72, 176–79; Müller, *Revolution*, pp. 119, 122; Anton Fischer, *Die Revolutionskommandantur Berlin* (Berlin, [1919]), p. 9; Erwin Könnemann, *Einwohnerwehren und Zeitfreiwilligenverbände* (Berlin [East], 1971), pp. 57–58; and Ludwig Dierske, "Sicherheitskräfte in Preussen zu Beginn der Weimarer Republik," *Aus Politik und Zeitgeschichte/Das Parlament* (B 47/49; 22 Nov. 1969), p. 34; Eichhorn, *Januar*, pp. 13, 22–24; R. Müller, *Kaiserreich* 2:143–44. Cf. Eichhorn's proclamation, *Vossische Zeitung*, 11 Nov. 1918, in *Revolutions-Dokumente*, ed. Buchner, no. 162.

159. Kluge, *Soldatenräte*, p. 179; and "Januar-Unruhen," no. 4121B, p. 7862.

160. Peter Bucher, "Zur Geschichte der Einwoherwehren in Preussen 1918–1921," *Militärgeschichtliche Mitteilungen* 9 (1971), 18–21; Heinz Oeckel, *Die Revolutionäre Volkswehr 1918/21* (Berlin [East], 1968), p. 35. See also Dierske, "Sicherheitskräfte," pp. 35–36. For a comparison of the nature of the Einwohnerwehren in Bavaria with those in Prussia, see Bruno Thoss, *Der Ludendorff-Kreis 1919–1923* (Munich, 1978), pp. 86ff.

161. Schäfer, *Tagebuch*, p. 31; Severing, *SBVPrLV*, 2 Dec. 1920, vol. 11, cols. 14421–22.

162. Könnemann, *Einwohnerwehren*, pp. 45, 117; and Heinz Oeckel, *Revolutionäre Volkswehr*, pp. 63–67.

163. See Prussian Ministry of the Interior to provincial governors, 18 Mar. 1919, ZR-Arch./B-19. See also Bucher, "Einwohnerwehren," pp. 24–25.

164. See Heine's "draft," 8 Apr. 1919, O. Braun papers/106 (IISG); decree of 15 Apr. 1919, *Ministerial-Blatt für die preussische innere Verwaltung* (1919), pp. 199–200; Prussian Ministry of the Interior, "Circular Letter of 15 Sept. 1919," ZR-Arch./B-19. Cf. Kolb, *Arbeiterräte*, p. 387; Könnemann, *Einwohnerwehren*, p. 287; and Bucher, "Einwohnerwehren," pp. 29, 32.

165. See the proclamation of the SPD executive committee, "Hinein in die Einwohnerwehren," *Vorwärts*, no. 612 (30 Nov. 1919). On the commissioners' sabotage, see von Knebel (Döberitz) to Dewitz, 24 Apr. 1919, O. Braun papers/59 (IISG).

166. Ernst Hesterberg, *Alle Macht den Räten* (Breslau, 1932), p. 279 (entry for 17 Sept. 1919).

167. See the protest lodged by the district executive committee of the SPD in Pomerania, 12 Sept. 1919, Grzesinski papers/503 (IISG). Cf. also Könnemann, *Einwohnerwehren*, pp. 142ff.

168. Könnemann, *Einwohnerwehren*, pp. 139, 144ff. The Bavarian citizens' militias were the foundation of the Kahr regime in that state. See Thoss, *Ludendorff*, p. 112.

169. A copy of the proclamation is in NSStAH/122a/XXXVII/156. Prussian Ministry of the Interior to provincial governors, 20 Mar. 1920, ibid.

170. See Hirsch's statements in "Bericht des Staatshaushaltsausschusses," *DrSVPrLV*, vol. 4, doc. 1000, pp. 1476–77.

171. See Prussian cabinet to provincial governors and district directors, 11 Dec. 1919 and Prussian Ministry of the Interior, "General Instructions to the Prussian Ministries, Governors and District Directors," 15 Jan. 1920, LASH/301/5645.

172. *Freiheit,* 8 Oct. 1919; and Koch-Weser, diary entry for 10 Dec. 1919, Koch-Weser papers (BA). The USPD ministers of the Revolutionary Cabinet had refused to work with Berger, but were not able to force his resignation; Breitscheid could only get him to take a long vacation. See, Rosenfeld, *SBVPrLV,* 14 Nov. 1919, vol. 5, col. 6476; and *Freiheit,* 6 and 8 Oct. 1919.

173. Erger, *Kapp-Putsch,* p. 134; see also Kurt Rosenfeld's comments (USPD) in *SBVPrLV,* 16 Dec. 1919, vol. 7, col. 8145. Cf. Berger's appologia "Die Tätigkeit des Staatskommissars für die öffentliche Ordnung anlässlich des Staatsstreiches am 13.3.1920" (16 Apr. 1920), Heine papers/335 (IISG).

174. Berger to O. Braun, 8 Mar. 1920, O. Braun papers/95 (IISG).

175. *SBVPrLV,* 31 Jan. 1920. vol. 7, col. 9098.

176. See Severing to Lichtenstein, 29 Mar. 1923, and Braun to Severing, 21 Aug. 1929, Severing papers/81/80, 01/15 (Arch.SD).

177. Bucher, "Einwohnerwehren," p. 56; and Severing's statements in "Bericht des Hauptausschusses . . . Ministeriums d. Innern . . . 1920," 6 Nov. 1920, *DrSVPrLV,* vol. 10, doc. 3275, p. 5722. Cf. Könnemann, *Einwohnerwehren,* p. 315; and Thoss, *Ludendorff,* p. 146. The Reich Ministry of Interior was far slower than its Prussian counterpart in moving against the militias, and even then local Reichswehr commanders often proved uncooperative. Cf. the documents in NSStAH/12a/XXXVII/92 and 95. Bavaria also protested against the dissolution of the citizens' militias (ibid., pp. 151–52).

178. Ebert in the "Sitz.d.ZR," 31 Dec. 1918, *ZR-Protokolle,* no. 19, p. 119; and H. Müller, *November-Revolution,* p. 174; Kluge, *Soldatenräte,* pp. 278, 350–57; and Carsten, *Revolution,* pp. 65, 107.

179. Schulz, *Demokratie,* pp. 340–41, 347; Bucher, "Einwohnerwehren," and Eimers, *Verhältnis,* p. 228.

180. See decree of 11 Nov. 1920, Severing papers 11/94 (Arch.SD).

181. See the meeting with representatives of the Prussian government on 19 Sept. and "Kab. Sitz.," 22 Sept. 1921, Ak/Rk *Wirth,* docs. 94, 97, pp. 272–73, 278–80. See also the documentation and especially Stegerwald to Reich Ministry of the Interior, 8 Sept. 1921, LASH/301/5646. Cf. Erich Kuttner, *Warum versagt die Justiz* ([Berlin], 1921), pp. 59, 62, 91.

182. On the paramilitary groups throughout the Weimar years, see James Diehl, *Paramilitary Politics in Weimar Germany* (Bloomington, Ind., 1977).

183. For a detailed analysis, see Thoss, *Ludendorff,* pp. 120ff.

184. Ibid., pp. 123ff.

185. Paul Lüdicke, *Die sozialdemokratische Misswirtschaft in Preussen* (Berlin, 1921), pp. 7–10; *SBVPrLV,* 2 Dec. 1920, vol. 11, cols. 14424–28, 14444–45 (Severing).

186. See "The meeting with the provincial governors," 14 July 1920, Severing papers/88/11; and Ministry of the Interior to provincial governors, 15 Aug. 1920, ibid./88/16.

187. "Meeting," 14 July 1920. Three months after the putsch, the Reichswehr Brigade 9 (Schwerin), for example, was again preparing for the final confrontation with Bolshevism despite the calm that prevailed at the time. See "Berichterstattung der Reichswehrbrigade 9 (Schwerin)" to the provincial governor, 20 and 23 May 1920, LASH/301/3713.

188. *SBVPrLV,* 30 Mar. 1920, vol. 8, cols. 10504–08.

189. A. von Holtzendorff to Cuno, 1 Dec. 1918, Hap.Arch./I, II.

190. *SBVPrLV,* 6 July 1920, vol. 9, col. 11610; Erger, *Kapp-Putsch,* pp. 91, 134; and Brammer, *Jagow,* p. 33. Cf. Thoss, *Ludendorff.*

191. Erger, *Kapp-Putsch,* p. 191, and Thoss, *Ludendorff,* p. 118.

192. Eliasberg, *Ruhrkrieg,* p. 84; and Severing, *1919–1920,* p. 17.

193. Heine himself confirmed the unreliability of the Prussian Security Police after the putsch. See Heine to Eugene Ernst, 27 March 1920, Heine papers/no. 337.

194. "Besprechung," 14 July 1920. Cf. Ministry of the Interior, *Neuordnung des Polizeiwesens* ([Berlin], 1920); and Severing, *Lebensweg* 1:312–15.

195. Cf. *DrSVPrLV*, vol. 7, doc. 2282, p. 3629. See also Severing, *1919–1920*, p. 223.

196. Cf. von Wolff (former citizens' militia coordinator in the office of the provincial governor of Hanover) to provincial governor of Hanover, 26 Mar. 1921 (draft), NSStAH/ 122a/XXXVII/25. See also *Freiheit*, 10 Apr. 1920, and 20 Jan. 1921. For a discussion of the restructuring of the local police, see Dierske, *Sicherheitswehr*, pp. 46–55.

197. Heine to Ernst, 27 Mar. 1920, Heine papers/337; Kessler, *Tagebücher*, 232 (23 June 1920).

198. Cf. a discussion of the controversy in *Vorwärts*, nos. 177, 207, 208 (7 and 23 Apr. 1920); and *SBVPrLV*, 7 July 1920, vol. 9. cols. 11673–74.

199. Cf. the development of the Bavarian state police into a predominantly right-wing force in E. Schuler, *Die Bayerische Landespolizei* (Munich, 1964).

Chapter 5. Parties and Prussia, 1922—1925

1. Alfred Kastning, *Die deutsche Sozialdemokratie zwischen Koalition und Opposition 1919–1923* (Paderborn, 1970), p. 137.

2. See *Vorwärts*, nos. 210, 212 (6 and 7 May 1924).

3. Johannes Schauff, *Die deutschen Katholiken und die Zentrumspartei* (Cologne, 1928), p. 125.

4. For a detailed history of the Bund, see Uwe Lohalm, *Völkischer Radikalismus—Die Geschichte des Deutsch-Völkischen Schutz- und Trutzbundes* (Hamburg, 1970). Membership in 1922 is found on pp. 89–90.

5. See Dietrich Orlow, *The History of the Nazi Party 1919–1933* (Pittsburgh, Pa., 1969).

6. Jan Striesow, "Die Deutschnationale Volkspartei und die Völkisch-Radikalen," Ph.D. diss., University of Hamburg, 1977, p. 421.

7. See Graefe to Reich Minister of the Interior in *Ak/Rk Cuno*, no. 77, pp. 258–59; also the documents confiscated in a raid on the DVFP's offices in NL Severing 19/107 (Arch.SD).

8. Graefe to Cuno, Mar. 20, 1923, in *Ak/Rk Cuno*, no. 100, pp. 316–19.

9. On the Hitler coup, see Harold J. Gordon, Jr., *Hitler and the Beer Hall Putsch* (Princeton, N.J., 1972). The government of Chancellor Cuno was especially anxious to retain the good will of the DVFP (*Ak/Rk Cuno*, doc. 172, pp. 520–21, n. 2).

10. Lohalm, *Radikalismus*, p. 247.

11. Ibid., pp. 318–19.

12. Richard F. Hamilton, *Who Voted for Hitler?* (Princeton, N.J., 1982).

13. On the intraparty conflict, in addition to the secondary literature cited earlier, see Hoetzsch et al. to Hergt, 1 Sept. 1922; and Hoetzsch to Staatspol, AG, 24 Sept. 1922, Diller papers (Forst.Hbg.); and von Xylander to Hergt, 6 Sept. 1922, DNVP papers/7533/II (Forst.Hbg.).

14. Xylander to Hergt, 6 Sept. 1922.

15. Günther Arns, "Regierungsbildung und Koalitionspolitik in der Weimarer Republik 1919–1924," Ph.D. diss., Univeristy of Tübingen, 1971, p. 161; and Arns, "Die Krise des Weimarer Parlamentarismus im Frühherbst 1923," *Der Staat* 8 (1969), 185ff., 196–97.

16. Brüning's recollection (*Memoiren* [Stuttgart, 1970], pp. 104–05) that the "old aristocracy" showed an interest in a cabinet that included both the DNVP and the SPD was typical of wishful thinking on the part of the Catholic Conservatives.

17. Hans Siegfried Weber, "Preussische Koalition und Deutsche Volkspartei," *Der Tag*, 7

Sept. 1923. It has not been possible to identify the author further, but he was certainly not a "leading" member of the DVP. The DNVP paid little attention to the DDP since the German nationalists expected the left Liberals to be destroyed by the general drift to the right among the bourgeois voters.

18. *SBPrLT 1921–24*, 23 Nov. 1924, vol. 17, cols. 25812–14.

19. Ibid., col. 25811. Cf. also Friedrich Winckler, *Rede* (Berlin, 1924), p. 9.

20. Hergt, "Memorandum" (secret), 3 Feb. 1923, DNVP papers/7533/II (Forst.Hbg.).

21. See v. Haniel to Hamm, 7 May 1923 in: *Ak/Rk Cuno*, doc. 153, p. 466.

22. *Kreuzzeitung*, 12 Oct. 1922.

23. *Ak/Rk Cuno*, no. 74, p. 253, n. 9.

24. Cf. Marx's memorandum, in Marx papers 1070/60/28 (Stadtarch.Cologne); see also *SBPrLT 1925–28*, 16 Nov. 1925, vol. 3, col. 4527 (Hess).

25. The following is based upon Schlange-Schöningen's confidential "Denkschrift," 19 May 1924, Schlange-Schöningen papers/19 (BA), which Schlange-Schöningen sent to Alfred Hugenberg. Cf. his public utterances, *Wir Völkischen* (Stettin, 1923), pp. 10–11.

26. See *Deutsche Tageszeitung*, 6 Jan. 1924; and *Deutsche Zeitung*, 31 Jan. 1924.

27. See Bredt to Westarp, 30 June 1924, in Johann Victor Bredt, *Erinnerungen und Dokumente*, ed. Martin Schumacher (Düsseldorf, 1970), pp. 345–46; Haenisch, "Um Preussen," *Vorwärts*, no. 30, 18 Jan. 1925.

28. The dramatic scenes in the Reichstag on August 29 have often been described, and do not need to be repeated here. See Werner Liebe, *Die Deutschnationale Volkspartei* (Düsseldorf, 1956), p. 82ff; Anneliese Thimme, *Flucht in den Mythos* (Göttingen, 1969), p. 84; also Paul Moldenhauer, "Politische Erinnerungen," p. 150, in Moldenhauer papers/1 (BA).

29. Cremer to K. v. Kardorff, 29 Sept. 1924, K. von Kardorff-Oheimb papers/18 (BA). Cremer was a member of the Reichstag and executive secretary of the DVP. Cf. Axel Freiherr v. Freytag-Loringhoven, *Deutschnationale Volkspartei* (Berlin, 1931), p. 40; von Freytag was a leader of the DNVP's radical wing.

30. *Vorwärts*, no. 394 (22 Aug. 1924). Incidentally, the issue was not the merits of the Dawes Plan. The Prussian government, for its part, had serious doubts about its benefits for Germany. See Hagen Schulze, *Otto Braun* (Berlin, 1977), p. 462.

31. The radicals had close ties to the Pan German Association (ADV), and this account is based upon the minutes of a session of that organization's executive committee held on 25 and 26 Nov. 1924. The protocol is in the ADV papers/412 (Forst.Hbg.).

32. See *Raiffeisen—ein deutschnationaler Finanz- und Korruptionsskandal* (Stettin, [1930]); and Magnus Freiherr v. Braun, *Von Ostpreussen bis Texas* (Stollhamm/Olbg., 1955), p. 188.

33. Schlange-Schöningen to Graef, 25 Aug. 1924, Schlange-Schöningen papers/19 (BA). Winckler, an old-line Junker active in the Protestant lay movement, was among the more moderate members of the DNVP Landtag delegation.

34. Henry A. Turner, Jr., *Stresemann and the Politics of the Weimar Republic* (Princeton, N.J., 1963), p. 155; Carl Severing, *Mein Lebensweg* (Cologne, 1950), 2:8, 2:14 Schulze, *Braun*, p. 360; and *Königsberger Allgemeine Zeitung*, 6 Feb. 1924.

35. See the notes in Marx papers/1070/63/1–3 (Stadtarch.Cologne); and Turner, *Stresemann*, pp. 174–76.

36. Turner, *Stresemann*, pp. 157–60; and Roland Thimme, *Stresemann und die deutsche Volkspartei 1923–25* (Lübeck, 1961), p. 54.

37. Moldenhauer, "Erinnerungen," p. 145.

38. Cremer to Kathinka von Kardorff-Oheimb, 29 Sept. 1924, K. von Kardorff-Oheimb papers/18 (BA).

39. See Garnich's attempts to defend the grand coalition at a membership meeting of the

DVP in June 1923, Severing papers/19/143 (Arch.SD). Garnich was a leading member of the DVP's Landtag delegation.

40. *SBPrLT 1921–24*, 7 Nov. 1924, vol. 17, col. 24555.

41. *Nationalliberale Correspondenz*, 8 July 1923.

42. Turner, *Stresemann*, p. 155; On the threats to the coalition government in Prussia, see *Deutsche Tageszeitung*, 6 Jan. 1924; and *Deutsche Zeitung*, 31 Jan. 1924. Cf. the minutes of the Pan-German's executive committee meeting, 25, 26 Oct. 1924, ADV papers/412 (Forst.Hbg.); *Vorwärts*, no. 306 (2 July 1924), suspected that von Eynern was the leader of the group calling for a Prussian *Bürgerblock*. Cf. *SBPrLT 1921–24*, 7 Oct. 1924, vol. 17, col. 24234 (Heilmann).

43. Schulze, *Braun*, pp. 462–64. Cf. Erich Kuttner, *Otto Braun* (Berlin, [1932]), p. 82.

44. See the joint statement by Dominicus, Gerland, Grund, Neirath, and Schiffer to the DDP Executive Committee, 21 Oct. 1924, *Deutsche Allgemeine Zeitung*, 23 Oct. 1924.

45. See the discussion at the meeting of the DDP Landtag delegation, "DDP-Fr.Prot.," 4 Oct. 1922.

46. Cf. Marx papers/1070/63, pp. 9, 33 (Stadtarch.Cologne).

47. Werner Stephan, *Aufstieg und Verfall des Linksliberalismus* (Göttingen, 1973), pp. 282–83.

48. Bernhard Falk, "Aufzeichnungen," pp. 107–08, Kl.Erw./385 (BA).

49. Cremer to K. von Kardorff-Oheimb, 29 Sept. 1924.

50. For a detailed account of the founding and history of the WiP, see Martin Schumacher, *Mittelstandsfront und Republik* (Düsseldorf, 1972); and the same author's "Hausbesitz, Mittelstand und Wirtschaftspartei," in *Industrielles System und politische Entwicklung in der Weimarer Republik*, ed. Hans Mommsen et al. (Düsseldorf, 1977), pp. 823–35.

51. Schumacher, "Hausbesitz," p. 829.

52. Schumacher, *Mittelstandsfront*, p. 87.

53. *SBPrLT 1925–28*, 19 Feb. 1925, vol. 1, cols. 558–59.

54. Hugo Stehkämper, "Wilhelm Marx," in *Zeitgeschichte in Lebensbildern*, ed. Rudolf Morsey (Mainz, 1973), pp. 183–85.

55. Cremer to K. v. Kardorff-Oheimb, 29 Sept. 1924.

56. Stegerwald, "Vom deutschen 'Gemeinschaftsgeist,'" *Der Deutsche*, 23 May 1923. Cf. "Wahrheit und Klarheit," ibid., 9 Oct. 1923.

57. See Marx's notes dated 10 Nov. 1923, Marx papers/1070/55/36 (Stadtarch.Cologne).

58. Rudolf Morsey, *Die Deutsche Zentrumspartei 1917–1923* (Düsseldorf, 1966), p. 431; and Stegerwald's remarks, *Der Deutsche*, 1 Apr. 1922.

59. Marx to Count Praschma, 8 Apr. 1928, Marx papers/1070/68, pp. 34–40 (Stadtarch.Cologne). Actually, such plans were completely illusory; the DNVP and the Social Democrats rejected any coalition that included both of them.

60. Marx papers/1070/68, p. 3 (Stadtarch.Cologne). See also Albert Grzesinski, "Kampf," pp. 148–49.

61. Adolf Gottwald, *Ziele und Erfolge der Zentrumsfraktion des Preussischen Landtags 1921/24* (Berlin, 1924), p. 40.

62. Karl Rohe, *Das Reichsbanner Schwarz-Rot-Gold* (Düsseldorf, 1966), pp. 279ff.

63. Gerhard Schulz, *Zwischen Demokratie und Diktatur* (Berlin, 1963), 1:513.

64. See Ulitzka, "Der deutsche Osten und die Zentrumspartei," *Nationale Arbeit—Das Zentrum und sein Wirken in der deutschen Republik*, ed. Karl Anton Schulte (Berlin, 1929), pp. 141–53.

65. See Paul Nieborowski, "Denkschrift über die Folgen des oberschlesischen Autonomiekonfliktes für das deutsche Zentrum," Jan. 1923, Severing papers/81/69 (Arch.SD).

66. Severing to the Cabinet, 25 May 1922, O. Braun papers/323 (IISG).

67. See Count Praschma to Marx, 11 Apr. 1925, Marx papers 1070/68, p. 47 (Stadt-archiv.Cologne). See also, Schulze, *Braun*, p. 468.

68. See the results of the roll-call vote, *SBPrLT 1925–28*, Feb. 20, 1925, vol. 1, cols. 693–698.

69. Papen described himself as a "German Nationalist within the Center Party." Quoted by Rudolf Morsey, "Franz von Papen," in *Zeitgeschichte in Lebensbildern*, ed. Rudolf Morsey (Mainz, 1975), 2:78. He also felt it appropriate to justify his political actions to the former crown prince. See Jürgen A. Bach, *Franz von Papen in der Weimarer Republik 1918–1932* (Düsseldorf, 1977), pp. 77–78.

70. Bach, *Papen*, pp. 68–69.

71. See *Germania*, 18 Feb. 1925.

72. Marx papers 1070/66, p. 3 (Stadtarch.Cologne); Bach, *Papen*, p. 83; *Vorwärts*, nos. 92, 101 (24 Feb. and 2 Mar. 1925).

73. Bach, *Papen*, p. 85, 100–01. Papen provides his own account of this episode in his memoirs, *Der Wahrheit eine Gasse* (Munich, 1952), pp. 131–32. Like much of the book, it is full of factual errors.

74. Carl Severing, "Koalitionsfragen," *Sozialistische Monatshefte* 57 (Dec. 15, 1921), 1082.

75. *SBPrLT 1921–24*, Nov. 10, 1921, vol. 3, cols. 4156–57.

76. Severing, "Kiel—Ein Nachwort zum Parteitage," *Gesellschaft* 1 (1927), 4; Donald R. Tracey, "Reform in the Early Weimar Republic: The Thuringian Example," *Journal of Modern History* 44 (June 1972), 211; Arno Scholz, *Null vier—ein Jahrgang zwischen den Fronten* (Berlin-Grunewald, 1962), pp. 69–70; Theodor Buddeberg, "Das soziologische Problem der Sozialdemokratie," *Archiv für Sozialwissenschaft und Sozialpolitik* 49 (1922), 128–29, discusses opposition to this trend.

77. Kurt Koszyk, *Zwischen Kaiserreich und Diktatur—Die sozialdemokratische Presse von 1914–1933* (Heidelberg, 1958), p. 150; and Fritz Bieligk et al., *Die Organisation im Klassenkampf* (Berlin-Britz, 1932), p. 56.

78. Rudolf Breitscheid, "Am Vorabend der Einigung," *Sozialist* 8 (29 July, 1922), 402.

79. *Vorwärts*, no. 330, 15 July 1922; *Protokoll über die Verhandlungen des Parteitages der SPD . . . Augsburg, Gera und Nürnberg* (Berlin, 1922).

80. Kastning, *Sozialdemokratie*, pp. 78–79.

81. Gustav Noske, *Erlebtes aus Aufstieg und Niedergang einer Demokratie* (Offenbach a.M., 1947), p. 227.

82. See Curt Geyer, *Drei Verderber Deutschlands—Ein Beitrag zur Geschichte Deutschlands und der Reparationsfrage von 1920 bis 1924* (Berlin, 1924). The "destroyers" in the title are Stinnes, Helfferich, and Havenstein.

83. See the report on two SPD membership meetings, *Volksblatt für Spandau und Havelland*, 31 Oct. 1923; and *Hamburger Echo*, 23 Nov. 1923. Cf. Eduard David's comments cited in Kastning, *Sozialdemokratie*, p. 80; Scholz, *Null vier*, p. 88; and David Morgan, *The Socialist Left and the German Revolution* (Ithaca, N.Y., 1975), p. 436.

84. See Severing to Beims, Feb. 25, 1924, in Severing papers/23/69 (Arch.SD); and Bieligk, *Organisation*, p. 57.

85. Günter Arns, "Die Linke in der SPD-Reichstagsfraktion im Herbst 1923," *Vierteljahrshefte für Zeitgeschichte* 22 (Apr. 1974), 197–99, 201.

86. Severing to Beims, 25 Feb. 1924; Hilferding to Kautsky, 19 July 1924, Kautsky papers/D-XIII/636 (IISG).

87. A Braun to Kautsky, 2 Jan. 1924, Kautsky papers/D-VI/412 (IISG). Such attitudes led to strange and self-defeating policy decisions. The SPD refused to give Cuno's de facto *Bürgerblock* cabinet a vote of confidence in late 1922, yet Rudolf Hilferding, a prominent former leader of the USPD, noted in a private conversation that if Cuno actually intended to resign as chancellor, this

would have to be prevented by tying him to his chair. See Gaertner to Cuno, 20 Feb. 1923, *Ak/Rk Cuno,* doc. 80, p. 269.

88. Otto Braun, *Von Weimar zu Hitler,* 2d ed. (Hamburg, 1949), p. 62.

89. Hilferding to Kautsky, 19 July 1924, Kautsky papers/D-XIII/636 (IISG). Cf. also Grzesinski to Scheidemann, 28 Apr. 1925, Grzesinski papers/304 (IISG).

90. On the Leinert scandal, see: SPD executive committee to the district leadership in Hanover, 13 Oct. 1924, NSStAH/310 II/A7; cf. also *Vorwärts,* nos. 424, 442 (9 and 19 Sept. 1924). The scandals of Richter,Heilmann, and others (by no means limited to SPD politicians) all led to the appointment of parliamentary investigative committees which conducted lengthy hearings. The Barmat hearings are analyzed by Winfried Steffani, *Die Untersuchungsausschüsse des Preussischen Landtages zur Zeit der Weimarer Republik* (Düsseldorf, 1960), pp. 165–66. As an example of the toll taken by overwork, Severing came close to suffering a breakdown in 1924–25. See Spektator, "Der Staatsmann Otto Braun," *Politische Wochenschrift,* no. 26 (28 June 1929), p. 619.

91. Kasting, *Sozialdemokratie,* p. 137.

92. Paul Herz to Kautsky, 22 May 1924, Kautsky papers/D/XII/412 (IISG).

93. Hilferding to Kautsky, 29 Dec. 1924, ibid./D/XII/638, 640.

94. Severing to Landsberg, 16 June 1924, Severing papers/23/72 (Arch.SD).

95. Only about a third of the delegates voted for a resolution calling for a return to "uncompromising class struggle between the bourgeoisie and the proletariat." See *Protokoll des Sozialdemokratischen Parteitages 1924* (Berlin, 1924), pp. 134ff. Cf. Kastning, *Sozialdemokratie,* p. 142.

96. Hilferding to Kautsky, 19 July 1924, Kautsky papers/D-XII/636 (IISG). See also *Vorwärts,* no. 306 (2 July 1924).

97. See Haenisch's article, "Vergesst Preussen nicht," *Vorwärts,* no. 560 (27 Nov. 1924).

98. Ibid., nos. 497, 532 (21 Oct. and 11 Nov. 1924).

99. *SBPrLT 1921–24,* 23 Oct. 1924, vol. 17, col. 25602 (Heilmann).

100. For detailed accounts of the party's history, see Werner T. Angress, *Stillborn Revolution* (Princeton, N.J., 1963)—the later German edition *Die Kampfzeit der KPD* (Düsseldorf, 1973) contains additional and updated material; and Hermann Weber, *Die Wandlung des deutschen Kommunismus* (Frankfurt a.M., 1969).

101. Angress, *Kampfzeit,* pp. 139ff.

102. Rudolf Breitscheid, "Die drohende Stinnes-Koalition," *Sozialist* 7 (5 Nov. 1921), 953.

103. The SPD's national chairman, Hermann Müller, subsequently described the Saxon coalition as a "misfortune" for the German republic. See the meeting of the SPD Reichstag delegation, 31 Oct. 1923, Keil paper/Verschied./24 [Arch SD]. Cf. Noske, *Erlebtes,* p. 235. On the KPD's accusations, see Raimund Wagner, "Zur Frage der Massenkämpfe in Sachsen vom Frühjahr bis zum Sommer 1923." *Zeitschrift für Geschichtswissenschaft* 4 (no. 2, 1956), 247.

104. See the ADGB's pamphlet, *Ist eine Einheitsfront mit den Kommunisten möglich?* (Berlin, 1922); minutes of the Reich cabinet meeting, 8 Sept. 1922, *Ak/Rk Wirth,* vol. 2, doc. 369, p. 1087. Cf. the letter to the editor by Willi Beuk, *Hamburger Abendblatt,* 1 Nov. 1973. Beuk headed a "Vereinigung Republik" in Hamburg that included KPD and SPD members.

105. See the minutes of a joint meeting of representatives from political parties and labor unions, 1 July 1922, *Ak/Rk Wirth,* vol. 1, doc. 307, p. 929.

106. Wagner, "Frage," pp. 246–64; Cuno to the Ministry of Foreign Affairs, 23 May 1923, *Ak/Rk Cuno,* doc. 164, pp. 496–500; and Mehlich to Severing, 23 Mar. 1923, Severing papers/19/1920 (Arch.SD).

107. Breitscheid, "Zur Frage der Koalitionspolitik," *Sozialist* 7 (no. 51, 24 Dec. 1921), 1098.

108. Cf. *Bericht über die Verhandlungen des VIII. (8.) Parteitages der Kommunistischen*

Partei-Deutschlands . . . Leipzig. 28. Januar bis 1. Februar 1923 (Berlin, 1923), pp. 51–52, 211ff.

109. For details, see Angress, *Kampfzeit*, pp. 483ff.

110. See the notes of the secretary to the Prussian cabinet, Nobis, 31 Aug. 1923; and Reich Minister of Finance to Prussian Minister of Finance, Sept. 1923, O. Braun papers/347, 344 (IISG).

111. Otto Braun responded to congratulations by his friend Johannes Timm (member of the Bavarian Landtag) by remarking that "condolence would almost be more appropriate." See Braun to Timm, 25 Nov. 1921, O. Braun papers/293 (IISG).

112. *SBPrLT 1921–24*, 10 Nov. 1921, vol. 3, col. 4157. On the lack of common ideological ground, see also the draft of the letter written by the SPD delegation to the president of the Prussian Landtag, 16 Feb. 1925, Grzesinski papers/1284 (IISG); and Heilmann to Marx, 16 Feb. 1925, Marx papers/1070/67/28 (Stadtarchiv.Cologne). Cf. ibid./1070/66/8–10.

113. Friedrich Grebe, "Die grosse Koalition in Preussen," *Allgemeine Rundschau* 18 (19 Nov. 1921), 640–41.

114. Carl Severing, "Koalitionsfragen," *Sozialistische Monatshefte* 57 (15 Dec. 1921), 1081. The Conservative *Kreuzzeitung*, 2 June 1922, noted bitterly that the cabinet's first programmatic declaration could just as easily have been delivered by Hirsch or the previous Braun cabinet; the presence of the DVP in the government did not seem to influence the contents.

115. The quotation is from Hugo Sinzheimer's article, "Der sozialistische Staatsbegriff," *Die Glocke* 7 (6 Feb. 1922), 1268. The prime minister underlined this and similar passages in his personal copy of Sinzheimer's article. See O. Braun papers/618 (IISG).

116. See Otto Buchwitz, *50 Jahre Funktionär der deutschen Arbeiterbewegung*, 2d ed. (Berlin [East], 1973), p. 84; and Schulze, *Braun*, pp. 388–92.

117. See the correspondence between Severing and v. Krause, Severing papers/23/56 (Arch.SD).

Chapter 6. Crises and Coalitions, 1922–1925

1. This subject and its ramifications has become a major tumbling ground of revisionism in the historiography of modern Germany in recent years. For a judicious assessment of the major viewpoints, see Peter Krüger, "Das Reparationsproblem der Weimarer Republik in fragwürdiger Sicht," *Vierteljahrshefte für Zeitgeschichte* 27 (Jan. 1981), 21–47.

2. For Prussian support of the policy of fulfillment, see Braun's comments at a meeting of the Reich chancellor with the prime ministers of the states, 27 Mar. 1922, *Ak/Rk Wirth*, vol. 1, no. 232, p. 645.

3. See Prussian Prime Minister to Foreign Ministry, 15 Dec. 1922, in *Ak/Rk Cuno*, vol. 1, no. 22, pp. 68–70, n. 3.

4. See the minutes of a meeting of the Reich chancellor with the Prime Ministers of the states, 20 Jan. 1922; "Chefbesprechung," 25 Aug. 1922; and "Besprechung des Reichskanzlers mit Vertretern der Länder," 28 Aug. 1922, ibid., vol. 1, no. 192, pp. 524–25; vol. 2, nos. 355, 357, pp. 1055, 1062. See also, Adolf Gottwald, *Ziele und Erfolge der Zentrumsfraktion des Preussischen Landtages 1921/1924* (Berlin, 1924), pp. 8–9.

5. See Richter's speech to the Königsberg DVP organization, *Königsberger Allgemeine Zeitung*, 29 June 1923.

6. See the minutes of the Reich cabinet meetings, 9 Jan., 6 Feb. 1923; and Cuno to press secretary of the Reich government, 23 Feb. 1923, *Ak/Rk Cuno*, vol. 1, nos. 37, 65, 82, pp. 122–23, 217–18, 272.

7. See Reich cabinet meeting 17 July 1923, ibid., no. 218, pp. 644, 644, n. 1.

8. Ernst Laubach, *Die Politik der Kabinette Wirth 1921–22* (Lübeck and Hamburg, 1968), pp. 293–94.

9. Ernst Troeltsch, *Spektator-Briefe,* ed. Hans Baron (Tübingen, 1924), p. 229 (9 Nov. 1921).

10. State Secretary Meister to Severing, 25 Apr. 1924, Severing papers/22/28 (Arch.SD).

11. See, for example, Winckler to Marx, 13 Feb. 1925, Grzesinski papers/1283 (IISG).

12. Johannes Fischart (pseud. of Erich Dombroski), *Neue Köpfe,* 4th ed. (Berlin, 1925), p. 233.

13. Weismann, who had succeeded Berger as State Commissioner for the Supervision of Public Order, became cabinet secretary in 1923.

14. "Grundsätze für die Erledigung von Geschäften des Staatsministeriums," 16 Dec. 1921, PrGStAB/Rep. 90/1367. Cf. Enno Eimers, *Das Verhältnis von Preussen und Reich in den ersten Jahren der Weimarer Republik (1918–1923)* (Berlin, 1969), p. 312.

15. Hagen Schulze, *Otto Braun* (Berlin, 1977), p. 371. The ministers did agree, however, that members of the cabinet needed to receive the prime minister's approval before discussing questions of general political significance with their counterparts in the Reich. See "Sitz.PrStMin.," 18 Sept. 1923, O. Braun papers/B/A/19a (PrGStAB).

16. *Tägliche Rundschau,* 6 Nov. 1921.

17. A. Dominicus, "Der Versuch einer Grossen Koalition in Preussen," *8-Uhr Abendblatt,* 8 Nov. 1921.

18. See the undated draft in Severing papers 12/17 (Arch.SD).

19. Dominicus, "Versuch." See also Schulze, *Braun,* p. 393.

20. Otto Braun, *Von Weimar zu Hitler,* 2d ed. (Hamburg, 1949), p. 42; and Schulze, *Braun,* p. 393.

21. O. Braun, *Weimar,* p. 112; and Braun, "Weimar MS," pp. 194–95. Braun's manuscript version of his memoirs is much more detailed and less restrained than the printed version.

22. Carl Severing, *Mein Lebensweg* (Cologne, 1950), 1:336.

23. See "DDP-Fr.Prot.," 23 May 1922, R 45 III/64 (BA).

24. Severing, "Koalitionsfragen," *Sozialistische Monatshefte* 57 (15 Dec. 1921), 1082.

25. See the notes Marx made in mid-February 1922, Marx papers/1070/53/9–11 (Stadtarchiv.Cologne); and "Besprechung des Reichskanzlers mit dem Interfraktionellen Ausschuss," 10 Feb. 1922, *Ak/Rk Wirth,* vol. 1, no. 205, pp. 562–68. See also Henry A. Turner, Jr., *Stresemann and the Politics of the Weimar Republic* (Princeton, N.J., 1963), p. 96.

26. *Die Zeit,* 28 June 1922.

27. Ibid., 13 Sept. 1922; see also, von Campe to Kardorff, 9 Sept. 1922, S. von Kardorff papers/8 (BA).

28. Laubach, *Politik,* pp. 293–94.

29. Ibid. On the complex financial difficulties facing Germany in these years, see Karl-Bernhard Netzband and Hans-Peter Widmaier, *Währungs- und Finanzpolitik der Ära Luther* (Tübingen, 1964); and, for a judicious contemporary analysis, the report of the Second Socialization Commission, "Entschliessung der Sozialisierungskommission zur gegenwärtigen Lage der Valutafrage," 14 Oct. 1922, Kautsky papers/G-13/120–24 (IISG).

30. See Carl Severing, "Das Gebot der Stunde," and "Das Ziel des Kampfes," *Sozialistische Monatshefte* 60 (Jan. 1923), 1–3; ibid., 61 (Mar. 1924), 151–55. Cf. G. Stieler (Center party representative in the Prussian Landtag) to Gronowski, 18 Jan. 1923, Severing papers/14/2 (Arch.SD); Friedrich Stampfer, *Die vierzehn Jahre der ersten deutschen Republik,* 3d ed. (Hamburg, 1953), p. 311.

31. See Gerhard Anschütz, *Das preussisch-deutsche Problem* (Tübingen, 1922), pp. 19–22; Schulze, *Braun,* pp. 410–11; and Eimers, *Verhältnis,* p. 428.

32. See Wachhorst de Wenthe to Severing, 30 May 1922, Severing papers/01/120 (Arch.SD).
33. "Sitz.Pr.StMin.," 2 Oct. 1924, O. Braun papers/287 (IISG); and *SBPrLT 1921–24*, 17 Oct. 1924, vol. 17, cols. 25426ff.
34. See, for example, Köster to Foreign Ministry, 2 Jan. 1922, RK 43 I/2305 (BA); and Gerhard Schulz, *Zwischen Demokratie und Diktatur* (Berlin, 1963), p. 529.
35. Schulze, *Braun*, pp. 404–05; "SitzPrStMin.," 31 May 1924, O. Braun papers/A/19a (PrGStAB), and 24 July 1924, Braun papers/286 (IISG). See also *Vorwärts*, no. 354 (30 July 1924).
36. On the complicated negotiations and motivations of the various participants in the fall 1922 crisis, see Laubach, *Politik*, p. 298; Hugo Stehkämper, in "Konrad Adenauer und das Reichskanzleramt während der Weimarer Zeit," in *Konrad Adenauer* (Cologne, 1976), pp. 422–23; Gotthard Jasper, *Der Schutz der Republik* (Tübingen, 1963). pp. 90–91; *Ak/Rk Wirth*, vol. 2, no. 408, pp. 1169–70; the report of the SPD Reichstag caucus, 13 Nov. 1922, Giebel papers/II/3/219 (Arch.SD); Stampfer, *Vierzehn Jahre*, p. 287; and the 1941 correspondence between Wirth and O. Braun, ed. Hagen Schulze, *Vierteljahrshefte für Zeitgeschichte* 26 (Apr. 1978), 168, 173.
37. Some left-wing members of the SPD Reichstag delegation had illusions that Wirth would be succeeded by Otto Braun as head of a left-of-center Reich cabinet. See Harry Graf Kessler, *Tagebücher 1918–1937*, ed. Wolfgang Pfeiffer-Belli (Frankfurt a.M., 1961), p. 346 (14 Nov. 1922); Reich cabinet meeting, 14 Nov. 1922, *Ak/Rk Wirth*, vol. 2, no. 408, pp. 1169–70.
38. Hans Luther, *Politiker ohne Partei* (Stuttgart, 1960) p. 90. Ebert had suggested him for a cabinet post as early as 1920. See Cuno to Ebert, 22 Sept. 1920, Hap.Arch./Pol. 1.
39. Those who disliked Cuno spoke of his "soft and florid manner" (Willy Hellpach, *Wirken im Wirren* [Hamburg, 1949], 2:313).
40. Cuno to DVP state organization in Hamburg, 31 Jan. 1920, Cuno to Holtzendorff, 23 Jan. 1920, and Reich offices of the Center party to Cuno, 12 May 1920, Hap. Arch./Pol. 1, Ber. 1; Cuno to Otto Fischer, 2 Jan. 1926, ibid./Pol. 3.
41. See Stegerwald, "Keine Legendenbildung," *Germania*, 9 Dec. 1922; and *Berliner Tageblatt*, no. 553, 5 Dec. 1922.
42. See Goslar's note to Braun, Dec. 1922 O. Braun papers/252 (IISG); and Marx papers/1070/53/90 (Stadtarch.Cologne).
43. Campe to Severing, 29 Apr. 1923, Severing papers/19/139 (Arch.SD).
44. See Goslar's note, Dec. 1922; and Goslar's and Braun's marginalia on a clipping from the *Frankfurter Zeitung*, 23 Dec. 1922, O. Braun papers/252 (IISG).
45. Severing to Campe, 2 May 1923, Severing papers/19/140 (Arch.SD). This correspondence is also found in Severing, *Lebensweg*, 1:399–400; K. M.[aretsky?], "Das preussische Idyll," *Der Tag*, 8 Dec. 1922.
46. *SBPrLT 1921–24*, 4 May 1923, vol. 12, cols. 16925–30.
47. Braun, *Weimar*, p. 51.
48. Mehlich to Cuno, 19 July 1923, Severing papers/14/29 (Arch.SD). This letter is also in Severing, *Lebensweg* 1:417–19.
49. See Hamm's report on the situation in the Ruhr, 29 July 1923, *AkRk Cuno*, no. 221, pp. 650–51.
50. "Sitz.PrStMin.," 3 July 1923, O. Braun papers/275 (IISG).
51. Reich cabinet meeting, 25 July 1923, *Ak/Rk Cuno*, no. 223, p. 661.
52. See the report of the session, RK 43 I/677 (BA).
53. *Germania*, 27 July 1923.
54. Günter Arns, "Regierungsbildung und Koalitionspolitik in der Weimarer Republik

1919–1924" (Ph.D. diss., University of Tübingen, 1971), p. 151. Cf. the commentaries in *Ak/Rk Cuno,* no. 233, p. 695, n. 1.

55. See "Besprechung mit Parteiführern der Arbeitsgemeinschaft," 12 Aug. 1923, *Ak/Rk Cuno,* vol. 1, no. 248, pp. 743–45.

56. See Richter to Severing, 13 Aug. 1923; Severing to Richter, 20 Aug. 1923, Severing papers/20/180; 181.

57. See "Ministerbesprechung," 12 Aug. 1923, *Ak/Rk Cuno,* p. 733.

58. "Kritische Bedenken," *Die Zeit,* 24 July 1923.

59. *SBPrLT 1925–28,* 14 Oct. 1925, vol. 3, col. 4363 (Severing); Severing, *Lebensweg* 1:425. See also Schulze, *Braun,* p. 433. Of course, the enthusiasm of some party leaders should not obscure the fact that there remained considerable opposition to the grand coalition. In the vote on the motion of confidence for the Stresemann cabinet, 19 of 53 DVP delegates, and 53 of 171 SPD members of the Reichstag abstained. See Julius Leber's articles in *Lübecker Volksbote* (8, 13 Aug. 1923), in *Ein Mann geht seinen Weg* (Berlin, 1952), pp. 166–68; and Turner, *Stresemann,* p. 115.

60. Alfred Kastning, *Die deutsche Sozialdemokratie zwischen Koalition und Opposition 1919–1923* (Paderborn, 1970), p. 123; and "SPD-Reichstagsfr.-Sitz.," 31 Oct. 1923, Giebel papers/II/259 (Arch.SD); ibid., Keil papers/Verschied./24 (Arch.SD).

61. Roland Thimme, *Stresemann und die deutsche Volkspartei 1923–1925* (Lübeck, 1961), p. 20.

62. The best description of the October crisis is in Arns, "Regierung," pp. 162–70, although the author largely ignores the Prussian component.

63. On Stresemann, see Marx's article, 17 Nov. 1923, Marx papers/1070/55/37–38 (Stadtarch. Cologne); Stegerwald's arguments are found in "Handeln statt Reden," *Deutsche,* 3 Oct. 1923. Cf. Papen to Porsch, 28 Oct. 1923; Marx's article, 29 Sept. 1923, Marx papers/1070/58, 66–67 (Stadtarch.Cologne); and Hermann Ullmann, "Das Essener Programm," *Deutsche Rundschau* 76, no. 11 (1950), 901–02.

64. Turner, *Stresemann,* pp. 134–35; on the planned purge of the civil service, see H. Müller's statements at the "SPD- Reichstagsfraktions-Sitz.," 30 Nov. 1923, Giebel papers/II/273 (Arch.SD); and Thimme, *Stresemann,* p. 24.

65. See Marx's notes, Marx papers/1070/58/1 (Stadtarch.Cologne); and Albrecht Philipp, *Von Stresemann zu Marx* (Berlin, 1924), p. 28.

66. Central Reich offices of the DVP, *Die Deutschnationalen und wir* (Berlin, 1924), p. 11; and *Hamburger Fremdenblatt,* 29 Nov. 1923.

67. Stresemann to Marx, 28 Nov. 1923, Marx papers/1070/58/2 (Stadtarch.Cologne).

68. "DDP-Fr.Prot.," 4 Nov. 1923 (Schreiber).

69. Ibid., 29 Nov. 1923.

70. See Marx's notes [Nov. 1923], Marx papers/1070/58/1 (Stadtarch.Cologne); and *Nationalliberale Correspondenz,* no. 129, 20 Dec. 1923. Cf. Schulze, *Braun,* p. 436; Thimme, *Stresemann,* p. 28; *Deutschnationale und wir,* p. 11.

71. Cf. Marx's notes on the meeting with Porsch, 29 Nov. 1923; and Marx's notes on a "Landtagsfraktions-Sitz.," Marx papers/1070/58/4–5 (Stadtarch.Cologne); see also Marx to Praschma, 8 Apr. 1925, ibid., 1070/68/39–40.

72. *Deutschnationale und wir,* pp. 10–11; and *Vorwärts,* no. 226 (15 May 1924).

73. "DDP- Fr.Prot.," 29 May 1924; *Vorwärts,* no. 232 (18 May 1924); Paul Moldenhauer, "Politische Erinnerungen," p. 145, Moldenhauer papers/1 (BA); and Turner, *Stresemann,* p. 167.

74. See his confidential memo to Hugenberg, 19 May 1924, Schlange-Schöningen papers/19 (BA).

75. Michael Stürmer, *Koalition und Opposition in der Weimarer Republik 1924–1928*

(Düsseldorf, 1967), p. 46; *Vorwärts,* no. 259 (4 June 1924); Marx's notes, Marx papers/1070/57/12 (Stadtarch.Cologne).

76. *Deutschnationale und wir,* p. 12; and Moldenhauer, "Erinnerungen," p. 146; "DDP-Fr.Prot.," 20 May 1924. See also *SBPrLT 1921–24,* 30 May 1924, vol. 16, col. 22368; and Stürmer, *Koalition* p. 46.

77. *Deutschnationale und wir,* p. 12.

78. Otto Rippel, "Die Deutschnationalen als Regierungspartei," *Politische Praxis,* ed. Walther Lambach (Hamburg, 1926), p. 66.

79. Crown Prince Wilhelm to Freiherr von Hünefeld, 11 Nov. 1924, Hap.Arch./Pol. 3. Incidentally, former Chancellor Cuno agreed (Cuno to Hünefeld, 9 Dec. 1924, in ibid.).

80. Severing, *Lebensweg* 2:14; Marx papers/1070/60/47 (Stadtarch.Cologne).

81. O. Braun, *Weimar,* p. 78; Severing, *Lebensweg* 1:456–57; and Schulze, *Braun,* p. 460.

82. Severing to Campe, 6 Aug. 1924, Severing papers/22/9 (Arch.SD). See also Severing, *Lebensweg* 2:14.

83. In order for the agreements to become effective under German domestic law, a number of constitutional changes were necessary, and those required a three-fourths majority in the Reichstag. Without the votes of at least a portion of the DNVP delegates, the Dawes Plan would remain in unratified agreement.

84. Marx papers/1070/60/72 (Stadtarch.Cologne).

85. See Hergt to Guérard, 29 Aug. 1924; and Guérard's and Lammer's explanation, 23 Oct. 1924, ibid./1070/63/7, 27; Moldenhauer, "Erinnerungen," p. 150; Graf Kanitz (Reich food minister) to Marx, 4 Oct. 1924, Marx papers/1070/63/10–11; Marx's own recollections, ibid./60/72; and the "Erklärung" by Guérard and Lammers, ibid./63/27–29.

86. *Vorwärts,* nos. 407 (29 Aug. 1924) and 512 (30 Oct. 1924); and *DNVP-Bericht Okt. 1924,* p. 3. The latter document is the official report of the German Nationalist representatives on a new set of negotiations in October, to be discussed later, but it contains information on the earlier discussions as well.

87. The word was used by the *Deutsche Zeitung,* 2, and 4 Sept. 1924.

88. See the clear-sighted analysis by Vockel, *Rundschreiben Nr. II des Reichsgeneralsekretariats des Zentrums,* 17 Sept. 1924 (confidential), Marx papers/1070/61 (Stadtarch.Cologne); and Lindeiner-Wildau to Goldacker, 13 Sept. 1924, cited in Stürmer, *Koalition,* p. 287.

89. Moldenhauer, "Erinnerungen," p. 154.

90. *SBPrLT, 1921–24,* 4 and 7 Oct. 1924, vol. 17, cols. 24099–106, 24187–90.

91. *DNVP-Bericht Okt. 1924;* Marx papers/1070/60/75, 63/2–3 (Stadtarch.Cologne). See also Stürmer, *Koalition,* pp. 75–76.

92. *Vorwärts,* no. 582 (10 Dec. 1924); ibid., no. 587 (13 Dec. 1924).

93. Schulze, *Braun,* p. 464; Stürmer, *Koalition,* p. 85.

94. Marx papers/1070/63/4–5 (Stadtarch.Cologne); Stürmer, *Koalition* p. 79.

95. Thimme, *Stresemann,* p. 100.

96. Bernhard Falk, "Aufzeichnungen," p. 176, typescript, BA/Kl.Erw./385.

97. Axel Freiherr von Freytag-Loringhoven, *Deutschnationale Volkspartei* (Berlin, 1931), p. 29.

98. See Severing to Cuno, 14 June 1923, *Ak/Rk Cuno,* no. 188, p. 559. In retrospect it is clear that the Prussians were wrong. Poincaré and the French government were primarily interested in reparation payments, although some influential French politicians did see another chance to establish at least an independent Rhenish state. See the synopsis of the debate in Gerald D. Feldman and Heidrun Homburg, *Industrie und Inflation—Studien und Dokumente zur Politik der deutschen Unternehmer 1916–1923* (Hamburg, 1977), p. 129.

99. See Karl Dietrich Erdmann, *Adenauer in der Rheinlandpolitik nach dem Ersten Weltkrieg* (Stuttgart, 1966), pp. 79–80.

100. See the minutes of a meeting between Hamm and Braun, 30 Apr. 1923; a session of the chancellor with the prime ministers of the states, 1 and 2 May 1923, *Ak/Rk Cuno*, nos. 145, 146, pp. 446, 453; and Max von Stockhausen, *6 Jahre Reichskanzlei*, ed. Walter Görlitz (Bonn, 1954), p. 63. The minister of the interior of the state of Baden even accused the Reichswehr of supporting acts of sabotage. See Remmele to Cuno and Gessler, 15 June and 27 June 1923, O. Braun papers/H/B-2/87 (Forst.Hbg.).

101. On these secret ties, see Severing to Reich Ministry of Economics, 14 June 1923, *Ak/Rk Cuno*, no. 188, pp. 560–62.

102. See the letters from Fröhlich (prime minister of Thuringia) and Braun to Reich chancellor, 5, 7 May 1923, RK 43 I/2730.

103. Cf. notes for a speech by the Reich commissioner in the Ruhr to the prime minister of the states, 12 Jan. 1923, ibid., no. 42, pp. 138–39.

104. See the meeting between Hamm and Braun, 30 Apr. 1923, *Ak/Rk Cuno*, no. 145, p. 446; and Schulze, *Braun*, p. 428. According to Hans J. L. Adolph, *Otto Wels* (Berlin, 1970), p. 210, the executive secretary of the SPD had demanded negotiations as early as January 26.

105. See *SBPrLT 1921–24*, 7 Oct. 1924, vol. 17, col. 24255 (von Campe).

106. The quotation is from Carl von Reibnitz, "Preussen und das Reich," *Sozialistische Monatshefte* 61 (26 Mar. 1924), 170. The Prussian prime minister warned the defense forces not to accept elements that wished to destroy the state; the apparent united front that such a move presented could not justify the danger to the republic that it entailed. See the notes on a meeting between Braun and the Reich press secretary, 30 Apr. 1923, *Ak/Rk Cuno*, no. 145, p. 446.

107. See Hamm's account of the internal security situation, 19 Apr. 1923, ibid., no. 131, pp. 407–10.

108. See, for example, "Sitz.PrStMin.," 10 Apr. 1923, Braun papers/B/A/19a (PrGStAB). Prussian Prime Minister to Reich Commissioner, 11 Jan., 3 and 26 May 1923, *Ak/Rk Cuno*, nos. 40, 143, 173; pp. 131–32, 439, 523.

109. Severing, *Lebensweg* 1:389–91.

110. "Sitz.PrStMin.," 27 March 1923, O. Braun papers/273 (IISG). The cabinet's resolution read, "The actions of the Minister of the Interior are regarded as necessary and justified and [the cabinet] unanimously approves his policies." An abstract of the minutes is in *Ak/Rk Cuno*, no. 108, pp. 334–41.

111. See Severing's marginalia on a copy of the *NL Correspondenz*, no. 26, 28 Mar. 1923, Severing papers/19/109. The *NL Correspondenz* had criticized Prussia's moves, assuming that Prussia had not informed the Reich prior to the action.

112. "Besprechung im RJM," 14 Apr. 1923, *Ak/Rk Cuno*, no. 119, pp. 371–72.

113. Graefe to Cuno, 25 Mar. 1923, ibid., no. 106, pp. 330–32.

114. Ibid., p. 331, n. 5.

115. On the concessions from industry, see Feldman and Homburg, *Industrie*, p. 150.

116. *Ak/Rk Stresemann*, vol. 2, no. 179, pp. 776–80.

117. Braun, *Weimar*, p. 54; Eugen Meyer, *Skizzen aus dem Leben der Weimarer Republik* (Berlin, 1962), p. 35; Luther, *Politker*, p. 179.

118. See Marx's notes, Marx papers/1070/54/44 (Stadtarch.Cologne); Bernhard Falk, "Aufzeichnungen," pp. 158–59, BA/K1. Erw./385; Giebel, "Aufz. über d. SPD Reichstagsfr.-Sitz.," 2 Nov. 1923, Giebel papers/II/268–72 (Arch.SD); Wilhelm Keil, "Notizen über die Fraktionssitzung der SPD-Reichstagsfraktion," 2 Nov. 1923, Keil papers (Arch.SD); "DDP-Fr.Prot.," 11 Sept. 1923; Turner, *Stresemann*, p. 147; Erdmann, *Adenauer*, pp. 127ff.

119. Reich cabinet meeting, 20 Oct. 1923, *AK/RK Stresemann*, vol. 2, no. 156, p. 671. Cf. Erdmann, *Adenauer*, p. 85.

120. The following discussion is based on the "Stenographischen Bericht über die Besprechung mit den Vertretern der bestzten Gebiete in Hagen," PrGStAB/Rep. 90/222. The

report is printed in *AK/RK Stresemann,* vol. 2, no. 179, pp. 761–826. Cf. Hans Luther, *Politiker,* p. 178; and Erdmann, *Adenauer,* pp. 89ff.

121. See "Sitz.PrStMin.," 30 Oct. 1923, PrGStAB/Rep. 90/103;M[ehlich] to Severing, 4 June 1923, Severing papers/79/13 (Arch.SD). See also Feldman and Homburg, *Industrie,* p. 160.

122. Werner Freiherr von Rheinbaben, *Kaiser, Kanzler, Präsidenten—Erinnerungen* (Mainz, 1968), p. 221. Politically Adenauer apparently envisaged an autonomous, demilitarized Rhenish State under British protection to thwart French ambitions in the area. See, Marie-Louise Becker, "Adenauer und die englische Besatzungsmacht (1918–1926)," in *Adenauer,* ed Stehkämper, pp. 11–18.

123. Hirtsiefer to Braun, 30 Nov. 1923, PrGStAB/Rep. 90/222. and Dr. Piesbergen, "Besprechung über die Rheinlandfrage . . . in Heidelberg 22. November [1923]," pp. 4, 6, ibid. The Prussian minister of commerce later admitted that the committee's powers were so broadly stated that it could assume the right to conduct political negotiations. See Ministry of Commerce to Prime Minister, 8 Jan. 1924, PrGStAB/Rep. 90/103.

124. "Sitz.PrStMin.," 30 Oct. 1923, PrGStAB/Rep. 90/103.

125. Haenisch to Severing, 24 Oct. 1924, PrGStAB/Rep. 90/222.

126. Mehlich to Severing, Severing papers/14/32 (Arch.SD).

127. Hirtsiefer to Braun, 30 Nov. 1923, PrGStAB/Rep. 90/222. Prussian Ministry of the Interior to Foreign Office, Prime Minister and Prussian cabinet, 7 Nov. 1923; Richter to Braun, 3 Dec. 1923, ibid.

128. Prussian Ministry of the Interior to Foreign Office et al., 7 Nov. 1923.

129. At the end of November, political leaders from Hessen and Baden met at Heidelberg to discuss the new situation. They concluded that if the Reich and Prussia were in fact to institute the policy of abandonment, other German states would also be free to take matters into their own hands. See "Piesbergen Bericht," 22 Nov. 1923.

130. "Sitz.PrStMin.," 3 Dec. 1923, PrGStAB/Rep. 90/222.

131. For the DVP resolution, see *Die Zeit,* 27 Jan. 1924.

132. See *Ak/Rk Marx,* vol. 1, no. 6, pp. 30–34; and Braun's explanation in *SBPrLT, 1921–24,* 5 Dec. 1923, vol. 14, cols. 20018–23. Cf. Schulze, *Braun,* pp. 339–41.

133. Reich cabinet meeting, 13 Dec. 1923, *Ak/Rk Marx,* vol. 1, nos. 1–5, pp. 1–30. See also Marx papers/1070/54/44 (Stadtarch.Cologne); and Prussian Ministry of Finance to Prime Minister, 8 Jan. 1924, PrGTtAB/Rep. 90/103.

134. Prussian Ministry of the Interior to Prime Minister and Cabinet, 18 Dec. 1923, PrGStAB/Rep. 90/222.

135. Braun to members of the Reich Cabinet and Prussian Cabinet, 28 Jan., and Marx to Braun, 5 Feb. 1924, PrGStAB/Rep. 90/178; and "Sitz.PrStMin.," 18 Mar. 1924, O. Braun papers/B/A/19a (PrGStAB).

136. Freund to Adenauer, 17 Jan. 1924, Severing papers/01/7 (Arch.SD).

137. The discussion that follows is based upon Lohmeyer, "[Denkschrift]," 8 Sept. 1923, O. Braun papers/I/4/3 (Arch.SD); and Gessler to Petersen, 1 Feb. 1924, in Otto Gessler, *Reichswehrpolitik in der Weimarer Zeit* ed. Kurt Sendtner, (Stuttgart, 1958), pp. 495–98. On Lohmeyer, cf. Walther Vogel, *Deutsche Reichsgliederung und Reichsreform in Vergangenheit und Gegenwart* (Leipzig, 1932), p. 172.

138. Severing, *Lebensweg* 2:8.

139. Michael Geyer, "Die Wehrmacht der Deutschen Republik ist die Reichswehr," *Militärgeschichtliche Mitteilungen* 14, no. 22 (1973), 163.

140. On Braun's and von Richter's views, see "Sitz.PrStMin.," 3 Dec. 1923 and 4 Mar. 1924, O. Braun papers/281, 285 (IISG). Cf. Schulze, *Braun,* p. 452; the Center party's position is found in Gerhard Senger, *Die Politik der Deutschen Zentrumspartei zur Frage Reich und Länder von 1918–1928* (Hamburg, 1932), p. 77.

141. "Sitz.PrStMin.," 21 Oct. 1924, Braun papers/B/A/19a (PrGStAB).

142. Cf. *SBPrLT 1921–24*, 24 Sept., 1 Oct., 3 Oct., 10 Oct. 1924, vol. 17, cols. 23591–96, 23886–900, 24012–32, 24480–506. See also the criticism of Boelitz's personnel policies in *Vorwärts*, no. 574 (5 Dec. 1924); O. Braun to Marx, 9 Nov. 1924, and Marx to Braun, 15 Nov. 1924, O. Braun papers/570 (IISG); O. Braun, *Weimar*, pp. 73–74; Schulze, *Braun*, p. 459.

143. See Südekum to State Secretary Walther, Nov. 10, 1924, in Südekum papers/101/II (BA).

144. See Grzesinski's handwritten coalition calculations (not dated, but written after 7 Dec. 1924), Grzesinski papers/1286 (IISG). See also Severing, *Lebensweg* 2:36; *Vorwärts*, no. 681 (10 Dec. 1924).

145. *Vorwärts*, no. 607 (25 Dec. 1924).

146. The resignation of Dominicus and other right-wing members from the party strengthened the DDP's willingness to work with the SPD. See Werner Schneider, *Die Deutsche Demokratische Partei in der Weimarer Republik 1924–1930* (Munich, 1978), p. 85; on the question of the Economics party joining the coalition, see "DDP-Fr.Prot.," 5, 6, 7, 14 Jan. 1925. See also Marx papers/1070/60/78 (Stadtarch.Cologne).

147. Johann Victor Bredt, *Erinnerungen und Dokumente*, ed. Martin Schumacher (Düsseldorf, 1970), pp. 188, 345–46; and Martin Schumacher, *Mittelstandsfront und Republik* (Düsseldorf, 1972), p. 118.

148. Braun, "Weimar MS," pp. 265–66.

149. *Vorwärts*, no. 7 (5 Jan. 1925).

150. One day before there was still no crisis atmosphere in the cabinet. The only point on the agenda of the cabinet meeting was a set of instructions for the Prussian delegate to a conference on interstate waterways in Heidelberg. See O. Braun papers/B/A/19a (PrGStAB).

151. *Was wir deutschen Männern und Frauen vor dem 7. Dezember sagen müssen* (DNVP pamphlet no. 185, Berlin, 1924), p. 5; and Karl Hans Kickhöffel, *Das System Severing* (DNVP pamphlet no. 184, Berlin, 1924), pp. 38–41.

152. When Herold suggested this on 5 January, von Campe replied that the DVP was "not opposed." See Grzesinski's notes, Grzesinski papers/1286 (IISG). Cf. Richter's almost passionate statements in *SBPrLT, 1925–28*, 5 Jan. 1928, vol. 1, cols. 1582–83.

153. When Braun expressed the hope that the grand coalition would soon return at a meeting of the multipartisan committee two leading DVP members, Stendel and Schwarzhaupt, but not von Campe, "violently shook their heads." See Grzesinski's notes, Grzesinski papers/1286 (IISG).

154. The SPD's *Vorwärts*, no. 100 (28 Feb. 1925), registered the phenomenon with approval.

155. See Schreiber's comment at the session of DDP's Landtag delegation, 5 Jan. 1925, "The People's Party wants to destroy the grand coalition" ("DDP-Fr.Prot.," 5 Jan. 1925). The precedent of 1919 did not support the DVP's position. In March 1919, the government decided, "The cabinet will not resign before the Constitutional Convention has met." "Sitz.PrGStMin.," 23 Mar. 1919, Braun papers/B/A/19a (PrGStAB).

156. Neither felt comfortable with the decision. In their final statements to the cabinet, the DVP ministers stressed their appreciation of the collegial cooperation within the government, and underscored that their resignation in no way represented a disavowal of the policies pursued by the grand coalition in the last three years. See "Sitz.PrStMin.," 6 Jan. 1925, RK 43 I/2286 (BA); and the statement released by the official Prussian press service, 6 Jan. 1925, Marx papers/1070/67/3–4 (Stadtarch.Cologne). Cf. Severing, *Lebensweg* 2:39–40.

157. The quotation is taken from a letter from Braun to Kuttner, cited in Erich Kuttner, *Otto Braun* (Berlin, 1932), p. 86.

158. The DVP knew that the Prussian SPD was more than willing to revive the grand

coalition at this time. See Carl Severing, "Für die Grosse Koalition," *Sozialistische Monatshefte* 62 (5 Jan. 1925), 1–2.

159. That von Campe had some such scenario in mind was confirmed indirectly in a conversation between the district director of Lüneburg, Krüger (SPD) and a DVP member of the Landtag, Rose, See Krüger to Severing, 18 Oct. 1925, Severing papers/25/16 (Arch.SD).

160. *SBPrLT 1925–28*, 14 Jan. 1925, vol. 1, cols. 79, 92.

161. Ibid., 23 Jan. 1925, col. 398.

162. Grzesinski to Tejessy, 24 Jan. 1925, Grzesinski papers/322 (IISG); and *Die Zeit*, 24 Jan. 1925; *SBPrLT 1925–28*, 23 Jan. 1925, vol. 1, col. 378. The leader of the Center party, Herold, who was suspected of wanting to form a government with the DNVP, declared afterwards that he had missed the vote by mistake. He emphasized that he would have voted against the vote of no confidence. See ibid., 30 Jan. 1925, vol. 1, cols. 415–16.

163. Braun's claims that he urged the cabinet's resignation (*Vorwärts*, no. 42 [25 Jan. 1925]) does not seem to be accurate. See Grzesinski to Tejessy, 24 Jan. 1925, Grzesinski papers/322 (ISSG).

164. *Kreuzzeitung*, 24 Jan. 1925; *Vorwärts*, no. 46 (28 Jan. 1925); Leber, *Mann*, p. 37 (24 Jan. 1925).

165. Grzesinski to Tejessy, 2 Feb. 1925, Grzesinski papers/322 (IISG); *Vorwärts*, no. 61 (5 Feb. 1925).

166. Braun suffered a collapse (Schulze, *Braun*, pp. 469–70); Severing was close to a nervous breakdown (Severing to Grassmann, 28 Jan. 1925, Severing papers/25/6 (IISG): Grzesinski to Tejessy, 2 Feb. 1925; and Severing to Braun 5 Feb. 1925, Braun papers/I/1/3 (Arch.SD).

167. Grzesinski to Tejessy, 2 Feb. 1925; *Vorwärts*, no. 61 (5 Feb. 1925).

168. Horion to Marx and Hess, 31 Jan. 1925, Marx papers/1070/67/17–21 (Stadtarch.Cologne); and *SBPrLT 1921–24*, 6 Oct. 1924, vol. 17, col. 24188 (Hess); Marx papers/1070/66/1–2, 71 (Stadtarch.Cologne).

169. See Stegerwald to Marx, 8 Feb. 1925, ibid./23.

170. Ibid./1–2; *SBPrLT 1925–28*, 18 Feb. 1925, vol. 1, col. 518 (Waentig).

171. Grzesinski to Tejessy, 12 Feb. 1925, and Grzesinski's handwritten notes, Grzesinski papers/322, 1286 (IISG); see also Haenisch to Severing, 1 Apr. 1925, Severing papers/25/8 (Arch.SD); Marx papers/1070/66/2, 8–10 (Stadtarch.Cologne); *Vorwärts*, no. 70 (11 Feb. 1925). See also the outcome of a discussion between Hess, Grzesinski, Göhre, and Schreiber, n.d., Grzesinski papers/1286 (IISG); and Severing, *Lebensweg* 2:41.

172. Marx papers/1070/66/8–10 (Stadtarch.Cologne); *SBPrLT 1925–28*, 2 Apr. 1925, vol. 1, col. 1346 (v.d. Osten).

173. Von Campe later criticized Marx for giving up too soon. The DVP leader was convinced the DNVP's hard-line position was only its opening gambit and not meant as a final position. *SBPrLT, 1925–28*, 18 and 19 Feb. 1925, vol. 1, col. 522 (von Campe), cols. 563–65 (Marx), col. 567 (Schlange-Schöningen), cols. 610–11 (von Campe).

174. The preliminary list of ministers contained the following names: Hirtsiefer (Economics), Steiger (Agriculture), am Zehnhoff (Justice), all from the Center party; Severing (Interior), SPD; Dr. Schreiber (Commerce), and Höpker-Aschoff (Finance), both DDP. The state secretary in the Education Ministry, Becker, who did not belong to any party, was named minister of education. See *SBPrLT, 1925–28*, 18 Feb 1925. vol. 1, cols. 504–05 (Marx). On the policy declaration, see "DDP-Fr.Prot.," 18 Feb. 1925 (Schmiljan); the declaration itself is in *SBPrLT, 1925–28*, 18 Feb. 1925, vol. 1, cols. 504–13.

175. *Vorwärts*, no. 80 (17 Feb. 1925).

176. See Hanns-Jochen Hauss, *Die erste Volkswahl des deutschen Reichspräsidenten* (Kallmünz, Opf., 1965) for a detailed analysis of the 1925 election.

177. See "Erste vorbereitende Sitzung zur Präsidentenwahl . . . ," 12 Feb. 1925, Hap.Arch./ReiPrä 25.

178. Hauss, *Volkswahl*, p. 43; *Vorwärts*, no. 118 (11 Mar. 1925).

179. "Erste Sitzung," 12 Feb. 1925.

180. Hauss, *Volkswahl*, p. 43.

181. Hellpach, *Wirken* 2:254–64, 269; Georg Schreiber, "Innenpolitik des Reiches," *Politisches Jahrbuch* 1 (1925), 50.

182. On the negotiations of the two parties, see Thimme, *Stresemann*, pp. 109–10; Hauss, *Volkswahl*, pp. 41ff.; Bredt, *Erinnerungen*, pp. 38–39.

183. Braun, *Weimar*, p. 83; Hauss, *Volkswahl*, p. 57; and Hartmut Schustereit, *Linksliberalismus und Sozialdemokratie in der Weimarer Republik* (Düsseldorf, 1975), pp. 107–08.

184. Typical was Julius Leber's attempt to classify the supporters of Jarres and Braun: "The black-white-red groups will march for Jarres. The workers' battalions will parade for Braun" (Leber, *Weg*, p. 38).

185. Detailed results in Hauss, *Volkswahl*, p. 74.

186. On the potential breach between the Catholics and Conservatives, see Karl Holl, "Konfessionalität, Konfessionalismus und demokratische Republik—Zu einigen Aspekten der Reichspräsidentenwahl von 1925." *Vierteljahrshefte für Zeitgeschichte* 17 (July 1969), 259, the possibility of a coalition government is discussed in Praschma to Marx, 2 Apr. 1925, Marx papers/1070/68/37–38 (Stadtarch, Cologne); and Walther Graef, "Der Werdegang der Deutschnationalen Volkspartei," in *Der nationale Wille*, ed. Max Weiss, (Berlin, 1928), p. 47.

187. Marx papers/1070/67/86–89 (Stadtarch.Cologne); *Vorwärts*, nos. 145, 148 (26 and 28 Mar. 1925). Cf. complaints by the DNVP, *SBPrLT, 1925–28,* 2 Apr. 1925, vol. 1, cols. 1338–40.

188. Heinrich Brüning, always ready to see conspiracies around him, suspected that the Center party's nomination of Marx in the first round had involved a secret deal with the SPD. See Brüning to Gessler, 31 Jan. 1955 (Gessler, *Reichswehr*, pp. 507–08). It was also noteworthy that in his campaign Braun had been very sparing in his criticism of Marx. See Hauss, *Volkswahl*, p. 72; and Schustereit, *Linksliberalismus*, p. 110.

189. "DDP-Fr.Prot.," 31 Mar. 1925; and Werner Stephan, *Aufstieg und Verfall des Linksliberalismus 1918–1933* (Göttingen, 1973), pp. 282–83.

190. Bredt, *Erinnerungen*, pp. 178–79.

191. See Cuno to Angerpointner (BVP), 21 Apr. 1925, and Cuno to Jarres, 22 Apr. 1925, Hap.Arch./ReiPrä 25.

192. Praschma to Marx, 2 Apr. 1925, Marx papers/1070/68/37–38 (Stadtarch.Cologne); Leber, *Weg*, p. 39 (entry for 7 Apr. 1925); and Hauss, *Volkswahl*, pp. 127–29, 275.

193. See Marx, "Bemerkenswertes aus dem Wahlkampf," n.d., Marx papers/1070/68/1–3. (The account is published in Hauss, *Volkswahl*, pp. 180–81.) See also ibid., p. 129.

194. A detailed analysis of the election results is in Hauss, *Volkswahl*, pp. 135ff.

195. *Vorwärts*, nos. 113, 116 (7, and 10 Mar. 1925); see also "DDP-Fr.Prot.," 10 Mar. 1925; Winckler to Marx, 13 Mar. 1925, Marx papers/1070/67/65 (Stadtarch.Cologne).

196. Marx to Praschma, 8 Apr. 1925, ibid./68/39–40.

197. *SBPrLT 1925–28,* 31 Mar. 1925, vol. 1, col. 1240.

198. The Center party's opposition to Braun is seen in Grzesinski to Scheidemann, 4 Apr. 1925, cited in Grzesinski, "Kampf," pp. 154–55.

199. *Vorwärts*, no. 156 (2 Apr. 1925); Grzesinski, "Kampf," p. 151; and "DDP-Fr.Prot.," 3 Apr. 1925.

200. Grzesinski, "Kampf," p. 151, *SBPrLT 1925–28,* 3 Apr. and 13 May 1925, vol. 1, cols. 1423–25, vol. 2, col. 1895; see also *Vorwärts*, no. 158 (2 Apr. 1925).

201. Grzesinski to Scheidemann, 4 Apr. 1925, Grzesinski papers/146 (IISG). See also Grzesinski, "Kampf," p. 151.

202. *SBPrLT 1925–28*, vol. 1, col. 1380.

203. Severing, "Der 2. Wahlgang," *Sozialistische Monatshefte* 62 (14 Apr. 1925), 198; and *Vorwärts*, no. 159 (3 Apr. 1925).

204. See *Mitteilungsblatt zur Vorbereitung der Reichspräsidentenwahl*, nos. 7, 8 [*sic*] (25 Mar. 1925).

205. Marx to Praschma, 8 Apr. 1925, Marx papers/1070/68/39–40 (Stadtarch.Cologne). See also Ernest Hamburger, "Betrachtungen über Heinrich Brünings Memoiren," *Internationale Wissenschaftliche Korrespondenz*, no. 15 (Apr. 1972), p. 27, n. 24.

206. Max Cohen-Reuss, "Deutsche und preussische Regierungsprobleme," *Sozialistische Monatshefte* 62 (2 Mar. 1925), 138.

207. *SBPrLT 1925–28*, 29 Apr. 1925, vol. 1, cols. 1557–58. Grzesinski expected that new elections would be held in the fall at the latest, but felt that mid-June was more likely (see Grzesinski to Tejessy, 27 Apr. 1925). Heilmann agreed (*SBPrLT, 1925–28*, 29 Apr. 1925, vol. 1, cols. 1529–30).

208. Ibid., col. 1558.

209. "DDP-Fr.Prot.," 8 May 1925.

210. *SBPrLT 1925–28*, 28 Apr. 1925, vol. 1, cols. 1467–70.

211. Hess emphasized that the Center party solidly supported Braun; "No one can doubt that," ibid., 29 Apr. 1925, vol. 1, col. 1488.

212. Ibid., cols. 1557–58.

213. See the results of the roll-call vote in ibid., 8 May 1925, vol. 2, cols. 1669–74. Of the two earlier renegades in the Center party, Loenartz voted for the cabinet, and Papen was excused because of illness.

Chapter 7. Personnel, Security, and Administrative Policies, 1922–1925

1. Paul Moldenhauer, "Politische Erinnerungen," manuscript, p. 18, Moldenhauer papers/1 (BA).

2. Carl Severing, *Mein Lebensweg* (Cologne, 1950), 1:336.

3. See Wolfgang Runge, *Politik und Beamtentum im Parteienstaat—Die Demokratisierung der politischen Beamten in Preussen zwischen 1918 und 1933* (Stuttgart, 1965), p. 203; State Commission for Public Safety to Ministry of the Interior, Reich Commissioner et al., 16 Mar. 1922, RK 43 I/676 (BA); and Ferdinand Friedensburg, *Lebenserinnerungen* (Frankfurt, 1969), 1:109ff. See also the articles on the conflict surrounding the removal from office of the East Prussian Landräte Auwers and Braun, *Königsberger Hartungsche Zeitung*, 14 Dec. 1922.

4. Runge, *Politik*, pp. 142, 235–37.

5. Severing changed Dominicus's blanket rule against Communist state and local civil servants to a case-by-case review policy (Ministry of the Interior to provincial governors and district directors, 8 Dec. 1921, NSStAH/122a/IX/2f). See also Severing, *Lebensweg* 1:337. In April 1922 the Reich Supreme Court rejected a suit against a cabinet decree of 15 Dec. 1920, which, it will be recalled, had reduced the mandatory retirement age for civil servants to sixty-five and for judges to sixty-eight.

6. See Severing, *Lebensweg* 1:336.

7. Runge, *Politik*, p. 197. Cf. the criticism of Freund in the *Kreuzzeitung*, 2 June 1922.

8. "Die Personalpolitik in Preussen," *Der Tag*, 1 June 1922. The unnamed author was identified only as "a member of the Prussian parliament," but Severing took the piece seriously enough to place a copy of the article in his personal papers. See Severing papers/85/7 (Arch.SD).

Cf. Arnold Brecht, *Aus nächster Nähe—Lebenserinnerungen 1884–1927* (Stuttgart, 1966), p. 315.

9. Werner Becker, *Demokratie des sozialen Rechts* (Göttingen, 1971), p. 90; Brecht, *Nähe*, p. 364; and "Sitz.PrStMin.," 17 Oct. 1922, Braun papers/B/A/19a (PrGStAB).

10. Hess and Herms to SPD executive committee, 7 Dec. 1921, Zentralrat-Archiv/B-41/1/B; "Severing werde hart!" *Der freie Beamte* 3 (11 Mar. 1922).

11. SPD executive committee of the Berlin district to Paul Herms, 15 Dec. 1921, Zentralrat-Archiv/B-41/1.

12. See Severing to Oeser, 8 Jan. 1922, Severing papers/80/66. Cf. Hans Peter Ehni, "Zum Parteienverhältnis in Preussen 1918–1932," *Archiv für Sozialgeschichte* 11 (1971), 252.

13. Grzesinski, "Kampf."

14. See Fritz Rathenau, "Als Jude im Dienste von Reich und Staat," typescript, p. 97 (LBI).

15. For example, the government prohibited all reunions of regimental veterans organizations, since experience had shown these often turned into antigovernment demonstrations. At the same time the cabinet remained mindful of civil rights and sentimental concerns. It refused to prohibit visits to the grave of the former empress (see Felix Stössinger to Severing, 28 June 1922 and Severing to Stössinger, 30 June 1922, Severing papers/13/21 (Arch.SD). Cf. the decree of the Ministry of the Interior, 15 July 1922, *Ministerialblatt für die preussische Verwaltung* 83 (12 July 1922), cols. 663–64.

16. Erich Kuttner, *Otto Braun* (Berlin [1932]), p. 80; and Severing, *Lebensweg* 1:352–53.

17. Rathenau, "Jude," p. 53.

18. Adam Remmele, *Staatsumwälzung und Neuaufbau in Baden* (Karlsruhe, 1925), p. 129.

19. Runge, *Politik*, p. 142.

20. See Curt Rosenberg, "Schutz der republikanischen Staatsverfassung," *Sozialistische Monatshefte* 62 (31 Oct. 1921), 944–48; and Braun's statements in "Chefbesprechung," 29 June 1922, Ak/Rk Wirth, vol. 2, nos. 304, 920.

21. See Erich Kuttner, *Warum versagt die Justiz?* ([Berlin] 1921), p. 17; and Junius, "Politische Chronik," *Neue Rundschau* 33 (1922), 220.

22. See Kuttner, *Justiz*, p. 96; *Vorwärts*, nos. 12, 39, 45 (7, 24, and 27 Jan. 1922); Erich Wende, *C. H. Becker* (Stuttgart, 1959), p. 130; and "Sitz.PrStMin.," 7 Nov. 1922, O. Braun papers/269 (IISG).

23. *PrGS* (no. 32, 1922), 207–08, (no. 1, 1923), 1. See also *SBPrLT 1925–28*, 23 Oct. 1925, vol. 4, cols. 5150–51 (Heilmann).

24. A small but telling sign: the director of the State Bureau of Engraving reported a flood of orders for new rubber stamps with Republican insignia in the summer of 1922. See decree of 19 July 1922, LASH/301/3161. Cost-conscious as always, the post-1918 governments had permitted use of the rubber stamps with royal insignia until they were worn out.

25. See A. Braun to Kautsky, 14 Feb. 1923, Kautsky papers/D-VI/40 (IISG).

26. Gerhard Schulz, *Zwischen Demokratie und Diktatur* (Berlin, 1963), p. 318; and Runge, *Politik*, p. 142. The attempt to avoid partisan attacks extended to the parties as well. See *Der Preussische Landtag 1921–1924*, ed. Paul Hirsch (Berlin [1924]), p. 59.

27. Ministry of the Interior to provincial governors in Hanover and Kassel, 17 Apr. 1923, NSStAH/122a/IX/2f; and Severing to Schulz, 28 Mar. 1923, Severing papers/14/22 (Arch. SD).

28. "Sitz.PrStMin.," 18 Feb. 1923, O. Braun papers/272 (IISG).

29. "Sitz.PrStMin.," 24 July 1923, O. Braun papers/B/A/19a (PrGStAB).

30. See, for example, Richter to Severing, 13 Aug. 1923, and Severing to Richter, 20 Aug. 1923, Severing papers/20/180–81 (Arch.SD).

31. Siehr to Severing, 9 Nov. 1925, ibid./23/75. Three years later Ferdinand Friedensburg became deputy police chief in Berlin. For Friedensburg's own account of the difficulties that faced him in East Prussia, see his *Lebenserinnerungen*.

32. Christian Engeli, *Gustav Böss* (Berlin, 1971), p. 67.

33. See "Sitz.PrStMin.," 6 Nov. 1923, PrGStAB, Rep. 90/739.

34. Cutbacks are described in Minister of Finance to Prime Minister and Cabinet, 27 Nov. 1923 and the related documentation, Grzesinski papers/773 (IISG). On the cabinet's lack of new programs, see Constantin Stein, "Verwaltungsbericht des Preussischen Landkreistages für das Jahr 1922/23," in *Die deutschen Landkreise,* ed. Constantin Stein and Erwin Stein (Berlin-Friedenau, 1926), 2:273.

35. See the circular of the civil servants' organization of Liegnitz (Silesia) to the provincial governors and district directors, 27 Feb. 1924, LASH/301/4410.

36. Cf. Reich Ministry of Finance, "Entwurf: Beschluss der Reichsregierung vom 10. Oktober 1923," Grzesinski papers/775 (IISG). On the strong position of the Ministry of Finance in the post-1918 period, see Hans-Peter Ehni, *Bollwerk Preussen?* (Bonn–Bad Godesberg, 1975), p. 36.

37. "Sitz.PrStMin.," 16 Oct. 1923, O. Braun papers/276 (IISG). See also minister of finance to prime minister et al., 23 Oct. 1923, LASH/301/4410; and the documents in Grzesinski papers/773 (IISG). Severing had originally objected to granting Richter plenipotentiary powers, but a majority of the cabinet, including Otto Braun, sided with Richter (Severing to cabinet, 13 Nov. 1923, PrGStAB, Rep. 90/739).

38. On the minister of finance's discretionary powers in carrying out personnel reduction decisions see, "Sitz.PrStMin.," 4 Jan. 1924, Braun papers/B/A/19a (PrGStAB).

39. See the "Notiz über eine Besprechung d. MdF, OPrä u. RPrä," 18 Feb. 1924, LASH/309/19370.

40. See the documentation in ibid./301/4410; Severing to Stendel, 22 Jan. [1924]; and "Notiz d. Amtl. Preuss. Pressedientes," 12 Feb. 1924, Severing papers/23/60, 74 (Arch.SD).

41. Cf. the documentation in Grzesinski papers/771–77 (IISG); and PrGStAB, Rep. 90/739, 790.

42. See "Sitz.PrStMin.," 6 Nov. 1923, PrGStAB/Rep. 90/739; "Sitz.PrStMin.," 14 Nov. 1923, O. Braun papers/279 (IISG).

43. Ministry of Finance, "Verordnung," 21 Feb. 1924, LASH/301/4410. Cf. Runge, *Politik,* p. 145.

44. "Sitz.PrStMin." 8 Jan. 1924, O. Braun papers/283 (IISG).

45. Cf. the documentation in LASH/309/19370; Grzesinski to Otto Ziska (of the metal workers' union), 12 Mar. 1924, Grzesinski papers/667 (IISG).

46. The figures are based on "Zusammenstellung der Ergebnisse des Abbaus nach dem Stande am 1.5.1924," sent to the Committee for Reduction of the Civil Service of the Landtag by the Ministry of Finance, 8 July 1924, Grezinski papers/774 (IISG).

47. Wende, *Becker,* p. 215.

48. Reinhold Schoenlank to Bruno Schoenlank, 31 Aug. 1931, Schoenlank papers (LBI).

49. Severing to Grassmann, 28 Jan. 1925, Severing papers/25/61 (Arch.SD).

50. As an example, see the evaluation of the Landräte in the district of Schleswig (district director of Schleswig, "Verzeichnis der Landräte," 21 Jan. 1924, LASH/301/4410).

51. Wende, *Becker,* p. 215; and Grzesinski to Lüdemann, 25 Apr. 1924, Grzesinski papers/770 (IISG). Cf. Prussian Ministry of Finance to Reich Ministry of Finance, 15 July 1922, PrGStAB, Rep. 90/739.

52. Wende, *Becker,* p. 215.

53. "Sitz.PrStMin.," 24 July 1924, O. Braun papers/286 (IISG).

54. Cited in Adolf Gottwald, *Ziele und Erfolge der Zentrumsfraktion des Preussischen Landtages 1921/1924* (Berlin, 1924), pp. 18–20.

55. Runge, *Politik,* p. 85.

56. Severing to G. Trittel, 26 June 1924, Severing papers/22/21 (Arch.SD).

57. Runge, *Politik,* pp. 144–45.

58. *SBPrLT 1921–24,* 28 May 1924, vol. 16, cols. 22281–82 (Heilmann). Cf. Severing's attack on the KPD, ibid., 4 July 1924, cols. 23128–32; and Baumhoff's (DVP) criticism of the DNVP, ibid., 24 Sept. 1924, vol. 17, cols. 23597–602. For a different point of view, see Hans-Karl Behrend, "Zur Personalpolitik des Preussischen Ministeriums des Innern," *Jahrbuch für die Geschichte Mittel-und Ostdeutschlands* 6 (1957), 178.

59. See the draft of the letter of the SPD Landtag delegation, 16 Feb. 1925, Grzesinski papers/1284 (IISG). and Heilmann to Marx, 16 Feb. 1925, Marx papers/1070/67/28 (Stadtarch.Cologne). See also ibid./66/8–10.

60. See "Besprechung des Reichskanzlers mit Vertretern der Länder," 4 Apr. 1922; and "Chefbesprechung," 3 July 1922, *Ak/Rk Wirth,* vol. 2, nos. 239, 309, pp. 666, n. 2, 669, n. 9, 932.

61. The best survey and analysis of the problem is James Diehl, *Paramilitary Politics in Weimar Germany* (Bloomington, Ind., 1977).

62. See Buck (Prime Minister of Saxony) to Reich Chancellor, 4 Jan. 1923, Ak/Rk Cuno, no. 35, p. 118.

63. See Georg Bernhard to Severing, 20 Mar. 1922, the memorandum of 18 Mar. 1922 included in this letter, and Severing to Jänicken, 17 Nov. 1921, Severing papers/81/76, 79 (Arch.SD).

64. Severing to Mehlich, 29 Mar. 1923, Höpker-Aschoff to Severing, 21 July 1923, Severing to Höpker-Aschoff, 29 Aug. 1923, and Severing to Brentano (Minister of the Interior of Hessen), 17 Sept. 1923, ibid./20/150, 19/123.

65. "Sitz.PrStMin.," 27 Mar. 1923, RK 43 I/2286.

66. Ibid.; and Severings' interview with the newspaper *Svenska Dagbladet,* 5 Apr. 1923, Severing papers/21/189 (Arch.SD).

67. Severing to Gessler, 20 Dec. 1922, O. Braun papers/500 (IISG); Severing to Gessler, 5 Jan. 1923, O. Braun papers/I/1/3 (Arch.SD). See also Otto Gessler, *Reichswehrpolitik in der Weimarer Zeit,* ed. Kurt Sendtner (Stuttgart, 1958), p. 240.

68. Braun to Ebert, 24 Aug. 1922, O. Braun papers/492 (IISG); and Reich Ministry of Defense to Reich Chancellor, 6 Apr. 1923, *Ak/Rk Cuno,* no. 117, p. 368.

69. Seeckt to Severing, 19 Aug. 1922, Severing papers/01/98 (Arch.SD). See also Severing, *Lebensweg* 1:365–66.

70. *Ak/Rk Cuno,* no. 61, pp. 207–08. See also Abegg's testimony before a Reichstag investigating committee, 8 July 1927, Severing papers/78/46 (Arch.SD).

71. Severing, *Lebensweg* 2:117; Gustav Adolf Caspar, *Die sozialdemokratische Partei und das deutsche Wehrproblem in den Jahren der Weimarer Republik* (Frankfurt a.M., 1959) p. 42. Cf. also Gessler's criticism of the Prussian policies, Gessler to Cuno, 6 Apr. 1923, *Ak/Rk Cuno,* no. 117, pp. 368–69.

72. Severing to Hamm, 8 June 1923, *Ak/Rk Cuno,* no. 184, pp. 550–51. Some high-ranking Reichswehr officers called upon both the regular army and the paramilitary organizations to be ready for an "inevitable" armed conflict with France. See the report by Colonel von Stülpnagel cited in Bruno Thoss, *Der Ludendorff-Kreis 1919–1923* (Munich, 1978), p. 269.

73. See Höpker-Aschoff to Severing, 21 July 1923, Severing papers/20/149 (Arch.SD). As strange as it may sound, a dictatorship of Seeckt and Severing was regarded as a matter of course by many. See Waldemar Schütze (a high official in the Prussian Ministry of the Interior) to retired State Secretary Zimmermann, 25 Feb. 1923, RK 43 I/676.

74. Severing to Gessler, 9 May 1923, Ak/Rk Cuno, no. 155, p. 489; and Severing to Gessler, 14 June 1923, Severing papers/19/125 (Arch.SD). Other state governments were also

concerned about this relationship. See Prime Minister of Baden to Cuno, 23 Feb. 1923, *Ak/Rk Cuno,* no. 81, p. 270; and Lipinski's statements at the "SPD Reichstagsfraktionssitz.," 27 Feb. 1923, Giebel papers/II/226 (Arch.SD).

75. Severing, *Lebensweg* 1:385–86. See also Severing to Mehlich, 29 Mar. 1923, Severing papers/19/120 (Arch.SD).

76. Severing to Gessler, 14 June 1923, *Ak/Rk Cuno,* no. 188, pp. 562ff. See also Caspar, *Wehrproblem,* p. 41.

77. See "Besprechung," 27 May 1923, *Ak/Rk Cuno,* no. 170, p. 517; and Gessler to Cuno, 6 Apr. 1923, ibid., no. 117, pp. 368–69.

78. The constitutional debate is noted in Severing to Gessler, 23 Apr. 1923, Severing papers/19/124 (Arch.SD).

79. Severing to Gessler, 14 June 1923, ibid.

80. See Abegg's statements to a Reichstag investigating committee, 8 July 1927, ibid./78/46.

81. Outside the cabinet room, especially among some DVP leaders, the decision was more controversial. See Josef Buchorn's article in the *Hannoverscher Kurier,* 6 Apr. 1923; Severing to Buchorn, 13 Apr. 1923, Severing papers/21/196 (Arch.SD); *Die Zeit,* nos. 119, 124 (26 May and 1 June 1923); and Garnich's statements at the "DVP-Mitgliedervers.," 29 June 1923, Severing papers/19/143 (Arch.SD); Boelitz to Becker, 23 June 1923, Becker papers, Korr. (PrGStAB). See also the exchange of letters between Severing and von Campe, Severing, *Lebensweg* 1:421–22; and the "Sitz.PrStMin.," 17 Apr. 1923, O. Braun papers/B/A/19a (PrGStAB). The dissolution order is found in "Sitz.PrStMin.," 27 Mar. 1923, O. Braun papers/273 (IISG). An excerpt of the minutes is in *Ak/Rk Cuno,* no. 108, pp. 334–41.

82. Oeser to State Secretary of the Reich Chancellory, 7 Oct. 1923, RK 43 I/677.

83. On the role of the Rossbach Organization in the rightist conspiratorial circles, see Thoss, *Ludendorff,* pp. 276ff.

84. See "Sitz.PrStMin.," 27 Mar. 1923; and the documentation, O. Braun papers/I/3 (Arch.SD); *Ak/Rk Cuno,* no. 105, pp. 328–29. See also Thoss, *Ludendorff,* pp. 283–84.

85. "Sitz.PrStMin.," 27 Mar. 1923 (IISG).

86. Rossbach contended that both Cuno and Seeckt were fully aware of his intentions. Rossbach also had to admit, however, that the chancellor acted "reserved and disinterested" toward him, while Seeckt refused to receive the lieutenant. See "Bericht eines Rittmeisters im 14. Reiterregiment," 21 Mar. 1923, Severing papers/18/92 (Arch.SD); and Rossbach to Cuno, 15 June 1923, *Ak/Rk Cuno,* no. 190, pp. 570–72. See also ibid. p. 331, n. 5.

87. Severing papers/14/34 (Arch.SD).

88. Severing, *Lebensweg* 2:129–30.

89. The Prussian cabinet attempted—unsuccessfully—to convince the Reich authorities to lift the decree earlier. See, "Sitz.PrStMin.," 20 Nov. 1923, O. Braun papers/280 (IISG); and Severing to Noske, 30 Nov. 1923, Severing papers/20/166 (Arch.SD). It might also be noted that in implementing the national state of emergency for its own territory, Prussia attempted to follow as far as possible the spirit of the constitution. Before issuing its decrees, for example, the cabinet consulted with the executive committee *(Ständiger Ausschuss)* of the Landtag. See Gottwald, *Ziele,* p. 14.

90. See "Verordnung des Reichspräsidenten," 8 Mar. 1924, LASH/301/5646.

91. Severing to Senator Sense (Hamburg), 12 Oct. 1923, Severing papers/20/175 (Arch.SD); Prussian Ministry of the Interior to district director of Schleswig, 21 Jan. 1924, LASH/301/5646. Cf. Friedrich Stampfer, *Die vierzehn Jahre der ersten deutschen Republik,* 3d ed. (Hamburg, 1953), p. 361; and Hagen Schulze, *Otto Braun* (Frankfurt a.M., 1977), p. 455.

92. "Sitz.PrStMin.," 9 Nov. 1923, O. Braun papers/278 (IISG); Severing, *Lebensweg* 1:447. Cf. Severing's handwritten note on Chrispien's letter to Severing, 15 Dec. 1923: "exemplary work by the police" (Severing papers/01/28 [Arch.SD]).

93. See the documents in Severing papers/20 (Arch.SD).

94. See "Sitz.PrStMin.," 10 Oct. 1923, O. Braun papers/B/A/19a (PrGStAB); and 20 Nov. 1923, O. Braun papers/280 (IISG). See also Severing, *Lebensweg* 1:442.

95. J. Kleinmeyer (SPD Reichstag delegate), "Preussische Verwaltungsprobleme im vierten Jahr der Republik," *Neue Zeit* 40 (17 Mar. 1922), 593.

96. See "Sitz.PrStMin.," 2 Oct. 1924, O. Braun papers/287 (IISG); and Engeli, *Böss,* pp. 175–76, 204–05.

97. See Paul Franken, "Die neue preussische Städteordnung," *Unser Weg 4* (15 July 1922), 274–77; and SPD, *Pr. Landtag 1921–24,* pp. 93- 99.

98. See the documentation on a meeting between Hess, Grzesinski, Göhre, and Schreiber, n.d., Grzesinski papers/286 (IISG).

99. See the draft in LASH/301/4949.

100. See, for example, the commentary by the district director of Schleswig to the provincial governor of Schleswig-Holstein, 31 May 1923, and the documentation in ibid.

101. See the documentation in LASH/301/4952. Cf. Severing, "Preussen-Probleme," *Neue Zeit* 39 (no. 14, 1 July 1921), 313–14; and Gottwald, *Ziele,* p. 17. Under Severing's plan no provincial governors would actually have lost their jobs since the minister of the interior intended to reappoint all of them as district directors.

102. [Kürbis?], "Grundsätze . . . Vereinfachung der Staatsverwaltung . . ." [23 Sept. 1921], LASH/301/5646; and Hörsing to Severing, 5 Aug. 1926, Severing papers/30/47 (Arch.SD).

103. For example, in June 1922 eight of the representatives from the East Elbian provinces in the Reichsrat voted against the "Law for the Protection of the Republic" which had been proposed by the Reich government and supported by the Prussian Cabinet in response to the Rathenau murder. See Friedrich Tischbein, "Aus dem Reichsrat—Erinnerungen. . .1919–1934," p. 52 (BA/K1.Erw. 295).

104. Gerhard Senger, *Die Politik der Deutschen Zentrumspartei zur Frage Reich und Länder von 1918–1928* (Hamburg, 1932), pp. 99–100.

105. Konrad Adenauer, "Konrad Adenauer als Präsident des Preussischen Staatsrates," in *Konrad Adenauer, Oberbürgermeister von Köln,* ed. Hugo Stehkämper (Cologne, 1976), pp. 355–404.

106. Even members of the coalition parties frequently voted with the opposition in the Staatsrat against the cabinet when provincial interests seemed threatened. See Adenauer, "Präsident," pp. 380–94; and SPD, *Pr. Landtag,* p. 84. On the conflicting points of view, cf. Enno Eimers, *Das Verhältnis von Preussen und Reich in den ersten Jahren der Weimarer Republik (1918–1923)* (Berlin, 1969), p. 319.

107. Cf., "Chefbesprechung," 12 May 1922, *Ak/Rk Wirth,* vol. 2, no. 271, pp. 781–82.

108. See Otto Braun, "Preussen und das Reich," *Berliner Tageblatt,* no. 595 (25 Dec. 1921); see also Braun in the "Besprechung des Reichskanzlers mit den Ministerpräsidenten der Länder," 6 Dec. 1922, *Ak/Rk Cuno,* no. 13, p. 43; and *SBPrLT 1921–24,* 10 Nov. 1921, vol. 3, cols. 4151ff.

109. Fröhlich to Severing, personal communication, 24 Feb. 1922, Severing papers/13/9 (Arch.SD).

110. On the negotiations between Hamburg and Prussia, see Südekum to Severing, 30 June and 30 Sept. 1922, ibid./01/109, 13/32; Lamp'l to Abegg, 18 Sept. 1922, LASH/301/5652; *Hamburger Volksblatt,* 17 Oct. 1922; and Werner Johe, "Territorialer Expansionsdrang oder wirtschaftliche Notwendigkeit? Die Gross-Hamburg-Frage," *Zeitschrift des Vereins für Hamburgische Geschichte* 64 (1978), 149–80.

111. On the activities of the association, see Severing papers/80/42–56 (Arch.SD).

112. On the Guelph agitation and the cabinet's countermoves, see ibid./22/28 and 80/57, 59, 60; and NSStAH/Rep. Heimatbund Niedersachsen/Vorl. 9/373.

113. *Vorwärts*, no. 233 (19 May 1924).

114. The separation of Upper Silesia from Prussia is discussed in: Ministry of the Interior to chairman of the Central Office for the Reorganization of the Reich, 22 May 1922, O. Braun papers/323 (IISG); and "Die wirtschaftlichen Folgen einer Verselbstständigung Oberschlesiens" (memorandum prepared by the Ministry of Commerce with the cooperation of the Ministry of Agriculture), n.d., O. Braun papers/323, 331 (IISG). It will be recalled that the leader of the autonomy movement was the head of Upper Silesia's Center party organization, Father Carl Ulitzka. See his article, "Der deutsche Osten und die Zentrumspartei," *Nationale Arbeit—Das Zentrum und sein Wirken in der deutschen Republik*, ed. Karl Anton Schulte (Berlin [1929]), pp. 141–53. As we have seen, ever since 1919, various Reich cabinets had at least implicitly supported the establishment of a new *Land* in Germany's southeastern corner.

115. Oeser to Severing, 5 Jan. 1922, Severing papers/81/65 (Arch.SD); *Kreuzzeitung*, 28 Mar. 1922.

116. Carl Severing, "Provinzialautonomie?" *Neue Zeit* 42 (4 Nov. 1921), 121.

117. O. Braun, "Akten-Notiz," 5 Jan. 1922; typescript of an interview with Braun, n.d. [about 25 Mar. 1922]; and Braun to Reich Chancellor, 14 Jan. 1922, O. Braun papers/318, 327, 330 (IISG).

118. Braun interview, 25 Mar. 1922.

119. Ibid.; wire service report on Braun's address, 20 Mar. 1922, O. Braun papers/342 (IISG).

120. Ph.H. [sic], "Ein schwarzer Tag für Oberschlesien," *Oberschlesische Zeitung*, 20 Mar. 1922; and *Oberschlesische Volksstimme*, 25 Mar. 1922; cf. the headline in the *Vossische Zeitung*, 20 Mar. 1922: "The address provides the foundation for the federal state!" The *Frankfurter Zeitung* was also critical (22 Mar. 1922).

121. See *Volkswacht für Schlesien*, 22 Mar. 1922.

122. *Kreuzzeitung*, 28 Mar. 1922.

123. *PrGS*, no. 31 (1922), pp. 205–06. Even this statute met opposition from the centralists. See Braun to Severing, 3 July 1925, Severing papers/01/10 (Arch.SD). Cf. Schulze, *Braun*, pp. 413–14.

124. See Ernst Siehr, "Denkschrift," 18 Apr. 1922, O. Braun papers/338 (IISG).

125. See "Chefbesprechung," 24 May 1922, *Ak/Rk Wirth*, vol. 2, no. 281, pp. 822–23.

126. See Reich cabinet meeting, 25 Apr., 27 Sept. 1922, ibid., nos. 255, 379, pp. 735–36, 1109–10, n. 4.

127. Siehr, "Denkschrift," p. 22.

128. SPD, *Pr. Landtag*, p. 13.

129. Eimers, *Verhältnis*, pp. 326–27.

130. See the resolutions of the Schleswig-Holstein provincial legislature, 29 Nov. 1923, R 43 I/677.

Chapter 8. Conclusion

1. This is the title of Luther's autobiography (Stuttgart, 1960).

2. The quotation is from Otto Boelitz, *Der Aufbau des preussischen Bildungssystems nach der Staatsumwälzung*, 2d ed. (Leipzig, 1925), p. 126.

3. Michael Stürmer, *Koalition und Opposition in der Weimarer Republik 1924–1928* (Düsseldorf, 1967), p. 278.

4. The most recent additions to this school of interpretation are Hans-Peter Ehni, *Bollwerk Preussen?* (Bonn–Bad Godesberg, 1975); and Horst Möller, *Parlamentarismus im Preussen der Weimarer Republik* (Berlin, 1978).

5. Discussions of this thesis run through much of the literature on the *Reichsreform*. A good

contemporary statement is Arnold Brecht's *Federalism and Regionalism in Germany* (New York, 1945), pp. 22, 133. More recently, Enno Eimers, *Das Verhältnis von Reich und Preussen in den ersten Jahren der Weimarer Republik* (Berlin, 1969), restated the position on the basis of new documentation and post-war conceptualizations.

6. Incidentally, the evolution of the Social Democrats to something closer to the traditions of the British Labour party was not limited to Prussia. It was true of the state-level party organizations in other *Länder* as well. See Sigmund Neumann, *Die Parteien der Weimarer Republik* (Berlin, 1932, rpt. Stuttgart, 1965) p. 40; also Friedrich Holdermann, "Badische Erfahrungen und die deutsche Gegenwart," *Hilfe* 24 (19 Sept. 1918), 453.

7. See Herbert Hömig, *Das preussische Zentrum in der Weimarer Demokratie* (Mainz, 1979); and the vehement criticism by a leader of the Center party's right wing, Franz von Papen, *Der Wahrheit eine Gasse* (Munich, 1952), p. 131.

8. This is true even of such a refreshingly revisionist work as Manfred Rauh, *Die Parlamentarisierung der Deutschen Reiches* (Düsseldorf, 1977), pp. 470–82.

9. Cf. the very emotional and strongly autobiographical account by Rudolph von Campe, the leader of the DVP in the *SBPrLT 1921–1924*, Oct. 7, 1924, vol. 17, col. 24254.

10. Jan Striesow, "Die Deutschnationale Volkspartei und die Völkisch-Radikalen" Ph.D. diss., University of Hamburg, 1977, p. 289.

11. Braun to Severing, Aug. 1, 1925, in Severing papers/01/12 (Arch.SD).

12. Ministry of the Interior to District Director of Hildesheim, Oct. 8, 1925, NSStAH/122a/IX/9. Cf. the documentation in LASH/309/17650.

13. *Der preussische Landtag 1921–1924,* ed. Paul Hirsch (Berlin [1924]), p. 13.

Glossary

Alldeutscher Verband (ADV)	Pan-German Association; an extreme right-wing, *völkisch,* and anti-Semitic organization.
Bürgerblock	Any parliamentary coalition that included only middle-class parties, excluding the SPD, USPD, and KPD.
Deutscher Beamtenbund (DBB)	German Association of Civil Servants; a professional association of Prussian civil servants with close ties to the SPD.
Deutsche Demokratische Partei (DDP)	German Democratic party; a left-wing liberal party.
Deutsch-Nationale Volkspartei (DNVP)	German National People's party; a right-wing, monarchist political group, successor to pre-war conservative parties.
Deutsche Volkspartei (DVP)	German People's party; a right-wing liberal party.
Einwohnerwehren (EW)	Citizens' militias; government-sponsored paramilitary organizations. Originally founded to keep order in the waning days of World War I, the *EW* soon became active in extreme right-wing politics.
Guelph movement	Hanoverian political party seeking the province's separation from Prussia.
Interfraktioneller Ausschuss (IFA)	Multipartisan Committee of the Reichstag organized by the reformist parties during World War I to coordinate their policies vis-à-vis the government.
Kommunistische Partei Deutschlands (KPD)	Communist party of Germany. Originally part of the USPD, the KPD split off in 1918, adopted a Marxist-Leninist ideology, was a member of the Comintern, and maintained close ties to the Russian Bolsheviks.
Land	State; basic territorial unit of the German Reich.
Landrat	County executive; chief of administration in each of the approximately four hundred Prussian counties, appointed by the minister of the interior with the advice of the county legislature.
Landtag	First chamber of the Prussian legislature; after 1918, elected by universal suffrage.

Nationalsozialistische Deutsche Arbeiterpartei (NSDAP)	National Socialist German Workers' Party, or Nazi party; extreme right-wing, *völkisch,* and anti-Semitic party headed by Adolf Hitler.
Nationalversammlung	National Assembly; the German National Constitution Convention in Weimar that met in 1919 to draft the Weimar constitution.
Oberpräsident (OPrä)	Governor; chief executive officer in each of the twelve Prussian provinces.
Preussische verfassungsgebende Landesversammlung (PrVLV)	Prussian state constitutional convention; a combined constitutional convention and state legislature that met in Berlin from 1919 to 1921.
Rätekongress	National Congress of Workers' and Soldiers' Councils, which met in Berlin in December 1918.
Rat der Volksbeauftragten (RVA)	Council of People's Plenipotentiaries; the provisional Reich government established in November 1918. Originally composed of three representatives each from the SPD and USPD, it remained in office until replaced by the parliamentary Reich cabinet in 1919.
Reichskommisar für die Überwachung der öffentlichen Ordnung	Reich Commissioner for the Supervision of Public Order; agency charged with reporting on the activities of political extremists. Until after the Kapp Putsch, it was staffed with officials sympathetic to the extreme right.
Reichsrat	Federal Council; the second chamber of the German national parliament. Delegates were not popularly elected, but appointed by the state governments.
Reichstag	First chamber of the German national parliament. Delegates were elected by universal suffrage.
Regierungspräsident (RPrä)	District director, chief of administration in each of the thirty-four Prussian territorial districts, responsible to both the provincial governor and the minister of the interior.
Sozialisierungskommission	Socialization (or nationalization) commission. A group of economists, labor and political leaders, headed by Karl Kautsky, who were appointed by the Rätekongress to make recommendations on the feasibility of structural changes in the German economy after World War I.

Sozialdemokratische Partei Deutschlands (SPD)	Social Democratic party of Germany; the largest of the socialist groups that emerged from the split of the German socialist movement in 1917. Although professing a Marxist ideology, the party was also committed to parliamentary democracy.
Staatsrat	Second chamber of the Prussian legislature; delegates were appointed by the provincial diets.
Unabhängige Sozialdemokratische Partei Deutschlands (USPD)	Independent Social Democratic party of Germany; left-wing socialist party resulting from the split of the socialist movement in 1917. The USPD itself split in 1920, with most of its leaders rejoining the SPD, while the bulk of the membership went over to the KPD.
Vollzugsrat	Executive Committee of the Workers' and Soldiers' Council of Greater Berlin, formed in November 1918.
Zentralrat	Executive Committee of the National Congress of Workers' and Soldiers' Councils, elected in December 1918.

Bibliography

Unpublished and Archival Sources

Amsterdam. International Institute for Social History (IISG)
Archiv des Zentralrates der Deutschen Republik
Eduard Bernstein papers
Otto Braun papers
Albert Grzesinski papers
Wolfgang Heine papers
Paul Herz papers
Karl Kautsky papers
Erich Kuttner papers

Berlin. Preussisches Geheimes Staatsarchiv (PrGStAB)
Akten des Finanzministeriums (Rep. 151)
Akten des Innenministeriums (Rep. 77)
Akten des Justizministeriums (Rep. 84a)
Akten des Ministeriums für Handel and Gewerbe (Rep. 120)
Akten des Ministeriums für öffentliche Arbeiten (Rep. 93)
Akten des Ministeriums für Volkswohlfahrt (Rep. 191)
Akten des Staatsministeriums (Rep. 90)
Carl Heinrich Becker papers (Rep. 92)
Otto Braun papers (Rep. 92)
Adolf Grimme papers (Rep. 92)
Friedrich Trendelenburg papers (Rep. 92)

Berlin. Archiv der Historischen Kommission (Arch.HiKo)
Restakten des Allgemeinen Deutschen Gewerkschaftsbundes (NB 65/0053)
Otto Hörsing papers

Berlin. Mendelssohn Archiv (Arch.Mendelssohn)
Albrecht Mendelssohn-Bartholdy papers

Bonn-Bad Godesberg. Archiv der sozialen Demokratie (Arch.SD)
Otto Braun papers
Wilhelm Dittmann papers
Karl Giebel papers
Ernst Heilmann papers
Wilhelm Keil papers
Paul Levi papers
Hermann Molkenbuhr papers
Hermann Müller papers
Gustav Noske papers
Carl Severing papers

Cologne. Stadtarchiv (Stadtarch.Cologne)
Wilhelm Marx papers

Hamburg. Forschungsstelle für die Geschichte des Nationalsozialismus in Hamburg (Forst.Hbg.)
Akten des Alldeutschen Verbandes (412)
Akten der Bürgervereine (451 and 452)
Akten der Parteien (740)
Akten der Verbände (7533)
Heinrich Class papers
Alfred Diller papers

Hamburg. Hapag-Archiv (Hap.Arch.)
Wilhelm Cuno papers
Arndt von Holtzendorf papers

Hamburg. Staatsarchiv (Staatsarch.Hbg.)
Carl Petersen papers

Hanover. Niedersächsisches Hauptstaatsarchiv (NSStAH)
Akten der SPD. Bezirk Hannover (Rep. 310 II)
Akten des Heimatbundes Niedersachsen
Akten des Oberpräsidiums Hannover (Rep. 122a)
Akten des Regierungspräsidiums Lüneburg (Rep. 80)

Koblenz. Bundesarchiv (BA)
Akten der Reichskanzlei (R 43 I and II)
Bestand DDP (R 45 III)
Bestand DVP (R 45 II)
Bestand Kleine Erwerbungen
Bestand Parteien- und Verbandsdrucksachen (ZSg 1)
Bestand Stahlhelm (R 72)
Eduard David papers
Hermann Dietrich papers
Eduard Dingeldey papers
Anton Erkelenz papers
Otto Gessler papers
Georg Gothein papers
Rudolf ten Hompel papers
Wolfgang Jaenicke papers
Siegfried von Kardorff papers
Kathinka von Kardorff-Oheimb papers
Erich Koch-Weser papers
Wilhelm Külz papers
Friedrich von Loebell papers
Hermann Luppe papers
Paul Moldenhauer papers
Friedrich Saemisch papers
Otto von Schlange-Schöningen papers
Gustav Stresemann papers (microfilm)

Albert Südekum papers
Gottfried Traub papers

New York.   Leo Baeck Institute (LBI)
Heinrich and Julie Braun-Vogelstein papers
Ernst Feder papers
Paul Hirsch papers
Kurt Kersten papers
Philipp Loewenfeld papers
Fritz Mauthner papers
Fritz Rathenau papers

Schleswig. Landesarchiv Schleswig-Holstein (LASH)
Akten des Oberpräsidiums Schleswig-Holstein (Rep. 301)
Akten des Provinzial-Schulkollegiums (Rep. 302)
Akten des Regierungspräsidiums Schleswig (Rep. 309)

Primary Sources

Documentary, Legal, and Parliamentary Publications

Akten der Reichskanzlei. Das Kabinett Cuno 22. November 1922 bis 12. August 1923. Ed. Karl-Heinz Harbeck. Boppard a.Rh., 1968.
_____. *Das Kabinett Bauer Juni 1919–24. Juni 1920.* Ed. Anton Golecki. Boppard a.Rh., 1980.
_____. *Das Kabinett Fehrenbach 25. Juni 1920 bis 4. Mai 1921.* Ed. Peter Wulf. Boppard a.Rh., 1972.
_____. *Die Kabinette Marx I und II,* Ed. Günter Abramovski. 2 vols. Boppard a.Rh., 1973.
_____. *Das Kabinett Müller 1, 27. März bis 21. Juni 1920.* Ed. Martin Vogt. Boppard a.Rh., 1971.
_____. *Das Kabinett Scheidemann 13. Februar bis 20. Juni 1919.* Ed. Hagen Schulze. Boppard a.Rh., 1971.
_____. *Die Kabinette Stresemann I und II.* Ed. Martin Vogt. 2 vols. Boppard a.Rh., 1978.
_____. *Die Kabinette Wirth I und II 10. Mai bis 26. Oktober 1921. 26 Oktober 1921 bis 22. November 1922.* Ed. Ingrid Schulze-Bidlingmaier. 2 vols. Boppard a.Rh., 1973.
Aktenstücke zum Reichsvolksschulgesetz, Ed. Walter Landé. Leipzig, 1928.
Allgemeiner Deutscher Gewerkschaftsbund. *Protokolle der Verhandlungen der Kongresse der Gewerkschaften Deutschlands.* Berlin, 1919, 1922, and 1925.
Allgemeiner Kongress der Arbeiter- und Soldatenräte Deutschlands, 16.–21. Dezember 1918— Stenographische Berichte. Ed. Adolf Kunze et al. Berlin, 1919.
Aufrufe, Verordnungen und Beschlüsse des Vollzugsrates des Arbeiter- und Soldatenrates Gross-Berlin. Berlin, 1918.
Die Deutsche Revolution 1918–1919. Ed. Gerhard A. Ritter and Susanne Miller. Frankfurt a.M., 1968.
Die deutsche Revolution in der Darstellung der zeitgenössischen Presse. Vol. 1: *Im Zeichen der roten Fahne.* Ed. Eberhard Buchner. Berlin, 1921.
Dokumente and Materialien zur Geschichte der deutschen Arbeiterbewegung, Reihe II: 1914–1945. Ed. Institut für Marxismus-Leninismus beim ZK der SED. Berlin, 1958–   .

Die Entwicklung der deutschen Revolution und das Kriegsende in der Zeit vom 1. Oktober bis 30. November 1918. Ed. Kurt Ahnert. Berlin, 1919.

Gesetz über die Bildung einer neuen Stadtgemeinde Berlin. Ed. Paul Hirsch. Berlin, 1920.

Der Interfraktionelle Ausschuss 1917/18. Ed. Erich Matthias and Rudolf Morsey. 2 vols. Düsseldorf, 1959.

Der Lebedour-Prozess, 19. Mai bis 23. Juni 1919. Ed. Georg Lebedour. Berlin, 1919

Militär und Innenpolitik im Weltkrieg 1914–1918. Ed. Werner Deist. 2 vols. Düsseldorf, 1970.

Ministerial-Blatt für die preussische innere Verwaltung. Vol. 79ff. Berlin, 1918–   .

Politische Justiz 1918–1933. Ed. Heinrich Hannover and Elisabeth Hannover-Drück. Frankfurt a.M., 1966.

Protokoll der Sitzung des [SPD] Parteiausschusses 8. und 9.12.1920. Berlin, 1920.

Quellen zur deutschen Schulgeschichte seit 1800. Ed. Gerhardt Giese. Göttingen, 1961.

Rechenschaftsbericht vom 1. Juni 1914 bis 31. Mai 1919. Ed. Generalkommission der Gewerkschaften Deutschlands. Berlin, 1919.

Die Regierung der Volksbeauftragten 1918/19. Ed. Susanne Miller and Heinrich Potthoff. 2 vols. Düsseldorf, 1969.

Sammlung der Drucksachen der verfassungsgebenden Preussischen Landesversammlung. 15 vols. Berlin, 1919–1921.

Sammlung der Drucksachen des Preussischen Landtages, I. Wahlperiode. 18 vols. Berlin, 1921–1924.

Sitzungsberichte der verfassungsgebenden Preussischen Landesversammlung. 13 vols. Berlin, 1921.

Sitzungsberichte des Preussischen Landtages, I. bis II. Wahlperiode. 17 vols. Berlin, 1924–1928.

Statistisches Jahrbuch für den Preussischen Staat. Ed. Preussisches Statistisches Landesamt. vol. 13ff. Berlin, 1915–   .

Statistisches Jahrbuch für das Deutsche Reich. Ed. Statistisches Reichsamt. Berlin, 1918–   .

Stenographische Berichte der Verhandlungen der Deutschen Nationalversammlung. Berlin, 1919.

Stenographische Berichte der Verhandlungen des Deutschen Reichstags. I.–III. Wahlperiode. Berlin, 1920–1924.

Die Verfassung des Freistaates Preussen vom 30. November 1920. Ed. Paul Hirsch. Berlin, 1921.

Der Zentralrat der Deutschen Sozialistischen Republik 19.12.1918–8.4.1919. Ed. Eberhard Kolb and Reinhard Rürup. Leiden, 1968.

Zentralrat der sozialistischen Republik Deutschlands: Vom I. Rätekongress zur National-versammlung. Ed. Gustav Heller. Berlin, 1919.

Zentralstelle für die Einigung der Sozialdemokratie: Protokoll der Konferenz der Einigung der Sozialdemokratie 21.–23. Juni 1919. Berlin, 1919.

Zwei Jahre Regierungsarbeit in Preussen. Ed. Presse-Abteilung des Preussischen Staatsministeriums. Berlin, 1921.

Zweiter Kongress der Arbeiter-, Bauern- und Soldatenräte Deutschlands am 8. bis 14. April 1919. Berlin, 1919.

Memoirs and Diaries

Amelunxen, Rudolf. *Ehrenmänner und Hexenmeister—Erlebnisse und Betrachtungen.* Munich, 1960.

Barth, Emil. *Aus der Werkstatt der deutschen Revolution.* Berlin, 1919.

Baumgart, Winifred, ed. *Von Brest-Litovsk zur deutschen Novemberrevolution;: Aus den Tage-büchern von Paquet, Gröner und Hopmann, März bis November 1918.* Göttingen, 1971.

Blos, Wilhelm. *Von der Monarchie zum Volksstaat: Zur Geschichte der Revolution in Deutschland insbesondere in Württemberg.* 2 vols. Stuttgart, 1922–1923.

Böhm, Gustav. *Adjudant im preussischen Kriegsministerium Juni 1918 bis Oktober 1919— Aufzeichnungen.* Ed. Heinz Hürten and Georg Meyer. Stuttgart, 1977.

von Braun, Magnus Freiherr. *Von Ostpreussen bis Texas—Erlebnisse und zeitgeschichtliche Betrachtungen eines Ostdeutschen.* Stollhamm (Oldb.), 1955.

Braun, Otto. *Von Weimar zu Hitler.* 2d ed. Hamburg, 1949.

Brecht, Arnold. *Aus nächster Nähe—Lebenserinnerungen 1884–1927.* Stuttgart, 1966.

_____. *Mit der Kraft des Geistes—Lebenserinnerungen 1927–1967.* Stuttgart, 1967.

Bredt, Johann Victor. *Erinnerungen und Dokumente 1914 bis 1933.* Ed. Martin Schumacher. Düsseldorf, 1970.

Brüning, Heinrich. *Briefe und Gespräche 1934–1945.* Ed. Claire Nix, Reginald Phelps, and George Pettee. Stuttgart, 1974.

_____. *Memoiren.* Stuttgart, 1970.

Buchwitz, Otto. *50 Jahre Funktionär der deutschen Arbeiterbewegung.* 2d ed. Berlin, 1973.

Cleinow, Georg. *Der Verlust der Ostmark—Die deutschen Volksräte des Bromberger Systems im Kampf um die Erhaltung der Ostmark beim Reich 1918/19.* Berlin, 1934.

D'Abernon, Viscount. *Memoiren.* Trans. Antonina Valletin. 3 vols. Leipzig, 1929–30.

David, Eduard. *Das Kriegstagebuch des Reichstagsabgeordneten Eduard David 1914–1918.* Ed. Erich Matthias and Susanne Miller. Düsseldorf, 1966.

Ebert, Friedrich. *Schriften, Aufzeichnungen, Reden.* Ed. Friedrich Ebert, Jr. 2 vols. Dresden, 1926.

Eichhorn, Emil. *Eichhorn über die Januar-Ereignisse—Meine Tätigkeit im Berliner Polizeipräsidium und mein Anteil an den Januar-Ereignissen.* Berlin, 1919.

Erzberger, Matthias. *Erlebnisse im Weltkrieg.* Stuttgart, 1920.

Feder, Ernst. *Heute sprach ich mit . . . Tagebücher eines Berliner Publizisten 1926–1932.* Ed. Cecile Lowenthal-Hensel and Arnold Paucker. Frankfurt a.M., 1971.

Fischer, Anton. *Die Revolutionskommandantur Berlin.* Berlin, 1919.

Friedensburg, Ferdinand. *Lebenserinnerungen,* vol. 1. Frankfurt a.M., 1969.

Friedrich Ebert und seine Zeit—Ein Gedenkwort über den ersten Präsidenten der Deutschen Republik. Charlottenburg, 1926.

Friedrich von Berg als Chef des Geheimen Zivilkabinetts 1918—Erinnerungen aus seinem Nachlass. Ed. Heinrich Potthoff. Düsseldorf, 1971.

von Gerlach, Hellmut. *Ein Demokrat kommentiert Weimar—Die Berichte Hellmut von Gerlach an die Carnegie-Friedensstiftung in New York 1922–1930.* Ed. Karl Holl and Adolf Wild. Bremen, 1973.

_____. *Meine Erlebnisse in der Preussischen Verwaltung.* Berlin, 1919.

_____. *Von Rechts nach Links.* Ed. Emil Ludwig. Zurich, 1937.

Gessler, Otto. *Reichswehrpolitik in der Weimarer Zeit.* Ed. Kurt Sendtner. Stuttgart, 1958.

Geyer, Curt. *Die revolutionäre Illusion—Zur Geschichte des linken Flügels der USPD—Erinnerungen.* Ed. Wolfgang Benz and Hermann Graml. Stuttgart, 1976.

Grimme, Adolf. *Briefe.* Ed. Dieter Sauberzweig and Ludwig Fischer. Heidelberg, 1967.

Groener, Wilhelm, *Lebenserinnerungen.* Ed. Friedrich Freiherr von Gaertringen. 2d ed. Osnabrück, 1972.

Grzesinski, Albert C. *Inside Germany.* Trans. Alexander S. Lipschitz. New York, 1939.

Haase, Ernst, ed. *Hugo Haase—Sein Leben und Wirken.* Berlin-Frohnau, 1929.

Hahn, Paul. *Der rote Hahn—Erinnerungen aus der Revolution in Württemberg.* Stuttgart, 1922.

Haussmann, Conrad. *Aus Conrad Haussmanns politischer Arbeit.* Frankfurt a.M., 1923.

_____. *Schlaglichter—Reichstagsbriefe und Aufzeichnungen.* Ed. Ulrich Zeller. Frankfurt a.M., 1924.

Hellpach, Willy. *Wirken in Wirren, 1914–1925.* 2 vols. Hamburg, 1949.

Hesterberg, Ernst. *Alle Macht den A.—und S.—Räten—Kampf um Schlesien.* Breslau, 1933.

Heuss, Theodor. *Erinnerungen 1905–1933.* Tübingen, 1963.

Hirsch, Paul. *Der Weg der Sozialdemokratie zur Macht in Preussen.* Berlin, 1929.

Hoefer, Karl. *Oberschlesien in der Aufstandzeit 1918–1921—Erinnerungen und Dokumente.* Berlin, 1938.

Hoffman, Adolph. *Episoden und Zwischenrufe aus der Parlamentszeit und Ministerzeit.* Berlin, 1924.

Hoffmann, Josef. *Journalist in Republik, Diktatur und Besatzungszeit—Erinnerungen 1916–1947.* Ed. Rudolf Morsey. Mainz, 1977.

Hofmiller, Josef. *Revolutionstagebuch 1918–19.* Ed. Hulda Hofmiller. Leipzig, 1938.

Höpker-Aschoff, Hermann. *Unser Weg durch die Zeit.* Berlin, 1936.

Keil, Wilhelm. *Erlebnisse eines Sozialdemokraten.* 2 vols. Stuttgart, 1947–48.

Kessler, Harry Graf. *Tagebücher 1918–1937.* Ed. Wolfgang Pfeiffer-Belli. Frankfurt a.M., 1961.

Köhler, Heinrich, *Lebenserinnerungen des Politikers und Staatsmannes 1878–1949.* Ed. Josef Becker. Stuttgart, 1964.

Köster, Adolf. *Der Kampf um Schleswig.* Berlin, 1921.

Lange, Friedrich C.A. *Gross-Berliner Tagebuch 1920—1933.* Berlin-Lichtenrade, 1951.

Leber, Julius. *Ein Mann geht seinen Weg—Schriften, Reden und Briefe.* Berlin, 1952.

Lemmer, Ernst. *Manches war doch anders—Erinnerungen eines deutschen Demokraten.* Frankfurt a.M., 1968.

Levi, Paul. *Zwischen Spartakus und Sozialdemokratie—Schriften, Aufsätze, Reden und Briefe.* Ed. Charlotte Beradt. Frankfurt a.M., 1969.

Löbe, Paul. *Der Weg war lang.* 3d ed. Berlin, 1954.

Luppe, Hermann. *Mein Leben.* Ed. Stadtarchiv Nüremberg and Mella Heinsen-Luppe. Nuremberg, 1977.

Luther, Hans. *Politiker ohne Partei—Erinnerungen.* Stuttgart, 1960.

Mayer, Eugen. *Skizzen aus dem Leben der Weimarer Republik—Berliner Erinnerungen.* Berlin, 1962.

Mayer, Gustav. *Erinnerungen—Vom Journalisten zum Historiker der deutschen Arbeiterbewegung.* Zurich, 1949.

Meinecke, Friedrich. *Autobiographische Schriften.* Ed. Eberhard Kessel. Stuttgart, 1969.

Michaelis, Georg. *Für Staat und Volk—Eine Lebensgeschichte.* 2d ed. Berlin, 1922.

Müller-Meiningen, Ernst. *Aus Bayerns schwersten Tagen—Erinnerungen und Betrachtungen aus der Revolutionszeit.* Berlin, 1923.

Müller, Hermann. *Die November-Revolution.* Berlin, 1928.

Müller, Richard. *Vom Kaiserreich zur Republik.* 2 vols. Berlin, 1924.

Noske, Gustav. *Erlebtes aus Aufstieg und Niedergang einer Demokratie.* Offenbach a.M., 1947.

————. *Von Kiel bis Kapp—Zur Geschichte der deutschen Revolution.* Berlin, 1920.

Oehme, Walter, *Damals in der Reichskanzlei—Erinnerungen aus den Jahren 1918–1919.* Berlin, 1958.

————. *Die Weimarer Nationalversammlung—Erinnerungen.* Berlin, 1962.

von Papen, Franz. *Der Wahrheit eine Gasse.* Munich, 1952.

Payer, Friedrich. *Von Bethmann Hollweg bis Ebert—Erinnerungen und Bilder.* Frankfurt a.M., 1923.

Preuss, Hugo. *Staat, Recht und Freiheit—Aus 40 Jahren deutscher Politik und Geschichte.* Tübingen, 1926. Reprint. Hildesheim, 1964.

Radbruch, Gustav. *Der innere Weg—Aufriss meines Lebens.* Stuttgart, 1951.

Rathenau, Walther. *Tagebuch 1907–1922.* Ed. Hartmut Pogge-v. Strandmann. Düsseldorf, 1967.

von Rheinbaben, Werner Freiherr. *Kaiser, Kanzler, Präsidenten—Erinnerungen.* Mainz, 1968.

Riezler, Kurt. *Tagebücher, Aufsätze, Dokumente.* Ed. Karl-Dietrich Erdmann. Göttingen, 1972.
Schäfer, Heinrich. *Tagebuchblätter eines rheinischen Sozialisten.* Bonn, 1919.
Scheidemann, Philipp. *Memoiren eines Sozialdemokraten.* 2 vols. Dresden, 1928.
_____. *Der Zusammenbruch.* Berlin, 1921.
Schiffer, Eugen. *Ein Leben für den Liberalismus.* Berlin, 1951.
Schmidt-Ott, Friedrich. *Erlebtes und Erstrebtes 1860–1950.* Wiesbaden, 1952.
Scholz, Arno. *Null vier—Ein Jahrgang zwischen den Fronten.* Berlin-Grunewald, 1962.
Schreiber, Georg. *Zwischen Demokratie und Diktatur—Persönliche Erinnerungen an die Politik und Kultur des Reiches 1919–1944.* Regensburg, 1949.
Sender, Toni. *The Autobiography of a German Rebel.* London, 1940.
Severing, Carl. *Mein Lebensweg.* 2 vols. Cologne, 1950.
_____. *1919/1920 im Wetter- und Watterwinkel.* Bielefeld, 1920.
_____. *Wie es kam!* Berlin, 1920.
Sollmann, Wilhelm. *Die Revolution in Köln—Ein Bericht über Tatsachen.* Cologne, 1918.
Stampfer, Friedrich. *Mit dem Gesicht nach Deutschland—Aus dem Nachlass Friedrich Stampfers.* Ed. Erich Matthias. Düsseldorf, 1968.
Stegerwald, Adam ["Aus meinem Leben"]. In *25 Jahre christliche Gewerkschaftsbewegung 1899–1924.* Berlin, 1924 pp. 132–52.
von Stockhausen, Max. *6 Jahre Reichskanzlei—Erinnerungen und Tagebuchnotizen 1922–1927.* Ed. Walter Görlitz. Bonn, 1954.
Stresemann, Gustav. *Reden und Schriften 1897–1926.* Ed. Rochus Freiherr von Rheinbaben. 2 vols. Dresden, 1926.
_____. *Vermächtnis—Der Nachlass in drei Bänden.* Ed. Henry Bernhard et al. 3 vols. Berlin, 1932.
von Thaer, Albrecht. *Generalstabsdienst an der Front und in der O.H.L.—Aus Briefen und Tagebuchaufzeichnungen 1915–1919.* Ed. K.G. Rönnefarth and Siegfried Kaehler. Göttingen, 1958.
Ulrich, Carl. *Erinnerungen.* Ed. Ludwig Bergsträsser. Offenbach a.M., 1953.
Wachenheim, Hedwig. *Vom Grossbürgertum zur Sozialdemokratie.* Ed. Susanne Miller. Berlin, 1973.
Warburg, Max M. *Aus meinen Aufzeichnungen.* New York, 1952.
Wermuth, Adolf, *Ein Beamtenleben—Erinnerungen.* Berlin, 1922.
Werner, Paul [Paul Frölich]. *Die Bayerische Räte-Republik—Tatsachen und Kritik.* 2d ed. Leipzig, 1920.
Winnig, August, *Am Ausgang der deutschen Ostpolitik—Persönliche Erlebnisse und Erinnerungen.* Berlin, 1921.
_____. *Urkunden über mein Verhalten zur Gegenregierung.* [Königsberg, 1920.]
Wolff, Theodor. *Der Marsch durch zwei Jahrzehnte.* Amsterdam, 1936.

Official and Semiofficial Party Publications

GERMAN DEMOCRATIC PARTY (DDP)
Bericht über die Verhandlungen des 2. ausserordentlichen Parteitages der Deutschen Demokratischen Partei . . . Leipzig vom 13.–15. Dezember 1919. Berlin, [1920].
Jansen, Robert. *Die grosse Koalition in Preussen.* Berlin, [1921].
_____. *Der Berliner Militärputsch und seine politischen Folgen.* Berlin, 1920.
_____. *Die Regierungsbildung in Preussen.* Berlin, 1921.
Lantzsch, Rudolf. *Die Agrarpolitik der Deutschen Demokratischen Partei.* Berlin, 1928.
Lewin, Bruno. *Die Aufgaben der Jugend im neuen Deutschland.* Berlin, 1919.
Nuschke, Otto. "Wie die Deutsche Demokratische Partei wurde, was sie leistete und was sie ist."

In Zehn Jahre Deutsche Republik—Ein Handbuch für republikanische Politik, ed. Anton Erkelenz, pp. 24–41. Berlin, 1928.

Die Programme der Deutschen Demokratischen Partei. Berlin, 1920.

GERMAN NATIONAL PEOPLE'S PARTY (DNVP)

Beamtenpolitik im Preussenhaus Deutschnationale Flugschrift no. 63. Berlin, 1920.

Hergt, Oskar. *Auf zum Preussenkampf!* Deutschnationale Flugschrift no. 183. Berlin, 1924.

Kickhöffel, Karl Hans. *Das System Severing.* Deutschnationale Flugschrift no. 184. Berlin, 1924.

Klingemann, Karl. *Wer verschuldete den Schmach- und Hungerfrieden?* Deutschnationale Flugschrift no. 25. Berlin, 1919.

Koch, Julius, *Deutschnationale Kirchenpolitik in der Preussischen Landesversammlung.* Deutschnationale Flugschrift no. 65. Berlin, 1920.

Lambach, Walther, ed. *Politische Praxis 1926.* Hamburg, 1926.

Lüdicke, Paul. *Die sozialdemokratische Misswirtschaft in Preussen.* Deutschnationale Flugschrift no. 83. Berlin, 1921.

Negenborn, Karl Georg. *Aus der Werkstatt Severings.* Liegnitz, 1924.

Philipp, Albrecht. *Von Stresemann zu Marx.* Berlin, 1924.

Regierungskrise und Reichstagsauflösung—Bericht der Unterhändler der Reichstagsfraktion, (Confidential; printed as a manuscript.) Berlin, 1924.

von Richthofen-Mertschütz, Freiherr. *Die Aufgaben der Deutschnationalen Volkspartei gegenüber der Landwirtschaft.* Berlin, 1919.

von Schlange-Schöningen, Ernst. *Wir Völkischen.* Stettin, 1923.

Thomas, Oskar. *Demokratie, Landwirtschaft und Landarbeiterschaft.* Deutschnationale Flugschrift no. 29. Berlin, 1919.

Was wir deutschen Männern und Frauen vor dem 7. Dezember sagen müssen. Deutschnationale Flugschrift no. 185. Berlin, 1924.

Weiss, Max, ed. *Der nationale Wille—Werden und Wirken der Deutschnationalen Volkspartei 1918–1928.* Berlin, 1928.

Winckler, Friedrich. *Rede . . . 4. November 1924.* Berlin, 1924.

GERMAN PEOPLE'S PARTY (DVP)

Bericht über den zweiten Parteitag der Deutschen Volkspartei am 18., 19. und 20. Oktober 1919 in Leipzig. Berlin, 1920.

Die Deutschnationalen und wir. Flugschrift der DVP no. 44. Berlin, 1924.

COMMUNIST PARTY OF GERMANY (KPD)

Bericht über die Verhandlungen des 8. Parteitages der Kommunistischen Partei Deutschlands . . . Leipzig 28. Januar bis 1. Februar 1923. Berlin, 1923.

————. *Frankfurt a.M. . . . 7. bis 10. April 1924.* Berlin, 1924.

Der Grüdungsparteitag der KPD—Protokoll und Materialien. Ed. Hermann Weber. Frankfurt a.M., 1969.

Protokoll des III. Kongresses der Kommunistischen Internationale. Moscow 22. Juni bis 12. Juli 1921. Moscow, 1921. Reprint. Milan, 1967.

SOCIAL DEMOCRATIC PARTY OF GERMANY (SPD)

Braun, Adolf, et al. *Das Programm der Sozialdemokratie—Vorschläge für seine Erneuerung.* Berlin, 1920.

David, Eduard. *Wer trägt die Schuld am Kriege? Rede . . . 6.6.1917 in Stockholm.* Berlin, 1917.

Haenisch, Konrad. *Kulturpolitische Aufgaben.* Berlin, 1919.
Heilmann, Ernst. *Die Noskegarde.* Berlin, 1919.
Heine, Wolfgang, *Wer ist Schuld am Bürgerkriege?* Berlin, 1919.
Kampfmeyer, Paul, *Wer ist Schuld an Not und Elend?* Berlin, 1922.
Keil, Wilhelm. *Die Sozialdemokratie und die Erneuerung Deutschlands.* Stuttgart, 1918.
Klühs, Franz. *Die Spaltung der USPD.* Berlin, 1920.
Krüger, Franz. *Diktatur oder Volksherrschaft—Der Putsch vom 13. März 1920.* Berlin, 1920.
——————. *Sozialdemokratie und Revolution—Leitfaden für Parteifunktionäre.* Berlin, 1918.
Kuttner, Erich. *Von Kiel bis Berlin.* Berlin, 1918.
——————. *Die deutsche Revolution.* Berlin, 1918.
Die Preussische Landesversammlung—Tätigkeit der sozialdemokratischen Fraktion. Ed. Gustav Heller. Berlin, 1920.
Der Preussische Landtag 1921—1924—Handbuch für sozialdemokratische Wähler. Ed. Paul Hirsch. Berlin, 1924.
Protokoll der Parteikonferenz in Weimar am 22. und 23. März 1919. Berlin, 1919.
Protokoll über die Verhandlungen des Parteitages der Sozialdemokratischen Partei Deutschlands . . . 1919. Berlin, 1919.
——————. *Kassel . . . 1920.* Berlin, 1920.
——————. *Görlitz . . . 1921.* Berlin, 1921.
——————. *Berlin . . . 1924.* Berlin, 1924.
Protokoll über die Verhandlungen der Reichkonferenz der Sozialdemokratischen Partei Deutschlands . . . Berlin . . . Mai 1920. Berlin, 1920.
Protokolle der Sitzungen des Parteiausschusses 1914—   . Berlin, 1914—   .
Die Reichstagsfraktion der deutschen Sozialdemokratie 1898—1918. Ed. Erich Matthias and Eberhard Pikart. 2 vols. Düsseldorf, 1966.
Schulz, Heinrich. *Kirchenschule oder Volksschule?* Berlin, 1927.
Sozialdemokratisches Handbuch für die preussischen Landtagswahlen. Berlin, 1921.
Stampfer, Friedrich. *Das Görlitzer Programm.* Berlin, 1922.

INDEPENDENT SOCIAL DEMOCRATIC PARTY OF GERMANY (USPD)
Preussen unter der Koalitionsregierung. Ed. Bezirksverband Berlin-Brandenburg, Berlin, 1921.
Protokoll über die Verhandlungen des ausserordentlichen Parteitages vom 2. bis 6. März 1919 in Berlin. Berlin, 1919.
——————. *Leipzig . . . 1919.* Berlin, 1920.
——————. *Halle . . . 1920.* Berlin, 1920.

CENTER PARTY AND BAVARIAN PEOPLE'S PARTY (CENTER AND BVP)
Bericht über die Verhandlungen des Parteitages der Rheinischen Zentrumspartei . . . Köln 15.—18. September 1919. Cologne, 1919.
Die Beteiligung des Zentrums an der Regierung. Ed. Aufklärungsdienst des Landessekretariat der preussischen Zentrumspartei. Berlin, 1919.
Dezemberwahlen 1924. Ed. Generalsekretariat d. BVP. Munich, 1924.
Gottwald, Adolf. *Die Arbeit der Zentrumsfraktion des Preussischen Landtages 1921/1924.* Flugschriften der Preussischen Zentrumspartei no.2. Berlin, 1924.
——————. *Ziele und Erfolge der Zentrumsfraktion des Preussischen Landtages 1921/1924.* Flugschriften der Preussischen Zentrumspartei no. 1. Berlin, 1924.
Klöckner, Alois. *Der erste preussische Landtag.* Berlin, 1921.

_____. *Wahl des Reichspräsidenten*. Berlin, 1925.

_____. *Die Zentrumsfraktion in der preussischen Landesversammlung*. Berlin, 1919.

Offizieller Bericht über den Ersten Reichsparteitag des Zentrums . . . Berlin 19. bis 22. Januar 1920. Berlin, 1920.

Offizieller Bericht des Zweiten Reichsparteitages der Deutschen Zentrumspartei . . . Berlin . . . 15. bis 17. Januar 1922. Berlin, 1922.

Handbooks and Bibliographic Aids

Biographisches Lexikon des Sozialismus. Ed. Franz Osterroth. Hanover, 1960.

Die bürgerlichen Parteien in Deutschland 1830–1945. Ed. Dieter Fricke et al. 2 vols. Leipzig, 1968–1970.

Chronik der deutschen Sozialdemokratie Ed. Franz Osterroth and Dieter Schuster. 2 vols. 2d ed. Bonn–Bad Godesberg, 1975.

Conze, Werner. "Zur deutschen Geschichte 1918–1933." *Neue Politische Literatur* 2 (1957): 926–35.

Die deutschen Landkreise. Ed. Constantin Stein and Erwin Stein. 2 vols. Berlin-Friedenau, 1926.

Erdmann, Karl-Dietrich. "Die Geschichte der Weimarer Republik als Problem der Wissenschaft." *Vierteljahrshefte für Zeitgeschichte* 3 (1955), 1–16.

Gatzke, Hans W. "The Stresemann Papers." *Jounal of Modern History* 26 (March 1955), 49–59.

Geyer, Michael. "Die Wehrmacht der deutschen Republik ist die Reichswehr—Bemerkungen zur neueren Literatur." *Militärgeschichtliche Mitteilungen* 14 (1973), 152–99.

Handbuch der deutschen Gewerkschaftskongresse. Ed. Salomon Schwarz. Berlin, 1930.

Handbuch der Nationalversammlung. Ed. Bureau der Nationalversammlung. Berlin, 1919.

Handbuch der Politik. Ed. Gerhard Anschütz, Fritz Berolzheimer et al. 6 vols. 3d. ed. Berlin, 1920–1922.

Handbuch der preussischen verfassungsgebenden Landesversammlung. Ed. Bureau der Landesversammlung. Berlin, 1919.

Handbuch der Revolution in Deutschland. Ed. Heinrich Marx. Berlin, 1919.

Handbuch des preussischen Landtages. Ed. Bureau des Landtages. Berlin, 1921–1925.

Handbuch über den Preussischen Staat. Ed. Preussisches Staatsministerium. Berlin, 1922–1926.

MdR—Biographisches Handbuch der Reichstage 1848–1933. Ed. Max Schwarz. Hanover, 1965.

Der Nachlass des Reichskanzlers Wilhelm Marx. Ed. Hugo Stehkämper. 4 pts. Cologne, 1968.

Reichshandbuch der deutschen Gesellschaft. 2 vols. Berlin, 1930.

Reichstagshandbuch. Ed. Bureau des Reichstages. Berlin, 1920–25.

Tarumi, Setsoko, and Hartfried Krause. "Bibliographie der USPD–Broschüren 1917–1922." *Internationale Wissenschaftliche Korrespondenz* 10 (1974), 457–71.

Übersicht über die Bestände des Geheimen Staatsarchivs in Berlin-Dahlem. Ed. Hans Bramig et al. Berlin, 1967.

Übersicht über die Bestände des Deutschen Zentralarchivs Potsdam. Ed. Helmut Lötzke. Berlin, 1957.

Verzeichnis der schriftlichen Nachlässe in den deutschen Archiven und Bibliotheken. Ed. Ludwig Bannicke and Wolfgang Mommsen. 2 vols. Boppard a.Rh., 1969–71.

Wähler und Wahlen in der Weimarer Republik. Ed. Alfred Milatz. 2d ed. Bonn, 1968.

Wahlen in Deutschland. Ed. Bernhard Vogel et al. Berlin, 1971.

Wahlen und Abstimmungen 1918–1933—Eine Bibliographie. Ed. Martin Schumacher. Düsseldorf, 1976.

Wahlstatistik in Deutschland—Bibliographie der deutschen Wahlstatistik 1848–1975. Ed. Nils Diederich et al. Munich, 1976.

Periodicals

Allgemeine Rundschau
Die Arbeit
Beiträge zur Geschichte der deutschen Arbeiterbewegung
Berliner Tageblatt
Correspondenzblatt der Generalkommission der Gewerkschaften Deutschlands
Deutsche Rundschau
Der Deutschen-Spiegel
Der Firn
Das Freie Wort
Freiheit
Germania
Geschichte und Gesellschaft
Die Glocke
Hamburger Echo
Die Hilfe
Internationale Wissenschaftliche Korrespondenz
Der Klassenkampf
Mitteilungen der SPD-Bezirksorganisation Gross-Berlin
Mitteilungsblatt des Bezirksverbandes Berlin-Brandenburg der USPD
Mitteilungsblatt des Reichsblocks zur Vorbereitung der Reichspräsidentenwahl
Mitteilungsblatt der SPD
Nationalliberale Correspondenz
Neue Rundschau
Die Neue Zeit
Der Sozialist
Sozialistische Monatshefte
Sozialistische Parteikorrespondenz
Der Tag
Unser Weg
Vorwärts
Die Zeit

Secondary Sources

Abraham, David. *The Collapse of the Weimar Republic*. Princeton, N.J., 1981.
Adenauer, Konrad. "Konrad Adenauer als Präsident des Preussischen Staatsrates." In *Konrad Adenauer,* ed. Stehkämper. Cologne, 1976, pp. 355–404.
Adler-Rudel, S. *Ostjuden in Deutschland 1880–1940*. Tübingen, 1959.
Adolph, Hans J. L. *Otto Wels und die Politik der deutschen Sozialdemokratie 1894–1939*. Berlin, 1970.
Albertin, Lothar. "German Liberalism and the Foundation of the Weimar Republic: A Missed Opportunity?" In *German Democracy and the Triumph of Hitler,* ed. Erich Matthias and Anthony Nicholls. London, 1971.
_____. *Liberalismus und Demokratie am Anfang der Weimarer Republik*. Düsseldorf, 1971.
_____. "Die Verantwortung der Liberalen Parteien für das Scheitern der Grossen Koalition im Herbst 1921." *Historische Zeitschrift* 205 (Dec. 1967), 566–627.
Angress, Werner T. "Juden im politischen Leben der Revolutionszeit." In *Deutsches Judentum in Krieg und Revolution 1916–1923,* ed. Mosse. Tübingen, 1963.

――――――. *Die Kampfzeit der KPD 1921–23*. Düsseldorf, 1973.

Anlauf, Karl. *Die Revolution in Niedersachsen*. Hanover, 1919.

Anschütz, Gerhard. "Der deutsche Föderalismus in Vergangenheit, Gegenwart und Zukunft." In *Der deutsche Föderalismus—die Diktatur des Reichspräsidenten*, ed. Gerhard Anschütz et al. Berlin, 1924 pp. 11–32.

――――――. *Das preussisch-deutsche Problem*. Tübingen: 1922.

Apelt, Willipalt. *Geschichte der Weimarer Verfassung*. 2d ed. Munich, 1964.

Arns, Günter. "Die Krise des Weimarer Parlamentarismus im Frühherbst 1923." *Der Staat* 8 (1969), 181–216.

――――――. "Die Linke in der SPD-Reichstagsfraktion im Herbst 1923." *Vierteljahrshefte für Zeitgeschichte* 23 (Apr. 1974), 191–203.

――――――. "Regierungsbildung und Koalitionspolitik in der Weimarer Republik 1919–1924." Ph.D. diss., University of Tübingen, 1971.

――――――, ed. "Erich Koch-Wesers Aufzeichnungen vom 13. Februar 1919." *Vierteljahrshefte für Zeitgeschichte* 17 (Jan. 1969), 96–115.

Back, Jürgen A. *Franz von Papen in der Weimarer Republik*. Düsseldorf, 1977.

Bahne, Siegfried. "Die KPD im Ruhrgebiet in der Weimarer Republik." In *Arbeiterbewegung an Rhein und Ruhr*, ed. Reulecke. Wuppertal, 1974.

Bär, Adolf. "Wie die Bestimmungen des Artikels 148 der Reichsverfassung . . . in den deutschen Ländern amtlich ausgeführt werden." *Vierteljahresschrift für philosophische Pädagogik* 7 (1926–27), 85–103, 125–243.

Barmeyer, Heide. *Andreas Hermes und die Organisation der deutschen Landwirtschaft*. Stuttgart, 1971.

Basler, Werner. *Deutschlands Annexionspolitik in Polen und im Baltikum 1914–1918*. Berlin, 1962.

Bäumer, Gertrud. "Die Überwindung des Klassenkamfes." *Die Hilfe*, Mar. 14, 1918, pp. 114–19.

Beck, Hermann, ed. *Wege und Ziele der Sozialisierung*. Berlin, 1919.

Becker, Marie-Luise. "Adenauer und die englische Besatzungsmacht (1918–1926.)" In *Konrad Adenauer*, ed. Stehkämper. Cologne, 1976, pp. 99–121.

Becker, Werner. *Demokratie des sozialen Rechts—die politische Haltung der Frankfurter Zeitung, der Vossischen Zeitung und des Berliner Tageblatts 1918–1924*. Göttingen, 1971.

――――――. "Die Rolle der liberalen Presse." In *Deutsches Judentum in Krieg und Revolution 1916–1923*, ed. Mosse. Tübingen, 1963, pp. 67–135.

Behrend, Hans-Karl. "Zur Personalpolitik des Preussischen Ministeriums des Innern—die Besetzung der Landratsstellen in den östlichen Provinzen 1919–1933." *Jahrbuch für die Geschichte Mittel- und Ostdeutschlands* 6 (1957), 173–214.

Benz, Wolfgang. *Süddeutschland in der Weimarer Republik*. Berlin, 1970.

Berglar, Peter. *Walther Rathenau*. Bremen, 1970.

Bergsträsser, Ludwig. *Geschichte der politischen Parteien in Deutschland*. 6th ed. Mannheim, 1932.

Berlau, Abraham Joseph. *The German Social Democratic Party*. New York, 1949. Rpt. New York, 1970.

Bermbach, Udo. *Vorformen parlamentarischer Kabinettsbildung in Deutschland—der Interfraktionelle Ausschuss 1917/18 und die Parlamentarisierung der Reichsregierung*. Cologne, 1967.

Bernstein, Eduard. *Die deutsche Revolution*. Berlin-Fichtenau, 1921.

Bessmertny, Alexander, and M. Neven du Mont, eds. *Die Parteien und das Rätesystem*. Charlottenburg, 1919.

Biegert, Hans H. "Gewerkschaftspolitik in der Phase des Kapp-Lüttwitz Putsches." In *Industrielles System und politische Entwicklung in der Weimarer Republik*, ed. Hans Mommsen, Dieter Petzina, and Bernd Weisbrod. Düsseldorf, 1974.

Bieligk, Fritz, et al. *Die Organisation im Klassenkampf.* Berlin-Britz, 1932.

Bischof, Erwin. *Rheinischer Separatismus 1918–1924.* Bern, 1969.

Bleuel, Hans Peter. *Deutschlands Bekenner—Professoren zwischen Kaiserreich und Diktatur.* Bern, 1968.

Bleuel, Hans Peter, and Ernst Klinnert. *Deutsche Studenten auf dem Weg ins Dritte Reich.* Gütersloh, 1967.

Boelitz, Otto. *Der Aufbau des preussischen Bildungswesens nach der Staatsumwälzung.* 2d ed. Leipzig, 1925.

Bölling, Rainer. *Volksschullehrer und Politik.* Göttingen, 1978.

Born, Karl Erich. *Staat und Sozialpolitik seit Bismarcks Sturz.* Wiesbaden, 1957.

Brammer, Karl. *Das Gesicht der Reaktion 1918–1919.* Berlin-Halensee, 1919.

_____. ed. *Fünf Tage Militärdiktatur.* Berlin, 1920.

_____. ed. *Verfassungsgrundlagen und Hochverrat: Der Jagow-Prozess.* Berlin, 1922.

Brant, Sebastian. "Politische Chronik," *Neue Rundschau* 32 (1921), 552–59, 660–67, 768–74, 880–86, 995–1002, 1108–14, 1221–27.

Brecht, Arnold. *Federalism and Regionalism in Germany.* New York, 1945.

Brüggemann, Fritz. *Die Rheinische Republik.* Bonn, 1919.

Bucher, Peter. "Zur Geschichte der Einwohnerwehren in Preussen 1918–1921." *Militärgeschichtliche Mitteilungen* 9 (1971), 15–59.

Buchheim, Karl. *Geschichte der christlichen Parteien in Deutschland.* Munich, 1953.

Buddeberg, Theodor. "Das soziologische Problem der Sozialdemokratie." *Archiv für Sozialwissenschaft und Sozialpolitik* 49 (1922), 108–32.

Buse, D. K. "Ebert and the German Crisis 1917–1920." *Central European History* 5 (Sept. 1972), 234–55.

_____. "Ebert and the Coming of World War I: A Month from His Diary." *International Review of Social History* 13 (1968), 430–48.

Carsten, Francis L. *Revolution in Central Europe 1918–1919.* Berkeley, Calif., 1972.

Caspar, Gustav Adolf. *Die sozialdemokratische Partei und das deutsche Wehrproblem in den Jahren der Weimarer Republik.* Frankfurt a.M., 1959.

Chanady, Attila. "The Disintegration of the German National People's Party 1924–1930." *Journal of Modern History* 39 (1967), 65–91.

Cohen-Reuss, Max. "Deutsche und preussische Regierungsprobleme." *Sozialistische Monatshefte* 62 (2 Mar. 1925), 135–38.

_____. "Der politische Sinn des Görlitzer Beschlusses." *Sozialistische Monatshefte* 57 (10 Oct. 1921), 865–69.

Comfort, Richard A. "The Political Role of the Free Unions and the Failure of Council Government in Hamburg, November 1918 to March 1919." *International Review of Social History* 9 (1964), 47–64.

Conze, Werner. "Die Krise des Parteienstaates in Deutschland 1929/30." *Historische Zeitschrift* 168 (Aug. 1954), 74–83.

Coper, Rudolf. *Failure of a Revolution.* Cambridge, Mass., 1955.

Cunow, Heinrich. "Die preussische Landtagswahl und die Parteien." *Neue Zeit* 39 (4 Mar. 1921), 537–41.

_____. "Der preussische Verfassungsentwurf." *Neue Zeit* 38 (2 Apr. 1920), 1–6.

Czisnik, Ulrich. *Gustav Noske.* Göttingen, 1969.

Deak, Istvan. *Weimar Germany's Left-Wing Intellectuals.* Berkeley, Calif., 1968.

Deutz, Josef. *Adam Stegerwald.* Cologne, 1952.

Dierske, Ludwig. "Sicherheitskräfte in Preussen zu Beginn der Weimarer Republik." *Aus Politik und Zeitgeschichte (Das Parlament)* B47/69 (22 Nov. 1969), 31–55.

Döhn, Lothar. *Politik und Interesse—Die Interessenstruktur der Deutschen Volkspartei.* Meisenheim am Glan, 1970.

Dona Westfalica—Georg Schreiber zum 80. Geburtstage dargebracht von der Historischen Kommission Westfalens. Münster, 1963.

Ehni, Hans-Peter. *Bollwerk Preussen—Preussens Regierung, Reich-Länder Problem und Sozialdemokratie 1928–1932.* Bonn–Bad Godesberg, 1975.

—————. "Zum Parteienverhältnis in Preussen 1918–1932." *Archiv für Sozialgeschichte* 11 (1971), 241–88.

Eimers, Enno. *Das Verhältnis von Preussen und Reich in den ersten Jahren der Weimarer Republik (1918–1923).* Berlin, 1969.

Einhorn, Marion. "Zur Rolle der Räte im November und Dezember 1918." *Zeitschrift für Geschichtswissenschaft* 4 (1956), 545–59.

Eisner, Freya. *Das Verhältnis der KPD zu den Gewerkschaften in der Weimarer Republik.* Frankfurt a.m., 1977.

Elben, Wolfgang. *Das Problem der Kontinuität in der deutschen Revolution.* Düsseldorf, 1965.

Eliasberg, George. *Der Ruhrkrieg 1920.* Frankfurt a.M., 1974.

Engeli, Christian. *Gustav Böss.* Stuttgart, 1971.

Epstein, Klaus. *Matthias Erzberger und das Dilemma der deutschen Demokratie.* Berlin, 1962.

Erdmann, Karl Dietrich. *Adenauer in der Rheinlandpolitik nach dem Ersten Weltkrieg.* Stuttgart, 1966.

—————. "Die Geschichte der Weimarer Republik als Problem der Wissenschaft." *Vierteljahrshefte für Zeitgeschichte* 3 (1955), 1–18.

Erger, Johannes. *Der Kapp-Lüttwitz Putsch.* Düsseldorf, 1967.

Eschenburg, Theodor. "Carl Sonnenschein." *Vierteljahrshefte für Zeitgeschichte* 11 (Oct. 1963), 333–61.

Fechenbach, Felix. *Der Revolutionär Karl Eisner.* Berlin, 1929.

Feldman, Gerald D. "Arbeitskonflikte im Ruhrbergbau 1919–1922." *Vierteljahrshefte für Zeitgeschichte* 28 (Apr. 1980), 168–223.

—————. *Army, Industry and Labor in Germany 1914–1918.* Princeton, N.J., 1966.

—————. "Big Business and the Kapp Putsch." *Central European History* 4 (1971), 99–130.

Feldman, Gerald D., and Heidrun Homburg. *Industrie und Inflation.* Hamburg, 1977.

Felix, David. *Walther Rathenau and the Weimar Republic.* Baltimore, 1971.

Fischart, Johannes (Erich Dombrowski). *Neue Köpfe—Das alte und das neue System.* 4th ed. Berlin, 1925.

Fischer, Kurt Gerhard, ed. *Politische Bildung in der Weimarer Republik.* Frankfurt a.M., 1970.

Flemming, Jens. "Parlamentarische Kontrolle in der November-Revolution." *Archiv für Sozialgeschichte* 11 (1971), 69–139.

—————. "Landarbeiter zwischen Gewerkschaften und 'Werkgemeinschaft.' " *Archiv für Sozialgeschichte* 14 (1974), 351–418.

von Freytag-Loringhoven, Freiherr. *Deutschnationale Volkspartei.* Berlin, 1931.

Fricke, Dieter, and Hans Randandt. "Neue Dokumente über die Rolle Albert Südekums." *Zeitschrift für Geschichtswissenschaft* 4 (1956), 757–65.

Friedlander, Henry Egon. "Conflict of Revolutionary Authority." *International Review of Social History* 7 (1962), 163–76.

Friedländer, Saul. "Die politischen Veränderungen der Kriegszeit und ihre Auswirkungen auf die Judenfrage." In *Deutsches Judentum in Krieg und Revolution 1916–1923,* ed. Mosse. Tübigen, 1963, pp. 27–65.

Frye, Bruce B. "The German Democratic Party 1918–1930." *Western Political Quarterly* 16 (Mar. 1963), 167–79.

Führ, Christoph. *Zur Schulpolitik der Weimarer Republik.* Berlin, 1970.

von Gablentz, Otto Heinrich. "Vom Patriotismus zum Nationalismus." In *Staat, Wirtschaft und Politik in der Weimarer Republik—Festschrift für Heinrich Brüning*, ed. Ferdinand A. Hermens and Theodor Schieder. Berlin, 1966, pp. 3–21.

Gabel, Walter. *Die Wahlrechtsfrage in der Geschichte der deutschen liberalen Parteien 1848–1918*. Düsseldorf, 1958.

Gast, Helmut. "Die proletarischen Hundertschaften als Organe der Einheitsfront im Jahre 1923." *Zeitschrift für Geschichtswissenschaft* 4 (1956), 437–65.

Gay, Peter. *The Dilemma of Democratic Socialism: Eduard Bernstein's Challenge to Marx*. New York, 1952.

Geiger, Theodor. "Panik im Mittelstand." *Die Arbeit* 7 (1930), 637–54.

von Gerlach, Hellmut. *Der Zusammenbruch der deutschen Polenpolitik*. Berlin, 1919.

Geyer, Curt. *Drei Verderber Deutschlands*. Berlin, 1924.

Giesecke, Hermann. "Zur Schulpolitik der Sozialdemokraten in Preussen und im Reich." *Vierteljahrshefte für Zeitgeschichte* 13 (Apr. 1967), 162–77.

Glees, Anthony. "Albert C. Grzesinski and the Politics of Prussia 1926–1930." *English Historical Review* 89 (Oct. 1974), 814–34.

Goldschmidt, Hans. *Das Reich und Preussen im Kampf um die Führung—Von Bismarck bis 1918*. Berlin, 1931.

Gordon, Harold J., Jr. *Hitler and the Beer Hall Putsch*. Princeton, N.J., 1972.

Grebe, Friedrich. "Die grosse Koalition in Preussen an der Arbeit." *Allgemeine Rundschau* 19 (14 Jan. 1922), 15–16.

—————. "Die grosse Koalition in Preussen." *Allgemeine Rundschau* 18 (19 Nov. 1921), 640–41.

—————. "Die Landtagswahlen in Preussen." *Allgemeine Rundschau* 18 (5 Mar. 1921), 109–10.

—————. "Preussen und das Reich." *Allgemeine Rundschau* 18 (1 May 1921), 218–19.

—————. "Die Regierungsbildung in Preussen." *Allgemeine Rundschau* 18 (26 Mar. 1921), 154–55.

—————. "Stegerwald preussischer Ministerpräsident." *Allgemeine Rundschau* 18 (16 Apr. 1921), 193–94.

—————. "Das Ministerium Stegerwald." *Allgemeine Rundschau* 18 (7 May 1921), 266–68.

Grebing, Helga. *Geschichte der deutschen Arbeiterbewegung*. Munich, 1966.

—————. "Die Linke in der Weimarer Republik." *Politische Studien* 18 (1967), 334–40.

—————. "Weimarer Portraits." *Politische Studien* 6 (1956), 17–35.

Groh, Dieter. *Negative Integration und revolutionärer Attentismus—Die deutsche Sozialdemokratie am Vorabend des 1. Weltkrieges*. Frankfurt a.M., 1973.

Grosser, Dieter. *Vom monarchischen Konstitutionalismus zur parlamentarischen Demokratie*. The Hague, 1970.

Grünthal, Günther. *Reichsschulgesetz und Zentrumspartei in der Weimarer Republik*. Düsseldorf, 1968.

Haenisch, Konrad. *Neue Bahnen der Kulturpolitik*. Stuttgart, 1921.

—————."Ein offener Brief an Professor Saenger." *Neue Rundschau* 20, pt. 1 (1919), 17–27.

—————. *Die deutsche Sozialdemokratie in und nach dem Weltkriege*. Berlin, 1916 .

—————. *Staat und Hochschule*. Berlin, 1920.

Hamburger, Ernest. "Betrachtung über Heinrich Brünings Memoiren." *Internationale Wissenschaftliche Korrespondenz*, no. 15 (Apr. 1972), 18–39.

—————. *Juden im öffentlichen Leben Deutschlands*. Tübingen, 1968.

—————. "Die Neugliederung des Reiches und die auswärtige Politik." *Sozialistische Monatshefte* 54 (31 May 1920), 450–58.

Hamel, Iris. *Völkischer Verband und nationale Gewerkschaft—Der Deutschnationale Handlungsgehilfen-Verband 1893–1933*. Frankfurt a.m., 1967.

Hartenstein, Wolfgang. *Die Anfänge der Deutschen Volkspartei 1918–1920*. Düsseldorf, 1962.

Hartfield, John, et al. *Illustrierte Geschichte der deutschen Republik*. Berlin, 1929. Reprint. Frankfurt a.m., 1970.

Hauser, Oswald. *Politische Parteien in Deutschland und Frankreich 1918–1939*. Wiesbaden, 1969.

Hauss, Hanns-Jochen. *Die erste Volkswahl des deutschen Reichspräsidenten*. Kallmünz/Opf., 1965.

Heberle, Rudolf. *Landbevölkerung und Nationalsozialismus*. Munich, 1963.

Heckart, Beverly. *From Bassermann to Bebel: The Grand Bloc's Quest for Reform in the Kaiserreich*. New Haven, Conn., 1974.

Heidegger, Hermann. *Die deutsche Sozialdemokratie und der nationale Staat*. Göttingen, 1956.

Heile, Wilhelm. "Die deutsche Revolution." *Die Hilfe*, 14 Nov. 1918, 541–43.

————. "Der Streik." *Die Hilfe*, 14 Feb. 1918, 63–64.

Heine, Wolfgang. "Die Beamten der Republik." *Sozialistische Monatshefte* 63 (Sept. 1926), 610–14.

Heinemann, Hugo. *Die sozialistischen Errungenschaften der Kriegszeit*. Chemnitz, [1916].

Heinemann, Manfred, ed. *Der Lehrer und seine Organisation*. Stuttgart, 1977.

Hellpach, Willy. *Der deutsche Charakter*. Bonn, 1954.

Hentschel, Volker. *Wirtschaft und Wirtschaftspolitik im wilhelminischen Deutschland*. Stuttgart, 1978.

Herlemann, Beatrix. *Kommunalpolitik der KPD im Ruhrgebiet 1924–1933*. Wuppertal, 1977.

Herschel, "Oberschlesien und Zentrum." *Allgemeine Rundschau* 18 (7 May 1921), 233–35.

Herzfeld, Hans, and Gerd Heinrich, eds. *Berlin und die Provinz Brandenburg im 19. und 20. Jahrhundert*. Berlin, 1968.

Hirsch, Paul. "Die Verfassung des Freistaates Preussen." *Neue Zeit* 39 (19 Nov. 1920), 184–89.

Holl, Karl. "Konfessionalität, Konfessionalismus und demokratische Republic–Zu einigen Aspekten der Reichspräsidentenwahl von 1925." *Vierteljahrshefte für Zeitgeschichte* 17 (July 1969), 254–75.

Holt, John B. *German Agricultural Policy 1918–1934*. Chapel Hill, N.C., 1936.

Hunt, Richard N. *German Social Democracy 1918–1933*. New Haven, Conn., 1964.

Ist eine Einheitsfront mit den Kommunisten möglich? Denkschrift über die Verhandlungen der Gewerkschaften mit den Arbeiterparteien über den Schutz der Rebublik. Ed. ADGB. Berlin, 1922.

Jacke, Jochen. *Kirche zwischen Monarchie und Republik—Der preussische Protestantismus nach dem Zusammenbruch von 1918*. Hamburg, 1976.

Jaeger, Hans. *Unternehmer in der deutschen Politik (1890–1918)*. Bonn, 1976.

Jasper, Gotthard. *Der Schutz der Republik 1922–1930*. Tübingen, 1963.

Jones, Larry. "Adam Stegerwald." *Vierteljahrshefte für Zeitgeschichte* 27 (Mar. 1979), 1–29.

Junius. "Politische Chronik." *Neue Rundschau* 33 pts. 1–2 (1922), 102–09, 214–21, 324–330.

Kaelble, Hartmut, ed. *Probleme der Modernisierung in Deutschland—Sozialhistorische Studien zum 19. und 20. Jahrhundert*. Opladen, 1978.

Kaltefleiter, Werner. *Wirtschaft und Politik in Deutschland—Konjunktur als Bestimmungsfaktor des Parteiensystems*. 2d ed. Cologne, 1968.

Kastning, Alfred. *Die deutsche Sozialdemokratie zwischen Koalition und Opposition*. Paderborn, 1970.

Kehr, Eckart. *Der Primat der Innenpolitik*. Ed. Hans-Ulrich Wehler. Berlin, 1965.

Kittel, Helmuth. *Die Entwicklung der pädagogischen Hochschulen 1926–1932*. Belin, 1957.

Kittel, Helmuth, ed. *Die Pädagogischen Hochschulen—Dokumente ihrer Entwicklung 1920–1932*. Weinheim, 1965.

von Klass, Gert. *Hugo Stinnes*. Tübingen, 1958.

Klatt, Rudolf. *Ostpreussen unter dem Reichskommissariat 1919/1920*. Heidelberg, 1958.

Klein, Peter. *Separatisten an Rhein und Ruhr*. Berlin, 1961.

Kluge, Ulrich. *Soldatenräte und Revolution*. Göttingen, 1975.

————. "Essener Sozialisierungsbewegung und Volkswehrbewegung im Rheinisch-Westfälischen Industriegebiet 1918/1919." *Internationale Wissenschaftliche Korrespondenz*, no. 16 (Aug. 1972), 55–65.

Knapp, Thomas A. "The German Center Party and the Reichsbanner." *International Review of Social History* 14 (1969), 159–79.

Knütter, Hans-Helmuth. *Die Juden und die deutsche Linke in der Weimarer Republik*. Düsseldorf, 1971.

Kocka, Jürgen. "The First World War and the 'Mittelstand.' " *Journal of Contemporary History* 8 (Jan. 1973), 101–23.

————. *Klassengesellschaft im Krieg 1914–1918*. Göttingen, 1973.

Koenen, Wilhelm. "Zur Frage der Möglichkeit einer Arbeiterregierung nach dem Kapp-Putsch." *Beiträge zur Geschichte der deutschen Arbeiterbewegung* 4 (1962), 325–52.

Kohler, Eric D. "Revolutionary Pomerania, 1919–20." *Central European History* 9 (Sept. 1976), 250–93.

Köhler, Henning. *Autonomiebewegung oder Separatismus?—Die Politik der Kölnischen Volkszeitung 1918/1919*. Berlin, 1974.

Kolb, Eberhard. *Die Arbeiterräte in der deutschen Innenpolitik 1918–19*. Düsseldorf, 1962.

————, ed. *Vom Kaiserreich zur Weimarer Republik*. Cologne, 1972.

Kollman, Eric C. "Eine Diagnose der Weimarer Republik—Ernst Troeltschs politische Anschauungen." *Historische Zeitschrift* 182 (Oct. 1956), 291–319.

Könnemann, Erwin. "Zwei Denkschriften der Kapp-Putschisten über ihr Verhältnis zur Sozialdemokratie." *Beiträge zur Geschichte der Arbeiterbewegung* 9 (1969), 490–500.

————. *Einwohnerwehren und Zeitfreiwilligenverbände*. Berlin, 1971.

————. *Der Kapp-Putsch und der Kampf der deutschen Arbeiterklasse*. Berlin, 1972.

————. "Zum Problem der Bildung einer Arbeiterregierung nach dem Kapp-Putsch." *Beiträge zur Geschichte der Arbeiterbewegung* 5 (1963), 904–21.

Könnemann, Erwin, ed. "Protokolle Albert Südekums aus den Tagen nach dem Kapp-Putsch." *Beiträge zur Geschichte der Arbeiterbewegung* 8 (1966), 262–78.

Kosthorst, Erich, et al. *Jakob Kaiser*. 3 vols. Stuttgart, 1967.

Koszyk, Kurt. *Zwischen Kaiserreich und Diktatur—Die sozialdemokratische Presse von 1914–1933*. Heidelberg, 1958.

Kotowski, Georg. *Friedrich Ebert*. Vol. 1: *Der Aufstieg eines deutschen Arbeiterführers 1871–1919*. Wiesbaden, 1963.

Koza, Ingeborg. *Die erste deutsche Republik im Spiegel des politischen Memoirenschrifttums*. Wuppertal, 1971.

Kranold, Hermann. "Nach den preussischen Landtagswahlen 1921." *Sozialistische Monatshefte* 56 (28 Feb. 1921), 169–72.

Krause, Hartfried. *USPD*. Frankfurt a.M., 1975.

Krauss, Erving. "Some Perspectives on Social Stratification and Social Class." *Sociological Review*, n.s. 15 (July 1977), 129–40.

Krüger, Peter. "Das Reparationsproblem der Weimarer Republik in fragwürdiger Sicht." *Vierteljahrshefte für Zeitgeschichte* 27 (Jan. 1981), 21–47.

Kunze, Otto. "Die Grosse Mitte." *Allemeine Rundschau* 18 (1 Oct. 1921), 539–41.

Küppers, Heinrich."Weimarer Schulpolitik in der Wirtschaft und Staatskrise der Republik." *Vierteljahrshefte für Zeitgeschichte* 28 (Jan. 1980), 20–46.

Kuttner, Erich. *Otto Braun*. Berlin, [1932].

───────. *Warum versagt die Justiz?* Berlin, 1921.

Lamp'1, Walther. *Die Revolution in Gross-Hamburg*. Hamburg, 1921.

Laubach, Ernst. *Die Politik der Kabinette Wirth 1921/22*. Lübeck, 1968.

Lebkowics, Herman. *Social Conservatism and the Middle Classes in Germany 1914–1933*. Princeton, N.J., 1969.

Ledebour, Minna, ed. *Georg Ledebour—Mensch und Kämpfer*. Zürich, 1954.

Lehmann, Hans Dietrich. *Der "Deutsche Ausschuss" und die Abstimmungen in Schleswig 1920*. Neumünster, 1969.

Lerner, Warren, *Karl Radek*. Stanford, Calif., 1970.

Linneborn, Johannes. "Zentrum und Preussenkonkordat." In *Nationale Arbeit—Das Zentrum und sein Wirken in der deutschen Republik*, ed. Schulte. Berlin [1929], pp. 225–34.

Lohalm, Uwe. *Völkischer Radikalismus—Die Geschichte des Deutsch-Völkischen Schutz- und Trutz-Bundes*. Hamburg, 1970.

Lösche, Peter. *Der Bolschewismus im Urteil der Sozialdemokratie 1903–1920*. Berlin, 1967.

Lucas, Erhard. *Frankfurt unter der Herrschaft des Arbeiter- und Soldatenrats 1918/19*. Frankfurt a.M., 1969.

───────. *Märzrevolution im Ruhrgebiet*. Frankfurt a.M., 1970.

Luckemeyer, Ludwig. "Die Deutsche Demokratische Partei von der Revolution bis zur Nationalversammlung 1918–1919." Ph.D. diss., University of Erlangen, 1975.

Ludewig, Hans Ulrich. *Arbeiterbewegung und Aufstand: Zum Verhalten der Arbeiterparteien in den Aufstandsbewegungen der frühen Weimarer Republik 1920–23*. Husum, 1978.

Lüth, Erich, and Hans-Dieter Loose, eds. *Bürgermeister Carl Petersen*. Hamburg, 1971.

Luther, Karl-Heinz. "Die nachrevolutionären Machtkämpfe in Berlin November 1918 bis März 1919." *Jahrbuch für die Geschichte Mittel- und Ostdeutschlands* 8 (1959), 187–221.

Mann, Golo. "Otto Braun: 'Von Weimar bis Hitler.'" *Geschichte und Geschichten*. Frankfurt a.M., 1961, "Otto Braun: 'Von Weimar bis Hitler.'" In *Geschichte* pp. 50–56.

Matthias, Erich. "German Social Democracy in the Weimar Republic." In *German Democracy and the Triumph of Hitler*, ed. Matthias and Anthony Nicholls. London, 1971.

───────. *Die deutsche Sozialdemokratie und der Osten 1914–1944*. Tübingen, 1954.

Matull, Wilhelm, ed. *Ostdeutschlands Arbeiterbewegung*. Würzburg, 1973.

Mehnert, Gottfried. *Evangelische Kirche und Politik*. Düsseldorf, 1959.

Meier-Welcker, Hans. "Die Stellung des Chefs der Heeresleitung in den Anfängen der Republik." *Vierteljahrshefte für Zeitgeschichte* 4 (1956), 155–60.

Meinecke, Friedrich. "Verfassung und Verwaltung der deutschen Republik." *Neue Rundschau* 30, pt. 1 (1919), 1–16.

Mellen, Sidney L. W. "The German People and the Postwar World." *American Political Science Review* 37 (Aug. 1943), 601–25.

Menges, Franz. *Reichsreform und Finanzpolitik*. Berlin, 1971.

Menzel, Hans. *Carl Severing*. Berlin, 1932.

Metzmacher, Helmut. "Der Novembersturz 1918 in der Rheinprovinz." *Annalen des Historischen Vereins für den Niederrhein*, nos. 168/69 (1967), 135–265.

Meyer, Folkert. *Schule der Untertanen*. Hamburg, 1976.

Miller, Susanne. *Burgfrieden und Klassenkampf*. Düsseldorf, 1974.

───────. *Das Problem der Freiheit im Sozialismus*. 2d ed. Frankfurt a.M., 1964.

───────. *Die Bürde der Macht*. Düsseldorf, 1968.

Mitchell, Allan. *Revolution in Bayern*. Munich, 1967.

Mittmann, Ursula. *Fraktion und Partei—Ein Vergleich von Zentrum und Sozialdemokratie im Kaiserreich.* Düsseldorf, 1976.

Möller, Horst. "Parlamentarisierung und Demokratisierung im Preussen der Weimarer Republik." In *Gesellschaft, Parlament und Regierung*, ed. Gerhard A. Ritter. Düsseldorf, 1974, pp. 367–87.

Mommsen, Hans. *Arbeiterbewegung und nationale Frage.* Göttingen, 1979.

Mommsen, Hans, et al., eds. *Industrielles System und politische Entwicklung in der Weimarer Republik.* 2 vols. Kronberg/Taunus, 1977.

Mommsen, Wolfgang. *Max Weber und die deutsche Politik.* 2d ed. Tübingen, 1974.

Morgan, David W. *The Socialist Left and the German Revolution—A History of the German Independent Social Democratic Party.* Ithaca, N.Y., 1975.

Morsey, Rudolf. "Franz von Papen." In *Zeitgeschichte in Lebensbildern—Aus dem deutschen Katholizismus des 20. Jahrhunderts*, ed. Rudolf Morsey. Mainz, 1973, 2:75–87.

———. *Die Deutsche Zentrumspartei 1917–1923.* Düsseldorf, 1966.

Mosse, Werner E., ed. *Deutsches Judentum in Krieg und Revolution 1916–1923.* Tübingen, 1963.

Motschmann, Claus. *Evangelische Kirche und preussischer Staat in den Anfängen der Weimarer Republik.* Lübeck and Hamburg, 1969.

Müller, Hermann, et al. *Zehn Jahre deutsche Geschichte 1918–1928.* 2d ed. Berlin, 1928.

Müller, Richard. *Was Arbeiterräte wollen und sollen.* [Berlin, 1919.]

Muth, Heinrich. "Die Entstehung der Bauern- und Landarbeiterräte im November 1918." *Vierteljahrshefte für Zeitgeschichte* 21 (Jan. 1973), 1–38.

Naumann, Horst, and Günter Bebel, eds. "Protokoll der Berliner Arbeiterräte am 19. November 1918 im Zirkus Busch." *Beiträge zur Geschichte der deutschen Arbeiterbewegung* 10 (1968), 1033–56.

Naumann, Horst, and Günter Bebel, eds. "Protokolle der Sitzungen des Vollzugsrates . . . und der Vollversammlung der Berliner Arbeiterräte vom 16., 17. und 19. November 1918." *Beiträge zur Geschichte der deutschen Arbeiterbewegung* 10 (Sonderheft 1968), 133–50.

Netzband, Karl-Bernhard, and Hans-Peter Widmaier. *Währungs- und Finanzpolitik der Ära Luther 1923–25.* Tübingen, 1964.

Neumann, Siegmund. *Die Parteien der Weimarer Republik.* Berlin, 1932. Rpt. Stuttgart, 1965.

Newmann, Karl J. *European Democracy Between the Wars.* London, 1970.

Niekisch, Ernst. *Politische Schriften.* 2d ed. Cologne, 1966.

Niewyk, Donald L. *Socialist, Anti-Semite and Jew—German Social Democracy Confronts the Problem of Anti-Semitism 1918–1933.* Baton Rouge, La., 1971.

Nipperdey, Thomas. *Die Organisation der deutschen Parteien vor 1918.* Düsseldorf, 1961.

Nowka, Harry. *Das Machtverhältnis zwischen Partei und Fraktion in der SPD.* Cologne, 1973.

Nusser, Horst G.W. *Konservative Wehrverbände in Bayern, Preussen und Österreich.* Munich, 1973.

Oeckel, Heinz. *Die Revolutionäre Volkswehr 1918/19.* Berlin, 1968.

Oestreich, Paul. *Es reut mich nicht! Schulpolitische Kämpfe zwischen Revolution und Kapp-Putsch.* Leipzig, [1920].

Opel, Fritz. *Der deutsche Metallarbeiterverband während des ersten Weltkrieges und der Revolution.* Hanover, 1957.

Osterroth, Franz. "Der Hofgeismar Kreis der Jungsozialisten." *Archiv der Sozialgeschichte* 4 (1964), 525–69.

Patemann, Reinhard. *Der Kampf um die preussische Wahlreform im Ersten Weltkrieg.* Düsseldorf, 1964.

Petzina, Dietmar. *Die deutsche Wirtschaft in der Zwischenkriegszeit.* Wiesbaden, 1977.

Pikart, Eberhard. "Preussische Beamtenpolitik 1918–1933." *Vierteljahrshefte für Zeitgeschichte* 6 (Apr. 1958), 119–37.

Pollock, James K., Jr. "The German Party System." *American Political Science Review* 23 (Nov. 1929), 859–91.

Portner, Ernst. *Die Verfassungspolitik der Liberalen 1919*. Bonn, 1973.

Prager, Eugen. *Geschichte der USPD*. 2d ed. Berlin, 1922. Rpt. Glashütten i.T., 1970.

Puhle, Hans-Jürgen. *Agrarische Interessenpolitik und preussischer Konservatismus im Wilhelminischen Reich (1893–1914)*. Hanover, 1966.

————. *Von der Agrarkrise zum Präfaschismus*. Wiesbaden, 1972.

Rauh, Manfred. *Die Parlamentarisierung des Deutschen Reiches*. Düsseldorf, 1977.

Rausch, Bernhard. "Regierungsbildung in Preussen und die Sozialdemokratie." *Neue Zeit* 39 (18 Mar. 1921), 589–95.

Reinhardt, Walther. "Aus dem Nachlass des Generals Walther Reinhardt." Ed. Fritz Ernst. *Welt als Geschichte* 18 (1958), 39–65.

Reisberg, Arnold. *An den Quellen der Einheitsfront—Der Kampf der KPD um die Aktionseinheit in Deutschland 1921–1922*. 2 vols. Berlin, 1971.

Remmele, Adam. *Staatsumwälzung und Neuaufbau in Baden*. Karlsruhe, 1925.

Reulecke, Jürgen, ed. *Arbeiterbewegung an Rhein und Ruhr*. Wuppertal, 1974.

Reuter, Ernst. "Reform der Berliner Verwaltung." *Sozialistische Monatshefte* 70 (14 Apr. 1930), 344–49.

Ribhegge, Wilhelm. *August Winning*. Bonn-Bad Godesberg, 1973.

Ritter, Gerhard A. *Arbeiterbewegung, Parteien und Parlamentarismus—Aufsätze zur deutschen Sozial- und Verfassungs-geschichte des 19. u. 20. Jahrhunderts*. Göttingen, 1976.

————, ed. *Entstehung und Wandel der Modernen Gesellschaft—Festschrift für Hans Rosenberg*. Berlin, 1970.

Ritter, Gerhard A., and Susanne Miller, eds. *Die deutsche Revolution 1918–1919—Dokumente*. Frankfurt a.M., 1968.

Roth, Guenther. *The Social Democrats in Imperial Germany*. Totowa, N.J., 1963.

Runge, Wolfgang. *Politik und Beamtentum im Parteienstaat*. Stuttgart, 1965.

Rupieper, Hermann J. *The Cuno Government and Reparations, 1922–1923: Politics and Economics*. Boston, 1979.

Rürup, Reinhard. *Probleme der Revolution in Deutschland*. Wiesbaden, 1968.

Sachse, Otto. "Was tut Stegerwald?" *Allgemeine Rundschau* 17 (19 Nov. 1921), 639.

Saenger, Samuel. "Politische Chronik." *Neue Rundschau* 35 (1924), 1300–05.

Schäfer, Friedrich. "Zur Frage des Wahlrechts in der Weimarer Republik." In *Staat, Wirtschaft und Politik in der Weimarer Republik—Festschrift für Heinrich Brüning*, ed. Ferdinand A. Hermens and Theodor Schieder. Berlin, 1967.

Scharlau, Winfried B., and Zbynek A. Zeman. *Freibeuter der Revolution—Parvus-Helphand*. Cologne, 1964.

Schauf, Johannes. *Die deutschen Katholiken und die Zentrumspartei*. Cologne, 1928.

Scheibe, Wolfgang. *Die reformpädagogische Bewegung, 1900–1932*. Weinheim, 1969.

Schiffers, Reinhard. *Elemente direkter Demokratie im Weimarer Regierungssystem*. Düsseldorf, 1971.

————. *Der Hauptausschuss des Deutschen Reichstages 1915–1918*. Düsseldorf, 1979.

Schmidt, Gustav. "Effizienz und Flexibilität politisch-sozialer Systeme—Die deutsche und englische Politik." *Vierteljahrshefte für Zeitgeschichte* 25 (Apr. 1977), 137–87.

Schmitz, Hermann. *Revolution der Gesinnung*. Neubabelsberg, 1931.

Schneider, Werner. *Die Deutsche Demokratische Partei in der Weimarer Republik 1924–1930*. Munich, 1978.

Schorr, Helmut J. *Adam Stegerwald*. Recklinghausen, 1966.

Schreiber, Georg. "Innenpolitik des Reiches." *Politisches Jahrbuch* 1 (1925), 35–75; ibid., 2 (1926), 49–91.

Schulte, Karl Anton. "Die Auseinandersetzung mit den ehemals regierenden Fürsten." *Politisches Jahrbuch* 2 (1926).

Schulte, Karl Anton, ed. *Nationale Arbeit—Das Zentrum und sein Wirken in der deutschen Republik.* Berlin, [1929].

Schulz, Gerhard. *Zwischen Demokratie und Diktatur.* Berlin, 1963.

Schulz, Heinrich. *Kirchenschule oder Volksschule?* Berlin, 1927.

_____. *Der Leidensweg des Reichschulgesetzes.* Berlin, 1926.

Schulze, Hagen. *Otto Braun.* Berlin, 1977.

_____. *Freikorps und Republik 1918–1920.* Boppard a.Rh., 1969.

_____. "Der Oststaat-Plan 1919." *Vierteljahrshefte für Zeitgeschichte* 18 (Apr. 1970), 123–63.

_____, ed. "Rückblick auf Weimar: Ein Briefwechsel zwischen Otto Braun und Josef Wirth im Exil." *Vierteljahrshefte für Zeitgeschichte* 26 (Jan. 1978), 144–85.

Schumacher, Martin. *Mittelstandsfront und Republik.* Düsseldorf, 1972.

Schumann, Wolfgang. *Oberschlesien 1918/19.* Berlin, 1961.

Schüren, Ulrich. *Der Volksentscheid zur Fürstenenteignung 1926.* Düsseldorf, 1978.

Schustereit, Hartmut. *Linksliberalismus und Sozialdemokratie in der Weimarer Republik.* Düsseldorf, 1975.

Schwarz, Gotthart. *Theodor Wolff und das Berliner Tageblatt.* Tübingen, 1968.

Schwarz, Jürgen. *Studenten in der Weimarer Republik.* Berlin, 1971.

Senger, Gerhard. *Die Politik der Deutschen Zentrumspartei zur Frage Reich und Länder von 1918–1928.* Hamburg, 1932.

Sering, Max, et al. *Die deutsche Landwirtschaft.* Berlin, 1932.

Severing, Carl. "Für die Grosse Koalition." *Sozialistische* Monatshefte 62 (5 Jan. 1925), 1–3.

_____. "Koalitionsfragen." *Sozialistische Monatshefte* 57 (15 Dec. 1921), 1081–84.

_____. "Preussenprobleme." *Neue Zeit* 39 (1 and 8 July 1921), 313–16, 337–41.

_____. "Provinzialautonomie?" *Neue Zeit* 40 (4 Nov. 1921), 121–24.

_____. "Ein Wort zum sozialdemokratischen Parteitag 1921." *Sozialistische Monatshefte* 57 (19 Sept. 1921). 785–88.

_____. "Der 2. Wahlgang." *Sozialistische Monatshefte* 62 (14 Apr. 1925), 197–99.

Siemann, Joachim. "Der sozialdemokratische Arbeiterführer in der Weimarer Republik." Ph.D. diss., Univ. of Göttingen, 1955.

Sinzheimer, Hugo. "Der sozialistische Staatsbegriff." *Die Glocke* 7 (6 Feb. 1922), 1262–68.

Spethmann, Hans. *Die Rote Armee an Ruhr und Rhein.* Berlin, 1930.

Stampfer, Friedrich. *Die vierzehn Jahre der ersten deutschen Republik.* 3d ed. Hamburg, 1953.

Staudinger, Hans. *Der Staat als Unternehmer.* Berlin, 1931.

Steffani, Winfried. *Die Untersuchungsausschüsse des preussischen Landtages.* Düsseldorf, 1960.

Steffen, Hans. *Otto Braun.* Berlin, 1932.

Stegmann, Dirk. *Die Erben Bismarcks.* Cologne, 1970.

Stehkämper, Hugo, ed. *Konrad Adenauer Oberbürgermeister von Köln.* Cologne, 1976.

Stephan, Werner. *Aufstieg und Verfall des Linksliberalismus 1918–1933.* Göttingen, 1973.

zu Stolberg-Wernigerode, Otto Graf. *Die unentschiedene Generation.* Munich, 1968.

Striesow, Jan. "Die Deutschnationale Volkspartei und die Völkisch-Radikalen." Ph.D. diss. University of Hamburg, 1977.

Ströbel, Heinrich. *Die deutsche Revolution.* Berlin, 1920.

Stump, Wolfgang. *Geschichte und Organisation der Zentrumspartei in Düsseldorf 1917–1933.* Düsseldorf, 1971.

Stürmer, Michael. *Koalition und Oppostion in der Weimarer Republik 1924–1928*. Düsseldorf, 1967.

————, ed. *Das kaiserliche Deutschland*. Düsseldorf, 1970.

Thadden, Rudolph von. *Fragen an Preussen*. Munich, 1981.

Thieme, Hartwig. *Nationaler Liberalismus in der Krise*. Boppard a.Rh., 1963.

Thieringer, Rolf. "Das Verhältnis der Gewerkschaften zu Staat und Parteien." Ph.D. diss. University of Tübingen, 1954.

Thimme, Anneliese. *Flucht in den Mythos*. Göttingen, 1969.

————. *Gustav Stresemann*. Hanover, 1957.

Thimme, Friedrich, and Carl Legien, eds. *Die Arbeiterschaft im neuen Deutschland*. Leipzig, 1915.

Thimme, Friedrich, and Ernst Rolffs, eds. *Revolution und Kirche*. Berlin, 1919.

Thimme, Roland. *Stresemann und die Deutsche Volkspartei 1923–25*. Lübeck, 1961.

Tormin, Walter. *Geschichte der deutschen Parteien seit 1848*. 3d ed. Stuttgart, 1968.

————. *Zwischen Rätediktatur und sozialer Demokratie*. Düsseldorf, 1954.

Tracey, Donald R. "Reform in the Early Weimar Republic: The Thuringian Example." *Journal of Modern History* 44 (June 1972), 195–212.

Troeltsch, Ernst. *Spektator-Briefe*. Ed. Hans Baron. Tübingen, 1924.

Turner, Henry A. *Faschismus und Kapitalismus in Deutschland*. Göttingen, 1972.

————. "The Ruhrlade: Secret Cabinet of Heavy Industry in the Weimar Republic." *Central European History* 3 (Sept. 1970), 195–228.

————. *Stresemann and the Politics of the Weimar Republic*. Princeton, N.J., 1963.

Ullmann, Hermann. "Das Essener Programm." *Deutsche Rundschau* 76 (1950), 897–903.

Unger, Emil. *Politische Köpfe des sozialistischen Deutschlands*. Leipzig, 1920.

Varain, Heinz-Josef. *Freie Gewerkschaften, Sozialdemokratie und Staat*. Düsseldorf, 1956.

Vogel, Walther. *Deutsche Reichsgliederung und Reichsreform in Vergangenheit und Gegenwart*. Leipzig, 1932.

Volkmann, E. O. *Revolution über Deutschland*. Oldenburg, 1930.

Wachtling, Oswald. *Joseph Joos*. Mainz, 1974.

Wagner, Raimund. "Zur Frage der Massenkämpfe in Sachsen vom Frühjahr bis zum Sommer 1923." *Zeitschrift für Geschichtswissenschaft* 4 (1956), 246–64.

Waldman, Eric. *The Spartacist Uprising of 1919 and the Crisis of the German Socialist Movement*. Milwaukee, Wis., 1958.

Wehler, Hans-Ulrich. *Krisenherde des Kaiserreiches*. Göttingen, 1970.

————. *Sozialdemokratie und Nationalstaat*. 2d ed. Göttingen, 1971.

Wehler, Hans-Ulrich, ed. *Moderne deutsche Sozialgeschichte*. Cologne, 1966.

Wells, Roger H. "Partisanship and Parties in German Municipal Government." *National Municipal Review* 8 (Aug. 1928), 473–81.

Wende, Erich. *C. H. Becker*. Stuttgart, 1959.

Wheeler-Bennet, John W. *The Nemesis of Power—The German Army in Politics*. New York, 1964.

Wilhelmus, Wolfgang. "Die Rolle der Räte in Vorpommern." *Zeitschrift für Geschichtswissenschaft* 4 (1956), 964–89.

Williamson, John G. *Karl Helfferich*. Princeton, N.J., 1971.

Winkler, Heinrich August. *Mittelstand, Demokartie und Nationalsozialismus*. Cologne, 1972.

Witt, Peter-Christian. *Die Finanzpolitik des Deutschen Reiches von 1903 bis 1913*. Lübeck, 1970.

Wolf, Heinrich. *Die Entstehung des Jungdeutschen Ordens und seine frühen Jahre*. Munich, 1970.

Worgitzki, Max. *Geschichte der Abstimmung—Der Kampf um Ermland und Masuren*. Leipzig, 1921.

Wright, Jonathan R. C. *"Above Parties": The Political Attitudes of the German Protestant Church Leadership*. New York, 1974.

Wulf, Peter. "Die Auseinandersetzung um die Sozialisierung der Kohle in Deutschland." *Vierteljahrshefte für Zeitgeschichte* 25 (Jan. 1977), 46–89.

Zeender, John K. "German Catholics and the Concept of an Interconfessional Party, 1900–1922." *Journal of Central European Affairs* 23 (Jan. 1964), 424–39.

Ziebill, Otto. *Geschichte des Deutschen Städtetages*. Cologne, 1955.

Zmarzlik, Hans-Günter. *Bethmann Hollweg als Reichskanzler*. Düsseldorf, 1957.

Zwing, Karl. *Soziologie der Gewerkschaftsbewegung: Gewerkschaften und Wirtschaft*. Jena, 1925.

Index

357